Praise for Transformational Leadership in Banking

Dr Anil K. Khandelwal is a respected banking figure who has earned his stripes through his well-recognized work at Bank of Baroda (BOB). In this book, Dr Khandelwal makes a powerful case for urgent and integrated reforms in the banking sector. This compilation by him offers timely solutions by focusing on issues that I couldn't agree more with and are needed for a strong governance structure and nurturing the right talent. I highly recommend this book for those who want to seriously understand the challenges faced by banks in India.

Deepak Parekh, *Chairman HDFC Ltd*

Dr Anil K. Khandelwal's edited book on transformational leadership in banking is both timely and instructive, with excellent perspectives on the issues of governance, leadership and HR in a digital environment. The book is a blueprint for transformation and reforms, especially in public sector banks, and will be of immense value to policymakers, regulators, board members, CEOs, researchers and to all those in leadership roles and the public at large.

G. C. Chaturvedi, *Former Secretary, Government of India and Chairman, ICICI Bank and National Stock Exchange*

Dr Khandelwal is a living legend for BOB. He has been a distinguished former chairman who pretty much invented a new template of an HR-driven transformation in terms of managing public sector banks, and BOB was his laboratory. This book, edited by Dr Khandelwal, not only brings fresh insights from his pen but is also an outstanding curated collection of essays and observations that encompass the broad spectrum of issues that confront banks today. As we face another crisis since COVID-19, there is no doubt that the answers to our problems must be in new ways of working and talent management. I am confident that all readers of this book would come away educated, enlightened and wiser.

Sanjiv Chadha, *Managing Director and CEO, BOB*

This book by Dr Khandelwal, who is a thought leader and authority on leadership and governance, is quite timely. What makes the book exceptional is its focus on intangibles such as leadership, governance and talent in transforming banks, which are normally ignored. Strong board leadership is needed to pilot internal reforms to make individual banks technology-driven and customer-centric. The book is strongly recommended to policymakers, senior bankers and academics as rich source material for reforms.

Shyamala Gopinath, *Chairman, HDFC Bank,*
and Former Deputy Governor, RBI

With the unique perspective of someone who has weathered it all as a head of not one, but two public sector banks, Dr Khandelwal provides a compelling, thought-provoking narrative and practical know-how on transformational leadership in the high-octane banking industry. This multifaceted account provides powerful examples of case studies, best practices and experiences of governance, change management and innovation by seasoned professionals and CXOs in systemically critical organizations. I feel the book will be of immense value to the C-suite, academics, regulators and policymakers alike. This is a must-read for every forward-thinking leader and HR practitioner.

Rajnish Kumar, *Former Chairman, State Bank of India*

This book provides invaluable insights into the world of banking and guides us on what is required to succeed in these turbulent times. There is no better person than Anil Khandelwal to draw from his rich experience and understanding of the sector in putting together this collection of writings—a must-read for all.

Naina Lal Kidwai, *Ex-chairman HSBC India and*
Director on the Board of HSBC Asia Pacific

Leadership is all about converting adversity into an opportunity for transformation. The twin forces of technology and a global pandemic are a perfect setting to unlock the potential of public sector banks in India. As usual, Anil Khandelwal has curated an excellent set of chapters, case studies and interviews, and he offers a roadmap to transformational leadership for Indian banks.

Jagdish N. Sheth, *Charles H. Kellstadt*
Professor of Business Goizueta Business School,
Emory University Atlanta, USA

This timely collection of chapters, interviews and case studies on the role of leadership and people development in contemporary Indian banking, provides insightful perspectives on how the banking sector can become an engine for India's economic development.

Rishikesha T. Krishnan, *Director, Indian Institute of Management (IIM) Bangalore*

Dr Anil Khandelwal's edited book on transformational leadership is a great contribution especially in the banking sector, where operational perspectives have guided leader's decisions at a time when market insights, customer centricity, agile technologies and processes and talent development should have been the priorities. This book's strength is an excellent amalgam of academic research and practice. Dr Khandelwal himself is a transformational leader, and hence, this book will be a great contribution to our understanding of the transformation process and leadership in the banking industry.

Rajan Saxena, *Former Vice Chancellor, Narsee Monjee Institute of Management Studies, Mumbai*

This exceptional book probes the structural issues framing public banks and suggests mechanisms that will improve the health of the financial system. Bank nationalization did raise India's savings rate, but finance was intermediated inefficiently. This landmark book focuses on governance, the composition of bank boards, tenure of CEOs, compensation, leadership pipeline and talent management, and provides insights as to how public sector banks can become strong and profitable institutions. Policymakers would do well to act fast on these recommendations.

Errol D'Souza, *Director, IIM Ahmedabad*

Comprehensive, focused and immediately useful, the book is an articulate and highly readable synthesis on leadership practices and a framework to apply in real-life situations.

Dr Anil K. Khandelwal has beautifully intertwined the ideas of governance, transformational leadership and human capital management in the ever-evolving Indian banking landscape by bringing together carefully commissioned chapters and case studies by leading experts and domain leaders in this book.

S. S. Mallikarjuna Rao, *Managing Director and CEO, Punjab National Bank*

This book holds up a mirror to the Indian banking industry. It offers a holistic picture of the current issues the industry faces and rightly focuses on the most critical missing piece of the puzzle—the need for transformational leaders. Transformational leadership is rare but so compelling in terms of an organization's ability to re-energise and reinvent. This book offers excellent insights into what is required to achieve this in a rapidly evolving industry.

Rakesh Makhija, *Chairman, Axis Bank*

The main thrust of banking regulatory structure is to ensure that banks play a positive role in India's development. Unfortunately, this structure has not lived up to its expectations, at least in case of public sector banking. In the preface to the excellent collection of chapters by academics and eminent practitioners that Dr Anil Khandelwal has compiled, he makes a strong case for moving away from an overly technical regulation of the banking sector to one where banks get excellent transformational leadership, extensive operating autonomy, flexibility in HR policies to get talent in specialist areas and a board with the needed diversity in expertise. Dr Khandelwal knows what he is talking about. He was CMD of BOB during 2005–2008. As a board member, I observed that he practised a highly effective, innovationist and transformational leadership. He succeeded beyond expectations. His message and the views of the other contributors to this book need to be taken seriously. I wish the book all success.

Pradip N. Khandwalla, *Former Director, IIM Ahmedabad*

Banking today is witnessing a revolution globally, and this selective collection of ideas, collated by Anil Khandelwal, from the best minds in Indian banking, brings to the forefront possible futures.

Gita Piramal, *author of bestsellers Business Maharajas, Business Legends and Managing Radical Change*

Transformational
LEADERSHIP
IN BANKING

Transformational
LEADERSHIP
IN BANKING

Challenges of Governance, Leadership and HR in a Digital and Disruptive World

Edited by

ANIL K. KHANDELWAL

Los Angeles I London I New Delhi
Singapore I Washington DC I Melbourne

First published in 2021 by

SAGE Publications India Pvt Ltd
B1/I-1 Mohan Cooperative Industrial Area
Mathura Road, New Delhi 110 044, India
www.sagepub.in

SAGE Publications Inc
2455 Teller Road
Thousand Oaks, California 91320, USA

SAGE Publications Ltd
1 Oliver's Yard, 55 City Road
London EC1Y 1SP, United Kingdom

SAGE Publications Asia-Pacific Pte Ltd
18 Cross Street #10-10/11/12
China Square Central
Singapore 048423

Published by Vivek Mehra for SAGE Publications India Pvt Ltd. Typeset in 11/13.5pt Bembo by Fidus Design Pvt Ltd, Chandigarh.

Library of Congress Control Number: 2021930982

ISBN: 978-93-5388-756-8 (HB)

SAGE Team: Neha Pal, Sandhya Gola, Sonam Rana, Aishna Bhatt and Rajinder Kaur

In the memory of two contributors to this book who passed away during the writing of the book.

Dr Pritam Singh, Former Director, IIM Lucknow and MDI Gurgaon

My teacher and friend of five decades

Dr N. Balasubramanian, Former Professor, IIM Bangalore

An inspiring mentor

Thank you for choosing a SAGE product!
If you have any comment, observation or feedback,
I would like to personally hear from you.

Please write to me at **contactceo@sagepub.in**

Vivek Mehra, Managing Director and CEO, SAGE India.

Bulk Sales

SAGE India offers special discounts
for purchase of books in bulk.
We also make available special imprints
and excerpts from our books on demand.

For orders and enquiries, write to us at

Marketing Department
SAGE Publications India Pvt Ltd
B1/I-1, Mohan Cooperative Industrial Area
Mathura Road, Post Bag 7
New Delhi 110044, India

E-mail us at **marketing@sagepub.in**

Subscribe to our mailing list
Write to **marketing@sagepub.in**

This book is also available as an e-book.

Contents

Part 2: Case Studies

Part 3: Perspectives from Experts

List of Abbreviations

3Cs	Clear, consistent and credible
ABG	Aditya Birla Group
ABs	Associate banks
ACC	Appointments Committee of the Cabinet
ACCA	Association of Chartered Certified Accountants
ACT	Atria Convergence Technologies
AGM	Assistant general manager
AI	Artificial intelligence
AIBEA	All India Banking Employees' Association
ATIs	Apex training institutes
ATMs	Automated teller machines
ATS	Applicant tracking system
AUD	Ambedkar University Delhi
BBB	Banks Board Bureau
BFSI	Banking, financial services and insurance
BMSB	Baroda Manipal School of Banking
BOB	Bank of Baroda
CDO	Chief digital officer
CDS	Career Development System
CEO	Chief executive officer
CFO	Chief financial officer
CGM	Chief general manager
CHROs	Chief human resources officers
CII	Confederation of Indian Industry
CLO	Chief learning officer
CMD	Chairman and managing director
CoE	Centre of Excellence
CPUs	Central processing units
CSEB	Crowdsourced employer branding
CVP	Customer value proposition
CXO	Chief experience officer
DALL	Disciplinary Action at Local level
DFI	Development finance institution
DFS	Department of Financial Services
DGMs	Deputy general managers
DL	Deep learning

DMD	Deputy managing director
DPDs	Disciplinary proceedings departments
EASE	Ease of Service Excellence
EBE	Employer brand equity
EMI	Equated monthly instalment
ER	Employee relations
ESG	Environmental, social and governance
ESRC	Economic and Social Research Council
EU	European Union
EVA	Electronic virtual assistant
EVP	Employee value proposition
EZIPL	Egon Zehnder International Private Limited
FCA	Financial Conduct Authority
FMCG	Fast-moving consumer goods
GM	General manager
GNPA	Gross non-performing assets
GPUs	Graphics processing units
HR	Human resources
HRA	Human resource accounting
HRCPC	Human Rights and Consumer Protection Cell
HRD	Human resource development
HRM	Human resource management
HRMS	Human resource management system
HUL	Hindustan Unilever Limited
IA	Inquiring authority
IBA	Indian Banks Association
IC	Intellectual capital
IDPs	Individual development plans
IFBI	Institute of Finance, Banking and Insurance
IIM	Indian Institute of Management
IIMA	Indian Institute of Management Ahmedabad
IIT	Indian Institute of Technology
IMA	ICICI Manipal Academy
IO	Inquiry officer
IR	Industrial relations
ISTD	Indian Society for Training & Development
IT	Information technology
JD	Job description
JMC	Junior management cadre

KRAs	Key responsibility areas
KYC	Know your customer
L&D	Learning and development
L&T	Larsen & Toubro
LDPs	Leadership development programmes
LEAP	Leadership Enhancement and Appreciation Programme
LHI	Learning Health Index
LMS	Learning Management System
LXPs	Learning Experience Platforms
MD	Managing director
MDI	Management Development Institute
ML	Machine learning
MMC	Middle management cadre
MOF	Ministry of Finance
MSR	Management, spirituality and religion
NPA	Non-performing asset
NPA	Non-performing asset
OD	Organizational development
PMS	Performance management system
PNB	Punjab National Bank
PO	Probationary officer
PR	Prescribed responsibilities
PSB	Public sector bank
PSD2	Payment Systems Directive 2
RBI	Reserve Bank of India
RFP	Request for proposal
ROE	Return on equity
ROI	Return on investment
RPA	Robotic process automation
RRBs	Regional rural banks
SBI	State Bank of India
SBILD	State Bank Institutes of Learning and Development
SDGs	Sustainable Development Goals
SMC	Senior management cadre
SME	Small and medium enterprise
SOIL	School of Inspired Leadership
STEP	Semantic testing platform
STEPS	Service, transparency, ethics, politeness and sustainability
STU	Strategic training unit

TAT	Turnaround time
TCS	Tata Consultancy Services
TL	Transformational leaders
TO	Trainee officer
TQM	Total quality management
UoTM	Universe on the Move
VECV	Volvo Eicher Commercial Vehicles Ltd
VMVSs	Vision, mission and value statements
VOB	Voice of Barodians
WFH	Work from home
WYSIATI	What you see is all there is
YBPs	Yoga-based practices
YONO	You Only Need One

Foreword

India's public sector banks have delivered consistently over the last five decades. They have provided the foundation for every significant economic activity required to propel growth and build the much-needed infrastructure on which the edifice of a modern economy can be built. Every time that the need has arisen, these banks have more than met the clarion call of the hour and supported entrepreneurs desiring to set up major enterprises. When called upon, they have more than adequately met credit requirements, irrespective of the tenor of the loan, the sector seeking credit and the size of the investment. From small ticket personal loans to huge exposures in major infrastructure projects, their footprint can be seen, pan India. However, despite having a 70 per cent share in Indian banking and undertaking all the heavy lifting to fulfil the multifaceted challenges to meet varied, complex and development priorities of the country, they are also the favourite whipping boys of the public—both informed and uninformed.

The travails, inadequacies and shortcomings of public sector banks stare us in the face. We have set up committees and task forces practically in every five-year plan, however, the maladies that afflict the banks continue with distressing regularity. Indian banking is at a crucial point in terms of its performance and future trajectory. It faces challenges arising from three sources: legacy banking practices, future of banking and economic priorities likely to come out of COVID-19. It requires a comprehensive analysis of the pitfalls that banks face and a toolkit designed to provide 360-degree coverage of reform measures. Who could have attempted it better than Dr Anil Khandelwal, who has seen it all, done it all from the 'shop floor' and even attempted a reform package whilst being a member of the Banks Board Bureau? Dr Khandelwal was responsible for the turnaround of Bank of Baroda; he chaired the committee of HR initiatives for public sector banks and was a member of the first Bank Boards Bureau set up by the government. He has the impeccable credentials to put together a book with contributions from distinguished experts.

It must be said to the credit of successive governments that they did recognize the nature of the problem-facing public sector banks and set up expert committees to suggest measures to overcome the problems. While the intent was conspicuously perceptible, alas, the desire to implement the suggestions was equally conspicuously absent. It must be said to the credit of the NDA government that they took the appropriate decisions in trying to identify and professionalize the executives through attractively worded projects such as Gyan Sangam, Indradhanush and PSB Manthan; however, they could not address the core issues such as neglect of intangibles, lack of professional culture, talent, application of sound HR principles to board functions, leadership and, most importantly, a hands-off approach of the majority stakeholder. Despite the creation of the Banks Board Bureau to recommend the appointment of the top leadership of banks, 'the appointments happen not through the process of governance but the process of government.'[1] The need for an integrated, consistent and sustained transformation in areas of professional capability and culture, talent and board-driven PSB banking is long overdue. Discernibly, such a transformation will not only alleviate many of the legacy challenges but will also prepare public sector banks towards the emerging future of banking, which is likely to be based on technologies (digitalization), talent and proper use of artificial intelligence. Culture and HR are the common interventions, whether our focus is on legacy or emerging challenges.

This book, edited by Dr Khandelwal, contains rich material obtained through carefully commissioned and researched articles and discussions with practitioners, experts, academicians, consultants and senior leaders of the banking industry on what should the new reform agenda look like, how the policymakers should go about implementing it and where the immediate priorities should be. The book has three main sections: (a) chapters, (b) case studies and (c) interviews. These three forms of narration provide a different lens to the various aspects of banking challenges, success stories and would appeal to audiences with different objectives and interest areas. They cover a vast swathe of issues such as the lack of transformative reforms, governance issues, leadership factors and the need for apposite talent.

While complex governance is a recognized bottleneck area, particularly in the context of public sector banks, this book differs in how the application of HR principles to board matters and functioning could make a significant difference. The range of reform agendas covers issues such as the appointment of board members (it is still done under the 50-year old Nationalization Act), the competence of the appointed board members in the new emerging digital context, it's autonomy in deciding the board composition, CEO and full-time directors, and their tenures and compensation, etc.

Yet another way in which this book contributes importantly to the reform agenda is through sharing insights from one-on-one interviews with senior

---

[1] Chapter 1, 'The Changing Context of Governance and Leadership in PSBs', by M. S. Sriram.

banking leaders (who earlier led some great institutions in multinational and private sector companies), who were in significant leadership roles and have seen the constraints through the objective lens. This type of grounded practitioners' insights in a volume is an invaluable contribution not only as education to most on what ails the banking sector currently but also for what needs to change and why.

The contributors have written in a simple and lucid style for readers to get to the core of issues and understand them without thick layers of jargon. The book maintains a bias towards actionable agenda and the practitioner's world, and hence, is a must-read for policymakers, regulators, practising leaders and managers, academicians, researchers and anyone interested in the banking sector. It is full of practical insights and suggestions with a roadmap for the future. The banking sector is in an urgent need for integrated reforms and intangibles (including culture, leadership, talent and governance) that would provide the maximum upside and returns for a long time to come. There are hardly any books on these themes, and it should trigger interest among bankers to discuss these themes. Time is of the essence. Public sector banks are here to stay, maybe in smaller numbers through consolidation, and will, therefore, assume a pivotal role for driving India's economic development.

This book is a landmark contribution at a time when such inputs are so critically required. The book provides 'a ready to implement' reform package and will prove to be an asset to policy planners and a reference resource for all the banking professionals in the field of governance and talent management.

Vinod Rai, Former Secretary, Department of Financial
Services, Former CAG of India and
Former Chairman, Banks Board Bureau

Preface

This book is a product of the COVID-19 pandemic. In early March, while shuffling through my bookshelf, I picked up my own book, *Human Resources Development in Banks* (1988), and reflected on the progress of the human resource development (HRD) function in public sector banks (PSBs) over the decades that have passed. The HRD function was taking off in the 1980s, and in that context, the book advocated its potential in PSBs' journey ahead. The book also specified roles at various levels, including that of the top management in making HRD a powerful instrument for business policy implementation and improving services. However, the book had argued, 'only a concerted and a well-orchestrated effort can help in establishing management credibility and create a climate for any worthwhile initiative in HRD'.

In the last three decades, while banking has taken rapid strides, such as the introduction of technology, retail banking orientation and, more recently, the amalgamation of 10 PSBs into 4, the HR function continues to suffer from neglect, resulting in its failure to become a mainstream function like any other banking commercial function. HR has experienced only incremental changes, such as the introduction of technology in HR administration, adoption of e-learning, rehash of training systems and some marginal improvements in other HR subsystems. A concerted and well-orchestrated HR strategy, both at the government and bank level, is still a pipe dream.

Key HR reforms that are fundamental to create substantial changes in the quality of talent, a strong leadership pipeline and a pro-active culture seem to have eluded PSBs. The strategic issues crying for changes as recommended by the Khandelwal Committee (2010) have remained unimplemented just like the fundamental changes suggested by the Naik Committee (2016) on governance. Undifferentiated compensation pattern and reward mechanisms, lack of professionalization, lack of solid steps in HR governance, short tenures of CEOs and full-time directors continue to deny the system the opportunity to break the trap of stagnancy in the HR function and develop any long-term HR vision. HR has not become a central and strategic issue for neither the government nor the boards or CEOs. Many of the current problems of the PSBs face can be attributed to this casual and rather peripheral positioning of this important function.

In the new digital environment, many facets of banking are changing and competition is really heating up. With weak balance sheets and mounting stressed assets, PSBs seriously need major reforms and initiatives in leadership, governance, culture and HR capabilities, in order to become robust and resilient entities. In times to come, the banks will be challenged by these drivers of business and the health of the PSBs will, to a great measure, depend on these critical issues.

The present book is backed by this thought and concern. It is my belief that time is running out for PSBs. If their falling market capitalization is any indication of their diminishing competitive positioning versus private banks, it is time to act, and act rather decisively. The book aims to challenge the existing ways of putting these strategic initiatives on the low-priority list and argues for leading initiatives in these critical areas as an unpostponable agenda.

Acknowledgements

This book is an outcome of the contributions of many outstanding professionals from the academic and practitioner's domains. I have been fortunate to have come in contact with many outstanding experts during my professional life, who willingly agreed to contribute to this book. They have been very gracious and accommodative in listening to my ideas and suggestions in writing their chapters.

I thank all my writers for their contributions.

The book has a special section featuring six interviews with the icons. Three of them are Arun Kumar (KPMG), who gives a helicopter view of strategic change agenda for the boards post COVID-19, Professor H. Krishnamurthy—a well-known name in PSBs for helping many banks transform their technology—shares challenges of the digital journey, and Professor T. V. Rao—a pioneering HRD academic, who understands HR issues in banking quite well—shares his angst as well as vision for HRD work in the PSBs.

Three outstanding professionals, namely Ajay Nanavati (former managing director of 3M), Ravi Venkatesan (former chairman, Tata Cummins India Ltd jointly with Professor Biju Varkkey, Indian Institute of Management [IIM] Ahmedabad) and Kewal Handa (former managing director, Pfizer Ltd, India), share their experiences of working as a non-executive chairman of three PSBs. With their backgrounds as CEOs in multinational/private sector, they share useful insights about the culture, governance and leadership issues that need prioritized attention by the government. I am truly grateful to them for their time and insights.

I am grateful to my friend Professor Rajen Gupta (former faculty member, IIM Lucknow and Management Development Institute, Gurgaon) for always being there to discuss issues, conceptualize and help in designing any academic or research work that I undertake. He suggested some young and leading researchers whom I approached, and their contributions appear in this book. I would like to especially mention one such scholar–practitioner Dr Anujayesh Krishna, a PhD from IIM Ahmedabad, who not only contributed two significant chapters (one jointly with me) but also became my sounding board for ideas that I was trying to focus on in this book. His experience in the UK banking industry and academic insights helped me sharpen my understanding of some issues. His contributions are too numerous and varied at every stage to list here. During this project, we also co-authored two articles on governance in PSBs. Thank you, Anuj.

I would also thank my friend Sushil Saluja (former senior managing director for financial services, Accenture, UK, and a contributor to this book) for his encouraging help in understanding the impact of digitalization in banking and its impact on structure, strategies, leadership and culture. It sharpened my understanding of multifold changes that the PSBs are confronted with. Thank you, Sushil for your grace and time. Likewise, my young friend Rajiv Jayaraman, a contributor to this book and an author of a well-regarded book on digital, helped me understand the role of digital technology in HR management and undertaking leadership training. Thank you, Rajiv.

I am also grateful to State Bank of India, Bank of Baroda, ICICI Bank and Union Bank of India for sharing their work in HR and leadership, which appear as case studies in this book.

I cannot express in words my gratitude to Vinod Rai, who graciously agreed to write the foreword. He has been a role model who has always guided me in my professional journey.

Editing a book is much like making a movie, requiring coordination with many actors (contributors), nudging them (direction) to align their acting (writing) to fall in line with the overall theme of the movie (book), pruning manuscripts (editing), music (create a rhythm in the script of the book, harmonizing the chapters to overall objectives), launching the film (book) through marketing, social media, reviews, etc. In this movie, I have played many roles. Hopefully, the movie (book) will impact the audience (bank management boards and policymakers).

I must admit that I have been a rebel husband, who continues to break promises to lead a peaceful retired life, and I thank my wife, Vandana, for her patience and support. This is my fourth book post retirement, and the entire credit goes to her unwavering support. My son, Umang, and daughter-in-law, Neha, who worked from home during COVID-19 pandemic, kept the spirits high and helped create a positive environment around, which helped me complete the project.

Towards the final stage of completing the manuscript, Meghna joined me as my support and helped me with the computer work to create a manuscript. Thank you, Meghna. My house support, Manoj, always makes sure that my culinary tastes and erratic demands from the kitchen are met from time to time. Thank you, Manoj.

Finally, I thank Commissioning and Editorial teams comprising Manisha Mathews, Neha Pal and Sandhya Gola for their support at every stage of the project.

INTRODUCTION

Indian banks cover the varied, intricate and dynamic banking needs of one of the biggest, complex and diverse economies in the world. According to a report, India has the highest number of commercial bank branches in the world (0.12 million, Jain, 2016). Indian banking employs close to 1 million employees. Around 70 per cent of this banking is being done by public sector banks (PSBs). According to the Database on the Indian Economy, Reserve Bank of India, the total deposits and advances of PSBs as of March 2019 were ₹84,862,140 million and ₹59,262,860 million, respectively. In the last five decades, PSBs have made exceptional contributions towards nation-building. They have also been entrusted with developmental priorities of governments over the last several decades. In the recent times, PSBs have contributed towards financing of rural sector, SMEs and the infra sector. PSBs also rose to the challenge in times of demonetization and implementation of some of the ambitious programmes of the government, such as the Jan Dhan Yojana and MUDRA loans.

Banking Challenges

The aforementioned successes, however, have been despite many constraints and challenges that PSBs face. Some of these challenges are well known and include the size of non-performing assets (NPA), poor credit growth and low market capitalization. Important stakeholders such as the government and the regulator have tried to address these challenges through recapitalization, regulations, rules and compliance-based processes, and mergers/amalgamations. There were also few progressive initiatives such as establishment of Banks Board Bureau and operationalization of EASE I and II. However, the effectiveness of these measures remained limited because of their ad hoc, fragmented and piecemeal nature. Such interventions mask the fact that at a deeper level, the successes of PSBs have not been without diluting the risk management systems, internal controls and neglect of their human resource (HR) policies and internal governance. The focus on immediate commercial goals coupled with the weakening of such internal controls, governance and leadership has contributed significantly to banking challenges.

The need for banking transformation arises not merely due to legacy governance and management challenges. As important as they are, the future of banking is likely to be even more transformational with newer technologies, novel business models, cyber risks and demographically heterogeneous customers. This emerging future of banking will make the banking context of the 1970s—and the management processes, leadership, mindsets and governance linked with it—not only ill-fitting (which is already the case) but also counterproductive because the 'traditional' reform methods may delude us into solving wrong problems in the wrong way. The COVID-19 situation has already redefined leadership challenges, and these new leadership challenges need new approaches and mindsets towards building resilient banks. If the objective is to address the 21st-century banking challenges and prepare for the future of banking, it is important to build governance, leadership and organizational mindsets that are aligned to the organizational frameworks of the future banking challenges. The book suggests that financial and business matrices are a deeper manifestation of organizational processes. Any ad hoc and piecemeal attempts to improve poor business and commercial matrices, as has been the trend so far, without considering governance, organizational and leadership processes that underpin them will, at best, offer costly short-term advantages. This is already showing up in different ways. For example, NPAs of PSBs are higher than their combined net worth, and PSBs' total market capitalization is lesser than the recapitalization funds infused in them.

Reform Trajectory and Outcomes

It is not that there is lack of concern, thinking or even initiatives on banking reforms. Over the last one decade, the government has appointed two committees of experts to look into the problems of HR (Khandelwal Committee, 2010) and governance (Nayak Committee, 2014). Both the committees have submitted their recommendations to revamp and strengthen PSBs. The government has taken some steps to implement the recommendations. For example, the position of the chairman and managing director is split into non-executive part-time chairman and managing director (MD) and chief executive officer (CEO, as recommended by both, the Khandelwal Committee and the Nayak Committee), created Banks Board Bureau as a replacement of appointment board for appointing whole-time directors and non-executive chairman. It has also taken other steps as a part of its Indradhanush programme (2015) for recapitalization of PSBs, policy of non-interference by the government in the running of banks, announcing framework for accountability and new performance measurement criteria based on key performance indicators. The government followed its intent to reform the banking sector by organizing Gyan Sangam (2015), a retreat of bankers which was also attended by the finance minister and addressed by the prime minister. The Gyan Sangam discussed issues of risk management, digitizing process, measures to strengthen risk management, financial inclusion and aspects of improving managerial performance. This was followed by another retreat (PSB Manthan, 2017) of whole-time directors and the senior management of PSBs on whose recommendations a PSB reform agenda called Ease of Service Excellence (EASE) was announced. It encapsulates the synergistic approach to ensuring prudential and clean lending, better customer service, enhanced credit availability, focus on micro, small and medium enterprises and better governance. Later, an EASE index was developed, and the bank's performance was monitored on various parameters. Although it is a good initiative to start with as a mechanism to build operational excellence, there is a risk that such an oversight could prove tactical, as it does not build better governance through an empowered board and could reduce board's role to an observatory status.

In spite of these initiatives, the problems in the Indian banking sector seem to be getting worse, or at least not going away. The NPA ratio of state-owned banks range from 5.56 per cent (SBI) to 20.50 per cent (Central Bank of India; Khan et al., 2020). The common equity tier 1 ratio for nine state-owned banks remains below 10 per cent (Khan et al., 2020). The Standing Committee on Finance (2017–2018) in its 68th report quoted the *BusinessLine* news (17 May 2018) to state, 'Muted growth in assets, steep losses and erosion in capital have led to the build-up of high leverage (ratio of assets to capital) in the banking system, particularly for public sector banks'. A recent paper (Acharya & Rajan, 2020, p. 2) argued,

> India's credit market outcomes are full of paradoxes. The country's credit to GDP ratio remains low, even by the standards of emerging markets, at less than 60% … the country's banking system has among the highest gross non-performing assets (GNPA) to total assets ratio globally…. The GNPA ratio stood at 8.5% even pre-COVID for the banking sector as a whole, 11.3% for public sector banks … 4.2% for private sector banks.

The Financial Stability Report by RBI in July 2020 estimates that post-COVID-19 could lead to an aggregate GNPA ratio of 12.5 per cent to 14.7 per cent. Since 2010, close to ₹4 trillion has been injected to recapitalize PSBs (Acharya & Rajan, 2020). The valuations of PSBs have fallen significantly more than the private sector banks, since the beginning of January 2020.

Missing Banking Reforms

The Indian banking sector is at a critical point given the COVID-19 challenges, economic slowdown and changing future of banking. The limited progress made through reforms thus far suggests that something crucial is missing from the process. The book argues that this 'something' is the lack of banking architecture based on governance, leadership and talent to create a meritocratic and forward-looking culture. For this to happen, there is a need for urgent reforms in the areas of governance, culture and human capital management. Previous reform efforts have missed out on these areas even though they are the common thread in the varied challenges that banks face. The central message of this book is that the banking sector needs urgent, integrated and substantive reforms, which can be accomplished only through transformational leadership with a focus on building governance, talent, culture (intangibles) and human capital management. The book aims to raise such issues and addresses a range of stakeholders such as practitioners, leaders, employees, regulators, government, shareholders, trade unions, academicians, researchers and industry associations, who are interested in health and believe in the potential of the Indian banking sector.

Governance

The book argues that application of sound and progressive HR principles into board matters could create a strong and business-aligned board membership and leadership leading to an effective governance. While banking governance is a well-covered area in the legal context, the role of HR in building strong governance through cutting-edge HR practices and norms with regards to board memberships, leadership, performance context and reviews, empowerment and autonomy have not received much attention and discussion. The financial markets have become very complex and competencies needed in each bank differ depending on the strategy and the bank's overall profile. The old method of selecting boards based on representation to different categories, whilst aligned to the previous banking context, is ill-suited to the needs of the 21st-century PSB. The existing practice also leads to delays in fulfilling critical board membership slots. An important reform in this space is for the government to relinquish the rigid guidelines on board composition and empower boards in line with Securities and Exchange Board of India's Listing Obligations and Disclosure Requirements. Using the HR principles into board matters can also alleviate other areas of concerns such as short MD and CEO tenures, lack of succession planning and contemporary appraisal processes for board and senior leaders, as well as the lack of HR flexibility to recruit at lateral levels and pay market compensation to name a few.

Leadership

As the banking industry undergoes changes, so will the quality and nature of leadership needed to guide PSBs. The weight of legacy banking challenges and emerging digitalized, competitive, multi-generational banking points to the need for transformational leadership. A sad reality is that the banking industry continues with the mindset of an operational banker focused on the immediacy of commercial goals. Banks have significant leadership gaps at various levels, and leadership needs are met through short-term ad hoc and floating plans. With few exceptions, there is no systematic grooming process for developing leadership bench strength. A bank may have a CEO and all its EDs from different banks, and they could be on short tenures for 2–3 years. In this context, the stakes are limited and the drive for cultural transformation may be lacking.

Transformational leaders are strategic individuals who can use their resources, perspective and influence to initiate the process of cultural change. To be truly transformational, leadership should engage all stakeholders (particularly employees) and change the focus from rules, controls and compliance to empowerment, flexibility and innovation. Such a transformation means bringing culture at the centre of the reform process. The importance of culture is best summarized by Peter Drucker, who was one of the original thinkers and source of management wisdom, when he reportedly said, 'Culture easts strategy for a breakfast' (Rick, 2014). Reform processes, so far, have focused on regulation, rules, controls and compliance, and they have reached a stage of diminishing returns. A unique characteristic of cultural transformation is the change from fixed mindset (accepting constraints as a 'given' and fixed/limited possibilities for improvement) to growth mindset (exploring different ways to improve through engagement of employees, new vision and innovative thinking; Dweck, 2016). When this cultural transition happens, change becomes self-sustaining in nature and sets off a chain reaction of positivity and alignment to bigger cultural goals. This is not an easy change and requires commitment, energy and long-term view. Banking sector is at a critical point in its reform process. Given that other approaches, such as regulation, control and compliance, have already been tried, it is imperative that the three strategic actors in the banking industry, namely government, regulators and boards/CEOs should now assiduously champion and encourage transformational cultural change and transition from fixed to growth mindset in banks. Through carefully commissioned essays from leading experts and case studies, the book aims to provide insights and frameworks on the performance upside and process involved in implementing such a change.

Human Resources

The Indian banking system employs close to 1 million employees, and some of the big banks have over 100,000 employees. The recent mergers of PSBs have created large and complex banking entities, which need good quality talent to ensure safe, resilient and forward-looking banking. Banks need more specialized skills in areas such as risk management, data analysis, digital technology, credit analysis and relationship management. The rise of complex, specialist skill sets, which are also in high demand in banking, raises the stakes for HR, as such talent will require very different HR strategies in terms of recruitment, training, engagement, compensation, retention and career progression. The future of banking will not only entail new technology and workforce, but also a different governance, cultural and leadership approach. This will in turn need a transformational shift in the way HR is seen at the board and CEO levels. It is also aligned with the emerging international trend to focus on culture as an alternate pathway to build strong banks. Culture is unique to each bank, and internal stakeholders, including boards, are in the best position to develop it. Viewed in this framework, effective culture is an outcome when governance, leadership and talent get aligned.

$$\text{Culture} = \text{Governance} + \text{Leadership} + \text{Talent}$$

Structure of the Book

To present various perspectives, ideas and implementable agenda, this book is divided into three main parts. Part 1 presents chapters by leading practitioners and academicians on the future of banking, governance, leadership and talent. These 21 chapters shed light on different aspects that are key to the banking reform process. Part 2 presents four banking case studies that cover the strategic role played by the HR function in banks not only in the transformation of the HR function itself, but also in facilitating the business transformation process. The inclusion of these case studies bolsters one of the main ideas of the book that when reforms in the human capital areas are undertaken, they facilitate good banking. Part 3 presents individual (one-on-one) interviews with various industry leaders and other experts in board effectiveness, human resource development and digitalization. Unsurprisingly, these leaders view the intangibles including better governance, culture, human capital and talent as areas where reform is urgently needed.

Part 1: Collection of Essays

The collection of essays in Part I is organized into four sections, each with its own theme. Together, these themes, namely future of banking environment, governance, leadership and talent, cover various priority areas that could make banks robust and safer.

Section 1 covers the future banking environment. Although there exists a great deal of material on the current challenges and the need for change in the banking sector, most of this material is centred on past practices and legacy issues. There is an urgent need for reform for the additional, perhaps more serious, reason that the future of banking is likely to be very different, and Indian banks are ill-equipped to deal with it. M. S. Sriram, in his chapter, 'The Changing Context of Governance and Leadership in Public Sector Banks', examines the issue of transformational leadership from the perspective of ownership of PSBs and argues that unless the fundamental structure of ownership, both de facto and de jure, is changed to make it truly accountable to the market structures, a transformational leadership would be unlikely. Sushil Saluja's chapter titled, 'Banking on Change: The Digital Revolution Is Now Here', discusses how technology is shaping our lifetimes like no other force and how the COVID-19 pandemic has accelerated the adoption of digital technology. He argues that the role of leader changes from being an enterprise-level supervisor to guide and coach for the organization. Akhil Handa, in his chapter, 'Future of Work in BFSI Organizations', presents the scenario for future workplace post digitalization and identifies three steps for creating banking workforce of the future, namely reimagining work to better understand how machine and man can collaborate, pivoting the workforce to areas that create new forms of values and scaling up new skill initiatives to enable people to work with intelligent machines. The author concludes by saying that the biggest driver of change has to be top management.

Section 2 deals with governance issues and discusses ways in which we need to reframe the discussion on it. While governance is a well-travelled territory from the perspective of corporate law, the application of HR principles to develop board leadership has been a significant missing piece in the current discussions. Indeed, as many interviews in Part 3 suggest, this could be one of the most important part of the banking reform process. N. Balasubramanian's chapter, 'Human Capital and Ethical Bank Governance: Some Perspectives from India', discusses the importance of soft factors such as personal ethics and organizational culture in ensuring effective banking governance apart from regulatory surveillance. The chapter examines to what extent human capital policies and practices engage the attention of board of directors in the overall governance framework. Anujayesh Krishna's chapter, 'Leadership Choices in Building Better Governance: Regulation or Culture', argues that banks need a qualitatively different organizational approach based on culture, because banking regulations do not always yield desired results and the future of banking is changing in a transformative way. To transform their cultures, banks need a strategic pivot and transform their existing cultures, which are primarily characterized by bureaucracy, rules, compliance and control processes, to a culture which is characterized by flexibility, risk-taking, empowerment, performance focus and willingness to take initiative. Krishna argues that this transformation is a complex leadership challenge. Key stakeholders can facilitate the process by including cultural assessments in their reviews, and regulators and government can initiate industry research and database on cultural best practices and variations within the sector. Anil K. Khandelwal and Anujayesh Krishna, in their chapter, 'Strategic Human Capital Management and Banking Governance: An Unexplored Symbiotic Relationship in PSBs', look at the HR challenges in PSBs and propose a set of HR reforms that should engage the attention of the board and provide a pathway to build resilient and robust banks. They also propose a draft human capital reporting template for use by individual banks arguing that it is in line with emerging international best practices and provide 'organizational health benefits'. Atul Kumar's chapter titled, 'Honouring Legacy while Embracing Evolution: The Ethics Narrative in SBI', throws light on the importance and relevance of ethics in the context of a large bank with a rich history and the structure and processes that seek to cement the ethical dimensions into business conduct.

Section 3 focuses on leadership, the crucial link that has a key role to play in practically every challenge that banks face today. While there is no dearth of material on leadership, there is conspicuous lack of material on leadership that is rooted in the Indian cultural and banking context and is practice driven. Anil K. Khandelwal's chapter titled, 'Banking Transformation as a Leadership Experience: Fifteen Actionable Insights from the Trenches', fills in this much felt gap. Based on his own personal experience as chairman and CEO of Bank of Baroda, the chapter shares the success story of transformation in a large-size, geographically dispersed, highly unionized and government-controlled bank in India. He argues that the focus on intangibles, such as fostering responsible culture, fixing accountability all across, deflating internal bureaucracy, respecting field wisdom, rejuvenating HR function, and innovations in customer service can bring dramatic transformation in the fortunes of the bank. The chapter provides 15 actionable insights from direct experience from the field. Pritam Singh and Asha Bhandarker's chapter, 'Organizational Transformational: Agenda for Indian Banks', brings out the role of transformational leaders as enablers, excellence seekers, direction setters, visionary strategist as well as role models to transform their banks. Abinash Panda's chapter, 'Grooming leaders in Public Sector Banks: Proposing a Leadership Development Process', argues that leadership development and succession planning remain Achilles' heel for PSBs. The author suggests a six-stage leadership development framework and process for leadership development for PSBs. Raj Bowen's chapter, 'Coaching and Mentoring: The Unsung and Underutilized Warriors of Leadership Development', discusses the criticality of coaching and mentoring at the heart of leadership development strategy and argues that this needs attention at the board and CEO levels. The next chapter covers the bank's culture using a 'field lens'. In the chapter titled, 'Crafting and "Living" the Bank's Culture: Notes from the Field', Anil Sachdev and Shyam Viswanathan argue that leadership development and crafting of enabling cultures are key business processes that require the attention of the board so that talent risk is given as much importance as financial risk in banks. Based on many decades of experience in assisting major Indian and global firms including banks in their transformation journeys, the authors define a seven-step process for building inspiring cultures that could transform these institutions. In the next chapter, 'Leadership in Times of Crisis: Lessons from COVID-19 Crisis', Prasenjit Bhattacharya discusses the central concern about employee wellness post COVID-19 and how ambiguity, fear, stress and work from home can add to the negative impact on health and wellness. Gordhan K. Saini, in his chapter, 'Employer Branding to Build Human Capital Advantage', argues that employer branding has a significant relevance to the service sector, including the banking sector, as revenues and profits depend on quality and customer satisfaction. Kuriakose Mamkoottam in his chapter, 'Trade Unions in the Digital Economy with Special Reference to the Banking Sector in India', examines some of the special features of digital economy and future role of trade unions with special reference to the banking sector in India.

Section 4 deals with the issues surrounding talent in the banking sector. Nishchae Suri's chapter, 'Skilling Is a New Currency: Are You a Learning

Organization?', argues that in these unprecedented and challenging times learning fitness or learning health of organizations provides collective ability to perform. The author shares his study on organizational learning health and shares that banking, as an industry, is ranked among the lowest when it comes to learning health. Rajiv Jayaraman's chapter, 'A New Manifesto for CHROs in the Era of Digital Change', focuses on the role of HR leadership in the digital change process and presents key methodologies that HR leaders can use to engage the organization and build future-ready capabilities and foster a culture that sustains successful digital initiatives. Rajeshwari Narendran's chapter, 'A Journey from Transactional to Transformational Function: HR Research Value Add in Banking', argues that it is imperative that HR function and strategies are based on reliable data and insights about the people issues. M. Mahapatra, in his chapter, 'Challenges of HR in Indian Public Sector Banks: Reflections and Confessions of a CEO', describes through an interesting parable the challenges of HR in PSB. Prakash Ranjan, in his chapter, 'A Passionate Journey of Continuous Transformation in HR', travels through a journey spanning more than two decades in different organizations and shares how the professional practice of HR function has created better business outcomes. In the final chapter, 'Wellness and Yoga: Investment for the Bankers', Ashish Pandey argues for the importance of well-being amidst the tumult of the banking sector and proposes that yoga-based practices and meditation may be effective in dealing with these challenges with their positive impact on physical, psychological and spiritual well-being.

Part 2: Collection of Case Studies

Although Indian banking is beset with numerous challenges, there have been a few transformational initiatives to build banks for the future. Part 2 of the book contains four such case studies from leading banks, namely State Bank of India (SBI), Bank of Baroda, ICICI Bank and Union Bank of India. It is hoped that through these case studies the best practices in this area will get wider currency, recognition and adoption.

The first case study covers the transformation process at SBI, the largest bank in India. Its transformation efforts have spanned across many areas of HR as well as facilitated the business goals of the bank. The areas of HR transformation covered in this case include initiatives such as 'Saksham', 'Abhivyakti', 'Sanjeevani', 'Nayi Disha' and 'SBI GEMS'. This case study covers the training and development within SBI including its comprehensive infrastructure and training initiatives. The case study also covers the role played by HR in the merger process and digital transformation.

The second case study on Bank of Baroda covers the professionaliza-tion of HR function. It covers the change process within the HR function itself, including how the foundation laid in 2005–2008 by the then CEO was carried forward and the scaling up of the HR philosophy and processes was continued. One of the highlights of the professionalization within the HR function was setting up of the steering committee of the board on HR. This has not only resulted in strategic thinking and leader-ship towards the HR function but also has downstream benefits like higher visibility to the HR function and leadership development.

The case study on ICICI Bank shows the role of organizational DNA anchors in building contemporary HR processes. The case study sheds light on building industry academia partnership, a key initiative, and the role it played in strengthening the leadership and HR processes.

The fourth case study on Union Bank of India describes the digitalization within the HR function. This digital transformation covered six key levers of HR, namely (a) way of working, (b) training, (c) employee engagement, (d) talent management, (e) culture and (f) employee relations.

Part 3: Collection of Interviews

The third part of the book presents the individual (one-on-one) interviews from the senior leaders and observers (academicians) from the banking industry. These leaders and observers were involved with banking sector for decades and have seen it up and close. Their insights on how the banks function, their constraints and areas where reform is needed are both deep and fundamental to the ways we should think about banking in the future. Taken altogether, these insights make a compelling reading as well as a case for reform in the areas of intangibles.

The first interview with Kewal Handa (former non-executive chairman, Union Bank of India) points out the serious risk posed by the talent gaps in PSBs and the need to have both autonomy and differentiation in policies to leverage on human capital. In Handa's view, the future of PSBs depends on how independent and how flexible they are in terms of hiring, compensation and creating performance culture. He strongly feels that it is time to free PSBs from administrative clutches to build an independent board, to which the top management must be made accountable.

In his interview, Ajay Nanavati (former non-executive chairman, Syndicate Bank) laments the lack of a customer-centric mindset and a culture of risk-taking and modern systems of HR, especially recruitment methodolo-gies, compensation mechanisms and continuity of leadership at the top level.

HR function needs total transformation with professionalization of HR. In Nanavati's view, PSBs require an empowered and independent board, CEOs with minimum tenure of 4–5 years, differentiated policies for compensation and autonomy for lateral recruitment for the senior level.

Ravi Venkatesan (former non-executive chairman, Bank of Baroda) and Biju Varkkey (professor, IIM Ahmedabad) suggest the need for serious reform measures in the area of HR and governance. They point out that a whole lot of factors, such as low trust systems, unwillingness to take risk, hierarchical issues and learning gaps, limit the potential of PSBs. They observe that the HR function requires complete overhaul. They opine that considering the challenges of digital banking, incremental reforms will not produce desired outcomes.

H. Krishnamurthy (chief research scientist (retired), Indian Institute of Science, Bengaluru) looks at the symbiotic relationship between technology and human capital, and how they could reinforce each other, if done in the right way. He feels that the technology and HR specialists as members of the board can bring in tremendous value addition for strategic decision-making.

T. V. Rao (former professor, IIM Ahmedabad) has seen the high and low points in the growth of human resource development in the banking industry as well as in the country itself. Rao feels that the record of PSBs in remodelling HR function is not encouraging except for some prime banks such as SBI and Bank of Baroda. The HR function has remained merely an administrative function. Rao feels that CEO is the driving force for building HR function and future of the bank and this task cannot be delegated. Similarly, professionally qualified and trained HR professionals are required for continuity. He laments the fact that excessive regulations and bureaucracy have obfuscated the development of HR function. Banks need a new breed of leaders to build such a culture.

In the last interview of this series, Arun Kumar (chairman, KPMG India) stresses the urgency before CEOs and feels that never before have CEOs and their teams been more in need of foresight and seasoned judgement. He points to the untapped human potential in PSBs and feels that for HR to make a true contribution, it needs to be an agile business partner. Referring to the current pandemic, his message is that HR has a big role to play to foster and advance the agenda of keeping people at the centre of firm's consideration.

The book comes at a time when Indian banking is undergoing crisis. It gives a strong message that unless banks become robust institutions by addressing governance, leadership, talent and culture, the sector is likely to remain in a perpetual crisis mode. It is expected that this book will empower practitioners, leaders and employees and provide food for thought and reflection to other stakeholders such as regulators, government, shareholders, trade unions and industry associations.

References

Acharya, V. V., & Rajan, R. (2020). Indian banks: A time to reform?

Dweck, C. S. (2016). *Mindset: The new psychology of success.* Ballantine Books.

Jain, M. A. (2016, November 24). Infographic: Little known facts about India's banking network. *The Hindustan Times.* https://www.thehindubusinessline.com/economy/infographic-little-known-facts-about-indias-banking-network/article9381949.ece

Khan, Z., Raghuvanshi, G., Taqi, M. A. (2020, September 13). Low valuation, rising bad debt limit India state banks' capital-raising options. S&P Global. Market Intelligence. https://www.spglobal.com/marketintelligence/en/news-insights/latest-news-headlines/low-valuation-rising-bad-debt-limit-india-state-banks-capital-raising-options-60241062

Khandelwal Committee. (2010, June). Report of the committee on HR issues of public sector banks. https://financialservices.gov.in/sites/default/files/HRIssuesOfPSBs.pdf

Rick, T. (2014). Organizational culture eats strategy for breakfast, lunch and dinner. Meliorate. https://www.torbenrick.eu/blog/culture/organisational-culture-eats-strategy-for-breakfast-lunch-and-dinner/

PART 1

Essays from Academics and Practitioners

CHAPTER

1

The Changing Context of Governance and Leadership in Public Sector Banks

M. S. Sriram

Introduction

The Indian financial system, which is dominated by the banking system, is a curious amalgam of multiple types of players, and we have listed the banking sector in Table 1.1 to provide a flavour of the range of institutions operating within this space. We locate the public sector banks (PSBs) in this larger rubric in order to clearly understand what ails them. It is not that all PSBs perform badly, neither is it that a given PSB performs very well consistently for a reasonable period of time. Therefore, the problem of governance and leadership in PSBs is a complex issue that should be unbundled. There have been visionary and transformational leaders in this space, but we still need to ask the question as to whether these leaders were there by design, or did they just use the opportunity that came their way to make a difference out of an individual initiative. If we were to classify the Indian banking space into the ownership categories of predominantly state owned and privately owned and do a sub-classification under these categories, we get a complex jigsaw that is detailed in Table 1.1.

For the purpose of this chapter, we shall only look at the banks that are broadly in the control of the state and, in particular, the PSBs that were nationalized in 1969 and 1980, respectively. While a total of 20 banks were nationalized, we now have 11 of these after a series of mergers, the first being

Table 1.1 Structure and Ownership of Banking Structure in India

Ownership	Category		Description
Privately Owned		Foreign Banks	There are 46 scheduled foreign banks either as wholly owned subsidiaries or branches.
		Local Area Banks, Small Finance Banks and Payment Banks	There are 3 local area banks, 10 small finance banks and 6 payments banks incorporated as corporations.
		New Gen Pvt Banks	There are eight new-generation private sector banks.
		Old Generation Private Banks	Old private sector banks that were incorporated, licensed and in operation prior to nationalization of the banks in 1969 and were not nationalized. We now have 13 old-generation private sector banks. At the time of nationalization, there were more than 15 private sector banks that were not nationalized.
State Owned	State Controlled	Incorporated under the Companies Act	IDBI Bank. This was initially a Developmental Financial Institution under the IDBI Act. It was converted into a company in December 2003. The conversion of the bank to a company still provided the state power to ensure that it had protection from some provisions of the Banking Regulation Act, including not seeking a licence from the regulator—RBI (GOI, 2003). For a brief while there was also Bharatiya Mahila Bank, which was later merged with State Bank of India.
	Incorporated under Special Legislations		Regional Rural Banks (RRBs) that operate under the RRB Act of 1976. At the peak, there were 196 RRBs. In the past decade after a series of mergers we now have 45 RRBs.
			PSBs nationalized under the Bank Nationalisation Act in two phases, 1969 and 1980. While the total number of banks that were nationalized was 14 and 6, respectively, we currently have 11 banks after a series of mergers.
			SBI under the State Bank of India Act. Till recently, its associate banks were also a part of the group. SBI was nationalized in 1955 and the associate banks in 1959. They were all merged into a single entity in 2017.

Local area banks operate in a limited geographical area and are restricted from opening urban branches. Small finance banks are expected to have half of their portfolio in loan sizes less than ₹2.5 million and 75 per cent of their portfolio in priority sector. Payment banks can do remittances, can accept savings up to ₹100,00 but cannot lend.

Of these, Yes Bank which got into financial difficulties is currently having a majority stake from the state-owned entities.

Of the above, Nainital Bank is 99 per cent owned by Bank of Baroda. The Government of India and the Government of Jammu and Kashmir (now Government of India) have a 59 per cent stake in the J&K Bank. DCB Bank was a co-operative bank that was converted into a corporation. Some of the old banks such as Bank of Madura and Bank of Rajasthan were taken over by ICICI Bank, Vysya Bank was taken over by Kotak Mahindra Bank and United Western Bank was merged into IDBI Bank.

It was declared as a private sector bank with effect from January 2019.[1] While it is categorized as a private sector bank, it is still indirectly owned by the state through a set of state-owned entities including Life Insurance Corporation of India, which is a majority shareholder in the bank. It has serving officials of the Government of India on the board.

The ownership is divided between PSBs (sponsor banks), the union government and the respective state government where they are present. The RRB Act was recently amended to open up the possibility of private shareholding with the proviso that the combined shareholding of the union and state governments and the sponsor banks would not go below 51 per cent (GOI, 2015).

Initially, the ownership was fully vested with the Government of India. Currently, the state has a majority stake in these banks with the rest being held by public and institutional investors.

Initially, the ownership was divided between RBI and the Government of India but now, while the Government of India owns nearly 59 per cent of the shares, the rest of the shares are held by public and institutional investors (SBI, 2020).

[1] https://www.idbibank.in/idbi-bank-history.asp

New Bank of India merging with Punjab National Bank (PNB) and in the past two years, a series of banks have integrated into a smaller number. In addition, there are now reports that the state would be satisfied in having only five banks under its control and would seek to divest its stake and privatize the other banks as a part of its future strategy.[2] There is also news that the Reserve Bank of India (RBI) has recently advised the government to cut its stake in PSBs to 51 per cent,[3] thereby increasing the participation of the markets in the capital structure.

Governance Structure of PSBs

The governance structure of PSBs is a marvel in theory and a nightmare in practice. While it is quite normal to call something that is not workable a theoretical possibility, in the real world, this is much more nuanced. Good theory is an abstraction of practice and good practice is an articulation of the theory. These two constantly inform one another. However, why do we say that the PSB governance is a marvel and a nightmare at the same time? For this, it would be good to understand the regulatory and legal ecosystem in which the banks operate.

1. The 11 PSBs are governed by the Bank Nationalisation Act and are not incorporated under the Companies Act. While they are listed and have public shareholding, operate as for-profit corporations and for all practical purposes behave like a company, they are not governed by the Companies Act. Therefore, any change in the regulatory ecosystem need not always automatically apply to these banks. They are exempt from certain provisions of the Banking Regulation Act and other statutes, sometimes implicitly and sometimes explicitly, making these entities accountable more to the ministry to which they belong to, rather than the regulatory dharma. This arrangement is a statutory arrangement and has little to do with the majority ownership of the entities. While the level of public shareholding dictates the number of directors on the board that can represent the minority shareholders, the rest of the appointments are done by the state. Similarly, the State Bank of India (SBI) is governed by a separate State Bank of India Act, and IDBI Bank and J&K Bank are

[2] https://www.livemint.com/industry/banking/govt-plans-to-reduce-number-of-psu-banks-to-just-five-report-11595243683640.html

[3] https://www.business-standard.com/article/finance/cut-stake-in-top-public-sector-banks-to-51-in-12-18-months-rbi-to-govt-120080300047_1.html

designated as companies under the Companies Act. We restrict a more detailed examination of banks under the Bank Nationalisation Act.

2. The writ of the regulator does not equally apply to all the banks, and, therefore, there are limitations in the actions that the RBI could take as a regulator. This was highlighted by the former governor of RBI, Urjit Patel, in his speech wherein he had highlighted the limitations of the functions of the regulator (Patel, 2018).[4] Banking, being a function of leverage by public deposits, has to have a stronger supervisory framework as against other financial institutions, and, therefore, under the Banking Regulation Act, the regulator (RBI) has the power to remove directors, supersede a bank board, force a merger, put banks under moratoriums, revoke the licence or even liquidate a bank.

3. The governance structure—the board of a bank could be called a marvel—because it represents all the diversity and interests that need to be included—people with larger public interests, minority shareholders, workmen and officers, representative of the Ministry of Finance and that of the RBI, wholetime directors, a professional chartered accountant, all these appointments are done at the behest of the state. The representative from the ministry usually has a disproportionate say, essentially because it is the line department that controls the institution and the ministry has a direct line of communication with the management of the bank which bypasses the board. This is where the marvel becomes a nightmare.

4. The nomination and remuneration committee checks for the fit-and-proper criteria of independent directors representing minority shareholders but has no say in the appointment of the other directors who are placed by the government through an order. The writ of RBI does not apply to either appointment or the removal of these directors.

Appointment Process of the Management

The appointment process of the management, the managing director and the wholetime directors, is largely done outside of the board. Earlier, this used to be done by the Ministry of Finance, with a panel representing the ministry, RBI and invited experts. The recommendations of the panel had to go through checks for vigilance and would eventually be approved by the Appointments Committee of the Cabinet (ACC; Nayak, 2014).

[4] https://www.rbi.org.in/scripts/BS_SpeechesView.aspx?Id=1054

While the panel is no longer in operation, it has been replaced by the Banks Board Bureau (BBB) which has members serving for a term. They recommend the appointments which are then considered by ACC. Ultimately, the appointments happen not through the process of governance but through the process of government. Usually, the appointments to the post of the wholetime directors happen from a pool of qualified general managers or equivalent of all the PSBs (including SBI). Similarly, the appointments for the post of managing director and chief executive officer (CEO) happen from the pool of wholetime directors. This has multiple challenges that have been discussed as follows.

Culture: This process of appointment means that neither the wholetime directors nor the CEO would be from the bank they are appointed to. If it happens to be the same bank, it is more of a chance than a choice. Therefore, the leadership takes time to assimilate the culture and working style of the banks and takes time to understand the strengths of the team they are working with.

Tenure: Both the positions have short tenures, and, therefore, it is difficult for the incumbent to build a long horizon as there is a constant churn. This is particularly true of PSBs. In case of SBI, the practice has been to have all the wholetime directors and the chairman from within SBI, which has given the bank years of stability and the incumbents are largely from the ranks of the bank. If we see a marked difference between the work culture of other PSBs and SBI, this may be one of the reasons.

Accountability: As we indicated earlier, the accountability of the management is naturally towards the appointing authority, which in this case is the state, and not to the governing board. Thus, the governing board is a relatively weaker player in the hierarchy, having been appointed by the same authority that appoints the management. While BBB created a layer of insularity between ACC and the bank, in effect, the shots are called by the state even on operational matters when they are of public interest.

Regulatory writ: We have already seen that the governor RBI had in the past indicated that the regulatory writ of RBI does not equally apply to PSBs. It is not only about appointments and removal of top management or replacement of the board but also the basic function of licensing banks, imposing moratoriums, mergers and appointing administrators—all actions that a regulator could undertake, cannot be undertaken essentially because the law of incorporation is different and the law that enables the regulator—the Banking Regulation Act—is blunted in this case. In this sense, the management of the bank is insulated from the regulator to a large extent.

Market incentives: While the management is accountable to the markets as entities that are listed and each of them go through the motions of disclosure, their existence does not get threatened if there is a loss of value in the market. Every time there is an erosion of the market value, they need not necessarily go back to the market for recapitalization. That recapitalization could come from the state or through entities owned or controlled by the state. The recent example of IDBI Bank (albeit being classified as a private sector bank) being bailed out by LIC of India is an example as to how the state-owned banks could bypass the market discipline and the loss of value does not affect the existence or growth of the bank. This leaves little for the management to be accountable for, much less the governance system.

Implications of the Current System

Much has been written about the implications of the current system on banking. The predominant argument has been recently provided by the former governor of RBI, Urjit Patel, who calls this a trilemma, that there is a dominant state-owned banking system, that there is limited fiscal space with the state and these two turn out to be a combination that could affect the market principles of efficiency and profitability negatively (Patel, 2020). While Patel sees this largely as a challenge for an independent regulator (that explains the trilemma), who is also largely under the state, it is much more than that. We need to look at this aspect from multiple policy choices and look at the broader intent of the state, and therefore the actions to be taken.

State-owned Institutions as Tools of Development and Growth

If we were to look at the history of banking in India, till we embarked on market-based reforms in 1991, the thinking of the state has been largely within the realm of the state. That intent was expressed explicitly in the nationalization of banks in 1969 and in the second round of nationalization in 1980. While there were a few banks left in the private sector, all the big banks came under the fold of the state. The logic that is apparent in the process of the ownership is that the state then controls not only the ownership but also the operational details of how these institutions operate. The state determines the priorities that serve the its agenda and carries them out through both the ownership and the strategic, tactical and operational control of the institutions. This is in one sense what Patel calls fiscalization of banking, making the line between the developmental objective of the state and the commercial objective of a bank rather blurred. If the state also announces the credit budgets (Patel, 2020), then these decisions are taken on the priorities of the state and not necessarily on the commercials. If we assume no cronyism in the decisions, even then, the decisions are based more on the priority of the state. There is also an argument that this fiscal dominance is a result of the twin deficits, the fiscal deficit and the current account deficit, which results in the crowding out of the corporate sector getting into low productivity traps (Acharya, 2020).

This is fine if we do not distinguish between the special purpose vehicles of the state as an extended arm of the state without the need for market participation. For instance, it is quite possible that we have a commercial entity substantially owned by the state with no significant competitors either by choice or by design such as Hindustan Aeronautics Limited or semi-autonomous organizations like the Indian Space Research Organisation, then it is evident that the discipline of the market does not necessarily apply. This was the case for Air India before the aviation sector was opened up to private players and this has been the case for PSBs as well. However, once the sector is opened up for market-based players and competition, the rules of the game substantially change unless we continue to treat the state-owned institutions as special institutions with a special purpose.

When we moved towards the process of finding market-based solutions in 1991 through the process of liberalization, the rules of the engagement changed fundamentally even for the banks. With the licensing of new PSBs, there was a large overlap in the areas where both the public and the private banks operated, and therefore competed. While the private banks did not have to carry the cross of the developmental agenda of the state, the state-owned banks continued to have this responsibility of not only carrying the credit budget of the finance minister (Patel, 2020), but also of implementing several schemes that were oriented towards inclusion and the poor.

Is it necessary for the state to use the ownership and control of banking institutions to further its developmental agenda, or is it possible for the state to treat its banks as commercial market-based institutions competing with the new banks and achieve the developmental agenda through any other means? This is an interesting question. The state has routinely addressed the developmental agenda through market-based institutions and the ownership of the banks is not really necessary. The branch licensing policy and the priority sector lending policy are a testament to achieve some developmental agenda through policy and regulatory interventions. In addition, the state could specifically subsidize certain activities that it considers important by providing for the viability of those activities, like opening and maintaining

Jan Dhan accounts. Therefore, the logic that was applicable at the time of nationalization—of having a dominant share in the banking activities—is no longer valid. In fact, as the private sector keeps gaining market share, any developmental agenda that the state-owned banks take up ends up hurting their ability to compete and eats into the profits and makes them more and more dependent on the state. This is a vicious circle and reduces the degrees of freedom that the management can exercise, even if they were to do so. With the value destruction they cannot exercise the option (if they had) of approaching the markets; every time the State pumps in resources, it imposes additional conditionalities and takes away more and more operational autonomy. This is a structural problem.

Private Banks and Developmental Agenda

As the market share of the private banks grow, they tend to take away the best of the clients and the most profitable portfolios. The private banks have the flexibility, agility and the power to make quick decisions. They are unifocal on the bottom line and are able to provide better pricing (because of efficiency triggered by low administrative cost) and better services (because of technology). However, the private banks do not have a direct line of command from the Ministry of Finance, their functioning is through the governance of the board of directors; the CEOs get a decent tenure and when they are found wanting, are let go. They are accountable to the market and the earliest signs of being lax show up in the valuation, which gives them an opportunity to auto correct. Since these institutions are completely focused on the bottom line, all developmental agenda is taken up either through an agency approach or is adhered to minimally or innovated to fetch profits. Let us review three examples.

In order to reach the smallest customers, the microfinance sector is serving many private banks who have acquired microfinance companies. The modus operandi is similar: Acquire a large enough microfinance institution, transfer the portfolio to the bank's books but keep the entity as a wholly owned subsidiary which works as an outsourcing agent to the bank. The staff of the erstwhile microfinance institution get compensated at lower levels and continue to generate the portfolio that sits in the bank's balance sheet. So they get the advantage of not only the low administrative costs but also that of high pricing for these loans. This model could be replicated by PSBs, but the pricing would naturally be questioned because they are public institutions and are not only answerable to the shareholders but also to the Parliament through the standing committees. So the pricing flexibility, although is theoretically available, would be constraining due to the public nature of ownership and the multi-accountability framework.

Try and work around risky loans through innovative collaterals. Agri gold loans, formation of joint liability groups and aggregation of transactions through arrangements with output buyers through tied contracts are several of the tricks that these institutions manage.

The third strategy is to look at the rule in its letter and pick up the most lucrative portfolio that qualifies for meeting the targets. Instead of doing crop-based agricultural loans, make loans for collateralized purposes like tractors, look at livestock with an insurance cover and agro-processing. They also constantly engage with the regulator to define and redefine the bucket so that they continue to work in the margins. And of course, any shortfall beyond that could be filled in through a securitization deal or through the purchase of priority lending certificates.

So, in a way, the profit-focused enterprises are actually leaning on the state-owned banks to do the dirty work and operate at the margins. In the process, the state-owned banks not only lose the portfolio that has intense market competition and margins but are also left with a more and more cost-intensive portfolio. Eventually, the portfolio of the state-owned banks is pre-decided because of the nature of its ownership.

Ownership or Leadership: The Conundrum

Till now, we have argued why the root cause of the problem of the PSBs is the ownership. Is this completely true? Are we then saying that the state system does not provide effective leaders? How does this explain some exemplary commercial institutions working under the overall supervision and ownership of the state? Is the ownership preventing good leadership from coming up? Why are several scholars as well as practitioners advocating the privatization of banks as a possible solution (Acharya & Rajan, 2020)? These are some questions that we need to address.

Let us look at this conundrum from within the banking sector first and then look at the interventions to see transformation of leadership. When we unbundle this, we find some of the elements or constraints are related to the way the ownership of the banks are structured and, therefore, how this ownership structure defines the position of a CEO. Some of the elements pertain to the person who is occupying the position which defines the elements of leadership embedded in the person.

If we were to look at SBI, which was nationalized much earlier than the other banks, it seems to perform fairly well, amongst all the nationalized banks. What is it that makes SBI distinct from the other banks? Why is the market perception (in terms of market capitalization in relation to its business size) more favourable in the case of SBI compared to that of the other banks? If we were to break it up and see, we would find some fundamental differences.

SBI due to its size has many more leadership positions as against the other PSBs. Apart from having an executive chairman, it also has multiple managing directors and several deputy managing directors. In general, the leadership role of SBI has always been from within the ranks. Therefore, there is no unexpected instability at the top, unlike the other PSBs where the whole-time directors come in from another bank and move on to another bank (if they have age on their side) or retire in a short duration. The board of SBI also has representatives of the ministry and the regulator at a much more senior level (secretary and deputy governor, respectively), and, therefore, we surmise that there is a much greater consideration on the direction in which the bank has to move. Since this also happens to be the banker of first choice for the state, there is a lot of business that comes its way naturally. Therefore, the bank is seen from a different lens as compared to the other PSBs. This is one case where the ownership has not affected the leadership role of the bank and, in general, SBI is valued as among the best state-controlled banks by the market. Its market capitalization is the best, both in terms of absolute numbers and as a relationship to the total business from among the state-controlled banks. However, being the largest bank in India with regard to business size, its market capitalization is the third largest, falling behind a relatively smaller bank like the Kotak Mahindra Bank (see Table 1.2). Interestingly, IDBI Bank, which is state controlled but declared as a private bank, has a much greater market capitalization in comparison to its total business which is an interesting signal for us to read. Both these banks seem to indicate that ownership per se might not be a limiting factor, but the structure of leadership and the framework in which they operate seem to be having some implication.

In the past, there has been much debate on whether the ownership of banks should continue with the state and if it were possible to insulate the banks from the operational control of the state. While the overwhelming argument has been that the state should have control over a smaller number of banks and move towards disinvestment in the rest of the banks as a first step and let go of the operational control irrespective of ownership, this has not received adequate traction from the state. There have been instances where the state has moved in this direction but has quickly stepped back to status quo *ex ante*. Starting with the Narasimham Committee of 1991

Table 1.2 Total Business Size and Market Capitalization of Various Banks (₹ in Billion)[5]

Public Sector/State Controlled	Business	Mcap	Old Private Sector Banks	Business	Mcap	New Private Sector Banks	Business	Mcap
IDBI Bank	3,520.59	200.35	City Union Bank	747.60	95.59	Kotak Mahindra	5,102.79	2,565.31
IOB	3,442.85	116.54	CSB Bank	271.57	20.55	AU Small Finance Bank	531.56	155.92
SBI	56,484.72	1,757.70	RBL Bank	1,158.18	69.01	Bandhan	1,237.11	327.94
UCO Bank	2,943.78	89.86	DCB Bank	557.15	29.49	HDFC Bank	21,898.78	4,732.62
Canara	15,200.00	385.61	Federal Bank	2,771.01	81.84	Ujjivan Small Finance bank	248.24	47.35
Bank of Maharashtra	2,369.22	51.89	Dhanlaxmi Bank	174.00	4.07	ICICI Bank	15,070.31	2,101.50
PNB	17,940.00	304.43	Karur Vysya	1,051.73	16.19	Yes Bank	2,767.44	281.76
Union Bank	14,590.00	231.92	Lakshmi Vilas	352.71	3.69	Axis Bank	12,251.16	1,070.39
Central Bank	4,661.54	69.66	Karnataka Bank	1,287.49	13.10	IDFC First Bank	1,506.74	119.69
Bank of Baroda	16,797.68	247.43	South Indian Bank	1,474.73	10.42	IndusInd Bank	4,088.10	243.55

Bank of India	9,280.31	105.68
Indian Bank	8,080.00	48.68
J&K Bank	1,621.85	8.85
Punjab & Sind	1,480.79	7.82
Total	158,413.32	3,626.41	9,846.18	343.97	64,702.24	11,646.01

[5] The market capitalization figures and the business numbers are as of 31 March 2020. However, in case of Punjab National Bank, Canara Bank, Indian Bank and Union Bank of India, which were in the process of merger with other banks, the total business numbers are not available as on 31 March 2020. Therefore, the numbers used are based on the individual balance sheets of each of the banks proposed in the merger plan and added to the merged entity based on the numbers of 31 March 2019. Since we are not making a granular statistical analysis, these numbers are a fair indication of the ballpark figures that are used for the larger argument. The source of all the numbers is https://www.moneycontrol.com/stocks/marketinfo/marketcap/bse/bank-private.html where the database of the banks is maintained.

and 1998 and several committees that followed, such as the Khandelwal Committee, the Raghuram Rajan Committee and the Nayak Committee, have all suggested that the state should reduce the controlling stake and provide more autonomy to the banks. However, each of the committees has been guarded in its approach of approaching the issue gradually. Selling off the banks or privatizing them in a big way would unnecessarily create controversies. As a result, there are many intermediary mechanisms that have been suggested.

For instance, the Khandelwal Committee among other issues suggested that there needs to be succession planning in the top management and a fixed tenure for CEO in addition to several measures of capability building and planning which were a mechanism of developing a longer term vision for the bank (Khandelwal, 2010). The Nayak Committee made a nuanced distinction between the government as an investor, as an owner and as a sovereign, and highlighted the conflation of issues when these were mixed. They suggested divestment of stake to less than a majority stake and in the interim have an intermediary mechanism of a Bank Investment Company and BBB (Nayak, 2014). The state on its part has varyingly implemented some of the recommendations made by the experts, but never has it bitten the bullet of the question of ownership and control.

The best attempt for the reform of the banking system came in when the new government took over in 2014. It appeared for a while that the intellectual discourse was being met by political action and the state was willing to let go of the operational control of the banks. Early indications of this action came in January 2015 when the government organized the first Gyan Sangam—a retreat of the directors of PSBs in the National Institute of Bank Management in Pune, in which the prime minister participated personally. In August 2015, the project Indradhanush was announced, highlighting a seven-point agenda for reforming the banks. For the first time after the Narasimham Committee had articulated reforms, it appeared that the state was moving ahead with some changes at the structural level rather than at the operational level of changing prudential norms and capital adequacy. The Indradhanush plan was followed up by announcing the first BBB in the finance minister's budget speech in February 2016 where it was mentioned that 'The Bank Board Bureau will be operationalized during 2016–17 and a roadmap for consolidation of Public Sector Banks will be spelt out'.[6] The setting up of BBB was preceded by some actions that coincided with the announcement of project Indradhanush, the roles of the

---

[6] https://www.indiabudget.gov.in/doc/bspeech/bs201617.pdf

chairman and managing director of PSBs were split. The state went ahead and appointed CEOs laterally from the private sector for two large banks—Canara Bank and Bank of Baroda. Bank of Baroda even got a non-executive chairman from the private sector.[7] These actions indicated that the state was taking the intermediate steps to make these institutions market facing. BBB became operational in April 2016 (for a discussion on the chronology of these reforms see George (2020)).

The next indication of the political discourse being at variance with the intellectual discourse came in when BBB started expressing concern about its limited autonomy and its inability to fundamentally change the governance system to be market facing. Of the various mandates that were sought by BBB, the following mandates were not granted to it.[8]

1. Recommendations be placed directly before the Appointments Committee of the Cabinet.
2. Search and selection of non-executive directors on PSB boards.
3. To develop a road map for transition of the government shareholding into a bank holding company.
4. A specific mandate on stressed asset resolution strategies.

The compendium further states that there is much more to be done in order to get the governance of these banks in order, including aspects like 'The non-executive Directors nominated/appointed by the Government on PSB Boards may not fulfil the criteria of Independent Directors'.[9] This compendium is a document that not only reveals that the steps needed for governance reforms were not being taken but also indicates that the intent to move in that direction seemed to be lacking. Here is a quote, 'These recommendations were made by the Bureau on March 15, 2017. The Bureau awaits latest updates from the DFS on the status of these recommendations'. The quote is from the compendium placed in the public domain a year later. Clearly, the reforms at the governance level do not pass the test of intent of the state. The reasons for this are obvious and not exclusive to the banking institutions. The state would not like to cede control of a set of institutions that are working for its larger welfare and redistributive objective, bearing the costs of those objectives through a lesser profitability.

---

[7] https://financialservices.gov.in/sites/default/files/PressnoteIndardhanush.pdf
[8] The compendium of recommendations made by BBB placed on 19 March 2018 on the website of BBB. https://banksboardbureau.org.in/WhatsNew/Details?id=13
[9] https://banksboardbureau.org.in/upload/PDF/Chapter5_190318.pdf

If ownership and control are essential to undertake a developmental role of the banking sector, the move is understandable. However, this is not a narrative that we have heard from the state to justify the policy moves. Therefore, even CEOs who came from outside and tried to bring some transformational changes (George, 2020) had limited tenures and moved on and the system regressed to its old methods.

Looking at the above issues, we can safely conclude that the leadership issue is predicated upon the ownership and control issues. Therefore, it is important to address these issues before one addresses the issue of transformational leadership in a systemic manner.

Other Shortcomings of Ownership and Control

Concerns of Concentration

The world over, it is accepted that banks are special institutions and concentrated ownership of banks is not good from a governance point of view. In fact, the bank licensing policy in India prevents not only concentrated holdings, by making it compulsory to pare down the ownership within a certain timeframe, but also ensures that the voting right of any shareholder is capped at 10 per cent, irrespective of their holding. The banking policy also prevents providing banking licences to large industrial houses. These are based on sound arguments of the need to have a diversified ownership structure to ensure that nothing gets railroaded in an institution that is so dependent of depositor's trust. In this context, having banks with a predominant owner, even if it is the state, is problematic unless there is a specific and well-articulated developmental purpose.

Broader Accountability Framework

In addition to the risks of being predominantly owned by the bank and the resultant fiscalization, there are other issues of concentrated ownership to be considered. The so-called Chinese walls between the regulatory function, the ownership function, the profit function and the developmental functions get very blurred. Therefore, the predominant owner can bypass all the governance-level checks and balances and get things done as per the writ of the government of the day.

With government as an owner or controller (it is quite likely that the state could reduce its holdings to below 50% and still continue under the Bank Nationalisation Act, which makes it a controller), the banks would be bound by most of the heightened accountability norms that apply to public institutions. These include being subject to vigilance clearance and being governed the Prevention of Corruption Act and being answerable to the sovereign through the parliamentary committees. While we could show SBI as an exception where it has managed to do relatively well and be perceived so by the markets, the market capitalization of SBI is nowhere near the size it should justify. Therefore, the signalling that the state could intervene operationally in the affairs of a banking institution in itself is a negative signal to the markets.

Signalling the Intent Rather Strongly

The current approach of the state is consistently giving mixed signals. In the first instance, the state accepted the Nayak Committee report in essence and formed BBB. However, it did not move ahead with the Bank Investment Committee. It tried to focus on leadership and governance of the banks but only for a short duration. When the banks needed capital, instead of approaching the market, the state itself invested in the recapitalization process several times, and, thus, increased its holdings in a creeping manner. The state has responded positively to some of the prudential norms specified by Basel and has done several activities in the name of reform, such as consolidating banks, but has not done things that are structurally important. If we go by the recent press reports, it appears that apart from the ownership of 5–6 large banks, the state is willing to divest its holdings in other banks. But a formal announcement to this effect has not come yet. What would be the best path for the state in this context? We look at the framework for leadership in a comprehensive manner.

The state can no longer pretend that there is a developmental imperative that justifies its ownership of the banking system. There is ample evidence that the market-based institutions are not only growing at the cost of the state-owned enterprises, but they are also growing both in collecting deposits and provision of credit services. The potential of their growth is partly reflected by the faith reposed in these institutions by the markets. Irrespective of the performance on fundamentals, the private sector organizations are getting a consistently better valuation, which may indicate a perception that irrespective of the performance, the state may use its power on multiple axes to direct the banking sector to undertake activities that further its agenda, by announcing credit budgets and increasing fiscalization. Therefore, there has to be a clear signalling of the shrinkage of the role of the state in universal banks. If the state wants to own five large banks strategically and divest its holdings in the others, it is a matter of detail.

The first step in signalling this is to put the banks (including SBI) on a regulatory-level playing field. This would include repealing the respective acts under which they are incorporated and moving them to the Companies Act. The template of IDBI Bank is now readily available to the state.

The second step in signalling is that the state indicates that all incremental capitalization of the banks are to be done through the market route. Which essentially means that the holding of the state remains where it is (if it is a rights' issue) or use the market route not only to augment resources for the banks but also to use it for block sale of its ownership to the public at large.

The third step would be to have truly independent boards, which can be achieved by subjecting the state-owned (or controlled) banks to all the regulatory requirements of licensing that the RBI has—cap on voting rights, timeframe for disinvestment to make it widely held, and a fit-and-proper test for the governance structure and the key management personnel. This step is predicated on the first step.

The fourth step, as suggested by the Khandelwal Committee, is to look at each institution as an independent institution with its own culture, management and governance structure. This means that there would be no multi-institution-level wage settlement agreements for employees (Khandelwal, 2010). It also means that there would not be any lateral movements within the banks in a closed loop at senior level, but all movements would be in an open marketplace where leadership could come out of the loop as well.

The concern about the developmental function of the banks should be applied on a non-discriminatory basis for all institutions, as we see in the current applicability of priority sector targets and subsidy or defrayal of costs if needed.

While discussing the state-owned banks, there is another category of banks that needs some attention—these are the old private sector banks that pre-existed the nationalization era and were not nationalized because of their size. These banks continue to show middling performance and are more comparable to the state-owned banks in terms of their market capitalization. These banks, post liberalization, have not shown the appetite to grow. Some of them got taken over by the larger players, such as ING Vysya being taken over by Kotak Mahindra Bank, and Bank of Rajasthan and Bank of Madura taken over by ICICI Bank. There may be a case for the consolidation of these banks as well, as they are neither achieving scale nor serving a special niche that could be seen as unique.

While the above are the steps that could be taken for state-owned commercial banks, RRBs which continue to have a larger developmental agenda, with limited area for growth and restrictions on operating largely in rural areas with a heightened requirement of priority sector lending could continue to be state owned and controlled. The case for marketization of RRBs can be made only with significant urbanization of its catchment area and the willingness of the private sector to participate in the agenda. We do not see this happening in the near future, except for a few cases. In general, RRBs continue to have a justification for a state-driven developmental agenda.

Conclusion

Recently, the former governor and the deputy governor of RBI, in a co-authored paper, have suggested some drastic measures to reform the banking system. Some of the measures were initiated when they were in office, some to do with internal systems, but at the structural level, they have been advocating the market route as a strong measure of reform. However, their argument looks at insulating banking from the state, including a radical suggestion of closing the Department of Financial Services (DFS; which deals with banking) in the Ministry of Finance. They talk about re-privatization of banks—both, from the perspective of getting market discipline and as a prudent fiscal measure (Acharya & Rajan, 2020). However, this argument does not emanate out of a debate on the public policy imperative for the state in continuing to use banking as a tool for development. If we see the history of reforms, we find that the state had clearly adopted all the 'reforms' that do not affect control, be it adhering to Basel norms, prudential standards and capital adequacy. However, the issues of structural reforms that take away the operational control of the state have always been short changed. The best attempt was setting up of BBB, but even that has been rendered ineffective. This is because the state continues to use PSBs for delivering its developmental objectives. The campaign to open Jan Dhan accounts is a recent example of this.

In conclusion, we have to break up the agenda of the government into two broad imperatives: participating in the market place for financial services, for which a handful of significant institutions under the control of the state could operate effectively as market intervention, and disciplining institutions.

SBI performs this role currently, and there could be a few more large banks. The argument for reform, therefore, has to come with shifting the developmental agenda to niche institutions (including RRBs) which could be periodically recapitalized. These efforts will not only be decentralized but also will not have a similar fiscal burden. There has to be an acknowledgement of the fact that these institutions perform a public and developmental purpose in difficult and non-lucrative markets and these developmental imperatives should continue through non-market-facing special institutions like RRBs.

References

Acharya, V. V. (2020). *Quest for restoring financial stability in India.* SAGE Publications.

Acharya, V. V., & Rajan, R. (2020, September 25). *Indian banks: A time to reform?* https://faculty.chicagobooth.edu/-/media/faculty/raghuram-rajan/research/papers/paper-on-banking-sector-reforms-rr-va-final.pdf

George, R. G. (2020, January 1). Bank of Baroda: Governance challenges of a public sector institution no. IMB 801. https://hbsp.harvard.edu/product/IMB801-PDF-ENG?Ntt=rejie&itemFindingMethod=Search

GOI. (2003). *The Industrial Development Bank (Transfer of Undertaking and Repeal) Act, 2003.* Author. https://www.idbibank.in/pdf/about-us/repealact030709.pdf

GOI. (2015). *The Regional Rural Banks (Amendment) Act 2015.* Author. https://financialservices.gov.in/sites/default/files/163855_0.pdf

Khandelwal, A. (2010). *Report of the committee on HR issues in public sector banks.* Ministry of Finance, Government of India.

Narasimham, M. (1991). *Report of the committee on the financial system.* Government of India.

Narasimham, M. (1998). *Report of the committee on banking sector reforms.* Government of India.

Nayak, P. (2014). *Report of the committee to review the governance of boards of banks in India.* RBI.

Patel, U. (2018, March 14). Banking regulatory powers should be ownership neutral. https://www.rbi.org.in/scripts/BS_SpeechesView.aspx?Id=1054

Patel, U. (2020). *Overdraft: Saving the Indian saver.* Harper Business.

SBI. (2020). *Annual report 2019–20.* State Bank of India. https://www.sbi.co.in/documents/17826/35696/23062020_SBI+AR+2019-20+%28Time+16_3b11%29.pdf/a358b5ec-1d32-a093-d9ac-13071fda9ff6?t=1592911831224

Banking on Change

The Digital Revolution Is Now Here

Sushil Saluja

Introduction

Technology is shaping our lifetimes like no other force. The recent COVID-19 pandemic has accelerated the adoption of digital technology, reinforcing many of the trends that previously existed. We now live in a world where online education has been established literally overnight, physical supermarkets have given ground to online retailing and many people use social media as their primary source of news.

Customer needs and expectations are changing fast, banks are no longer the sole providers of financial services. You only have to look at the number of new digital banks in the world plus the moves of retailers and other industries to see that the traditional role of a retail bank is under threat. Survival of these retail banking institutions is by no means guaranteed.

Traditional forms of customer inertia cannot be relied upon, and the barriers to entry for new entrants will continue to get lower in the years ahead, catalysed by the introduction of 'open banking' and the Payment Systems Directive 2 (PSD2). The needs of the consumer are set to accelerate and financial institutions need to transform to keep up or risk extinction.

One myth is that digital illiteracy in countries such as India will prevent this, or at least slow it down. There is no doubt that many countries such as India, Indonesia and some Western provinces in China all suffer from low levels of literacy, economic wealth, access to infrastructure and, therefore, digital literacy.

However, WhatsApp now has nearly 500 million users in India, and its use accelerated during the lockdown period. This is around 20 times the number of WhatsApp users in the USA. With the forthcoming introduction of 5G mobile technology and the blurring of lines with Facebook (the owner of WhatsApp and having around 350 million users in India), WhatsApp seems to be part of an unstoppable force to accelerate digital adoption at all levels of society.

Look at the introduction of WhatsApp payments, allowing one citizen to transfer money to another using the country's UPI scheme, and the role of the bank in payments is suddenly undermined. The threat for banks does not lie in the future, it is here, now.

Furthermore, as we move from adoption of individual technologies to combination of technologies, the opportunities and threats become exponentially greater. For example, many banks now consider branches to be unnecessary to serve their customers. Robotics, which started off as a capability for back office efficiency, is fast moving to be a support tool for customer service agents. Combined with speech recognition and artificial intelligence (AI), we have the makings of exemplary customer service as well as reduced need for direct human interactions. Data analytics and machine learning (ML) were all once considered to be separate activities and outside the banking arena. This is no longer the case with core activities such as customer proposition development, credit risk scoring and the convergence of social media becoming an unstoppable force. Imagine, for example, going to a retailer of electrical goods and wishing to purchase a fridge with a small loan. What if the retailer could use social media credit scoring, not financial records, to make an instant decision on whether to loan you some of the money to purchase the fridge with no bank involved? This is not fiction, it is in place already today and set to accelerate as technologies combine.

> 'Longevity in this business is about being able to reinvent yourself or invent the future.'
>
> —Satya Nadella, CEO of Microsoft Corporation

The consequences for existing banks are profound and widespread. It is no longer about only online delivery, apps and smart user interfaces, it is now also about the core business model, the underlying human capital and, of course, the leadership in the digital age. It is also about the speed and agility of change, which further reinforce the need for effective leadership and governance in the digital age.

Institutional strategies that have proved effective for the past 10 years are no longer valid and need to be recast. It is not just about remaining relevant for customers, whilst meeting expectations for shareholders and employees, it is also about making stark choices that can lead to success, failure or simply survival. So, what will differentiate the winners from the losers?

The objective of this chapter is to set out some of the considerations for leaders of large-scale financial services. I looked at the technological context-driving change and have highlighted key questions that leaders should look at to assess how to steer the changes that lie ahead:

1. Who owns the customer, and what's digital customer service?
2. What about workforce and leadership implications?
3. How does governance change?
4. What about cyber and risk management?

Let me start with an example from the Indian banking industry that will illustrate many of the points put across in this chapter (Box 2.1).

The ease of entry for new players in this technology-enabled industry also means that the industry is increasingly competitive (Boxes 2.2 and 2.3).

Box 2.1   HDFC Bank: From Transactions to Experience, a Story of Digital Excellence

The bank, over the years, has seen a rise in transactions through digital channels. This rose to 55 per cent by 2015. User-friendly platforms made customers feel increasingly comfortable while banking online and through their phones. Their overwhelming response encouraged us to push for the digitization of all transactions. By the end of FY 2016, when digital transactions had grown to 71 per cent, we shifted our focus to digital journeys. To be recognized today as the 'best digital bank' in India at Asiamoney Best Bank Awards 2019 is truly humbling.

Customer centricity is at the heart of everything we do. Our aim is to now move from providing convenience to delivering differentiated customer experiences. Over the past 25 years, we have strived to re-evaluate how customers interact with the bank and how their needs and expectations have evolved over time. Today, our customers are part of a 'market of one' and we have repositioned ourselves into a day-to-day lifestyle bank; an approach that goes beyond transactions and to journeys. Our customers are individuals with diverse needs and preferences. The one-size-fits-all approach is no longer relevant and customization is the need of the hour. With this in mind, we make it a priority to build digital capabilities that ensure customer experiences are characterized by intuition, context and relevance immediacy hyper-personalization.

To do this, we bring next-generation technology into play, namely AI.

AI is fuelled by data, specifically customer data, to generate tailor-made solutions. This is similar to a salesperson observing a customer's preferences and recommending them products they may like. As our customers interacted and transacted across our digital platforms, we were able to gather insights on their transactional and behavioural data. AI-based technologies could then harness the massive troves of data and analyse it to understand their needs, and use

(Continued)

(Continued)

that understanding to create a unique, highly personalized banking experience for everyone.

In 2017, we launched electronic virtual assistant (EVA) across all our digital channels. Customers can chat with this virtual assistant 24 × 7 and easily obtain the information they need. Today, EVA, through seamless integration with Google Assistant and Alexa, offers our customers ease of accessibility. For instance, if a customer wants information on our FD interest rates, all they have to do is say, 'Alexa, what is the interest rate on an FD for a year?' and EVA responds with the necessary information.

Source: HDFC Annual Report 2018–2019.

Box 2.2   Digibank

Mobile-only Digibank was launched by Singapore's DBS in spring 2016. It offers a broad range of products, including savings/deposits, investments, insurance, loans, cards and remittances.

At the time of the launch, it announced plans to onboard five million customers and a deposit base of ₹500 billion ($7.4 billion) over five years.

Digibank offers a simple account opening process: download the app, register in 90 seconds and get access to an e-wallet immediately. Provide your income tax permanent account number and your Aadhaar number with your biometric information (Aadhaar is a 12-digit individual identification number issued by the Unique Identification Authority of India), visit one of the 500 local Café Coffee Day outlets for biometric verification, and you're all set to use your 'paperless, signatureless' bank account.

Digibank's customers also get a physical Visa debit card to withdraw cash from 200,000 automated teller machines (ATMs) nationwide.

By spring 2019, the bank had over 2.5 million customers across India.

Box 2.3   YONO

YONO, which stands for 'You Only Need One' is an integrated digital banking platform offered by the State Bank of India to enable users to access a variety of financial and other services such as taxi bookings, online shopping and medical bill payments.

It was launched in November 2017.

Via the YONO app, users can get the standard banking services, such as account opening, fund transfers, bill payments and loans. The app can also be used to make ATM withdrawals.

In addition, YONO offers services from 60+ e-commerce companies including online shopping, travel planning, taxi booking, online education and offline retail.

This is good for consumer choice and innovation, but can also mean that existing players get left behind if they do not transform themselves sufficiently quickly.

Technological Context

Many of us can remember the time when laptops were not prevalent or when mobile phones were not in common usage. It is hard to imagine that iPhone was launched just over 10 years ago. Those who own a smartphone are rarely without it, thereby establishing it as one of the new consumer 'control point' of the 21st century. Even more profound is the way devices such as the smartphone have helped to redefine our expectations for the ease of access and price for digital services using portable devices.

Yet the mass adoption of the smartphone is only one of the many changes in technology that has occurred and will occur in the coming months and years (wearables, cloud, AI, etc.). This is in many ways the continuation of a trend that has been underway for some years now. Douglas Arner, of the University of Hong Kong, and colleagues, have catalogued the three waves of technological disruptions in finance:

- The first wave of technology (Fintech 1.0) was prompted by the completion of the first transatlantic telegraph cable in 1866 and saw finance gradually shift from analogue to digital.
- This was followed by a second wave of technological innovations in financial services, starting with the advent of ATM in 1967 (Fintech 2.0).
- Fast forward and we are now witnessing a third wave of increasing technological pervasiveness in finance coupled with the emergence of new actors and channels for the provision of finance (Fintech 3.0).

To understand the scale of change underway, you only have to look at the level of investment in fintech in recent years and indeed the huge valuations commanded by those technology-based companies promising innovation despite limited financial performance. There are perhaps the following five key technologies to consider for financial services.

Big data and analytics: Big data is used to describe a massive volume of both structured and unstructured data that is so large that it is difficult to process using traditional database and software techniques. Increased computing power for processing and storage over the past decade means that it is now possible to process and analyse such data more effectively.

The financial services industry is one of the largest generators and users of data, as billions of financial transactions flow each and every day. This data can now be used to analyse and anticipate customer needs and behaviours, thereby allowing financial institutions to provide more effective propositions and services.

Through a combination of predictive analysis, behavioural profiling and real-time detection, big data analytics can enable financial institutions to conduct fraud detection at a rate that was not previously possible.

Robotic process automation (RPA): RPA refers to software that can be easily programmed to do basic tasks across applications just as human workers do. The software robot can be taught a workflow with multiple steps and applications such as taking received forms, sending a receipt message, checking the form for completeness, filing the form in a folder and updating a spreadsheet with the name of the form and the date filed. RPA software is designed to reduce the burden of repetitive simple tasks on employees.

All financial services companies have many teams and employees dedicated to administrative and processing activities that can be reduced in volume using robotics. Initially, most applications of RPA were in the back office to automate administration and improve productivity. However, more recently, use cases have shifted towards more customer-facing activities such as supporting call centre operators to complete more activities whilst talking to a customer, thereby improving customer service as well as productivity.

AI and ML: AI is the broader concept of machines being able to carry out tasks in a manner similar to the way humans think and act. ML takes this one step further by settling on the core idea that we should be able to give machines access to data and let them learn for themselves.

It is no surprise, therefore, that there are a large number of applications being developed and deployed in financial services: chatbots that bring together basic elements of RPA, credit decisions, risk management, fraud prevention, trading and increasing inclusion of themes such as sentiment analysis.

Cloud computing: In its simplest form, cloud computing is the provision of massive amounts of computer power (processing and storage) in remote locations and accessible on demand over the internet or dedicated networks. Given the increase in availability of data and the demand for further processing power, this is perhaps one of the greatest accelerators of change in the near future.

Recent times have seen the emergence of several large-scale providers of cloud computing services, which offers companies the ability to convert fixed costs to variable costs as well as access world-class levels of security. For organizations that adopt cloud effectively, it can lead to reduced technology costs, improved flexibility and scalability as well as greater responsiveness to changing customer needs.

Blockchain: Blockchain is based upon distributed ledger technology. By allowing digital information to be distributed but not copied, blockchain technology created the backbone of a new type of the internet. Although it was originally used for the digital currency bitcoin, its use has moved on considerably to other applications separate from currency.

Using cryptography to keep exchanges secure, blockchain provides a decentralized database, or 'digital ledger', of transactions that everyone on the network can see. This network is essentially a chain of computers that must all approve an exchange before it can be verified and recorded.

The technology can work for almost every type of transaction involving value, including money, goods and property. Its potential uses are almost limitless: from collecting taxes to enabling migrants to send money back to family in countries where banking is difficult.

Blockchain can streamline banking and lending services, reducing counterparty risk and decreasing issuance and settlement times. It allows authenticated documentation and know your customer/anti-money laundering data, reducing operational risks and enabling real-time verification of financial documents.

Although still in the early days of its deployment, many believe that longer term blockchain will truly transform financial services for corporates and other institutions.

Future Business Models

The Basel Committee on Banking Supervision recently published analysis on the implications of fintech for banks and supervisors. The report considers five stylized and non-mutually exclusive scenarios in which technology and fintech could impact banks, with a particular focus on: (a) who manages the customer relationship or interface and (b) who provides the services and takes the risk.

These comprise the following.

- **Scenario 1—Better bank:** Incumbent banks digitize and modernize themselves to retain the customer relationship and core banking services, leveraging enabling technologies to change their current business models. For example, new technologies such as biometry, chatbots or AI could help banks maintain a value-added remote customer relationship. Banks could further innovate payment services and digitize the lending process through more efficient interfaces and processing tools.
- **Scenario 2—New bank:** In this scenario, incumbents are unable to survive the wave of technology-enabled disruption and are replaced by new technology-driven banks (e.g., 'neo-banks') with full-service 'built-for-digital' banking platforms. We have seen examples of such banks around the world, such as Atom Bank in the UK, Bunq in the Netherlands, WeBank in China and Varo Money in the USA.
- **Scenario 3—Distributed bank:** A third scenario considers the possibility of financial services becoming increasingly modularized. Incumbents are able to carve out enough of a niche to survive, but other financial service providers 'plug and play' on the digital customer interface. A large number of new businesses emerge to provide specialized financial services. For example, the adoption by consumers of mobile wallets developed by third-party technology companies, such as Android Pay, Apple Pay or Samsung Pay, is an example of the distributed bank scenario.
- **Scenario 4—Relegated bank:** Incumbent banks become commoditized service providers and cede the direct customer relationship to other financial service providers. Fintech and big tech companies use front-end customer platforms to offer a variety of financial services from a diverse group of providers. In contrast, banks would be relegated to providing only commoditized functions such as operational processes and risk management, while other service providers would own the customer relationship.
- **Scenario 5—Disintermediated bank:** The final scenario would see incumbent banks becoming irrelevant because there is no longer a need for balance sheet intermediation, as customers interact directly with individual financial service providers. In this scenario, customers may have a more direct say in choosing the services and the provider, rather than sourcing such services through an intermediary bank. One example is peer-to-peer lending platforms, wherein individual customers can directly take on the role of the lender or the borrower.

Who Owns the Customer and What Is Digital Customer Service?

The real significance of digital customer service is not the application of technology, it is the ability to meet customers' needs that themselves are fast evolving. In a world where there is convergence of industries in meeting daily customer needs (such as retail and financial services), who owns the customer becomes a key strategic question for banks in addition to a strategic factor for underlying business and economic model of an existing bank.

Layered on top of this is the dramatic acceleration of mobile usage and hence user-centric design and user-centric customer service, enabled by technology. Both are inextricably linked and indivisible through the eyes of the consumer.

Let us first explore the key question of who owns the customer. The traditional paradigm of banks owning customers is under threat:

- Expectations changing, and financial services being part of a broader transaction or lifestyle event
- Other industries being able to transact and offer banking services

New entrants in many parts of the world are competing on customer service as well as rates. For example, Revolut and Monzo in the UK and N26 in Germany—large numbers of new customers acquired often with no branches and account opening reduced from weeks to minutes.

Open banking/PSD2 in the UK and Europe has laid the foundation for convergence of industries, with non-banks able to offer financial services and banks being forced to decide the balance of the customer relationship/distribution versus manufacture they wish to adopt.

At its simplest form, this is a key strategic decision for banks: maximize distribution (and potentially sell other banking products) or become a pure manufacturer for other companies to cover, or a mix-and-match model in between. But underpinning this is also the reality of the business and economic model that is at the core of the bank. For example:

- Will banks be able to continue to rely on net interest margin for the primary source of their profitability, or will they need to move to a service-based charge for some customer segments?
- Will banks be willing to distribute products from other financial institutions that are able to manufacture them at lower cost, and if so, will they provide customer service and generate the value add (margin) as per expectations?

This then brings us to the subject of customer service for institutions in the digital age. An efficient operation is critical but no longer sufficient for a successful customer service function. Customer service needs to shift from an 'inward out' mindset focused on product and service to an 'outward in' mindset focused on customers' journeys and needs.

The key difference is whether the customer fits into the bank's offerings or whether the bank fits into the customer's needs. The latter is increasingly dominating the landscape, as witnessed by the shift to needs–based service undertaken by sbiINTOUCH, and the increasing number of banks defining customers' journeys as their starting point. You only have to look at Lloyds Bank in the UK and La Caixa and BBVA in Spain to get some clear examples.

The key objective of customer service shifts further towards driving consumer acquisition, retention and loyalty through service. Integration of multiple channels, like integration between physical and digital channels, is taken for granted as customers are increasingly expecting a 'mobile first' service with high availability and integration, breadth and depth of other channels when required (see Box 2.4).

Not every bank can invest the amount of money Bank of America does in technology and digital applications. It is important to prioritize digital

---

Box 2.4   Bank of America

Technology remains a top priority for many banks in the USA, where technology adoption is far advanced. For example, Bank of America as it invests $3 billion annually in technological initiatives. Typical of most large US banks, Bank of America is committed to continuous innovation to meet digital consumer needs.

For instance, the bank has an app that lets consumers to apply for a mortgage on the bank's mobile app or online, potentially receiving conditional approval within a day. Applicants can personalize their loan terms, lock in interest rates and 'save and resume' an application in process. Users also have access to a platform designed to track loans, monitor user actions, upload documents and review and acknowledge disclosures from a smartphone.

'The Digital Mortgage Experience is about ... making things easy, intuitive, simple and fast', Michelle Moore, head of digital banking at Bank of America, said in a statement. 'It's the latest example of our high-tech, high-touch approach to serving clients'.

Bank of America has high consumer ratings in many of its digital offerings, with the speed at which customers could perform typical banking tasks being most critical.

investment to maximize the positive impact on the greatest number of consumers. This may involve the elimination of frustrations as much as the addition of functionality.

Allowing a consumer to open a new account online and with a mobile app without requiring a branch visit is a great example of eliminating a frustration. In addition, being able to access capabilities like viewing past statements, transferring funds with a single click or simplifying the process of setting up a fraud alert will improve mobile banking account growth and engagement.

Finally, all of the largest banks are aggressive in their communication to customers about the benefits of mobile banking. They use email, text alerts, online marketing and even direct mail to reinforce the use of digital channels.

This has led to the rise of banks with no branches, often providing very high levels of customer service and cost-efficiency. For example, Starling Bank in the UK prides itself on being a digital-first bank for small and medium enterprise (SME) customers with quick account opening, highly effective and relevant products plus access to physical branches through a tie-up with the post office when required. How existing banks match this level of service, given legacy and inertia, is not clear unless there is significant transformation.

To make matters more challenging, mobile banking users don't compare their digital experience with the experience in a branch. They compare mobile banking to the experience received on non-financial services apps such as Amazon, Uber, Best Buy and other leaders in digital engagement.

Historically, branches have been the mainstay of retail banks. However, changing consumer needs enabled by technology now means that it is increasingly commonplace for banks, particularly new challenger banks, to have no branches. For example, Fidor in Germany provides two-way conversations via social media. Starling, Monzo and Revolut in the UK provide banking services for retail and SME customers without branches. Starling uses local post offices to enable physical connectivity as required by customers.

One of the consequences of the strategic choices over customer, distribution and product is the consequence for ecosystem. For example, does a bank need to form alliances with other banking product manufacturers or non-financial services distribution channels? These are not alliances that banks have typically sought previously.

Added to this, there are further strategic questions around the approach to adoption of fintech, and what this means for operating model as well as ecosystems required. For example, many of the functions of a bank can increasingly be undertaken by fintechs. Often small and fast moving, they can be innovative and cost-effective in what they do. But they also require the organization to be adept at changing its operating model. Building the correct ecosystem of such organizations is as important as the ecosystem required to deliver new services for evolving customer needs.

What about the Workforce and Leadership Implications?

The traditional paradigm of banks owning customers is under threat: expectations changing and financial services being part of a broader transaction or lifestyle event. Furthermore, other industries are able to transact and offer banking services now.

Herein, the implications for the workforce are equally important. The number of people required to deliver services to the customer will undoubtedly reduce over time, at varying speeds, depending on geography. Process automation and the introduction of AI will increasingly help financial services institutions move from functional orientation (e.g., for processing) to customer-centric processes with far greater emphasis on helping customers through their 'journeys', providing moments of delight at key points.

However, the greater shift is likely to be the emphasis on behaviours and motives versus competences and experience. To be agile and effective in a customer-centric world, for example, it will be increasingly important to have intellectual curiosity and be comfortable with ambiguity.

Future needs for motives and behaviours are often innate and not learned or educated for raising the question of how to attract, motivate and retain talent in the digital age. One thing is for sure that previous paradigms of looking solely at academic qualifications and experience are likely to be insufficient for many roles.

In a report by Cognizant on 'Going Digital: What Banking Leaders Need to Know', several key imperatives for organization and talent are drawn out. These are as follows.

- **Break down organizational barriers:** How do you dismantle line of business silos and enable sharing of customer data and processes? Cross-functional groups are a start. Assembling teams from HR, finance and marketing branches plays an important role in uniting the patchwork of fragmented efforts that exist in most banks.
- **Take a new approach to talent:** Proactive workforce planning is as essential to banks' digital evolution as acquiring new expertise is. Technology is an obvious place to begin. Attracting top talent will require a strategy to counter the job market's perception of banking as technologically conservative.

- **Develop incentive structures that work:** Inspiring bank employees to adopt customer-centric approaches across multiple platforms is a key challenge. Banks are replacing metrics like average call handling time with benchmarks such as net promoter score, which rewards proactive approaches and values customers' best interests.
- **Cultivate a digital culture:** Culture always plays a role in large transformation programmes, and digital is no exception. But it's well worth the effort: successfully negotiating digital cultural shifts is a competitive differentiator for banks. An intense customer focus coupled with the ability to innovate and act quickly is difficult for competitors to emulate.
- **Be purposeful in what you say and do:** Reinforce customer focus at every opportunity by asking the question, 'How does this impact the customer?'.

The extent of change to some attributes of strong leadership in the digital economy cannot be underestimated. For example, leaders must not only have strong digital savviness themselves (e.g., understand implications even if they are not experts), but they must also be able to balance the inherent tensions that exist in securing and operating in the digital world (e.g., do I invest for profit or invest for future positioning and growth?).

The strategic choices are pivotal to the success of the organization on a multi-year basis, even if often seeming to be separate from short-term operational business performance. For example:

- Setting a clear vision for the organization extends far beyond establishing a galvanizing mission statement into questions around future customer value proposition, implications for business model and operating model.
- Resource allocation of both tangible capital (e.g., investment $) and intangible capital (highly skilled individuals) become critical to the decisions that have to be taken. Failing to invest in IT in the short term may reduce operating costs but may also make the transition to digital customer services much more difficult.
- Leading a workforce with two, three, and possibly four generations of employees presents a new challenge, particularly when the range of employee expectations is so broad, from job security and progression for older generations to work-life balance and broader social goals such as climate change for younger generations.
- Creating an internal culture of reinvention becomes one of the key attributes for any transformative leader, along with carefully judging the pace of change required for the organization and its employees.

Traditionally, leaders in legacy organizations have been rewarded for strong financial performance but sometimes this mindset can also lead to blind spots. For example, there are notable case studies in recent history of blind spots leading to significant corporate consequences:

- In the 1950s, Kodak had the lion's share of the US amateur film market. In 1981, came digital which disrupted the company's equilibrium by shifting the meaning associated with cameras and allowing newcomers such as Sony to bypass one of Kodak's distribution network. Should it have acted faster?
- Prior to iPhone, Nokia was renowned for innovation globally, but then failed to respond at this key point. Was this another example of management blind spot with dire consequences? Identifying and overcoming these blind spots in the digital age is a critical prerequisite for effective leadership.

Future leaders need to maintain their clear focus on having a clear vision and high performance, whilst leading from the front. Moreover, they increasingly need to be purpose driven, nurture passion and work across boundaries. Handling ambiguity and taking longer-term bets become more critical so the need to be more data-driven in key judgements goes up.

> '90% of CEOs believe the digital economy will impact their industry, but less than 15% are executing on a digital strategy.'
>
> —MIT Sloan and Capgemini

How Does Governance Change?

Governance for any large organization remains key, particularly those operating in regulated environments such as financial services. But the role of governance and the way it is delivered become more sophisticated and more business-critical manner.

Safeguarding the future interests of the bank and its customers remains of paramount importance, as we have seen in the way that governance has been strengthened over the past 10 years since the financial crisis.

However, acting as long-term stewards for the organization and directing management where appropriate for the digital age take on greater significance.

- The time horizon for which a board needs to think and guide decisions increasingly becomes longer, with the consequences of key decisions sometimes only manifesting themselves after the term of individuals involved.
- Learning to steer organizations through an increasingly connected world with more regular geopolitical risks requires a different level of judgement (making good decisions in the face of radical uncertainty).

Each of these brings greater need for being comfortable with ambiguity as well as having greater insight into future customer needs and how they can be served particularly through the application of technology. From a world where standard operating procedures and policies may have been sufficient for many forms of governance, we are entering an era in which clarity of outcomes and good judgements become increasingly important.

In a report by Cognizant on 'Going Digital: What Banking Leaders Need to Know', several key imperatives for organization and talent are drawn out. These are as follows:

- **Focus on operating models and governance:** These are the essential planning tools to bridge your bank's strategy and organization. The operating model connects a bank's digital strategies with its organizational design. It defines accountability and responsibility for all activities, from business processes and data quality management to application development.
- **Rethink your reporting structure:** Instead of top-down project planning, digital capabilities demand dynamic, discovery-oriented approaches that free teams to quickly test ideas and learn from data and outcomes.

Knowing when to invest in items beyond the current digital transformation requires further insight and courage. It's hard to say today the extent to which an organization's long-term survival is dependent upon shifting to sustainable finance, even harder to redirect resource and focus away from performing in today's world and accelerating towards the digital world.

In a report by MIT and Capgemini Consulting on 'Governance: A Central Component of Successful Digital Transformation', the authors highlight that governance often goes beyond organizational structures to include specific leaders. These new roles include 'digital czars' who lead digital transformation at the firm or business level as well as less senior liaison roles.

Digital Czars

In March 2012, Starbucks Coffee Company announced the hiring of a chief digital officer (CDO), Adam Brotman, reporting to the firm's CEO. According to Brotman, '[Digital] has been an essential part of how we build our brand and connect with our customers… there's been such a seismic shift [in our interactions with customers] that we needed to pull it all together and make it a priority'.

Areas of responsibility for these 'digital czars' vary from one company to another according to the strategic priorities of the firm towards digital. Brotman at Starbucks has responsibility for web, mobile, social media, card, loyalty, e-commerce, Wi-Fi and the Starbucks Digital Network, as well as company's emerging in-store digital and entertainment teams.

Digital Liaisons

Some of the companies we interviewed have positioned liaisons in business units to lead digital transformation at a local level. Spanish media group Prisa has assigned CDOs in each division to lead implementation of the digital transformation in their division and to coordinate with the corporate CDO. A global insurance group executive said that in his company, 'The role of [digital liaisons] is first to help business units to take the digital dimension into account and second to encourage the use of central resources'.

Some liaisons have knowledge sharing rather than leadership roles.

Nestlé's 'digital acceleration team' hosts people from all countries to develop their digital expertise and take it back to their home offices. For example, Nestlé's Digital Acceleration Team hosts people from multiple countries to develop their digital expertise and take it back to their home offices. With people from multiple markets with an interest or existing experience in digital, Nestlé is able to build and share expertise as well as propagate local innovations.

What about Cyber and Risk Management?

With increasing advancement of digital comes the greater advancement of cyber capabilities and cyber activities. This is compounded by the fact that cyber is a global topic, not confined to geographic or industrial boundaries.

India's central bank, the Reserve Bank of India (RBI), has revealed that it discovered around 50,000 cyber frauds in the country's scheduled commercial banks in 2018–2019 fiscal.

'In an endeavour to strengthen the cybersecurity posture of Indian banks, focused and theme-based IT examinations are planned during 2018–19. Targeted scrutiny, as and when required, would also be conducted for appropriate policy and supervisory intervention', RBI stated in its annual report.

It is increasingly important for leaders to make sure that their investments and advancements in digital capabilities are matched by their emphasis in cyber. The initial thought process for most organizations is to focus on ensuring that the organization is secure and protected from cyber activity. Customer reputation impact, legislation and regulatory fines have raised the bar for this. This is a critical defensive tactic and not to be underestimated.

However, there are also offensive responses as well. Banks have generally invested more in cyber protection than their small corporate customers. A bank that not only keeps itself safe, but also helps keep its smaller corporate customers safe, is an attractive bank. Insurers who are able to underwrite and insure against cyber losses have the opportunity to grow their business significantly, particularly if they can provide market-leading expertise to help corporate clients evaluate and protect against risks with rapid response to remediate in the event of breach.

These move cyber from being an area of investment to sustain core business to being one of the means of strong differentiation in the digital age.

Cyber is but one facet of the broader risk management framework that any organization should consider. Indeed, traditional risk management moves from a few well-established dimensions to a more multi-dimensional (and more complex) framework for assessing and driving the performance of the organization forward.

Traditional areas of evaluation such as credit, financial and operational risk remain as critical as ever, but these are enhanced by technology, providing not only business opportunity but also new technology-specific risks.

Additionally, risk management for an organization has often been confined to evaluating risks facing an organization within its institutional boundaries. However, with the increasing reliance upon third parties (especially fintech) and increasing convergence across industries, it now moves to external orientation also. The systemic risks around an institution are often harder to understand, let alone manage, but these are clearly of greater significance in the digital world.

Risk management must keep pace with technology-driven change and take the front seat in helping banks to achieve digital ambitions. The revolution in technology demands that every bank reinvents itself, and risk management has a critical role to play in this transformation: adapting to a risk environment and risk profile that is changing faster and more intensively than ever, leveraging risk management to enable business transformation and sustained growth, dealing with risk management effectively and efficiently and managing through and recovering from disruptions.

Risk management still needs to maintain a focus on protecting the enterprise. However, increasingly, it also has to take a central role in the evolution of a firm's digital and IT strategy, and to be credible, it needs to be involved from the initial planning to implementation. Traditional risk management frameworks have a strong bias towards risk reduction or avoidance, so new approaches are needed to enable risk management professionals to support and enable growth.

Conclusion

With some change and so many choices, how does one sift through the dynamics and priorities facing institutions as they seek to accelerate their transformation?

Fortunately, some things don't change.

- Customers remain key, and meeting their needs remains a key imperative for all organizations. New business and sales are a measure of customer engagement as opposed to being the primary goal for the organization.
- People still matter and need to be treated as a key asset even when there is much change ahead.
- The fundamentals of business economics in banking do not change considerably, that is, capital adequacy, financial prudence and financial disciplines continue to matter.

The skill is adapting to the art of leadership in the new digital and sometimes uncertain world that we now live in.

'You can't delegate digital transformation for your company... You and your executives have to own it! Executives need to engage, embrace and adopt new ways of working with the latest and emerging technologies.'

—Barry Ross, Ross & Ross International

Future of Work in BFSI Organizations

Akhil Handa

After COVID-19, the world around us will be changed forever. In a matter of weeks, work from home (WFH) has become the norm, not the exception. The virus has forced a reckoning of how we view work, undertake travel, and engage with the ecosystem. It has led to a proliferation of technologies that has made all of this possible.

Before the pandemic, digital transformation was optional for many organizations. When COVID-19 took hold, necessity dictated that all organizations 'become digital'. Like demonetization accelerated the digital payments adoption by 2 years, COVID-19 is expected to accelerate the digital adoption by 1–2 years as well, depending upon how long the pandemic lasts or a cure/vaccine is found.

In fact, banking, financial services and insurance (BFSI) organizations, classified as 'essential services' under the Indian Central Government Order, have been driven to hasten the grouping of men, material and technologies with digitization at its front and core. The entire banking ecosystem and the way consumers interact with financial organizations are being remodelled as a result of COVID-19.

In much of the pre-COVID-19 era, BFSI digital transformation was driven by the desire to enhance customer experience with the use of data and advanced analytics, front-end innovation and technology. It was clear that industry leaders knew what needed to be done, and in many cases, how to proceed. What was missing was the *urgency* to rapidly transform. This has changed with the onset of COVID-19. We are sure to look back on this period as a tipping point between the fence sitters moving up the digital adoption curve.

More importantly, the adoption is not just going to be based on *how we put our off-line processes online,* but rather, *how we fundamentally rethink—HOW we are doing EVERYTHING*—and turn it into nothing but clicks. How do we get there fast? Frankly, this should have been the focus all along. COVID has perhaps provided a rather painful dose of clarity.

While there is uncertainty for envisaging the post-coronavirus world, there is one reality that has been proven without a doubt. Change can happen in an instant. The key is to imagine possible outcomes and set in motion those initiatives that can position the organization most advantageously. The most important of these changes is human capital development, that needs to be made more adaptable and agile in its orientation and delivery as we move towards a decentralized and deconstructed environment, moving from monoliths to components. To understand the needs of reskilling, we need to better understand the underlying currents of digital-driven change.

Extent of Automation in Banking Accelerating

Before COVID-19, the banking industry did a great deal of talking about 'becoming digital', but less than 15 per cent of BFSI organizations considered themselves digital transformation leaders. In fact, during the long-lasting recovery and prosperity experienced for more than a decade post the great financial crisis of 2008, very few organizations 'bit the bullet' of building a digital-ready bank.

When the coronavirus pandemic hit, everything changed overnight. Organizations were forced into providing the digital banking alternatives not only to consumers but to the employees as well. For those organizations that were not prepared, new business opportunities were lost, customer satisfaction suffered and employee productivity dramatically dropped.

Broadly, there have been two parts to solving this, that is, increasing digitization for the following:

1. Internal processes
2. Customer facing process and service delivery

Internal Processes

This involves improving seamless and secure remote operational capabilities including IT operations, security, enabling hybrid cloud, data analytics and data centre infrastructure. BFSI organizations need robust workflow and project management applications. These are all available off the shelf in the market today. Examples include virtual desktop infrastructure, monitoring tools and hybrid cloud options (indeed Office 365 is on cloud today in Bank of Baroda [BOB]).

To complement this, we need productivity and collaboration tools such as video calling, remote attendance marking, project tracking, document sharing, management application and online proofing. In fact, BOB deployed Microsoft Teams for collaboration and video conferencing. The scale and pace of adoption of Microsoft Teams is something I have never witnessed in my career before. In the face of digital document sharing, do we really need a huge number of sub-staff in the banks? Wouldn't it be better to upskill them to perform the roles of officer cadre instead?

Getting back, these tools are required for seamless interaction with colleagues and clients. Task-related tools need to have features like the ability to create tasks and subtasks, templates for different types of projects, guidelines, milestones, notifications, baselines, critical path and automatic project scheduling, all of which promotes the feeling of being connected and helps managers stay on top of workstreams.

Until recently, most news about artificial intelligence (AI) tools has focused on its potential as a job killer. The truth is that AI is the latest in a long line of productivity-driving tools that will replicate what productivity growth has always done over the course of history: create net growth in employment and more wealth for more people.

AI can be leveraged to drive digital transformations in banks. Industry 4.0 emphasizes the importance of automation to fast track the development and deployment of products in the banking and finance sector. Automation and AI have redefined work and enabled the digital workforce to free their time for more creative and innovative tasks. J. P. Morgan has hired a separate head for AI and machine learning (ML) services. They are recruiting engineers from big tech firms, such as Google and Facebook, to be part of the team. Similar positions are emerging at top Wall Street banks such as Goldman Sachs, UBS and Bank of America Merril Lych for ML and AI strategies.

Hedge funds, such as Two Sigma and Citadel, are hiring utilizing AI and ML to build ML, neural network, deep learning for financial products and trading.

I've kept aside many of the business unit-specific core applications, for example, Human Resource Network for Employee Services or Treasury software or cash management solution. These applications also need to move to cloud native environments, which is possible in the next gen of the available solutions in the market. This is relatively easier.

Customer Facing Process and Service Delivery

This is trickier, for it involves balancing technology adoption with the customer's requirements of also being able to physically walk into and discuss matters with the officers of the bank, especially in the rural/semi-urban parts of our operations. However, in terms of digital delivery readiness, should a customer so require, we estimate there are over 200 services a retail bank branch offers, and each of these services, barring a few physical ones (such as locker operation, know your customer (KYC) updation and mobile number updation), could be delivered electronically through mobile banking, internet banking and contact centre through process redesign. Even the contact centres can now be manned by voice bots and no longer require the first level of human contact, which has generally relayed over from the interactive voice response set-up. Voice bots can be lot more efficient and offer personalized service to the calling customer. Globally, the role of design officers is gaining momentum. Using agile methods, they re-engineer business processes to make them more efficient. For instance, Lloyds Banking Group has a created the role of 'chief design officer' focusing on human-centred design, as the bank's strategy of transforming for success in a digital world generates pace.

Further, the asset-creation processes also need to move towards digitaliza-tion, for that is where the customer is expected to be. For the same purpose, Bank of Baroda has created a Digital Lending Department to consolidate all digital journeys across retail—micro, small and medium enterprises; agri and fintech into one core corporate vertical. This can lead to almost 90 per cent productivity gains as per our internal calculations.

But huge efforts are required for human skill development, for there are new job families that need to be created. For instance, this requires officers to:

1. Process different kinds of data points, such as credit bureau records, bank account records, social media activity and public records to assess users' creditworthiness, more quickly
2. Pre-empt defaulters and fraud by analysing a variety of data points such as income levels, demographics, credit history, payment history and usage patterns
3. Automate and speed up loan application processes using advanced ana-lytical models
4. Provide personal wealth management services, improving credit health and improving savings through robo-advisory services
5. Deliver personalized banking and digital marketing

Once we have successfully set up the new processes, we have to take a good look at every job role—in administrative offices, back offices and customer facing roles—and need to fundamentally challenge the assumptions, including:

1. That there is a need to be present physically (and in some cases at all) to effectively perform the job.

2. Weighing it against a competing technology solution to enhance productivity, reduce errors and upskill employees and reduce drudgery. This would be especially the case for our service hubs and shared services unit for whom repetitive tasks can be performed using robotic process automation (RPA).

For instance, the current task of rescheduling and providing for equated monthly instalment (EMI) moratorium could be handled by an RPA tool—right from sending out an SMS to reading its response, calculating the new EMIs, changing the tenure appropriately in core banking solution and sending the feedback back to the client and the branch.

Legacy banking models through on-premise servers can prove to be a limitation to delivering agile solutions to customers. Simply put, traditional servers cannot support the needs of next generation on demand products and business models. Some banks are taking notice. For instance, Goldman Sachs knew that public cloud is gathering pace and has consequently developed a 'Sky Team' to manage the transition. It is now looking at roles that can help them deploy faster. The blue-blooded Goldman Sachs, an investment bank and a marquee financial services company, is not looking for number crunching bankers but rather engineers and developers for its core engineering division. These are fundamental shifts.

Directionally, jobs that require a lot of repetitive tasks will most likely be eliminated, if they haven't been already. Examples include keypunch operators, many back-office finance roles, customer support personnel and even some branch employees' roles. Some may only require a change in skills as opposed to the removal of the job, but that requires retraining. This requires a movement from repetition to more strategic roles that require critical, empathetic thinking or the creative engagement of a human.

Change Has Been in the Making for a While Now

Many traditional physical banking skills such as tellers, branch customer service officers and loan processing officers were witnessing a paradigm shift in the pre-COVID-19 era itself. However, physical distancing instructions have made digitalization more important than ever. In the evolving context, traditional banking skills will be required to be upgraded to digital skills.

The banking landscape has been undergoing technological changes since 2010. New-generation fintechs are coming up with products and services that are directly competing with bank products. Various classes of fintechs including insurtech, regtech, payments fintechs among others are acting as direct substitutes for banks and in certain conditions even replacing banks. Not surprisingly, these fintechs have been more adept at managing the remote working situation given their digital-first approach. The fintechs have been able to leverage emerging technologies such as AI and ML efficiently to deliver services.

Bank of Baroda provides various alternate delivery channels such as ATM, debit card, mobile banking, internet banking, cash recycler, self-services passbook printer, e-lobby and cash management services and many new customer-centric digital products. Some of these products are considered the best in the industry. Mobile banking currently provides 170+ services to the customer to transact from the comfort of their home. Not surprisingly, the BOB mobile banking product is rated within the top three in the banking industry. However, to further spread awareness and market the products, the digital skills of bank's staff need to be digitally reskilled. There needs to be a complete reskilling, right from digital sourcing to digital processing of the request/application to the digital communication, product management and reporting.

Fintechs have been actively helping reshape the banking service delivery landscape. The relationship to incumbents run over collaboration on one end to competition on the other. Fintechs operate in lending automation, robo-advisory, regtech, identity solutions, robotic process automation, digital payments, cybersecurity, etc.

One area where fintechs have been dominant and have secured a leap over banks is digital payments. As per data reported by National Payments Corporation of India, unified payment interface has been growing exponentially and consistently logging over 1 billion transactions a month from October 2019 (barring the month of April 2020). Over 80 per cent of these digital transactions are now originated over fintech payment applications.

Digital payments call for new job families, including designing user interface/user experience, managing product, cyber security, merchant engagement, digital campaigning, architecture lead, tech development, etc. It also has had a direct impact on the cash industry, including an impact on requirement of less cash dispensers, tellers, cash vans, etc. vis-à-vis the growth in the economy. In some cases, even cash dispending is being remodelled in innovative ways, for example, enabling mobile ATMs or enabling distributed Cash@POS. This again requires an ability to be able to speak the digital language to conduct effective business.

The Future Workplace in Banking Post Digitalization (and COVID-19)

Near to medium term, there will be cross-pollination between fintechs and traditional lenders to optimize the resource and skill mix. In fact, I am an example of this cross-pollination—having run my fintech company before joining Bank of Baroda.

There are and will be new roles that will get created in response to the changing organizational and technological structure, including:

- Chief fintech officers
- Chief partnerships and alliances role
- Digital trust and security officer
- Crypto and blockchain roles
- Advances analytics and AI champions, data science
- Finance engineers, who will bridge between AI and traditional legacy
- Digital evangelists, embedded within business
- Open banking experts
- Developing and supervising automation will require humans

The overarching theme in the above roles is the use of AI to augment human skills. AI is likely to transform the world of business and the everyday lives of people as profoundly and beneficially as any of the great innovations of the past. It is the fifth revolution. And it is likely to do so in a much shorter timeframe, forcing incumbents into quick action. The impact will be industry wide and enterprise wide so it makes sense to have an enterprise strategy and enterprise-level leadership dedicated to AI.

An analysis by Accenture indicates that between 2018 and 2022, banks that invest in AI and human–machine collaboration could boost their revenue by an average of 34 per cent and, critically, their employment levels by 14 per cent.

Upskilling: A Call to Reorient Human Resources to Respond to the Need of the Moment

Three steps will be essential for creating the banking workforce of the future:

1. Reimagine work to better understand how machines and people can collaborate.
2. Pivot the workforce to areas that create new forms of value.
3. Scale up 'new skilling' initiatives to enable people to work with intelligent machines.

Technologies which were till yesterday textbook subjects have gone live and are making significant impact on the traditional banking systems and legacy work environments.

1. **Hybrid cloud:** According to IBM, cloud computing is quickly on its way to become mainstream in banking, with most banks searching for the optimal mix of traditional IT, public and private clouds.
2. **Application programming interface platforms:** The bank will serve as a platform on top of which third-party companies can build their own applications using the bank's data.
3. **RPA:** RPA is helping banks and credit unions accelerate growth by executing pre-programmed rules across a range of structured and unstructured data. This intelligent automation gives processes the power to learn from prior decisions and data patterns to make decisions by themselves, reducing the cost of administrative and regulatory processes by at least 50 per cent while improving quality and speed.
4. **AI and ML:** A team of Harvard pathologists developed an AI-based technique to identify cancer cells. It did well, scoring 92 per cent accuracy, but it still fell short of human pathologists who typically achieve precision rates of around 96 per cent. The biggest surprise came when humans and AI combined forces. Together, they accurately identified 99.5 per cent of cancerous biopsies, indicating that their diagnostic contributions were to some degree complementary, not duplicative. AI, when combined with human ingenuity and creativity, will allow both, humans and corporations to achieve much more. Used in this way, banks will gain the ability to solve complex challenges, develop new products and services, and break into or create new markets by inspiring entirely fresh revenue streams. Because the workforce, too, is such a critical enabler of future growth, it is important that planning and investing in it is a top priority. New skills, new roles and new ways of working will be needed.
5. **Blockchain:** Distributed ledger technology could be used for a range of applications in BFSI space from trade finance to central KYCs to even grounds up core banking solutions.

'Today's bank officer can be imagined to be using the *hybrid cloud* to download and upload statements while making digital transfers for customers through *fintech partners enabled via APIfication*. Their mundane daily activities such as clearing, posting of transactions and compliance statements will be handled through a pre-programmed RPA. They will be routinely deploying AI and ML algorithms to look for emerging business avenues.'

Table 3.1	Automation of Various Roles
Probability of Automation by Role	
Cashiers	97%
Brokerage clerks	98%
Loan officers	98%

Source: Accenture, Future Workforce Survey–Banking.

Basically, a stand-alone credit officer or an operations officer will be a thing of the past. All that multi-tasking will be aided and abetted by technology. And data supports the fact that stand-alone jobs shall be candidates for elimination (see Table 3.1).

Every single role can be reimagined through digital technologies. A few examples are given in Table 3.2.

Table 3.2	Reimagining Various Roles through Digital Technologies
Today	**Tomorrow**
A contact centre agent answers customer calls and messages, handling both minor and major issues.	Virtual agents and automation take care of simple queries and issues, allowing the human workforce to manage relationship portfolios and deal with exceptions and major issues involving complexity and sensitivity.
A communications specialist reads comments about the bank on social media and responds to those likely to have the greatest impact.	Supported by comprehensive scanning of social media, the specialist develops a strategy for optimizing the bank's profile and trains intelligent machines to respond to comments, rapidly and at scale.
A credit supervisor reviews loans granted to ensure loan criteria have been met and risk minimized.	AI reduces duplication of effort by flagging marginal credit decisions and highlighting problematic issues.
A risk and operations professional manually updates and checks various types of compliance reporting and controls for a business or functional area.	AI platforms, using ML and predictive analytics, simplify and drive efficiency in data gathering, raise the quality of controls, augment the risk and ops professional, and free up time for them to focus on analysis.

(Continued)

(Continued)

Today	Tomorrow
A financial advisor spends a significant amount of time onboarding a potential customer, taking personal details and interrogating their financial situation. Then they go away to do the research and hopefully secure the relationship.	The prospective customer goes online and uses AI to onboard themself. They complete the other administrative requirements and provide relevant research which they have sourced. This allows the financial advisor to focus on the true value of their offering: building the relationship and providing quality advice.

Source: https://financialservicesblog.accenture.com/new-ai-powered-roles-emerge-in-the-workforce-revolution

Response to the Lockdown: Some Initiatives Will Permanently Alter the Way We Work

Before the pandemic, the discussion about working from home for most banking employees was just a discussion. At best, it was an exception allowed for a few due to illness or for those who were associated with outside sales. Usually, requests to WFH were dismissed out of concern for loss of productivity. When COVID-19 hit, working from home became a necessity for almost everyone.

While the initial 7–10 days were anything but smooth, most workers who never had experienced the challenges of working with an entire family at home had to settle into a new routine. This entailed getting new equipment, creation of new working environments, setting up new work schedules, etc.

Banks will need to have preparedness and business continuity planning has to be recast and reworked to handle COVID-type disruptions in the future, which will include pushing physical service delivery spaces like branches to digital delivery, reworking traditional banking workflows, working from remote locations, co-working spaces like 'WeWork' can be a new working cubicle for administrative staff, etc.

As we look to the future, some workers will return to the traditional office when the coronavirus crisis subsides. But ideally, many should not be required to. We believe offices will not die out completely. But the notion of spending 60–70 hours there a week will. The office was a product of the third Industrial Revolution. The fourth one really took off as the virus hit—and the office could be a casualty. So will many ways of performing work. (see Table 3.3).

Table 3.3		BFSI Industry Members with Their Response to Lockdown with WFH Announcements
Company	**Country**	**Announcement**
J. P. Morgan	USA	10 per cent of staff to WFH
Morgan Stanley	USA	90 per cent of staff to WFH
Citibank	USA	All non-essential staff except traders and few operations staff
RBI	India	Only essential staff in office (~10%), all else to WFH
Bank of Baroda	India	Every staff member at its corporate centre and its branch establishments will work from office/home on alternate days
Canara Bank	India	40–50 per cent of circle office employees
State Bank of India	India	Every staff member at its corporate centre and its branch establishments will work from office/home on alternate days
Central Bank	India	WFH for staff at central office and zonal administrative offices/training colleges/centres
Axis Bank	India	Two-thirds of employees in headquarter to WFH
Uni Credit	Italy	Two-thirds of staff in Italy to WFH
Credit Suisse	Swiss	Split into teams and alternate days office/WFH/ separate locations
SocGen	France	Only staff working in 'critical operations' will be allowed on site. This includes traders in its global markets operations who have been split into sub-teams working in segregated offices.
Credit Agricole	France	Only employees whose activity is considered critical and who cannot operate remotely will come to work either in the bank's premises or in the recovery sites.
BNP Paribas	France	Operating 'split teams' and encouraging home working
BBVA	Spain	Close to 100 per cent employees WFH
Kookmin Bank	South Korea	Agents of the bank distributed across eight different locations to avoid mass infection
National Australian Bank	Australia	75 per cent of the workforce worked from home, bank reported a 5–7 per cent increase in productivity
Woori Bank	South Korea	Complete (100%) call centre work force enabled to WFH through remote telephony systems

(Continued)

(Continued)

Company	Country	Announcement
TCS	India	75 per cent of workforce to be shifted to WFH mode by 2025
Tech Mahindra	India	94 per cent of the work in COVID lockdown period has been performed from home and 25 per cent of work force shall work from home in the long term
BSE	India	90 per cent employees working from home during lockdown period
Intel	India	More than 95 per cent employees WFH during lockdown
Twitter	USA	Allowing all its employees indefinite WFH
Shopify	Canada	Allowing all its employees indefinite WFH
Facebook	USA	Allowing all its employees indefinite WFH
Microsoft	USA	WFH until September 2020
HCL	India	50 per cent staff to WFH permanently

Source: Data compiled by the author from various sources.

Leadership Leading the Way

Perhaps the most important—and indeed the most difficult—change ahead for traditional banks is a change of mindset. The digital age is fundamentally impacting culture as it forces banks to shift from a product-centric point of view to a client-centric one, from a place where the current IT set-up is doing the job to a tech-savvy mindset, from planning cycles to 'test and learn' and from silos to inclusiveness.

The biggest driver of this change has to be the top management. All decisions and communications should thrust towards digital. As the management dives into digitization, initial results could be disappointing. Implementation is often slower than expected. It's difficult to scale digital initiatives across the institution. Dearth of talent with the necessary digital and analytics skills is an impediment. The organization doesn't want to change. And the impact on the bottom line is much smaller than they thought it would be. As a result, initial enthusiasm wanes over the course of the project.

But the focus has to remain. A radical idea of engaging a *chief cultural transformation officer* can be looked at. Reorienting business processes to serve the customers digitally should be the way forward.

CHAPTER

4

Human Capital and Ethical Bank Governance

Some Perspectives from India

Late N. Balasubramanian

It is truly enough said that a corporation has no conscience. But a corporation of conscientious men is a corporation with a conscience.

—Henry David Thoreau

By this profound statement, Thoreau ([1849], 2015, p. 3), the 18th-century American essayist and philosopher, whose writings influenced the likes of Leo Tolstoy and Mahatma Gandhi, lifted the legal veil hiding and shielding the people who act in the name of the corporation. In so doing, he also highlighted the key role of the human dimension in corporations, the value systems people operate under and their great potential to build or destroy their corporations' perceived reputation.

The importance of human capital in any business, of course, cannot be gainsaid, but its imperative need in knowledge-based, people-dependent service industries such as banking and finance can perhaps do with some reiteration. Human capital management is gaining momentum in terms of investors' interest too; a 2020 survey indicates that 54 per cent of the respondents mentioned human capital management as the second top sustainability topic that institutional investors will focus on when engaging with boards (Sodali, 2020).

This is, of course, not to say that worthwhile human capital initiatives are not in place in banks; in many cases, to varying degrees, they are and some measure of board-level interventions also happen. It is just that worldwide, regulatory disclosure requirements and practices in this key area are woefully inadequate (except perhaps with regard to top-level executive compensation matters) and a wake-up call seems eminently appropriate.

To what extent do (and should) key human capital policies and practices engage the attention of board of directors in the overall governance framework is the main focus of this chapter.

Trends in Corporate Governance and Stakeholder Capitalism

In corporate governance, questioning shareholder primacy and advocating stakeholder interests are not new. While established case law in the US was quite unequivocally in favour of shareholder primacy,[1] the questioning of this primacy was also already in progress.

In the 1960s, when some industry leaders began to talk about social responsibility of corporations, famous economist, Milton Friedman, reacted, 'Few trends could so thoroughly undermine the very foundations of our free society as the acceptance by corporate officials of a social responsibility other than to make as much money for their shareholders as possible' (1962, p. 133).

Internationally, there are at least three other major developments in the last couple of years endorsing stakeholder capitalism.

- The Business Roundtable—the influential industry organization of leading corporations in the USA—came out with its Statement on the Purpose of the Corporation (Business Roundtable, 2019) sharing their 'fundamental commitment to all our stakeholders' and to 'deliver value to all of them, for the future success of our companies, our communities, and our country'.
- A few months later, the World Economic Forum followed suit: in December 2019, with its Davos Manifesto 2020, it declared, 'The purpose of a company is to engage all its stakeholders in shared and sustained value creation. In creating such value, a company serves not only its

---

[1] Ford v. Dodge (1919) 204 Mich.459, 170 N.W.668, 3 A.L.R. 413; the case related to Henry Ford's proposal to cut prices of cars, even while earning substantial profits; on a plaint by minority shareholder, Dodge, the court held, 'A business corporation is organised and carried on primarily for the profit of stockholders', and as such reducing the price for the benefit of customers was not within the powers of the board. This century-old judgment has not been overruled till date, even though judicial attitudes towards stakeholder interests have softened worldwide!

shareholders, but all its stakeholders – employees, customers, suppliers, local communities and society at large' (World Economic Forum, 2020).

- The British Academy, UK's premier and prestigious body for humanities, based on its 2018–2019 research for the Future of the Corporation project, revisited the contract between business and society, and promoted accountability in all constituencies (The British Academy, 2019, p. 32).

India was among the very few countries (the other being the UK[2]) to legislate boards' responsibility to promote the interests of relevant stakeholders besides their traditional fiduciary duties to the company and its shareholders.[3] The reality is key stakeholders' interests had to be (and were) taken care of if corporations were to succeed in producing sustainable profits for the shareholders, a situation that Harvard Professor, Lucian Bebchuk, calls *'enlightened shareholder value'*.

Human Capital: The 'X' Factor in Bank Governance

Listed banks are subject to the regulatory and supervisory jurisdiction of the country's central bank, Reserve Bank of India (RBI), in addition to the capital markets regulator, Securities and Exchange Board of India. Notwithstanding such supervision, there are several instances of bank frauds and misdemeanours.[4] This is a clear indication that regulatory surveillance alone is not the answer, but soft factors like personal ethics and organizational culture play a role, especially in banking.

Like any other service business but arguably to a much greater extent, the reputation and success of banks depend upon the quality and capacity of

---

[2] Section 172(1) of the UK Companies Act, 2006 (as amended) stipulates: 'A director of a company must act in the way he considers, in good faith, would be most likely to promote the success of the company for the benefit of its members as a whole, and in doing so have regard (among other matters) to … (b) the interests of the company's employees, (c) the need to foster the company's business relationships with suppliers, customers and others, (d) the impact of the company's operations on the community and the environment, …'

[3] Section 166(2) of the Companies Act, 2013, lays down: 'A director of a company shall act in good faith in order to promote the objects of the company for the benefit of its members as a whole, and in the best interests of the company, its employees, the shareholders, the community and for protection of environment'.

[4] Domestic private sector *Yes Bank* is the latest addition to the long list of public and private sector banks embroiled in sub-optimal and allegedly fraudulent management decisions on lending, insider trading, conflicts of interest and so on. Although RBI's reputation as an effective regulator has been targeted from time to time, RBI's own stand has been that its disciplinary powers to be more effective are inadequate.

their human capital. Since banks deal with ready money and have access to the confidential personal data of their clients, it would be fair to conclude that banks should have a strong human resources function that would ensure high levels of integrity and ethical behaviour traits in its employees.

The following discussion covers three hierarchical levels: employee in much of the 'rubber meets the road' kind of transactions that take place in business on an ongoing basis, the chief executive and their suite of key personnel, and the directors.

Ownership of an Organization Culture

There are many definitions and descriptions of what culture actually means. Culture is also driven by the explicitly stated or customarily implied 'purpose' and the ethical values the conglomeration or the individual stands by and for.

Among the leading business corporations in India, there are several that are identified as good and trustworthy in terms of products and service, transparency, working environment and profitable performance. We looked at the published statements of purpose, values, ethics and so on of two such entities, the multi-product-and-services Tata Group and the IT major, Wipro.[5] The Tata Group enumerates five *core Tata* values, which underpin the way they do business, as: integrity, responsibility, excellence, pioneering and unity. Wipro refers to the *spirit of Wipro* as their *beacon* that gives direction and a clear sense of purpose, and it is comprised of four principal values: being passionate about clients' success, being global and responsible, treating each person with respect and exercising unyielding integrity in everything they do.

A close look at these two statements offers a striking commonality of intent to a large extent: ethical behaviour, integrity, responsibility, excellence, innovation, entrepreneurial drive, respect for the individual, clients' and customers' success and delight and so on.

Leading by Example

The sceptic would, perhaps not without reason, make light of such statements of intent as 'easily written but hardly followed in practice'. Well-produced statements are indeed no substitute to the top living up to them.

---

[5] tata.com/about-us/tata-values-purpose; wipro.com/about-us

If an organization, like Wipro, mandates economy class by air for all domestic travel and the company chairman himself abides by that rule, its signalling effect is significant.

Tata group also offers, at a corporate level, an instance of leading by example: in line with their stated policies, the group largely appears to have steered clear of practices that would not satisfactorily stand the 'test of public scrutiny'. The response of J. R. D. Tata, the Group chairman who steered the Group's affairs for several decades, is a classic in walking the talk:

> What would have happened if our philosophy was like that of some other companies which do not stop at any means to attain their ends. I have often thought of that and I have come to the conclusion that if we were like other groups, we would be twice as big as they are today. What we have sacrificed is a 100 per cent growth, but we wouldn't want it any other way. (Lala, 2004, pp. 201–202)

Organizational Justice

Another important component of any initiative to establish credibility and ensure buy-in of postulated ethical and value principles is to ensure that any breach by anyone is promptly dealt with and punished as appropriate.

Jack Welch, when confronted with questions on how he managed to cope with GE's scandals and remain unscathed, said:

> I figured out that I cannot personally police perfect behavior of this organization. I can, though, have a set of values. Integrity. We have talked about it at every meeting. A violation of integrity. There's no discussion. You are gone. And we have example after example where people are just taken right out the door … Immediately. (Slater, 1999, p. 249)

Harsh words, but necessary for the due enforcement of prescribed rules. Nearer home, the managing director of Tata Finance, a Tata Group Company, a highly rated performer with a bright future in the Group, had to step down on charges of deals that reeked of self-dealing, which apart from being illegal, were a violation of the Tata code of conduct and its values (Lala, 2004, p. 215).

Training and Development

Periodical training of managers and staff on company values is another important mechanism to refresh and reiterate the company's message. In a vast majority of such instances, individuals could be indifferent or use the rationalization 'that is how business is done here'.[6] But for other consci-entious people, there are options. Decision-making is a lonely process; it is entirely up to the individual to take a call on which of these options is the right one in their personal circumstances. Organizations' training and counselling functionaries ought to equip their employees to think through such options maturely and help them to reach right decisions.

Is Whistleblowing Ethical?

Is it 'right' for an employee or anyone else who gets to know of some wrongdoing to disclose it to others? At the same time, a righteous person is also troubled that what is happening is not 'right' and needs to be stopped, even if it meant blowing the whistle. Both views have ethical overtones. In cases of material corporate misbehaviour, one should be guided by the fact that to be aware of it and yet not acting up on or against it can make the person an accessory after the crime. Preet Bharara (2019, p. 193), the US attorney for the prestigious Southern District of New York, writes:

> In the shadow of most massive frauds and cover-ups are lurking all manner of enablers—people who were helpful either to the perpetration of the crimes or to their concealment … People are too often afraid to confront power. Why? Because that is the culture of so many institutions.

Walking the Yellow Line

In a regulatory context, the 'line' refers to what one cannot breach in terms of legislative or regulatory mandates. Most well-governed companies would want to be safely well away from that line but there are many who would want to get away with impunity. Such people and institutions seem to revel in doing so to maximize some edge or profit, beat competition or internal 'stretch' target achievement. It is no different from Gordon Gekko's 'greed is good' sermon in the 1987 film, *Wall Street*. The truth is greed is not good, as so many have found in their utter ruin time and again.

---

[6] Sadly, that is the path often taken by many organizations, especially multinational corporations with a good record of ethical conduct in their home countries, willing to look the other way in reputedly corrupt Third Word host countries, so long as their hands are not visibly dirtied!

Human Capital Development and Reporting in Banks

We now turn to exploring to what extent this invaluable human capital is being nurtured to its full potential in banks, and to what extent banks' boards of directors are involved in overseeing the managements' performance in this regard. For this purpose, we use two representative entities: Charlotte, North Carolina based Bank of America, and Mumbai-headquartered State Bank of India (SBI), both adjudged[7] as the 'Best Banks in 2019' respectively in the world category and in India, by the *Global Finance* magazine (October 2019). The banks' respective websites were then accessed for necessary information. Annexure 4.1 sets out key statistics and practices as gleaned from their published reports and proxy statements as well as from additional inputs received from the banks.[8] The following is a summary discussion of the banks' overall corporate governance and its oversight role with regard to their human capital management related practices.

Bank of America

On Overall Governance

A Board size of 17 members (including chief executive officer [CEO]) may seem, at first sight, somewhat unwieldy, however, it may be justified by the bank's size (revenues of $91 bn in calendar 2019), its diversity (6 women, 3 coloured/ethnic); besides, there seems to be reasonable distribution of committee work without too many cross memberships. Four of these sixteen external directors have 10+ years of tenure, which may be seen as likely to be eroding their independent status; the mitigating factor is that they constitute just 25 per cent of all the independent directors, and, thus, board independence overall may still be of a very high order.

The bank is committed to stakeholder capitalism, environmental, social and governance (ESG) reporting and the Sustainable Development Goals

---

[7] Shortlisting criteria included: knowledge of local conditions and customer needs, financial strength and safety, strategic relationships and governance, competitive pricing, capital investment and innovation in products and services, all weighted for their importance. Final criteria included: scope of global coverage, size of staff, customer service, risk management, range of products and services, execution skills and use of technology. In case of a tie, bias towards local provider than a global institution; towards privately owned, not government owned; towards the best, not the biggest; and towards providers of service needs of corporates engaged in global business.

[8] The support provided by the two banks is gratefully acknowledged.

(SDGs), with the board overseeing progress towards their achievement.[9] The board's oversight processes are very well articulated; board committees (e.g., the one dealing with human capital) are geared to overseeing performance through equivalent management committees charged with the responsibility of supervising and administering plans and programmes.[10]

On Board Governance of Human Capital Management and Development

By definition, corporate boards only oversee, direct, control, counsel and contribute on policies and programmes brought up for their review and support; of course, they ought also to monitor performance at regular intervals and suggest course corrections as required. Directors with requisite domain knowledge or experience can challenge management's plans and bring to bear their expertise to make the presented proposals more robust. As board deliberations are not usually accessible, there can be no precise assessment of board contribution in any such specific detail. But it is possible to get a sense of the effectiveness of board oversight processes by looking at the agenda the board and its committees set for themselves. From this point of view, Bank of America's articulation of the board's oversight list is praiseworthy.[11] For example, the oversight covers the following with specific reference to human capital:

- Management's identification, measurement, monitoring and control of risks including compliance risk and conduct risk
- Establishment, maintenance and administration of appropriate compensation programmes and plans
- Maintenance of high ethical standards and effective policies and practices to protect the bank's reputation, assets and business
- ESG initiatives which include human capital management policies and practices

The board and its committees are reported to play a key role in the oversight of the bank's culture, setting the tone at the top and holding management accountable for maintaining high ethical standards. They do this by:

---

[9] See Bank of America Annual Report 2019, pp. 24–26.
[10] See Bank of America Annual Report 2019, p. 64 for a graphic description and commentary.
[11] See Bank of America Annual Report 2019, p. 6 for a fuller description.

- Reviewing and providing an oversight of the Bank's human capital management strategies, programmes and practices, including diversity and inclusion goals and progress
- Regular briefings from senior management on these issues and meeting with key managers below the senior-most management levels to assess for themselves how conduct and culture expectations cascade throughout the organization

On Leadership Development and Human Capital Benefit Programmes and Policies

Annexure 4.1 sets out some of these programmes but it is important to highlight two aspects of the initiatives:

- The number of leadership development programmes that focus on female employees and those belonging to ethnic and coloured minorities are truly inspirational in furthering gender equity and social cohesion.
- Some of the benefit programmes such as life event services that provide physical, emotional and financial support in cases of domestic violence, terminal illness or loss of loved ones (this last one covers retirees as well) are iconic in their concept. The results are there to see: employee turnover runs at 11 per cent in 2019 and employee engagement scores are at a more than healthy 85 per cent level.[12]

State Bank of India

On Overall Governance

Based on an analysis of the 2019 Annual Report, one finds that the board sized at 14 directors is satisfactory enough; its average age of non-executive directors as (roughly 66) arguably makes it one of the youngest boards among the top 100 companies; the average tenure of the board at just 1.37 years. Only 4 of its 14 directors meet the listing norms of independence, being directors elected by shareholders; and on gender diversity too, with only 2 women directors (1 of them a full-time executive) board diversity could likely be seen as relatively low[13] (Note: In the year 2020, the central

---

[12] Bank of America Annual Report 2019.

[13] Research suggests that a critical mass of three women directors, preferably all of them qualifying as independent, is ideal for board effectiveness. It may also be noted that SBI being state owned and controlled, appointment of directors (other than those elected by minority shareholders) is the prerogative of the Government of India and not SBI's board.

board comprised of 14 members, including a woman director). The bank is committed to stakeholder capitalism, ESG reporting and SDGs, with the board overseeing the progress made towards their achievement.[14] The board's oversight processes are very well articulated.

On the Board Oversight of Governance around 'Intangibles'

Although SBI does not currently have a board committee on human resources, its leadership is geared to overseeing performance through the management committee, charged with the responsibility of supervising and administering plans and programmes.[15] They cover a range of areas such as ethical standards, conduct risk, customer protection, cyber security management systems, employee benefits and wellness plans, diversity and inclusion, and ESG initiatives.

Ethics, Customer Service and Conduct Governance

The bank's culture over the decades has stemmed from its core values—service, transparency, ethics, politeness and sustainability. SBI was the first in the Indian public sector to start an independent 'ethics and business conduct vertical' and the first to constitute the position of chief ethics officer. In 2017, SBI took this seminal initiative and created the position of the chief ethics officer to establish and oversee an independent ethics and business conduct.

SBI's customer grievances redressal mechanism is designed to redress customer grievances courteously, promptly and satisfactorily. The bank was the first in India to introduce a code of fair banking practices in India called Towards Excellence. The bank has effective mechanisms for identification, measurement, monitoring and control of 'conduct' risk. It has also designed a robust fraud and cyber security management system aimed for protection against internal and external breaches.

Human Capital Mechanisms

SBI has taken a number of initiatives towards employee wellness and benefits, diversity and inclusion, and training, and development. The bank's human capital management efforts are centred on improving the welfare as well as wellness of its employees. Few specific measures include reimbursement of broadband charges, entertainment expenses, scholarships

---

[14] See SBI Annual Report 2019, pp. 24–26.
[15] See SBI Annual Report 2019, p. 64 for a graphic description and commentary.

for wards, staff loans at subsidized rates, leave travel concessions, festival advance etc. SBI also introduced a scheme called 'Atoot' to provide immediate support to families upon the death of employees while in service. It provides financial support for funeral expenses and assistance in transportation of mortal remains, when required. Yet another employee-centred mechanism is the 'Sanjeevani' helpline. It provides means to staff members in order to seek redressal of their grievances and later extended to retired employees as well.

SBI has a communication initiative called 'Nayi Disha', which was designed to communicate the macro-concerns of SBI with its vast employees. Phase II was designed and delivered during the FY 2019–2020 around four important cornerstones: building customer relations, selling solutions, service with compliance and growing our service reputation.

SBI is an equal opportunity employer and provides fair and equal compensation to its employees irrespective of their gender. SBI has mechanisms towards the well-being and fair opportunities for its women workforce. Women make up over 25.28 per cent of SBI's total workforce, and over 3,500 branches are headed by women. Measures taken towards this include, but are not limited to, special provisions related to their transfer and posting, leaves, health and medical requirements. The bank has a zero-tolerance policy in place on discrimination and sexual harassment. The bank has launched an online platform on its intranet for filing of sexual harassment complaints titled 'Garima'. The portal is a one-of-its-kind initiative in public sector banks.

The bank has a widespread training infrastructure comprising of 6 top-notch apex training institutes and 51 Regional State Bank Institutes of Learning and Development. The bank has shown its leadership credentials by pioneering the implementation of apprenticeship training through a pilot programme. This has lent support to the Government of India's 'Skill India Mission' for creating a skilled talent pool in the banking, financial services and insurance sector.

Sustainability

To enhance sustainability practices in the bank in a formalized manner, the bank has put in place a board-approved 'sustainability and business responsibility policy'. The bank has entrusted the deputy managing director (HR) and corporate development officer to oversee the bank's overall sustainability vision. SBI introduced a dedicated online tutorial 'ASTITVA' for its employees on sustainability issues pertaining to bank's internal sustainability measures and the UN SDGs.

A key part of sustainability initiative is Carbon Neutrality Project. Few initiatives under it are as follows:

- An approach paper is in place where the bank envisages achieving the 'carbon neutral' status by the year 2030. The initiative of remote monitoring based solar power system at branches (rural/semi-urban) in lieu of generator sets is being taken.
- SBI Green Fund—for all their digital channel customers, the bank is offering Green Reward points—which can be redeemed for credit—to SBI Green Fund, the proceeds of which will be utilized for sustainable activities.
- Green bonds—integration of environment and social management systems in their credit assessment process and business decisions has assumed critical importance. During the reporting period, the bank issued additional green bonds of USD 100 million, which add up to the aggregate green bond size of the bank at USD 800 million.

The Road Ahead

There are strong winds of change around the world towards the view that one cannot narrowly define corporate responsibility exclusively in terms of share owners. Banks are no different; if anything, their stakeholder involvement is of a much higher degree as most of its financing needs are met by depositors. Offered below are some specific suggestions towards this end.

On Bank's Corporate Purpose

Very few banks in India seem to have deliberated and articulated their main purpose.

Internationally, many banks seem to believe their role as advancing the well-being of the society, as contributing to the preservation and protection of the environment, some specifically in terms of climate change, and so on. In a developing country like India, there will be many niche spaces which banks can explore as their purpose.

In India, consolidation through the merger of some banks provides both, a challenge and an opportunity to redefine their purpose. Banks can choose their unique identity within that overarching umbrella purpose of the state-owned brands. Foreign-owned banks operating in India similarly have an opportunity to identify their local purpose within the broad group purpose.

On Board Governance

Board independence and gender/ethnic diversity need to be strengthened. It is important to ensure that 'fit and proper' criteria are strictly followed in the selection or election of the directors.

There is a pressing need to have on board independent directors with specialist expertise in human capital management. In fact, in a 2019 Securities and Exchange Commission consultation on improvements in governance disclosures in the USA, the need for such expertise on boards has also been included for comment. Nothing needs to come in the way of individual banks constituting a board-level committee to address this need.

On Human Capital and Leadership Development

Ethical governance in banks critically depends upon committed participation of employees and managers at all levels. Articulation of policies, close monitoring of their compliance at the operating level, and appropriate training and counselling programmes need to be introduced/strengthened with expert assistance. Documented evidence[16] seems to suggest ad hoc and person-dependent tactical measures being adopted to manage this trade union dominated industrial relations have an important function and are an existential asset, with very little long-term strategizing for this important function; perhaps, this situation has changed now, with increasing competition in banking business. In any case, time is opportune for bank boards to step in urgently and set up institutionalized mechanism for the management for developing this key resource.

Banking has increasingly become a specialized-knowledge-dependent business with widespread adoption of modern technology and quantitative analytics. While the advent of artificial intelligence is a giant step, it brings with it collateral risks, all of which need dedicated experts to satisfactorily address them (Zetzsche et al., 2020). Policies that radiate an approach of

---

[16] Illustratively, Khandelwal (2018, p. xix); 'For too long, IR was considered, at best, a nuisance to deal with or to live with, and management initiatives were few in terms of strategic planning for effective management of IR'.

care and consideration for the employees are the ones that create everlasting bonding.

A large proportion of bank employees in India are unionised at an industry level. While ethical leadership, by creating an ethical work culture, can positively influence the industrial relations culture, the scope in banking may be constrained by union and management behaviour. Since most of the benefits and other programmes would be negotiated at an overall banks–unions level, CEOs and top managers should seek to establish a personal working relationship based on trust, respect and care.

By the very nature and size of the work involved, banks tend to be large scale *inorganic* employers. A great deal of banks' transactional and other administrative work is outsourced to other entities, either due to cost or expertise considerations. It is important that banks ensure that the human capital of such entities do not adopt practices that the banks' own employees are not subjected to.

On Human Capital Disclosures

Despite the significant bulk of information listed corporations provide to their investors and others, there is very little that is known of this invaluable asset, human capital, except some top management compensation-related disclosures and employee numbers. A few companies, including banks, globally do provide some information voluntarily, especially after the stakeholder capitalism movement had gained some traction. Large investors around the world have begun to seek some information on corporate policies on how this key asset was managed. Leadership companies, and banks among them, ought to take the lead in this matter (without regulatory interventions) to share in public domain their human capital policies and programmes. And most importantly, disclosures should cover the role of the board in the formulation and effective administration of the company's policies and programmes including managing the 'conduct' risk associated with ethical breaches.

Annexure 4.1	*Human Capital Governance in Bank of America and SBI*

(The information below is an illustration of areas and practices under governance and human capital initiatives. The idea behind the analysis below is not to imply a technical or general comparison.)

Category	Criterion	Bank of America Calendar 2019	SBI FY Ending March 2020
Performance	2019 revenue (billion)	$91.2	$18.94
	2019 net income (billion)	$27.4	$1.92
	2019 total shareholder returns % (S&P Index/NSE Index %)		
	One year	46.2 (31.5)	–39%
	Three years	68.6 (53.1)	–32%
	Five years	114.1 (73.8)	4%
	2019 employee turnover (%)	11.0	
	Number of employees—about	200,000	249,448
Board oversight on human	Board membership independence (%)	94	42.86
	Women on board (%)	35	7
	CEO experience in board membership (%)	65	14.28
	Human capital experience in board membership (%)		
Capital management	Board oversight relating to human capital management:	Yes	Yes
	Management's identification, measurement, monitoring and control of 'conduct' risk	Yes	Yes
	Maintenance of high ethical standards and effective policies and practices to protect bank's reputation, assets and business	Yes	Yes
	Establishment, maintenance and administration of appropriately designed compensation programmes and plans	Yes	Yes

(Continued)

(Continued)

Category	Criterion	Bank of America Calendar 2019	SBI FY Ending March 2020
	ESG initiatives which include human capital management policies and practices	Yes	Yes
Select human capital and development initiatives	EP for EW[16]: Women's pay average as % of men's	99+	100
	For business leadership/C-level executive potential employees:		
	Women's next level leadership programmes	Yes	
	Women's executive development programmes	Yes	
	Leader development forum	Yes	
	Emerging leader programme	Yes	
	Manager excellence consultants	Yes	Yes
	Creating opportunities for personal growth and development	Yes	Yes
	Learning hub—for personalized learning plans tailored to their roles and interests	Yes	
	Tuition reimbursement programmes plus individualized academic advisory services	Yes, depending on eligibility criteria and norms	Through various programmes and initiatives, digital and e-training, and apprenticeship training
	Pathways to new appointments and reskilling	Yes (Career Path Tool and MyCareer)	
	Supporting physical, emotional and financial wellness		
	26 weeks parental leave, 16 of which are fully paid	Yes	Yes

[16] EP for EW = Equal pay for equal work; covers operations in the USA, the UK, France, Ireland, Hong Kong and Singapore.

Category	Criterion	Bank of America Calendar 2019	SBI FY Ending March 2020
	Centre-based and in-house back-up care for children and adult family members		
	Confidential free access to specialists for counselling during difficult moments for employee and family	Yes	Yes
	Reimbursement for adoption, fertility and/or surrogacy expenses	Yes, subject to policy	No
	Life event services:		
	Counselling and other support for events like		
	• Terminal illness of employees/family members	Yes	Yes
	• Domestic violence—support and connection to resources	Yes	No
	• Retirement—support for preparation	Yes	Yes
	• Medical workplace accommodation—for needy employees	Yes	No
	• Bereavement support—to employees and retirees for loss of loved one	Yes	Yes
	• Critical event support such as natural disasters, violence and house fire	Yes	Yes

Bibliography

Bharara, P. (2019). *Doing justice: A prosecutor's thoughts on crime, punishment and the rule of law.* Bloomsbury Publishing.

Business Roundtable. (2019). Statement on the purpose of the corporation. https://opportunity.businessroundtable.org/wp-content/uploads/2020/03/BRT-Statement-on-the-Purpose-of-a-Corporation-with-Signatures.pdf

Freeman, R. E. (1982). *Strategic management: A stakeholder approach.* Cambridge University Press.

Friedman, M. (1962). *Capitalism and freedom.* University of Chicago Press.

Global Finance. (2019, October). World's best banks 2019: Bank of America named best bank in the world. https://www.gfmag.com/magazine/october-2019/worlds-best-banks-2019-bank-america-named-best-bank-world

Khandelwal, A. K. (2018). *CEO: Chess master or gardener? How game-changing HR reforms created a new future for Bank of Baroda.* Oxford University Press.

Lala, R. M. (2004). *The creation of wealth: The Tatas from the 19th to the 21st century* (Rev. ed.). Penguin-Viking.

Morrow, S. (2020). *5th institutional investors survey 2020.* https://morrowsodali.com/uploads/insights/attachments/83713c2789adc52b596dda1ae1a79fc2.pdf

Slater, R. (1999). *Jack Welch and the GE way—management insights and leadership secrets of the legendary CEO.* McGraw-Hill.

The British Academy. (2019). *Principles for purposeful business: How to deliver the framework for the future of the corporation.* The British Academy.

Thoreau, H. D. [1849] (2015). *Civil disobedience* [Digital edition]. Xist Publishing (Original title: *Resistance to civil government*).

World Economic Forum. (2020). Davos manifesto 2020: The universal purpose of a company in the fourth industrial revolution. https://www.weforum.org/agenda/2019/12/davos-manifesto-2020-the-universal-purpose-of-a-company-in-the-fourth-industrial-revolution/

Zetzsche, D. A., Arner, D. W., Buckley, R. P., & Tang, B. (2020). Artificial intelligence in finance: Putting the human in the loop. https://papers.ssrn.com/sol3/papers.cfm?abstract_id=3531711

Leadership Choices in Building Better Governance

Regulation or Culture

Anujayesh Krishna

Banking is considered a key sector in the development and growth of economy and, by implication, the well-being of the society. The economy and society have become more complex and interconnected over time, and it now presents banks with a mix of challenges and priorities, which are qualitatively and quantitatively different from the legacy issues and challenges that banks traditionally addressed. To meet these challenges and priorities, banks require an organizational approach that is also qualitatively different from the legacy-based (regulations, rules and control) frameworks that they are most familiar with. The purpose of this chapter is to assess the role and impact of regulations in modern-day banking and build the case for culture in meeting governance challenges as well as building better banks in the future.

Governance through Regulations: Road Travelled So Far

The banking sector is considered a key sector for many reasons. Banks are 'funded' by the depositors in addition to their shareholders. Building trust and governance is, therefore, critical to ensure banks' survival and progress. Banks also provide financing solutions to all industries and customers (including depositors), and therefore, are crucial to the smooth functioning of the economy. Banking is also part of a complex ecosystem and is considered systemic in nature, that is, a failure in one bank could have a disproportionate impact on the whole banking system.

Given this key role, it is not surprising that the banking sector is regulated to ensure that it functions safely and smoothly. This has led to the leadership approaches, cultures and organizational design templates that are built on rule-based, bureaucratic and control frameworks. While such approaches have had their 'silent' successes in preventing failures, the rise of new-age banking (which is fast, complex and unpredictable) and the changing banking environment (overlapping ecosystems, emerging technologies, multi-generational employees and newer business models) call for a reassessment of the effectiveness of regulatory, rule- and control-based approaches, and if necessary, supplementing it with additional organizational approaches.

Nature, Scope and Effects of Regulation

Since the financial crises of 2008, the banking sector internationally has seen a phenomenal rise in regulation. The last 10 years have also provided time to reflect and understand their effectiveness from the experiential perspective. It is being argued increasingly that regulation and its reliance on control and compliance alone are not very effective in controlling bad banking practices and behaviours. For example, Filabi (2018) noted that legal 'requirements are often a porous and complex series of rules that are frequently gamed, or fall short of the regulatory goals of long-term safety and soundness' (pp. 38). In addition, 'rules may incentivise firms to follow the letter and not the spirit of the Law' (Financial Conduct Authority, 2018, pp. 12).

Similarly, Wheatley (2014) quoted Steare (2011) and pointed out, 'at their worst, laws, regulations and red tape have a tendency to multiply because they remove our responsibility for deciding what's right…that governments tend to respond to scandal with regulations, without considering that it is this 'obedience culture' that often fails in the first place'. Wheatley used the example of the UK regulators' experience and argued, '…if we take the FSA as just one example of this culture. You see its guidance increasing by some 27% during 2005–08, a period that coincides with many of the most explosive crises we're dealing with today'.

Regulation, with its emphasis on rules, control and compliance processes, is usually based on past experiences, crises and governance challenges, and therefore, is likely to be effective if the context and industry does not change much. In a dynamic and constantly evolving industry, these are very difficult conditions to meet. The rear-mirror nature of regulation was articulated by Martin Wheatley (2014), the then chief executive of Financial Conduct Authority (FCA), in his address:

> Two key areas of focus that I want to touch on tonight: First, the importance of creating effective, future-proofed regulation. Second, the importance of effective self-regulation.
>
> On the first, our priority issue at the FCA has been, and will continue to be, moving the regulator away from a low value culture of reacting to events … For the official sector, this problem has been particularly acute. Around the world there's been a culture of reacting to conduct issues; whether mini-bonds in Hong

Kong, currency swaps in Korea, structured agricultural products in Australia or of course PPI in the UK.

Given their reactive nature, regulations deal more with the 'known knowns' instead of the 'known unknowns'. They are based more on a rear-mirror view as opposed to a GPS view. When the context changes, regulations start losing their relevance and become less of a force for good. This is especially important in an industry like banking where both the context and the industry itself change continuously with new firms, business models, products and platforms.

Regulations could also result in unintended consequences when firms try to mitigate the impact of regulation, rule and control processes in unexpected ways. For example, the bonus cap rule in the European Union, which required that bonuses of identified staff in banking firms falling under the scope of rule should not be more than twice of fixed pay, led to an increase in the fixed pay of identified staff generally in the form of role-based allowances (European Banking Authority, 2014).

Behavioural Implications

Rules, compliance and control processes are critiqued for the costs (Deloitte, 2017) and the resource 'burdens' they put on banks. While stakeholders are aware of out-of-pocket costs, the intangible costs and their consequences are equally compelling.

Speaking from an experiential point of view, rules and control processes are perceived as tactical and 'controlling' in nature as opposed to being an 'enabler'. Rules, compliance and control provide guardrails against wrong practices and bad behaviours, but in doing, they are also likely to breed a culture of fear, control, obedience, risk aversion and lack of initiatives. In an extreme case, regulations also run the risk of leading to 'regulatory overbearance', bureaucracy, stifling of initiatives and an environment of negativity, where fear and lack of decision-making become rampant. In Indian banking, the Nayak Committee (2014) on banking governance drew attention to it, and the Khandelwal Committee (2010) stressed on the need of cultural transformation.

An equally important implication is the unstated belief (or illusion) that control and compliance equal good banking. Behavioural research on in-attentional blindness raises the possibility that leaders may develop tunnel vision and (false) confidence that meeting regulations and rules is same as building great banks. While prevention of wrong practices and behaviours is essential to build safer banks, good banking is also about 'enabling' capabilities around customer focus, innovation and effective risk management processes.

Kahneman (2012), in his landmark book, *Thinking, Fast and Slow*, referred to WYSIATI (What you see is all there is) rule, which he used to explain several biases in human judgement and choices. WYSIATI rule states: 'You cannot help dealing with the limited information you have as if it were all there is to know'. In the banking sector, the prevalence of rules and control processes and the constant focus on regulation have the psychological effect of creating a make-believe reality that it is the only approach. Even when leaders are aware of human bias created by 'availability heuristic', emphasis on rules and controls leaves them with not enough bandwidth to focus on 'enabling capabilities'.

Culture as an Alternate Pathway

The above discussion suggests that regulations, rules and control either do not always achieve their purposes or there is a high organizational cost in terms of resources and culture that they engender. The point is not that regulations are to be abandoned, rather it is mistaking that they are the only way to build safer and better banks, and the risk that they become an end in themselves. Culture, as an alternate approach, is 'crowded out' because of Kahneman's WYSIATI rule. Since most discussions happen around rules, compliance and control, they are seen as the only choices.

Given the experience from regulatory front lines, international bodies, such as Financial Stability Board, Group of Thirty and the FCA (one of the two regulators in the UK with responsibility for market integrity and fair competition) have started focusing on culture as an alternate pathway to build better banks.

The role of culture was highlighted by the Group of Thirty in their July 2015 report on 'Banking Conduct and Culture'. The report makes the point that a 'great deal rests on culture' (Group of Thirty, 2015, pp. 5) and 'Poor cultural foundations and significant cultural failures were major drivers of the recent financial crisis, and continue to be factors in the scandals since then...' (pp. 11). Similarly, in its stocktake report on governance frameworks (May 2017), Financial Stability Board (2017) noted that the culture 'of an institution can defeat its formal governance. Indeed, overtime the culture of a firm can be a major influence on its governance framework' (pp. 5).

The case for culture becomes additionally strong when the features of new-age banking are considered. The future of banking is likely to be driven by new technologies, business models, complex ecosystems, a multi-generational workforce and new economic and financing needs. Effective banks in this context need to be driven by flexible cultures that have initiative and risk-taking, experimentation, organic structures and collaboration as their dominant features. A culture that is based on rules, control and bureaucracy is not well adapted to this new-age banking and likely to encounter new risks and failures.

While attention to culture in the banking context by regulators is a recent and welcome phenomenon, organizational culture is a well-recognized concept with strong research support. Culture has been identified in varied forms as an ingredient in organizational success in the seminal works of researchers, such as William Ouchi (1981), Pascale and Athos (1986), Peters and Waterman (2015) and Jim Collins (2001). Recently, Sackmann (2011) conducted a meta-analysis of 55 studies and concluded that 'most studies support a direct link between corporate culture and firm performance'.

The relationship between regulations and culture is more nuanced than simply a choice between the two approaches to build better banks. Depending on how the discussion is framed, these two approaches can be seen as complementary or competitive. The discussion below covers three different areas, where both approaches wield influence, albeit in different ways.

Accountability and Governance

Regulations with their focused attention on safety and financial soundness are generally seen as the main way to build effective governance and better banks. However, as we have seen in previous sections, regulations are not always effective. Following its own experience, FCA (one of the two UK regulators), in the recent past, shifted its focus towards culture as the pathway to transform banks. In its publication containing various perspectives on the topic, FCA stated:

> Culture in financial services is widely accepted as a key root cause of the major conduct failings that have occurred within the industry in recent history, causing harm to both consumers and markets… Given its impact and the role it needs to play in re-building trust in financial services, firms' culture is a priority for the FCA. (Financial Conduct Authority, 2018, pp. 3)

To the FCA, accountability is an important aspect in the relationship between regulation and culture building. As the FCA document notes,

> So, how can regulation promote healthy culture? Two fundamental concepts underpin our thinking about culture and regulation. The first is that regulation

has to hold the individual as well as the firm to account… The second concept is that leaders can manage culture even if they can't measure it very well. This is deeply embedded in the Accountability Regime too. The regime aims to hold firms' leadership to account for their own behaviour and for taking reasonable steps to manage the behaviour of those in their areas of responsibility. (Financial Conduct Authority, 2018, pp. 3–4)

Similarly, a joint report by the Association of Chartered Certified Accountants (ACCA) and the Economic and Social Research Council (ESRC) in the UK noted, 'ACCA believes that a healthy corporate culture is a prerequisite of good governance and sound risk management' (Association of Chartered Certified Accountants, 2014, pp. 2). In its research report titled, 'A Duty to Care? Evidence of the Importance of Organizational Culture to Effective Governance and Leadership', CIPD referred to scandals across sectors and noted, 'In all cases … Boards in these situations overlooked, or were not aware of, data and insights which may have highlighted upcoming cultural and operational threats…' (CIPD, 2016, pp. 3).

Asymmetric Nature of Influence

Regulations, when they are effective, can prevent bank failures and wrong-doings; however, implementing regulations is not always the same thing as delighting customers or building innovative banking products. Culture, however, is more symmetric in its influence. While a good culture could facilitate building strong firms, a bad culture could harm the firm in multiple ways, even when rules and processes are in place. Martin and Cialdini (2016) argued, 'organisational environments (created by leaders who encourage or just allow the use of unworthy practices or questionable tactics) can experience a triple whammy of internal consequences: reduced employee performance; higher employee turnover and increased malfeasance' (pp. 99). Viewed in this context, stakeholders do not have a choice between regulations and culture. Building great culture is necessary in its own right, even when the focus is on regulations, as bad culture could harm the bank and jeopardize the governance efforts.

Locus of Control: Internal or External

Regulations are externally imposed and provide limited, if any, choice to the banking firm. This is in contrast to culture building, where leaders have more leverage, including, unfortunately, the choice not to pay attention to it. There is research to suggest that we credit achievements to our own efforts and attribute failures to external factors. There is also research that suggests that when change is chosen, as opposed to being imposed, it is likely to be more effective. These insights suggest that culture is more suited to the challenge of building great banks. Regulators, however, can support the culture-building process in banks by building platforms for research, sharing best practices and including progress on culture in their review processes.

Leadership Challenges and Choices in Exploring Culture

The decision to use culture as an alternate pathway despite its appeal is not an easy one. Cultural change represents one of the most formidable leadership challenges. Building the right culture is not a short-term engineering problem and it impossible to prescribe a precise rule book or a 'user manual' that contains a step-by-step process to do it. Because it is intangible, complex and hard to accomplish, culture provides competitive advantages that cannot be easily copied. This argument serves as a business case for culture (assuming values are not by themselves sufficient) and calls for leaders and senior managers to invest efforts in it.

Culture in Banking Sector

Banking cultures, due to a focus on risk-management and compliance processes, are increasingly perceived as risk-averse and control cultures. There is paucity of research on banking cultures, though research interest in this area is developing.

The Khandelwal Committee report (2010), on human resource (HR) issues of public sector banks (PSBs), pointed out in the context of HR function that the 'present arrangement has promoted high level of standardization and rule orientation … Standardization has created a culture of lack of initiative, innovation and professionalization in HR area. Overall, all these have not been conducive to rendering effective customer service' (pp. xxv). One implication is that banking culture needs reassessment and change towards a performance-driven culture that recognizes risk and initiative taking, and HR policies and processes have a pivotal role to play. The Nayak Committee report (2014) on the 'Governance of Board of Banks in India' noted a similar challenge in Indian PSBs noting that there is a 'perverse' belief in banks that avoidance of 'personal initiatives and discretion' helps in career-building.

General Cultural Road Maps

Transforming culture requires leadership to make choices on the type of culture to work towards and understand the trade-offs involved. Current banking cultures, as noted above, are likely to be characterized by bureaucracy, rules and control-driven behaviours. The limitations of this type of culture are likely to be accentuated by new-age banking, which is likely to be technology driven, fast paced and with a multi-generational workforce.

Organization theory is rich in research that suggests that effective culture varies with the organizational environments. If the environment is complex, unpredictable and varied, as banking environments are, then a culture characterized by differentiation, empowerment, flexibility, experimentation, risk-taking and open communication is more effective.

In addition, in its ACCA-ESRC project report (2014), ACCA identified the following 14 distinct cultural trade-offs for the boards to consider.

- Values as a wealth-driver versus values as a protector
- Openness to mistakes versus zero tolerance
- Leadership versus followership
- Conformity versus challenge
- Independence versus involvement
- Enforcing versus avoiding or exploiting regulation
- Common sense versus rules and procedures
- Empowerment versus rules and tight rules versus loose rules
- Quantitative measures versus qualitative measures
- Innovation versus control
- Risk seeking versus risk avoiding
- Trust versus accountability
- Human capital versus human cost

Yet another, and perhaps more useful from a practical standpoint, way to understand culture is to understand its nature. While there is rich literature available on cultural properties, the following are features that stand out from a practical perspective.

- 'Culture is not optional; it exists whether we like it or not' (Financial Conduct Authority, 2018, pp. 10)
- Each firm's culture is unique, and there is no 'one-size-fits-all culture', though healthy cultures share a few common characteristics
- Leadership plays a key role in setting the culture and sets the 'tone from the top'

- Culture is dynamic and requires a shift from linear thinking (simple cause-and-effect relationships) to a holistic perspective (a whole system that consists of innumerable visible and invisible parts constantly interacting with each other)

The above principles can be used by leaders to think deeply about their existing and desired cultures and build their own transformational journeys.

Implications

Cultural transformation is not an easy challenge, particularly in large-sized banks with legacy processes, structures and sub-cultures in place. This section presents implications that could facilitate this complex process of change.

Implications for Regulators

Culture is unique and intrinsic to an organization, and as the FCA argued, there is no 'one culture fits all' model. Given this, it is a difficult challenge for regulators to assess and provide a cultural goalpost (or framework) for the firms to follow. This presumably limits the role of regulators and raises important questions. Filabi (2018, pp. 38) posed these questions in the following way:

> In the context of financial sector regulation, this raises a specific question—how can prudential and conduct regulators who intend to influence the culture of supervised firms use tools other than enforcement processes to motivate firms to more proactively manage their culture (Bailey, 2017)? In other words, can regulators effectively and fairly bring an enforcement action against a firm for not having the 'right' culture? And, if culture can't be regulated and enforced in the traditional ways, what specific tactics should the regulator take to advance this important topic?

Notwithstanding the above challenges, emerging experience suggests that regulators can help in promoting culture through industry-level strategic interventions and firm-based interventions.

1. **At the strategic/industry level**, regulators may consider the following:

    - Prioritize cultural assessment at the same level as prudential management, governance practices and risk management in their review process. Regulators could help build a 'culture of culture', that is, an operating environment, where 'culture' becomes a strategic priority and it is normal to talk about it.

- Make accountability a key part of cultural assessment and mandate use of responsibility maps and prescribed responsibilities for senior and key roles as had been done under the accountability regime in the UK.

  The UK regulators introduced the Senior Managers and Certification Regime to hold senior managers accountable for their own behaviours as well as those in their areas of responsibilities. The framework also includes two prescribed responsibilities (PR)[1] specifically on a firm's culture. They are as follows:

  o PR(h) on the 'responsibility for overseeing the adoption of the firm's culture in the day-to-day management of the firm' (p. 4);
  o PR(i) on the 'responsibility for leading the development of the firm's culture by the governing body as a whole' (p. 4)

  PR(h) remains with the executive, usually the chief executive officer (CEO), while PR(i) is usually with the chair of the board. The framework expects CEO and the chair to review regularly the progress on firm's culture including the factors that drive behaviour.

  Recently, Australia has also introduced a similar framework called Banking Executive Accountability Regime, which seeks to ensure higher and effective accountability for banking leaders. Such initiatives consider accountability a key component of banking culture.

- Accelerate the industry learning curve through investing in research-based practices. The need for a knowledge base on culture in the Indian banking sector is long overdue. This is not a novelty idea. Tom Reader (2018) argued, 'In other industries where cultural practices related to risk and ethics are key to institutional prosperity (e.g. aviation, oil, healthcare, rail, nuclear), more formalised and customised approaches have been taken to describing and measuring organisational culture' (pp. 24).

  To start with, such research initiatives could focus on various dimensions of culture across various types of banks, how they relate

---

[1] PR refers to specific responsibilities that firms need to give to their senior managers to ensure that there is a clear accountability for that responsibility. https://www.fca.org.uk/firms/ senior-managers-certification-regime/dual-regulated-firms Prudential Regulatory Authority, one of the two UK regulators, included the culture-related PR in its rule book. The two PR cited are on Page 4, but this could change if the rule book is edited later. https://www. bankofengland.co.uk/-/media/boe/files/prudential-regulation/policy-statement/2018/ ps2618app1.pdf

to effectiveness and how various dimensions could be improved and progress against them measured. This analysis could also build a repertoire of questions and insights on culture as different banks go through their experiences and learn from each other.

- Build their own surveillance systems to ensure that behaviours, drivers and outcomes are being picked up with higher accuracy, timeliness and detail, as the industry and individual firms traverse their culture-building trajectory. Experientially, observations indicate that symptoms of firm's governance and performance problems show up as 'behavioural symptoms' at an early stage, which if attended to in time, reduce the need for a major 'surgery' or intervention later.

Table 5.1 presents stages of governance challenges that could be mapped to various cultural markers.

2 **At the firm level**, regulators may formally require banks to do the following:

- Reassess and professionalize the HR function, particularly in PSBs. As the Khandelwal Committee report (2010) on HR issues in PSB notes, there is an urgent need for strategic and progressive HR systems and processes, and that HR itself has become a potential risk to the system.
- Understand their existing culture and values, and how they relate to day-to-day organizational life, preferably using the resources developed through industry-specific research.
- Develop their own short- and long-term cultural plans and interventions. This will include review and improvise organization design and management processes to support culture and accountability (similar to the UK's accountability regime), transparency and customer impact.
- Institutionalize processes to record, critique and learn from cultural failings including provision of means, like whistle blowing, that could proactively help to prevent bank failings.

Implications for Banking Leaders

An important implication for leaders is to take a broader view and recognize that meeting regulatory requirements, compliance standards and control processes is essential, but it does not automatically equate to building a great bank. Building a bank requires an organizational approach and culture that is different from the 'control'- and 'compliance'-driven culture.

Table 5.1 Cultural Markers to Stage Governance Challenges: An Exploratory Banking Culture Model

(This model is based on anecdotal and experiential observations, and the underlying assumption is that before governance failures show up through financial/quantitative matrices, they can be tracked in time and cost-efficient ways using qualitative/cultural matrices. Since the aim is to prevent failures, this model focuses on challenges and does not include stages of successes.)

Stage	Stage Name	Main Symptoms	Main Stakeholder Impacted	Dominant Features	Cultural Markers
Stage 1	Management failures (May or may not be localized)	Customer service problems	Customers	Customer process failures Poor customer practices. (Mis-selling, sharp practices)	• Poor and opaque customer service • Aggressive culture • Overly focused on targets
Stage 2	Malignant leadership failures	Above and Employee Ethics/ Motivation Problems	Above and Employees	Above and Egregious products	Few or all of the above and • Disengaged employees • Difficulties in hiring good people • Compartmentalized businesses/ functions • Number-driven performance focus • Unclear communication channels
Stage 3	Challenged governance	Above and Internal management reporting problems	Above and Reputation and shareholders	Above and Profiteering through common sharp customer and/or bad organizational practices.	Few or all of the above and • Conduct issues suspected • Open/vacant key/senior roles • Disengaged leadership at the middle • Opaque culture

	Audit issues		Systematic, in a division or bank itself, and could spread	• High attrition at key/senior roles • Diffused responsibilities • Lack of accountable structures • Ineffective/unchallenging board and apathy
Stage 4 Institutional governance failure	Above **and** Regulatory and fiduciary reporting problems Funding (transactional) problems Survival problems	Above **and** Sector/Industry (depending on bank's size)	Above **and** Lack of transparency in financial statements Financial statements not passing 'smell test' and cannot be trusted Frequent 'adjustments' in statements	Few or all of the above **and** • Leadership dependence/hero worshipping • Bank split into various islands • Access to leadership seen as exclusive and privileged • Growth and promotion criteria opaque • Open knowledge of board-level concerns and differences • No takers for key/senior positions
Stage 5 Systemic governance failure	Above **and** Capital/Revival/Turnaround problems External capital providers not interested	Above **and** Banking ecosystem/economy (depending on bank's size)	Above **and** Accountability at both system and individual levels, misconduct, errors of commission Difficult to establish review trails	Few or all of the above **and** • Organization-wide disengaged employees • High turnover at all levels • Board-level issues

Few additional implications are as follows:

- New-age banking environment is likely to be dynamic, unpredictable, varied and complex. Research and anecdotal experience suggest that cultures, which provide for empowerment, flexibility, risk-taking, open communication and experimentation are more effective. Given the legacy context of Indian PSBs, building such a culture is a significant challenge and requires transformational leadership.
- Desired culture has higher likelihood of getting institutionalized, if it is given the same primacy as business priorities, and reviewed in formal and informal ways just like any other business priority.
- Relationship between business targets and cultural values is complicated and contextual. While an effective culture should, in theory, prevent wrong practices, this is not always the case, particularly under conditions of tough targets, survival pressures and inappropriate reward structures.
- Cultures, which are driven by a singular (business) focus, for instance, business targets or obsession with control processes, could, under certain conditions, force employees to choose between what is good for them and what is right for the bank.

Conclusion

This chapter argues that banks need a qualitatively different organizational approach based on culture, because banking regulations do not always yield desired results and future of banking is changing in transformative ways. This is broadly the experience of international firms and regulators. To transform their cultures, banks need a strategic pivot and transform their existing cultures, which are primarily characterized by bureaucracy, rules, compliance and control processes to a culture which is characterized by flexibility, risk-taking, empowerment, performance focus and willingness to take initiative. This is not an easy change, and both regulators and banking leaders need to play a transformational role to institutionalize culture as a go-to approach to build great banks.

Bibliography

Association of Chartered Certified Accountants. (2014). *Culture and channelling corporate behaviour: A joint research project by ACCA and the ESRC* [online]. http://www.accaglobal. com/content/dam/acca/global/PDF-technical/corporategovernance/5-mins-on-culture-and channelling-corporate-behaviour.pdf

Bailey, A. (2017). Culture in financial institutions: It's everywhere and nowhere. Speech. HKMA Annual Conference for Independent Non-Executive Directors. https://www.fca.org.uk/news/speeches/culture-financial-institutions-everywhere-nowhere

Cialdini, R. (2016). *Pre-suasion: A revolutionary way to influence and persuade.* Simon and Schuster.

CIPD. (2016). *A duty to care? Evidence of the importance of organizational culture to effective governance and leadership.* Author. https://www.cipd.co.uk/Images/a-duty-to-care_2016-evidence-of-the-importance-of-organisational-culture-to-effective-governance-and-leadership_tcm18-14220.pdf

Collins, J. (2001). *Good to great.* Random House Business Books.

Deloitte. (2017). Regulatory Productivity. https://www2.deloitte.com/us/en/pages/regulatory/articles/cost-of-compliance-regulatory-productivity.html

European Banking Authority. (2014). Opinion of the European Banking Authority on the application of Directive 2013/36/EU (Capital Requirements Directive) regarding the principles on remuneration policies of credit institutions and investment firms and the use of allowances. EBA/Op/2014/10. https://eba.europa.eu/documents/10180/657547/EBA-Op-2014-10+Opinion+on+remuneration+and+allowances.pdf

Filabi, A. (2018). Carrot or stick? Culture as a regulatory approach. In *Transforming Culture in Financial Services.* Discussion Paper DP 18/2. https://www.fca.org.uk/publication/discussion/dp18-02.pdf

Financial Conduct Authority (2018). *Transforming culture in financial services.* Discussion Paper DP 18/2. https://www.fca.org.uk/publication/discussion/dp18-02.pdf

Financial Stability Board. (2017). *Stocktake of efforts to strengthen governance frameworks to mitigate misconduct risks.* https://www.fsb.org/wp-content/uploads/WGGF-Phase-1-report-and-recommendations-for-Phase-2.pdf

Group of Thirty. (2015). *Banking conduct and culture: A call for sustained and comprehensive reform.* http://group30.org/images/uploads/publications/G30_BankingConductandCulture.pdf

Kahneman, D. (2012). *Thinking, fast and slow.* Penguin Books.

Khandelwal, A. (2010). Report of the committee on HR issues of public sector banks. https://financialservices.gov.in/sites/default/files/HRIssuesOfPSBs.pdf

Martin, S., & Cialdini, R. (2018). Influence, culture and change. In *Transforming culture in financial services.* Discussion Paper DP 18/2. https://www.fca.org.uk/publication/discussion/dp18-02.pdf

Nayak, P. (2014). Report of the committee to review governance of boards of banks in India. https://rbidocs.rbi.org.in/rdocs/PublicationReport/Pdfs/BCF090514FR.pdf

Ouchi, W. G. (1981). *Theory Z.* Addison-Wesley.

Pascale, R. T., & Anthony, J. A. (1986). *The art of Japanese management.* Penguin.

Peters, T., & Waterman, R. H. (2015). *In search of excellence: Lessons from America's best-run companies.* Profile Books.

Reader, T. W. (2018) Identifying and measuring organisational culture in financial services. In Transforming culture in financial services. Discussion Paper DP 18/2. https://www.fca.org.uk/publication/discussion/dp18-02.pdf

Sackmann, S. A. (2011). Culture and performance. In. N. M. Ashkenasy, P. M. Wilderom, & M. F. Peterson (Eds.), *The handbook of organizational culture and climate* (pp. 188–224). SAGE Publications.

Steare, R. (2011). *Ethicability: How to decide what's right and find the courage to do it.* Roger Steare Consulting Limited.

Sutherland, J. (2018). Why regulation alone will not influence firm culture and consumer outcomes and what else is needed. In *Transforming Culture in Financial Services*. Discussion Paper DP 18/2. https://www.fca.org.uk/publication/discussion/dp18-02.pdf

Wheatley, M. (2014, 4 March). Ethics and economics. Speech. Worshipful Company of International Bankers. https://www.fca.org.uk/news/speeches/ethics-and-economics

Strategic Human Capital Management and Banking Governance

An Unexplored Symbiotic Relationship in PSBs

Anil K. Khandelwal and Anujayesh Krishna

There is an increased emphasis on improving the governance in banking given its role in the economic and social development. Lack of effective governance in banks was considered one of the main reasons behind the global financial crises of 2008 and a few other banking failures (UK Parliament, 2013). In the Indian context, governance challenges in both private and public sector banks have in the past plagued banking performance and on more than a few occasions, caused panic among depositors and concerns with the regulators and the government. The standard and default approach to improving banking governance has been the use of regulations and control processes. While intuitively appealing and aligned to traditional command and control structure, regulations and control processes have their limitations. They are costly to enforce and implement (particularly for small and mid-size banks), discourage innovation and risk-taking initiatives, have unintended consequences and by themselves do not solve the full range of governance challenges. This is one of the factors that has led to international financial bodies including the Financial Conduct Authority (FCA, one of the two financial services regulators in the UK) to focus on culture as an alternate pathway to build better banking governance (Financial Conduct Authority, 2018). This is also a recognition of the role that intangibles or soft factors play in building strong governance within banks.

Although human resources (HR) capital is a key factor in building robust governance, it has until now remained unattended and unexplored at the higher echelons, where it is relegated to a departmental concern. This has led to a transactional view of the human capital, and importantly, its limited applicability in improving banking governance. This chapter explores the strategic roles, competencies of HR functionaries, including the role of the board and the government to build the HR function, and associated accountability at various levels to strengthen the architecture of governance in public sector banks (PSBs).

Changing Nature of Banking

A bigger challenge to using regulation to improve governance comes from the larger, systemic shifts taking place in the banking sector. Banking has become complex, fast-changing and technologically driven industry, and this trend is likely to accelerate further. Using regulations, with its focus on rules, control and compliance, in a fast-changing and complex industry, runs the risk of using a rear mirror-approach, as opposed to GPS-approach to reach a desired goalpost. The future of banking, driven mostly by technology and human capital, poses different governance challenges. These challenges are discussed below at the level of industry and individual banks.

1. **Systemic changes at the macro level:** While it is not possible to predict the specifics of the new banking, it is possible to make few observations about the direction of changes in the banking sector. The future of the banking sector is likely to be more technologically driven and have multi-generational employees and customers. The advances in technology and higher innovation will also give rise to a variety of business models and new products and services, which will lead to a complex, interconnected and dynamic banking ecosystem.

The emerging complexity, variety (business models, products and services, customer needs) and interconnectedness in the banking ecosystem will make it difficult to apply a standard regulatory approach to improve governance, as each business model has its unique risk fingerprints and a different asset profile. The pace and complexity of change also make it difficult to have a regulatory, rear-mirror-focused approach to governance, as the context changes continuously and it is not likely that same risks will reappear frequently. However, in this variety and unpredictable pace of change, there is a common asset class, namely HR, which remains a constant. An active engagement of HR, who are on the front lines of various changes in the industry, could provide a GPS and forward-looking governance. Inclusion of mandatory reporting on HR will, therefore, add strength to the regular and standard reviews that the board and other stakeholders perform. Since most regulations are around managing asset-related decisions and risks, it is urgent now to ensure that the same, if not more, governance spotlight is directed towards HR.

2. **Future of banking at the individual bank level:** While capital and branches (physical infrastructure) were main assets in the past, the future of banking is likely to be driven more by technology and intangibles assets (e.g., trust and reputation, leadership, customer service and innovation, KPMG, 2019; Lal et al., 2019; PricewaterhouseCoopers, 2014). This shift in the nature of assets (from capital and physical infrastructure to technology and intangibles) has deep implications in terms of underlying drivers of growth, nature of risks and the governance priorities. The growing complexity in the banking sector and advances in technology make role the of human capital and culture more important in the following two main ways.

First, an increase in the complexity in various banking functions such as risk management, treasury, credit, compliance and HR makes it likely that the lack of requisite expertise could result in bad banking decisions, which individually or cumulatively could over time lead to governance failures. In fact, the Khandelwal Committee (2010), appointed by the Government of India, to look into the HR issues in PSBs, identified HR as possibly the biggest risk in the banking sector. This risk unfortunately is likely to get much bigger in the emerging future of banking. With higher automation (through technology) of standardized and routine functions, the importance and premium on non-standard, complex and strategic decision-making are likely to significantly go up. The availability and quality of human capital will, therefore, play an important role in shaping whether or not banks are exposed to poor decision-making, strategic and operational failures, and other similar risks.

Second, the future of banking suggests that the competitive and strategic advantages will increasingly accrue through the superior management of intangible assets. Various intangible assets, such as customer service, innovation and digitalization are more, if not exclusively, amenable to HR as opposed to financial and physical capital. HR are the only asset class that could influence and control intangible assets (including technology). Viewed in this context, 'traditional' risks such as poor credit decisions, obsolete technology and failure to manage non-performing asset (NPA) levels need to be reframed as shadows or derivatives of the 'real' risk, namely inadequate human capital and rigid and bureaucratic culture. This makes it both necessary and urgent at senior (board) and strategic levels to drive accountability with respect to use and effectiveness of human capital. As argued above, any failures and weaknesses in human capital could have a downstream growth and risk impact through other intangible assets.

Current HR Challenges in PSBs: Gap Analysis

The previous section highlighted the role of human capital in building better governance. The need for this accountability becomes self-evident and urgent when a gap analysis is done between the current HR practices (in PSBs) and desired practices, given the emerging future of banking (Table 6.1). This comparison focuses mostly on PSBs, as they cover 70 per cent of the banking in India.

Table 6.1	*Gap Analysis between Current (Mostly in Public Sector) and Future HR Challenges*	
HR Areas	**Summary Description of Current HR**	**Desired State (Given the Changing Context and Future of Banking)**
HR Accountability		
Role and objectives	Maintenance of HR within the framework of government guidelines and industry-level agreements. Limited scope for discretion and initiatives	Customized HR policies and practices depending on the needs of individual bank and its strategic priorities. Differentiated policies to achieve desired HR outcomes in terms of culture, compensation, engagement and motivation
Oversight	In most cases, typically below board or even CEO level	Board-level regular oversight and review, just like any mainstream business function within the bank
Main stakeholders	HR head, CEO, employees, industry, government	Board and other stakeholders (including regulators and shareholders), CEO, trade unions, employees, industry, research and academic institutions

HR Areas	Summary Description of Current HR	Desired State (Given the Changing Context and Future of Banking)
Accountability process	Mostly internal to bank, tactical and need-based reporting	Formal board and senior-level reviews; mandated reporting on key HR matrices, external review and benchmarking
HR Culture		
Salient cultural aspects	Mostly bureaucratic; largely, rule-based culture with compliance orientation	Meritocratic; empowerment, risk and initiative taking, experimentation, innovation
Approach towards change	Piecemeal and often lacking an integrated approach; relatively, few instances of sustainable transformational change. Key areas of focus are under-prioritized	Change process and mindset embedded in culture; dynamic and ongoing adaptation to context and needs; major focus of change on diversity, inclusiveness and building an architecture of intangibles
Flexibility and empowerment	Limited flexibility and empowerment in adapting HR policies to the need of individual bank	Flexible HR practices; high empowerment to differentiate HR to suit individual bank's need
HR Assets		
Professionalization and training/ background of HR team	Professionalism by exception (islands of professionalism in some cases)	Professionalism is the norm; professionally trained HR functionaries; focus on integrity, process sensitivity and humaneness; additionally, business understanding; HR is accorded priority like any other critical business function
Digitalization of HR function	Varies with the bank; in general, potential of digitalization is underutilized	Use of digitalization to build meritocratic bank; digitalization drives all processes to create HR value and experience

(Continued)

(Continued)

HR Areas	Summary Description of Current HR	Desired State (Given the Changing Context and Future of Banking)
Structure and nature of HR function	Mostly centralized, HR functionaries thinly spread and underoptimized	Decentralized with high-level guidance; customized to the needs of the individual and groups; HR structure in alignment with business of the bank; HR functionaries well-aligned and optimized to meet HR goals
Board and strategic support	Tactical, conditional upon CEO's approach	Strategic and ongoing

PSBs are instrumentalities of the country's economic development. Their robustness and stability are critical to the economic and financial stability of the country, particularly in the context of the COVID-19 challenge. PSBs are large systems with over 0.1 million bank employees in each of the 5 large banks excluding the State Bank of India (SBI), which has over 0.25 million employees. Although massive in terms of employee and asset size, unfortunately, HR in PSB has received casual attention from all the stakeholders in the system, such as owners and regulators, as well as the banks themselves. They have been discussed in piece-meal manner from time to time, mostly in terms of constraints, however, solutions have deluded the system.

In 2009, the government made some serious attempts to study the HR issues in PSBs and appointed a committee under the chairmanship of Anil Khandelwal, former CEO, Bank of Baroda (one of the authors) and an HR specialist. The report, which is widely known as the Khandelwal Committee report, made seminal recommendations (numbering 105 recommendations) and commented that given the prevailing state of affairs and neglect of HR functions, HR would be a new risk factor. The government accepted 55 recommendations, and some significant recommendations were kept pending, which even after 10 years have not been implemented.

The current challenges in the HR function in PSBs could be summarized using three broad categories, namely HR accountability, culture and HR assets.

1. **HR accountability:** The HR function co-existed with industrial relations (IR) function, which had trade unions and officers' associations as key stakeholders and influenced the decision-making with regards to employment and service conditions. While the role and influence of trade unions was eclipsed by the economic liberalization and advances in technologies, the personnel function, even with the change of name to human resources, did not evolve as a strategic partner to the business due to multiple factors [please also see Professor T. V. Rao's interview (Interview 5) in this book].

The dominance of transactional mindset towards HR function without room for innovative and professional thinking has led to the neglect of HR as a strategic function. The implementation of rules had become an end in itself and, therefore, accountability is established more in terms of compliance and control than contribution to the business. This is in evidence, perhaps very strongly, in the HR structure itself, where in most cases, boards (or even CEOs) do not see HR function as being strategic enough to be accountable to them. This lack of strategic oversight at board and CEO levels creates a vicious cycle of low expectations, low contributions and low accountability. The result of this reduced accountability is a serious opportunity loss for all stakeholders including boards, regulators and the employees. In the emerging context of banking, this could also mean a serious governance risk, as employees are the assets that manage, influence or control all other risks.

2. **Culture in PSBs:** The rule- and control-based approach in PSBs over time has led to a bureaucratic culture marked by lacking in risk-taking, initiatives, experimentation, innovation and employee development. The rise of NPAs and other governance failures as well as approaches used to address them have the unfortunate effect of developing fear-psychosis and a preference for not taking any initiative. The Nayak Committee report (2014) on the 'Governance of Board of Banks in India' noted that there is a 'perverse' belief in banks that avoidance of 'personal initiatives and discretion' helps in building the career.

The prevalence of bureaucratic, risk averse and static culture is due to multiple reasons, which includes government's ownership and control, lack of empowerment/autonomy in designing its own HR policies and processes and legacy banking system. As a result, HR in PSBs are mainly seen as implementer and enforcer of compliance and standardization (one-size-fits-all HR processes across all PSBs), mostly required by the government. Over the years, this approach has led to rigid processes that are ill-suited to the context, needs and challenges of individual banks. The Khandelwal Committee report on HR issues of PSBs pointed out that the 'present arrangement has promoted high level of standardization and rule orientation' (pp. xxv). This is evident in the HR policies with regards to recruitment processes, promotions, manpower planning, ability to offer market compensation and incentive schemes. This standardization and rigidity reinforce the bureaucratic culture. Given the emphasis on culture by international financial bodies (such as Group of Thirty and Financial Stability Board) as a pathway to build better governance, cultural reform presents one of the most serious challenges in PSBs.

3. **HR assets:** Building a strategic HR function depends on many factors including the support, resources and infrastructure made available to the HR function. These aspects are collectively referred to as HR assets in this chapter. The requirement to implement the standard HR policies in PSBs does not provide the opportunity to professionalize the HR function and build professional capabilities. The lack of autonomy to design HR initiatives also does not align well with the aspirations of professional HR managers. Similarly, PSBs do not have opportunities to use latest HR practices and techniques, unless there is a CEO or senior HR leader, who is committed to transformational agenda. In the context of intangible assets and culture, latest HR practices and approaches need to be seen as invaluable assets, particularly when the aim is to improve governance and accountability.

While digitalization and use of high-end technology-driven HR tools such as predictive analytics, artificial intelligence, machine learning and other approaches are becoming common, PSBs lag behind, and in many cases, are non-starters in their usage. Use of latest technology can provide resources and means to add strategic value to business and improve employee experience. Finally, an important asset for the HR function in PSBs is support from the board and business leaders. In the current context, it is largely tactical and conditional upon the willingness of CEO and the board. This deprives HR function of a valuable asset that could help it in building credibility and strategic partnerships within the bank.

Human Resources Design: Integration of Governance and HR

The triad of HR accountability, culture and HR assets comes together through HR design. There are five main principles to consider while designing the HR function in PSBs for the future of banking. These are: role of CEO in building HR function, governance and structure of HR function, building HR competencies in HR leaders, autonomy to design HR initiatives suited to individual banks and focus on digitalization in HR function.

1. **Role of CEO in building HR function:** The future of banking is increasingly going to be reliant on intangible assets such as human capital, culture, innovation, customer services and good risk-management processes. These intangible assets are at their strongest when the HR function is accorded priority like any other critical business function by CEO. The context in PSBs, however, does not make it easier, as there is a constant focus on performance based on 'numbers' and limited scope for discretion and initiatives in terms of HR design. Building a strong HR function is also complicated, if not discouraged, by the short CEO tenures and uncertainty. However, in some banks such as SBI and Bank of Baroda (please see Professor T. V. Rao's interview (Interview 5) in the book) have had leaders at different point of times who contributed to building HR foundation and processes. In such cases, the short tenure was a constraint, but not a stop traffic light for building a strong HR function.

As the various interviews and case studies in this book indicate, transformational leaders recognize that the overall legacy processes and culture need to adapt to the future of banking. They recognize culture and HR as areas that could deliver maximum value in building the banks for tomorrow. They also have a strong sense of values and ethics, as well as a belief in the role and significance of intangible assets including human capital. They see the results (the performance 'numbers') as the by-product of intangible successes (such as engaged employees, innovation and an effective use of HR). Cultural transformation and building HR are therefore seen as a key priority, which, in turn, raise their profile and influence with other business leaders. Such CEOs lead the process of designing and implementing HR strategies and building the 'business' of HR.

Khandelwal's research (2018) on CEO's strategies in IR and HR reveal that the IR/HR function in banks is centralized around CEO, who is the key designer of HR/IR strategies. In the changed context of banking, Khandelwal (2018, pp. 322) observed that the key role of CEO is to build HR competencies of the highest standards, appropriate structure, culture and mechanisms to ensure a professional approach to HR to link it to business goals (Box 6.1).

Box 6.1 Key Roles of CEO in HR

- Policy formation in HR (in relation to various sub-systems of HR)
- Upgrade and support the role of HR function
- Develop appropriate HR structure for HR function
- Appoint the best in class and professionally trained HR head
- Integrate IR–HR function
- Encourage innovations in HR
- Develop big picture for HR contributions for effective business development
- Take effective steps for developing leadership pipeline and succession for critical roles
- Develop robust and engaged culture
- Crusader for inclusiveness and diversity
- Develop institutionalized compassion
- Put in place a HR governance system and an architecture of integrity
- Greater emphasis on the issues of 'employee wellness, diversity and socially disadvantaged'.

---

2. HR governance: Role of government—two key concerns

a. **Autonomy and differentiation of HR practices:** As majority shareholder of PSBs, human capital management should be a key concern of the government more so when PSBs are undergoing myriad problems relating to business and leadership deficit. Many of the former non- executive chairmen of PSBs (see interview section) have also observed that HR and leadership deficit remain the principle problems of PSBs and have suggested government to take reform majors. There are some critical areas in HR for the government to decide.

PSBs today are required to follow the industry-wide wages and service conditions following the industry-wide collective bargaining arrangement. This approach ignores the ground reality that each bank's context and priorities vary, sometimes significantly, from that of the other banks. These settlements are restrictive in staff deployment as per business needs and in some ways restrict motivation of performing staff by not permitting variable pay concept. Such industry-level arrangements need to be reviewed to allow bank-wise arrangements in line with the recommendations of the Narasimham Committee I (1991), the Narasimham Committee II (1998) and the Khandelwal Committee (2010). This will help banks to carve out compensation system in line with their capacity to pay and drive motivation in the employees, apart from individual banks owning greater responsibility in designing their HR strategies. The standardization and lack of autonomy currently do not allow HR function to customize HR initiatives that add business value at the bank level.

Post COVID-19, banks need to be given autonomy in introducing flexible work formats which are going to be the norm and which will help in the lowering of costs and bring greater efficiencies. Instead of having rigid work formats, variable working and/or on-demand workers are going to increasingly be the norm rather than exceptions. Banks, therefore, need to be given flexibility around introducing these new employment practices now. Different work formats will require differentiated service conditions which the present industry-level Bipartite Settlement do not provide for. Similarly, banks have to start thinking of differentiated compensation practices and levels for different work formats and types of employees in the bank.

b. **Micro-managing HR:** Besides the restrictions experienced by the individual banks to design their HR policies, they also face problems because of the increasing number of guidelines issued by the government on various HR matters.

One can appreciate the concern of the government to maintain uniformity in HR policies/systems across the PSB space but in the changing environment on account of competition and digitalization, each bank is at a different stage of growth with unique business problems and culture which require innovative HR initiatives in all areas such as recruitment, compensation, deployment of staff and performance management systems. Today, PSBs are constrained by the industry-level common wage payment system and service conditions as well as government guidelines on recruitment (methodology of recruitment of clerical and subordinate staff), deployment of married female staff (posting at the same place that of husband), common performance management system, calculation of vacancies of general managers and chief general manager on a defined business criteria and even formation of interview panels for selection of top management. HR is a key lever for building culture of performance and engagement, but it is preoccupied with compliances and administration, and the developmental work becomes a peripheral concern.

In a competitive and digitally disruptive environment, restrictive HR policies and structures designed over five decades back have become not only irrelevant but also counterproductive. They are not conducive to the digital journey of banks requiring new structures, specialized critical talent and modern people processes based on differentiation in performance and compensation systems. The existing systems of HR which are standardized and unrelated to performance are like an old socialist pattern and evidently out of date in a market economy and competition triggered by a rapid wave of technology. Reforms in HR systems and structures have waited for too long and have created a restrictive environment for better productivity and performance. The HR and governance reforms are now unpostponable and could be bigger risks than non-performing financial assets. Together, they have the potential to give a killer dose and the system is not very far from it. Incremental reforms have failed to show the desirable outcomes.

To begin with, the government should give complete autonomy to banks in their HR strategies formulation and withdraw their existing guidelines except for constitutional obligations of reservations of socially disadvantaged at the entry level of appointments. It can issue broad guidelines such as use of ethics, fair play and equity in managing HR function and make them accountable to annual HR audit to be undertaken by an accredited external agency. The use of vanilla and standardized HR practices makes it harder, even impossible, to compete with the private sector and could even make PSBs unsustainable in the near future of banking. To become an effective function, the rate of change within HR (and indeed the bank themselves) should be consistent with the rate of change outside the bank. Standardization and rigidness in policies and culture do not allow this important principle to take roots and HR function to adapt meaningfully. Differentiation and customization of HR to the banks' need are an important need of the hour, and when this autonomy and expectation are embedded, HR can become a strategic partner and contribute to effective governance (Box 6.2).

3. **Role of board committee on HR:** One key reform, already recommended in the Khandelwal Committee report and referred to above, relates to the activation and/or constitution of steering committee of the board on HR. This committee should, inter alia, look into the following at the minimum on a regular basis (Box 6.3). While some banks have set up these committees and are doing an excellent job of rejuvenating their HR systems, many other banks either do not have such committees or the meetings of these committees are irregular.

Box 6.2   Reform Measures in HR by the Government

- Urgent measures should be undertaken to encourage the five large banks (to begin with) to decide their own system of compensation and reward mechanisms in line with the recommendations of various committees from time to time
- Autonomy in HR to respective boards of the banks
- Appointment of an exclusive full-time director for HR in large banks
- Appointment of an independent director in five large banks with HR background
- The government should advise all PSBs to activate boards committee on HR to develop a long-term strategic plan for human capital management of respective banks
- Major reforms in the compensation structure of the full-time directors and at key management levels
- Promote professionalization of HR function

Such committees can make great contribution in pursuing critical issues such as leadership development and employee engagement (please see Case 2, 'Sustainable People Processes and Leadership Development in Bank of Baroda', by Joydeep Dutta Roy).

Box 6.3   Role of Board Committee on HR

- Develop an HRD policy document which should cover a long-term strategy for talent management.
- Review talent management framework and ensure that adequate number of people are available for critical positions.
- Review training arrangements for new competencies and for the new business plans.
- Review employee engagement strategy.
- Review performance management system and the rating behaviour.
- Review manpower planning and resourcing strategies.
- Review HRD policies in the context of best practices in the industry.
- Review HRD audit and take corrective measures.
- Review learning infrastructure in the bank.
- Initiate effective measures for developing leadership pipeline (Khandelwal Committee, pp. 73)

Besides, the committee also discusses and decides the use of digitalization in HR functions.

Finally, each bank is to set up an HR research cell within the HR department to undertake periodical employee engagement surveys, HR climate studies and areas of grievances, and build effective linkages with academic institutions for cooperation on research relevant to a bank.

4. **Competencies in the HR leaders in PSBs:** There is also a need to allow HR function to become more professional through the hiring of professionally trained HR specialists, who are familiar with modern HR methodologies and HR technologies (Box 6.4). One of the key recommendations of the Khandelwal Committee was to professionalize the HR function in banks by appointing professionally qualified HR professionals who can provide continuity and help in the implementation of innovative HR policies.

Banks should carve out a long-term strategy for talent management, review learning infrastructure, initiate effective measures for leadership pipeline and many other relevant issues. This will require a competent HR professional and team to thrive the change in the right direction.

5. **Digitalization of HR function:** Since the future of banking is likely to be technology based, it is important that HR functions themselves are seen as having a digital mindset. Digitalization requires new culture,

---

| Box 6.4 | Desirable Competencies in HR Leaders |

- Understanding of human processes to create motivation and engagement among employees for organizational growth
- High personal reputation in terms of integrity, authenticity and credibility
- Soft corner for socially disadvantaged and lower rung employees at the start of ladder
- A catalyst for organizational change
- An astute negotiator with collectives to design new paradigm of relationship based on understanding
- Result driven, task focused, but compassionate
- Willing to take up leadership in business roles
- Expert knowledge and networked in the HR profession
- Understanding the context of industry: How business is conducted, basic knowledge of various verticals
- Digitally savvy and developmental orientation
- Articulate, innovative and transfunctional in their approach and style
- A professional who can speak up, confront on issues of principles, a champion for what is right

skills and architecture of capabilities. Fundamentally, digitalization will cause change in the work, the worker and the workplace. This will entail newer challenges for the function including reskilling of workforce, new organizational design and culture, hiring challenges, more differentiated performance management and compensation, and employee retention and engagement (see Chapter 17). This will raise the expectations and demands on the HR function in terms of processing more data, understand employees more meaningfully, formulate data-driven HR strategies and offer services in a customized and timely manner. Digitalization will require a radically reformed HR that can respond to the aspiration of a diverse workforce, focus on the development of different groups, such as women and socially disadvantaged groups, and help build intangible capital. Digitalization will also provide resources and tools to ensure more HR accountability through analytics, faster data availability, real-time communication and engagement pulse surveys, and opportunities to engage with employees in multiple ways.

Additionally, the recent merger of banks has increased the number of employees in each bank, and digitalization provides the tools to scale up HR function in effective and strategic ways. Although few banks have taken initiatives in digitalization, given the advances and opportunities offered by technology, digitalization in HR should be a strategic agenda as it provides an effective route to build data-driven HR function.

The above principles (namely role of CEO in building HR function, governance and structure of HR function, competencies of HR leaders, autonomy to design HR initiatives suited to individual banks and focus on digitalization in HR function) and the triad of HR accountability, culture and HR assets (discussed in the previous section) identify various areas and details about the what, how and why of the HR reform process. For HR to contribute to improved governance, they need to be radically reformed, and this change could be facilitated through mandated HR reporting. The analysis so far provides a road map on various information items that could be included in this mandatory reporting.

A Case for HR Reporting: The Concept, Context and Rationale

As previously noted, the future of banking is likely to be steered by digitalization, complexity, specialist skill sets, innovation and multi-generational employees' base. These 'intangible' factors are likely to play a significant role in banks' performance and risk profile than had been the case in the capital- and branch-driven banking context so far. In the emerging future of banking, the role of human capital as an asset class is more significant. It is an asset class in itself (in terms of skill set availability, performance delivery, etc.) and an asset that manages and controls other assets, particularly technology and multi-generational employees. This role and distinction were not crucial in the legacy context because capital and physical assets played a primary role in banking performance. In the emerging future of banking, intangible assets, which are more prone to human interventions, will play an influential role. It, therefore, follows that building effective governance requires a recognition of the important, and changed, role of human assets as a source of banks' strengths and potential vulnerabilities.

The core idea that HR reporting will lead to more accountability towards human capital utilization, and therefore, better overall governance has some peripheral support to it. In the aftermath of 2008 financial crises, remuneration was seen as a contributing factor to the crisis. This has over the years led to higher remuneration disclosure requirements under the Pillar 3 disclosure (Bank for International Settlements, 2017). The remuneration regulations in the European Union (EU, European Banking Authority, 2015) require higher remuneration reporting standards as part of overall remuneration governance reform process. The idea was that higher disclosure requirements and transparency will allow governance oversight towards them to improve. Similarly, the growing concern about rising gender pay inequality has led to the mandated gender pay gap reporting in the UK. The gender reporting in a short time has led to economy-wide analysis (Office for National Statistics, 2019). In the USA, firms now do reporting on pay ratios.

Given the thrust on enlightened stakeholder management philosophy, many leading banks have started publishing a detailed HR capital report as the best practice initiative. Such reports are called by different names, but in nearly all cases provide a line of sight to the state of human capital inside the firms. There could be multiple reasons for such reporting including organizational health benefits to the firm itself.

The above trend in human capital reporting is also accompanied by an increase in the reporting of other aspects of a firm behaviour, which may not have any immediate impact on governance or performance but is seen as a sign of responsible corporate citizenship behaviour. These aspects include, besides mandatory financial reporting, reporting on environmental, social and governance; environment, health and safety; and corporate social responsibility.

The rationale to require mandatory HR reporting is anchored in two principal arguments. First, as argued above, HR are an important asset and risk in the emerging context of banking. Any governance initiative that excludes HR oversight, therefore, represents an incomplete governance process. It can be argued that this will not just be a procedural oversight; rather, it would represent a deeper conceptual and strategic blind spot in not tuning in with the changes in banking and, therefore, ignoring one of the most important items from the governance process. Second, when properly assessed, human capital risks can also be a front runner of underlying deeper governance failures and, therefore, could save costly and late interventions into governance failures that show up suddenly at a later stage.

Additional 'Organizational Health' Benefits of Mandatory HR Reporting

In addition to building better governance, there are other 'health' benefits of making HR reporting mandatory in the annual reporting process.

To the extent there are success stories in PSBs in terms of a strong HR function, they are largely due to the efforts of a CEO or other senior HR leaders, who believed in transformational leadership and role of HR in building the banks. This was the case in the late 1970s and 1980s with SBI and later at Bank of Baroda (please see Case 2, which covers this journey and where the HR committee of the board was appointed in early 2003). As the SBI example shows, once such leaders move on, the momentum and indeed the interest gets eroded. The requirement to discuss HR at the board level and do mandatory reporting on key HR matrices removes the role of fortuitous factors like presence of good leaders to build a professional HR function. In principle, the role and importance of HR function should be institutionalized and not be totally leader dependent. The very process of collating, analysing and debating issues, even if forced by mandatory requirement, could give health benefits in terms of institutionalizing the role of HR function. Over time, this could lead to improved internal HR processes, awareness of blind spots and generation of strategic empathy towards the function.

Increasingly, investors as well as other stakeholders are becoming interested in understanding banks' strategy, plans and progress not only in terms of milestones but also in terms of the risks, resource utilization and broader stakeholder engagements. The reporting on HR proactively meets these three requirements. It allows external stakeholders, including shareholders and regulators, to assess the risks posed by the state of HR function including the culture in it and provide inputs and 'nudges' based on that.

Organizational Citizenship

Since the financial crises of 2008, there is an increased emphasis on stakeholder management, which looks at organizational membership in a society in terms of how well obligations to all stakeholders including its employees are met. In this context, HR reporting is seen as a sign of organizational transparency and commitment to human resources. Leading global banks such as Citi Group, Bank of America and Deutsche Bank have started publishing their own human capital (or equivalent report).

International Norms and Practices in HR Reporting

International reporting practices on non-financial reporting (under which HR reporting falls) are at a general level and vary depending on the country and organization that recommends the reporting. The survey below is suggestive in nature, since practices evolve and change continuously.

The UK government published a new regulation in 2013 that requires strategic reporting (Financial Reporting Council, 2018) from publicly listed firms, which includes, among other things, information about the employees, but only when it is considered necessary to understand the position, performance or development of the company's business. The EU (2014) non-financial reporting and diversity directive requires firms to disclose information, among other things, on employee-related matters in terms of ensuring gender equality, implementation of fundamental conventions of the International Labour Organization, working conditions, respect for the right of workers to be informed and consulted, and health and safety at work. *The International (IR) Framework* on integrated reporting (International Integrated Reporting Council includes human capital as one of the six capitals, namely, financial, manufactured, intellectual, human, social and relationship, and natural). It recommends reporting human capital 'in terms of alignment with and support for governance framework, risk management approach and ethical values … ability to understand, develop and implement on organization's strategy…[and] loyalties and motivations for improving processes, goods and services, including their ability to lead, manage and collaborate' (International Integrated Reporting Council, 2013, pp. 13). The Global Reporting Initiative's reporting framework encourages HR reporting on various aspects that include standard benefits for permanent employees, safety and injury data, average training provided, total headcount and turnover, etc.

Notwithstanding the above reporting norms and practices, some of which are voluntary, there are international banks, such as Bank of America, Citibank and Deutsche Bank, which publish a separate report or section on aspects of HR that provides context and information of HR practices within them.

Scope and Range of HR Reporting

Let us illustrate and understand the aspects of HR that are reported by some leading banks (as mentioned above) in their human capital report.

Citi Group in its report has focused on the diversity, and how various HR processes (such as recruitment, pay, learning and growth) are increasingly used to achieve the goals of employee diversity. This illustrates the power of various HR processes when they are integrated and work in synergy to achieve a given goal.

The *Human Capital Management Report* of Bank of America is broad-based with a view on building a great place to work. The report provides rich information on the diversity including, like Citi report, use of various HR processes to build diversity as well as a great place to work. The report also includes a message from the chairman and CEO. The range of thinking on diversity is very broad and includes areas such as intergenerational employee groups and cognitive and developmental disabilities. The report also provides information on the support provided on various areas of employee well-being including domestic violence, critical life events and mental and emotional well-being. There is also information on the employee engagement scores since 2012. The quantitative information in many cases covers multiple years, which allows a dynamic trend view of progression on reported matrices.

Deutsche Bank's report covers the full range of HR processes starting from recruitment to turnover, but it also includes additional information in the form of an interview with the member of management board and global head of HR on the future of work. The report also covers the business transformation and HR approach towards it. The range of information covers the routine HR activities and less covered items such as suggestions made by employees and savings from them, age and average length of service for different regions/years, initiatives on digital HR and internal mobility across divisions/intra-divisions for different years at the officer/non-officer levels. While it provides information on culture, the report goes a step further and provides information response rate, employee commitment index and enablement index.

The Way Forward and Recommendations

While there are some lessons to be gained from the international experience in HR reporting, it is important to develop an approach keeping in mind the unique context of Indian banking, particularly PSBs. There are three important considerations to keep in mind while making the recommendations.

First, with certain exceptions, most HR reporting has been stymied by the use of terminology and vague prescriptions on what firms could voluntarily decide to publish. This has led to inconsistent and incomparable disclosures. Interestingly, where the requirements were more prescriptive and specific and less reliant on voluntary disclosures, such as Capital Requirements Directive IV remuneration requirements in the EU and gender pay gaps in the UK, the quality, consistency and comparability of information have been significantly higher. This suggests that the key to getting expected benefits from HR reporting is in being specific, prescriptive and making disclosure mandatory. Having a specific format also allows comparisons, benchmarking and industry-level research into the effective and not-so-effective HR practices.

Another challenge relates to the confidentiality of information. If it is to be argued, as this chapter has done, that human resources are key assets, then disclosure of HR practices and matrices could potentially weaken the competitive benefits in using them well. While this is a valid challenge, it ignores the nuances and hard work involved in making HR tick. Although best practices exist, the complexity of HR does not make it easy to use the plug and play approach from competitors' best practices, particularly if the information is provided at the headline basis.

Finally, as mentioned at the beginning of this section, it is important that the format should reflect the unique aspects of India, mostly, public sector banking. The Khandelwal Committee report contains a rich analysis on the most important HR control matrices in the context of PSB, which is used in this chapter to develop a HR reporting format (Annexure 6.1). This format can be considered as a start point to develop the final format, which can be used for the mandatory HR reporting. It is suggested that this should be a dynamic and on a three-year rolling basis, except for the first two years.

Conclusion

The current state of HR function and culture in PSBs needs radical reforms, as it is out of tune with the current banking context. This misalignment is likely to get bigger and riskier when banking will increasingly rely on human capital, which is the biggest risk (or the weakest link) in PSB performance. HR can contribute to building stronger PSBs and better governance, only if function is moved from the periphery of banking oversight into the central nervous system of PSB's activities, performance and governance.

The recommendations on mandatory HR reporting are in line with the slowly emerging trends. Indian regulators and banking can take a lead in this important area and establish it as a benchmark internationally. This could also contribute towards the reputational capital of Indian PSBs on a global level.

Based on international trends, emerging focus on enlightened stakeholder management and challenges in the banking system, one can say that mandatory HR reporting is an idea whose time has come.

Annexure 6.1. Proposed Format for Mandatory HR Reporting

(Note: The formation and information below is presented as an idea bank from which most relevant information items could be selected, or improvised, to develop best practices in the field of mandatory HR reporting).

Human Capital Report (Illustrative Format)
(On a rolling three-year basis, except for the first two years)

Section 1. About the Bank and Business

Name of the bank	
Year	
Business strategy and focus areas	
Main business areas	
Geographical spread	
Business turnover	
Profits	
CEO name, start date and tenure	

Section 2. HR Information about the Board

Number of board members	
HR background, if any, of board members	

HR committee of the board (excluding remuneration committee)	• Active/Inactive
If active,	
name of members	
Gender diversity ratio	
External/Internal members	
Number of meetings held during the reporting year	
Key areas of focus and decision-making of the committee	
• HR strategy	
• Learning	
• Diversity	
• Communication and engagement	
• Succession planning	
Actions and key decisions taken	

Section 3. HR Information at the Bank Level

Name of the HR head	
Who the HR head reports to	
Details of chief human resource officers: Qualifications, professional training in HR	
Brief structure of HR function at corporate level/zonal/regional level	
Total number of HR functionalists including number of specialists (grade wise)	
Total number of employees	Permanent, contract and others
Employee attrition (at various employee levels), retirements during the year category wise including terminations and dismissals	
General HR Overview	
HR strategy	
HR initiatives	

Main HR risks and remediation plan	
Updates on IR	
Any innovations in any sub-system of HR introduced during the year	
Any incubation projects	
Employee engagement	
Main cultural features (based on survey, if available)	
Main cultural failings, challenges	
Use and progress in technology/ digitalization in different HR areas	
Employee inputs	Number of grievances Number of suggestions
External HR advisors	Name Specialist area Period of appointment Compensation
Ethical Issues (Corporate Value and Ethics)	
Complaints on POSH (Prevention of Sexual Harassment)	
Machinery for sensitizing and improving ethical orientation of employees	
Details of frauds attributable by the employees	

Section 4. Manpower Planning and Recruitment

	Total Number of Positions	Positions Filled	Average Number of Applications per Position	Average Lead Time
Top management				
Junior management				
Non-management				
Total				

Section 5. Talent Pyramid

	Head Count	Percentage
Top management		
Junior management		
Non-management		
Total		

Section 6. Employee Demographics

S. No.	Category	Sub-category					
1.	Top Management	CGMs	GMs	DGMs	SC	ST	Females
a.	Number						
b.	Average age						
c.	Percentage of total employees						

2.	Senior Management	Chief Manager	Assistant General Manager	SC	ST	Females	Number of Disabled Employees
a.	Number						
b.	Average age						
c.	Percentage of total employees						

3.	Middle Management	Scale II	Scale III	SC	ST	Females	Number of Disabled Employees
a.	Number						
b.	Average age						
c.	Percentage of total employees						

S. No.	Category	Sub-category				
4.	Junior Management	Scale I	SC	ST	Females	Number of Disabled Employees
a.	Total					
b.	Average age					
c.	Percentage of total employees					

Section 7. Learning and Capability Development

1. Budget spent
2. Amount spent as a per cent of net profit
3. Training infrastructure for building new skills and capabilities. Major steps taken to build new capability in technology, risk management, corporate credit and treasury. Adequacy of trained executives in critical functions
4. E-learning and certifications
5. Areas of deficit talent
6. Spend on training of employees as a percentage of operating profit
7. Total man-hours of training clocked

   a. Classroom
   b. Digital
   c. External training for senior management in India and abroad

8. Total man-hours of training per person

Clerical	Junior Management	Middle Management	Senior Management

9. Total number of employees covered under learning programmes

Section 8. Diversity and Inclusiveness

1. Gender diversity ratio

Overall	Clerical	Junior Management	Middle Management	Senior Management

2. Women in leadership roles (senior management and above) = %
3. Inclusiveness ratio
   Disability (as a % of the total workforce)
   LGBTQIA (LGBTQIA refers to lesbian, gay, bisexual, transgender, queer or questioning, intersex, and asexual or allied)
4. Special measures for improving diversity and inclusiveness
5. Human resource development initiatives for women and socially disadvantaged
6. Specific steps undertaken to improve women's representation in senior and top management cadre including facilitative HR policies. Similarly, for socially disadvantaged

Section 9. Leadership and Talent Development

1. Talent review board: Key initiatives and actions
2. Hours of learning exchange (internal) by top leadership team in developing junior–middle management leaders
3. Steps initiated to build leadership at junior and middle levels
   a. Hiring of young professionals
4. Steps initiated for building leadership in senior management cadre
   a. Mentoring
5. Steps initiated for developing top management cadre with specific details of coaching and
   a. Mentoring
6. Spend of leadership development of senior and top management as a percentage of operating profit

Section 10. Succession Planning

1. Details of steps for succession planning for critical positions
2. Details of policy on succession planning approved by the board/boards committee on HR
3. Top 50 positions: ready now, ready in 12–24 months, ready in 24–36 month

Section 11. Employee Engagement

1. Whether any employee engagement survey is undertaken and if yes, details and the key findings and the steps taken
2. Number in percentage of employees who participated in engagement survey

3. Employee satisfaction quotient/Score/per cent
   • Zone wise
   • Region wise
   • Employee segment wise

Employee Communication

1. Steps to improve upward communication
2. Steps to keep employees informed about key developments and the business of the bank
3. Communication sessions held on POSH awareness
4. Communication sessions held on corporate values and ethics

Employee Grievances

1. System of employee grievances (details and content analysis of grievances) and the steps taken to resolve them.

Section 12. Industrial Relations

1. Pattern of collective bargaining in the bank on wages and service conditions
2. Details of trade unions of both workmen and officers
3. Machinery to resolve issues
4. State of IR like work stoppages or strikes

Section 13. Wages, Incentives, Welfare and Wellness

1. Business per employee
2. Profit per employee
3. Staff cost to income
4. Direct salary cost to indirect cost

Reward Mechanism Including Employee Stock Ownership Plans for Various Levels (Details)

Employee Welfare and Wellness

1. Any specific welfare measures initiated during the year over and above the industry-level mechanism
2. Any benefits to employees over and above the government guidelines
3. Steps taken to encourage physical wellness in employees
4. Steps taken to improve emotional wellness of employees

128 / **Anil K. Khandelwal and Anujayesh Krishna**

References

UK Parliament. (2013, June 12). Changing banking for good. Report of the Parliamentary Commission on Banking Standards. Vol. 1. *Summary, and conclusions and recommendations.* https://www.parliament.uk/documents/banking-commission/Banking-final-report-volume-i.pdf

Financial Conduct Authority. (2018). *Transforming culture in financial services.* Discussion Paper DP 18/2. https://www.fca.org.uk/publication/discussion/dp18-02.pdf

PricewaterhouseCoopers. (2014). *Retail banking 2020 evolution or revolution?* https://www.pwc.com/gx/en/banking-capital-markets/banking-2020/assets/pwc-retail-banking-2020-evolution-or-revolution.pdf

KPMG. (2019). *The future of digital banking.* https://assets.kpmg/content/dam/kpmg/au/pdf/2019/future-of-digital-banking-in-2030-cba.pdf

Lal, A., Chiarella, D., Han, F., Romanelli, G., Röhrig, M., Zheng, V., & Liu, X. (2019, August). The power of many: Corporate banking in an ecosystem world. McKinsey & Company. https://www.mckinsey.com/industries/financial-services/our-insights/the-power-of-many-corporate-banking-in-an-ecosystem-world

Khandelwal, A. (2010, June). Report of the committee on HR issues of public sector banks. https://financialservices.gov.in/sites/default/files/HRIssuesOfPSBs.pdf

Nayak, P. (2014, May). Report of the committee to review governance of boards of banks in India. https://rbidocs.rbi.org.in/rdocs/PublicationReport/Pdfs/BCF090514FR.pdf

Narasimhan Committee II. (1998). Action taken on the recommendations. https://rbidocs.rbi.org.in/rdocs/PublicationReport/Pdfs/24157.pdf

Bank for International Settlements. (2017). Pillar 3 disclosure requirements—consolidated and enhanced framework. https://www.bis.org/bcbs/publ/d400.htm; https://www.bis.org/bcbs/publ/d400.pdf

European Banking Authority. (2015, December 21). Final Report. Guidelines on sound remuneration policies under Articles 74(3) and 75(2) of Directive 2013/36/EU and disclosures under Article 450 of Regulation (EU) No 575/2013. EBA/GL/2015/22. https://eba.europa.eu/sites/default/documents/files/documents/10180/1314839/1b0f3f99-f913-461a-b3e9-fa0064b1946b/EBA-GL-2015-22%20Final%20report%20on%20Guidelines%20on%20Sound%20Remuneration%20Policies.pdf

Official for National Statistics. (2019). Gender pay gap in the UK: 2019. https://www.ons.gov.uk/employmentandlabourmarket/peopleinwork/earningsandworkinghours/bulletins/genderpaygapintheuk/2019

Financial Reporting Council. (2018, July). Guidance on the strategic report. https://www.frc.org.uk/getattachment/fb05dd7b-c76c-424e-9daf-4293c9fa2d6a/Guidance-on-the-Strategic-Report-31-7-18.pdf

EU. (2014). Directive 2014/95/EU of the European Parliament and of the Council of 22 October 2014 amending Directive 2013/34/EU as regards disclosure of non-financial and diversity information by certain large undertakings and groups Text with EEA relevance. https://eur-lex.europa.eu/legal-content/EN/TXT/PDF/?uri=CELEX:32014L0095&from=EN

International Integrated Reporting Council. (2013). *The International <IR> Framework.* https://integratedreporting.org/wp-content/uploads/2013/12/13-12-08-THE-INTERNATIONAL-IR-FRAMEWORK-2-1.pdf

Honouring Legacy while Embracing Evolution

The Ethics Narrative in SBI

Atul Kumar

Board on Boardwalk: Making Ethics Matter

Late in August 2016, the boardroom of State Bank of India (SBI) on the 18th floor of State Bank Bhavan was charged up. That day, the merger of SBI with its five associate banks and Bharat Mahila Bank was on the table. The directors were deliberating on the agenda. SBI has a pedigree of ethical grandeur surpassing generations and geographies. The issue at hand was how to preserve this iconic vintage with its distinctive ethos after the merger is over. How to foster a sociocultural integration with the inbound entities in a way to generate an organizational culture that reverberates SBI in its quintessential character and flow? The directors knew that identity shaping in the post-merger phase is a complex process of engaging with several disparate audiences and constituencies, each with its own set of expectations and priorities, through a synergy of values, emotions and leadership. Most obviously, it calls upon a behavioural process which must be built from within and integrated across the organization through spoken and unspoken forces of culture and people. It seemed uphill to steer the bank into the contemplated direction, especially in the human side of the enterprise, after completing the biggest banking merger that ever happened in Indian corporate history.

At first glance, it might arguably look odd why the board of directors was so concerned with the bank's pulse soon after its amalgamation when ethics have all time been central to its culture. To gather a better perspective, let us turn the pages of history. Modern banking started in India with the formation of the Imperial Bank, the parent bank of SBI, in the first decade of the 20th century. Few people know that the Imperial Bank was a brainchild of John Maynard Keynes, the most influential economist of our times, who also headed the bank in the initial years. His idea that economics is a subject of ethical judgements shaped the institutional culture of the Imperial Bank of India in its formative phase. Although the Imperial Bank was rechristened as State Bank of India in 1955, the Keynesian legacy continued and permeated through the organization yielding an unbeatable reputation for being the most trusted bank of the nation. As a result, SBI of today is a massive national institution and not merely a commercial bank. Yet a challenge was slowly building up on the vistas. Public trust in banks, worldwide, was declining precipitously and the headwinds were tapping the Indian shores. For this very reason, maintaining public trust in the amalgamated SBI and upholding its brand reputation was a topic du jour for the boardroom.

The directors were carefully weighing in on the whole matter. Trust is ultimately the product of integrity—a consistent commitment to do what one says. Ethical conduct based on the practice of the espoused values and principles is, therefore, the key to earning trust. The bank has been legendary in this regard, undeniably. Still, the far more important question was how to blend and refresh what SBI stands for in its bigger and more diversified version? The bank was passing through a digital makeover and repositioning itself as a modern and agile bank in a rapidly transforming India. The challenges around shifting structures, processes, employee demographics and generational trends were emerging inside while readjusting socio-economic realties, aspirational milieu of a younger India and social media were rewriting the customer expectations from outside the bank. Post-merger, close to 70,000 personnel from diverse work cultures were to stack the deck and exacerbate the cultural diversities. An ever-increasing reliance on technology was stretching the potential for amoral behaviour. In the midst of such conundrums, the competitive landscape was shrinking as well.

After exhaustive discussions on all these specifics, the directors finally resolved that although ethics have been a constituent force in the bank since birth, the time has come to actively trend it as a cultural premise for spawning the post-merger bank into a future-ready organization. Values are key building blocks of an organization's identity and culture and, therefore, sharing of values is consequential not only for an upbeat sociocultural integration but also for a neat identity construction in the combined entity, both at individual and organizational levels. That was well-nigh to say that the ethical imagination would have to be stirred up among the rank and file all the time in the post-merger bank.

To chauffeur the initiative, the board decided that an independent ethics and business conduct function should be set up in the bank that redefines values and embeds them with the operational fabric of the merged organization. The task was to be entrusted with a sufficiently senior functionary in the chief general manager grade to lend not only gravitas but also status and effectiveness to the role. Accordingly, the Ethics & Business Conduct function in the bank came into existence on 9 March 2017 with the joining of the chief ethics officer. The position of the chief ethics officer was the only one of its kind in the Indian public sector, as aptly tweeted then by one famous banking journalist, that SBI has bequeathed the first chief ethics officer to Indian banking. The message was unmistakable. In creating the position of chief ethics officer, the board had underscored the importance it attached to the highest standards of ethics in SBI.

The Role, Reporting Lines, Organizational Structure and Relationships

Broadly, chief ethics officer was expected to play a key role in promotion of a strong ethical culture in the bank for an enhanced brand equity and market reputation. They had to set up a structure, namely the Ethics & Business Conduct Department at Corporate Centre and develop and oversee an ecology of consequences administration in the bank. On the ethics side, chief ethics officer was to set a wide mandate centring around nurturing the ethical reflection in daily conduct both from individual and institutional viewpoints. For example, responsibilities comprised developing a code of ethics, defining and propagating the expected behaviours, assessing and mitigating inherent and residual ethical risks in business activities and products, spotting ethical vulnerabilities, providing corrective guidance, etc. Designing and conducting the capacity building programmes on ethical awareness and decision-making for all the employees—existing or onboarding— periodical impact assessment surveys, etc. were also in the role. In the business conduct area, the role mainly involved making the discipline man-agement ecosystem more humane and efficient in the bank by setting up a focal point at Corporate Centre for monitoring of non-vigilance business misconducts. It also called for assessing the structural and systemic deficien-cies in the consequences administration and standardizing the related policies, processes, procedures and skills for improving the operational efficacy.

Initially, chief ethics officer had to report directly to the managing director (MD, compliance and risk) having key interactions with the chairman, other MDs and the deputy managing director (DMD, HR) & chief digital officer (CDO). Later, it was decided to shift their reporting to DMD (HR) & CDO for better synchronization with the human resources function. An oversight of the central board as well as the chairman was present through half-yearly and quarterly reporting mechanisms. The activities were also subject to an annual review by the management audit. The department with two cells,

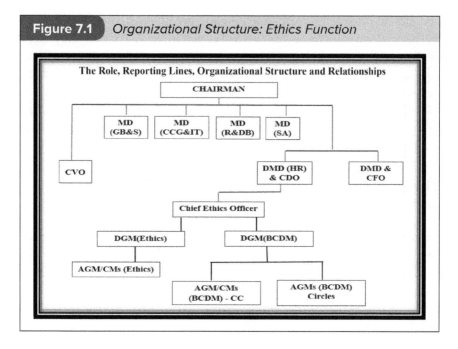

Figure 7.1 *Organizational Structure: Ethics Function*

ethics and business conduct, each headed by one deputy general manager with two or three support resources had to be structurally lean and digital savvy for functional agility keeping in mind the original nature of mandate. Organization wise, ethics cell had no downward linkages, whereas business conduct and discipline management (BCDM) cell had a three-layered structure—Corporate Centre, business groups and administrative offices (see Figure 7.1).

The Journey Begins

The journey of Ethics & Business Conduct function started with the minimal manpower of one chief and two support officers. Although the role sheet of chief ethics officer itemized several responsibilities, all the individual pieces such as policies, procedures, structures, strategies and goals that shape the ethical environment and culture were to be ideated and developed. Nevertheless, the team kicked off with communicating ethics messages to the employees, using a wide variety of channels, for introducing and stirring up ethics in their collective mind space. A sensitization campaign, namely e-nuggets was launched. It was in the form of sending a daily

SMS—a purposeful quote from chief ethics officer reminding everyone every day that ethics form the soul of banking—at 10 AM in the bank, right from the chairman to the assistant. The underlying idea was to ignite ethical thoughts just before the working day begins. As envisaged, the employees became curious and started wondering who chief ethics officer was? Something new seemed to be happening in the bank. Simultaneously, an email-based daily quiz 'What Is Your Ethics IQ?' simulating real banking scenarios about ethical dilemmas and four probable choices was introduced. One of the choices was an ethically correct one. A vibe generated in the first week itself. After one month, a stage came when the staff so keenly awaited the quiz every morning that if the email release got delayed even for one hour, enquiries poured in. Ethics had made its presence felt.

Ethical Diagnosis: Setting the Course of Action

Before preparing the policy groundwork for an ethical infrastructure, it was vital to have an honest diagnosis of the current state of play—the prevailing ethical climate in the bank. Thus, with the inaugural address of the chairman, an ethics pulse survey was launched which covered responses from over 16,000 employees from all cross sections, hierarchies and geographies in the bank. The survey was anonymous and focused on how employees view management and the bank, what ethical dilemmas and situations do they face and how they perceive the ethical climate in the bank. The findings gave an integrated view of the prevailing ethical climate at macro, meso and micro levels and provided insights both from employee and institutional perspectives. It was the first time that a pulse survey of such large sample size had been carried out by any public sector bank (PSB) or public sector undertaking in India, and that too, totally in-house. A similar climate assessment was carried out for the contractual employees. This data charted a course to set the framework and playbook for the rest of the ethics effort.

Rearticulating Vision, Mission and Values Statements

Now, the first step was to plan a code of ethics and other policies to determine the itinerary of ethics management. The code reflects the ethical principles of an organization as a policy statement. The process started with rumination. As an organization what was our aim or vision and how did we plan to realize it? What did we stand for? What was to be the moral frame of our behaviours? The existing vision, mission and value statements (VMVSs) could not provide the fitting answers as, crafted 10 years ago, they had lost their relevance. Over the last 10 years, the bank had undergone a colossal change in its personality and attitude as a progressive and contemporary bank. Consequently, it was decided to revisit VMVSs to make them truly resonate with the needs and aspirations of everyone, in addition to capturing the bank's new identity. A well-strategized exercise was set off with a participative approach converging on three types of value conversations. Staff members were asked to reflect on how we do things in the bank to explore their understanding of the past and how it impacts them today, and to share their hopes and dreams in the bank going forward. This process blended introspective, historical and aspirational aspects and, with overwhelming feedback from over 30,000 employees, the new VMVSs surfaced as the nub of the combined churn of workforce minds. A chain of presentations and discussions succeeded and ultimately the board concluded that the new vision of the bank is to be 'the bank of choice for a transforming India'. The action charter towards the vision was to be 'committed to providing simple, responsive and innovative financial solutions'. And core values of service, transparency, ethics, politeness and sustainability (STEPS) were to be the guiding lights in daily actions and decisions for accomplishing the mission and, in turn, translating the bank's vision into a reality.

Soon after redrafting the new VMVSs, an internalization campaign was launched across the bank by hosting a quiz set on the intra-site to gauge the awareness levels regarding the new VMVSs. Upon successful completion of the quiz, a certificate to the effect was generated. With a vibrant response, all the employees completed it within 90 days. The chairman drove the effort. For example, wherever on a visit in the bank, the chairman asked how many of the officers in the audience knew that what STEPS stand for? At times, they randomly questioned in meetings what are the new vision and mission of the bank. These actions helped in making STEPS the most famous acronym in the bank and fully integrating it with the organizational consciousness in a short time.

Playing the Playbook: The Code of Ethics, Communications and Trainings

A code of ethics was put together around the five values of STEPS. The code listed key ethical principle for each value. These principles were further broken down to the particular behaviours required to live them while discharging daily duties. Containing a decision-making guide to help make better ethical choices, the code was like an ethical toolkit with authentic banking examples illustrating potential dilemmas, along with practical sources of seeking advice and speaking up. It gave a simple message that corporate integrity depends on individual integrity and the employees are accountable for their behaviours. As the simple adoption of a code doesn't guarantee ethical improvement, a drive was commenced deftly to ensure maximum internalization of the tenets of code, with every staff member asked to read and understand the code and sign a statement to that effect. To ensure easy accessibility, the code of ethics was prominently hosted on the bank's intra-site in the chairman's corner. Also, one-page summary of the code was formulated and widely circulated within the bank with instructions to keep on every desk as a constant reminder of what bank expects from its staff members with respect to ethical conduct. The whole idea was to inoculate the core values in each and every staff member and make ethics a part of the daily discourse—to create a work environment in which values and ethical standards are as central as the economic purpose.

To shape behaviour in durable ways, values were continually reinforced through communications, trainings, employee townhalls, knowledge café sessions, power talks, annual reports, corporate videos, brochures, lift displays, bulletin boards and other means. One weekly blog 'Coffee with Aristotle' on ethical leadership was a mega hit. Master classes on ethics were conducted to make the employees understand how the code provisions apply and how to navigate ethical dilemmas and avoid wrongdoing through achieving a coherence between personal values and the values of STEPS. Formal ethics trainings were made part of the socialization process of the newcomers—all trainings characterized by exploration and expansiveness. The participants were prepared in advance for the trainings and made aware of the larger context of an overall corporate ethics effort. The trainings helped the participants see or recognize the latent ethical dimensions in not-so-evident situations. Every session aspired to fit the participants with moral lenses through which they will parse the ethics grammar of their worlds. Besides the ethics portal, an ethics helpline, parallel to the existing whistleblowing mechanism, was put in place for the employees to get advice or report concerns.

Towards a New Template of Business Conduct and Discipline Management

The problem in matters of conduct breaches and discipline is basically a problem of attitude, and hence, it is necessary to recognize the latent socio-psychological forces while dealing with such affairs. Service rules and penal provisions exist. Trainings for percolation of these take place regularly. Employees are aware of all these provisions. Even then, irresponsible and unethical behaviours emerge. Therefore, the initial premise, on the business conduct side, was that if the behavioural roots of conduct failings are understood and addressed, then such events could be minimized. For doing so, it was necessary to draw out the innate goodness, moral agency, of the employees and nudge them on the road to positive conduct. This was an atypical approach to the consequence management system and called for systemic interventions, both at the policy and structural levels.

At the time of joining of chief ethics officer, administrative and non-vigilance breaches were handled independently by the circles, business groups and other departments. There was no summit point for effecting corporate oversight or standardizing the processes. No consolidated data was accessible for offering a bank-level landscape of non-vigilance offences with the corresponding outcomes. Such fault lines made it hard to get a macro view of the organization-wide infractions or to assess the efficacy of deterrence processes from the policymaking stance. That being the case, having collated a data directory of non-vigilance and administrative cases for the previous three years, a study was conducted on the data to read institution-wide patterns from the on hand catalogue of human failures behind the disciplinary cases. As structures influence ethical behaviour through the creation of authority and accountability lines, a discursive report on the insights was then put up to the top management recommending action items for revamping the consequence management system. To illustrate, among others, all the disciplinary proceedings departments (DPDs) or cells in the bank were renamed as Business Conduct & Discipline Management departments or cells and brought under the direct oversight of the Ethics & Business Conduct Department at Corporate Centre. The name DPD strikes a hostile note in the minds of employees and helps produce a perception that is negative. And so, the name was changed to convey a pro-employee reverberation right at the outset. Such positive actions spoke louder than words in the area of conduct. See Boxes 7.1 and 7.2.

Box 7.1   Ethics First: Business Next

He was an outstanding branch manager, a star performer of the region. Always achieved budgets, popular among customers, smart, good speaker, effective team leader and known for his trouble shooter image. Seniors saw him as a model branch manager secretly aspiring to have him under their direct control. They banked on Shekhar Prasad* to meet the business shortfalls of the region and he never disappointed. One day, all of a sudden, his regional manager (RM) received a call alleging that Shekhar was involved in misusing the branch charges account and showing some of his personal expenses as business-related ones. RM was shocked and did not believe the caller. However, discreet verifications revealed within three days that the caller was truthful, no matter the sums were pretty small. It was already February. Year end was fast approaching. Last week only, RM had requested Shekhar to market some extra loans to compensate the shortfall of the region. He himself was due for promotion. He knew, without achieving the growth targets, promotion would be hard to come by. He was in a fix, whether to call Shekhar and counsel him as the involved amounts are very small, or just ignore the matter considering Shekhar's brilliant performance or tactfully wait and let March be over, so that the growth targets are met and the promotion chances remain unaffected as well. Action can be taken even after one month. RM had attended two ethics roundtables. Somehow, he didn't feel comfortable with either course of action and approached chief ethics officer for guidance through helpline. After discussing the issue, first he suspended Shekhar Prasad, sent a strong demonstrative message to others against unethical conduct and set off the process of disciplinary action immediately. Although he made concerted efforts to bridge the deficit, he could not succeed. When RM appeared for his interview, he was put a question about the then very famous case of Shekhar Prasad. RM responded with utmost sincerity, narrated his own conflicting lines of thoughts at the material time and how he could navigate the challenge. The board was much impressed with the honesty and ethical courage of the officer that he was promoted disregarding the fact of business shortfall.

* Shekhar Prasad is an imagined name.

| Box 7.2 | The Midas Touch of Ethics |

After one workshop on ethics, a senior officer called and thanked the chief ethics officer the next day. He made a small yet an impactful point. That executive stayed near Corporate Centre and daily went for an evening walk after work on his way back home. And at the time of leaving office, he mostly used to take one bottle of mineral water to sip while walking. The water bottles were provided by the bank to senior executives in those days. However, on the day of the workshop, when he was preparing to leave for the evening walk and home in the evening, and out of habit as he picked up the water bottle, it struck to him that it is wrong to use official water for personal purpose. He thought for a moment and then kept the bottle back. He came out of the office building, bought water from a roadside vendor for ₹12 and started his walk. Ethics made him reflect on his daily actions and nudged towards one small behavioural shift.

Tone from the Top: Demonstrating Consistent and Committed Ethical Leadership

Ethics is a top-down affair. Significant ethical change is difficult without the buy-in of top leadership. In an ethical organization, the structure provides the hardware, the culture and systems provide the software and the leadership provides the power supply. Although all are needed to ensure a healthy ethical climate, there is no escape from the fact that an organization can be only as ethical as its top leader wants it to be. Only those values they endorse explicitly are translated into everyday organizational practices

(Figure 7.2). That way, SBI's chairmen—current or earlier—have always been acting as the moral custodian of the function. The preceding chairman, who was instrumental for creation of the function, took a deep interest in modulating the upcoming ethics discourse in the bank. The current chairman is responsible for building and unleashing the systemic capacity around ethics promotion in the bank. For example, he never misses any opportunity to articulate the importance of the core values of STEPS in his meetings, addresses and other conversations.

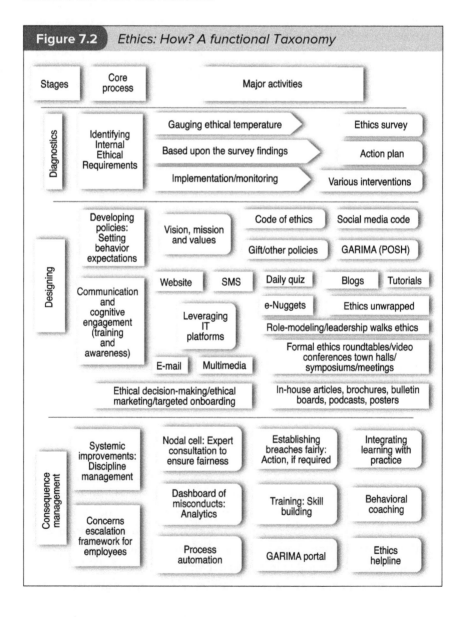

Figure 7.2 *Ethics: How? A functional Taxonomy*

Willingness to Be Willing: Exercising Normative Influence

In a substantive sense, advocacy is inevitable in an agenda of nudging changes in attitudes or behaviours. It is solely through the influence processes that the leaders pilot and lead change today. If the process is handled well, it can move people away from the negative choices and in more positive directions via the self-enforcing power of legitimacy as has happened in the bank. Legitimacy nurtures self-induced behaviours. Financial history demonstrates the limitations of punitive action. The discipline and enforcement cannot live up to their organizational promise on their own. Ethics have to join in and afford hope by ushering in potentially forceful behavioural constraints on individual and organizational decision-making, regardless of the countervailing influences. Therein lies the moral authority and efficacy of the ethics function in the bank.

Better Together: Coordination with the Vigilance Function

The chief ethics officer is expected to supervise only the violations of non-criminal or say non-vigilance nature. The bank has a position of chief vigilance officer for the transgressions of vigilance nature because of its public sector lineage. This ring-fencing prevents any potential or apparent conflict in the operational roles of the ones who are supposed to function complementarily on the vigilance and non-vigilance sides of misconducts. In practice, too, both departments act collaboratively. Even then, the conceptual inadequacy occasionally renders an impression that there is some dichotomy in the co-existence of vigilance and ethics in a public sector entity. This is because both the functions deal with the same gamut of human failures, engage with similar methodologies to reach their outcomes and, sometime, no doubt, overlap in their journeys as two sides of the same coin.

The exogenous statutory aspect lends vigilance function more enforcement potency from a narrower, punitive perspective. In contrast, the ethics function rests on the broader schema of self-induced pro-social behaviour and, at a deeper level, extends merely the purpose of establishing the vigilance oversight, if the preventative ingredients of vigilance are weighed up. Prescriptively again, vigilance aspires to promote a culture of probity by curbing corruption which is an alternative form of emphasizing on the culture of ethics. Behavioural sciences have told us that self-regulation is better than externally imposed sanctions. In this light, SBI experiment substantiates an inherent alignment in the aims of both the activities and makes a powerful case for creating the role of chief ethics officers in other PSBs as well for making a positive ethical difference in their cultures.

Who Will Guard the Guards: Ethics Committee of the Board or the Top Management?

Forming of an ethics committee of the board as a structural anchor was considered last year. But the idea was not pursued further as the chairman, who chairs the board, was himself guiding and steering the ethical infrastructure. All the other whole-time board members, namely MDs were also constantly involved in bolstering the ethics process in the bank. In that backdrop, the committee, in fact, would not have served any meaningful purpose in terms of value adding or oversight. Although the management audit carries out a formal review of the activities of the ethics and business conduct vertical once a year, the function remains practically under continual oversight of the top leadership round the year. Not only the reports to DMD (HR), MDs and chairman capture quantitative and qualitative appraisal of the undertaken works, but the Chairman also often reviews the performance and provides feedback as well as guidance. An annual evaluation of chief ethics officer takes place to assess how effectively they are meeting performance expectations and contributing to the achievement of organizational objectives both in the short and long terms.

What Do Eyes See and Ears Hear? Taking Ethics Seriously

Employees are the eyes and ears of an organization. By listening to them, a truer picture can be formed of whether the bank is living up to its values. Last year, an engagement survey was conducted with participation of almost 0.2 million employees which demonstrated that the employees have faith in the function and believe it was playing an important role in terms of improving the organizational context, conduct and consequences. This perception of employees is all the more notable as it maps the qualitative impact of interventions on the organizational culture. Informal conversations also reveal that the employees are now better aware of the requirements of an orderly conduct and repose more confidence in the organizational justice. Once upon a time, there used to be a frequent question in workshops, whether ethics are necessary for banking from the younger officials. They thought that a business decision and an ethical decision are two different things. Today, in roundtables, the employees conflate ethical and business considerations. Millennials even feel that without this ethics initiative SBI would have been a lesser place to work for.

Fostering Ethics: Yesterday, Today and Tomorrow

Looking at the journey so far, it had started with small steps and kept on building incrementally, with deep normative effect which has been modifying conscious and unconscious behaviours, tacit social order and mindsets in the bank. Yet it has not been a trajectory without its share of angst and despondencies. With no precedents, no resources, no persons to seek guidance and without professional support, it was too arduous to set the roll against a wide-spread scepticism among the senior managers as what purpose the new set-up would serve. How can ethics be taught or learned? It is fully formed and unchangeable. The people at SBI do know the difference between right and wrong. Even when invited to attend ethics roundtables, they tried to avoid feeling as if their personal ethics are being questioned. Attitudinal barrier was the biggest pain point. Other challenges such as to prepare appealing content on a regular basis, to get good speakers for workshops or to conduct pulse checks in a vast organization in-house proved to be less daunting in comparison.

Within two years, SBI was recognized as the second-most reputable banking brand globally by the Brand Finance's prestigious Reputation Report on Banking UK 2018. It was an external commendation of the impact of SBI's ethics effort in its swaying footprints. The Indian Institute of Banking & Finance, under the guidance of chief ethics officer, set out a paper on 'Ethics in Banking' last year for the JAIIB examination to spread ethical awareness among industry newcomers. The Ministry of Finance in Gyan Sangam of top executives in PSBs had formed a group to devise the ways for accentuating ethics in banking and, subsequently, a committee under the chair of the SBI chief ethics officer to ink a strategy document for extending the narrative all over PSBs.

Well begun is half done but there is a lot that is still to be done. To name a few, the website has to be made fully dynamic. One mobile app, Make Decision Ethically, is under ideation to empower employees to help clarify their dilemmas with a click on their mobile. A monthly ethics newsletter is in pipeline. The workshops and roundtables are being gamified along with preparation of one-minute video clips and corporate films on ethical issues. Emerging technologies are bringing an altogether new set of complex ethical challenges that are to be negotiated with in near future.

Organization Is a Noun and Ethics a Verb

Although an ethics infrastructure in which employees do not merely follow the rules but try to understand why they are following them and do so willingly is fairly entrenched in banks today, ethical breaches can only be avoided when the organizational integrity fuses with the individual integrity, continually pushing individuals to do the right thing through necessary incursions and steadfastly listening the organizational heartbeat. Applying ethical co-ordinates in large corporate settings like SBI is a demanding process and involves dynamic forces, making it easy for the ethics to slip between the cracks or fall into the blind spots, often unnoticed, until it is too late. The solution is not to ever disregard that ethics is a cultural process that is never finalized and that too on a road-less travelled.

As complexities evolve and challenges proliferate in an increasingly disruptive world, SBI has opened the window on an ethical exuberance of grandeur. Let the view not be wasted as it unmutes the organizational conscience in its elemental significance and holds out a moment of truth to many banks in their individual organizational lives. Their survival might as well depend on it in changing times.

Suggested Readings

Boatright, J. R. (2008). *Ethics in finance*. Blackwell.

Bowman, J. S., & West, J. P. (2015). *Public service ethics*. SAGE Publications.

Bruhn, J. G. (2001). *Trust and health of organizations*. Kluwer/Plenum.

Callahan, D. (2004). *The cheating culture*. Harcourt.

Chakarborty, S. K. (1996). *Management by values: Towards cultural congruence*. SAGE Publications.

Johnson, C. E. (2016). *Organizational ethics: A practical approach*. SAGE Publications.

CHAPTER

8

Banking Transformation as a Leadership Experience

Fifteen Actionable Insights from the Trenches

Anil K. Khandelwal

Introduction

One of the most remarkable aspects of organizational change efforts is their low success rate. According to McKinsey & Company, more than 50 per cent transformation efforts fail for a variety of reasons. In this chapter, the author shares a success story. It is about the transformation in a large, geographically dispersed and highly unionized government owned bank in India, the Bank of Baroda (BOB), with 2,800 branches and 40,000 employees in 2005. This transformation during 2005–2008 received accolades worldwide, especially in the financial world. The author, based on his first-hand experience in piloting this major transformation, has developed 15 insights for transformation. In the following pages, the author discusses these insights, how they relate to each other and the role they played in the overall transformation process. To understand these insights in an integrated context, it is useful to develop some familiarity with the concepts of transformation process, transformational leadership, restructuring and turnaround management.

Transformation: Concept and Approaches

In the recent past, transformation has become a common term, and as one McKinsey article noted, 'perhaps the most overused term in business' (Bucy et al., 2016). A recent article on transformation observed,

> Embarking on a transformation is one of the most critical decisions a CEO will ever make … Many CEOs will say that they have been involved in multiple transformation. But by our definition—an intense, organization-wide program to enhance performance and to boost organizational health—very few have delivered one sustainable, at-scale business transformation, let alone several'.
> (Bucy et al., 2016)

Transformation is frequently understood as a large-scale change process to turnaround, or significantly improve, the business performance. The need for such transformation is increasingly being felt because, 'In industry after industry, scenarios that once appeared improbable are becoming all too real, prompting boards and CEOs of flagging (or perhaps merely drifting) businesses to embrace the T word: transformation' (Bucy et al., 2016).

While transformation is a large-scale organizational change, and one of its key objectives is to significantly improve the performance, looking at it purely in terms of a bigger change process does not convey the essence, nuances and risks in it. The core of transformation is in changing the heart and soul, the mindset, of the entire organization through culture building, new intangibles and organizational capabilities as well as employee engagement. Transformation may also involve change in business model, digitalization and business structuring. However, when transformation is defined narrowly in terms of tangible outcomes, it also becomes vulnerable to a poor outcome, which probably explains its high failure rate. It is noted, 'Transformations typically degrade rather than visibly fail' (Bucy et al., 2016). A large-scale change process which focuses on improvements in tangibles is not as sustainable, lasting and meaningful to employees as transformation which changes the culture, mindset and organizational capabilities.

An organizational turnaround can be considered as one type of organizational transformation. Based on his research, Khandwalla (1991) made a distinction between surgical turnarounds and humane turnarounds. Surgical turnaround includes downsizing, changes in business strategy, management overhauls, tighter controls and financial restructuring. Humane turnarounds include employee involvement, cultural change, decentralization and engagement of internal and external stakeholders. Research showed that humane turnarounds though not well celebrated are effective change management strategies. Based on his research, Khandwalla (1992) proposed a typology of turnaround management, which included four types, namely surgical reconstructive, surgical innovative, non-surgical innovative and non-surgical transformational. A natural question here is: why are the humane turnarounds (or non-surgical turnarounds) not practised more?

Part of the reason could be that they are not as well-known and discussed. Kahneman (2012), in his landmark book, *Thinking, Fast and Slow*, mentioned WYSIATI (What you see is all there is) rule, which states: 'You cannot help dealing with the limited information you have as if it were all there is to know'. This rule gives rise to biases in human decision-making and choices. A possible reason for lack of information about humane turnarounds could be lack of stories and practical insights from the 'field'. There are not as many humane turnarounds as surgical turnarounds, and this makes for its low popularity, even though they are just as, if not more, effective. Yet another reason for the popularity of surgical turnarounds could be our preference towards 'star' leadership culture. Surgical turnarounds seem more aligned to our existing notions about 'star' leadership.

Among other things, 'star' leadership runs the risk of being misunderstood and misapplied. O'Reilly and Chatman (2020) argued, '…transformational leaders, especially those who are narcissistic, can also embody a dark side, mobilizing followers to pursue goals that are dangerous. A failure to understand these differences can put organizations at risk'. They recommended making a distinction between a transformational or narcissist leader.

Transformation: Role of Context and Social Environment

While transformation is a global phenomenon and there are seminal works like Kotter's (2012) eight 'accelerators' available to practitioners, it is important to realize that transformation is also very contextual and takes place in a unique social environment in which banks (or organization) are embedded. This may rule out certain choices (such as mass retrenchment and business restructurings in case of public sector banks [PSBs]) because of value systems, social preferences, government frameworks and similar factors. It is well known that Indian banks, particularly PSBs, work under governmental constraints and frameworks and, therefore, do not have the choices that private sector firms have. Organizational transformation is difficult even when all choices are available but becomes far more challenging and a leadership-worthy endeavour when there are constraints on the choices. In this context, there is a need to share more information on the transformation, so it can be used effectively.

Khandwalla (2001) discussed two distinct modes of restructuring, namely Western International Management Consultants (WIMC) mode of restructuring and process-based restructuring. Few main elements in the WIMC mode of restructuring are new vision of the corporate's future, maximizing shareholder value, sharper management focus and core competencies, emphasis on contracting out and networking, re-engineering processes, etc. In the process-based restructuring, participation of stakeholders (particularly internal ones) is emphasized and they remain salient in the implementation process. Creative restructuring implies:

> much trial and error, exploratory thinking ... effective implementation of the chosen path or solution ... Restructuring requires so many and so large changes that for creative restructuring, recourse must be had to many minds and points of view ... Many issues need to be tackled, including those that are not readily apparent.... (Khandwalla, 2001, pp. 11)

Khandwalla noted that unfortunately several of the WIMC have not worked too well.

The 15 actionable insights (Annexure 8.1) take into consideration the perspectives outlined above and aim to fill in some of the gaps that currently exist, particularly in the Indian context and PSBs. The author has developed these 15 actionable insights for transformation based on his 'real-life' experience at the bank. It is hoped that these insights will fill in an important space in the following ways:

- While transformation is a well-written area, there is still a dearth of material, which is contextually embedded, particularly with respect to Indian business and social environments, where humane (and non-surgical) transformations have a greater social and organizational value. It is important that a contextual and culture-specific approach relevant to the Indian framework is developed. This chapter is a step in filling the gap and contributing towards that goal.
- It seems that existing frameworks on transformations focus on why transformations fail and less on what works. Kotter's (2007) article on 'Leading Change', for example, draws attention to the eight errors why the transformation efforts fail. Identifying reasons why transformation does not work is a useful contribution to the field. However, leaders and practising managers are equally 'hungry' to know what works and why. The 15 insights in this chapter are based on the author's first-hand experience of leading the transformation process. They are therefore more about what works. They are also written in a way that practising leaders can relate to, reflect on and implement.
- The transformation at BOB is different from many other known accounts of transformation for the three main reasons:

o It was carried out under multiple constraints on choices owing to government ownership of the bank.

o The transformation ran a high risk of failure because of the unionized context.

o Finally, the limited chief executive officer (CEO) tenure (of three years) makes transformation effort more complex, as the author had additional pressure to ensure that it is completed during his own time, and his successor and employees do not have to deal with legacy challenges. The completion of transformation within this limited time also address a commonly held view that short CEO tenure is a hindrance. It is indeed the case that short and uncertain tenures do not help the transformation agenda; however, as the BOB case study shows, it is very much possible to accomplish the agenda in limited tenures of three years.

In the author's opinion, the successful delivery of transformation under such constraints and few choices (unlike those available to the private sector) make the lessons of transformation more valuable and worth sharing more broadly. They suggest that transformation is possible despite big constraints and challenges and in a limited time. Noted management scholar Professor Pradip Khandwalla (2011) observed:

> I see BOB's turnaround from decline in market share under Khandelwal as a transformational-creative turnaround … Khandelwal's leadership style and turnaround strategy was especially suitable in a public sector Indian bank in which firing people or closing facilities was very difficult. Case studies of leaders like Khandelwal reveal a lot of what is not taught or not stressed enough in our management programmes…. (pp. 375–378)

Transformation is a uniquely contextual experience and closely anchored in the broader cultural and social milieu of the organization. It is for this reason the 15 insights in this chapter are somewhat different from John Kotter's (2012) eight 'accelerators'. The insights by the author are different and unique as they have emerged from contextual factors specific to a developing country. Some factors not covered in Kotter's scheme pertain to improve the ability of an organization to manage large-scale transformation and build internal strength to cope with growing challenges. We are all aware that no two transformation challenges can be absolutely similar. Thus, these insights serve the purpose of a useful check list in a transformation process. It may be stressed that checklists cannot do away with the need for courage, wit and improvisation. These insights, based on a single case, should hopefully provide a guideline to any large organization's transformational effort. The insights describe how an organization can be transformed with a clear vision, execution discipline, employee engagement and customer centricity. The author believes that these insights are useful for any transformation process, especially those in large-sized organizations.

Bank of Baroda: Background and the Transformational Challenge

Established in 1908, BOB stands tall on a century-old foundation; its first brick was laid by Sir Sayajirao Gaekwad III, the visionary ruler of Baroda, a princely state of pre-Independence India. Starting off as a small-town bank, it had its presence all over India by the time the Government of India nationalized it in 1969. Fourteen major commercial banks were nationalized in India in 1969. With government control, the CEO of the nationalized bank is accountable to the Administrative Ministry, the Ministry of Finance (Government of India), shareholders and public at large. Their actions and the actions of their staff are subject to scrutiny by various government agencies and the Parliament. The wake of nationalization posed new challenges such as mass banking, rural banking, social banking and entrepreneurial banking. They were very efficiently managed by the bank. The financial fundamentals of the bank were always strong and sound.

BOB was one of the earliest banks in India to venture into international banking in 1953. The inherent strengths and resilience of the bank have helped it to weather many storms and post uninterrupted profits. By the turn of the century, it achieved the first position among the nationalized banks in the country. However, between 2000 and 2004, the bank encountered a sharp decline in business. Its stock price went down, the credit growth stagnated and it slid down to fourth position. During this period, peer banks moved and adopted a new technology. The bank lagged behind on this count due to opposition from militant unions who resisted the change. Unions opposed technology within the bank because of their love for a comfort zone and a desire to not disturb the apple cart and challenge the spirit to experiment with change. An accommodative and paternalistic culture towards employees and trade unions ushered in unintended consequences in terms of resistance to change and technology adoption rendering the very approach of friendly and paternalistic culture irrelevant and counterproductive. The bank continued with its normal routine pace in spite of massive changes which came into India after liberalization in the 1990s. It did not quickly tune into the newly emerging competitive pressures.

The author steered a dramatic transformation of the bank from a staid PSB to a valuable brand in a short period of just three years (2005–2008) when he was its chairman and managing director. This captured attention of various stakeholders. International publications highlighted the transformation and many case studies were written about it by leading academicians.

One of the main planks of the transformation was the focus on building intangibles such as fostering a responsive culture and fixing accountability all across, but more so in the senior and top management levels. This would have a knock-on effect on several parameters such as speed in decision-making, service delivery and employee education and engagement. It would enable an overhaul of the human resources (HR) function, create a distributive leadership, do brand building, lay extraordinary emphasis on innovations in customer service and facilitate a massive overhaul in operations through the use of technology. This transformation, by the author, was unique in many respects. Transformation usually conjures up the images of surgical turnarounds with closures, restructuring and lay-offs. The transformation at BOB was an example of leadership which practises toughness (directed towards business processes and practices) and compassion in the same breath. Toughness confronted the existing chaotic industrial relations (IR), the entrenched internal bureaucracy, a lack of concern for customers as well as for individual employees and a pedantic managerial mindset. Compassion used to resolve people's problems, encourage innovation and build a creative culture.

The results of the transformation were dramatic on two fronts: rejuvenation of the bank with modern technology plus service excellence and posting extraordinary business outcomes. The author covers the full, detailed story of the transformation in his book *Dare to Lead* (2011). In some ways, the foundation for a smooth transformation in 2005–2008 was laid during 2000–2003 when the author, as executive director, resolved IR conflict and regained management control in the workplaces to improve discipline, customer service and productivity. The total narrative about the IR conflict and management strategies to undertake reforms to regain control appears in the author's recent publication, *CEO—Chess Master or Gardener* (2018).

The transformation which mainly focused on strengthening processes, leadership, human capital, technology, innovations in customer centricity, new business models, image makeover and the likes enabled the bank to grow year after year helped it to regain an enviable position in the banking space in India. The transformation succeeded despite the many challenges it faced.

The bank was recently chosen by the Government of India for amalgamating two smaller PSBs with it. This reflects the strength of the bank and the trust it enjoys in the eyes of the government. After the amalgamation, the bank holds the second position in the public sector banking space in India. Today, analysts rate the bank very high for its strong balance sheet, leadership strength and ongoing upgradation of its technology.

The Fifteen Insights

1. **Reimagine the compelling future**

   The urge for transformation is always triggered by contextual considerations. A disruptive environment on account of technological changes, new competitive reality, new product innovations, changes in government policies, etc. may call for major shifts. From this may emerge the need for transforming the organization to make it more adaptive, innovative, digital centric and customer oriented. Transformation is essentially a leadership play. It must take birth in the mind of CEO who galvanizes the organization to change by painting a thrilling and exciting picture of the future across the organizational members.

   In our context, the change was triggered mainly by the post-liberalization environment in India which witnessed the emergence of some private banks. These banks used the latest technology and did not have any cultural baggage, and therefore, succeeded in drawing away customers and business. On the other hand, PSBs like ours had huge legacy issues such as absence of technology, rampant delays in customer service and restrictive practices actively encouraged by the trade unions, besides government ownership. As mentioned earlier, the bank had shown a downward trend between 2000 and 2004 in terms of business while its peer banks had moved ahead. Banking analysts had adversely commented upon the bank's capacity to face competition unless it adopted technology and moved along with the changing times. In the new scenario, we had no option but to change swiftly for our sheer survival and maintain our brand position—we were at the top only a few years back. As an insider, who had witnessed the growth of the bank all along the past decades except for this difficult time, the author felt a sense of duty and determination to arrest this tendency of decline and restore the bank on the growth tracks. All this meant reimagining the future and carving out a compelling vision that could portray the challenges posed by technology-driven banks, fierce competition and sky-high expectations. The challenge was to change, on many fronts, with alacrity and speed.

A new vision for the bank as a full-service technology-driven multi-specialist bank in next three years was finalized after a series of internal discussions and an exclusive board meeting. A document, Vision 2005–2010, was approved by the board. It also sanctioned the required budget to put in place the new technology. To top it all, the board gave the author *carte blanche* to go ahead with speed in implementing the new technology (core banking) and reselecting the lost clientele and the business; they provided all the support that was needed. This indeed was a great push towards deliverance. It called for quick steps for implementation of core banking and doubling the business of the bank in the next three years. There was unbridled clarity about the direction of change. As CEO, I had to be a challenger of status quo and weave a new tapestry of growth. My mandate, in short, was to create a happening bank, lifting it from the quagmire of stagnancy of growth, thought pattern and action. *Development of a compelling vision for the future is at the core of initiating any transformation programme.*

2. Harness the potential of digitalization

Technology can be a boon or a disaster depending on whether or not leadership takes charge and timely decisions to build new skills, talent and make it a new way of life for each member of the bank. Most transformation will be triggered by consideration of unleashing fullest potential of business through technology, fullest potential of staff and merit-based HR.

The BOB transformation was triggered by the bank's failed attempts to implement new core banking solutions (anytime, anywhere banking) due to the trade union's massive protests, which successfully stymied the process. The staff morale was at the lowest ebb as other banks were already ahead BOB in implementing core banking and we were losing customers.

After taking over, my first priority was to launch the tech project. My business managers were waiting for the go ahead from the board and we convened a special board meeting to get all the approvals to launch it. We took a number of actions such as sending top functionaries to all the zones to communicate and implement, creation of a project office at corporate level with a general manager heading project office and creation of specialized training set-up in Gujarat to train our front-line staff. Right from Day 1, we made business-owning tech project and most of the team members for core banking were drawn from the business side. We reviewed tech projects every week in our morning meetings. We created a steering committee of the top management. I chaired this and our tech expert board member, a professor at Indian Institute of Technology (IIT) Bombay, who was a member of the steering committee, also attended. His contributions were most valuable.

The task of putting a new system and simultaneously running the old system posed herculean problems, but the zeal in employees and passion to excel made us implement core banking in record time. In fact, the motivation in the teams was so great that in just 100 days, we implemented the project of installing 500 new ATMs. The bank was rebirthing and transiting from legacy-driven systems to modern architecture. In doubling the business in just three years, technology readiness played a key role and a collateral advantage was regaining the confidence of customers and heightened morale of all the employees.

During the transformation and later on, it is important for a CEO not to consider technology a separate specialist function and leave it to its own technical agenda. Digitalization requires CEO not only to make resources available (e.g., manpower, hardware choices, etc.), but more importantly, communicate their commitment to technology, building digital culture and mindset, stakeholder alignment, support to training and reskilling, and importantly, remove the roadblocks into the change management process. Digitalization is a field force that changes continuously and changes everything through newer technologies and applications. In the Indian context, the demographic profile of customers is varied, and it is important that customers understand the technology to benefit from it. The business benefits of digitalization start accruing only when there is a constant outreach and 'education' of customers, and they 'convert' to technology and use it regularly. Technology allows banks to develop synergy among business products, verticals and enables new product development and innovation. All of this requires full organizational capabilities and bandwidth. For this reason, digital transformation can happen truly only when the organizational design, HR processes including rewards, and culture are aligned to technology as an enabler rather than as a 'technical department'. This holistic change across the bank happens when the CEOs take charge to bring various stakeholders together to work towards unlocking the potential of digitalization for the bank.

3. **Mobilize support from the key stakeholders**

Any large-scale transformation needs complete support of and a mandate from its board of directors. Additionally, in the case of a public sector organization, support from the government is also crucial. The force of the environment is overarching. The efforts of CEO and the board's commitment to the new vision are critical factors for success of the transformation. In fact, the board before finalizing the future vision needs to discuss and debate it rigorously, allocate resources and set timelines for implementation. A mid-course review of the transformation is also necessary. One of the key roles of the board chair and CEO is to ensure that the board has relevant competencies to pilot the transformation programme.

The board of BOB had a key competency gap in the area of technology. As the bank had an ambitious plan to implement a technology-driven business transformation programme requiring huge capital investment, the presence of a board member with such competencies was an immediate requirement, more so when the bank itself had limited talent in this area. The author, after due process, persuaded an eminent professor of computer science, from a leading IIT, to join the board. This was a game changer in developing a technology vision for the bank. The bank was also fortunate to have on its board an internationally eminent management scholar, who also was the former director of a prestigious management institute in India. The board also had a progressive representative from the government.

One of the most critical and ticklish tasks in the context of the public sector is to deal with the government which has to factor in public concerns, union pressures and political interventions. It is common for the vested interest to stymie the process of transformation by raising many issues. The bank was no exception to this phenomenon. Vested interests, mostly trade union groups, frequently complained to the government about our various initiatives such as technology, brand building and HR initiatives just to name a few. They would raise frivolous and sometimes even scandalous objections with the sole intention to sabotage our efforts as they feared an identity crisis post the technology implementation. It required a spirited-cum-rigorous explaining to the government from time to time, with facts and data about our transformation initiatives. We needed government support on various actions we took including some unpleasant ones such as rationalization of branches, transfer of union officials and streamlining various unethical practices. In the public sector, support from and handholding by the bureaucracy are very important to successfully pilot the journey of transformation.

Undertaking transformation involving complex changes in a large-size organization may sometimes call for making bold moves and standing firm in spite of political pressures, even at the risk of one's job. Support is never spontaneous or automatic. It has to be negotiated. Cooperation from important stakeholders is a sine qua non in any transformation process. A CEO's grit and gumption play an important role in withstanding the pressures from those opposing and sabotaging transformation.

4. **Attack the tumour inside**

Organizations are usually bound by their culture. During transformation, key cultural factors can pose stumbling blocks to change efforts. No major change can be implemented and sustained without identifying and dealing with the key problems which may have remained unattended and have eventually become a part of culture, thereby causing major constraints in the process of change. These factors may include the trade unions' resistance to change, a soft work culture, restrictive practices, managerial inertia, high degree of internal bureaucracy, inconsistent HR policies, low morale in employees, lack of concern for customer service, poor levels of governance and suboptimal ethical standards. A critical roadblock to transformation is just to live with these problems and turn a blind eye to them. You need to resolve them.

IR in BOB, which had been a sore point for long, posed a major threat to the change process. This was the Achilles' heel; it could potentially sabotage our proposed transformation efforts. It was therefore a top priority to confront this problem head-on in order to clear the decks for implementation of a major technology-driven business transformation. In the bank, the management's past dealings with the trade unions had an accommodative stance. The trade unions in the past had stonewalled any efforts for major organizational changes. IR oscillated between confrontations to cosy collusive cohabitation. The resultant IR climate had manifested itself in the form of employee indiscipline and restrictive practices, which affected customer service. IR caused a major stumbling block to implement technology and undertake many other reform measures in customer service in delivering efficient service. This problem had to be dealt with, although it was considered quite risky as it would invite problems from trade unions. Between 2001 and 2004, in his role as an executive director, the author decided to confront this issue head-on (in spite of lack of support from CEO) and after facing a very difficult period personally, the author was able to successfully deal with IR problems, thereby clearing the decks for smooth implementation of technology. By this time, the author had also taken over as CEO and his efforts to streamline IR paid off handsomely and paved the way to take a variety of initiatives to transform the bank. Thus, it is important for the top management and CEOs to diagnose and deal with the major problems and constraints effectively for the smooth implementation of the transformation. The transformation, brought about after removal of major impediments, is bound to succeed.

5. **Sensitize all the employees about the cost of not undertaking change**

For the success of transformation, one of the biggest questions is how to get people aligned behind the organization's overarching goals. How do you create shared meanings and interpretations of reality to facilitate coordinated actions? How do you make employees understand the need for disturbing their comfort zone? How do you develop confidence and trust in them about the commitment and sincerity of leadership to design and lead the new future of the organization and finally how do you develop positive self-regard among employees to apply themselves fully to rise above and pull collectively for creating a new future for the organization and themselves?

So, it is very important to create an environment of employee education and involvement in the transformation process; it helps to build the momentum, ownership and passion for the transformation. Change is normally seen as a concern of the top management. Very often, adequate attention is not paid to the employees down below, even less to the foot soldiers. People at the lower rungs are often made recipients of the changes planned at the top. Because of this, many a time, they resist or cold shoulder a call for change. This happens when they are not made aware of the actual working of the organization on an ongoing basis and are often fed on a diet of 'all is well', even when it is not so. Thus, the real challenge is to ensure that people understand and accept the challenges of change. Where the management sensitizes the employees about the rationale and logic of the change and their consequences on the future of the organization, the results tend to be positive. The employees need to be explained not only the positive dimensions of change in terms of unleashing the new growth opportunities, but they also have to be made aware of the cost of not embracing the changes.

When we embarked upon the major change programme, our main concern was to sensitize the foot soldiers about the present reality of our business and services, which portrayed a dismal picture. We had to persuade them to be a partner in modernizing the bank—with technology, efficient service delivery and innovative products. I strongly believed in interacting directly with the employees and sharing our concerns about the decline in the bank's ranking on account of delay in technology implementation and mediocre level of service. We organized 10 town halls at different large business centres covering about 20 per cent of the 40,000 employees during my first 100 days of taking charge as CEO. In these meetings, I openly shared with employees the current market positioning, our vision for the next five years and our strategy to regain the first position among the nationalized banks in India. Through PowerPoint presentations, I explained the declining trend in our business and the weakening of the competitive position of the bank mainly on two counts—our failure to adopt technology and the competition we faced from the newly minted private banks which used technology to deliver anytime anywhere banking services. I also shared as to how and why we lost business and customers in key centres, why analysts adversely commented about the future of the bank and the resultant adverse movement in the bank's share price.

My message was direct and clear. I shared with employees that the bank is likely to go downhill unless we change our traditional ways of rendering services and doing things; going downhill would be disastrous for the bank and injurious to everyone. After my open sessions, I would freely entertain questions from employees and clarify any issue that bothered them. The employees would tell me that they were not aware about the state of the bank's health as they were always told by their unions that everything was hale and hearty on the business front. Lack of communication from the management about the reality had added to the problem.

In view of the fact that the workplace restrictive practices and an average customer service had taken strong roots in many centres, the employees were advised, both in such town halls and through circulars, about the management's policy of zero tolerance for indiscipline and restrictive practices. At the same time, assurance was given that genuine problems faced by employees would be dealt with urgency and compassion. Such a straight talk coming from CEO helped in disturbing the comfort zone and created a collective consciousness among our employees to rise to the occasion and be a partner in the change process.

These direct interactions created a huge impact and employees made a commitment to the transformation. The rest is history!!

The employees have an equal stake in the growth of the organization; their engagement is vital during the change process. Employees' problems, anxieties and concerns have to be understood and resolved both during and after the transformation.

6. **Constitute a rowing team**

Transformation time is not a business as usual. It requires an altogether different environment and ecosystem signalling a happening atmosphere. It needs critical attention from the CEO and the top management in terms of their time and efforts. There is always a tendency for the top management to remain bogged down with the routine activities of the organization. Therefore, it is important to constitute a team, with some rapid-fire band of individuals with appropriate skill sets and capabilities, who will remain committed to push the transformation on a day-to-day basis. The team members should be competent, collaborative and focused on actualizing the vision. This team has to be from across functions and needs to have a proven track record. The team has to be given freedom and should feel empowered. The size of the team would depend upon the nature of the change. Sometimes, persons with special talent/specialization may have to be inducted laterally. The project team bears the biggest responsibility; it has to ensure that the normal business of the company goes on without interruption and the agenda for change is also pursued simultaneously.

Our transformation programme was kick-started by identifying and carefully selecting a team from various functions, which comprised of some senior executives and some really young talent. We set up a special project team for implementation of technology. One of our former general managers, an expert in technology matters and an old hand in implementing changes in the bank, was hired as an advisor on contract basis to help and guide the project team. The project team was empowered to take important decisions and had direct access to CEO for any urgent consultations.

The project team did an excellent job in creating change by managers at various zonal/regional levels and in coordinating implementation of various projects under transformation. The team worked closely with the consultants engaged on various fronts, especially the one for introduction of core banking technology to provide 'anytime anywhere banking' without disrupting day-to-day delivery of service. The guidance by consultants and the cohesive working of the team with the consultants delivered many 'quick wins' for the bank.

Transforming an organization is never a solo affair. It needs hands-on problem solvers who work with empowered and engaged executives. Together, they push forward transformation. The process is akin to rowing a large boat in a turbulent river.

7. **Create a crucible for culture change**

Very often, more so in large organizations, due to hierarchies and internal bureaucracy, a certain inertia sets in for any change. It is subconsciously internalized and gets manifested as a pattern within the organization. This acts as a major stumbling block in bringing about any change.

One of the biggest challenges during transformation is the creative destruction of the legacy patterns and processes, especially those which cause delay in production and are obstructive to customer service. No large-size organization can succeed in its transformation unless efforts are directed to bust internal bureaucracy to the required minimum and create a hassle-free delivery system. Everyone needs to learn the new ways of doing things in a technological environment and develop a new attitude to serve customers. An agile, alert and accountable management can make a big difference in accelerating the transformation process.

The management of transformation can be at risk unless it is ensured that all the important operational units act in unison and in a coordinated way. There is also a need to create an ecosystem of learning, across all levels of management and employees, to help them to collectively take the organization ahead. It is akin to moving a big flywheel together.

The bank had multiple legacy issues like lack of timely response to customer issues, delays in decision-making, excessive internal bureaucracy contributing to delays, lack of accountability for speedy decision-making at the senior and top levels and lack of perspective to operate as a well-knit entity. The main problem was the culture at the senior and the top levels where the executives operated in their functional silos with restricted communication among themselves. This resulted in a lack of concern towards operating manager's urgent need to get decisions on key business issues, a big brotherly attitude towards those junior in the hierarchy, delay in resolution of issues, etc. My main challenge was to bring a culture change from paper-pushing to problem-solving, from hierarchy-based to team-based decision-making and ensuring a shift from risk aversion to collective risk-taking.

If the bank had to become customer focused and regain its admirable market positioning, the entire ecosystem of decision-making and its processes needed to be darned up. This required confronting attitudes, disturbing the comfort zone and drilling in a new attitude of being proactive with smart response to customer problems. To achieve this, a system of daily morning meeting was introduced with all the general managers, executive directors and CEO to discuss, debate and solve problems with speed and alacrity. Initially, the daily meeting of the top functionaries created a certain degree of tension but soon it was replaced by a team effort to work together and achieve together.

In this forum, live issues reported by the operating managers and the customers were deliberated upon and quick decisions were taken and communicated. The forum addressed issues of coordination among various functions of the Bank. The implementation of various projects was monitored on a daily basis and prompt corrective action was taken to ensure their hassle-free implementation. Tensions and disagreements were brought to the fore and discussed so that everyone was on board when major decisions were taken. We thought through and worked on the best ideas that could reposition the Bank. All the top executives learnt together, almost on a daily basis, with an attitude of problem-solving. This honed **our** collective leadership skills.

An ambitious 100-day agenda for implementation of many innovative steps was finalized in this forum which could be successfully achieved through the collective endeavours of the team. This greatly motivated the employees and gave them the confidence to achieve the vision of the bank. The morning meetings were the birthplace of many customer-centric innovations such as 8:00 AM–8:00 PM banking, 24-hours human banking, retail loan and small and medium enterprise (SME) loan factories, to name a few. Proposals were finalized for new strategies for international operations, retail and SME strategies, marketing and brand-building strategies and many such initiatives for improving operational excellence. The morning meetings became a forum for conceptualization, diagnosis of the problems, collective problem-solving and agenda setting for high-speed execution during transformation. It also provided opportunities for personal growth and leadership development for many in the top management; we all learnt leadership lessons centred around real-life issues.

Our decision to have a daily meeting of one hour to confront, negotiate, coordinate, challenge, persuade and build consensus on major issues and facilitate smart implementation was the greatest lesson in our transformation journey. This was the flag bearer of our commitment to create a team culture at the top that heralded a new environment of speedy decision-making, time-bound problem-solving, smart response and management accountability. We could create a new culture of facilitation and ownership through a daily investment of time and effort. One cannot change the culture merely through sermons or circulars. We need to collectively deploy ourselves for the common goal over a long stretch of time till it becomes habit to work together. This was the single-most important mechanism for success of the transformation.

This experience suggests that it is necessary to create a crucible experience, especially at the level of top management, to review organizational processes and to engage in ongoing learning from experience. This mechanism proved to be the biggest instrumentality for culture change.

8. **Move from an operational to an organizational mindset**

CEOs, especially in large organizations, often tend to get sucked into operational routine, in spite of their best intentions. They have to deal with mounds of paperwork that continuously flow in from various verticals. Similarly, frequent meetings also consume a lot of their time. As this leads to lack of time and focus on the transformation agenda, CEOs need to consciously, and sometimes even ruthlessly, break the trap of routine. They need to develop an organizational mindset, which involves focusing on strategic issues like the organization's future positioning, developing competence to meet the evolving competition and creating a reputation for innovations and leadership.

During our transformation process, I redefined my role with a greater accent on mentoring the top management team and resolving issues for smooth facilitation of various changes. Most operational issues were delegated to the next level. A major part of my attention and time went in rehashing the HR function and engaging with the consultants hired to work and implement the transformation. Besides this, I also focused on rehashing business strategies, innovations in product offering and service delivery, and technology implementation. I took steps to strengthen leadership bench strength and put in place a system of smart communication with employees and customers. My main emphasis was on building and developing a culture of accountability for achieving operational excellence.

Upon reflection, I note with great satisfaction that we could reposition the bank as India's international bank—a technology-driven modern entity. This was possible because we changed our track from an operational mindset to an organizational mindset.

During transformation, the top management should redefine its roles and priorities and spend more time on collective discussions on the major strategic issues that will prepare the organization for the future.

No organization can succeed if everyone in management is doing more of the same thing.

9. **Use field wisdom**

During transformation, a number of changes in business processes, new product innovations and review of the decision-making process became necessary. Diagnosis of issues and problems faced by the various stakeholders helps in understanding and planning the key areas of focus that require change.

The field staff, the people who are closest to the customers, are the farthest from the decision-makers. Similarly, customers too, are not connected to the top management. The customers' unvarnished feedback and concerns about the products, services and expectations often do not find their way to the top management. This happens for a variety of reasons. How do we make accumulated knowledge and ideas of the field staff and of customers available to top decision-makers?

In the bank, there existed weak links between customers' problems and the response and solutions from the management. Same was true for the employees also. We wanted to bridge this gap. We strengthened the voice of customers and our frontline employees. We regularly captured ideas from the field staff and the customers, discussed them in our morning meetings and connected this field wisdom with the corporate decision-making process. During our frequent interactions with the field staff in our regular town halls, we received some great insights about the unexplored opportunities in business, the processes that hindered business development and the modifications needed in our policies and procedures to develop a competitive advantage. We promptly implemented the changes based on such feedback. We made policy changes, wherever required. Our new retail loan policies and business loan policies were, in fact, greatly remodelled on the basis of feedback from the field staff and customers. We would also share our strategy for implementation of technology and get ideas of employees and customers with regard to their expectations and anxiety.

The transformation may be initiated at the top level, but its success depends upon using field wisdom and removing constraints faced by the field staff and the customers. The top management must respect the feedback, insights and inputs from the field staff and customers in formulating growth strategies for the future and while designing new products.

10. **Build intangibles**

Transformation is often misconstrued as undertaking certain specific change like adopting new technology or reorganization of structures or adjustments post mergers or acquisition. This is a myopic view of transformation. Transformation is an opportunity mainly to create a new future of the organization and this is best achieved by building intangibles such as human capital, leadership, customer centricity and technology infrastructure. Intangibles are those that cannot be measured in rupee or dollar terms. Delivering financial performance is one thing and creating a healthy organization is another. Soft-side strategy initiatives are the foundation stone of hard-side strategy successes.

I was clear in my mind that I had to prepare the bank for long-term competitiveness and develop it as a powerful brand; we could not allow ourselves to yield to the temptation of focusing on short-term business results. We needed to be far-sighted and take some foundation building steps such as developing architecture for the new capabilities, developing a culture of performance, responsive communication, collaboration, speed and compassion. Besides this, we needed to develop a new leadership for the future which was not only technologically savvy but also emotionally sensitive and inclusive. Interestingly, our unwavering emphasis on building architecture of intangibles for the stable, long-term growth of the bank delivered excellent business results, far beyond my expectations.

From my experience I feel that a CEO's main role is to continuously improve on building intangibles to ensure long-term sustainability of their organizations; this task cannot be delegated and cannot be undertaken as a part-time concern. In fact, I believe that 'the business of CEO is not to do business but to build intangibles which will drive business and create a sustainable organization'.

11. **Rejuvenate the HR function**

The HR function is most critical; it can either facilitate or obstruct the success of any transformation programme. It is concerned with the employees and the culture of an organization. Can employee relations be rated as supportive or obstructive? Are employees largely happy about the people processes? Do they possess the required capabilities for undertaking contemplated changes? Do they feel fairly treated by the management and are they emotionally connected to each other and the management? Do they feel let down by lack of care, compassion and motivation? Is HR decision-making ad hoc and are there bureaucratic delays and inconsistent application of rules, or is HR guided by a policy framework? Answers to these questions can tell about the employees' perceptions about the HR function in any organization. These perceptions are very critical in designing any transformation programme.

For effective transformation, the fundamental thing is to recognize the importance of employees and employee processes in creating a positive climate of trust. Employees often feel used and exploited by clever management through their pep talks and fake promises, and thus, deep work in building trust in the cadres is required. The main role of management is to lift the sight of employees from their limited mental mode to higher level of thinking about architecting the future of their organizations. The CEO has to ensure that HR function is reorganized and rehashed to build credibility with the employees and puts this function under their direct oversight during the transformation programme to ensure that employees are at the centre of attention to contribute to their maximum potential. Each vertical and functional head has to play the role of an effective HR manager as well for the people in that function. Mere operational skills and domain expertise are not enough at any time, much less during transformation.

The perception of HR function in the bank was far from positive. Employees wanted transparency, merit and objectivity in HR policies. The bank had a long period of patronizing and relationship culture. This culture manifested itself in different ways and in the process, performance always suffered. During periods of transition and transformation, this acted as a barrier. The relationship culture crippled the incentive to perform and one of the biggest challenges was to move from a relationship culture to a performance culture and to create a new growth-oriented mindset. My main focus was to create a HR culture that could seamlessly facilitate transformation—a culture that was an anti-thesis of the prevailing bureaucratic style of working which acted as a barrier to effective customer service and resolving the problems of customers. We believed that culture is a prerequisite for transformation—a new culture that can create enthusiasm and momentum for change. Innovations, risk-taking and excellence are the outcome of team and collaborative work. HR and its contributions were considered a key differentiator to achieve our vision and push growth momentum.

An integrated approach to human resource development (HRD) was introduced and a prodigious effort, right at the CEO level, to put the employee at the centre of our HR initiatives became the hallmark of our policies. A major focus of our efforts was directed at creating an enabling climate for everyone to work with confidence and without any fear. The key elements of our HR focus were to move from an IR to HRD paradigm. This entailed putting extraordinary focus on 'employees' wherein you build their morale, build new competencies in them, create employee motivation, build trust, build new capabilities related to the emerging environment, improve performance management, develop a performance culture, build a leadership pipeline in the executive cadre, improve performance through frontline engagement, de-bureaucratize the HR decision-making and make HR administration employee friendly through technology. It is important to ensure that the HR structure, system and processes complement each other to create a culture of continuous development, collaborative problem-solving and creating new mechanisms through which the employee voice can be heard right at the top.

As a first step, we activated the HR Steering Committee of the Board and ensured that it met every quarter. Under my chairmanship, the HR Steering Committee comprised of the executive director, two members of the board and two invited members—one an HR expert from the industry and one a leading academic on HR. The committee developed a prioritized agenda for HR transformation in the context of our vision 2005–2010.

Several new initiatives were taken which focused on the development side of HR by creating a new structure for HR which would be in alignment with our new thrust. The composite HR function was bifurcated into human resource management and HRD. Several other initiatives were also taken to reskill our HR functionaries into the developmental paradigm of HR and make HR administration employee friendly through technology. We undertook a talent identification exercise in all cadres, revamped various HR sub-systems improving performance culture and launched new leadership development strategies to groom 300 leaders for the future and set the stage for succession strategy in the senior cadre. We focused on developing in-house excellence in the training system and developing a pipeline of young talented managers. The frontline cadre was engaged with transformational objectives through monthly communication from CEO to 40,000 employees. Employees were reached out on all important initiatives of the bank such as initiating the core banking project, logo change and rebranding, recovery drive, special business campaigns and customer-centric initiatives. All the communications from employees were responded. I spent about 60 per cent of my time in directly engaging with remodelling of HR function and strategies.

With so many steps taken, we achieved an excellent management–employee connect than any other time and the employees' response to transformational initiatives was very positive and engaging.

One of the key factors in making the transformation successful was our relentless efforts in remodelling the HR function to build transparency, fairness and an organizational justice mechanism. Our emphasis on and initiatives for people's motivation were somewhat above the concern for business as we strongly believed that it is only the happy employees who can take back the bank to its past glory. The core orientation of our new HR was on responsiveness, fair dealings, compassion, new capability building and meritocratic career advancement. Much of our success under transformation can be attributed to our proactive HR function which took the lead in employee care and provided a fair and transparent system in HR management. In the post-COVID environment, the concern for employees' wellness and work from home must seize the attention of HR to design suitable policies.

Employees' response to transformation is directly related to their perception of HR function because employees experience the management through HR policies. Thus, the management needs to have a clear diagnosis of HR function—about its bureaucracy, its perception on the criteria of fairness, accessibility, emotional connect, listening to problems and the overall response and credibility to enable it to initiate prompt corrective action.

12. Micromanage excellence

As transformation takes place, the major focus of CEO and the top management often remains on managing the concrete deliverables. While this is imperative, often the other important aspects such as building end-to-end service excellence, hassle-free problem-solving mechanism for stakeholders, internal response mechanisms and frontline attitudes get relegated to the periphery. A good film is an outcome of perfect synergistic working among its various units such as acting, editing, lyrics, music, artwork and screenplay. In the same way, a sustainable transformation can be achieved by creating a tapestry of excellent service, positive mindset of the foot soldiers, proactive attitude in helping customers and a complete alignment of intent and action. Excellence can be measured by looking at issues such as how organizational members respond to stakeholders' issues, how customers are treated, how smooth are the internal processes, how swiftly customers and employees' issues are attended to, how caring is the organization towards its employees, how learning is promoted and how organizational discipline and decorum are maintained.

During our morning meetings, there was less focus on monitoring the business outcomes but greater accent on drivers of business such as the way we handled customer complaints, the way we responded to employee issues, the way our premises were kept, the issues of internal bureaucracy, the frontline attitudes, our overall response mechanisms and innovations in our product range and competitor's business strategies. The focus was on creating excellence in the smallest of things that mattered in creating a tapestry of excellence.

CEOs and top management have a special task cut out for them, on this count, during the transformation.

13. **Create emotional connect**

The cornerstone of a successful implementation of the vision and the transformation is the emotional engagement of the employees. Rational logic never drives people the way emotions do. The challenge is to focus on a common cause, build a sense of community and create a climate that enables people to tap into passion, energy and a desire to move together in a positive direction. In large organizations, employees are divided across socio-economic backgrounds, geography, language as also social and union affiliations. The challenge is to integrate them towards a common goal. In this, the human and emotional side of transformation assumes significance. This is far more challenging than seeking engagement at an intellectual level. Employees need to be connected through the feelings of affection, compassion, care and concern. They need to feel respected, visible and included.

During the period of the transformation process, we focused on reaching out to the employees at an emotional level so as to bring in them a sense of connectedness to the larger vision. As a HR professional and now CEO, I was psychologically sensitive to employees' deeper pattern of thoughts and emotions which manifested into occasional cynicism, negativity and lack of involvement. We had to, thus, reach out to the employees at a deep personal level and give them the confidence that they matter and that the management was there to address their problems and the related stress and anxiety.

We worked genuinely to reach out to them and responded to their personal problems by engaging with them to fulfil their hopes and aspirations and inspiring them for positive action. For this, a nucleus of HR specialists was created in the CEO's office to establish humanitarian connect with the employees. Prominent action mechanisms such as a direct hotline to CEO to enable the employees to reach out in times of distress, employee conclaves,[1] counselling services and several such initiatives were launched from the CEO's office. It was also our endeavour to act with empathy and fairness to solve long-standing problems and one such issue was the regularization of about 1,000 casual labour working for several years against permanent vacancies. Even the trade unions appreciated this gesture. The humane orientation to problem-solving in employees' matters greatly improved the overall trust level. Many such programmes became game changers not only in creating the emotional connection with the employees but also in instilling enthusiasm, which played an important role in the transformation success.

Transformation is emotionally demanding on a CEO; it is equally demanding on every employee. Thus, one of the most challenging parts of a CEO's work is to create an emotional ecosystem across the organization rather than merely seeking an intellectual consensus for transformation. This implies empowering employees and igniting them to deliver the transformation.

14. **Optimize business expectations**

Very often, the process of transformation calls for creative destruction of existing systems and processes which need to be replaced with new ways of working in a changed technological environment. The people at operating level face numerous problems during the process of migration from one system to another, especially in a technology-driven transformation. It is like creating a new building after demolishing the older one. The operating managers too face new challenges on account of the transition. In a customer-centric industry like banking or airlines, the problems get exacerbated as the service cannot be disrupted even for a moment during the process of transformation. Throughout this period, the top management has to restrain from its aspirational and aggressive

---

[1] Employee conclaves were conducted in an informal and non-threatening environment through behavioural science methodology involving a large group of around 100–120 participants drawn from a cross section of employees covering all cadres with the objective to ignite zeal and a positive image of themselves as also of the bank and to seek their commitment to the new vision.

business growth and avoid transmitting any unnecessary pressure down the line. Many a time, the transformation process suffers on account of the management's continued emphasis on aggressive business growth; such a pressure can be counterproductive. It must be stressed that the sole goal of transformation is to prepare the organization to handle more business in a hassle-free way. As we implemented the transformation, it was a conscious decision to sacrifice near-term growth to invest in building the basic pillars of growth, such as technology upgradation, building leadership bench strength, employee engagement and customer-centric innovations. Imagine our surprise when we realized that we were proved wrong as the bank's business started growing from the first year itself and towards the end of three years, the business not only doubled but on various parameters it achieved extraordinary results. The total business doubled (107%), credit showed a growth of 145 per cent, non-performing assets were down by about 6 per cent, net profit grew by 112 per cent, business per employee more than doubled, eight million new customers were added and international operations recorded more than 100 per cent growth.

This experience clearly shows that the appropriate initiatives combined with right intent and clarity on objectives can bring in dramatic business growth sooner than expected. Therefore, there is a need to create a balance between transformational and business objectives without becoming unduly anxious about the latter.

15. **Build a culture of governance**

Most transformations have a high failure record or at best they have a fragile and short tenure. The reasons for this are not difficult to fathom. Most of the times, it is the lack of effective governance across the organization that brings the transformation into disrepute. Governance is concerned with right and ethical ways in achieving corporate goals. It is also about serving the interests of key stakeholders. The questions asked are: Is the organization delivering smooth service with easy access to management? Do employees feel empowered in doing their duties? Do the shareholders feel happy about the growth and reputation of the organization? Internal governance and its architecture must be strengthened to withstand the compelling pressures of business in an evolving environment. A regular interface with various stakeholders and incorporating their expectations and constructive feedback into organizational processes systems and policies can positively help the process of institutionalization of governance.

Alongside our transformation, we introduced an effective mechanism to periodically receive feedback from our senior operating managers like zonal and regional managers about the implementation of our various initiatives in business and technology with special focus on understanding their constraints, if any. We also put in place an effective system to regularly communicate with all the staff to keep them informed about the various initiatives of the bank to enhance business and other relevant matters. A system of accountability for senior and top management was introduced for speedy response to decision-making.

Transformation must be institutionalized into the nervous system of the organization. This needs work in building culture, people, systems, a new communication pattern and a new accountability for top and senior managers which go beyond achieving business targets. Shortcuts and inconsistent policies in the name of business exigencies must be replaced by creating consistency and uniformity in policies across the organization.

Conclusion

Transformation is neither just a technology play nor just a business enhancement play; it is a leadership play in engaging, energizing and inspiring people to a larger purpose. Once trust is created in the leadership, my experience is that employees go out of their way in standing by the organization.

When the CEO leads transformation from the front, it sets the right tone and tempo for the change; it also helps consultants to continuously share the level of implementation and sort out problems. To sum it up, the transformation has to be driven by CEO; it cannot be outsourced to the consultant and HR. The stakes are very high and can only be ignored at their peril.

Transformation is not an end in itself, which shows to the world how smart the organization looks with its technology or its products. Its main purpose is to bring about a DNA change in the culture of the organization in terms of its impact on the society. Any transformation that only makes an organization an efficient machine to churn out better numbers will be taking a limited view of the purpose of transformation. It is for such reasons that a majority of transformation efforts fail.

Transformation must improve the health of the organization to align, execute and renew itself to create exceptional sustainable performance and build its reputation for its people and leadership, and make it more resilient and resonant. Transformation requires deep knowledge of people processes and an uncompromising commitment to engage employees. It may start with a limited purpose, but eventually, transformational leaders should be able to expand its purpose and focus on taking those foundational steps that continuously provide leaders who can carry the baton of change in this ever-changing reality. When this process takes roots, the transformation in future is almost on autopilot mode. When leadership is built, business also builds. When the focus is entirely only on business, without erecting strong pillars of culture and leadership, it is like building a mountain on a sandy foundation. When leadership ladder is properly put against the wall of challenges, you can climb onto any business challenge smoothly. In this growingly complex world, leadership represents the only sustainable competitive advantage for business organizations.

One of our top priorities alongside the technology-driven business transformation was to create leadership which was equally concerned about building a new culture which was service oriented, innovative, responsive, compassionate and creative at problem-solving.

Our efforts bore fruit when as many as a dozen alumni of this transformation project were eventually selected by the Government of India for CEO positions in other PSBs. Our emphasis on building leadership pipeline has made the bank stronger and respected in spite of the many challenges it faced.

One of the high points of our transformation programme was to reposition the bank as a marketing organization. Alongside the introduction of core banking and expansion of ATM network (which other peer banks had already initiated), the bank created a new identity altogether. The transition of the bank from an old, slow-moving, deposit-taking company (research revelation by AC Neilson & Co., a well-known marketing research firm) to a vibrant, innovative, customer-centric and technology-savvy bank was in many ways an endorsement by the public of our speed and alacrity in changing the perception about us through many customer-centric innovations, and in particular, undertaking a rebranding exercise through logo change and appointing a cricket icon as bank's brand ambassador. The new logo, the Baroda Sun, is a new symbol of change, dynamism and optimism. The bank was repositioned as India's international bank, which signified the intrinsic strength of the bank in the international operations in 22 countries around the globe and over 20 per cent profit coming from it.

Finally, the question, however, is if it is a leadership play, why do only few ventures go for all out efforts to undertake transformation of their organizations? What is it that makes many CEOs end up tinkering with a thing here and a thing there and remain cautious not to invite the fury of those who are affected by transformation? As Harvard professors, Heifetz and Linsky (2002), observed:

> Anyone who has stepped out on the line, leading part or all of an organization, a community, or a family, knows the personal and professional vulnerabilities. However gentle your style, however, careful your strategy, however, sure you may be that you are on the right track, leading is a risky business.

Unlike private and multinational organizations, the risks are far greater in the public sector because of the essential feature of accountability to public at large through the mechanism of parliamentary system. You are accountable for your action to investigative agencies, and so you should take steps out of line with established procedures, even in the larger interest of efficiency. My commitment to undertake this massive transformation was largely inspired by the great vision of the founder of the bank, who, 112 years ago, established BOB in a small town, and as an acknowledgement of the stellar efforts of my many predecessors who nurtured the bank over the decades. When leaders are driven by a higher purpose, risks appear dwarfed. Principles, passion and courage become the driving force for the leaders who venture to change the lives of people through their organizations. While transformation is largely risky, it is certainly worthy of the costs.

Transforming a large organization, as complex as BOB, in a highly unionized environment with hardly any discretion to incentivize employees through financial rewards, was like riding a tiger without any cover. What really worked was our unrelenting focus on higher order purpose, bold experiments and initiatives in people processes and, above all, an abiding faith in the collective passion of its 40,000 employees. Our efforts were focused to mobilize the emotional commitment of our employees through listening, empowerment, helping their personal growth and standing by them in their times of difficulty. We could demonstrate that trust is driven by the leader's own passion to the vision and relentless engagement with the reform and transformational agenda. My experience is perfectly echoed by Feser (2016) when he says:

> 'Inspirational leadership is the most effective approach to creating complex and dynamic situations in which people are "emotional" that is, under pressure and stressed, such as when an organisation is going through a transformation process.'

(*Note:* For this transformation, the author received the Asian Banker Leadership Achievement Award, 2007, for lifetime achievement and contribution to excellence in the financial services industry.)

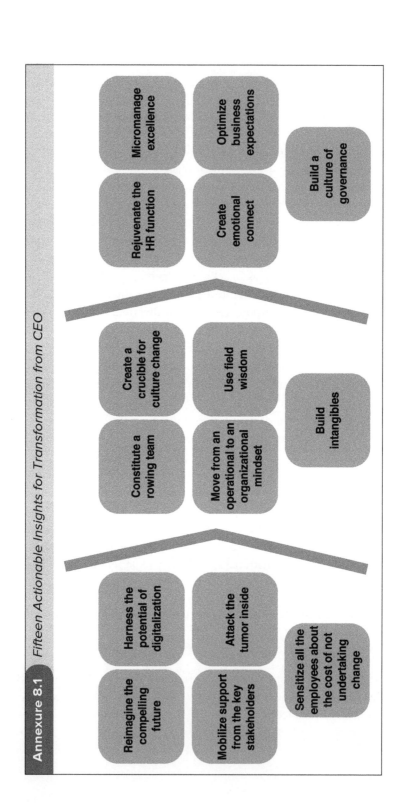

Annexure 8.1 *Fifteen Actionable Insights for Transformation from CEO*

Reimagine the compelling future

Harness the potential of digitalization

Mobilize support from the key stakeholders

Attack the tumor inside

Sensitize all the employees about the cost of not undertaking change

Constitute a rowing team

Create a crucible for culture change

Move from an operational to an organizational mindset

Use field wisdom

Build intangibles

Rejuvenate the HR function

Micromanage excellence

Create emotional connect

Optimize business expectations

Build a culture of governance

Bibliography

Bucy, M., Hall, S., & Yakola, D. (2016). Transformation with a capital T. McKinsey Quarterly. https://www.mckinsey.com/business-functions/rts/our-insights/transformation-with-a-capital-t

Cappelli, P., Singh, H., Singh, J. V., & Useem, M. (2010, March). Leadership lessons from India. *Harvard Business Review, 88*(3), 87–95.

Feser, C. (2016). *When execution is not enough: Decoding inspirational leadership.* Wiley.

Heifetz, R., & Linsky, M. (2002). *Leadership on the line—staying alive to the dangers of leading.* Harvard Business School Press.

Kahneman, D. (2012). *Thinking, fast and slow.* Penguin Books.

Khandelwal, A. K. (2007, June). Moving HRD from the periphery to the centre for transformation of an Indian public sector bank: Keynote address, 4th Asian Conference of the Academy of HRD. *Human Resource Development International, 10*(2), 203–213.

Khandelwal, A. K. (2011). *Dare to lead: The transformation of Bank of Baroda.* SAGE Publications.

Khandelwal, A. K. (2018). *CEO chess master or gardener.* Oxford University Press.

Khandwalla, P. N. (1991). Humane turnarounds. *Vikalpa, 16*(2), 3–16.

Khandwalla, P. N. (1992). *Innovative corporate turnaround.* SAGE Publications.

Khandwalla, P. N. (2001). Creative restructuring. *Vikalpa, 26*(1), 3–18.

Khandwalla, P. N. (2011). Khandelwal's leadership: An academic perspective. In A. K. Khandelwal (Ed.), *Dare to lead: The transformation of Bank of Baroda.* SAGE Publications.

Kotter, J. P. (2007, January). Leading change: Why transformation efforts fail. *Harvard Business Review.*

Kotter, J. P. (2012, November). Accelerate! *Harvard Business Review, 90*(11), 45–58.

O'Reilly, C. A., & Chatman, J. A. (2020). 'Transformational leader or narcissist? How grandiose narcissists can create and destroy organizations and institutions. *California Management Review, 62*(3), 5–27. https://doi.org/10.1177/0008125620914989

Organizational Transformational
Agenda for Indian Banks

Late Pritam Singh and Asha Bhandarker

Perusal of the growth and competitiveness of many successful organizations brings out that very few have been able to sustain their performance and growth over the decades. For example, 89 per cent of the companies which featured in the Fortune 500 list of 1955 had dropped from the list decades later (Perry, 2014). The first decade of the 2000s saw global giants such as American Airlines, Bank of America, Circuit City, HP, Merck, Motorola, Nokia, Rubbermaid, Scott Paper and Zenith fall from their hallowed positions as industry leaders.

Such examples clearly bring out that organizations cannot afford to be complacent and have to make sustained and strategic efforts to keep growing and stay successful. Various global, economic, political, sociocultural and national factors contribute to organizational growth and performance. Within the organization, however, the key enablers as well as (potentially) debilitating factors are technology, HR systems, leadership styles and work culture. There is no doubt that in order to achieve corporate transformation, all the levers (strategy, structure, systems, styles, staff, shared values and skills along with massive use of technology and artificial intelligence (AI)) must be activated and aligned with each other.

Public Sector Banks: The Context and Need for Transformation

This chapter proposes that Indian banks, particularly public sector banks (PSBs), sorely need to transform in order to become more aligned with the contemporary business context and better prepared for the future. PSBs constitute the financial backbone of the Indian economy and this is especially so, given the slowdown in the economy due to COVID-19. In addition, the need for transformation in PSB arises due to following factors:

- PSBs currently face serious competition from private sector banks who are steadily eating into their market share.
- The recent mega mergers of PSBs have thrown up many complex leadership and management challenges.
- The advent of digitalization requires a transformation in terms of human resources (HR) skills, methods of working and use of technology to deliver customer service.
- The rising percentage of millennials moving up the hierarchy and their workplace expectations, like those of other millennials (Singh et al., 2012), are also raising challenges for banks to handle.

In these times of transition, PSBs need visionary and transformational leaders who can enlist the involvement of this generation and groom and coach them. The deeply conservative and hierarchical style of operations of PSBs does not motivate and inspire millennials and certainly does not provide an enabling work culture. Although PSBs need to transform on multiple levels (mentioned above), the creation of an enabling work culture to unleash people power is critical for the success of the various initiatives. In fact, people and HR practices are least developed in PSBs as brought out by the 2010 Khandelwal Committee report (Press Information Bureau, 2010) which identified key HR challenges before PSBs: building capabilities for the future, improving productivity and performance cultures, building talent management practices and succession planning for important leadership positions.

Factors Affecting the Typical Indian Work Culture

Leaders planning to work on organization transformation in PSBs need to be aware of the following mindsets and attitudes of people and handle them appropriately, since they deeply impact the prevalent work culture in PSBs.

1. **The typical value predisposition of Indians:** Research found that Indian value predisposition is more status quo-ist than transformational, and it is displayed through the distancing behaviour of leaders, a position- and power-oriented behaviour and focus on rituals rather than results. Four typical value predispositions and mindsets (for detailed analysis at the cultural and psychosocial levels see Singh & Bhandarker, 2002) through which this predisposition is expressed have been presented below.

   a. **Clan orientation:** Executives in Indian organizations tend to affiliate around clans based on language, regions, caste, even divisions and departments in an otherwise diverse organization with people from different parts of the country.

b. **Hierarchical orientation:** Indians generally experience familial hierarchy as a part of their earliest socialization. As a result, people look up for clear direction from the top management. People tend to feel insecure when such clarity is missing, and they lapse into safety-seeking behaviour and become more rule bound and status quo–ist.

c. **Emotional orientation:** Childhood socialization predisposes Indians to be more emotional in orientation (Singh & Bhandarker, 1988). They seek emotional safety, and in its absence, they relapse into traditionally defined clans (regional, social caste and community affiliations) for psychological support, identity and a sense of belonging.

d. **Thought not action:** The major strength of Indians resides in their ability to think, assess, analyse and dissect. On the flipside, the major weakness is their poor focus on action.

Our experience in the corporate sector in the last few decades has shown us that the above four mindsets continue to hold good even today in typical Indian organizations including PSBs. For example, research (Singh et al., 2012) brought out that working executives (millennials) expressed that organizations are hierarchical and top-down, conformity centric, pay inadequate attention to unleash human creative potential, silo functioning and are less sensitive to people development.

The above-cited mindsets of Indian leaders and position holders result in a stifling work culture, which is indifferent to human talent, and therefore, promotes a culture of blind obedience rather than a robust culture of performance excellence. The changing expectation of millennials further makes it more imperative that leaders work to create a different work culture.

2. **Expectations of millennials from the workplace—challenge for Indian banks:** Research over the last decade (Ashok & Vinay, 2017; Jain, 2013; Yahiya, 2011) has brought out that as compared to the previous generation, the millennial generation has different mindsets, values and attitudes. A study (Singh et al., 2012) on 2,158 millennials across India's top engineering and management schools found that millennials would like to work in organizations which provide freedom to take initiative, opportunity to experiment and express views, performance-based recognition, equity and fairness, and opportunities for learning and development. These millennial expectations are diametrically opposite to the prevailing work culture of PSBs, hence the strong disconnect.

These findings have implications for the type of leadership which Indian banks need—leaders need to shift from the typical hierarchical orientation to a more egalitarian approach combined with a mentoring approach in line with prevailing values of the millennials.

Literature Review

This literature review examines findings of the research work done on both transformational leaders and corporate transformation.

Corporate Transformation: Role of the Transformational Leader

The core theme of this chapter is corporate transformation which can positively influence the creativity, growth and performance of organizations. According to Burns (1978), transforming leadership is a process in which 'leaders and followers help each other to advance to a higher level of morale and motivation'. Transformational leaders (TL) empower their followers to be problem-solvers, such that employees grow in their creativity by learning from their failures and experimenting with various options without the fear of failure (Jung, 2001; Jung et al., 2003; Shin & Zhou, 2003).

Transformational leadership is an important route to achieve lasting corporate transformation. This has been amply demonstrated in the Indian context in our research on seven leading Indian organizations which were transformed in the last decade. Findings revealed that change maestros (Singh & Bhandarker, 2011) demonstrated the characteristics of TLs. Whether they headed banks, telecom, conglomerates, steel or biotechnology companies, they were perceived by their followers as enablers, excellence seekers, direction setters, visionary strategists and entrepreneurial innovators, as well as role models and people with high credibility. This set of values and behaviours helped leaders influence their people and through a co-partnership with them, transform their organizations and prepared them to cope with the competition and sustain themselves for a longer period.

Work Culture

Schein (1982) defined organizational culture as a pattern of basic assumptions that the group learned as it solved its problems, that has worked well enough to be considered valid and is passed on to new members as the correct way to perceive, think and feel in relation to those problems. Chief executive officers' (CEOs) self-directive values (Berson et al., 2008) were found to be associated with innovation-oriented culture, security values were associated with bureaucratic culture and supportive values were associated with supportive cultures.

Bass (1985) demonstrated that leadership style has a significant impact on culture. Research suggests that leaders have a central role in shaping and controlling organizational culture, both being closely intertwined, and play a major role in nurturing appropriate culture which helped improve the implementation of specific government reforms.

Transformational Leaders

TLs have to work on developing the following aspects of work culture to mobilize people and make the organization more competitive and agile. Corporate transformation cannot occur when leaders show status consciousness, distancing behaviour, clan orientation and focus on thought not action—identified above as the key mindsets observed in PSBs. Based on all our consulting work in the corporate sector and banks as well as research on transformational leadership (Singh & Bhandarker 1989, 2002; Singh et al., 2012a) in the last three decades, it is possible to affirm that TLs have to become enablers, excellence seekers, direction setters, visionary strategists as well as role models to transform their banks. The value frame of TLs has to be more egalitarian, open and fairness centric, so that they create a work culture suitable for the millennial generation (Singh et al., 2012).

Dimensions of Corporate Transformation in Indian Banks

The journey of an organization to transform into a sustainable institution depends on creating and nurturing a great work culture which is unique to it, a culture where people can thrive and utilize their potential to build the organization, make it more agile, more customer savvy and robust enough to last.

Nine dimensions have been mapped out for transforming organizational culture in banks: create a winning vision; create new business models; create a customer-centric organization; nurture intellectual capital; soul of a startup, heart of a colossus; prepare today for tomorrow; creative destruction; ethical governance; and teamwork. These have been identified by examining the styles and approaches adopted by TLS of the corporate world. The following is based both on our extensive experience of consulting in organizations as well as a study of the research literature.

Create a Winning Vision

TLs of Indian banks need to create a winning vision full of excitement, which captures the imagination of people, provides them a sense of meaning and purpose to move collective energies for goal achievement, helps build strategy and clarifies the action priorities for building the organizational road map. Successful leaders influence organizational members through the power of the vision which they passionately believe in and share. For example, when Matsushita spoke about making electrical goods available as cheaply as water or Kaku spoke about living and working for the common good (Kotter, 1997), people followed because of the passion with which the leaders articulated and lived their visions.

When Khandelwal embarked upon transformation of Bank of Baroda (BOB), he developed a great vision to inspire people and this vision provided meaning, direction and focus to the energies of the collective in BOB (Khandelwal, 2011). In an unusual step, he decided to disseminate the vision across the organization through multiple approaches so that the last man standing understood where the organization is headed. It increased the passion, commitment and ownership—the key to mobilizing the collective towards the goals. Direction setting through active involvement of organizational members is critical to build a sense of ownership and commitment to the vision.

Create a Customer-centric Organization

Great organizations tend to focus on customer needs and try to anticipate and meet them. When ICICI leveraged the power of technology in the 2000s to serve the customer, it gave them a leading-edge vis-á-vis competitors and helped them become one of India's leading banks. It is high time that PSBs place the focus on the customer and reorient and realign their strategies. A dynamic interchange and interaction with the customer are required to understand the mind of the customer and get feedback about customer needs and expectations. In fact, banks need to co-create products along with customers, especially with the millennials. HDFC Bank is a great example of a private Indian bank that has retained its position by adopting customer-centric technology, a platform-based approach, efficient processes and new innovations.

The ability to provide value to the customer will define the competitiveness of an organization. Organizations need to have a grasp of both the present and the future needs of the customer to grow and effectively compete. PSBs need to make efforts to attract customers, retain and regain customers using the power of big data and AI to make targeted and customized efforts at different customer segments.

Create New Business Models

Indian PSBs are too busy fighting fires and handling crisis before them, rather than preparing their organizations to become more proactive. Their face is turned to the government and their back to the customer. This attitude needs to be reversed (e.g., HCL under Vineet Nayar).

The business model will then shift to become more proactive and give priority to customer needs to anticipate, be more efficient and agile to take care of their requirements. In order to become more agile and proactive, banks need to leverage the power of technology and AI. Lessons can be learnt from the telecom sector which is leveraging AI tech to study customer usage and top-up patterns to predict customer preferences, to design and offer personalized products to retain customers and deepen relationships with them, thus increasing revenue and customer stickiness.

In order to execute new business models, banks need high-quality talent. They need to use unconventional approaches to develop best-in-class talent as well as hire high-quality talent. Above all, they need to re-examine empowerment down the line which can enable them to become more responsive, agile and proactive. The organizational structure will have to also be aligned with the changed priorities and become flatter so that banks can respond faster to changing business requirements.

Nurture Intellectual Capital

Intellectual capital (IC) is the collective reservoir of wisdom, built on the basis of the accumulated experiences and knowledge of the institution. IC is the software which gives the company its key competitive advantage. The growth and effectiveness of companies is closely linked to their ability to evolve and learn so as to continually provide value to the customer. In order to nurture IC, companies must build systems that help them attract and retain talent; gather, share and retrieve knowledge and encourage people to be creative and innovative.

The hierarchical, seniority-centred styles of Indian companies must shift to a more open, idea-driven work culture that enables people to create knowledge, share knowledge and use it effectively to make decisions. Ironically, in Indian companies, the ideas of people at the frontline of the company are stifled. Systems are needed to tap into frontline information, keep people networked, share experiences, facilitating mutual learning and building brainstorming groups consisting of people across functions and hierarchy. CEOs of organizations must facilitate the big-picture thinking of their top teams by sharing and creating a collective cognitive map which influences decision-making and problem-solving.

The tendency of PSBs to completely outsource thinking to consulting firms is a cause for concern. Many transformation efforts have failed because they did not address basic issues. PSBs need to have certain selected talent who are groomed adequately for such key roles as internal partners to consultants. PSBs also need to develop their own think tanks which draw in high-quality talent to work for them using unconventional means.

Soul of a Start-up, Heart of a Colossus

The soul of a start-up refers to the entrepreneurial spirit that pervades and drives the company to be flexible and seek new opportunities; heart of a colossus indicates the staying power of the company to last out the competition, to invest and to use wisdom and experience. In the era of opportunity and competition, the quick footed and nimble, with their agility, flexibility and quick responses, have a better chance of winning than the dinosaurs that get slowed down by sheer size. Large PSBs are characterized by the twin perils of bureaucracy and hierarchy, which build inflexibility and rapidly threaten to convert them into inflexible dinosaurs. Indian banks are slothful bureaucracies where work culture is rule bound, precedence focused and activity driven, stifling individuality and creativity. They, however, have staying power, owing to government ownership which needs to be properly used for the long term.

The challenge for these large banks is to reinvent themselves, infuse the start-up spirit of speed and agility with focus on quality, and cost and closeness to the customer into their organization to revitalize their way of working. They must build the sense of ownership among the employees of the company. To build ownership, they need to break the operating structure of these behemoths into smaller, more manageable units with total empowerment, responsibility and accountability. The restructuring of ABB into 5,000 profit centres and 1,300 legal entities gave the company outstanding results. Introducing the profit centre concept can have a powerful impact on increasing the sense of ownership, an essential to drive opportunity-seeking behaviour. Successful CEOs need to recreate small company dynamism through profit centres. This is highly motivating for entrepreneurial and ambitious leaders at the middle level of the organization. Entrepreneurial executives flourish when they have the freedom and authority along with accountability.

Prepare Today for Tomorrow

This refers to the company mindset of both, exploring and exploiting the present opportunity, as well as implementing strategies with a future focus. In an era of increasingly short product cycles, companies have to constantly look ahead and prepare. If your action is focused on yesterday and today, then you may not have a tomorrow to deal with. As Michael Dell, CEO, Dell Computers, put it (Farkas & Backer, 1996), '…in this business there are two kinds of people really, the quick and the dead'.

Indian PSBs are presently teetering between life and death but are kept alive through regular capital infusion by the government, which keeps them afloat. Although they are changing, PSBs are still operating using past practices, slow to reorient themselves in a robust and decisive fashion. Reinventing products in response to customer requirements is the core strategic action which needs to be taken. This has been amply demonstrated by banks such as HDFC and ICICI.

Toyota Kirloskar is a great example of a company making a paradigm shift from viewing itself as an 'automobile company' to a 'mobility company', one that not just produces cars but also creates futuristic devices to assist in human motion. In anticipation of regulatory changes, the company had built a BSVI compliant plant years before the regulation came into play.

Anticipating sociocultural and political changes and their likely impact on PSBs is an important aspect which can help banks to prepare for tomorrow. Annual strategy brainstorming is a very important way to anticipating the above; niche experts should be involved in such meets so that best ideas and best practices can be discussed. The common routes taken by companies and banks to prepare for the future include painting alternate emerging future scenarios, building clarity on goals (not targets), regular meetings and feedback from within and outside the company.

Creative Destruction

'Life begins from death' goes the famous Indian saying. Creative destruction is the act of discarding those aspects, products and processes, for example, which are no longer relevant and adding value. It entails giving up old habits and ways of doing business and substituting them with new, more contemporary approaches. When organizations are clear and focused about their vision and direction, they can identify what is to be discarded and what is to be retained.

In order to operate successfully in the fast-changing business scenario, companies have to discard the feeling of infallibility. As Intel's ex-chief Andy Grove succinctly put it, 'only the paranoid survives'. Complacency born out of success gives companies a false sense of security which stops them from reflecting and getting rid of old patterns. This sense of superiority later becomes arrogance, overconfidence and rigidity. Such companies are destined to fail as brought by Jim Collins (2009) in his book *How the Mighty Fall*.

A major challenge for CEOs is to prepare people to move out of the 'comfort zone' of the known and familiar. Active involvement of the executives who will implement change is essential to make this creative destruction a success. Many organizations built great plans for organizational transformation but failed miserably because the implementers were not involved and committed to the process. The focus should be not only on what went wrong but also on how to win the future.

Teamwork

Working together is the basic building block for channelizing collective energy, empowering teams and collaborating to reach organizational goals. In order to nudge everyone towards teamwork, the leader has to show the same kind of respect to everyone, regardless of department, gender and geographical locations. The change in the working paradigm from centralized and individual to collective can be facilitated through an inclusive leadership style at the top. One of the earliest leaders to signal the change in work culture has been Jack Welch at GE. Many other Indian leaders followed suit in companies such as L&T, BOB, ICICI and Zensar Technologies. True to his style of intense companywide communication, Welch gave slogans which signalled the changeover in the work culture towards collaboration—break down the walls (across departments) and build bridges (MacLachlan, 1988). When the leader displays inclusivity, people down the line follow, provided the leader is an accepted one and there is trust and liking in the equation between leader and followers.

Evaluation and recognition are two techniques by which the company reinforces desirable pro-team and collaborative behaviour. Team-based reward systems are also making a reappearance in the form of profit sharing, gain sharing, team-based rewards, group incentives etc. The company management should work on long-term 'shared destiny' relationships between stakeholders, suppliers, manufacturers, employees and management, companies and customers—all working together to reduce cost and improve quality. This is a powerful example of using the higher goal for both management and union to work together. Efforts must be made by companies to tackle deficits in skills by rigorous training. A great example is from TCS which rolled two important initiatives to establish a good culture and promoting it widely within the organization: Mpower, people managers at different centres to deal with key employee issues and Maitree, which reaches out to employees' families and brings them together for various cultural events. This is one area where many PSBs such as State Bank of India (SBI), BOB and many others do a great job of bringing together work and family on important occasions. In the Indian context, with the cultural predisposition towards hierarchy and clannish orientation, it is extremely important for the leader to emphasize teamwork and bring people together.

Ethical Governance

The Hindu tenet *Satyameva Jayate*, the truth ultimately conquers, finds an echo in every world philosophy and underlines the importance of winning through the right means, where right is assessed by the extent to which it helps rather than hurts the interests of other stakeholders. Viewed from the socio-psychological perspective, the ethical mode of functioning reduces conflict within the organization and creates a healthy work atmosphere. It also helps increase individual commitment and motivation. Above all, it contributes to building organizational reputation and creates goodwill. It also makes the organization attractive to millennials, who are known to be socially more sensitive than the previous generation (Singh et al., 2012b).

Two important aspects of ethical organization functioning are: business ethics—ethical treatment of customers, community, environment, shareholders—and managerial ethics—ethical practices within the organization. In the Indian context, house of Tatas, Infosys and Wipro stand out for the ethical business practices they employ. Mahindra & Mahindra Ltd has contributed for various corporate social responsibility projects for education and improving green cover and protecting biodiversity in the country.

Worldwide, a shift is taking place on the ethical posture of companies because of public reaction against those companies that are perceived to be poor in discharging social responsibility to the community. The recent protests linked to climate change, various forms of discrimination including

LGBTQ, bring out that companies must sit up and take notice of the social-level shifts taking place. In the Indian context, companies need to spell out the work ethics regarding quality, performance standards, speed and cost standards. Such clarification is extremely important in the light of the Indian value system, which predisposes people to give priority to affiliative values rather than work values.

Leadership Development

PSBs must invest in leadership development at key levels in the organiza-tion. A deep leadership pipeline needs to be developed from general manager to at least chief manager level. Leadership talent can be identified both through their performance and the level of acceptance which lead-ers enjoy from their teams. They need to be provided all-round exposure by throwing them into challenging assignments, providing them opportuni-ties to attempt transformation on a small scale and continuously developing their confidence and capabilities through high-quality training and recogni-tion. The consistent and sustained work on all the above is evident in banks such as SBI and BOB which have produced some outstanding leaders over the years.

References

Ashoka, M., & Vinay, S. (2017). Customer acceptance of millennial generation banking services: Challenges and prospects. http://dx.doi.org/10.2139/ssrn.2929837

Bass, B. M. (1985). *Leadership and performance beyond expectations*. Free Press.

Berson, Y., Oreg, S., & Dvir, T. (2008). CEO values, organizational culture and firm outcomes. *Journal of Organizational Behavior, 29*(5), 615–633. https://doi.org/10.1002/job.499

Burns, J. M. (1978). *Leadership*. Harper & Row.

Collins, J. (2009). *How the mighty fall: And why some companies never give in*. HarperCollins.

Farkas, C. M., & Backer, P. De. (1996). *Maximum leadership: Five strategies for success from the world's leading CEOs* (p. 203). Perigee Business.

Jain, Y. (2013). Mobile banking: A study on adoption & challenges in Southern Rajasthan, India. *International Journal of Innovative Research and Development, 2*(4), 902–914.

Jung, D. I. (2001). Transformational and transactional leadership and their effects on creativity in groups. *Creativity Research Journal, 13*(1), 85–195.

Jung, D. I., Chow, C., & Wu, A. (2003). The role of transformational leadership in enhancing organizational innovation: Hypotheses and some preliminary findings. *Leadership Quarterly, 14*(4–5), 525–544.

Khandelwal, A. K. (2011). *Dare to lead: The transformation of Bank of Baroda*. SAGE Publications.

Kotter, J. P. (1997). *Matsushita leadership: Lessons from the 20th century's most remarkable entrepreneur*. The Free Press.

MacLachlan, R. (1988). Regeneration X. *People Management, 2*, 34–39.

Perry, M. J. (2014). Fortune 500 firms in 1955 vs. 2014; 88% are gone, and we're all better off because of that dynamic 'creative destruction'. https://www.aei.org/carpe-diem/fortune-500-firms-in-1955-vs-2014-89-are-gone-and-were-all-better-off-because-of-that-dynamic-creative-destruction/

Press Information Bureau. (2010). Khandelwal committee report. Ministry of Finance, Government of India.

Schein, E. H. (1982). *Organizational culture and leadership.* Jossey-Bass.

Shin, S. J., & Zhou, J. (2003). Transformational leadership, conservation, and creativity: Evidence from Korea. *Academy of Management Journal, 46*(6), 703–714.

Singh, P., & Bhandarker, A. (1988). Cultural ethos in organizational milieu: A framework for organization building. *Indian Management, 27*(10), 4–18.

Singh, P., & Bhandarker, A. (1989). *Corporate success and transformational leadership.* Wiley.

Singh, P., & Bhandarker, A. (2002). *Winning the corporate Olympiad: The renaissance paradigm.* Vikas Publishing House.

Singh, P., & Bhandarker, A. (2011). *In search of change maestros.* SAGE Publications.

Singh, P., Bhandarker, A., & Rai, S. (2012a). *In Search of Change Maestros.* SAGE Publications.

Singh, P., Bhandarkar, A., & Rai, S. (2012b). *Millennials and the workplace: Challenges for architecting the organizations for tomorrow* (p. 224). SAGE Publications.

Yahiya, S. (2011). *Prospects and challenges of electronic banking in Ghana—a case study of SG-SSB bank limited, ACCRA* (Thesis). Institute of Distance Learning, Kwame Nkrumah University of Science and Technology, Kumasi.

8 Conversation. 6 Indian companies that use great corporate culture to retain great employees. https://conversation.8card.net/great-indian-workplaces-corporate-culture/

Grooming Leaders in Public Sector Banks

Proposing a Leadership Development Process

Abinash Panda

Leadership: A Strategic Organizational Capability

In a hyper-competitive business environment, organizations cannot remain competitive without having a competent leadership team. McKinsey research has consistently shown that good leadership is a critical part of organizational health, which is an important driver of shareholder returns (De Smet et al., 2014). There is an increasing importance of effective leaders in organizations, irrespective of industry (Feser et al., 2017).

Most organizations view investment in leadership development as critical because they acknowledge leadership capability as the most important human capital issue their organizations face (McKinsey & Company & The Conference Board, 2012).

There is an increasing importance of effective leaders in organizations, irrespective of industry (Feser et al., 2017). Dennis Baltzley, global head of leadership development solutions at Korn Ferry Hay Group argues, 'The best thought-out business strategy will fail miserably if leaders within an organization do not have the skills to make it come to fruition' (ET Online, 2016).

Besides a strong leadership pipeline, organizations need to be agile to develop requisite organizational capabilities to be future ready. For instance, ICICI Bank, in recent times, has focused its attention in enabling its employees to deliver customer-centric solutions, nurturing leaders, cultivating domain skills and building a culture of data-enabled decision-making. In order to achieve that, the bank has identified three emerging capabilities, namely design thinking, data analytics and advisory skills (ICICI, 2018).

To summarize, organizations need leaders who are good at anticipating emerging challenges and responding to those proactively by developing requisite organizational capabilities. This has become more salient in recent times as leaders confront, among other things, digitization, the power of data analytics as a competitive weapon, and the ability of artificial intelligence to automate the workplace and enhance business performance.

Building a robust leadership pipeline and developing organizational capability are salient to creating a competitive and healthy organization. Leaders, in more than one way, build intangibles such as human capital, brand, marketing and leadership to contribute to brand/market value of the organization (Khandelwal, 2011, p. 357). Organizational leaders should be the architects to create an ecosystem that facilitates the learning of new and weeding out redundant capabilities and in the process making organizations future ready.

Leadership Talent Deficit in Public Sector Banks: Genesis and a Brief Overview

Although most banks consider 'leadership' as key to long-term organizational success of their organizations, the IBA McKinsey Bank Benchmarking Survey of 2016 has revealed the acuteness of a gap in leadership in public sector banks (PSBs) compared to private banks in India (Table 10.1).

The Government of India had set up a committee to study human resources (HR) in PSBs under the chairmanship of Khandelwal in 2009, popularly known as the Khandelwal Committee, to look into the various

Table 10.1	*Leadership Gap Created by Retirements (% of Employees)*					
	PSB Average			**Private Banks Average**		
	2015–2016	2017–2018	2019–2020	2015–2016	2017–2018	2019–2020
General manager	26	70	95	7	25	41
Deputy general manager	16	47	71	2	7	15
Assistant general manager	12	36	58	1	5	10

Source: Lok Sabha Secretariat (2018).

aspects of HR challenges in PSBs and recommend ways on how PSBs should deal with them.

The Khandelwal Committee recommended that PSBs should overhaul their HR systems and processes to address the challenges of weak leadership pipeline and gaps in organizational capabilities. There is a need to groom leaders across the leadership pipeline in a systematic manner; look into their talent management and development practices, along with their approach to succession planning for key roles; build intangibles such as HR, leadership, governance and integrity without being solely obsessed with operational performances.

The Standing Committee on Finance in its 68th report (2017–2018) also expressed concern about limited professional depth and functional expertise and urged PSBs to address the issues of talent deficit.

Most PSBs do not have any strategic framework for identifying and grooming leaders or a systematic succession plan for key positions (Khandelwal Committee, 2010, p. 57). Quick promotions without well-rounded grooming of bankers have become counterproductive. Leadership development and succession planning have been the PSBs' Achilles' heel that seems to be hindering them from achieving their market potential.

Banking, in the recent past, has become increasingly complex and skill intensive, with financial technology (fintech) becoming the prime disrupter. The challenge for PSBs is to make the best use of technology and innovation to bring down intermediation costs while protecting their bottom lines, which requires PSBs to tweak their business model to remain relevant by aligning their business strategies and products and service offerings with the customers' needs, without compromising operational efficiency. Developing talent pool for different areas of skills should be the prime agenda for the training systems of PSBs, though leadership development and succession planning in PSBs have not been as effective as they should be until now, barring a few exceptions like BOB.

Ineffectiveness in grooming leaders in PSBs is invariably attributed to the existing processes of appraisal, nebulous training and grooming and skewed exposures to different kinds of management development programmes in India and abroad. Such a piecemeal approach makes it difficult for the grooming process to keep up with changes in the organization's priorities and develop a critical mass of leaders ready to pursue them. Leadership development processes, in general, has not been effective as they should in many industry sectors. Why is it so?

Why Leadership Development and Succession Planning Have Not Been Effective and Best Practices in Leadership Development

Beer et al. (2016) have attributed ineffectiveness in training and developmental efforts in grooming leaders to the erroneous premise underlying training and learning interventions. The assumption is that performance and behavioural problems of organizations are rooted primarily in individual deficiencies. Hence, the learning and development efforts are directed towards individuals to equip them with desired knowledge, skills and attitudes. In reality, however, behavioural and performance problems of organizations stem from poorly designed and ineffectively managed systems. Hence, any learning and developmental intervention which is not supported by organizational systems and processes may not yield desirable results. Most organizations seem to be trapped in this erroneous logic. They focus on improving individual capability without creating right kind of systems and processes (e.g., talent management, performance assessment and management, succession planning, etc.). Additionally, organizations often fail to translate their company's strategy into a leadership model specific to their needs. They mostly offer leadership training as a quick-fix solution to groom instant leaders. Individuals, just by participating in a leadership development programme, with an overdose of classroom-based cognitive/theoretical inputs, rarely become competent leaders.

Pfeffer (2015) has observed that the leadership development interventions have an overdose of cognitive component and informational inputs, which do not automatically translate into internalization and change in behaviour in the real-world work context. Such a prescriptive approach fails to groom leaders. He further added that the design and delivery of leadership training and development are primarily guided by 'lay preaching'. Advice offered to participants in leadership development programmes (LDPs) is often based on the ideal world, not reality. Leadership development interventions, by design and the way they are facilitated, do not offer participants space and context to reflect, which make these interventions highly conceptual with an overdose of theoretical insights.

Leadership development process in India has not been as effective as it should be in grooming leaders because of (a) over reliance on classroom-based formal training, which tends to focus more on cognitive inputs and (b) organizational obsession for financial performance at the expense of employee development (Panda, 2018).

Organizations such as Hindustan Unilever Limited (HUL), Aditya Birla Group (ABG) and Tata Group are acknowledged to have an effective leadership grooming process. How is their process different from their peer organizations?

Best Practices in Leadership Development in Non-banking Sector

HUL has institutionalized an employee development-centric learning ecosystem. Its guiding philosophy, 'leaders build leaders', has made HUL to institutionalize an employee development-centric learning ecosystem. HUL has an integrated management development process which includes regular performance reviews underpinned by a common set of leadership behaviours, skills and competencies. There is a regular review of ways of working to drive speed and simplicity through their business in order to remain agile and responsive to marketplace trends (HUL, 2019, p. 21). 'Performance development planning' is an integrated process that includes performance evaluation, development and career progression of each executive. Individual development plans drawn out for each employee focus on building knowledge and skills for the immediate role, and preparing them for future roles. The leadership development approach at HUL blends experience-centric learning; coaching, mentoring and peer learning; and formal structured programmes in 70:20:10 ratio. It offers cross-functional and cross-geographical exposure to its leaders. Internal resource committees have responsibility for identifying future skills and capability needs, developing career paths and identifying the key talent and leaders of the future.

ABG offers its employees opportunities to learn, develop and grow as professionals. LDPs are primarily experiential in nature and leverage innovative methodologies to design and deliver learnings. Coaching and mentoring are also key to leadership development and capability building processes in the group. Besides LDP, functional training programmes are designed to enhance functional domain knowledge in line with the industry's best practices. Moreover, Gyanodaya, the Group's global centre for leadership learning, designs and delivers relevant and current knowledge and competence-building learning opportunities across the Group. Gyanodaya Virtual Campus, the Group's e-learning platform, has a robust learning management system serving 30,000+ active e-learners at various levels across the globe, which includes the e-learning modules from the very reputed Harvard Manage Mentor.

The leadership development architecture of the Tata Group is guided by Tata leadership practices that comprise 14 leadership competencies. Tata Group has three-tiered leadership development programmes: 'Tata Group Strategic Leadership Seminar' in collaboration with Harvard Business School, designed for enterprise level leaders with strategic roles; 'Tata Group Executive Leadership Seminar' in partnership with Ross School of Business, University of Michigan, designed to develop understanding of different functional levers of business to develop cross-functional understanding and an integrated action plan for business strategies and 'Tata Group Emerging Leadership Seminar' in collaboration with Fisher College of Business, Ohio State University, designed for high-potential managers moving into general management roles. The group through its corporate learning centre, Tata Management Training Centre, leverages technology-enabled platforms (live e-classroom, live video broadcast and self-paced e-learning programmes) effectively to deliver various programmes.

All three organizations discussed above identify key capabilities required to be developed in order to be competitive in the future. The key people processes such as talent spotting, grooming desired capability, performance assessment and management, learning and development besides succession planning are seamlessly integrated (usually via competency framework) to equip executives with potential and desired capabilities.

These organizations invest in developing a leadership talent pipeline with robust succession planning in place for critical roles/positions. They have systems and processes in place to identify talent (executives with potential). They become part of the talent pool to be groomed for key roles and leadership positions.

Each of the organizations has a robust leadership pipeline. They identify executives with potential at each level of organizational hierarchy with the help of robust performance management systems and assessment of demonstrated behaviour to achieve the performance goals.

Finally, these organizations curate portfolios of diversified experiences with developmental potential. These organizations leverage multiple approaches to groom leader, which include classroom sessions (both face to face and via e-learning platform), on the job, besides coaching and mentoring.

In summary, 'best in the class' organizations (a) contextualize leadership development programmes around their business strategy, (b) ensure developmental interventions are available and accessible to all across the organization, (c) ensure participants apply learning to improve on the job performance and (d) integrate the learning process with other people practices such as performance management and talent management systems that reinforce new capabilities and behaviours.

Let's look at what expert committees on banking have recommended to revamp the leadership development and succession planning in PSBs.

Recommendations of Expert Committees

Review of recommendations of various committees such as Khandelwal Committee, Gopalakrishna Committee[1] on capacity building and the Standing Committee on Finance and their suggestions on how PSBs should deal with HR challenges reveals the following:

HR strategy and planning must be aligned with the business strategy and planning, and identify and project skill gaps for future. Second, each PSB must have a leadership competency model, ideally consisting of 6–8 competencies, which should help the organization have a seamless linkage and integration among all people processes. Third, each PSB should build a pool of specialists in critical areas such as treasury, corporate credit, international banking, retail banking, social banking, technology, risk management, marketing, infrastructure financing, financial inclusion, etc. Fourth, a comprehensive, systematic and rigorous leadership development strategy should be in place to groom leaders internally, keeping the bank's strategic goals in mind. Fifth, in-house training colleges/centres should conduct relevant research and provide learning support to the management. Sixth, all banks should have a governing board on training/advisory committee to review the effectiveness of learning and development efforts. Finally, technology-enabled platforms should be leveraged to make learning content accessible to participants working in geographically dispersed branches.

Grooming Effective Leaders: Why and How?

Feser et al. (2017), on the basis of their study on 'What Is Missing in Leadership Development', have identified following characteristics of leadership development process that facilitate the building of a strong leadership pipeline in any organization:

---

[1] Reserve Bank of India's Gopalakrishna Committee on capacity building (July, 2014) was mandated to (a) identify capacity building requirements keeping in view the role of the financial sector and what it should deliver and (b) examine the skills required at various levels/operations to deliver on the required role.

1. The process focuses on inculcating leadership behaviour that executives believed was critical driver of business performance.
2. The scope of various interventions is broad-based to cover the whole organization.
3. The design of the interventions takes into account the organizational characteristics and business ecosystem.
4. The participants are encouraged to apply their learnings to their job.
5. Developmental interventions focus on the strength of participants rather than the areas of development; leverage coaching and mentoring process to encourage participants to reflect on experiences to learn and professionally grow.
6. Senior leaders are personally involved as project sponsors, mentors and coaches.
7. Learning and development process is integrated with other HR subsystems (performance management, talent management, talent acquisition and others) via a competency model.

Bersin (2012) has argued for a need to have leaders at all levels instead of having a highly competent leader at the top for enduring business performance, which begins with the identification of relevant leadership qualities needed to be effective in achieving organizational goals with a given strategy. Organizations also need a robust people development framework that facilitates the grooming of executives with potential to give peak job performance. Talent identification and development become salient as organizations must identify capabilities needed in future and develop those capabilities within. Organizations need to be very focused, systematic and intentional in their efforts to identify and groom leaders for the future.

Leadership Pipeline in PSBs

The leadership pipeline in any PSB consists of (a) junior management cadre (JMC) with mostly customer-facing roles, (b) middle management cadre (MMC) with operational roles and responsibilities and (c) senior management cadre (SMC) with strategic roles and responsibilities (Figure 10.1).

JMC: Bank officers in JMC hold front-line customer-facing roles. The Khandelwal Committee urged PSBs to have two-year mandatory integrated training and induction for employees in this cadre to provide systematic exposure to all aspects of banking besides mentoring by senior officers to

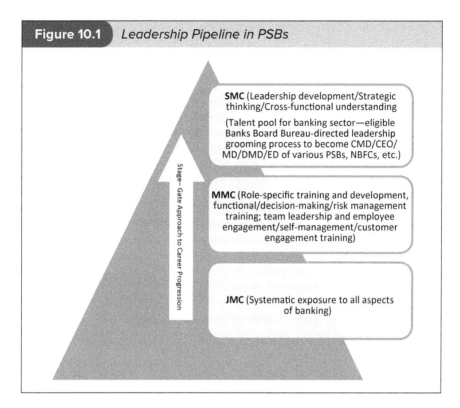

Figure 10.1 *Leadership Pipeline in PSBs*

SMC (Leadership development/Strategic thinking/Cross-functional understanding

(Talent pool for banking sector—eligible Banks Board Bureau-directed leadership grooming process to become CMD/CEO/MD/DMD/ED of various PSBs, NBFCs, etc.)

MMC (Role-specific training and development, functional/decision-making/risk management training; team leadership and employee engagement/self-management/customer engagement training)

JMC (Systematic exposure to all aspects of banking)

Stage– Gate Approach to Career Progression

develop functional expertise in one or two functional domains before they are promoted to MMC.

MMC: In MMC, executives should be given role-specific training with intent to develop leadership, decision-making, risk management skills and other relevant functional training. The Reserve Bank of India (RBI) has made it mandatory for all commercial banks and All India Financial Institutions in India to obtain a certificate course for various specialist roles such as treasury operations, risk management, accounting and credit management. The Khandelwal Committee has proposed that executives in this level should have successfully completed a leadership development intervention before they are considered for promotion from MMC to SMC.

SMC: Executives in SMC occupy critical roles, where they need to exercise leadership which is vital to achieving the goals. Executives in SMC cadre with leadership potential (assessed via Assessment Centre administered by Hay Consultant) are eligible to be a part of the talent pool who are groomed to occupy top management positions (whole-time director's positions) in various PSBs and financial institutions. Egon Zehnder International Private Limited (EZIPL) strategizes the leaders grooming process.

The Process of Grooming Leaders for Top Management Cadre

Indian Institute of Management, Bangalore, in collaboration with PSBs, Department of Financial Services, Government of India, Indian Banks' Association and EZIPL, has designed the customized leadership development programme to help PSBs have a competent leadership team at the top to deal with leadership challenges in a competitive marketplace. The Banks Board Bureau (BBB) takes the ownership of grooming executives for top management cadre. The participants go through a series of 30-day intervention over a period of nine months. The intervention leverages multiple approaches for grooming such as (a) exploration of self to become aware of self and (b) functional development through exposure to new knowledge, emerging processes in the areas of strategy, risk management and digital transformation. The participants also undertake a live (action) project as a part of leadership development process.

Six-stage Leadership Development Process: Putting Ideas into Practice in PSBs

BBB takes the ownership of grooming leaders for top management cadre of the banking and finance sector. The onus of grooming bank officers in JMC to take up senior management roles remains with each PSB. Leadership development initiatives to be effective and efficient should include (a) identifying relevant leadership competencies along with behavioural indicators, (b) spotting bankers with leadership potential (talent), (c) curating a bouquet of developmental and learning opportunities, (d) grooming leaders, (e) creating a psychologically safe and technologically enabled learning ecosystem and (f) having an integrated people processes.

Leadership Competencies for PSBs with Behavioural Indicators

A banker, to be effective and efficient in the current hyper-competitive banking sector, requires a complex mix of banking knowledge, functional skills, leadership capabilities and interpersonal qualities. PSBs, the Khandelwal Committee (2010, p. 58) felt, require tech-savvy, customer-savvy, execution-driven and bold decision-makers who are strongly focused on people. Following nine key leadership competencies would be required to be an effective leader in a bank context.

1. **Ownership and accountability:** Accepting one's own responsibility and be accountable for the outcomes of the decisions taken
2. **Leveraging relationships for business growth:** Building and nurturing trusted relationships using one's personal and professional networks for business growth
3. **Drive for result and performance management:** Garnering and utilizing resources to achieve business goals and managing the performance of the team
4. **Engaging employees:** Offering guidance and creating a psychologically safe ecosystem to help subordinates develop relevant competencies for personal and professional growth
5. **Learning agility:** Openness to experiment, explore and challenge self to acquire and leverage new competencies for more effective performance
6. **Exercising leadership:** Building and leveraging personal and professional credibility along with positional authority to mobilize resources to address business challenges
7. **Customer-value creation:** The ability to understand and effectively address customer issues and needs to build and nurture a credible and trusting relationship with customers
8. **Being technology savvy:** The ability to be smart with technology, to be informed about the latest technology; understand and leverage technology to enhance one's productivity and efficiency
9. **Risk assessment and management:** Being able to assess different kinds of risks through appropriate due diligence and take necessary actions to mitigate them.

Spotting Bankers with Leadership Potential (Talent)

Given that leadership development is a very resource-intensive process, identifying executives with leadership potential becomes key. PSBs need to spot bankers with leadership potential (talent) for grooming them for leadership roles. They should rely on multi-rater assessments or assessment and development centre for this purpose. Bank of Baroda has institutionalized a talent-spotting process titled KHOJ, which leverages psychometric assessment tools.

Curating a Bouquet of Developmental and Learning Opportunities

Classroom sessions offer conceptual and theoretical inputs, whereas on-the-job assignments provide opportunities to individuals to apply these insights on the job and learn from reflecting on these experiences. These reflective practices can also be simulated through live projects supplemented by real-time, interactive feedback from their chosen mentors and coaches. This approach helps executives to assimilate learning. At times, organizations rely on multi-rater assessments instead of live projects for reflective practices. Individuals become more self-aware.

Organizations may also rely on (action–learning) live projects, which offer opportunities to participants to apply the conceptual learning in work situations and develop new competencies. Siemens and HUL provide executives the opportunities to work on live projects.

HUL believes that an individual's learning and growth comes from the roles they handle at work, hence, it offers ample diversity in the experiences during induction and later through projects and short-term assignments. IBM strongly endorses its performance-supported learning in which learning occurs within the work task or work environment itself.

Organizations in India leverage more than one method by blending them judiciously to groom leaders. Table 10.2 summarizes various approaches used by organizations in India to groom leaders.

Some of the most prevalent approaches in organizations in India are: classroom sessions (both face to face and via e-learning platform), on the job, live projects with interactive and real-time feedback from mentors and coaches besides personal attention through formal and informal coaching and mentoring (Shyamsunder et al., 2011a, 2011b).

Table 10.2	*Leadership Development Approaches Leveraged by Organizations in India*
Approach/Method	**Organizations in India**
Classroom sessions (face to face and e-learning)	ABG, Bharat Electronic Limited, Ashok Minda Group, HDFC Bank, HUL, IBM, Murugappa Group, Tata Chemicals Limited
On-the-job assignments	Ashok Minda Group, Lupin, HDFC Bank, Infosys, Shoppers Stop, Siemens
Live projects with interactive and real-time feedback	BEL, Ashok Minda Group, IT Multinationals, Microsoft, Murugappa Group, Shoppers Stop, Siemens, Tata Chemicals Limited
Other people (mentoring and coaching)	ABG, HDFC Bank, HUL, Infosys, Microsoft, Siemens, Shoppers Stop

Source: Shyamsunder et al. (2011b).

The findings of Lessons of Experience, India, study have revealed that challenging assignments and role modelling are the most powerful learning experiences in the Indian context (refer to Box 10.1 for five significant developmental experiences). The study also revealed that classroom-based formal training is not as effective as one generally believes it to be (Panda, 2018).

What are the possible on-the-job experience-based developmental opportunities in a banking context?

Box 10.1	Five Significant Developmental Experiences in the Indian Context

1. **New initiatives:** Experiences related to starting something from scratch by seizing the opportunities available. It includes any green field projects, introducing new products, processes or system.
2. **Early life experiences:** Experiences one has gone through during early phase of life outside the work context (e.g., in schools and colleges).
3. **Role models:** Colleagues observe and emulate people, who they acknowledge as their role models. In the process, they learn significant leadership lessons.
4. **Fix it/Turnaround assignments:** The person is made responsible for assignments that fix problems or turn around a situation.
5. **Lateral/cross-functional moves:** Progression between functions, lines of business or departments. It may also entail changes in responsibilities within the existing position, role or function.

Developmental Opportunities in Banking Context

The following table presents an indicative list of on-the-job experiences with developmental opportunities available to participants in the banking context (Table 10.3).

Table 10.3	Indicative List of Experiences with Developmental Opportunities in Banking Context
Experiences with developmental opportunities	Specific examples from banking context
New assignments (being empowered and trusted)	Setting up a branch in a new locality

(Continued)

(Continued)

Fix it/Turnaround situations	Reviving a non-performing asset Influencing a defaulter to start paying instalments Turning around a loss-making branch Handling difficult customers/stakeholders
Stretch assignments	Mobilizing deposits/advances Negotiating with difficult stakeholders Rural assignments Increase in job scope
Hardships/Mistakes	Non-performing asset due to wrong due diligence Difficulty in loan recovery Dealing with trade unions
Other people	Role modelling through shadowing Mentoring through guided reflection Coaching

Grooming Process

Grooming process involves two aspects: first, agreeing on one's individual development plan and second, exposing the banker to a set of relevant developmental experiences in a targeted manner, keeping one's developmental needs in consideration.

Table 10.4 maps targeted developmental experiences corresponding to each of the desired leadership qualities with the assumption that when

Table 10.4 *Targeted Developmental Experiences for Leadership Qualities*

Leadership Competency	Targeted Developmental Experiences
Ownership and accountability	• Fix it/Turnaround situation (e.g., Reviving a non-performing asset, influencing a defaulter to start paying instalments, turning around a loss-making branch, handling difficult customers/stakeholders) • Starting from scratch/Being empowered and trusted (e.g., setting up a branch in a new locality)

Leadership Competency	Targeted Developmental Experiences
Leveraging relationships for business growth	• Challenging assignment, stretch target (e.g., mobilizing deposits/advances, dealing with difficult stakeholders), rural assignments/increase in job scope • Shadowing (role modelling) • Mentoring (through guided reflection)
Drive for result and performance management	• Shadowing (role modelling) • Mentoring (through guided reflection) • Coaching
Engaging employees	• Shadowing (role modelling) • Mentoring (through guided refection)
Learning orientation	• Behavioural laboratory • Challenging assignments • Hardship (failures/mistakes) • Mentoring (through guided reflection) • Coaching
Exercising leadership	• Challenging assignments • Shadowing (role modelling)
Customer value creation	• Lateral moves (job rotation) • Mentoring (guided reflection) • On the job (customer dealing assignments)
Being technology savvy	• Classroom intervention • On the job with mentoring
Risk assessment and management	• Classroom intervention • On the job with mentoring

a person goes through any developmental experience (mentioned in the second column), the banker is likely to develop leadership competency (mentioned in the first column).

Using 'Leadership Development Map' for Grooming Leaders in Banking Sector

The leadership development map presented in this section (Table 10.5) is an adapted version of Yost and Plunkett's (2010) framework for grooming

Table 10.5	*Leadership Map for Developing Leadership Capability in Banking Sector*		
Key Developmental Experiences	**Desired Leadership Qualities**	**Key Relationships**	**Learning Readiness of the Executive**
Being empowered and trusted (when an executive is genuinely empowered and is trusted by one's superior and organization to experiment and explore)	Ownership and accountability	Mentors (bosses) (guided reflection)	Cognitive capability
	Leveraging relationship for business growth	Stakeholders Role models (shadowing)	Openness to feedback
Rural assignment(s) (when a banker is posted in a rural branch)	Drive for result and performance management		Reflective capability
	Learning agility (learning to learn)		Open to experiment and explore
Starting new assignment (greenfield project)	Engaging employees		
	Exercising leadership		
Fix it/Turnaround situation	Customer value creation		
Increase in job scope	Being technology savvy		
Lateral moves	Risk assessment and management		
Hardship (challenging situations including dealing with trade unions in the bank)			

bank leaders. It is an integrated map that should help learning leaders of PSBs in India for grooming leaders by targeting appropriate developmental experience(s) and relationships, keeping the developmental needs of the banker, which have been identified using the competency model of PSBs.

The first column in the following table titled, 'Key Developmental Experiences', lists out a few frequently leveraged developmental assignments (experiences) to choose from. The second column titled, 'Desired Leadership Competencies', lists out each of the qualities an executive needs to be groomed with. The third column lists out the key relationships that play a critical role in developing required leadership qualities.

Finally, the fourth column titled, 'Learning Readiness of the Executive', mentions four key attributes. The participants should be intellectually (cognitively) capable to stretch oneself to deal with the challenges embedded in an assignment/experience, be open to experiment and explore new ideas without fear of failure or making mistakes, be receptive to and reflecting on feedback and finally be open to reflect on experiences and gain novel insights.

Creating a Psychologically Safe and Technologically Enabled Learning Ecosystem

Participants must be encouraged and guided to experiment and explore their ideas, apply new insights without any fear of failure and reflect on their experiences to learn and grow. Such a fearless environment must be psychologically safe for the participants, where genuine mistakes are not only tolerated but considered as learning opportunities. Senior executives act as mentors and coaches to offer genuine and timely feedback (Day, 2010) and guide the participants to reflect on it.

Besides, given the spread of each, PSBs in India must leverage technology-enabled platforms to achieve optimal efficiency. E-learning and other alternate technology-enabled delivery channels for learning must be extensively used for training and learning. Learning leaders must equip employees with required IT training so that they become digital-savvy.

Having an Integrated People Process

The success of leadership development depends on how leadership development process is integrated with other people processes such as performance management system, talent management system, career progression of employees, recruitment and selection process, and succession planning.

An integrated and holistic HR system is critical for reinforcing the required changes in employees' behaviour and mindset and ensuring employees acquire relevant competencies, and leadership competency model holds the key.

Accountability and Ownership of Leadership Grooming Process

The leadership grooming process should not only be well designed but also be well governed. The chief learning officer (CLO) should be responsible and accountable for ensuring effectiveness of leadership development process in grooming leaders. Robust leadership bench strength for key positions is the vital sign for an efficient and effective leadership development process of any PSB.

CLO is responsible for developing apt learning and development strategy in alignment with business strategy and deploying the strategy to achieve desired goal of grooming leaders. They must ensure that the training/learning centre(s) are conducting relevant research, developing teaching content, designing and delivering learning and development interventions, besides grooming facilitators, mentors and coaches. They should collaborate with various academic institutions to co-design and co-deliver various learning and development interventions; be in touch with key stakeholders such as Indian Banks' Association, RBI and others to identify institutions and courses that will meet the certification requirements for different specialized roles.

Without the support of the chief executive officer and the board, CLO alone cannot bring in sustainable change in the grooming process. The chief executive officer has to take the ownership of HR and people processes, which will ensure involvement of top leaders in employee development process. Each PSB should have a HR steering committee of the board, which should monitor overall effectiveness of the leadership grooming process.

Moreover, each functional area head should be held accountable for ensuring their team members are groomed with necessary competencies to deal with job challenges and perform up to their potential.

Summary

The readers, after going through this chapter, would have realized the urgency of grooming leaders in PSBs in India, given the leadership talent deficit each of them faces as on day. The banking sector in India has become highly competitive and customers are becoming more discerning. In this chapter, the author has presented the challenges faced by PSBs in India and has proposed a leadership development process, distilled out of learnings of various organizations which have been effective in grooming leaders.

References

Beer, M., Finnström, M., & Schrader, D. (2016). Why leadership training fails—and what to do about it. *Harvard Business Review, 94*(10), 50–57.

Bersin, J. (2012, July 30). It's not the CEO, 'it's the leadership strategy that matters'. *Forbes* [online] https://www.forbes.com/sites/joshbersin/2012/07/30/its-not-the-ceo-its-the-leadership -strategy-that-matters/#308f1f86db86

Day, D. V. (2010). The difficulties of learning form experience and need for deliberate practice. *Industrial and Organizational Psychology, 3*(1), 41–44.

De Smet, A., Schaninger, B., & Smith, M. (2014, April). The hidden value of organizational health—and how to capture it. *McKinsey Quarterly*.

ET Online. (2016). Majority in India rank leadership development efforts as fair to very poor. https://economictimes.indiatimes.com/small-biz/hrleadership/ leadership/ majority-in-india-rank-leadership-development-efforts-as-fair to-verypoor-study/ articleshow/55575467.cms

Feser, C., Neilson, N., & Rennie, M. (2017, August). What is missing in leadership development. *McKinsey Quarterly*, 1–5.

HUL. (2019). *Annual report, 2018–2019.* https://www.hul.co.in/Images/hul-annual-report-2018-19_tcm1255-538867_1_en.pdf

ICICI. (2018). *Annual financial report, 2018* (p. 21). https://www.icicibank.com/managed-assets/docs/investor/annual-reports/2018/annual-report-fy2018.pdf

Khandelwal, A. K. (2011). *Dare to lead: The transformation of Bank of Baroda.* SAGE Publications.

Khandelwal Committee. (2010). Report of the committee on HR issues of public sector banks. https://financialservices.gov.in/sites/default/files/HRIssuesOfPSBs.pdf

Lok Sabha Secretariat. (2018, August). *Standing committee on finance report, 2017–2018.* Sixty-eighth report. Ministry of Finance, Department of Financial Services, Lok Sabha Secretariat.

McKinsey & Company, & The Conference Board. (2012, October). *The state of human capital 2012—false summit: Why the human capital function still has far to go.* Author.

Panda, A. (2018). Experience-centric leadership development process: Challenges and way forward for organisations in India. *International Journal Indian Culture and Business Management, 16*(1), 99–116.

Pfeffer, J. (2015). *Leadership BS: Fixing workplaces and careers one truth at a time.* Harper Business.

Shyamsunder, A., Anand, S., Punj, A., Shatdal, A., Vyas, B. M., Kumar, B., Philip, B., Reddy, C. M., Sarmma, C., Mahapatra, G., Srikhande, G., Kartikeyan, V., Jaiswal, M. K., Chawla, N., Rao, P., Nair, P. K., Kaipa, P., Krishnan, R., Krishnan, R. T., Sar, R., Vasan, S. K. … Bhatnagar, D. (2011a). Leadership development in organizations in India: The why and how of it (Part I). *Vikalpa, 36*(3), 61–118.

Shyamsunder, A., Anand, S., Punj, A., Shatdal, A., Vyas, B. M., Kumar, B., Philip, B., Reddy, C. M., Sarmma, C., Mahapatra, G., Srikhande, G., Kartikeyan, V., Jaiswal, M. K., Chawla, N., Rao, P., Nair, P. K., Kaipa, P., Krishnan, R., Krishnan, R. T., Sar, R., Vasan, S. K. … Bhatnagar, D. (2011b). Leadership development in organizations in India: The why and how of it (Part II). *Vikalpa, 36*(4), 77–131.

Yost, P., & Plunkett, M. (2010). Developing leadership talent through experiences. In R. F. Silzer & B. E. Dowell (Eds.), *Strategy driven talent management: A leadership imperative.* Jossey Bass

Coaching and Mentoring

The Unsung and Underutilized Warriors of Leadership Development

Raj Bowen

Leadership remains one of the most widely discussed and researched subjects across nations, sports, business, armed forces and any venture that depends on a few igniting the passions and potential of many for common goals. Given how much has been shared on this area, we find it almost impossible to comprehend such a yawning gap between available knowledge and application on the ground. With $370 billion spent globally last year on training and development (Training Industry, 2019) by organizations, with alarm bells ringing all around, the situation should have all stakeholders very worried. As we delve deeper into exploring this divide between knowing and doing, we see Marshall Goldsmith's (2015, a globally acclaimed executive coach and leadership advisor) study which shows that when it comes to changing behaviours, humans are very good planners and very poor doers. So that is why help is needed to progress from the wider organization's process focus on leadership development, in order to 'coach and mentor' every employee for an organization to constantly renew and transform itself.

Success Stories

When we look at work being done in this area, for instance, by Unilever, which gets referred to as 'a leadership factory', we realize there is a complete leadership value chain that must be addressed to be able to do what they do for creating so many leaders for the larger world beyond their own organization. Unilever starts the talent development process at the junior-most levels. When a fresh management trainee joins the organization, they spend dedicated time in the field, in village markets, working with stockists and distributors, going from shop to shop and learning the basics of the fast-moving consumer goods (FMCG) business. 'Having employees work across functions and learning the complexities of the dynamic FMCG sales and distribution channel, that works through the smallest of retail/grocery stores, has helped create global leaders', according to B. P. Biddappa, global vice-president, human resources (HR), Home Care, New Business Models, Firm of the Future (Tandon, 2019).

> The fact that we give early big jobs from HUL—they work in operations, and in factories, sales and in the field, and we have people who do careers across functions … so, a human resources person will do both corporate and factory HR. They are given very strong, big jobs early on and that builds a strong sense of leadership and a good general management perspective.

Despite the dynamic changes in the world, Tata Consultancy Services (TCS) rarely, if ever, has felt the need to get leadership talent from outside at senior levels, and it continues to lead its industry in many ways, including almost 90 per cent retention in a workforce of around 450,000 employees. What makes their internal leadership development so effective? In the words of Ritu Anand, senior vice-president and chief leadership and diversity officer, 'There is something about the Indian way of leadership that is yet to be benchmarked and amplified. I realise that it is a combination of training, coaching, mentoring—all that affects the mind, body and soul'. A world-class leadership development programme can be adopted by any aspiring company, but it is the culture and values of the organization that decide the effectiveness.

Sustainable organization transformation is about facilitating the desired change of behaviours right across every employee, through individual coaching and mentoring. This is not very different from what happens with a top-notch cricket team, for instance. That is why the best teams not only have a team coach, they also have a batting coach, a bowling coach, a fielding coach and nowadays, a psychologist for mental toughness and stress coaching!

The Foundation for Coaching and Mentoring

When we reflect on what is common between the practices embraced by organizations such as Unilever and TCS, we see the need for a learning and development culture—the fabric that ties in how things are done in such organizations. Naturally, building such a culture will need the senior executives' role modelling at the highest level, but more importantly, it will involve the nurturing of an environment where employees trust one another completely. That is when the magic of collaboration starts becoming a multiplier of business results. This trust is not always easy to build. Forbes.com, in a research summary article published in 2018, mentions a *Harvard Business Review* survey, which reveals that 58 per cent of employees say they trust a stranger more than their own manager (Sturt & Nordstrom, 2018)! We can well imagine the implications of this across businesses in the current environment of massive change, disruption and turbulence.

Implications for the Banking Sector

If there is one sector in India that has been completely disrupted over the past couple of decades or so, it is the banking sector. The first mountain of technology-led disruption has, by and large, been managed and capital, as the lifeblood, is also getting reasonably managed, barring the monster of non-performing assets (bad loans, in simple language) which still need to be tamed.

Perhaps a good example of coaching future leaders is provided by Bank of Baroda (BOB), when CEO Anil K. Khandelwal (2005–2008) commenced a massive strategy for leadership development. One of the game-changing processes deployed by him was that of the 'daily morning meetings' around live organizational issues. These helped the top management in collaborative learning around real-life problems and in broadening perspective around ground realities. In a way, even without that formal label, this was as clear an example of small group coaching as any! Leadership development has continued as an integral way of life at BOB since then.

In a report published by FICCI along with KPMG (2013), the key drivers for the banking sector disruption have been called out beautifully: (a) changes in the regulatory framework, (b) rapidly changing customer expectations, (c) shift in employee demographics and (d) onslaught of technology enablement. The study goes on to identify a set of six core competencies that must get embedded into the learning and development culture across the bank: strategic leadership, change leadership, operational leadership, stakeholder leadership, talent leadership and customer leadership.

In view of the massive challenges faced by the banking system, the need for coaching and mentoring cannot be overemphasized. In fact, in a financial institution, where at various levels executives face daily dilemma situations, they need coaches and mentors to help them resolve the issues over a period so that a culture can be internalized wherein senior-to-junior and peer-level coaching becomes part of the developmental process. It is not always that you need a formal system of coaching and mentoring (in some cases, it may be necessary). Most potential leaders learn all the jobs by observing their colleagues and seniors and through a conscious effort of the organization to provide different job exposures. The State Bank of India (SBI) also stands out as an example of a very large bank that has implanted strong training and development practices, involving cross-function mentoring and location exposure to its talent and very robust processes that sustain the efforts, including their Leadership Institute at Kolkata—no mean achievement for a bank with around 25,000 branches and over 250,000 employees. They also made a massive investment in digitalization of operations, an agenda that was being led directly by former chairman, Rajnish Kumar. In fact, over the past 4–5 years, several managing directors (MDs) of other PSBs have come from SBI. In 2019, Anshula Kant, MD of SBI, was appointed as the MD and chief financial officer of the World Bank—a recognition of her experience of leading an organization with such large-scale and complex financial transactions. Now, a formal system for coaching all these individuals into where they reached may not always have been there, but the top leaders set such strong leadership benchmarks through their own conduct and created such a culture of learning that many younger managers, driven by their curiosity to learn and grow, learnt phenomenally by watching and working with them. As the author, Roy T. Bennett, writes, 'Great leaders create more leaders'.

India's leading private bank, ICICI Bank, relentlessly pursues talent development through multiple initiatives in parallel. The seeds from which this culture emerged were sown by K. V. Kamath, when he was the chairman. In his words, 'My journey into mentoring was a very conscious one' (Ganguly, 2012). 'We had a large pool of people, most of them in their 30s, but none of them at seniority levels required by the organisation. Each one's need is totally different'. This culture started by Kamath, continued years after he moved on.

Top-level Sponsorship

The mandate needs the executive sponsorship of the board itself. Only when the board focuses on and supports and reviews the CEO on these areas, does the impact start showing on the culture and the way things are done in the organization. One of the world's best-known CEOs, Jack Welch, when he headed General Electric, personally 'knew' the individual growth plans for almost a thousand senior executives headed towards larger and more complex roles in the firm. Just imagine CEO of a firm with $500 billion+ market capitalization, spending almost 50 per cent of his time on talent issues! He had a very sharp business purpose here. 'Companies that invest in leadership development deliver stock market returns five times higher than the returns of companies that place less emphasis on human capital', according to a major study by *Harvard Business Review* and McBassi & Co (Bassi & McMurrer, 2007). Surely, that would be of interest to any board!

The Coaching and Mentoring Imperative

Now we must remember that, at the last mile, it is not what every individual in the firm 'knows' about leadership but what he 'does' on a day-to-day basis. That is why it is said, 'The notes you get from any bank are the same. What makes the difference is the teller'! That is why the development effort must reach the personal effectiveness of every employee. Now, the organization has to move beyond aggregating employees into groups or levels and realize that 'every single employee is unique in their own way' and the transition from knowing to doing must be different for everyone. Most organizations miss this point, and huge and well-intentioned organization-wide development efforts and investment go completely waste if this final link in the chain is not put in place with the same rigour and commitment. This is the vital link of coaching and mentoring!

In fact, the existence of coaching is as old as humankind itself—across history, mythology, politics, religion, sports and now in the corporate world. In fact, countless agencies and individuals have jumped into this terrain that has no entry barriers—anyone can be a coach. In addition, as happens in any 'industry' in the unregulated early growth stage, there are all sorts of coaching options being sold—business coaching, personal mastery coaching, life coaching, transition coaching, millennial coaching, retirement coaching etc. In addition, there are many 'certifications' on offer, including fast-track models that award 'global' certificates over a 1–2-day workshop. Imagine a pilot getting certified through such a 'crash course'- the pun is surely intended!

A reputed case study helps illustrate the powerful impact of coaching. Anderson's (2001) study (known as 'the Metrix-Global Survey') was designed for a Fortune 500 firm and a coaching group to determine the business benefits and return on investment (ROI) of coaching. Results revealed that coaching had a 'significant to very significant' benefit on nine key business measures. Although specifics are not mentioned, the authors concluded that coaching produced a 529 per cent ROI and significant intangible benefits. When employee retention was included as a benefit, ROI increased to 788 per cent.

However, the authors do advise to select coaches carefully; provide strong organizational support and measure, and communicate the impact to reproduce similar results in other organizations. For instance, an executive coach who is engaged to work with a bank's cluster manager, who is being promoted to a larger regional role, is not supposed to be an advisor to the person. Instead, they must know how to ignite the person's excitement so that it overpowers their apprehensions, stresses and fears of failure. It is not a surprise that the founder of Microsoft, Bill Gates, has gone on record with his assertion that 'everyone needs a coach' in a talk featured on YouTube in 2013.[1]

Some Current Trends

As we explore even deeper to understand the ground realities around how coaching is or is not being leveraged effectively, we seem to see a 'build and/or buy' approach. Organizations that see leadership development as something that runs on a track parallel and separate from business never derive the benefits that other organizations do. There is one clear difference that separates the former from those who do—the vital glue that makes leadership development stick, an internal culture of coaching. The former sees coaching as something that must be 'outsourced', either to the most convenient and/or cheapest resource if the target audience is mid-level or to fancy brands that look good in the HR head's list of achievements for senior leaders' coaching. Organizations committed to leadership development as a core part of their business strategy invest in building an internal culture of coaching that becomes a core behaviour for leaders that is both mandated and monitored. There is plenty to learn from such organizations.

The Untapped Opportunity Inside the Organization

While the conventional understanding of 'coaching' points more towards the task of engaging external coaches to work with selected senior individuals, we must remember that internally there are massive opportunities for managers to coach their team members towards the fulfilment of their

---

[1] https://www.youtube.com/watch?v=XLF90uwII1k

potential. Bersin & Associates (a global HR research firm, later acquired by Deloitte in 2013) published their research in 2007 (Josh Bersin, 2007) and their findings were eye-opening, the single talent process which delivers the greatest business impact is coaching, implementing a process for executive and management coaching throughout the organization. This process scored higher than much of what we consider sacrosanct: setting goals, aligning goals in the organization, understanding critical competencies and high-performing recruiting. They found that while 70 per cent of organizations claim they coach their employees, many managers lack coaching skills, and only 11 per cent of senior leaders actively coach regularly. This by itself establishes the need for organizations to ensure that managers are trained formally on 'coaching skills'.

Are coaching and mentoring the same? Now the question: While the need for coaching seems solidly established, where does 'mentoring' fit, and how is it different from coaching? A coach works with an individual to help build the capacity in the person to 'discover' their own effectiveness that makes them far more successful. To that extent, an external coach remains a relatively detached resource, where the magic is not so much about them but what they can enable in the employee being coached. On the other hand, when an employee has access to a mentor, the experience is heavily influenced by the sheer experience of the latter and becomes very immersive. However, we must keep in mind that, in such cases, the employee is learning how their mentor solved similar problems or what they would do, if they were in the employee's situation. Necessarily, it is important that the mentor is completely familiar with the internal organization context, which cannot always be grasped that intimately by an external coach.

What to Use When and Where

Organizations committed to leadership development deploy all three avenues intelligently: hiring external coaches, managers coaching their next lines and experienced internal mentors paying back through their experience and superior business understanding. Naturally, this sort of commitment calls for continued support right through from the board, CEO and chief human resource officer down to all the managers in the organization. Only a handful of organizations are able to initiate, implement and sustain this lifelong process, which does not get short circuited by vagaries of business or leadership changes at the top—the two most common disruptors of talent development efforts in most organizations.

The Emergence of 'Reverse Learning'

The culture that makes it natural for leaders to learn from each other without egos is what helps both formal and informal coaching and mentoring reach the lowest level in the firm. In fact, with a sharp decline in the average age of the workforce now, the senior leaders are feeling the need to seek out and learn from their juniors who often seem far better connected with contemporary business needs than they are—times have just changed so fast. In a discussion featured on YouTube in 2018, Narayan Murthy, the founder of Infosys, shared that when they designed the first leadership development programme at Infosys, all the top leaders sat down to learn selling skills and finance from their own junior team members.[2] Several industry-leading organizations have formalized this opportunity and call it 'reverse mentoring'. The *Economic Times*, in an article published in May 2017, reported

> Companies such as PepsiCo, GSK Consumer Healthcare India, Jubilant FoodWorks, Microsoft, Vodafone and Mindtree, are championing reverse mentoring—getting young employees to mentor senior, and even top leadership—on everything from technology, ways of working, social media and engagement. GSK Consumer Healthcare India started the reverse mentoring initiative in November 2016 and has put the entire India leadership team through the process.

Wake-up Call for Senior Leaders

While many organizations are formally and informally encouraging this practice, others are still mired in old mindsets and egos of senior leaders which can be a major obstacle here. A few years ago, I was coaching the Asia Pacific Head of R&D of a large chemical industry multinational, a brilliant individual who had worked his way up the organization over 28 years. In one of our sessions, I found him very distracted, disturbed and restless. On probing, he shared that he had not slept for two nights, disturbed over the behaviour of a young engineer trainee assigned to his team, who had just joined the firm a week before. A couple of days ago, he was in his cabin, working late, when this girl ran by his office, opening the door and with a breezy 'bye boss, see you tomorrow', went home! I could not understand what the problem was. It was only after he explained his feelings more that I understood. His issue was that when he had joined the firm as an engineer trainee 28 years back, he would have to seek an appointment

[2] https://www.youtube.com/watch?v=vLNwGMmDUn0

with his manager through a secretary, and he could not leave the office till his manager had left, just in case he was called for some work. It took time for me to coach him to let go his ego-driven barriers on how to relate to a much younger workforce and the need to alter his outdated mindset (I do hope the learnings have continued!).

What Does Not Work

Some time back, I was invited to coach the chief financial officer (CFO) of a global multinational organization by the head HR who had been tasked by CEO (assume delegation here) to get a coach to work with the executive as his aggressive and abrasive behaviour was becoming a problem for his team and peers. The project ran almost over a year. The individual truly benefited, and his team and peers also reported significant changes. The catch was that the problem was somewhere else—the head HR was actually the root cause of the problem, conniving constantly to find ways to derail the CFO's effectiveness. I was not surprised when the coaching candidate joined a competitor at a much wider portfolio, almost immediately after the coaching engagement! So who lost in the game? The organization, and just because the CEO delegated a part of his job that he was accountable for. It would be naive to believe that he was not aware of the interpersonal dynamics at play.

What Works

In the other instance, I was invited to coach a set of executives reporting to CEO of a global multinational, who had the tough task of leading an organization culture and performance turnaround. At the first stage itself, the CEO insisted that we first conduct a 360-degree feedback assessment for the team, including himself as one of the first candidates to be assessed. He addressed the entire team on the criticality of the whole process, and despite his extremely demanding business schedules, he completed the feedback for every member of his team with complete integrity. He remained involved with me on everyone's personal development plan, making very detailed notes of where he and his chief operating officer needed to change their behaviours. The exercise had started with a doubt around some team members, whether they were to be retained or let go. As the project got extended over the next line of leaders, not one member of the senior team had to leave and everyone went on to willingly take on and achieve far more than they had ever planned! The organization today boasts of a leadership coaching 'culture' as one of its business advantages. If I were to pick the most critical aspect of the engagement that made all the difference here, I would pick (a) the organization had a clear strategy to build the leadership of its top talent and (b) CEO held himself personally accountable for making this happen. As the organization now ramps up its growth, all senior leaders have the additional key responsibility area of coaching and mentoring the teams below them and design their own succession plans in the process.

The personal role modelling of CEO and sharing his own vulnerability, seeking feedback from the teams on where he needed to improve, made a big difference to the culture of the organization—the leaders started trusting each other.

They still have a long way to go till a leadership development culture gets institutionalized, but the foundation has been laid. Was it only 'coaching' that was at play here? Not at all. The bigger change that happened is that once leaders (and their teams) started trusting each other, they started communicating across a host of issues—personal as well as professional. They started seeking help as well as helping each other. The reason I bring this up is that, going beyond the stimulus of external coaching, internally, the leaders started mentoring, coaching, advising, counselling, sharing and supporting and that made all the difference for a culture transformation. Now academics will (and rightly so) point out differences among all these skills, but the fact is that an effective leader needs to use all these, as he builds more leaders. No wonder, most leaders struggle to build the next line. The bigger issue is for them to be personally convinced and be passionately committed to do it. Once that happens, building the skills of coaching, mentoring, feedback, counselling, etc. is easy. Seeing these role models in the organization, managers across the levels start seeing themselves as 'talent builders' and that is a huge thrust to an organization's drive for leadership excellence.

The Massive Impact of Change

A popular term now is VUCA (volatile, uncertain, chaotic and ambiguous). If this is the environment, organizations will have to function in, there are no ready answers to new problems. It becomes direct responsibility of the CEO to ensure that the organization has a culture where employees at every level take accountability for decisions that help them and the larger organization move consistently ahead with the agreed goals. This is not an easy task and needs a rigorous process implanted across the organization, which links intent with the business execution of the firm.

Given that one of the largest service industry employers in the country is the banking sector with around 1,400,000 employees in 2018 (Tripathi, 2019), we can well imagine the phenomenal opportunity that exists here to raise the game of leadership development, spearheaded by formal and informal coaching and mentoring. Of course, this will take a massive coordinated effort, pooling resources of multiple stakeholders and backed solidly by the Reserve Bank of India and the finance ministry.

The Diagnostic Checklist

Banks that truly build the connections between leadership development, coaching and mentoring show certain traits and this may well be a useful checklist for readers to assess where their bank stands on this aspect (while this checklist is developed keeping the scale and rapidly evolving challenges in the banking sector, the same applies to any organization that aspires to reach its business potential by truly exploding its talent potential):

- Does the board endorse leadership development, coaching and mentoring as a key input to succession planning actively?
- Does the CEO review the documented individual leadership growth plans for at least two levels below? Is this on their calendar as a schedule for the full year? Do they seek feedback in a structured manner for their own development? Do they share their personal growth plan with their team?
- Does the CEO work with the HR team to identify and plan the leadership development of all the high potential talent? Do they hold their respective managers accountable for the coaching and mentoring of these individuals? Are all personal development plans linked with organization outcomes?
- Are senior leaders held accountable for moving high potential talent across functions and beyond their teams?
- Does the CEO support the HR team so that all managers are trained on how to 'coach' their teams? Are these managers held accountable to share their 'internal coaching' results with their managers in a structured process?
- Does the bank encourage a culture where employees actively seek out and work on feedback for their self-development?
- Do at least 80–90 per cent of key senior roles get filled by internal candidates? (There would be exceptions for new banks in the start-up stage and niche roles, e.g., data scientists and digital technology specialists that have not been part of the plan earlier)

- Does the bank identify and make mentors accessible to those needing/seeking help? Is this monitored and progress tracked?
- Does the bank consistently invest on making external executive coaching available to identified leaders? Is there a clearly laid down method of selecting coaches? Are the coaching candidates' managers personally involved from the start to closure of each coaching journey with a documented system to manage the same?
- Is there a clearly communicated mechanism for coaching and mentoring to reach the junior-most employee in the firm?

When you honestly rate your bank on these 10 core requirements on a 10-point scale, you will easily know if there is more work to be done to feel secure about your company's future and which areas need to be focused on for enabling true sustainable transformation. Good luck on this fascinating journey!

Bibliography

Anderson, M. C. (2001). Case study on the return on investment of executive coaching. Metrix-Global, LLC.

Bassi, L., & McMurrer, D. (2007). Maximizing your return on people. https://hbr.org/2007/03/maximizing-your-return-on-people

FICCI & KPMG. (2013, July 24). *Public sector banks—profiling the leadership landscape*. Author.

Ganguly, D. (2012). What makes KV Kamath India Inc's most prolific CEO guru. https://economictimes.indiatimes.com/what-makes-kv-kamath-india-incs-most-prolific-ceo-guru/articleshow/12637350.cms

Goldsmith, M. (2015). *Triggers*. Crown Publishing Group.

Josh Bersin. (2007). Coaching: An imperative for leaders. https://joshbersin.com/2007/06/coaching-an-imperative-for-leaders/

Sturt, D., & Nordstorm, T. (2018). 10 shocking workplace stats you need to know. https://www.forbes.com/sites/davidsturt/2018/03/08/10-shocking-workplace-stats-you-need-to-know/

Tandon, S. (2019). Spotlight on Indian talent with Unilever's new hires. https://www.livemint.com/companies/news/spotlight-on-indian-talent-with-unilever-s-new-hires-1552845514697.html

The Economic Times. (2017). To tap into Gen Y ideas, leaders become mentees. https://economictimes.indiatimes.com/jobs/to-tap-into-gen-y-ideas-leaders-become-mentees/articleshow/58582916.cms?from=mdr

Training Industry. (2019). The leadership training market. https://trainingindustry.com/wiki/leadership/the-leadership-training-market/

Tripathi, K. (2109). Top heavy: Indian banks have more officers than clerks; how the situation changed in just 15 years. https://www.financialexpress.com/industry/banking-finance/banking-jobs-top-heavy-indian-banks

Crafting and 'Living' the Bank's Culture*
Notes from the Field

Anil Sachdev and Shyam Viswanathan

Some leadership teams create an organization that they would be delighted for their children to join as employees. Others leave behind a legacy that they would not wish their children to be a part of. It boils down to the culture created by the leaders of the company. The culture of an enlightened organization is a paradox—always in a state of 'dynamic equilibrium'. It is the constant and consistent frame of reference by which the organization conducts itself. Specific to leadership in the Indian banking sector, let us consider this aspect of leadership in the context of events observed in the recent past.

An Important Role in Nation Building

Since independence, banks have played a vital role in the development of the Indian economy. Public sector banks (PSBs) have shouldered a lion's share of this responsibility. The State Bank of India was nationalized in 1955, and over the next couple of decades, many more PSBs were created. Our PSBs took banking services to the remotest and financially most unviable corners of the country. Apart from paying their share of corporate taxes, PSBs have also been a steady and reliable source of dividend income for their biggest shareholder—the Government of India. From priority sector lending to implementation of the government's welfare schemes, the social mandates are far more heavily loaded on our PSBs than on the private sector banks. Almost 80 per cent of the 350 million bank accounts opened under the Pradhan Mantri Jan-Dhan Yojana scheme have been opened by the PSBs, 16 per cent by the regional rural banks and a mere 4 per cent (a little more

---

* The contents of this article reflect the personal views of the authors and do not reflect the viewpoint of any organization that they may be associated with.

than 10 million accounts) by the private sector banks. Therefore, it would be unfair to compare the business performance of our PSBs and the larger private sector banks on the same set of evaluation parameters.

Leadership in Indian PSBs

Notwithstanding their pivotal role in nation building, PSBs and their leaders face significant challenges. Employees have long—sometimes, more than 10 hours a day—working hours, particularly in branch operations. Frequent transfers from one city to the other play havoc with family and personal life. Impatient, demanding, and often, unreasonable retail customers bring their own stress, as do the risks associated with dealing in money and money-related products, where tolerance for error is minimal.

New developments such as mergers, increased regulatory oversight, lack of digital skills at senior levels, retirements and attritions at senior levels have thrown up urgent leadership challenges. Private sector competitors and new entrants into the digital banking arena are making rapid progress in areas such as digitization, scenario planning and risk-management practices. In the post-COVID era of distributed information availability, processing and deployment—driven by tech-savvy mid-level managers—require PSBs to move from 'command and control' to employee engagement. With a large majority of PSB employees likely to be millennial soon, the present hierarchical structure and practice of PSB leadership is untenable. Lateral recruitment of quality talent and accelerated growth of existing talent are not easy in a unionized environment.

Late Professor Sumantra Ghoshal spoke of the 'smell of the place'. He said that certain companies had the smell of 'Kolkata in summer'—hot, humid, stifling and exhausting. These companies develop a culture of constraint, compliance, control and contract, whereas certain other companies had the smell of 'Fontainebleau forest in spring—crisp, fragrant and irrepressible. The positive energy and innovative approach to work, driven by employee engagement, is palpable in the premises of these companies. Unfortunately, many of our banking institutions, particularly our PSBs, have created within themselves what Professor Ghoshal referred to as 'summer-time Kolkata'.

Cultural Challenges in the Banking Sector

There have also been many disheartening and debilitating developments in the banking arena over the past couple of decades, and these need to be addressed if transformational leadership is to be achieved.

The recent history of banking in India is not exactly a tale of glory. The industry has seen governance and performance issues including lack of leadership credibility, and we have not seen a reduction in the speed of this downward slide. As per the RBI, almost 7,000 cases of fraud—totalling more than ₹700,000 million—were detected in the FY 2019, an 80 per cent increase over the previous year. The recent global history of banking and financial services is not very heartening either. Leading banks such as Wells Fargo and Deutsche Bank have experienced culturally challenging times. A lot of these dysfunctional behaviours can be traced to the culture and process of reward and recognition—both formal and informal—that have evolved in the banking industry. But this is only a part of a bigger malaise.

Leadership to Foster an 'Inspiring' Culture

A bank, like any other institution, has two sides to its manifestation. Its *left-hand side* or its *doing*—what it *does* and the business activities it performs. These are tasks such as accepting deposits, lending, selling and managing instruments of investments such as mutual funds. Then there is its *right-hand side* or its *being*—what it *becomes* in terms of its institutional character—demonstrated by its employees' behaviours with each other and with other stakeholders. The right-hand side also influences the leaders' decisions, particularly under stressed business conditions, and is more commonly referred to as the 'value system' or 'culture' of the organization. Two banks with similar left- hand side in terms of product portfolio, business strategy, geographical presence and finances may exhibit dramatically different right-hand sides!

The left-hand side is the 'smartness' of the bank—strategic thinking in terms of competitive edge, geographical presence, customer segmentation and analytics, technology, product portfolio, pricing, alliances, etc. The right-hand side is the sustainable 'health' of the bank. A lot of our banking institutions, both PSBs and in the private sector, have focused on the left-hand side of their development and have ignored the right-hand side. The outcome is a leadership ethos that inspires fear of authority rather than love, admiration and respect.

The right-hand side is important, not just for the organization to be a pleasant entity to deal with or an employee friendly place to work. The 'Fontainebleau forest in spring' culture attracts and retains superior quality of talent and gets the best out of them—consistently. This, as global corporate history demonstrates over a period of time, stimulates a positive and sustainable impact on the left-hand side of the organization in terms of the 'commercial vitals' of the enterprise in covering revenue, profit, market share, quality, return on capital employed and market capitalization.

Some organizations have, with earnest intentions, commenced initiatives to articulate and deploy, across the enterprise, their preferred culture or right-hand side. Unfortunately, they have permitted themselves to get derailed at varying stages of the journey.

Root causes of the derailment are many. Every positive transformational effort, initiated by a well-intentioned CEO or top management, will run into an opposing force of cynicism and scepticism, in the initial stages. This negative force, combined with the normal human inertia and resistance to change, creates a powerful opposing force. Fortunate are those institutions which are able to reach a *critical mass* of employees who are either champions of the new initiatives or disciplined soldiers of the organization, who throw their weight behind the mandate of the top management. If the number of employees working, covertly or overtly, against the change (or are indifferent to the new initiative) overwhelms those in favour, the organization fails to reach *critical mass*. Hence, the articulation of the culture must be simple, easily understood by the least literate employee and measurably *linked to the role* of every employee. The process of deployment, to critical mass and then to full institutionalization, must be carefully designed and meticulously executed, learning from the failures and successes of many other organizations that have attempted this journey before.

Mitigating the likelihood of these negative forces calls for training and expert handholding of the CEO and the apex leadership team in visualizing, articulating and deploying the preferred culture of the bank. How can this be done with a higher probability of success?

Culture: A Seven-step Journey

Having worked for a few decades as faculty and consultants with a number of private and PSBs, non-banking financial companies and Indian corporations from other industries, we have developed a reasonable familiarity with many of the means by which culture can be reimagined, fostered and enshrined by a committed leadership. These approaches are not unique to the banking industry. We draw upon insights gathered during the course of our intense journeys, in the company of the top management of a diverse set of Indian organizations—one of the top three multi-business conglomerates with a huge portfolio of businesses in the financial products and services domain; arguably the largest e-commerce player; three of the main life Insurance

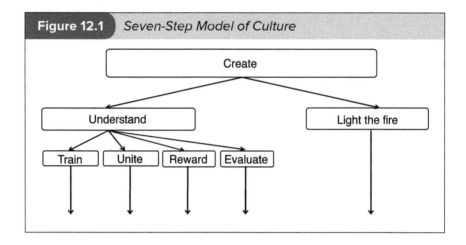

Figure 12.1 *Seven-Step Model of Culture*

providers; a major manufacturer of commercial vehicles; a leading producer of agri-vehicles and equipment; the Indian arm of a giant global telecom company; and a couple of prominent educational institutions.

The seven-step model that we have prototyped, experimented with and refined over the past many years is easily remembered by the acronym CULTURE (Create; Understand; Light the Fire; Train; Unite; Reward; Evaluate) (Figure 12.1).

Step 1: Create Clearly and Tangibly

Stephen Covey said, 'All things are created twice—first mentally; then physically.' We prefer to do Step 1 of mental creation with the apex leadership team of the organization. The advocacy and active participation of the CEO or managing director is a must. Most organizations, at some point in their history, have attempted to articulate their 'values framework' or 'culture' in terms of words such as 'integrity' or 'bias for action'. They even add a few words of 'definition'. Sadly, these are often found to exist as colourful posters on the office 'walls' rather than 'experienced' as day-to-day behaviours in the office halls.

Tried and tested methods are available to help the leadership team agree upon and 'articulate' their 'preferred' organization culture, not just as words or definitions but as 'everyday stakeholder experience'. Culture is not merely a 'promise' made by the organization. It's what the stakeholder 'experiences'. If the leadership team wants 'bias for action' to be associated with their cultural DNA then, in Step 1, they debate and converge on the actual and 'vital few' visible behaviours that every employee *will always or will never* demonstrate with each different key stakeholder (employee, customer, channel partner, vendor, member of the community, etc.) of the organization. The specific and 'vital' behaviours are articulated as precise statements (norms) that can be easily evaluated as visibly apparent 'bias for action' by the stakeholder based on their personal experience of every interaction. Similarly, for every one of the carefully chosen words or phrases that the apex leadership would like key stakeholders to associate with the organization's culture. This process of debate and co-creation is, very often, a much-needed opportunity for the senior-most leadership to rediscover their reason for existence as an organization. After this exercise, we have heard many a chief experience officer confide in us that it was a journey back to the 'basics' of why they chose their profession and what inspired them to give their best in the early years of their career. It is also, surprisingly, a rediscovery of home truths that had lost sight over many years of chasing targets, deliverables, deadlines and personal career goals. See Box 12.1.

Over the next few years, L&T became a role model in all three dimensions!

Box 12.1   Total Quality Management (TQM) in L&T

Many years ago, Anil Sachdev was involved with a large transformation programme in L&T. S. D. Kulkarni was the MD of the company and he personally led the initiative by investing a lot of time in the programme. As the founder and CEO of Eicher Consultancy Services, Anil Sachdev, co-author of this paper, was facilitating this programme along with his colleagues. The entire top management personally participated in a three-day-programme on TQM—the model that we were using as the vehicle for change.

L&T also initiated a retreat of the top team every quarter, like the GE 'work outs', in which they spent two days. In the unique design that was developed for these meetings, spouses of the top team were invited, and several joint sessions were held with them based on the assumption that conversations at home would reinforce the transformation efforts and the impact was very heartening!

We also facilitated a company-wide visioning exercise involving thousands of people to energize the company on its aspirations to not only grow but transform the entire customer experience to make L&T a benchmark organization. A few years after the first programme of change, A. M. Naik became the CEO and invited us to do another exercise on revisiting the vision and values of the company in light of the global environment and the intense competition they were facing then.

This led to energizing the work force towards a global vision and standards, and brought shareholder value creation to the fore along with customer delight and employee engagement.

The behaviour 'norms' which are co-created in Step 1 by the apex leadership are very different from the Ethical Code of Conduct documents created by many large companies. Ethics are moral principles laid down or accepted in a society which apply to all corporate entities and Ethics Code of Conduct is the expected behaviour to comply with those principles. But norms of behaviour mandated by the culture of the company build the authentic and consistent image of what the company uniquely and deeply believes in, and will not compromise under any circumstances. These are not mandated by society but mandated by the leadership of the organization to differentiate themselves uniquely within their industry and among their competition.

Step 2: Understand and Link to Employees' Roles

In Step 1, the apex leadership reimagined the organization's culture and articulated it as simple and visible behaviours that lead to the desired 'interaction experiences' of each key stakeholder. In Step 2, this organizational 'intent' is understood, internalized and 'committed to' by the next two or three levels of leadership who, as role models, will inspire the rank and file to align with the desired culture and who, as 'warriors', will fight the inevitable battles against inertia, cynicism and scepticism.

In the 'understand' stage, expertly facilitated conversations are held with cohorts of senior executives, where the culture-articulation process of the apex leadership is shared. Apprehensions and alternative points of view are welcomed, discussed, debated and the 'intent' is clarified. The objective is to arrive at a common leadership understanding of the 'culture imperatives' and their impact on the business health of the organization as well as on employee engagement. During these conversations, the 'intent' of the apex leadership is understood in terms of 'behavioural norms' for every role.

Time and space are created for leaders to bring the 'skeletons' out of the cupboard. They are encouraged to talk about the real-life 'blocks' that are likely to hinder the implementation of the stated norms. These 'blocks' could be historical practices or habits in the organization, existing processes (or absence of necessary processes) and dilemmas where an employee is torn between conflicting demands of business mandates and behavioural norms. These discussions are facilitated such that they do not take the form of 'crib sessions' and are channelized into collaborative problem-solving leading to implementable resolutions. See Box 12.2.

Box 12.2	Visioning Future in Volvo Eicher Commercial Vehicles Ltd (VECV)

In the recent past, the authors were engaged in a major transformation Programme in VECV.

As part of this programme, we enabled the entire workforce reimagine the organization of the future by first discovering their 'gifts' by learning from stories of their 'joyful best' performance; leveraging these to create a powerful 'dream' for the future; designing the future by focusing on new priorities and ways of working; and delivering the same by first energizing the entire workforce, celebrating new success stories and linking values and behaviours to all the HR systems. This enabled each person to appreciate how the person's role impacted the work of his or her team and that of the entire organization and had major positive impact both in terms of tangible output and employee and customer experience.

Step 3: Light the Fire, Enterprise Wide

Having gained a deep and common understanding of the culture 'intent' and the behaviour norms, the senior and top management team sets about the evangelization process.

This is done in two main ways.

Walking the Talk

Employees emulate the 'video' that they see every day of their senior leaders' decisions and behaviour. And they emulate these decision-making practices and behaviours rather than the 'audio' speeches that the leaders may make in their address to the employees. If leaders at the senior level do not practice their preaching, on a day-to-day basis, they lose both respect and credibility to expect adherence to cultural norms by the rank and file.

In an exercise we did with Indus Towers, this was done in a unique way. Design thinking was used to observe and study how leadership behaviours impacted the culture, and the top team personally defined the dos and don'ts of behaviour to live the values and gave personal commitments to start and do more of positive behaviours as well as reduce or eliminate the undesirable ones. The top team regularly introspected on the same and invited feedback from other employees to learn and transform. This enabled the organization to win the Best Workplace award from Gallup for many years and created the foundation that won them the Deming Prize.

Visual and Omnipresent Communication

The 'culture promises' made by the apex leadership and the daily 'stakeholder experiences' (the 'proof of the pudding') are displayed in prominent locations across the physical and digital premises of the organization including all their offices and their intranet portals. Every employee encounters, many times a day, visual reminders of the 'cultural promises' and their personal role in making the 'stakeholder experience' a reality. The internal communications teams brainstorm, prototype and experiment with different creative means of doing this and evaluate the effectiveness of their efforts by measuring employee 'recall' and 'impact' of the messaging.

In a worldwide initiative that the co-authors facilitated with Aditya Birla Group, this was done with great imagination and creativity. A unique simulation was designed and facilitated to enable all employees own and internalize the cultural attributes, which resulted in a huge positive impact. Values were included among important criteria to reward and recognize individuals and teams in the chairman's awards function, attended by hundreds of employees and watched live, globally, by 120,000 people.

Step 4: Train through Leaders as Culture Champions

A few culture champions are selected from among the senior leaders who have undergone Step 2 to take the message to the middle and junior levels of the organization. They do this through short training modules, of less than a day, for existing employees. They also conduct these sessions for new recruits as part of the induction process. Their seniority ensures that their audience will take them seriously. Additional criteria for their selection as champions are communication skills (they should be able to hold the attention and interest of their audience); credibility (they should be acceptable to the audience as role models qualified to talk about organization culture, based on their past behaviour) and passion (they should volunteer to be a culture champion and to play a role beyond their job description to craft the future of their organization). Using 'instructional design' methodologies, simple and engaging training modules are created and handed over to the culture champions and a brief 'train the trainer' session helps them to deliver these interventions thereafter.

Every employee undergoes a short online annual 'recertification' process where they are tested for their understanding of the norms of behaviour and the impact on key stakeholders and the business.

In Aditya Birla Group, nearly 400 leaders were trained as 'value champions' to facilitate transformational learning.

Step 5: Unite through Participation, Recruitment and Onboarding

As an ongoing process, employees at all levels are encouraged to continuously highlight day-to-day 'blocks' that hinder 'living' the culture, along with suggestions on how to neutralize these blocks. Many organizations create the office of a 'culture ombudsperson' to act as a conscience keeper to the board and to the apex leadership, as well as a sounding board to every employee.

The culture mandate is also brought into the recruitment process. Leaders are equipped with skills, 2 such as Behavioural Event Interviewing, which help them look for 'markers' that indicate the likely fit of the candidate within the 'cultural DNA' of the organization. If recruitment interviews only evaluate technical or functional capabilities, without assessment of the culture match, the organization is likely to bring in employees who are good in job-related competencies but may, later, turn out to be misfits in terms of the expected behaviours. Leaders are urged to drop, from the consideration list, functionally competent candidates who do not show a predisposition to resonate with the company's culture.

Many times, it may not be possible to reject candidates on the grounds of likely cultural misalignment due to recruitment pressures and a shortage of talent pool. In this situation, the organization needs a powerful and effective 'onboarding process' that 'inducts' the new employee into the 'culture' and behaviour norms of the company. Ideally, there should be both a 'culture filter' at recruitment stage as well as effective 'onboarding'. In a less than ideal situation, at least one of these should be strong enough to compensate for any deficiency in the other.

A Whistle Blower Protection policy is created to encourage employees to call out violations of the stated norms, in confidence, without the fear of backlash. Step 5 leads to a unified organization of many like-minded people who feel safe enough to call out deviant behaviours and nip dysfunctionality in the bud. Anil Sachdev and his team worked closely with Mahindra Group in the Rise initiative which involved setting up design teams to transform all critical HR processes, ranging from recruitment and onboarding to communication and performance management so that the culture pillars of 'accept no limits', 'alternate thinking' and 'driving positive change' came alive in the hearts and minds of people.

Step 6: Reward and Discipline

Goldratt once observed, 'Tell me how you will measure me, and I will tell you how I will behave.' If employees' compensation and career growth is not directly and significantly linked to their observable conduct and is measured against the cultural norms expected, then the initiative derails quickly. If the leadership pays lip service to cultural norms of behaviour and rewards *only* functional deliveries, the employee quickly learns that culture is for 'posters on the office walls' and proceeds to do whatever it takes to get rewarded. Adherence to behaviour norms must have an equal (or greater) impact on compensation and career growth as a functional performance.

This step sees the entry of the culture elements and behaviour norms into the performance management and succession planning activity.

Also, in Step 6, the organization configures rituals to celebrate those employees who stand by the culture norms, even under stressful circumstances.

See Box 12.3.

It is also essential to identify individuals who 'depart from' or 'violate' the cultural norms. A 'departure' is a minor transgression that calls for a counselling conversation with the immediate supervisor. But a 'violation' is usually a deliberate act in defiance of the organizational behavioural or decision-making mandate; and this must attract a harsh response.

In all the examples given above, the performance management and reward systems were redesigned to include values in the competency framework of the company that received significant weightage in deciding rewards.

Box 12.3   Culture Articulation in a Multi-business Conglomerate

In a large multi-business conglomerate, where we were closely involved in the culture articulation and deployment exercise, we started an annual ritual of the Values Awards Night. The award winners were not nominated by their supervisors or by the management. Instead, all employees were invited to send in, anonymously, stories about colleagues who they had observed standing by the company's values, even under very difficult circumstances. From the hundreds of stories that came in, the most impactful ones were selected by a jury, the facts verified and the heroes were recognized publicly on the Awards Night. The lobby of the hotel where the function was held displayed huge panels with the award winners' photograph and the story to inspire all employees who attended the function with their families.

Step 7: Evaluate Frequently

Since care is taken, in Step 1, to articulate the 'culture' as norms of easily observable behaviour, they are converted into survey statements which can be rated on a behaviourally anchored rating scale. Surveys are frequently administered among the key stakeholders and they rate the behaviours they have observed in their interactions with the company's representatives. This 'quantifies' the culture-based data gathered from the 'moments of truth' where stakeholder meets company and is a great decision-support tool for the leadership to identify areas of development and take corrective action.

These aspects of building culture are rooted in an effective talent-management framework that the co-authors have used in many organizations including the ones described before.

Our philosophy and approach are based on Whole Person Leadership which derives its power from ancient wisdom, traditions and Indian spiritual ethos.

It is our belief that human beings have four fundamental capacities—to learn, think, relate and act.

The capacity to learn is the 'mother' capacity that derives its power from the 'consciousness' or the life-giving force within all of us. It is the silent witness within us that enables us to observe our past and learn about what we need to do differently—*introspection*. It helps us to observe our actions, emotions and thoughts, in the present, to appreciate what is enabling us to learn and what is coming in the way of our learning—*reflection and contemplation*. It is what gets us into the *'flow'* of new experiences so that instead of fearing the unborn future, we develop the child like curiosity to learn!

Our values serve as multipliers to these capacities. The power of our values in action, our character gives us the strength to take on new challenges, learn from failures and get out of our comfort zones to source inspiration and put in sustained efforts to make the desired future manifest.

With this approach in mind, our interventions 'discover' capacities, observe values in action and derive insights on the unutilized capacities or potential—all of which were extremely useful inputs to design individual development plans for leaders.

Conclusion

Culture is the glue that makes all employees rise together to serve the 'purpose' of an organization. It is the reason that makes people go the extra mile to perform and contribute. It inspires people to come to work every day and imparts a level of pride that makes work itself the biggest motivator. In organizations that have cultures that create ownership, people find more meaning in their lives and they carry this energy to their homes and community.

Most of us spend a large part of our waking hours at work. In the recent COVID environment of working from home, this aspect is even more visible. Organizations that have enabling and inspiring cultures like Dr Reddy's, Tata Steel, Fab India and Volvo Eicher are giving their employees the strength to cope with this crisis and emerge stronger. They are the ones who have worked consciously on developing their ways of working with careful thought to leadership development, succession planning, fair performance management and reward systems as well as responsive and transparent communication.

If India must become a truly globally competitive nation, it must urgently reform the banking system in the country. They key to do this is to make culture building, talent management and leadership development the biggest priority of the board. Banks must not only measure and report risk in their loan portfolio but also the risk in their talent portfolio and 'practiced' culture. The nominations and remuneration committee of the board must redefine its scope to assess how the bank is building a culture of meritocracy and renovating its talent management process to measure potential. The committee also needs to revisit how career and succession planning is being done; how the process of matching talent with strategic initiatives is being done to build capability; how exposure is being given to new technology and expertise; how leaders are using bank's projects as curriculum to conduct impactful education; how leaders take responsibility to develop the right kind of talent; how rewards are being given to advance the right talent, and finally, how the leadership team tracks the culture to manifest a 'high-performance and high-touch' organization that creates the highest quality of customer and employee experience to make the bank an organization of consequence.

13

Leadership in Times of Crisis
Lessons from COVID-19 Crisis

Prasenjit Bhattacharya

If you are the CEO of a company, this is your time. People may not remember your predecessors, but they will never forget you!

What were you doing or not doing when your company was hit by the COVID-19-induced tsunami? This will be a question that will follow you for the rest of your life.

We spoke to over 250 organizations and many CEOs to find out what the leaders of the best workplaces had been up to. This article is a primer based on what we observed.

Dealing with the Crisis

We, at Great Place to Work, interact with some brilliant leaders. All of them have business continuity plans or contingency plans. For many multinationals, these plans are tested every quarter in some geography or another, be it in the form of economic upheaval, natural calamities or political turmoil.

None of them were even remotely prepared for this crisis.

The first case was tracked in China on 17 November 2019. By 1 December, this information was known to others. Not since the Spanish flu of 1918 had the world seen a pandemic like this.

India declared COVID-19 a notified disaster only on 14 March and the lockdown was announced on 24 March 2020.

True to style, many leaders of corporate India had figured out the implications about a month ahead, around the end of February. In fact, Times Network had already started 'work from home' drills well before the lockdown (and no, according to them, they did not have any inside information!)

What did these leaders do in March?

Many things. Some of the common strategies were as follows.

Scenario Planning

Meticulously prepared budgets for the new financial year were kept aside. They prepared a COVID budget. 'How do you reduce fixed cost, and how do you protect people?' These were the two questions that Patu Keswani of Lemon Tree Hotels started with. His team came with three scenarios— different levels of demand destruction, leading to different levels of cost reduction. In the beginning of March, even they had not anticipated a scenario four—the entire country going through a lockdown.

The result? As I write this chapter, Lemon Tree's revenue went down by 80 per cent and costs went down by 70 per cent. Did Patu succeed in his aim of protecting people? At the time of writing this chapter, no layoff had been announced and the salaries of 8,000 employees were being paid. And the hotel is still achieving close to cash break-even!

How?

Apart from pulling back all discretionary expenses like hotel renovation, the top 1,000 managers have taken salary cuts to the tune of 65 per cent. (Remember, salary costs are a significant part of costs for a hotel.)

This is not the first time that they are doing it. When they took salary cuts in 2008, they got back the cut money with 12 per cent interest when the business rebounded!

Work from Home Transition

While most organizations were waiting to see if the immediate disruptions in the phase 1 of lockdown was just a temporary phase, Sumit Mitra, CEO of Tesco Global Services, had no such doubts. He ordered 1,000 laptops for people working from home, transported office equipment including furniture to employees' homes, took permission from the government to operate an international business from home and quarantined his data service centres. 'Most people were waiting for the peak to flatten out, I was preparing for the peak. Now we are ready for the long haul.'

The result? Headquarters of Tesco, recognizing the proactive steps taken by Sumit and his team, relied on them to cater to the gaps in delivery. (At one time, over 50,000 employees of Tesco in the UK were quarantined or under medical leave.) Tesco Global Services business, in India, saw a 50 per cent jump.

Work from home was not a part of the disaster recovery plan for most businesses. It required management principles to be clearly articulated. Tesco in India is, again, a case study. These are some of the things they did:

1. **Stop random forwarding of WhatsApp messages in employee groups:** Reduce information to one or two credible sources like WHO (Sumit borrowed many ideas from Sun Tzu, the writer of the Chinese treatise, *The Art of War*. 'It is fitting that I borrow ideas from the Chinese to fight the virus that originated there,' he said, half in jest.)

2. **Focus even more on the core purpose:** More than ever, people need to feel that their work has meaning, it is not a job. Sumit could mobilize his people with one goal, 'We have to feed the nations we serve.'

3. **Be clear on the guiding principles:** Some examples are as follows.

   a. Protect the weakest; for example, senior management to take pay cuts before others.
   b. Safety of colleagues must be taken care of.
   c. Customer focus—hold on to your customers. Take care of existing customers before focusing on new customers.
   d. Daily conversation—feedback must be given in real time.
   e. Focus must be on brilliant basics and not discretionary items.

   Guiding principles come to one's aid when the situation is uncertain and unpredictable. For example, one company had a guiding principle called 'one family'. When the CEO was asked when people would be able to start air travel or travel using public transport, his answer was, 'When we are comfortable with an adult family member of our family doing the same.'

4. **Communication: Use this transition as an opportunity to inspire your people**—Leaders have understood the need for daily conversation. As I write this, over 500 branches of Mahindra Finance have opened and many are yet to open. Every day, people get to know about inspiring stories from these branches. Kotak Mahindra Bank has all their branches operating with reduced staff. The fact that one employee took the initiative to drop emergency medicines at the home of a senior citizen, who is a customer, might have been missed in normal circumstance. Not right now. Such stories go all the way up to the CEO and MD.

   In a war, you need a command structure, clear strategy, simple and consistent communication, feedback from the front line and fast decisions that cut through the hierarchy. This is not the time for committees.

Manpower/Cost Rationalization

The inevitable consequence of demand and supply destruction is cost reduction. Lemon Tree Hotels always had better ratios compared to most other five-star hotels. They expect that their operating leverage will increase by 10 per cent and staffing per hotel will reduce by 20 per cent after this crisis. Unlike many other hospitality chains, Lemon Tree is not laying-off people yet. It is planning to expand! 'We have always been a bit paranoid since we do not have a sponsor like many other Groups. We will be the last man standing in any crisis!'

M. K. Anand, the CEO of Times Network, makes no secret of the fact that every year there is a set of forced attrition cases based on performance (the famous or notorious forced ranking). There are no lay-offs planned at Times Network. That is because they did not wait for COVID-19 to create an efficient organization. 'Any CEO who was waiting for Corona virus to strike to reduce people, was not doing a competent job,' is the rather overarching comment he makes.

Unlike Times Network, for most organizations, a 20–25 per cent reduction in staff cost seems feasible now, even at last year's volumes. In other words, post COVID-19, staff cost will be reduced for most organizations.

Is it worth it?

That would depend on your industry. If it is IT services or staffing companies, staff cost is the single biggest cost in their books. You will hear more about IT services because they offer jobs on their rolls, while staffing companies have multiple models of employment.

If you are a large oil and energy company like Indian Oil Corporation Limited, National Thermal Power Corporation Limited or Reliance Industries Limited, then staff cost is low, in single digits. You have other costs to worry about.

But is there a good way to rationalize employee cost? Here are some pointers from the best employers.

1. First, protect your customer base.
2. Question the business model: real cost savings is in looking at changing the assumptions of the business model, for example, we need to meet the customer to sell.
3. Make an emergency plan for cash conservation.
4. Reduce real estate cost by taking advantage of remote working.
5. Zero based budgeting: minimum viable cost of replacement as a benchmark for salary cost (not compensation surveys). Most good-to-have costs will be variable; only the must-have costs will be fixed.
6. Try to ensure minimum impact on most vulnerable.
7. Humane graded lay-offs—try to save the majority.
8. Re-assess every business line—segregate between short-term cost benefits and long-term implications.

Despite best efforts, lay-offs might be necessary. Great Place to Work® has identified the following as good practices:

1. Listen to employees
2. Support managers in doing these conversations—do not outsource it to human resources who may not know the context of individual employees
3. Communicate transparently to the whole organization
4. Offer support to colleagues being laid-off
5. Engage employees who stay on your rolls
6. Follow up with those who have been laid-off and offer support, if possible, to those who need it

In the last recession, organizations like Google and Intel, along with many other best workplaces, laid-off people. What distinguished them was how they did it.

Employee Issues

While there have been some benefits for employees, namely, reduction/elimination of travel time, opportunity to spend quality time with family members and a plethora of online learning opportunities with no or low commercial investment employees in our surveys have reported several challenges.

Key issues impacting many employees are as follows.

Ambiguity and Some Fear

Employees of the best workplaces are used to leaders who know where the business is going and how to get there. They are struggling with a situation where the leaders know where to go, but not necessarily the details of how to get there.

In such situations, the best employers are compensating by making their communication more frequent. Line managers are now in touch with all their team members daily and helping them define priorities on a weekly basis.

Fear is also being produced by financial insecurity among employees. The best workplaces are trying to reduce this by instituting transparent communication.

Stress and Work-life Balance

Contrary to popular opinion, low work-life balance does not necessarily lead to stress. A significant spurt in activity which does not result in tangible outcomes leads to stress. This seems to be more pronounced for working women who are managing home and office without regular domestic staff. Family fault lines are getting accentuated and personal relationships are being tested.

The number of reported cases of anxiety, depression and domestic violence has increased. As we know, reported cases are just the tip of the iceberg.

Inadequate Infrastructure at Home

There are reports of employees sitting on the floor, staring at a computer screen for long hours without a break, not having reliable internet access and not having the privacy required to do sensitive work. Most organizations are yet to address the fundamental challenge that homes have not been designed to be offices.

Takeaways for Management

Leadership across organizations had to address the following issues:

1. The unit of engagement is not just the employee, but also his/her immediate family and context
2. Support home infrastructure
3. Do not lose your customer focus
4. Increase focus on employee wellness, including counselling
5. Monitor productivity, collaboration and speed
6. Assess enhanced risks arising out of work from home
7. Ensure continuous feedback

Refer to the Annexure 13.1 for some of the significant changes post-COVID-19 which are impacting employees.

One of the biggest realizations that leaders now have is the key role played by the line manager in ensuring that all employees are connected to the organization. Remote working means that the line manager has become the key driver to connect, inspire and develop employees.

The Opportunity for Business Transformation

Leaders at the best workplaces have been quick to spot opportunities for business transformation. The digital account of Kotak Bank—811 in the first 10 days of May—saw around 14,000 accounts being opened per day!

While everyone is selling products and services digitally, some have used this as an opportunity to fundamentally change its business model. A well-known bank is radically reimagining its customer acquisition and customer care process to enable all sales and upselling using technology and digital nudges.

Demand and supply destruction for some industries is an opportunity for supply acquisition for others. Expect such consolidation to happen in hospitality, airlines, retail and even in manufacturing. Many promising start-ups will be available for acquisition.

One of the biggest changes witnessed by most organizations is the merging of multiple generations like millennials, Gen Z, Gen Y, Gen X and others into one—the post-COVID generation!

Post-COVID generation is agile, digitally adept, comfortable with remote working and productive. They understand that the only way to increase compensation is to continuously increase their skills so that their market value is slightly ahead of their compensation.

The good news is that employees are more eager than ever before to explore new ways of working. Years of mindset change and change management work has been done in a month due to COVID-19.

Are you a leader who is willing to take this once in a lifetime opportunity to transform your business, or are you only content with cost-cutting and running your business as usual?

Leadership Dilemmas and Principles

COVID-19 is the world's most effective leadership development program. Real leaders are emerging in all organizations. Hierarchy has broken down. For example, each hotel manager in Lemon Tree is now a mini-CEO. By now, most CEOs know who their real leaders are.

Are the CEOs themselves real leaders?

No corporate leader has faced a global pandemic of this magnitude in their lifetime. However, most have faced multiple crisis situations.

Some of the principles articulated by leaders of great workplaces are:

1. **Define your priorities:** For example, customer service versus employee safety. Atria Convergence Technologies (ACT), a Bangalore-headquartered company defined their order of priority as follows:

    1. Employee's health and safety
    2. Uninterrupted service to customers
    3. Attending to new customers

2. **Leaders must be a role model:** ACT's CEO, Bala Malladi, and his senior managers went out in the market to be with their field employees who were servicing customers since internet connectivity is an essential service.

3. **Establish direct and continuous channels of communication with employees—keep the focus on the purpose:** Tesco India has a daily communication process with all its employees and is able to calculate their Employee Net Promoter Score on a daily basis. The messages of the leadership reach all employees, daily.

4. **Focus on employee health, safety and wellness:** The immediate response of many leaders is to focus largely on revenue and cost. While that is a priority for the management team, it is a mistake to make that as the priority for your internal communication. Focus on employee health, safety and wellness before you talk about revenue and productivity.

5. **Ensure you have a process to measure productivity and implementation of strategic plans:** Many organizations are falling into the activity trap. Managers who were comfortable taking and giving targets are now falling back on showing activities, as opposed to outcomes. Leaders must hold their key managers accountable for both activities and outcomes.

6. **Take a backseat!** After the first few weeks of leading from the front, many CEOs have figured out that this is an opportunity to develop the second line. Career and succession plans are being dusted and potential CEO successors are being identified. If you are a leader at any level within the organization, here is your opportunity to prove your leadership mettle.

7. **Do not lose sight of the future:** The impact of every crisis is overestimated while you are in the middle of it. It is important to remember that most things in the world did not change fundamentally after the Spanish flu, or even after the Black Death, when we did not have the scientific knowledge that we have now.

8. **Every decision is an opportunity to build trust:** Keep the organization's core values at the centre of your decisions. What you do now will impact your future relationship with all key stakeholders—customers, suppliers and employees. If your customer is not able to pay the EMI for their car loan, there is little to be gained by seizing their asset. Try and help them. Most customers are honest. They will pay back in time. What is more, they will remember you for good reasons.

When your employee is taking a salary but not pulling their weight, find out what is happening with them or their family. Are they dealing with anxiety of some kind? Your employee might be finding it difficult to pay their Estimated Daily Instalment (EDI) (yes, employees pay EDI every day for the salary they take once a month).

Some may find it easy to squeeze a supplier or an employee during a crisis; do so knowing that you are withdrawing from the trust account between you and the stakeholder, also known as goodwill.

Key Conclusions for India

There are broadly two strategies being adopted by countries trying to contain COVID-19—social isolation or massive testing or a combination of the two. Unfortunately, both have had only limited success in India. Our peak kept on being pushed back month after month, as cases kept on increasing. Last, I know, a TV channel, which was proudly advertising their superior analytics claiming 20 June as the date for the peak, has stopped updating their projection for the peak. My conclusions are not based on this or many other 'scientific' studies. It is based on discussions with around 250 organizations that he contacted. It will be a big relief if I am proved wrong for some of them.

1. **Pray for a good rainfall and uptake in rural economy:** We had a bumper year in rabi crops. Even though supply chains are disrupted, rural India has food. Monsoon is predicted to be normal. This augurs well for the rural economy. The government must increase its capital expenditure and invest in infrastructure which will help create many rural jobs.

   Any social and economic distress in rural India has severe implications for the middle class in urban India, not just the political class.

2. **Key challenges in education and health will not be addressed:** The current crisis has exposed our public health infrastructure. Atmanirbhar Bharat, like its previous avatar, Make in India, will require radical reform in skills training.

   Not happening. The current bureaucracy can give daily dictates on ever changing instructions to 1.3 billion Indians but cannot transform education and health. This forces the political class to regularly manufacture various distractions.

   Once the current crisis is reduced, the rich will go back to their exclusive private healthcare and foreign education. The middle class will have to pay far more for their medical insurance. Corporates will benefit and masses will remain focused on emotional distractions.

3. **India is not going to replace China as a manufacturing powerhouse:** Those talking about these are deluded and haven't spoken in private with reputed manufacturers. The top reasons for India not being able to replace or even come close to China in manufacturing are as follows.

a. Arbitrary or frequent policy changes
b. Infrastructure, including unavailability of skilled manpower
c. Robust and healthy supply chain of micro, small and medium enterprises
d. Unfair and non-simplified labour laws (as opposed to arbitrary scrapping of labour laws en masse)

Developed economies are aware of macroeconomic and political risks. Investments of millions of dollars in manufacturing will not come without political and economic stability. Indian entrepreneurs are donating but not investing. Unlike in the past, a globally dispersed supply chain will not be viewed as a sign of sophistication.

4. **India can be the global back office for the world:** Unlike manufacturing, where supply chain risks are tangible and real, this crisis has shown that India can come to the rescue when it comes to using technology to run operations around the world. Our IT and IT services industry will rebound and thrive. India will be the global office. What is more, the bulk of the employees in this industry will no longer be in the large metros. Bharat will be the back office for India, even as India becomes the back office for the world.

5. **Informalization of work and long-term prospects:** The 7 per cent of workforce in the formal sector (excluding government sector or public sector enterprises) will shrink even more. However, the enterprise of Indian people will lead to a rebound next year. This will be led by a slew of young and new entrepreneurs who will extensively use digital platform models to bring together millions of workers in the unorganized sector.

The New Normal

It is now a truism that we have to live with Corona virus. A lot of what seems to be significant changes, will look less significant in future. What will, however, be likely to be different in future?

1. **Physical versus digital battle is over.** Digital has won. While the future is likely to be hybrid, digital will be the dominant medium.

2. **Some new behaviours will stay.** Wearing of masks may stop in time, but personal hygiene like hand washing will not. Social distancing in public places will stay longer. As a result, routine infectious diseases like the common flu might reduce.

3. **Large cities will reduce in importance** as centres of employment as remote working makes it feasible for most employees to work from anywhere, preferably their hometowns.

4. **Customers will not demand physical meetings for many products.** Digital sales will take off. A new breed of sales and marketing professionals will emerge for whom technology and customer analytics will be a key tool.

5. **Mindset change and differences in various generations will be less of an issue in change management.** The post-COVID generation will be more open to change. They will move from passive to active in building their market skills and not be dependent on the employer.

6. A very large percentage of employees used to being told what to do will experience **increased levels of stress, anxiety and disengagement**. This will be compounded by lack of or dysfunctional personal relationships. Our surveys of employees show financial concerns, anxiety and work-life balance as top three concerns of employees just now. Organizations, on the other hand, will have more intrusive and ubiquitous ways of measuring productivity. To ensure a healthy and productive employee, organizations will increase their focus on employee wellness, manifold.

7. **Organizations are not ready for all the risks associated with remote working.** While technology is also mitigating such risks, it cannot eliminate human related risks with family members overhearing and being privy to matters which would have been confined to offices. Expect a few major blow-ups.

Imagine you are addressing the students of all the Ivy League management colleges one year from now. They are listening with rapt attention as you talk about your journey during COVID-19 pandemic and post that.

What will you say?

Employee Experience & Engagement in the Post-COVID World

IN THE PAST

Work and life mostly analogous
- Conducting work and life mostly in person
- Physical workplace
- Work from home was mostly an exception rather than a norm
- The talent market for organizations was limited by geographical and physical constraints.
- Accommodation concerns of employees in the place of employment.

Demographic classification of workforce
- Generational classification
- Gender based classification
- Customized people practices tailored to cater to these different employee cohorts and constituencies

Fixed workforce operating out of fixed location / workplaces
- Place of work was fixed
- Comprised mostly of permanent employees, on the rolls of the company
- Employment terms were fixed
- People practices related to the physical workplace were therefore crucial

Set pace of work and business cycles and conventional measures for cost efficiency, productivity
- Effort / input as well as impact both visible
- Cyclical / episodic feedback from employees and customers
- Business as usual meant most businesses operated with 15% to 33% inflated costs

THEN

COVID – 19 Happened

SO NOW

Work and life mostly digital
- Conducting work and life through screens
- Virtual workplaces mostly
- Work from home becomes a legitimate employee expectation for many roles.
- The talent market is now much larger for organization and somewhat boundaryless. Talent can be hired from anywhere, regardless of geography, location.
- No accommodation concerns of employees.

Demographic classification of workforce rendered irrelevant
- Due to accelerated digital migration, demographic classification based on generation has lost relevance. It is now one homogenous group – the post COVID generation.
- Gender classification has blurred significantly
- People practices need to be now tailored to suit this homogeneous virtual workforce.

Dispersed workforce operating virtually
- Virtual workforce, remote working, not just WFH. (Remote working could be from any city)
- Gradually lesser fixed staff and more temporary staff
- Short term engagement / project to project contract (gig economy) is slated to blossom) leading to less control over workforce.
- People managers who manage small or large team will become crucial and people management skills will become premium.
- **People managers pull far more weight in a post-Covid world, than HR practices.**

Mental and psychological well-being of employees becomes a key employee benefit, a necessary part of the employee value proposition [EVP]
- Social distancing, need for temperature checks changes the purpose of the office from physical workplace to a place for occasional social interaction and community space.
- The demarcation between work-life and personal life are blurred and hence looking out for the mental and psychological well-being of employees will be the onus of the organization / employer. (What happens at home has a direct impact)

Mental and psychological well-being of employees through real-time, in person social interactions at the physical workplace
- Humans biologically wired for social interaction as a means of mental and psychological wellness and the quality of the human experience at the work-place ensures that to an extent mental and psychological well-being possible
- Clear demarcation possible between work-life and personal life (What happens at home was 'Personal')

Need for agility and adaptability, uncertain and shorter business cycles leading to unconventional measures for cost efficiency, productivity
- Only impact visible with very limited control on effort / input. Only remote monitoring
- Continuous and real-time employee and customer feedback
- Zero based budgeting e.g. minimum viable cost of replacement as opposed to compensation survey based salary fixation.

Source: Great Place to Work (2018).

14

Employer Branding to Build Human Capital Advantage

Gordhan K. Saini

'A brand is not built by accident but is the product of carefully accomplishing—either explicitly or implicitly—a series of logically linked steps with consumers.'
—Keller (2011, p. 125)

Employer Branding: Definition and Characteristics

Though human capital is considered as the main source of sustained competitive advantage (e.g., Becker et al., 2001), organizations continue to face two major challenges on this front: first, challenges in hiring due to intense competition for skilled talent; and second, retention of talented employees. These challenges have become more complex due to the changing demographics of the workforce, multigenerational workforce and diverse expectations of millennials and generation Z[1] employees (Randstad, 2019). These challenges could be alleviated by using a novel approach from marketing discipline known as employer branding. 'Employer branding is an activity where principles of marketing, in particular the 'science of branding', are applied to HR activities in relation to current and potential employees' (Edwards, 2010, p. 6).

Although previously, employer branding was defined mainly in terms of benefits (e.g., set of various benefits provided by employment and identified with the employing company), scholars now look at the term more holistically. In doing so, they posit employer branding to refer to 'identifiable and unique employer identity' that differentiates a firm from its competitors (Backhaus & Tikoo, 2005,p. 502), 'a targeted, long-term strategy to manage the awareness and perceptions of employees, potential employees, and related stakeholders' (Sullivan, 2004) and an internal and external

---

[1] Generation Z has age between 18 and 24 years, while millennials have age between 25 and 34.

promotion of 'what makes a firm different and desirable as an employer'. (Lievens, 2007, p. 51).

The emergent holistic perspective allows us to delineate a few characteristics of employer branding. First, it makes the case for the application of marketing and branding principles in HR context; second, it points to the need for a well-designed, targeted and long-term strategy for talent management; third, it focuses on both internal employees and external candidates; fourth, the holistic perspective suggests the need to differentiate the employer with other employers in the mind of current and potential employees, and relevant stakeholders.

It is important to clarify the difference between employer brand and employer branding terms. The employment or employer brand 'highlights the unique aspects of the firm's employment offerings or environment' and 'is a concept of the firm that differentiates it from its competitors' to attract, motivate and retain the firm's current and potential employees (Backhaus & Tikoo, 2004, p. 502), while 'employer branding describes the process of building an identifiable and unique employer identity' or more specifically, 'the promotion of a unique and attractive image' as an employer (Backhaus & Tikoo 2004, p. 502).

Cable and Turban (2001) proposed that the brand equity concept of marketing can be generalized to recruitment contexts and argue that an employer's efforts towards candidates are similar to an organization's efforts to attract consumers.[2] Based on the premise of consumer brand equity, the concept of employer brand equity (EBE) has emerged. EBE of a firm is the outcomes of the individual's employment decisions (such as decision to apply, accept job offers, remain with the company) that are attributable to the employer brand of the organization (Collins & Stevens, 2002).

Cable and Turban (2001) proposed three major dimensions of employer knowledge (or EBE): employer familiarity, employer reputation and employer image. Employer familiarity is the job seeker's awareness or ability to recognize an organization as a prospective employer. The employer's reputation is the job seeker's belief regarding how other individuals affectively view the organization as an employer. Employer image is the job seeker's beliefs about the attributes and associations related to the organization as an employer. In addition to employer awareness, Cable and Turban (2001) and Collins and Stevens (2002) also use the term 'surface brand associations,' measured in terms of organizational attractiveness and 'complex brand

---

[2] Banerjee, P., Saini, G. K., & Kalyanaram, G. (2018) find exception to this in certain situations.

associations' represented by job and organizational characteristics to define the EBE construct.

Benefits and Advantages of Employer Brand

Researchers have shown that developing an employer brand can be an effective organizational strategy to differentiate an employer from competitors and gain a competitive advantage in the talent market (App et al., 2012; Collins & Stevens, 2002; Lievens & Highhouse, 2003) and respond to recruitment and retention challenges (Martindale, 2010). A recent research report by Randstad (Randstad, 2019) cited that 91 per cent companies believe employer brand and reputation can even impact revenue (CareerArc, 2017).

Broadly, the benefits of an employer brand can be classified into two categories based on the target audience. First, benefits associated with potential/external employees; and second, benefits associated with existing/internal employees. These two categories are discussed below.

Employer Brand and Talent Attraction

An organization with a strong employer brand is considered to have several advantages related to talent attraction. Organizations with strong employer brand send signals to potential employees, create positive reputation, thereby attracting more candidates. For example, a well-managed employer brand attracts 3.5 more applicants per job. It also reduces the cost-per-hire by 50 per cent (Sundberg, 2020), and the best employers get nearly twice as many applications per employee as compared to other organizations (Hewitt, 2009). Further, job application decisions are significantly influenced by employer reputation. For example, 96 per cent of 527 MBA students, in 12 top business schools in the US, Europe and Asia, said that reputation was an important factor in their choice of potential employer (Auger et al., 2013). Empirical research shows that organizations attracting more qualified applicants have a larger applicant pool, leading to the greater utility of the organization's selection system (Lado & Wilson, 1994).

A strong brand can help in attracting talent in a competitive talent market in what is called the 'war for talent' scenario (Michaels et al., 2001). As per the consulting firm Manpower Group's survey, 2019, 63 per cent employers in India said they can't find the talent with desired skills.[3] In fact, skills

---

[3] https://www.manpowergroup.co.in/talent-shortage.html

shortage is a major concern that requires the attention of business and HR leaders. Reports from consulting organizations and academic research converge that employer branding can minimize the negative effects of the talent shortage problem by leveraging the power of the brand. Randstad Report (Randstad, 2019) cites that 99 per cent of employers believe that managing employer brand and reputation is important when attracting top talent.

Employer Brand and Talent Retention

Branding within organization has an important role in employee engagement and organizational citizenship behaviour as well as in retaining employees and building a talent brand, which subsequently attracts prospective job seekers (Raj, 2018). Employer branding is considered a useful staff retention strategy by influencing employment experience of employees thereby increasing job engagement and reducing voluntary turnover (Riley, 2009).

Employer brand research report (2019) by Randstad shows that 'a fifth of the global workforce has changed employers in the past year [i.e., 2018] and a third plans to do so in the coming year [i.e., 2020].' 'With workforce on the move, employers are forced to come up with ingenious ways to attract and retain talent and need tailor-made approaches to accomplish this' (Randstad, 2019). We believe offering a customized and compelling employee value proposition (EVP), similar to customer value proposition (CVP), can be a response to talent attrition challenges. EVP is an important employer-branding tool which involves offering an employment package that is relevant to employees and different than what is provided by other employers.

Relevance of Employer Branding in Banking Organizations

In the banking sector, revenues and profits depend on the quality of services and customer satisfaction. Empirical research (Afsar et al., 2010) shows that main determinants of customer loyalty in banking sector are perceived to be quality, trust, satisfaction and commitment. The concept of service-profit chain suggests that satisfied employees will create satisfied customers and finally, positive business results (Hesket et al., 2008). Therefore, managing existing employees very well, through employer branding strategies, can be an important source of competitive advantage in services sector including banking.

Employer brand employs customer brand experience framework in managing employees. HR touchpoints such as recruitment process, orientation, employee communication, shared services, reward, employee engagement surveys, performance management and employee development are various HR areas using which distinctive employer brand experience can be created (Mosley, 2007). Employer brand can facilitate the translation of brand ethos into the everyday experience of employees, which reinforces the organization's ability to deliver consistent and unique customer brand experiences (Mosley, 2007).

Scholars have suggested that employer branding can play a key role in the creation, protection and promotion of corporate reputation (Burke et al., 2011; Walsh & Beatty, 2007). In fact, 'employer branding should reflect the bank's identity, culture, image and reputation; and position the bank as an employer of choice for effective talent attraction, engagement and retention' (Maheshwari et al., 2017, p. 754).

In the banking sector, employees are less likely to look for alternative employment opportunities and they prefer job security and career growth opportunities within the organization (Wallace et al., 2014). Employer branding can provide holistic employment experience by fulfilling psychological contract and it can be a tool to enhance employee engagement through the employment package provided in the form of economic, psychological and functional benefits (Barrow & Mosley, 2005). Employers can differentiate in the competitive labour market through psychological benefits (e.g., feeling good at the workplace) which are likely to contribute in employee engagement (Barrow & Mosley, 2005).

Employer attractiveness is another area where employer branding can be useful in the banking sector. Various reports show that the banking sector is not among the most preferred sectors for job seekers (financial services was 6th most preferred sector while services was 10th most preferred sector among a total of 13 sectors (Randstad, 2019)]. Using the employer branding approach, banks can identify the employment attributes which are distinct and relevant to the new-age (Generation Y and Z) job seekers and can amplify them in their recruitment communications, such as campus relations and career websites. This could enhance the attractiveness of the bank relative to the competitors and possibly other industries as well.

Designing Compelling EVP

The concept of EVP is an integral part of employer branding. This is similar to the CVP that marketers use for customer. EVP represents the package of reward features or employment advantages and benefits offered to employees, consistent with organizational values, characteristics and attributes. Eisenberg et al. (2001) suggest that the value proposition provides the central message that is conveyed by an employer brand and it truly represents what the firm offers to its employees.

EVP development and communication process can broadly be divided into three steps. First, the identification of expectations of target audience (i.e., current and potential employees); second, the design and development of EVP considering the competitive scenario and company's values, culture and identity); third, communication of EVP to external and internal target audience including other stakeholders.

The first step in EVP design is much like customer research in the marketing field wherein the preferences of target audience are identified. In this step, the expectations of current and potential employees about their preferences for employment attributes are discovered. Several methods can be used for this. These include internal employee surveys, exit interviews, survey of job applicants in specific college campuses, employee engagement and job satisfaction surveys. Additionally, consulting organizations such as Randstad, Deloitte and KMPG regularly publish reports highlighting the employment preferences of both job seekers and employees and their sectoral preferences. Based on this data, an employer would know what is expected by the target audience from their (current or prospective) employer. The employer can prioritize the expectations of target audience and then assess its strength and weakness in each area, that is, how well the employer is positioned vis-à-vis the target audience's expectations.

The second step involves knowing the organization's culture, values and identity. In other words, to understand what the company is known for and what are its values. What is the culture of the organization? Understanding this is very important as EVP should be aligned with the company's values and its corporate brand because any difference will be starkly visible. The other important aspect in EVP design includes knowing about competitors and their offerings. The employer needs to identify the relevant competitors against whom they are competing for the same talent pool. An understanding about the competitors' offerings will facilitate a comparison between the employer and its competitors on each employment attribute that is relevant to the target audience. It would provide useful benchmarking data for assessing the employer's position vis-à-vis its competitors on employment offerings. An effective EVP includes a good mix of current strengths and future aspirations. Employer branding expert Mosley (Mosley, 2012) suggests that the main elements of an EVP include the core areas of employer brand, brand positioning, personality and pillars.

Third and final step includes the communication and promotion of the designed EVP to external and internal target audience. Considering that there are two major target audiences—current and prospective employees—for EVP communication, banks should identify separate communication messages and channels for each target group. For prospective employees, the employer can also identify the college campuses that it visits for hiring, and then design campus events for making job applicants aware about the EVP offerings. Studies (Gunesh & Maheshwari, 2019) have shown the use of career websites to disseminate the employer brand in the banking sector. The pre-placement talk sessions can highlight the EVP offerings clearly. For existing employees, internal communication channels such as induction orientation, intranet, newsletters, company magazines, customized emailers and company events can be used for disseminating EVP within the organization.

Two important things must be considered very carefully while designing and communicating EVP. First, EVP elements and their communications must be clearly aligned with the company's values, identity, culture and more specifically, its corporate brand. According to the LinkedIn Talent Solutions report (2016), 85 per cent of respondents consider that the organization's mission, culture and values can be the main elements of the employer brand. Second, EVP communications and signals across communication platforms must be clear, consistent and credible (3Cs). Scholars (i.e., Wallace et al., 2014; Wilden et al., 2010) have highlighted a significant role of 3Cs in employer brand creation.

EVP Positioning and Communication Framework

This section discusses the EVP and communication framework developed by the author. It is shown in Figure 14.1.

1. **Expectations of target audience:** These expectations cover preferences of job seekers such as compensation, better professional development, work–life balance, challenging work, opportunities for career advancement and work-culture. These can be identified through customized studies of current and prospective employees about their preferences for employment attributes. There are also readily available industry/consultant reports on employee preferences that can be used.

2. **Your offerings:** These include attraction and retention drivers of the organization for which EVP design is proposed. These can be discovered by in-depth interviews of employees at various levels and study of job seekers about the organization. Retention drivers could be job profile,

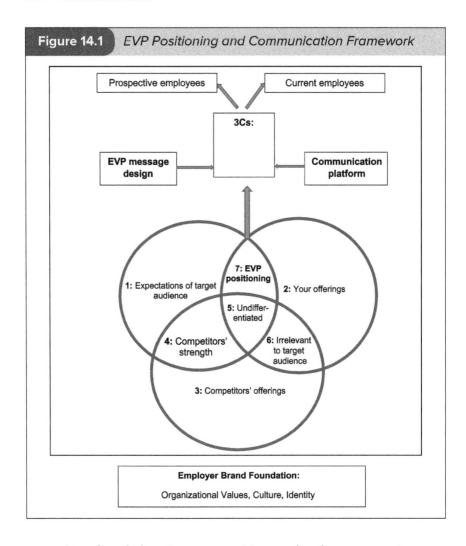

Figure 14.1 *EVP Positioning and Communication Framework*

quality of work, learning opportunities, work culture, supportive team members, flexibility and freedom at workplace. Attraction drivers could be a strong brand name, client-facing roles, opportunity to work with a diverse range of businesses, prospects to work with high quality talent, challenging work environment, friendly work culture, meritocracy and access to senior management.

3. **Competitors' offerings:** This will include the offerings from competitors such as compensation, career opportunities and work–life balance. Here, it is important to identify the relevant competitors in the talent market. The organization should understand its employees' views in defining their competitors.

4. **Competitors' strength:** These are the target audience's expectation areas where competitors are performing better than the organization. For instance, compensation, career opportunities and work-life balance may be better or perceived as better at a few competitors' banks.

5. **Undifferentiated areas:** These are the target audience's expectation areas where the organization and competitors are performing equally well. There are attribute areas which nearly all competing organizations provide to target audience. Examples include opportunities for career advancement and work-life balance.

6. **Irrelevant to target audience:** These include offerings by the organization and competitors which are not valued or expected by the target audience. In practice, it is difficult to identify such areas because no company offers something which is not valued by the target audience. Hence, it may be more useful to identify offerings which are important to the target audience.

7. **EVP positioning:** These are the target audience's expectations which are not fulfilled by the competitors' offerings and your organization has a competitive advantage. For instance, you may perform better than competitors in culture and values. In this, your organization should identify expectation areas of target audience where your organization is better than other relevant competitors. The EVP should be positioned in this area.

Guidelines for Practising Employer Branding

1. **Designing a comprehensive and integrated employer branding programme:** Currently, employer branding is practiced in a piece-meal manner. Minchington (2015) suggests that organizations view the employer branding as project-based rather than ongoing agenda. We recommend that employer branding should be seen as a long-term investment for talent management, and practised as an ongoing activity rather than a project-based strategy. Furthermore, it is important to take a multidisciplinary perspective. In fact, Minchington (2015) suggests that successful employer branding practice needs a deep collaboration between marketing, HR and communications.

2. **Aligning employer branding with corporate branding and product branding:** Empirical studies have shown that both product and corporate brands significantly influence talent attraction (Banerjee et al., 2020; Ewing et al., 2002; Harris & Chernatony, 2001; Kim

et al., 2011). Specifically, DelVecchio et al. (2007) found that applicants' evaluation of job characteristics is affected by consumer brand equity. Further, an underperforming product or service brand may have negative spill-over effects on employer brand. Scholars recommend that the employer brand should grow out of the established company brand, and talent framework should be fully embedded into the business (Banta & Watras, 2019).

3. **Segmentation approach to talent management and employer branding:** Considering the diverse workforce and its varying expectations from employers, the one-size-fits-all approach for EVP is unlikely to work in a dynamic talent market. Alnıaçık et al. (2014) recommend that HR practitioners need to understand the relevance of differentiated and customized EVPs and communicate the same through employer-branding communication channels. There is need to adopt the 'one-size-fits-one customized employment' approach (Fitz-enz, 2010).

4. **Managing crowdsource-based employer branding platforms:** Recently, a new form of employer branding known as crowdsourced employer branding (CSEB) has emerged (Dabirian et al., 2017). In CSEB, former and current employees voluntarily share their employment-related experiences on social network platforms such as Glassdoor (Kietzmann, 2017). Surprisingly, only 45 per cent of employers monitor and address those reviews (Talentnow, 2018). Hence, we recommend that firms should actively manage their employer brand and reputation on CSEB platforms.

5. **Effective use of social media for employer brand communication:** With the advent and proliferation of social media, a plethora of digital recruitment opportunities have opened up. We believe that the effective communication of a well-crafted employer brand on several social media channels can significantly impact the candidate's decision about its potential employer (Pant, 2019). It should be noted that 65 per cent of companies were able to increase their brand recognition from the employee advocacy posted on social media platforms (Hinge Research Institute, n.d.).

6. **Top management support and buy-in employer branding programme:** Any employer branding effort without top management support will be a waste. Barrow and Mosley (2005, p. 46) suggested that 'it can mean rocking the status quo, breaking down silos, establishing new roles and relationships and answering difficult questions on what the organizations stands for, and why?' Bondarouk et al. (2014) recommend that HR practitioners need to develop strategic thinking,

innovation and leadership skills for garnering necessary support for employer branding strategy.

7. **HR and employer brand managers need to think like a marketer:** Since EVP development process is very similar to developing a CVP, thinking like a marketer will help in designing a customer-oriented (i.e., current and potential employees focused) EVP. To follow marketing orientation philosophy, practitioners need to understand the key marketing and branding principles as well as traditional and social media-based communication methods for talent attraction (Bondarouk et al., 2013). The amalgamation of marketing and HR management theories and the consideration of potential and current talents as customers generates a customer-oriented employer branding (Jothi, 2010).

8. **Developing employees as brand ambassador:** Another useful strategy to generate a favourable attitude towards the employer brand is the use of a brand ambassador. Employer branding team can identify the employees who matter most or 'employees who make the brand … by creating a brand reputation and a work environment attractive to the potential hires who will improve brand equity even more' (Gelb & Rangarajan, 2014). Such employees can be designated as brand ambassadors for promoting the employer brand internally as well as externally, including at college campuses.

9. **Set your internal branding and communications right:** Employer brand managers should make use of internal communications to reinforce, periodically, to the employees that they are the brand. Internal branding should provide employees with a clear understanding of what the employer brand and its promises are. Bankins and Waterhouse (2019, p. 227) propose that, 'If current employees have better (poorer) perceptions of organizational identity, this will result in better (poorer) perceptions of organizational reputation and overall employer attractiveness.'

10. **Feedback and continuous improvement in EVP and employer branding:** Remember that the EVP once designed is not the EVP forever. The talent market is dynamic because of the changing composition and evolving requirements of the workforce. A prudent strategy to remain relevant is to differentiate in the talent market by incorporating the changing trends into the brand. One way to do this is through feedback from employees on important areas such as the company strategy, its purpose and current employment offer whilst imagining they were still looking at the organization as a potential place to work (Banta & Watras, 2019).

References

Afsar, B., Rehman, Z., Qureshi, J. A., & Shahjehan, A. (2010). Determinants of customer loyalty in the banking sector: The case of Pakistan. *African Journal of Business Management*, 4(6), 1040–1047.

Alnıaçık, E., Alnıaçık, U., Erat, S., & Akçin, K. (2014). Attracting talented employees to the company: Do we need different employer branding strategies in different cultures? *10th International Strategic Management Conference Procedia, Social and Behavioral Sciences*: Vol. 150 (pp. 336–344). http://doi.org/10.1016/j.sbspro.2014.09.074

App, S., Merk, J., & Buttgen, M. (2012). Employer branding: Sustainable HRM as a competitive advantage in the market for high-quality employees. *Management Revue*, 23(3), 262–278.

Auger, P., Devinney, T. M., Dowling, G. R., Eckert, C., & Lin, N. (2013, 19 March). How much does a company's reputation matter in recruiting? *MIT Sloan Management Review*, Spring 2013.

Backhaus, K., & Tikoo, S. (2004). Conceptualizing and researching employer branding. *Career Development International*, 9(5), 501–517.

Banerjee, P., Saini, G. K., & Kalyanaram, G. (2020), The role of brands in recruitment: Mediating role of employer brand equity. *Asia Pacific Journal of Human Resources*, 58(2), 173–196.

Bankins, S., & Waterhouse, J. (2019). Organizational identity, image, and reputation: examining the influence on perceptions of employer attractiveness in public sector organizations. *International Journal of Public Administration*, 42(3), 218–229.

Banta, K., & Watras, M. (2019, June). Why we need to rethink 'employer brand'. *Harvard Business Review*. https://hbr.org/2019/06/why-we-need-to-rethink-employer-brand

Barrow, S., & Mosley, R. (2005). *The employer brand: Bringing the best of brand management to people at work*. John Wiley & Sons.

Becker, B., Huselid, M., & Ulrich, D. (2001). *The HR scorecard: Linking people, strategy, and performance*. Harvard Business School Press.

Bondarouk, T., Marsman, E., & Rekers, M. (2014). HRM, technology and innovation: New HRM competencies for old business challenges? *Human Resource Management, Social Innovation and Technology Advanced Series in Management, 14*, 179–215.

Bondarouk, T., Ruël, H., Axinia, E., & Arama, R. (2013). What is the future of employer branding through social media? Results of the Delphi study into the perceptions of HR professionals and academics. *Social Media in Human Resources Management Advanced Series in Management, 12*, 23–57.

Burke, R. F., Martin, G., & Cooper, C. L. (2011). *Corporate reputations: Managing opportunities and threats*. Gower.

Cable, D. M., & Turban, D. B. (2001). Establishing the dimensions, sources and value of job seekers' employer knowledge during recruitment. *Research in Personnel and Human Resources Management, 20*, 115–163.

CareerArc. (2017). 29 surprising stats on employer branding—Infographic. https://www.careerarc.com/blog/2017/11/employer-branding-study-infographic/

Collins, C. J., & Stevens, C. K. (2002). The relationship between early recruitment-related activities and the application decisions of new labor-market entrants: A brand equity approach to recruitment. *Journal of Applied Psychology, 87*(60), 1121–1133.

Dabirian, A., Kietzmann, J., & Diba, H. (2017). A great place to work!? Understanding crowdsourced employer branding. *Business Horizons, 60*(2), 197–205.

DelVecchio, D., Jarvis, C. B., Klink, R. R., & Dineen, B. R. (2007). Leveraging brand equity to attract human capital. *Marketing Letters, 18*(3), 149–164.

Edwards, M. R. (2010). An integrative review of employer branding and OB theory. *Personnel Review, 39*(1), 5–23.

Eisenberg, B., Kilduff, C., Burleigh, S., & Wilson, K. (2001). *The role of the value proposition and employment branding in retaining top talent.* Society for Human Resource Management.

Ewing, M., Pitt, L., & De Bussy, N. (2002). Employment branding in the knowledge economy. *International Journal of Advertising, 21*, 3–22.

Fitz-enz, J. (2010). *The new HR analytics: Predicting the economic value of your company's human capital investments* (p. 67). AMACOM, American Management Association.

Gelb, B. D., & Rangarajan, D. (2014). Employee contributions to brand equity. *California Management Review, 56*(2), 95–112.

Gunesh, P., & Maheshwari, V. (2019). Role of organizational career websites for employer brand development. *International Journal of Organizational Analysis, 27*(1), 149–168.

Harris F., & Chernatony, L. D. (2001). Corporate branding and corporate brand performance. *European Journal of Marketing, 35*(3/4), 441–456.

Heskett, J. L., Jones, T. O., Loveman, G. W., Sasser, W. E., & Schlesinger, L. A., (2008, July–August). Putting the service-profit chain to work. *Harvard Business Review*, 118–129.

Hewitt. (2009). Point of view: What makes a company a best employer? http://www.aon. com/attachments/thought-leadership/pov_Best_Employer_Position_Paper.pdf

Hinge Research Institute. (n.d.) *Understanding employee advocacy on social media.* https:// hingemarketing.com/uploads/hinge-research-employee-advocacy.pdf

Jothi, V. (2010). HR marketing. Recruiting Blogs [Web log post]. www.recruitingblogs. com/profiles/blogs/hr-marketing

Keller, K. L. (2011). *Strategic brand management: Building, measuring, and managing brand equity.* Pearson Education.

Kietzmann, J. H. (2017). Crowdsourcing: A revised definition and an introduction to new research. *Business Horizons, 60*(2), 151–153.

Kim, J., York, K. M., & Lim, J. S. (2011). The role of brands in recruitment: A mixed-brand strategy approach. *Marketing Letters, 22*(2), 165–179.

Lado, A. A., & Wilson, M. C. (1994). Human resource systems and sustained competitive advantage: A competency-based perspective. *Academy of Management Review, 19*(4), 699–727.

Lievens, F., & Highhouse, S. (2003). The relation of instrumental and symbolic attributes to a company's attractiveness as an employer. *Personnel Psychology, 56*, 75–102.

Lievens, F., Van Hoye, G., & Anseel, F. (2007). Organizational identity and employer image: Towards a unifying framework. *British Journal of Management, 18*, S45–S59.

LinkedIn Talent Solutions. (2016). *2016 talent trends reports.* https://business.linkedin.com/ talent-solutions/job-trends/2016-talent-trends-home#all

Maheshwari, V., Gunesh, P., Lodorfos, G., & Konstantopoulou, A. (2017). Exploring HR practitioners' perspective on employer branding and its role in organisational attractiveness and talent management. *International Journal of Organizational Analysis, 25*(5), 742–761.

Martindale, N. (2010, February). Think before you leap. *Personnel Today*, 18–46.

Michaels, E., Handfield-Jones, H., & Axelrod, B. (2001). *The war for talent.* Harvard Business School Press.

Minchington, B. (2015). Who must lead employer branding? International waters-employer branding. *HR Future, 9*, 14–17.

Mosley, R. (2007). Customer experience, organizational culture and the employer brand. *Journal of Brand Management, 15* (2), 123–134.

Mosley, R. (2012). EVP development. In R, Mosley. (Ed.), *Employer rand management: Practical lessons from the world's leading employers* (pp. 123–142). John Wiley and Sons Ltd.

Pant, D. (2019). Crafting an employer brand that attracts talent. People Matters. https://www.peoplematters.in/article/employer-branding/crafting-an-employer-brand-that-attracts-talent-22972 1/6

Raj, A. B. (2018). Employee well-being through internal branding: An integrated approach for achieving employee-based brand outcomes. *Global Business Review, 21*(3), 1–22.

Randstad. (2019). Employer brand research 2019, global report. https://www.randstad.in/employer-brand-research/global-report-2019.pdf

Riley, C. (2009). Employment brands to protect against increased staff churn in recovery. *Keeping Good Companies, 61*(11), 688.

Sullivan, J. (2004, 23 February). Eight elements of a successful employment brand. *ER Daily*.

Sundberg, J. (2020). Employer brand vs. employee experience. Link Humans. https://linkhumans.com/employer-brand-employee-experience/

Talentnow. (2018). Recruitment statistics 2018: Trends & insights in hiring talented candidates. https://www.talentnow.com/recruitment-statistics-2018-trends-insights-hiring-talented-candidates/

Wallace, M., Lings, I., Cameron, R., & Sheldon, N. (2014). Attracting and retaining staff: The role of branding and industry image (pp. 19–36). In R. Harris, & T. Short (Eds.), *Workforce development*. Springer. https://link.springer.com/chapter/10.1007/978-981-4560-58-0_2.

Walsh, G., & Beatty, S. E. (2007). Customer-based corporate reputation of a service firm: Scale development and validation. *Journal of the Academic Marketing Science, 35*(1), 127–144.

Wilden, R., Gudergan, S., & Lings, I. (2010). Employer branding: strategic implications for staff recruitment. *Journal of Marketing Management, 26*(1–2), 56–73.

Trade Unions in the Digital Economy with Special Reference to the Banking Sector in India

Kuriakose Mamkoottam

Introduction

COVID-19 moved rapidly from one country to another, engulfing the whole of humanity in a short span of time. The pandemic and the consequent lockdown have changed the world in dramatic ways. It is likely to affect us much more deeply with its long-standing effect on the global economy. The epidemic is already beginning to redefine the way we live and work, the way we interact with each other, our consuming patterns, travel and entertainment preferences. In fact, the COVID-19 lockdown has opened a small window to view the future world of digital economy far beyond what we experience today. Digital technology is likely to dominate the world of work as well as our private lives much quicker and faster now.

Digital Technology and the Gig Economy

Digital technology, which is ushering in the 'fourth Industrial Revolution', is a combination of many things including the internet, robotics, algorithm, analytics, artificial intelligence (AI), big data, cloud computing, open source, online community and platforms. 'Gig economy' is a common term today. Innovative use of technology has contributed to the rapid proliferation of 'gigs' or one-off jobs. Different kinds of non-standard employment by creating digitally mediated labour marketplaces or labour platforms has led to the development of the gig economy. These platforms help connect workers with consumers for one-off tasks or jobs that are completed either virtually or in person by an on-demand workforce. This workforce operates with limited social and labour protections.

Impact of Digital Economy on Labour Market and Employment

There is a view that the fourth Industrial Revolution will create many new jobs. However, the reality is that it will destroy many more repetitive tasks, thereby making a large number of the existing labour force redundant and jobless. While 'jobless growth' had gained currency since the advent of computerized work processes during the 1980s, this time there is a real threat of a 'jobless future' (Ford, 2015). According to a study by Frey and Osborne (2013), around 47 per cent of total US employment is in the high-risk category and is likely to be lost. Similarly, 40–60 per cent of workforce in the European Union countries are likely to be impacted by advances in technology over the coming decades. However, others like Roubini (2015) claim that in a country like Germany the proportion of employees whose jobs are under threat from automation is not likely to be more than 12 per cent. Interestingly, the services sector which, not long ago, overtook other sectors as the main source of employment and revenue generations, is likely to be significantly impacted by digital technology.

Employment in the gig economy is not governed by the traditional norms of employment. The relationship is based on a partnership model governed by a contract of self-employment. In a way, the new form of employment may be seen as an addition to the unorganized sector, which is crying for legislative intervention. For example, if we examine the contract signed between Uber services and the 'customer' (the customer here being the transportation company) on the one hand, and that between the transportation company and the driver on the other, we find that the two contracts together cover, directly or indirectly, all four (major) concerned parties, namely Uber Services as a technology platform; the direct customer, who is a transport service provider; the driver, who delivers the service; and finally, the end user (passenger), who actually consumes the service (Uber, 2020a, 2020b). Uber enters into a business-to-business relationship with the transport company. The contract authorizes a transportation company (customer) to engage in transportation services in the areas of jurisdiction(s) in which it operates. In fact, Uber does not function as a transportation carrier or agent for the transportation of passengers. The agreement absolves Uber of any ownership or accountability in the entire process of the actual operation or chain of actions carried out for providing the transportation service to the end user (passenger). The status of employees, who are engaged in the gig economy, is ambiguous. The recent recommendation of the general counsel, who was appointed to the National Labour Relations Board by the US president, said in the memo dated 16 April 2019 that Uber drivers cannot be considered employees under (the US) Federal Labour Law because they own their own vehicles, set their hours and are free to work for the company's competitors. Freelance contractors are not treated as workers as they cannot become members of trade unions and are not entitled to the various protection under the law. Uber is an example, perhaps an important one, which treats its drivers as contractors; a model which became a trendsetter and spread to different parts of the world in quick time.

Legislation, in most countries, has classified employment into different categories, each with privileges and obligations. However, the new category of workers called 'crowd workers' and millions of those engaged in virtual platforms have thrown up a new challenge for the regulators to differentiate between genuine self-employment and the crowd workers of the gig economy.

Labour Response and Trade Unions

The gig economy could be a serious challenge for workers as existing models of unions and collective bargaining may not be of help, especially within the existing legislative framework. As more and more tasks are getting automated and digitized, both in the manufacturing and in the service sector, more jobs will be outsourced to crowd workers, who perform low-skilled and repetitive tasks. Such monotonous, low-skilled and low-paid work, with no spatial constraints, has very little or no marketplace bargaining power.

A recent survey of 120 platforms, such as Uber, Amazon, Flipkart, Zomato etc., across 23 countries—Europe, North America, South America, Asia (including India), and Africa—carried out by the Fairwork project (2020), found that the stakeholder focus was skewed in favour of shareholders, investors and customers compared to workers, even though it is the workers who constitute the foundation of the 'platform'. The main conclusion of the study was that the workers were most concerned about the assurance of pay to maintain their income level. With the exception of a few, platform-based enterprises did not accept such responsibility. Their primary focus has been on measures to protect customer interests with minimal efforts to protect that of the workers. Further, the study found that platform (companies) across the globe during the COVID-19 crisis were,

> Offering loans rather than grants to workers with financial difficulties; deferring rather than waiving loan repayments; simply telling workers to disinfect rather than monitoring that they do so; providing general health and safety guidance

information rather than bespoke personal advice; paying minimum sick pay rather than maintaining past earnings during illness.

It is against introduction of technology that trade unions fought major battles during the past decades with employers, most of which the unions may have lost. Trade unions, more than in any other institution in the world, have made the most significant contributions to improve wages, working conditions and the overall quality of life for the workers. At the same time, trade unions cannot be said to be among the quickest institutions to introspect and find solutions in response to new situations. Unions have not often been innovative enough in restructuring their organizations or re-visioning their strategies to deal with new challenges. Trade unions, at the same time, have also received the worst criticism from different sections of the society, including governments, employers/management, civil society and even the workers themselves. Trade unions are institutions of contradictions. This could partly be explained by the fact that they have been influenced by larger politics and political ideologies of different kinds.

Like in politics and political parties, values, goals and agenda of trade unions have been influenced by the leadership, may be unduly so. It is never easy for voluntary organizations like trade unions to remain focused on the goals and values of the large membership base, as the base itself may not have a shared set of goals and values on many issues. Perhaps, for this reason alone the leadership of trade unions have not found it easy to lead a unified front. By and large, it often gets guided and supported by a small percentage of its membership, leaving a large section of the members dissatisfied, and gradually, apathetic to the union and its operations. This, in turn, makes the union leadership oligarchic, serving the goals of a small coterie of individuals (Mamkoottam, 1982). On one hand, the oligarchic leadership distances the larger base of the membership, the limited interest and participation by the larger membership creates a self-serving oligarchy within unions on the other. This kind of vicious circle is commonly found in many voluntary organizations and political parties. The relevant question to ask here could be if the trade unions are ready and willing to face the challenge thrown up by the digital economy, the new workplace and the emerging labour market. Are the existing structures and strategies of trade unions capable of dealing with the rapidly changing world of the digital technology and the emerging gig economy? Unions have been asked similar questions many times at regular intervals in the past, more often and more sharply since the advent of computerization and automation of the workplace during the 1970s–1980s. As we know, the traditional trade-based unions, which were successful until the beginning of the 20th century, have been overshadowed, though not totally replaced by industrial unionism, peaking in the 1960s–1970s. So, there is a need and possibility for alternate and different forms of structures and strategies to emerge that can represent the workers of the digital technology and the gig economy.

The Case of Banking Sector

Much like other sectors of industry and business, the banking sector, too, has to reinvent itself in order to respond to technology. The digitization of the banking system demands reformulation of business strategies and organizational restructuring to achieve economy of cost and efficiency of operations. New business models and operating systems require the reimagination of customer experience and employee engagement. Digitized banking not only increases efficiency of operations but also, by introducing many new products and services, it takes the banking process closer to the customer empowering him/her to enjoy 24 × 7 banking services. A labour-intensive banking system will, gradually, become technology intensive. The process, while automating the routine and repetitive tasks, has transferred many of the tasks to the customer, which were traditionally performed by the banking employee, just as it happens in travel, tourism, hospitality or many other service sector activities.

The digitization process is based on major changes in the traditional systems of banking, both in terms of front-desk operations and back-office systems. These systems and processes, which are built on data, analytics and AI, facilitate the transfer of data, processing events and services throughout the enterprise, leading to automated decisions. The new systems and processes not only accelerate error-free and speedy responsiveness—an integral element of efficient process—but also leads to reduction of cost while increasing revenue. The banking sector across the world, including in India in a limited manner, has started to take advantage of the platform-based (gig) economy and use social media to reach out and stay connected with digital customers.

Trade Unions and the Future of Indian Banking

Issues relating to data confidentiality, security, regulatory compliance, inter-operability of standards and quality of services are of critical importance to banks. Legacy technology has made it difficult for most traditional banks across the globe to compete with new, tech-driven competitors. However, new solutions are expected to make banking institutions more agile and consumer-focused. It is predicted that the next big push in AI and machine learning will be able to extract data from within banks' own firewalls. Few banks in the world have, so far, deployed advanced technologies, such as platforms or AI to their advantage. Apart from investing in expensive technologies, banks may have to make major structural changes, staff restructuring and cultural adjustments in order to be able to embrace the digital or platform technologies.

Introduction of digital banking will lead to a dramatic reduction in the workforce. Often, business inertia, legacy, monetary policies and conservative shareholders may delay the banks from introducing innovation and change. In India, the banking sector is in a different situation as many of the large banks are in the public sector, that is, under the purview of the State. Some of the leading banks across the globe, including those in the private sector in India, have shown how investments in digital technologies could be critical, especially for customer retention, expansion and customer satisfaction. It is perhaps by adopting new technologies which allow data-driven decisions that the banks can become more flexible to find innovative solutions to reduce cost and offer quick and error-free services such as cashless transaction and many other personalized customer experiences in an extremely competitive environment.

A Capgemini report on 'Cloud Computing in Banks' (Sriram, 2011) enumerates numerous benefits such as cost saving and usage-based billing, business continuity, business agility and focus as well as green IT among major gains. Apart from avoiding heavy investments in hardware and software, cloud computing allows banks and financial institutions to choose services as required and pay for them accordingly. Instead of the banks, the provider becomes responsible for managing technology and the banks will benefit from higher levels of data protection, disaster recovery and so on. More importantly, cloud-based operating models allow for shorter development cycles, faster product development and quicker customer response. Above all, cloud computing is said to the reduce energy consumption and carbon footprint from the better utilization of physical infrastructures. It is clearly a matter of time as more and more confidence, trust and reliability develop in this new technology before financial institutions and banks will adopt them in good measure.

Similarly, a report by Deutsche Bank (2015) highlighted the urgency of adopting innovative IT in banking which has huge potential for cost saving, among other things. Customers are said to be leading the drive for

digitalization of banking. They constantly compare and expect global standards in terms of their needs being met, ease of transaction and how enjoyable
it was. What makes newer technology more attractive is its economic benefit
in terms of lowering costs while increasing revenue and security. However,
banks will need to develop strategies that optimize processes and costs while
being able to manage increased volumes of data and connect the data to the
business and fulfil the legal/ regulatory requirements. This entire process is
expected to continuously engage with customers, partners, employees and
investors (Sriram, 2011). In order to remain competitive, banks may have
no choice but to accept the challenges of (digital) structural change and
redesign their operating models. Many of the global banks are said to have
invested or set aside billions of euros or dollars for taking advantage of the
digital technology.

In India, the public sector banks have been playing a major role as they
contribute the largest share—as much as 70 per cent or more—of the Indian
banking system. The banking sector will continue to play a major role in
the future of the country's economy. Apart from rendering routine services,
banks are required to lend finance and facilitate growth and development of
the economy, be it through infrastructure or other new initiatives, and ensure
financial inclusion of the population in the market economy. Regardless
of their many achievements, the public sector banks have not been able to
keep up with their counterparts in the private sector, especially in terms of
new products and customer satisfaction. By responding better and quicker
to customer needs, the private sector banks have gradually eroded the market
share and traditional customer base of those in the public sector.

Human resources are among the most important assets for organizations
to be able to face the challenges of change, and banking is no exception. The
quality of employees, in terms of knowledge, skills and attitude, provide
the cutting edge to competition. Appropriate human resource management policies and practices are critical to attract, motivate and retain human
talent, enhance performance and enable the organization to be competitive.
The Khandelwal Committee report (2010) on 'HR Issues of Public Sector
Banks' identified some of the HR challenges before the public sector banks
and made several recommendations to make them more professional and
competitive.

> Capacity building for the future; improving productivity and performance culture;
> building talent management practices; building succession planning for key critical
> and leadership positions; developing ownership, accountability, professionaliza-
> tion and institutional mechanism for sustained human capital y management;

transforming HR function from legacy driven HR to developmental HR, etc.
(Khandelwal Committee, 2010)

are, undoubtedly, among important HR challenges before the public sector
banks.

Recruitment, retention and motivation strategies play a paramount role in
the management of all organizations. Reward, recognition and performance
management systems and practices are the cornerstones of a performing
organization, which consists of motivated and talented people driven by
energy, enthusiasm and are constantly impatient to innovate and improve.
Unfortunately, the existing system of HR practices prevalent in the public
sector banks in India lack imagination, if not archaic. Wages and service
conditions for employees up to the level of general managers of all banks
are settled through industry-wide negotiations between representatives of
the Indian Banks' Association, an apex organization of all the nationalized
banks, and a group of national trade unions (in total—nine) representing the
employees of the public sector banks. Interestingly, as much as 98 per cent
of banking employees from the public sector banks are represented by one
or the other of these unions. The single largest and the oldest among them
all is the All India Banking Employees' Association (AIBEA), established in
1946, which represents around 35 per cent of the employees of the public
sector banks.

In a telephonic conversation, Rajen Nagar, President of AIBEA for more
than two decades, was frank and forthcoming in sharing his views with me
on the future of banking, especially in view of technological changes and
other banking reforms under process. According to him, AIBEA, or for
that matter any other union, is not against automation or modernization
of banking. However, they are opposed to privatization and the increasing
trend in contracting out permanent jobs, thereby expanding the informal
sector. The union president deplored that, in some branches, the share
of permanent staff has become as little as 10 per cent of the total staff.
AIBEA is proud of its achievements to have created the culture of collective bargaining with the nationalized banks. The union is equally proud
that it has constantly helped improve wages and the working conditions
for employees. The unions have relentlessly fought to promote banking
in the public sector, ensuring stable employment and social security of
banking employees.

The union believes that banking should remain in the domain of the
government as banks deal with public money and should be engaged in
the development of social capital. The president of the AIBEA was

of the view that the so-called banking reforms that are being ushered by the government help only the private corporations, allowing them to borrow large amount of money and not return them with impunity. The union is also against the proposed amalgamation of many banks into four or five, as the process will destroy many jobs and other benefits to the country. The unions are not against automation or digitalization of banks. According to Nagar, although it may have been the ICICI bank which started with digitalization way back in 1996, it was public sector banks like the SBI which took the lead. Even today, a large percentage of the 280,000 ATMs in the country are established and maintained by the public sector banks. Unions do not oppose introduction of new technologies or restructuring of the banking process, however, they do not approve the increasing rate of the privatization and informalization of the banking sector. While the new technology brings new jobs along with it, these new jobs are invariably created outside the formal economy, thereby expanding the informal sector. What is not acceptable is the fact that as of today, trade union rights are not available to the employees of the informal sector. As a strategy to address the issues of the informal sector, AIBEA has started to organize the informal sector employees as well.

The Khandelwal Committee (2010) had observed in its report that the new thrust of banking is mainly on sales and marketing, and accordingly, the skill structure needed to change. The committee also observed that the HR policies are largely driven by external compulsions rather than by the banks' business objectives. Many banks are said to have major problems in redeployment of clerical staff, constrained by banks' own internal settlements as well as industry-level settlement. Similarly, several rural and semi-urban branches are understaffed, whereas they have pockets of excess clerical staff at metro and urban centres. The committee recommended the need to review policies that affect mobility, flexible utilization of staff, productivity, performance and customer service. In fact, the president of AIBEA is not against interbranch posting or transfer of the clerical staff, but it has to be decided on the basis of discussion and negotiation with the union representatives at the branch level.

In view of the increasingly competitive scenario of the emerging Indian banking sector, the Khandelwal Committee recommended that performance and productivity should not only be included but take the centre stage in the new agenda of union management negotiation. The unions are not against performance assessment. In the words of AIBEA president, in any case, all promotions are based on performance. After a person has been assessed and promoted, his/her salary cannot be based on further assessment. Moreover, trade unions do not agree to any local level bargaining or negotiation for wages. They believe that wages have to be negotiated and settled only centrally at the national level. According to him, wages and working conditions have to be standardized for all employees at all branches of the banks. One may, of course, argue that the current practice of wage settlement may have no bearing on the performance of the individual employee or that of individual banks. This system leaves little or no powers at the level of the head of the branch to reward or discipline a subordinate. The trade union assumes an extraordinary role to negotiate on matters of promotion, transfer and redeployment of employees.

The union president said that trade unions always embraced new technology but expressed concern at the anti-labour attitude of the government of the day. During COVID-19, labour, in general, and migrant labour, in particular, have been poorly treated. Trade unions have registered protests, though they cannot go on public protest or demonstration during this time. The unions have announced 3 July 2020 as the day of national public protest against anti-labour policies of the governments in the temporary suspension of some of the crucial labour laws which are fundamental to the livelihood and security of the labour force. In fact, since 2014, the current government has not approved the list of worker and officer representatives at the board level, which was a statutory practice. Although AIBEA made representation to approve the list of worker and officer representatives, the government has not acted. It returned the list saying that one of the worker representatives did not have the mandatory five-year experience. The union has once again sent a fresh list awaiting response from the government. The union has not planned any legal action, as they believe in discussions and negotiated settlements, not in legal course. It was when many senior managers were increasingly becoming anti-union (although officers too are members of the Bank Employees' Association), a consolidated (new) forum called United Federation Banking Unions was created in 1999 as an umbrella organization of all the banking unions.

In response to a question regarding strategies adopted by AIBEA to reach out and attract greater participation and involvement of the increasing number of young and women employees, the president of AIBEA was confident that the nearly 35 per cent of women employees, many at the officer level, are actively interested in union matters. Similarly, he was certain that the young employees have come to realize the importance of trade unions in the changing scenario. The case of a woman joint secretary of AIBEA was also cited as an example in this context. In fact, the union president went on to suggest that unions are not against technology; on the contrary, they themselves have adopted new technologies and social media for internal communication within the organization across different levels of its structure at the national, state and the unit level. According to Nagar, most of the bank digitization is focused at the urban centres and it is not the priority in the nearly 27 per cent of the rural banking today where customers are not ready and will not be in quite a long time. However, he cautioned by saying that it is worrying to see the organized sector across the world getting marginalized with the increasing level of digitalization. It is time for global collaboration and AIBEA maintains close ties with United Federation of Trade Unions as well as the European Trade Union Congress.

Human resources and the role of trade unions had drawn the attention of many experts who examined the Indian banking system during the past decades. The Narasimhan Committee, in 1991, had observed, among other things, that trade unions, while contributing to the improvement of service conditions of the banking employees, have created serious restrictive practices limiting the management's decisions on many areas of human resource management including transfer and promotion, adversely affecting discipline, work culture and productivity of the banking system. The unrestrained power of the unions has restricted and delayed timely introduction of technologies and rational policies in the Indian banking process. In fact, the Narasimhan Committee II once again, in 1998, recommended strongly that, given the new competitive environment, it was imperative for the public sector banks to recognize the specific conditions of individual banks and move to bilateral system of wage negotiation and settlement in place of the national-level negotiation process.

The Khandelwal Committee, in 2010, went a step ahead and strongly argued for decentralization and professionalization, especially with reference to human resources and industrial relations in the public sector banks. The committee made specific observations on the restrictive practices which limit management's freedom in critical decisions such as promotion and redeployment of clerical staff. For example, often, branches (banks) in rural areas suffer from understaffing, compared to excess staff in urban centers, due to the restrictions accepted in the internal and industrial-level settlements limiting the transfer of clerical staff within 100 kms. The committee had suggested the need for a new agenda of union management relations which should include performance management and productivity improvement while addressing redressal of employee grievances. The committee further emphasized on the need to replace the current system of industry-level wage negotiation with enterprise level negotiation based on the performance of individual banks and their capacity to pay. It is only such a decentralized process which could promote and encourage a culture of innovation and individual initiative which are important for survival in the current highly competitive environment. More importantly, a performance-based work culture could be most suitable to embrace the advantages of the digitalized economy.

In fact, it is very relevant here to refer to a recent book (Khandelwal, 2018) which is based on a detailed case study of one of the largest public sector banks. Khandelwal (2018) describes the top management policies of the public sector banks as highly centralized and the leadership strategies as ad-hoc and whimsical, almost always influenced by the expedient wishes of the political administration and the extra-constitutional power centres invested in the trade union leaders. The leader-centred trade unionism and the peace-seeking approach of the management not only make the union leaders powerful individuals but also make the operating managers powerless. The short-term and personally convenient strategies of the management combined with the personal influencing style of the trade union leaders do not allow formulation of strategic human resource policies or industrial relations practices which could benefit the larger section of employees and help promote a much more productive and dynamic banking system.

Given the above scenario, it could be far from easy for the public sector banks in India to adopt digital technologies to the level the private sector banks may be able to. A survey (ETBFSI, 2019) of more than 350 banks and financial institutions revealed that only 17 per cent of banks managed any kind of digital transformation in the banking systems, achieving higher scale of services. The major obstacles to the adoption of digital banking are said to be, as elsewhere in the world, the legacy technology and system integration challenges. In fact, only 39 per cent of banks surveyed had confidence in digital technology and believed that digital transformation could accelerate delivery of products and services. More interestingly, only 14 per cent of the banks accepted that they have been in a leading position to adopt innovation, while more than 50 per cent admitted that they have been lagging behind. Furthermore, about 50 per cent of the banks surveyed continue to operate with the traditional organizational structures across retail business and corporate banking segments, while a mere 26 per cent of them were preparing to gradually be able to work with platform or open banking models. In other words, many banks are not yet ready to apply any of the new technologies based on open platforms or advanced analytics.

Conclusion

While trade union density continues to decline all across the world, including Europe with visible differences among countries, the cases cited in this paper seem to suggest that the gig economy could offer an opportunity for the revival of the labour movement, at least in Europe. COVID-19 has suddenly awakened trade unions and found relevance in the UK. The trade union movement is likely to claim a place of importance as it did in the 1970s. Issues of health and safety at work, which has been of marginal interest to most people, most of the time, has suddenly come to claim everybody's attention.

However, the implications of digital technology and their impact on trade unions in India may have a different story to tell. In India too, trade union density declined during the past few decades following the liberalization and globalization of the Indian economy since the early 1990s. Trade unions continued to weaken as some of the public sector companies became sick with the restructuring and revamping of many others. In a country where the best and brightest minds preferred to join the government or work for a leading public sector organization, the trend started to change in the 1980s when better opportunities opened up in the private sector, including multinational companies. The scenario took a massive turn with the announcement of the second industrial policy of the country by Manmohan Singh in 1991. Apart from attracting indigenous entrepreneurs and existing businessmen to invest in India, leading MNCs set up their establishments in the newly liberalized India. The private sector of the post-liberalized India attracted professional talents, as the experienced among them chose to leave the public sector for better remuneration and working conditions. Further, the advent of the IT and communication sector witnessed a major shift in the mindset of the country in favour of the private sector.

The divestment of public sector undertaking on one hand, and the decline of blue-collar workers in the manufacturing sector on the other, has had a major impact, weakening the bargaining power of trade unions in the Indian organized sector. The disruptive power of trade unions, which peaked in the 1970s and attempted to return in the middle of the 1990s, primarily to protest against the liberalization process, has virtually become non-existent in India today (Mamkoottam, 2017). Having lost their bargaining base in the manufacturing sector, trade unions in India have, time and again, asserted themselves in many of the services sector organizations, especially in banking. As described earlier, administration and management of banking in India, which largely belong to the public sector, have not been among the most professional or forward-looking.

The digital economy, perhaps, offers a golden opportunity to the Indian public sector banking to reinvent their human resources policies and industrial relations strategies. Both unions and management may have to accept the reality that industrial relations based on an inclusive strategy of partnership and collaboration rather than confrontation and conflict could be the way forward. Efficiency and profit may best be seen as an outcome of accepting human resources as the critical variable and technology as the most important differentiator in the digital economy.

References

Chandrashekhar, A., & Pramanik, A. (2020). *IT's clicking: TCS seeks to be work from home bellwether.*, *The Economic Times*.

Deutsche Bank. (2015). *Digitalisation and the Future of Commercial Banking, Deutsche Bank AG* [Brochure].

ETBFSI. (2019, 18 October). Only 17% banks deployed digital at scale. *BFSI.com*. https://bfsi.economictimes.indiatimes.com/news/banking/only-17-banks-deployed-digital-at-scale/71650219

Fairwork. (2020). *The gig economy and Covid-19: Looking ahead* (Fairwork Report on Platform's Covid-19 Policies).

Ford, M. (2015). *Rise of the robots: Technology and the threat of a jobless future*. Basic Books.

Frey, C. B., & Osborne, M. (2015), *Technology at work: The future of innovation and employment*. Citi GPS. http://www.oxfordmartin.ox.ac.uk/downloads/reports/Citi_GPS_Technology_Work.pdf

Khandelwal, A. (2018). *CEO: Chess master or gardner*. Oxford University Press.

Khandelwal Committee. (2010). *Report of the committee on HR issues of public sector banks*.

Mamkoottam, K. (1982). *Trade unionism: Myth and reality*. Oxford University Press.

Mamkoottam, K. (2017). Changing labour markets and industrial relations, changing times: Make in India and ensuing labour reforms. *Management and Labour Studies*, *42*(1), 1–9.

Roubini, C. (2015). Precarious work and access to collective bargaining: What are the legal obstacles? *International Journal of Labour Research*, *5* (1), 133–151.

Sriram, S. (2011). *Cloud computing in banking*. Capgemini Financial Service.

Uber Technologies Inc. (2020a). Services agreement. https://www.uber.com/legal/en/document/?name=general-terms-of use&country=united-states&lang=en

Uber Technologies Inc. (2020b). Driver Addendum to Services Agreement. https://www.uber.com/legal/en/

CHAPTER

16

Skilling Is a New Currency
Are You a Learning Organization?

Nishchae Suri

Skilling is at the heart of transforming nations. It is, indeed, the biggest opportunity and challenge of the decade. The speed and scale at which organizations are able to upskill and reskill their workforce may well become their only competitive advantage. In this race, agility is a key transformation lever and organizations must invest time and money to reskill their workforce such that they can quickly adapt and adjust to this new order of work. Owing to the coronavirus pandemic, corporate mortality rates are expected to soar. With the frequent shifts in the market conditions and uncertain futures, continuous learning is integral to the 'future of work'.

The concept of a learning organization isn't new. In the 1990s, Peter Senge, in his book *The Fifth Discipline*, talked about the learning disabilities of an organization and the impact it has. It is interesting that the words 'whole' and 'health' come from the same root (the Old English *hāl*, as in 'hale and hearty'). The unhealthiness of our learning, today, is in direct proportion to our inability to see it as a 'whole'.

Organizations aspire to improve their overall learning health, knowing that it is next to impossible to build a culture of continuous learning, without having a healthy learning ecosystem, but they often forget that it takes a whole system's approach to achieve this.

Each organization must become a learning organization where employees exhibit lifelong learning behaviours if it is to survive, sustain and grow.

A learning organization has a compelling vision of employees skilled at creating, acquiring, transferring and applying knowledge. Such learning organizations are more agile and have the ability to respond faster to changing environments compared to their competitors. As a result, they continuously deliver higher performance.

In these unprecedented and challenging times, organizations need to learn more than ever before. Learning fitness or learning health is your collective 'ability' to perform. Research shows that organizations with a strong learning culture, significantly, outperform their competitors (Bersin, 2010).

1. 58 per cent more likely to have future skills to meet future demands
2. 34 per cent more likely to respond better and quicker to customer needs
3. 26 per cent greater ability to deliver 'quality products'
4. 37 per cent greater employee productivity
5. 17 per cent more likely to be have higher profitability and be market share leaders
6. 46 per cent more likely to be innovative, that is, first to enter the market

This chapter will address the need for skills development as the landscape of the banking industry evolves and technology transcends human effort. It sheds light on the current learning realities of the industry, the imponderables that learning practitioners grapple with and provide a set of guidelines that are the key to building smart, healthy and sustainable learning organizations.

Unchartered Waters: Navigating the Shifting Tides

While the global financial crisis of 2008 had changed the face of banking in a visible way, its macroeconomic impact managed to conceal the pervasive current of fundamental forces that continue to affect the industry, such as the imposition of tighter regulations with the enforcement of Basel III, evolving client needs, the digital revolution, disintermediation and globalization (Schwarz et al., 2015). As the ripples of the crisis are still being dealt with, the COVID-19 pandemic poses a new grave challenge to financial institutions. In the initial weeks of the pandemic, the sector witnessed a significant market value drop, reaching a level lower than during the 2008–2009 crisis (Accenture, 2020). Banks are recalibrating strategies for their survival and sustainability as the economic fallout spreads.

In a world where virtual teaming forms the base for working, financial services institutions are striving to keep the 'lights on' by keeping open their supervisory and compliance functions that were never designed for remote work and operationalizing distribution channels despite social distancing advice.

Harnessing strategic and operational agility is the need of the hour, as market forces and customer behaviours are bound to change post this crisis and change the face of the industry yet again.

The Future Is Where 'Human Meets Digital'

The banking sector is in a dynamic space and is transforming at a breakneck pace. Technology is becoming indispensable to homes but so are digital servicing domains. Customers are already beginning to trust artificial 'chat-bots' and the day is not far when the robots will be at their behest for their financial needs.

Financial institutions endeavour to leverage technology and innovation to lower intermediation costs along with protecting their bottom lines. Technologies like artificial intelligence (AI), machine learning (ML) and big data will be instrumental in detecting frauds, monitoring the use of funds by borrowers and tracking suspicious transactions. Detecting potential threats and taking pre-emptive action will be enabled by the power of advanced analytics and real-time monitoring of emerging cybersecurity risks. The larger goal of making a shift from human to digital in banking with these new innovations is to serve customers by reducing costs and providing a range of products with safe and secure access.

Race to Reskill

If the rate of learning is not greater than the rate of change you are experiencing, then you are bound to fall behind.

With a highly dynamic and changing environment as a backdrop, defining an effective strategy for talent management and mitigating the risks associated with it is fundamental for current and future business growth. A few years ago, I led an interesting study at Klynveld Peat Marwick Goerdeler that focused on assessing talent risks in organizations. We identified risks in five critical talent categories—capability, capacity, compliance, cost and connection. Capability related risks, which involve building the skills an organization needs to compete, now and in the future, are the breadth and depth of skills and capabilities present within a workforce and how well aligned these are to an organization's needs, which have emerged as top risks for organizations in India (Suri, 2013, p. 4). With the pandemic, capability risks have only accentuated further.

This definitely warrants for a more holistic approach to upskilling and reskilling in organizations to build the workforce of tomorrow. I believe in the new and ever-evolving world of work, learning professionals will be key in mitigating the risk of capability by acting as the following (EdCast, p. 60):

1. **Business leader:** Aligns decisions and spends on the short-term, medium-term and long-term needs of the business and people.
2. **Portfolio manager:** Optimizes the entire content portfolio and ascertains what generates maximum returns.
3. **Marketeer:** Makes known the value of learning, especially in times of business slow down, and embraces the opportunity to change the brand perception of learning.
4. **Technologist:** Drives adoption of remote working and digital learning tools and enables learning in the flow of work.
5. **Ambassador:** becomes a role model for the mindset and behaviours of an everyday learner.
6. **Data scientist:** Develops a robust framework of metrics and uses analytics to make data-driven decisions.
7. **Change maestro:** Leads and accelerates change efforts through proactive communication and stakeholder management.
8. **Scout:** Seeks and identifies experts in the organization and makes tacit knowledge explicit.
9. **Culture propagator:** Designs learning policies and processes (reward and recognition frameworks) to build a culture of continuous self-directed learning.

As the heat of competition rises in banking, it is vital for business leaders to understand the challenges and opportunities posed by digitization, making it essential to focus on talent development. Organizations in banking, financial services and insurance (BFSI) need to manage talent like capital and create a talent strategy which delivers value through the transformation of culture, process and structure (Maor, 2019). As per McKinsey, 43 per cent of all working hours in banking activities will be automated in the future—a massive shift from basic cognitive skills to socio-economic and technological ones awaits us (Maor, 2019). Reskilling is also recognized by 75 per cent of executives as being critical to adapting to the digital age, however, only about 10 per cent of roles are likely to be obviated, with the remaining majority likely to be modified to varying degrees by automation and digitization, allowing for upskilling and redeployment (Maor, 2019).

What is it that the organizations plan to do to bridge the skills gap? To hire the skilled or to reskill, that is the question. However, as the need for skills evolves, hiring cannot alone close the gap fast enough. PwC's 'Banking and Capital Markets Trends' report reveals that 40 per cent of organizations plan to invest in upskilling their internal talent pool, 23 per cent plan on hiring from firms in the same industry and 16 per cent plan to hire from outside, 16 per cent plan to bring in fresh talent through affiliations with higher educational institutions and only 5 per cent of organizations report changing the composition of the workforce by bringing in contingent workers to fill the gap (Gealy, 2019, p. 4).

Not only is reskilling critical from an organizational standpoint, if done right, it also has a transformative effect on employees. In one case, McKinsey documents that employee satisfaction rose from 70 per cent to 80 per cent during the process, which is a significant finding because 40 per cent of transformations fail because employees do not buy into the new approach (Maor, 2019).

Institutions need to refine and redesign job skill sets to equip individuals for higher-order work requiring intuitive, creative, interpretive and problem-solving skills. The new 'super jobs' that would be created due to this redesign will seek talent that can connect the dots between technology and business (Volini, 2019). Augmented by tech solutions, the banker of tomorrow will epitomize 'less doing, but more thinking' with a blend of composite skills and capabilities which span across complex finance, coding and behavioural skills.

In the words of Shantikanta Das, RBI Governor, 'The possibilities are enormous. We should be seized of the issues and act in time' (Economic Times, 2020).

As functioning and delivery of banking services evolve, it is equally essential for the workforce to transform itself to cope with these changes. Learning and development, as a function, need to play a key role in enabling employees in banking to reskill and upskill themselves in keeping up with the changing times and the transformational needs of the industry.

Looking in the Mirror

'Without data you're just another person with an opinion.'
—W. Edwards Deming

At EdCast, I conceptualized and led a study on organizational learning health, covering 104 organizations in India with the aim of building a deeper understanding of the present state of the learning proficiencies in organizations.

I also held interviews with 22 leading experts including chief learning officers (CLOs) with experience at some of the largest, most successful companies around the world to gain a perspective on the probable trajectory of L&D.

What's worrying is that the EdCast 'Learning Health Index (LHI) Study 2020' revealed that banking, as an industry, ranked amongst the lowest when it came to learning health with a score of 63 on a scale of 100 (EdCast, 2020, p. 62).

- In BFSI, 77 per cent of the organizations do not prepare and allocate learning budgets in a planned manner that is fully tied to the priorities of the business.
- In BFSI, 95 per cent of the organizations are not using advanced real-time analytics to measure the effectiveness of L&D interventions.
- Less than 10 per cent of organizations in BFSI report the curation of high-quality content internally and the integration of other HR systems with L&D.
- In BFSI, 86 per cent of organizations are yet to implement policies and processes that always encourage experimentation and are tolerant of failure.
- None of the organizations in BFSI completely personalize and democratize learning.
- No organizations in BFSI report the use of highly sophisticated learner-centric tools to provide learning at the point of need, to enable social learning and integration of HRMS elements.
- In BFSI, 9 per cent of organizations report that their L&D proactively scans the horizon of learning to leverage the latest developments and deliver a superior learner experience.

Early Warning Signs: 10 Signs You Should Watch Out for

It is common for an organization to exhibit early warning signs before deteriorating or dying. The key to optimal outcomes is recognition of these warning signs followed by an appropriate and timely response. Very often, the culmination of these signs shows up in lower engagement scores in which L&D scores are unfavourable, ultimately leading to high attrition. Research has evidenced that organizations that are recognized as 'best employers' offer differentiated career growth and learning opportunities to their employees.

Measuring and managing organizational learning health is critical. Many organizations are unaware of what is broken or missing (EdCast, 2020, p. 62).

1. Managers play a passive-defensive role in encouraging their team members to be everyday learners, which is likely to inhibit and impair learning, break employees' spirit and demotivate them.
2. Learning is primarily seen to be a compliance requirement and not driven by a culture of commitment, promoting behaviours where people act 'out of fear' and not 'out of performance'.
3. Learners are not recognized and rewarded for learning new skills and knowledge.
4. Leaders and managers do not show an interest to understand and appreciate the concerns, fears or what is most meaningful to an individual.
5. Leaders and managers do not invest their time in nurturing and developing talent.
6. Leaders and managers do not encourage holistic learning based on the wealth of knowledge in the universe but limit learning to role requirements.
7. Organization operates with a deficit mindset and encourages learning only to fix weaknesses and not build on strengths.
8. Leaders and subject matter experts in the organization do not invest their time in continuously upgrading their own knowledge and skills.
9. Individuals are not rewarded for their team behaviours wherein they contribute to how the team learns together as a group and helps others grow and develop.
10. Leaders are not actively promoting the cause of learning and the learner.

While the current state of L&D in banking is rather grim, it also provides the sector with the biggest opportunity to improve their organizational learning health. The industry needs a holistic approach to learning which facilitates a psychologically safe learning environment, institutes a set of concrete learning practices that allow free flow of knowledge and a leadership team that champions the need for learning and role models the right learning habits and behaviours.

New Frontiers of L&D: Embrace the Future with Grace

Over the last decade, the focus of the L&D function has taken an enormous leap from delivering compliance training to playing the role of a leadership and management development engine, which has paved the way for the rise of the Transformer chief learning officer with the growing demands being placed on organizations to bridge the skill gap, create a future-ready workforce and deploy learner engagement tactics to engage the modern-day learner.

As we transcend the new frontiers of L&D, let's look at what the CLOs are looking for, playing ushers to this epochal change.

Garnering Executive Sponsorship and Developing Learning Champions

According to the 2019 PwC CEO survey, 'CEOs' anxiety', the lack of essential skills has risen from 63 per cent in 2014 to 73 per cent in 2019. However, there are still not enough champions for the cause of learning. Research shows that 83 per cent of learning professionals report that executive buy-in is not a challenge, however, only 23 per cent of them regard CEOs as active champions of learning (LinkedIn Learning, 2020, p. 7).

Procuring Increased Learning Budgets

As senior leaders understand the increasing value of learning and reskilling, the phenomenon of scarcity in resources for L&D budgets is a fading myth with only 27 per cent of learning professionals citing budget constraints in 2020 (LinkedIn Learning, 2020, p. 7). The upward trend in L&D budget allocations from 2017, 2018, 2019 continues into 2020 as well, with more than a third of learning professionals globally and 72 per cent in India expecting growth year over year; 57 per cent of them plan to spend more on their online learning programmes (LinkedIn Learning, 2020, p. 7).

Measuring the Impact of Learning

This is ironic because only 6 per cent of organizations report measuring return on investment through the framework of metrics deployed to measure learning interventions (EdCast, 2020). There is no industry standard that defines a way to measure the impact of learning. While most organizations rely on telemetry—consumption related (lower-order) metrics, slow but gradual adoption of analytics can be witnessed. L&D is still grappling with the question of measuring what matters in a way where the data can be used to enhance coverage, improve the quality of learning programmes, impact talent strategy and make business decisions.

Building and Sourcing Compelling Content

Research shows that 57 per cent of learning professionals are spending more time with online learning than they did three years ago, indicating that online learning is playing a bigger part in blended learning programmes (LinkedIn Learning, 2020, p. 16). With large libraries of content available to help quickly curate and personalize learning recommendations, the time spent on building and sourcing content is expected to go down over time. However, since content strategy and architecture are at the heart of learning interventions, it will never cease to be a priority for CLOs.

Enriching Learner Experience

As many as 94 per cent of learners say they would stay at a company longer if it invested in their L&D, but 49 per cent report that they do not have the time to learn at work (Chelovechkov et al., 2019, p. 43). Given that time is of the essence, learners are craving a highly personalized learning experience that serves up the right learning at the right time, without having to dig for it. Learners across all generations also want to learn with their colleagues to exchange ideas, share insights and ask questions (LinkedIn Learning, 2020, p. 26). The top priority for CLOs is to consistently personalize learner journeys and aid them with well-defined, career development frameworks and optimize it through robust technology platforms which enable targeted upskilling.

Engaging the Modern-day Learner

Driving engagement has been a perennial challenge for learning professionals and with wider and dispersed demographics, it isn't getting any easier. Given that the L&D community is yet to converge onto a true north metric for engagement, learning professionals only spend 15 per cent of their time raising awareness about the learning offerings that are available to employees across their organizations (LinkedIn Learning, 2020). CLOs strive to build a brand of learning and engage learners by creating 'sticky learning experiences,' which will also serve as valuable metrics to gauge engagement and inculcation of the learning habit.

Leveraging Latest, Effective, Accessible and Pocket-friendly Technology

As many as 31 per cent of learning professionals prioritize teaching their employees how to use technology more effectively so that learning organizations are better able to provide their workforce with the resources and knowledge that they want at the time and place that it is most relevant, enabling learners to better manage their personal development journey (LinkedIn Learning, 2020). Given that only 28 per cent of employees are highly satisfied with the learning solutions offered by their company, Gartner's recent study reports that improving the user experience of technology is the foremost strategic priority of L&D professionals today (Gartner, 2019).

Fostering a Continuous Culture of Learning to Build Smart and Healthy Learning Organizations

As many as 42 per cent of learning professionals consider fostering a culture of continuous learning in their top three priorities for 2020 (LinkedIn Learning, 2020, p. 22). However, only 6 per cent of organizations deploy robust R&R frameworks to celebrate learning behaviours (EdCast, 2020). Learning culture is the lifeline of an organization's ecosystem. It drives an independent quest for knowledge and promotes shared learning directed towards the goals of the organization. To build an everyday learning culture, it is essential for individuals to feel responsible for their own development. Research shows that enabling self-directed learning with online learning solutions is the number one strategic focus area for learning professionals nationally (LinkedIn Learning, 2020, p. 15).

L&D Reset, Reboot, Renew: Building Blocks of a Smart and Future-ready Learning Organization

Building a smart and sustainable learning organization requires eight key building blocks that interact with one another to form a healthy learning ecosystem (Figure 16.1).

1. **Strengthen the partnership: Align learning with strategy**—Aligning learning strategy with business priorities is the starting point of leading a successful learning function. As strategic business partners, organizations must ensure that their capability development initiatives support the mission of the businesses they work with. To build alignment, L&D teams must:

   - Clearly articulate the few critical priorities and must-win battles to which the company and CEO are committed over the next three to five years.
   - Align current offerings with the strategic priorities mentioned in the CEO agenda.

Learning strategy and business planning: The extent to which the current and future needs of the business drive the learning strategy and plans in the organization. How are learning and development budgets prepared and allocated? How agile is the learning function to change course and respond to business requirements?

Learning culture: What importance does the organization place on learning? Who takes accountability and what are the consequences related to learning? How are learners recognized and rewarded in the organization? What role do leaders, managers and team members have to play?

Impact and measurement: What learning metrics are used to measure efficiency and effectiveness of learning? To what extent does an organization use data analytics, predictive modelling in taking decisions related to talent and learning?

Learner experience: Experience embodies a 'consumerized' approach that is hyper-personalized and multi-modal. Employees have the freedom to consume the knowledge when and where they want to, from a wide range of content resources, tailored to their learning needs, styles, preferences and interests.

L&D policies and processes: Learning processes involve the aggregation, creation, curation, collection, interpretation, dissemination and application of knowledge. They include experimentation to develop and test new products and services; intelligence gathering to keep track of competitive, customer and technological trends; disciplined analysis and interpretation to identify and solve problems; education and training to develop employees.

Tools and technologies: What technologies are being used and to what extent in leading, enabling, managing and supporting learning and development as well as the "learner" in the organization? How are learning technologies integrated with enterprise systems and with one another?

L&D portfolio: The nature, type and complexity of solutions and services the function is entrusted to carry out in the organization, e.g. performance consulting, knowledge management, change management, instructional design, business intelligence, content development etc.

L&D competence: The core skills and capabilities required by L&D professionals for leading and managing a high impact learning organization. At what level of proficiency is the L&D function operating within the organization? what are their strengths and areas of development?

- Get inputs and buy-in for the learning agenda from leaders in the rest of the business—all the way to the CEO level.
- Activate the learning agenda through programmatic activities and changes to the learning portfolio.
- Link all spend to performance metrics to ensure scrap learning is minimized and move to a near-zero learning inventory.
- Set up governance councils to review the functioning of L&D, periodically. A mix of HR, learning and business leaders in the governance councils can ensure balanced functioning.

2. **Impact assessment: Plays the role of a return creator**—Resources are scarce and ensuring the effectiveness of spend is critical. As Drucker said, 'If you cannot measure it, you cannot improve it.'[1] When learners can't put what they've learned into practice, time and money are wasted. L&D's responsibility is to not only impact change, but also make results measurable and visible by demonstrating commercial gains, productivity gains, 'and use data analytics, predictive modelling in taking decisions related to talent and learning.'

   At the end of the day, L&D's goal is to tie learning to results. If they get the objectives right, the design right and the delivery right, they will be able to get the effectiveness right.

3. **L&D policies and processes: Learning must be complemented by an aggregated input that spans across the complete employee lifecycle**—Learning processes involve the aggregation, creation, curation, collection, interpretation and dissemination of knowledge. They include experimentation to develop and test new products and services; intelligence gathering to keep track of competitive, customer, and technological trends; disciplined analysis and interpretation to identify and solve problems and education and training to develop employees. The underlying need to build core processes stems from the fact that effective learning cannot be the result of isolated capability-development initiatives.

   Organizations need to integrate not just HR systems but also the structures, processes, governance models and strategies to succeed. Borrowing from the Gestalt school of thought, 'The whole is, after all, greater than the sum of its parts.'

4. **L&D portfolio: 'Charter of learning' that clearly outlines the L&D function's reason for being raison d'être**—L&D functions should continue to upgrade the nature and quality of services and solutions

---

[1] https://mckinneylaw.iu.edu/iiclr/pdf/vol24p203.pdf, p. 4.

that they provide to meet the evolving and rapidly changing needs of the business. In many organizations, L&D is still tactical and operational, while a few have raised their game where they continuously reconfigure the learning ecosystem architecture, addressing both form and function, enable key performance outcomes through consulting, orchestrate and manage knowledge flows and exchange, drive change of learner behaviours and mindset, design learning experiences suited to the modern day learner, use instructional design to power specific learning outcomes, gather and mine business and employee data to improve the quality of decision making and curate content which is suited to the context of the organization.

5. **A lasting learning culture: Self-directed learning**—A philosophy where individuals feel responsible for their own development is essential to build an everyday learning culture, rather than an isolated training one. Learning initiatives must be intrinsically driven for ensuring commitment over compliance. Self-driven learning will come as a natural corollary to well-designed talent programmes that allow individuals to achieve mastery in fields of interest or appeal to their sense of purpose.

6. **The era of the learner: Batch size equals 1**—Learner experience is much more than a buzzword; it heralds a paradigm shift. With learner experience, you are not creating a curriculum; you are creating an experience, one that will translate to the single most differentiating factor.

    By making personalized content available to learners anytime, anywhere and on multiple devices, L&D departments have a realistic shot at significantly reducing the learning curve.

7. **Tools and technology: An ally in the journey of transformation**—We are currently witnessing a learning revolution of which technology is an integral part. Organizations are keen to switch to a 'single' system of record for their employees but are finding it difficult to identify one system that addresses all of their requirements. Organizations require a set of software to deliver a single-user interface, build and manage employee journeys, develop apps, create and monitor workflows and add forms of conversational interfaces to the mix to be able to meet business requirements and drive learner engagement.

    In their journey of transformation, organizations need to fuel the practice of continuous learning in the flow of work. According to the LHI Study 2020, 68 per cent of institutions from BFSI are yet to implement this and over a quarter haven't even seriously considered operationalizing it! The pursuit of lifelong learning should be far more than simply a noble aspiration. It requires equipping employees to direct their own paths by offering edification and expertise on a single platform, accessible on an anytime-anywhere basis. Sixty-nine per cent of HR functions believe that `learners in their organizations expect more intelligent systems that will anticipate their needs (Gartner, 2018). Self-serving learning enablement is done best when it is personalized with the help of cutting edge cognitive technologies like AI and ML that curate key learnings and insights daily, based on learner behaviours—goals, styles and preferences—and putting the learners in the driver's seat to steer their own development journey. By making learning available on the go through MobileFirst platforms, organizations can truly provide learning 'at the point of need'.

The introduction of the Learning Experience Platforms (LXPs) is designed to expand the range of training content that learners have access to, while also providing a more intuitive and personalized learner experience (Gartner, 2020). Fifty-one per cent of learning professionals intend to increase the investment in LXPs to meet learner expectations (Gartner, 2019). It's an additional layer of the training-technology stack that sits on top of the Learning Management System (LMS) with the Learning Record Store forming the bottom-most layer. The LXP fills up all the crevices that an LMS leaves open—multimedia library, AI-driven content recommendations, user generated content, personalized learning paths, contextual-on the job learning.

Today, a variety of tools and systems are being used by employees to carry out their day-to-day job activities which are integrated into the LXP to maximize productivity and efficiency. One of the biggest areas of opportunity is making learning available in workplace communication and collaboration tools. A 2019 study on work-life balance found that knowledge workers are checking communication tools an average of once every six minutes (Mackay, 2019). Digital adoption tools provide in-app guidance and training to help users get up to speed with a new solution or inform them of system changes and updates. An example of this is MyGuide, one of the products EdCast offers. By embedding learning in systems of productivity and business applications, CLOs can accelerate the 'flow of work' itself by enhancing productivity, quality of work and satisfaction.

8. **Developing the learning professional: An evolving role**—The role of L&D is that of a connector, connecting the learner to the learning, the learning to the business, the technology to design and the context to the content.

L&D is a function that holds the potential to craft life-changing experiences, impact productivity and engagement and drive change. But to do this in today's day and age, we need to go beyond the conventional and embrace the new.

L&D professionals, today, must have three emotions in their armour:

- **Business partners:** L&D professionals should treat business leaders as customers and must continuously challenge the business on needs and delivery methods and advise them on opportunities to impact business performance.
- **Empathy for the learner:** In the times of experiential learning where we strive to craft life-changing experiences, learning design and delivery cannot be done unless L&D understands the 'realities' of learners.
- **Love for technology:** For L&D to serve the modern learner in the age of modern learning, an appreciation of the role technology plays in the life of a learner is a must.

Learning is the New Working

We all know that to ascend the learning curve we need to tread the learning curve, but what is even more compelling today is that the learning curve is also the 'yearning' curve. Eighty-three per cent of employees believe it is their responsibility to reskill themselves (PwC, 2019). To enable individuals to make strides in their learning journey, it's imperative for organizations to keep their employees engaged by making available self-directed opportunities for growth in the flow of work that will not only contribute to their individual development, but also to the overall organizational success.

As culture is the core to strategy, developing a culture of learning is the key to making employees lifelong learners. At EdCast, I have been closely working with a global multinational bank that deems learning culture to be the lifeline of its learning ecosystem. The bank has defined a number of strategic themes that they are working on to transform learning in the bank including experience, capability, content, measurement and technology. The work is very specific, contextualized and defined. What they realized was that there is a critical overarching theme of learning culture. They invested in technology, set up measurement frameworks and relied on cues and direction from culture. They launched a Global Learning Week, where their most senior business executives led global events, a panel on the future of banking and interactive sessions on competencies such as nimble learning. They encouraged their leaders to use the 'language' of learning, talk openly about successes and learning from failures, being agile and experimenting. With the goal of making self-directed learning a reality, the bank took a step, rather a leap, in the direction by launching its newly minted LXP powered by EdCast for its employees worldwide.

The LXP is geared towards the learner with the aim of improving learning content, discovery and consumption (Gartner, 2020, p. 3). However, for its successful implementation and fruitful impact, organizations have to align LXP's objectives with organizational learning goals and harvest a healthy learning culture by weeding out outdated L&D strategies. Research has, evidently, established that learners crave inspiring and challenging learning experiences throughout their career. All we need to do now is create a conducive, healthy learning environment by leveraging technology to skill at scale and with speed which will not only help the learner, but also allow organizations to survive and succeed in the new-age work world, where learning is the new working.

Bibliography

Accenture. (2020, 26 March). *COVID-19: How banks can manage the business impact*. https://www.accenture.com/ro-en/insights/banking/coronavirus-banking-rapid-response.

Bersin & Associates. (2010). *High impact learning culture*. Author.

Chelovechkov, A., Spar, B., Lefkowitz, R., & Van Nuys, A. (2019). *2019 workplace learning report* (3rd Annual Report). LinkedIn Learning.

EdCast. (2020). *Learning health index study 2020*.

Gartner. (2018). *Gartner Digital Experience Benchmarking Survey*. Author.

Gartner. (2019). *Learning innovations survey*. Author.

Gartner. (2019). *Gartner global labor market survey*. Author.

Gartner. (2020, 29 April). *Learning experience platform (LEP): Features & implementation*. Author.

Gealy, S., Gemes, A., Hoffman, D., Jain, A., & Vido de, L. (2019). *Banking and capital markets trends 2019* (PwC's 22nd Annual Global CEO survey trends series). PricewaterhouseCoopers. https://www.pwc.com/gx/en/ceo-survey/2019/Theme-assets/reports/banking-capital-markets-trends-2019-report.pdf

LinkedIn Learning. (2020). *2020 workplace learning report* (4th Annual Report). Author.

MacKay, J. (2019, 24 January). *The state of work life balance in 2019: What we learned from studying 185 million hours of working time*. blog.RescueTime.com.

Maor, D. (2019, 3 May). *A strategic blueprint for making the most of banking talent*. McKinsey & Company. https://www.mckinsey.com/industries/financial-services/our-insights/banking matters/a-strategic-blueprint-for-making-the-most-of-banking-talent.

PWC. (2019). *CEOs' curbed confidence spells caution* (22nd Annual Global CEO Survey). Author.

Schwarz, J., Baumgärtner, C., Casale, G., Creyghton, A., Dany, O., Massi, M., Tang, T, Berg, P., & Halliday, K. (2015, 23 March). *Five trends disrupting the corporate banking landscape*. Boston Consulting Group. https://www.bcg.com/en-in/publications/2015/financial-institutions-business-unti-strategy-five-trends-disrupting-corporate-banking-landscape.aspx.

Suri, N., Outridge, P., Bolton, R., Croucher, L., Dlomu, N., Geke, M., Molino, P., Saran, C., Shirodkar, S., Payne, T., Spears, M., Svensson, R., Welsing, P., & Williamson, M. (2013, November). *Time for a more holistic approach to talent risk.* KPMG International.

The Economic Times. (2020, February 24). Changing landscape of banking industry will unfold: Shantikanta Das. https://economictimes.indiatimes.com/markets/stocks/news/changing-landscape-of-banking-industry-will-unfold-shaktikanta-das/articleshow/74288697.cms?from=mdr

Volini, E., Schwartz, J., Roy, I., Hauptmann, M., Van Durme, Y., Denny, B., & Bersin, J. (2019, 11 April). *Leading the social enterprise: Reinvent with a human focus* (2019 Deloitte Global Human Capital Trends). Deloitte Insights.

17

A New Manifesto for CHROs in the Era of Digital Change

Rajiv Jayaraman

Many years ago, Charles Dickens, in his novel, *A Tale of Two Cities*, said, 'It's the best of times, it's the worst of times.' Sometimes, reading these iconic lines makes one wonder if the author was talking about the digital age that we live in.

It is the best of times because we now have unprecedented access to resources at incredible prices at a click of a button. It is the age of instant gratification, ease and ultra-convenience. It is an age where an entire set of population is getting themselves heard through broadband and mobile phone access. The power is shifting squarely to the hands of individuals. It seems like we are all, finally, empowered to be at our creative best.

It is the worst of times because this is also an era of unprecedented change. Jobs are getting automated, workplace stress due to change is on the rise, we are connected on social networks but disconnected from the people next to us, social platforms are becoming battle grounds filled with trolls. There is a huge divide between digital-haves and have-nots.

It's no secret that we are now firmly in the middle of the fourth industrial revolution. Rapid changes are sweeping across various industries. Think about a few of these mind-numbing statistics:

1. 90 per cent of the world's information was created in the last two years, says an IBM report (ScienceDaily, 2013).
2. Pizza Hut, the global food giant, has launched a series of shoes called the Pie Top series. These shoes are equipped with digital buttons, pressing which you can get your favourite pizza delivered to where you are (Moscovic, 2018).
3. Automated cars are passé—now, we are talking about flying taxis.
4. People are volunteering to have microchips embedded inside their bodies (Ma, 2018).

Focusing specifically on the banking industry,

1. Banking has become a platform business where traditional banks are now starting to operate an open platform, where a plethora of Fintech companies are integrated into the platform to provide customers greater choice and convenience.
2. Banks are earning revenue by selling movie tickets and various other lifestyle products on their platforms, something we couldn't imagine a few years ago.
3. Banks are tapping into innumerable data points from the customer journey across various channels to enhance customer experience and unlock new revenue streams.

In the face of these rapid changes, there is a choice that organizations must make. Stay ahead of the curve and lead the way or be swept away by these changes and become redundant. When we peel the onion, we realize that, like any other major transformation, the success of digital transformation depends on the quality of the leadership team across levels in the organization, clarity in strategy, capabilities and culture. To ensure success, HR leaders of banks have an incredibly important role to play in the digital change process.

- The role of HR, in the digital change process, entails Aligning and engaging the organization on digital strategy
- Building future ready capabilities across levels in the organization
- Building a digital culture that sustains successful digital change initiatives

---

HR Imperatives in the Digital Age

Digital strategy + Digital capabilities + Digital culture = Digital outcomes

---

To realize these outcomes, HR leaders must use new digital approaches revolving around platforms, data analytics, design thinking and agile methodologies. In short, we need a new manifesto for HR leaders in the banking industry to prepare their organizations for the digital future.

Whether it turns out to be the best of times or the worst of times for an organization depends a lot on how HR leaders reimagine their roles for the digital age. Before delving into the manifesto, let's try to understand what's changing in the banking landscape.

The Four Blurring Lines in the Banking Industry

In my book *Clearing the Digital BLUR* (2019), I presented the concept of four lines that are getting blurred away in every industry, causing severe disorientation to organizations, often leading to disruption.

The Era of the Digital BLUR

Many business leaders are increasingly talking about experiencing lack of visibility and heightened uncertainty in their businesses in the digital age. In other words, they are experiencing a state of blur.

1. Consider the following examples. What do Uber, Skype and Airbnb have in common? Their business models are all about facilitating interactions through their digital platform without owning the physical infrastructure.
2. IBM Watson can detect malignant cancer better than the best human doctors (Steadman, 2013).[4]
3. According to the World Economic Forum, the time taken by an average unicorn to reach a billion-dollar valuation is roughly 4.4 years. The typical Fortune 500 company took 20 years to achieve this status (World Economic Forum, 2016).

These examples reveal an underlying shift that has happened in the last decade. We now live in the age of the digital BLUR—an age where many of the crucial lines that governed businesses in the past have started blurring away.

BLUR (Figure 17.1) is an acronym that stands for Boundaryless organizations, Limitless digitization, Unbounded innovation and Relentless iteration. Essentially, these are lines that separate an organization from the outside world, the physical world from the digital world, the industries and the now from the next.

Boundaryless Banks

Uber doesn't own any of the cars that operate in its network and its large number of drivers are not on its payroll. Airbnb doesn't own any of the rooms in its network. Skype doesn't own any network towers. These companies operate their business by orchestrating fluid networks of people and assets that are external to the organization.

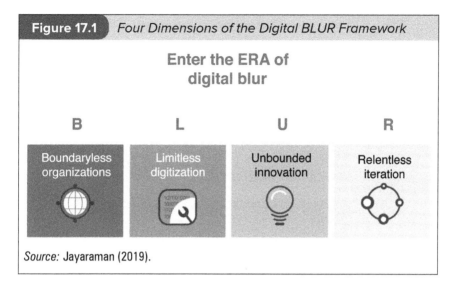

Figure 17.1 *Four Dimensions of the Digital BLUR Framework*

Enter the ERA of
digital blur

B	L	U	R
Boundaryless organizations	Limitless digitization	Unbounded innovation	Relentless iteration

Source: Jayaraman (2019).

In the digital age, the lines separating internal and external sources of value creation for an organization are fast blurring away. The lines within the organization are also blurring away. Internal silos present severe challenges for organizations to respond fast in the digital age. Consequently, the lines separating different functions within the organization are coming under scrutiny. ANZ Bank made an announcement in September 2017 that they are blowing up their internal hierarchies to structure themselves as 150 start-up teams and adopt agile work practices embraced by technology companies such as Google, Amazon and Facebook (Yeates, 2017). In this way, this large, well-established Australian bank has not only acknowledged the need to disrupt its traditional structures but also is taking the bold step to act.

Globally, the banking vertical is experiencing the great unbundling. The industry structure is starting to look as shown in Figure 17.2.

At the top of the stack is the experience layer for the customer where an omnichannel experience is provided across physical branches, mobile banking, ATMs, phone banking etc. Then comes the aggregation layer, where the bank starts to act like a platform that brings diverse set of financial services providers to add value to the customer. Then comes the process layer that uses robotic process automation, AI and internet of things in front-office, mid-office and back-office processes. This is then backed by the data layer where analytics helps organizations find value. At the base of it all, is the infrastructure layer which operates on a cloud platform.

Each layer of the bank is getting unbundled today with Fintech companies chipping away at the profitable layers without incurring huge overheads of

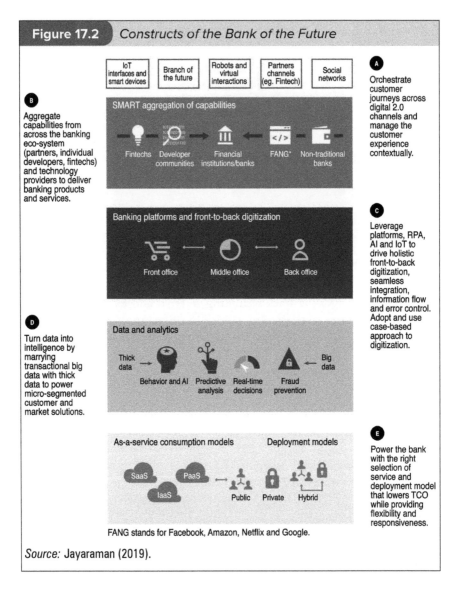

Figure 17.2 *Constructs of the Bank of the Future*

FANG stands for Facebook, Amazon, Netflix and Google.

Source: Jayaraman (2019).

running a full-service bank. LendingClub, for instance, focuses tightly on lending products as opposed to providing an end-to-end banking service.

Limitless Digitization

Lines separating the physical and the digital world are blurring away. The world around us is getting limitlessly digitized. Practically, every object we see in the physical space can potentially be digitized just by slapping a cloud enabled sensor on it. From movies to books to music to money, many things that used to exist purely in the physical form are now also available in the digital form. While there are about 7 billion people on the planet today, connected devices are estimated to be around 20.4 billion by 2020, outnumbering humans by a factor of 3 (Gartner, 2017).

Digitization has completely altered the concept of money and matters related to finance. Banks around the world are aggressively driving customer interactions to digital channels to lower the cost of doing business. Many banks experience a higher Net Promoter Score, a critical customer satisfaction metric, on digital channels as opposed to all other channels. It is a critical insight that digital not only reduces transaction and operating costs for the bank, but also increases customers' willingness to engage, and eventually, pay.

Banks are facing a sweeping change in customer habits with Gen Y migrating to online and mobile banking and Gen X demanding more consulting services with a human touch. Branch sizes are shrinking, and in fact, most of the banks find that 90 per cent of their customers haven't visited any of their branches. HSBC operates its digital bank, called Firstdirect.com, as a separate entity to deal with this dichotomy in customer expectations.

Founded in 2009, in Germany, Fidor Bank became the world's first Fintech bank, pioneering collaboration between traditional financial services and technology businesses. 'We are reimagining everything about banking, building from the ground up,' said Matthias Kröner, the CEO of Fidor Bank (Fidor Bank, 2019).

Fidor Bank provides modern products and services like crowdfunding, trading of virtual currencies and 60-second bank transfers. Fidor's banking concept offers consumers an online community in which they can give and receive financial advice, offering them rewards for the same.

Unbounded Innovation

Many digital innovations such as automated cars, bitcoins and the blockchain do not just impact one industry. Such unbounded innovations simultaneously cause deep disruptions across multiple industries. Many industry lines, therefore, are likely to get blurred away in the process.

Furthermore, the process of innovation is no longer happening purely within organizational boundaries. Today, customers, partners, suppliers and practically anyone can co-create innovations with an organization.

Limitless digitization is complemented by unbounded innovation in the banking industry. Digital innovations such as robo-advisory, which have almost zero to negligible registration fees, use algorithms to manage funds is turning out to be a boon to millions of people who don't have access to personalized financial advice.

Conventionally, banks have been focusing on product selling; be it loans, insurance or fund management, it was a static product selling model. Most modern banks are now transforming themselves into a multifaceted platform which is not only a virtual bank, but also a lifestyle kiosk selling movie tickets and other lifestyle products. Traditionally the gatekeepers of customers' money, banks are now also their lifestyle partner. In the digital age, banks are crossing industry boundaries and becoming ubiquitous.

Relentless Iteration

Lines between the now, new and the next are blurring away. While in the industrial age there was a concrete end-state for products and services, in the digital age, products and services undergo relentless iteration without a specific end-state. Things are blurring away in the time dimension. As a result, everything is becoming, everything is arriving.

Back in the day, software organizations launched a major version of their software once a year. Today, it is tough to keep up with the versions of software on the cloud and in the mobile app stores. Versions change overnight, and the consumer is blissfully unaware and doesn't care as long as the experience is stellar.

The same phenomenon is being seen in the world of physical products as well, thanks to 3D printing and rapid prototyping. These trends tremendously reduce the time it takes to prototype products, deliver product updates and achieve predictive maintenance.

A bank's digital footprint needs to be constantly worked upon to enhance customer experience. A mobile banking app, for example, cannot remain static for a long time; it needs to continue building a unique user experience every day. In fact, one of the challenges faced by most banks is that when a customer walks into a bank branch, employees at the branch often have no idea what the customer has experienced in the digital world. Herein lies the challenge of most modern banks of how to enable employees to provide a seamless customer experience across channels.

What Do These Changes Mean for HR Leaders in Banks?

It is quite evident that the HR function in banks needs to undergo dramatic transformation in the context of the changes we have discussed so far.

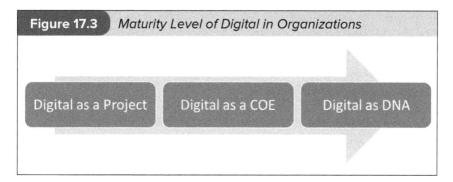

Figure 17.3 *Maturity Level of Digital in Organizations*

Digital as a Project · Digital as a COE · Digital as DNA

Depending on the evolution of the bank from a digital transformation perspective, one might find organizations dealing with digital as a project or digital as a Centre of Excellence (COE) or digital as DNA (Figure 17.3).

Digital, as a project, manifests as one-off implementations across the organization without an overarching governance model. This leads to non-standard ways of looking at digital technologies, customer value and digital business models.

As organizations move further along the evolution curve, they start to treat digital from a COE perspective. In this stage, you find organizations setting up a centralized digital team that governs digital projects across the board. In such organizations, you will find that most digital decisions are made by the COE, and in effect, this ends up becoming another silo in the organization.

When the organization moves into the next step of the evolution, they start to look at digital as their core DNA. In this stage, you will find organizations cascading their digital strategy across the organization, building capabilities across levels and business units, and establishing a supporting culture that ensures success of change initiatives. In other words, such organizations start to operate like a digital native.

Here are the principles that HR leaders must use as part of the new HR manifesto to deal with digital change.

1. Move away from a linear talent model to an ecosystem-based talent model where organizations get access to talent from within and outside the organization in a seamless fashion.
2. Use HR analytics to embrace data-enabled decision making that helps the organization meet critical business goals.
3. Use principles of design thinking to create employee journey maps to deliver wow experience to employees.
4. Embrace agile ways of working in the organization to promote a culture of experimentation and learn-fast environments.

Earlier, we established that HR leaders need to focus on three critical pillars to drive digital outcomes: strategy, capability and culture. Let us now delve deeper into these pillars.

Cascading Digital Strategy

Once the organization develops clarity on digital vision and strategy and formulates a game plan, it becomes the core responsibility of the HR team to create alignment across teams on the big picture and help cascade the vision, strategy and game plan to critical levels within the organization. In many organizations, lack of alignment on the purpose behind digital ends up ringing the death knell on this critical transformation process.

In a nutshell, organizations respond to digital BLUR in the following ways (Figure 17.4).

1. In response to boundaryless organizations, banks must embrace the ecosystem as part of their core strategy. In the banking industry, we see banks now operating open platforms where the focus is on building an ecosystem with Fintech companies actively taking part in the bank's platform.
2. In response to limitless digitization, banks must embrace data as part of their core strategy. In the banking industry, we find banks sitting on top of heaps of customer, financial and transaction data. Using state of the art analytics, banks are monetizing data in a big way.

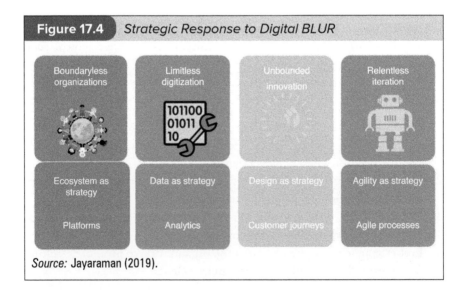

Figure 17.4 *Strategic Response to Digital BLUR*

Boundaryless organizations	Limitless digitization	Unbounded innovation	Relentless iteration
Ecosystem as strategy	Data as strategy	Design as strategy	Agility as strategy
Platforms	Analytics	Customer journeys	Agile processes

Source: Jayaraman (2019).

3. In response to unbounded innovation, banks must embrace design as part of their core strategy. In the banking industry, we find companies tracking customer journeys and designing an omnichannel experience across ATMs, bank branches and mobile banking.

4. In response to relentless iteration, banks must embrace agility as part of their core strategy. In the banking industry, we see companies reducing the time taken to approve loans, real-time advice on financial investments and transactions.

When the bank starts operating in a boundaryless fashion both internally and externally, HR functions must think about the process, policies and culture not just for the organization but for the entire ecosystem. This requires HR leaders to develop big-picture thinking, keeping the ecosystem in sharp focus. Internally, work is getting done through a network of competencies rather than through traditional rigid structures. HR function needs to incorporate principles of ecosystem thinking while designing the organization for the future of work. In effect, this entails building a fluid organizational design using artificial intelligence for talent acquisition and staffing for projects.

In a limitlessly digitized world, HR professionals need to start making use of data for talent analytics across the entire lifecycle of employees. The challenge in today's context is that employee data is tucked away in multiple systems and functions, robbing the bank of the opportunity to develop a single view of the employee. Using HR analytics, HR functions in banks can transition to becoming a performance assurance team with the mandate of ensuring that peak performance gets delivered.

In the unbounded innovation era, HR professionals must apply empathy maps and design employee journey maps to create wow experiences. While thinking around customer experience has evolved quite a lot, the same cannot be said about employee experience. Many leading thinkers assert that without stellar employee experience, customer experience is just a dream. To achieve stellar omnichannel employee experience, HR leaders must understand employee journey maps and use principles of design thinking and gamification.

In response to relentless digitization, HR needs to embrace real-time response and proactive action. In fact, wherever we use the word annual, it is safe to pause and think about why things cannot be real time. From onboarding to performance conversations to strategy planning to rewards, things can be a lot more real time and iterative.

Figure 17.5 shows the key focus areas for Highly Digital HR.

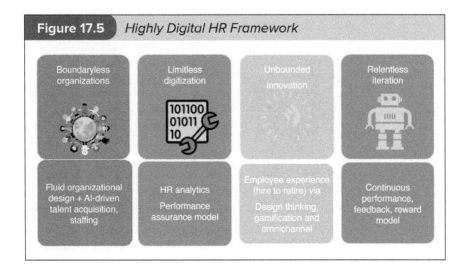

Figure 17.5 — *Highly Digital HR Framework*

Building Digital Leadership Capability to Ensure Readiness

Having a great digital strategy without upgraded leadership capabilities is a recipe for sure-fire failure. Digital leadership is significantly different from industrial-age leadership along various dimensions. Whereas industrial leadership was all about command and control and hierarchies, digital leadership is all about influencing through collaboration and networks. While industrial leadership relied on experience of the leader for crucial decisions, digital leadership tends to include data-enabled decision making as a core pillar of leadership. Industrial-age leaders tend to view the world through the lens of their own products, whereas digital leaders tend to view the world through the eyes of the customer. While industrial-age leaders placed a lot of emphasis on stability avoiding uncertainty, digital leaders have an agile mindset where change is incorporated into the heart of decision making.

The four digital leadership personas are listed in Figure 17.6.

HR leaders have the responsibility to build new-age leaders that are networked within and across organizational boundaries. They must focus on building sense-making as a critical capability in the VUCA (volatility, uncertainty, complexity and ambiguity) world. They must also build leaders who have the design acumen to create wow experiences for customer, employees and partners alike. Also, HR leaders must create a psychologically safe environment where leaders can embrace smart failure and rapidly iterate towards success. Without these crucial shifts in leadership capabilities across levels in the organization, chances of success are quite bleak.

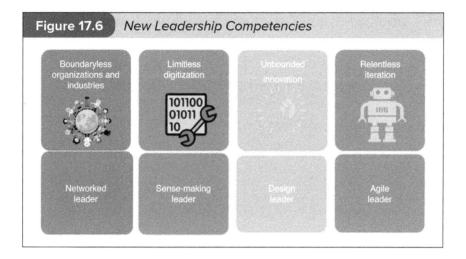

Figure 17.6 *New Leadership Competencies*

Fostering Digital Culture

The age-old saying 'Culture eats strategy for breakfast' rings true even in the digital age. While traditional organizations tend to have concentration of power at the top, digital organizations tend to have distributed power, and have an open, collaborative and sharing culture. Traditional organizations often get mired in bureaucracy and turf wars; digital organizations try to enable decision making through data. Traditional organizations tend to operate in silos, whereas digital organizations look at the world through an ecosystem-oriented lens to build a culture of diversity and inclusion. Traditional organizations have been averse to failures and rapid experimentation. In contrast, digital organizations promote smart failures and instil fail-fast or learn-fast cultures (Figure 17.7).

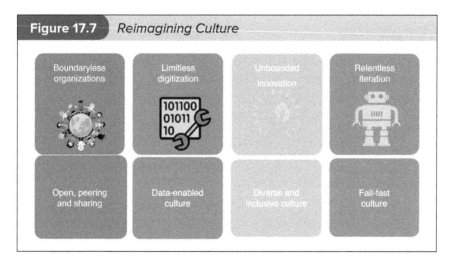

Figure 17.7 *Reimagining Culture*

HR Organizations of Future in the Banking Domain

Digital Recruiting

Digital recruiting can be defined as the use of modern technologies as a tool to attract and hire the most qualified talent for a job opening. HR in banks can use the following digital recruiting strategies to stay ahead of the game in the war for talent.

Leverage Social Media

About 94 per cent of talent acquisition managers are networking on social media sites in look out for the best talents (Betterteam, 2020). Going beyond LinkedIn, the professional networking site, recruiters are looking at Facebook, Instagram and Twitter to find new talent.

AI in Hiring

There are many manual, repetitive tasks that are involved in the hiring process—for example, CV screening, scheduling, tracking etc.—that can be taken care of by the new technology. Other AI-based technologies such as chatbots help you respond to different candidate questions on time and with greater accuracy. This improves candidate experience tremendously.

Axis Bank uses algorithm-based video interviews, along with aptitude tests, to hire around 2,000 customer service officers from a pool of more than 40,000 applicants.

Intelligent Applicant Tracking System

Today, about 70 per cent of recruiting companies are using some form of applicant tracking systems (ATSs) (Oswal, 2018). ATS helps document employee records and the associated recruitment history and activity. Most importantly, it helps ensure compliance under different state laws that government talent recruitment and onboarding processes. In addition to connecting with candidates, just when the need arises, it is important for HR leaders and talent acquisition experts to manage, nurture and engage talent so that they become the employer of choice when the need arises.

Onboarding

According to Gallup, only 12 per cent of employees strongly agree that their organization does a great job onboarding new employees (Gallup, n.d.).

Yet, onboarding is the first step toward delivering an effective employee experience, and in its absence, many employees don't stick around. Poorly designed onboarding processes are one of the reasons more than one-quarter of new employees quit within 90 days (Inc., 2018).

Many organizations are adopting Microsoft Teams for onboarding new employees. Through Microsoft Teams, new employees can immediately have access to past conversations and documents, or use chat, audio or video calling features to ask questions about the projects. The employee self-service bot within Microsoft Teams reduces the time employees spend searching for information to get their job done. Through this bot, new employees can access HR policies and processes like leave, benefits and payroll via chat.

Talent Development

A new wave of digital tools can help companies to focus not only on hiring but also on managing, retaining and developing employees. From a learning management system to content libraries and massive open online courses to learning in the flow of work on collaboration tools such as Slack or Microsoft Teams, today's HR leaders have plenty of digital tools to provide continuous learning options for employees.

Performance Management

Performance management used to be a once-a-year ritual in most organizations where goals were set, performance appraisals were done and feedback was provided to employees. Furthermore, many organizations today have dropped the traditional bell-curve approach to ranking employees to pave way for a more feedforward system that helps employees learn and grow. Using digital tools, organizations are empowering line managers to set agile goals, track performance on a regular basis around the year and provide real-time feedback to employees.

Succession Planning

One of the most important responsibilities fulfilled by HR leaders is ensuring sustainability of the organization through robust succession planning. While most of the focus has been on senior-leadership succession in the past, today, companies are investing in building a leadership pipeline across levels in the organization. HR leaders use sophisticated assessment tools and inputs from past performance to first identify top talent and then groom this talent in a systematic fashion to meet the needs of the now and the next.

Bank of Baroda: Growth and Empowerment Using Digital Platforms

Bank of Baroda is an Indian multinational, public sector banking and financial services company. It is the third largest public sector bank in India with 131 million customers and a total business of $218 billion. With a headcount of 85,000 employees, the bank has presence in every state in India with coverage of 90 per cent of all districts in India. The bank also has 100 overseas branches across various countries.

Less than a decade ago, the very organization of the human resource function was less than optimal to take advantage of the advancements in digital technologies. Earlier, the HR function was operating in silos and was, to a large extent, decentralized. Under the leadership of Shri. Joydeep Dutta Roy, Chief General Manager, Strategic HR, significant changes were ushered in to centralize the HR function. This enabled the bank to digitize core HR operations and perform 'hygiene tasks' including payroll, benefits, employee rosters etc. very efficiently in an automated fashion. Digitization of the HR process at a central level has also allowed the bank to operate at an elevated speed where volume of HR tasks can be handled uniformly without any human biases creeping in. In addition to HR operations, digitalization has since been introduced across the entire spectrum of an employee lifecycle at the bank be it recruitment, onboarding, performance management etc.

Creating growth and empowerment for employees at different levels is an important lever that the HR function can use to drive organizational performance. Earlier, the bank had an annual performance appraisal system that was prone to biases due to lack of real time actionable data. More importantly, the performance system did not do much to give insights to employees to improve their performance. It was merely a record keeping activity at that time.

Today, using a new-age system called Baroda GEMS (Growth and Empowerment Management System), the bank has made sure that daily performance conversations using real-time data is a possibility. Performance management is not merely an end-of-the-year assessment activity anymore. The system is geared to truly make the employees succeed on a daily basis. It is a real time, daily system that enables employees to make adjustments to their way of working in order to reach their targets. Using sophisticated algorithms, the Baroda GEMS platform gives timely inputs on performance, shares best practices followed by top performers across various regions. The Baroda GEMS platform is available 24x7 and is mobile enabled. By making the system accessible to everyone in the organization, the bank has successfully managed to bridge the data gap across levels and enabled managers as well as their direct reports to have an objective conversation around performance issues. The dashboard feature allows senior leaders to get a bird's eye view of organizational performance on a real-time basis.

Massive transformation of systems and platforms across the organization is by no means an easy task. Shri Joydeep, along with senior leaders in the organization, enabled training programmes for employees across level to understand the importance of the new system. They also appointed change champions across the organization to help other employees. Constant communication with employees demonstrating positive results of the platform was a key aspect to change mindsets of employees and to make the change stick.

Today, the bank has a well-oiled digital system that powers the entire HR function. Looking ahead, the bank is looking to use predictive analytics to mine existing data, draw patterns and inform critical decisions to create a future-ready bank.

Summary

- To sum up, here are the principles that HR leaders must use as a part of the new HR manifesto to deal with digital change: Move away from a linear talent model to an ecosystem-based talent model where organizations get access to talent from within and outside the organization in a seamless fashion.
- Use HR analytics to embrace data-enabled decision making that helps the organization meet critical business goals.
- Use principles of design thinking to create employee journey maps to deliver wow experience to employees
- Embrace agile ways of working in the organization to promote a culture of experimentation and a learn–fast environment.

HR leaders need to play a pivotal role in firmly establishing the pillars of digital strategy, digital capabilities and digital culture in order to ensure success in the digital transformation process.

References

Betterteam. (2020). Social recruiting tips. https://www.betterteam.com/social-recruiting-tips

Fidor Bank. (2019). Your partner of choice for your own banking project. www.fidor.com/story

Gallup. (n.d.). State of the American workplace. https://www.gallup.com/workplace/238085/state-american-workplace-report-2017.aspx?zd_source=hrt&zd_campaign=4035&zd_term=kaumildalal

Gartner. (2017). Gartner says 8.4 billion connected 'things' bill be in use in 2017, up 31 percent from 2016. https://www.gartner.com/en/newsroom/press-releases/2017-02-07-gartner-says-8-billion-connected-things-will-be-in-use-in-2017-up-31-percent-from-2016

Inc. (2018). The top 3 reasons why new employees quit in the first 90 days and how to prevent it. https://www.inc.com/adam-robinson/3-common-mistakes-that-make-new-employees-want-to-quit-in-first-3-months.html?zd_source=hrt&zd_campaign=4035&zd_term=kaumildalal

Jayaraman, R. (2019). *Clearing the digital BLUR*. Wiley.

Ma, A. (2018, May 14). Thousands of people in Sweden are embedding microchips under their skin to replace ID cards. *Business Insider*. https://www.businessinsider.in/tech/thousands-of-people-in-sweden-are-embedding-microchips-under-their-skin-to-replace-id-cards/articleshow/64161231.cms#:~:text=Thousands%20of%20people%20in%20Sweden,skin%20to%20replace%20ID%20cards&text=About%203%2C000%20Swedish%20people%20have,make%20their%20daily%20lives%20easier.

Moscovic, C. (2018). Don't miss a second chance of March madness: Pizza Hut® the pie tops II sneakers that order pizza and pause the game with the push of a button. http://blog.pizzahut.com/dont-miss-a-second-of-march-madness-pizza-hut-unveils-the-pie-tops-ii-sneakers-that-order-pizza-and-pause-the-game-with-the-push-of-a-button/

Oswal, N. (2018). The latest recruitment technology trends and how to really use them. https://www.pcworld.idg.com.au/article/633219/latest-recruitment-technology-trends-how-really-use-them/#:~:text=Today%2C%20about%2070%25%20of%20recruiting,associated%20recruitment%20history%20and%20activity

ScienceDaily. (2013). 90% of world's data generated over last two years. https://www.sciencedaily.com/releases/2013/05/130522085217.htm

Steadman, I. (2013, 11 February). IBM's Watson is better at diagnosing cancer than human doctors. *Wired*. https://www.wired.co.uk/article/ibm-watson-medical-doctor

World Economic Forum. (2016). *World Economic Forum white paper digital transformation of industries: In collaboration with Accenture*. http://reports.weforum.org/digital-transformation/wp-content/blogs.dir/94/mp/files/pages/files/digital-enterprise-narrative-final-january-2016.pdf

Yeates, C. (2017, 10 September). ANZ Bank restructure to create '150 start-ups'. *The Sydney Morning Herald*. https://www.smh.com.au/business/banking-and-finance/anz-bank-restructure-to-create-150-startups-20170906-gybxr8.html

CHAPTER

18

A Journey from Transactional to Transformational Function*

HR Research Value Add in Banking

Rajeshwari Narendran

Fierce global competition, augmented technologies, artificial intelligence, design thinking, changing structures, more aware customers, changing government priorities and policies, embracing new strategies in the volatile world and a further host of new challenges in the environment are forcing banking and financial institutions to evaluate constantly how they perform and sustain their businesses. The delicate dynamism of balancing the see-saw largely rests on the utilization of human capital and expandable human potential. The questions now are: How does HR function add value to business development? How long it can just remain transactional? How can HR, as a function, struggle to find a seat on the table, respectfully?

Dave Ulrich, the global icon of HR, in a webinar, on HR's Future Value Creation: Principles, Targets and Actions, held on 11 June 2020, stated an example of how a certain head of HR experienced short-lived excitement when he was consecutively invited three times into a board meeting, however, he was unfortunately dropped later as he could not convert this opportunity to add value in terms of talent, leadership or contributing to futuristic organizational design. Can we relate this example to HR in the banking sector?

HR should be closely linked to business strategy and it must be a seamless expertise system designed in attracting, retaining, deploying, developing and inspiring the talent as per the ever-changing demands of the business. Getting a seat on the table can never be easy unless HR speaks the language of business. HR, as business think tank, can provide strategies where organizational design and people can co-create competitive advantage and can

---

* The discussed points are a compilation of the author's experiences in the form of various interactions and personal experiences, which are suggestive in nature.

shoulder the responsibility towards stakeholders' value. For aligning the HR agenda and organizational agenda, the HR teams should have knowledge, insights, skills, experiences, and above all, a positive mindset to march with organizational expectations. Intellectual capital is identified as a significant strategic asset which provides long-term benefits and better performance. It is important to analyse to what extent intellectual capital is efficiently utilized in creating value for organizations (Chahal & Bakshi, 2016). Assimilation of human resource management (HRM) strategies with business strategies should be the primary worry of banks (Jha & Mishra, 2015).

Khandelwal (2010), in his report on public sector banks (PSBs), has clearly indicated that employee compensation package, skill sets, skewed age profile, restrictive deployment and performance management system are the major issues that are placing PSBs at a disadvantage.[1] Some of the major HR challenges before PSBs include—building capabilities for the future; improving productivity and performance culture; building talent management practices; building succession for key critical and leadership positions; developing ownership, accountability, professionalization and institutional mechanism for sustained human capital management; transforming HR function from legacy-driven HR to developmental HR etc., all of which have been creating many barriers. The mergers and acquisitions are also creating a vast cultural dissonance within and without addressing the deeper issues; the success of such major drives can easily put banks into stress.

The Movement of HR from Transactional to Transformation Leader

With the advent of HR technologies and HR analytics, the human function is reaching new heights and being recognized as a decision science (Lawler et al., 2006), just like any marketing decision science or financial decision science. The essence is the decision framework with systemic integration and use of measurements, data and advanced analytics to optimize the resources for the business as a meaningful contribution. HR decision science helps to deeply understand what is to be measured, ascertain return on investment (ROI) of HR processes and interventions using data, further improve the human capital dynamics in the organization and provide support in driving transformation through pooling right talent in right proportions.

The modern-day HR assures that a deeper research orientation with the perfect blend of analytics can produce precise and measurable impact on business development and overall results.

[1] Report on the committee on HR issues of public sector banks, June 2010.

This drive has improved the value proposition of HR outside the HR function. The growing economy has posed more challenges for HR managers to focus more on strategic policy formulation and utilize growth in the right direction for the business (Bhasin et al., 2020).

The banking sector plays a key role in the development of the Indian economy. Ever since the Government of India has adopted the economic, financial and banking sector reforms, the banking industry in India has undergone a major change. The healthy competition that has been posed by the PSBs has helped improve the quality of service of the PSBs and has also diversified products through innovation (Bhalla et al., 2018). To foster and nurture innovation and new-age banking practices, the banks need to be equipped with an inquisitive mindset in order to keep the fire alive in making human capital achieve its highest potential and create strategic value proposition. The Indian banking industry is facing multiple challenges at domestic and international market spaces and there is a subsequent need for a paradigm shift in HR practices. The bankers need to identify the missing links in researches which are crucial for the future of human resource development (HRD) as well as the performance of Indian banking system (Bhatt, 2012).

During the past three decades, there has been a huge change in the operation of banking services in India. In an industry like banking, which is service-oriented, the quality in service majorly depends on the effective HRD practices in banks. There is a significant change in the operations of the banking sector in India. Banks need to have passionate employees who strive to take their organization to greater heights (Sarangi & Srivastava, 2012). Various factors, such as changing socio-economic profiles of the customers, government policies, changes at national and international levels, have necessitated banks to strengthen their HR through effective HRD practices (Latha and Rao, 2019), which further necessitates its seed in deeper human-research orientation to create a sustainable impact.

The Big Picture

The banking systems in India are not engaged in any formal research, especially in HR. There is a felt need that when it comes to knowing deeper human effectiveness, banks adopt some international benchmarks and look up to engage global players such as McKinsey or BCG or depend upon Gallup matrices. It is heartening to know that there is a huge untapped potential for in-house dedicated research wing which can be a 'formal discipline' as a specialized function and should not be taken when only one needs to firefight. We therefore also need to institutionalize a system for regular HR research. For HR, research should be a way of life and provide inputs into strategic processes. We need a case for building a culture of HR research. How do we build this culture, and how do we get this message across? While the author does not question the engagements of international consultants or following global standards, it is a matter of import to check how effective or useful these tools can be in the Indian scenario as we are so culturally different. Simply put, what applies to horses cannot be applied to trees!

For example, the glass ceiling impact on women in leadership or work–life balance or the acceptance of LGBT (lesbian, gay, bisexual, transgender) at workplaces mean different things in our context! However, understanding these issues with a keen eye for research may pave the way for better practices with openness to transform.

There is a silver lining that leaders are waking up to the idea of—standardized research and analytics—, which are to be used for better decision making and meeting out future disruptions. The positive side is that India has large PSBs where such initiatives are always welcome. If Indian banking takes up research-based interventions in a serious way, then we can reimagine it reaching the global benchmark and brand. It may be relevant to mention that in the early 1980s, Bank of Baroda (BOB) undertook a unique initiative to recruit seven core faculty in its Apex Staff college at Ahmedabad in behavioural science, HR, general management, economics and operations research with a clear mandate to encourage research in these respective areas. One of the core faculty in HR was allowed to pursue his PhD in industrial relations (IR) on a topic relevant to the problem of the bank. According to this faculty, who later moved to the position of CEO of the bank, 'My research insights helped me to change the paradigm of Industrial relations to eventually facilitate a major transformation of the Bank' (Khandelwal, 2018, pp. 303–332).

An HR research unit can be housed in the training function or in the mainstream HR function. It is imperative to collaborate with academic institutions and research institutions to pave the way for writing case studies on Indian banks and to delve deep upon the seen and unseen issues and challenges through PhD researches in universities or B-schools. BOB, through its Apex Academy in Ahmedabad, in 2015, had set an example with a tie-up of sponsoring IIM Ahmedabad case centre to write and share the case studies from BOB for deeper intervention and to create a win–win for management education to learn from these cases. Banks are sitting on huge data, variety and key HR insights, waiting to be distilled and used for banking and HR transformation.

Recently, SBI has set up an SBI Institute of Leadership in Kolkata with state-of-the-art facilities, both in training and research. It has a number of researchers and faculty members to undertake useful research on the issues of banking and HRD. HR research and analytics could provide a great strategic leverage to individual banks, the industry as well as academic institutions, and a research base can enrich the training of senior executives.

The challenges in modern banking are complex and varied. Often, a problem starts in one HR function, such as simple job description or key responsibility areas, and later, the impact can be seen in other areas, such as performance or policy. During COVID-19, the focus of training shifted completely to webinars or online mode, which may impact human relations or learning adaptability or even employee health. We need to identify whether a deeper dent may be seen on the mental well-being, employee engagement or work culture or even overall productivity, both in positive or negative manner, in the future. The fact cannot be neglected that integration and inter-connection of functions, results and impacts may vary depending on the status of the economy, bank performance, leadership, strategy etc.

The Micro Perspectives on Transformative HR Research

For the purpose of writing this chapter, the author has done a dipstick study with HR and non-HR professionals in various public sector and private sector banks in India, in order to understand the texture of existing practices and challenges broadly. The idea was not prescriptive but to have a spectrum of understanding of the current challenges as well as prospects, and dive deep into the nitty-gritty of HRM/HRD practices. Some very interesting aspects and concerns were understood, and a review-based secondary research was used to support such conclusions.

It was rather a matter of concern to know that more than 50 per cent of executives or staff in HR do not hail from core HR.

There was a grave concern that the top leaders in other functions did not value HR and it is still considered more of a side function than core for business. While the top HR leaders expressed that they feel they can contribute much more, they continue to await an opportunity. The question here was how could HR bring that immense potential it has on the table of business strategy? The inputs and inferences from the conversations and discussion forums with middle and top positions in HR and non-HR functionaries in banks have created a base to develop a checklist of probable research-based interventions that can be the foundations for business development from the roots of HR.

Recruitment, selection and onboarding

It was understood that for PSBs, the Institute of Banking Personnel Selection conducts online exams to recruit officers and clerks and uses various aptitude tests for selecting suitable candidates. It would be interesting if these tests can be based on tailor-made needs, rather than being generalist and applicable for all.

The selection process can be helped with psychometrics, psychodynamic analysis and personality assessment tests to check compassion and emotional intelligence along with intelligence quotient of prospective candidates.

The employee onboarding is considered to be a boring function due its repetitive nature, however, a research-oriented mind can inculcate seeds of deep work culture with mindful games and exercises to assess interests and the hidden potential of employees.

The discussions also offered an insight about how most banks today face generation gaps and ego issues around it, however, a robust buddy mentor program with careful choice can create a wonderful, happy learning experience in the new blood, to give them the enthusiasm to work towards the glory of the organization. These baby steps can create a huge impact and make an umbilical connection in young entrants.

Employee connect and engagements

The preparation of next gen banking requires a tech-savvy environment for augmented technologies, artificial intelligence, chatbots, robotics and training-learning facilities. While most banks have training functions in place, they deal mostly with traditional technical functions and a few IT based interventions only. Here comes the role of research orientation where HR can give specifications with cross functional IT and specialized functionaries to help design and develop customized solutions for day-to-day banking and non-banking activities.

Talent and rewards

The talent management practices can be based on regular assessments of potential and to identify high performers, high influencers and highly motivated personnel from those who are moderate and lower in performance, inspiration and morale, in order to check and intervene timely and pull them from the fences. There can be a regular timeline research on retaining talents and what attracts the high performances, whether it is challenge, money, power or position that may attract talent to perform to the best of their capabilities or any other motive that leads to high performance.

The talent pool can be based on sustainable and competitive advantages so that a future oriented team can always look for innovative ideas to move fast forward.

The texture of banking is different in rural, urban and semi–urban settings, and thus, the research can be done on competencies to handle different clientele including languages and cultural sensitivities of the local needs. This can largely be taken care of while decisions on promotions and transfers are taken. There can be a business driver analysis based on ethnocentricity that whether the banking requirements of the locality is relationship driven, purely commercial and business driven, contribution driven or a mix, and accordingly, staffing competencies can be placed.

HR research can give useful clues about the interaction process between the field level staff and the customers and its impact on retention of customers. It can also give useful clues about the attitudinal issues, issues of discipline and restrictive practices. HR climate surveys in a particular territory and follow-up interventions can facilitate the organization development process.

Attitude as a challenge

The biggest issue that the discussion forums identified was 'attitude'. It is important to note that cross functional training for a beginner and job rotation in early career sets the tone for a deeper understanding of banking operations.

The gender gaps, generation gaps, the power- and politics-associated ego and stagnation in learning, work-hour efficiencies and relationship management, with both internal and external clients, are also some of the very important points for research.

It is apt to mention here that in one of the cooperative banks, there was a continuous problem of rising conflicts and non-performance along with very poor team spirit. The author administered a personal effectiveness scale developed by Professor Udai Pareek, the doyen of HR in India. The test hardly takes five minutes to complete and gives results based on self-disclosure scores, openness to feedback and perception. The administration of this simple psychometric test helped understand that the entire team had low scores on readiness to accept feedback; with deeper intervention, the same team could outperform their targets within a small span of time. 'This is magical,' was the exclamation of the regional head who then happily agreed to get OCTAPACE (Openness, Collaboration, Trust, Authenticity, Pro Action, Confrontation and Experimentation) tests done across the region and many insights were then used to make the entire region a success. This proves that where there is will, there is a way.

Promotions and transfers

Promotion and transfer is a major cause of employee disenchantment at various levels. Research can reveal the areas of concerns which can help improve motivation of people. Another significant area of research is about gender issues. This should help providing insights about issues such as why a large number of women refuse promotions, what policy intervention can help them to plan their careers and how HR policies can be redesigned to facilitate this process. Research can also help give insights about the issues of fairness in job rotations, transfers and different kind of biases that may be prevalent in operating policies. In short, research can help in creating a meritocratic system.

A robust HR accounting system based on internal survey research can definitely take care of over-staffing and under-staffing issues. Similarly, a structured HR information system can give much insight to employee competencies, deficiencies, areas for improvements and development paths for proper career management.

Conflicts and IR challenges

The challenges of handling social security, welfare activities, conflicts and biases around inclusion and diversity, discrimination, union behaviours, decision drivers for compensation, benefits and service conditions can also be researched to take better decisions around these challenges. A white paper on collective bargaining can pave the way for rationale for such major decisions which can make or mar the bank and its future by deciding the percentage spent on human capital and its development. It can be a research agenda to check whether any privileges lead to complacency or push performance to comfort zones.

Cultural aspects and ROI on HR

Organization culture is a reflection of people, their character and conduct. A research-based HR can always work on work ethics, values, norms, traditions, beliefs etc., to create a legendary culture. The organizational citizenship behaviour, camaraderie, team dynamics, interpersonal relations, trust and innovation are some flavours in HR which can create a huge implication on business results and can improve bottom-line and top-line targets attainment.

There is another interesting area which came through discussion about where all the violations in service rules happen and why people take short cuts or try to misuse a loophole in policies or procedures. Some people take transfer on compassionate grounds; do these grounds hold true even today or should there be continuous updating and checks for such takers and how can we minimize problems, both to employee and organization?

Redundancy of rituals procedural lapses

There are many rituals in banking HR practices which can be easily scrapped as they have lost their shine; these can be easily traced with simple surveys or small studies. According to a very senior banker, the suggestion boxes are a small token award associated with it, which is more of a ritual than a necessary exercise. Similarly, ranking and rating for the sake of performance appraisals and having the bell curve syndrome can be checked for its relevance. The gratis promotions in the fag end of the career, (almost on the verge of retirement) which are of no use to the organization, rather turn out to be only a face-saving exercise or pleasing a separating colleague.

The nominations in training programs just for the sake of nominations or formality can be identified by a research on utility of trainings on the job, which can paint a real picture and can save a huge amount spent on unnecessary and irrelevant L&D exercises. The HR research can focus on identifying such activities and can actually create a more value-based activity for better image and trust.

There are many such provisions like various allowances, house building loans, vehicle loans, other advances, reimbursement of medical bills and many such privileges extended to employees, however, there are number of misuses seen around it which an agile HR executive can research and create preventive measures for. This can be then measured in terms of monetary savings or costs or even to check the ROI of an agile HR.

Leaves holidays and festivals

It emerged from discussions that many leaves are overused, misused or never used which included even sabbaticals, maternity and paternity leaves, childcare leaves etc. A research-oriented mind in HR can look out for creating measures to optimize the leaves and benefits associated with it and can help the banks to turn these into business days. There was a suggestion to develop a framework of choice-based holidays where the employee can choose 10 days of their choice of leave in place of forced holidays.

Well-being

A research on work-life balance, quality of work life, mental well-being, employee health, long sitting hours and impact on health, stress and lifestyle diseases, infectious diseases like the Corona pandemic and bankers' risks etc., can not only prove to take corrective steps or preventive measures but also may generate health indices to go up.

Community development and role of banks

Online banking vis-à-vis human touch-point banking, compassion, care and role of banks in economic empowerment and human capital development, CSR based interventions, self-help groups, microfinancing and its human face, financial education and inclusion, access to bottom of pyramid and human development aspect are also few areas where HR can develop research to prove its worthy contributions to business development in the true and micro sense.

Building an Integrated HR Research Approach

The range and complexity of changes going on in the banking industry raises the significance and role of HR in different ways. It is, therefore, important to make the HR function a data- and research-driven function, which can inform decision making in the best possible ways. This will also contribute towards the professionalization of the HR function.

A good starting point for creating a HR research culture will be to build a research unit as part of the HR function. This research unit can add value in a variety of ways—it could create research designs for various studies relevant to the banking sector, conduct surveys and build interventions based on them, explore and understand the response to technological changes, setting-up studies on evaluation of leadership training etc.

At a broader level, banks can interface with academic institutions for joint research projects in HR areas, sponsoring PhD programmes on organizationally relevant problems, support case studies on important initiatives such as transformation and act as a sounding board for the management on HR issues and problems.

A research unit can also help in sharing and disseminating HR practices around and facilitate the change of the HR mindset both, among the HR employees as well as business managers and leaders. Given the diversity of Indian banking employees, in terms of age, backgrounds, digital literacy, social context, and other factors, research programs to understand the impact and best practices will facilitate the transformation process.

Summing Up

In the evolving world of banking and digitalization, many changes in the structure, processes and employment policies will be called for. Transformation will be almost on continuous basis. Yesteryears' HR policies based on ad hocism or outdated settlements between management and trade unions will call for replacement by installing a meritocratic system. Human resource policies will be an important lever for change and transition as it will help to develop HR policies based on research insights. This will not only motivate employees but also improve the credibility of HR functions and their functionaries. HR has to rise to the occasion.

References

Bhatt, P. (2012). HRD in emerging economies: Research perspectives in Indian banking. *Indian Journal of Industrial Relations, 47*(4), 665–672.

Chahal, H., & Bakshi, P. (2016). Measurement of intellectual capital in the Indian banking sector. *VIKALPA-The Journal for Decision Makers, 41*(1), 61–73.

Jha, R., & Mishra, M. K. (2015). A study of HRM and employees performance in banking sector in India. *International Journal of Advance Research and Innovative Ideas in Education, 1*(3), 24–28.

Khandelwal, Anil. (2018). *CEO, chess master or gardener?* Oxford University Press.

Latha, V. M., & Rao, V. N. (2019). Human resource development practices in Indian banking sector: An overview. *IOSR Journal of Business and Management, 21*(10), 35–39.

Lawler, E., Baudreau, J. W., Mohrman, S. A. (2006). Achieving strategic excellence an assessment of human resource organizations. Stanford University Press.

Sanjeev, Bhalla, N. S., Sidhu, T. S., & Shruti. (2018). Human resource practices and job satisfaction in selected new generation private banks: An empirical study of their relationship & their impact among executive employees. *Pacific Business Review International, 11*(6), 7–16.

Sarangi, S., & Srivastava, R. K. Impact of organizational culture and communication on employee engagement: An investigation of Indian private banks. *South Asian Journal of Management, 19*(3), 18–13.

Sujan, B., Bhasin, J., & Mushtaq, S. (2020). Reallocation of HR functions: A study of HR effectiveness in banking sector. *Jindal Journal of Business Research, 9*(1), 72–83.

Suggested Readings

- 'Recent Study Shows Impact of HR Competencies on Business Performance' by Wayne Brockbank, Dave Ulrich, Jon Younger and Mike Ulrich.
- Khandelwal Committee Report on Public Sector Banks, 2010.

Challenges of HR in Indian Public Sector Banks
Reflections and Confessions of a CEO

M. Mahapatra

The Beginning

The February morning was finer than expected. The right nip in the air, new foliage awaiting the spring which made my walk so invigorating, the usually delayed newspaper wallah delivering on time and all the servants and the gardener reporting for work. My wife was happy and offered me a steaming cup of tea with a beaming face. I could not have asked for better. I was in no mood to spoil the ambience by starting with the newspaper. Thus, I ambled into the garden chair and picked up my Wodehouse to read again of the wise counsel of Jeeves. The mirth of literature and the tonic of good bird's chirps did not last long though. The maid brought my phone to me outside, saying there were incessant rings! I saw four missed calls. Two from my friend Anil, a professor in the local management institute, and two from my general manager (GM; HR).

First, I decided to call the GM (HR).

He was all nerves. 'Sir, we must finalize the HR transformation request for proposal (RFP). I need your guidance. You have been reminding me, but I don't know where to start.'

I was irritated. The bank needed many redoes and re-jigs in HR. The bank also urgently required a lot of new things. I had been discussing this for the umpteenth time with the HR department. Many should have been done or started years ago. However, getting bogged down with routine, with little time to envision and plan, is common in organizations and even more so in public sector undertakings.

'But what have you been doing all these days? You have lost precious time you see!' I exclaimed.

'Sir, my plate is full. There are 12 positions of assistant general manager, deputy general manager and GM which need filling up. It is so difficult to find suitable people. There are too many young officers, they are not ready for credit or branch assignments. Regional managers and branch heads find it difficult to manage the youngsters. I did all permutations and combinations. IT, marketing and risk departments are asking for quick posting and training of officers as they don't trust the vendor and the consultant staff. Human resource management system (HRMS) has broken down three times last week and I don't know if we will be able to update the leave records and deductions. All lady officers want sabbatical leave and light work. Scheduled Castes/Scheduled Tribes association is blaming me of caste bias. All this time, the chief financial officer (CFO) is asking me to reduce staff as our productivity is low among peers. I am getting disoriented sir! I am a diabetic myself. I will be grateful if you change me and post a youngster in my place…!' He would have continued had I not interjected.

'My dear, you have just narrated the headings of the HR transformation RFP,' I interrupted.

'Sorry sir, I don't follow.' He sounded incredulous.

'Do you remember me telling everyone that a problem well defined is half the solution?' Please have a HR huddle jot down all the problems you have faced in HR in last three months, down to the minutest detail. We will finalize the RFP in no time.' I said, as the other phone started ringing. It was Anil.

'What has happened to you, boss? All well? You are too busy a CEO! I read your article. So nice! Do keep up with your reading and writing.' Anil was his friendly self.

'Sorry, could not call you back. How is your new book selling? And the classes in the college?' I asked.

'All well. Your *bhabhi* says namaste to you. By the way, my new upcoming book is a collection of writings from experts on human resources problems at workplace. I phoned to request you to write a piece.'

'Let me think and get back to you. Drop in for a drink. I've got some new wines,' I said, disconnecting.

I was amused at the coincidence. Probably, I could kill two birds in one shot? I would finalize the RFP for my GM (HR) and write the piece for Anil. I started walking back inside to get ready for the office, as I remembered what Nelson Mandela once said: 'It always seems impossible until it is done.'

Office affairs were routine. I scheduled the meeting with the HR for later in the afternoon. First with the HR team and then the HR team along with a friend Raman, with a background in HR consulting. As sincerely and honestly as they could, the HR team, led by their GM, listed down all the problems they had faced in the last three months. I asked them to narrate the interactions, what they thought to be the problems and what they thought other leading banks are doing. Essentially, I was trying to understand their grasp of the challenges and the best practices. There were a few routine experiences, however, we could shortlist a few challenges before my friend showed up to discuss and finalize the list of top 10 challenges and what our problem statement was when an interface happened with the intending partners of HR transformation. The list ran thus:

1. Challenge of purpose in HR
2. Challenge of organizational culture and politics
3. Challenge of ageing staff
4. Challenge of digitization and innovation
5. Challenge of skill and fit
6. Challenge of collaboration and friendship
7. Challenge of the millennial work force
8. Challenge of productivity
9. Challenge of social justice
10. Challenge of discipline

When Raman came later, we were able to discuss each one of these points in greater detail and find discussion points, as well as what has been done in the industry to get ready for the wider discussion. Our analysis was both stimulating and eye opening. So much is always achieved with an open yet informed, intellectual discussion!

Here are my notes, which I made for writing, later, the article that Anil had requested.

Challenge of Purpose

The main challenge before HR in public sector banks (PSB) today is the confusion about the purpose of HR. HR needs to continuously define and reposition itself both, in organization as well as the industry context. The understood purpose is to manage recruitment, transfer, postings, promotions, perquisites and discipline. The big pictures of HR purpose, that is, bringing employee empathy and transparency, making the HR future ready with aligned training, creating branding through HR, customer/market centricity designs are all aspirational purposes but are seldom discussed, debated or designed in PSBs. I asked, 'Do we have an HR vision for ourselves?' There were blank looks.

Raman asked, 'How should we ask things to begin?'

I said, 'Let us ask for a template of the road map for each one, what are the data points, what a translated HR big picture looks like and what are the measures of success of listed actions. Probably, the best place to begin shall be an articulation of best practices.'

Organizational Culture and Politics

By now, I had ordered coffee for everyone. Coffee led to a discussion on the debilitating effects of gossip and office politics. The culture of most PSBs is to block constructive and innovative ideas. This culture of staying in the comfort zone and lack of experimentation was quickly decided as a challenge. As Peter Drucker once said, 'Culture eats strategy for breakfast.' HR transformation must start with demolishing the culture of misinformed office politics and replacing it with frequent communication, articulation of benefits in both long and short term, and dialogue with employee-opinion leaders. The motto should be making employees love their organization instead of bad mouthing it! As Simon Sinek tells, 'Customers will never love a company until the employees love it first.' There must be clear responsibilities for seniors and social media must be effectively used, if necessary, with professional help and modern communication tools.

Ageing Staff

As I was expecting, this was a hot debate. Raman winked at me as the tempers rose. The youngsters were blaming oldies in the bank to be responsible for bureaucracy, slow to adapt and moored in the past. The seniors blamed youngsters as brash, inexperienced, not learning from mistakes and not understanding the value of good risk management.

I had to intervene. 'A bank needs the senior staff as much as the energy of the youngsters'. Ageing or aged staff is often cited as the main reason for PSB problems. But data, after large scale induction of youngsters, does not support this theory. Senior staff have proven to be more suited to credit, risk management and managerial roles. They were found to be little slow to adapt but proven to be more consistent after a while. Raman cited several examples from the manufacturing and IT sectors where seniors are in such short supply that the salary difference between a 30-year-old and a 50-year-old is almost 10 times! My own readings showed that both youngsters and older staff have similar life and career goals (Figure 19.1)!

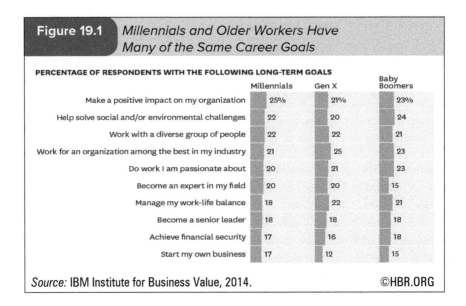

Figure 19.1 *Millennials and Older Workers Have Many of the Same Career Goals*

PERCENTAGE OF RESPONDENTS WITH THE FOLLOWING LONG-TERM GOALS

	Millennials	Gen X	Baby Boomers
Make a positive impact on my organization	25%	21%	23%
Help solve social and/or environmental challenges	22	20	24
Work with a diverse group of people	22	22	21
Work for an organization among the best in my industry	21	25	23
Do work I am passionate about	20	21	23
Become an expert in my field	20	20	15
Manage my work-life balance	18	22	21
Become a senior leader	18	18	18
Achieve financial security	17	16	18
Start my own business	17	12	15

Source: IBM Institute for Business Value, 2014. ©HBR.ORG

Therefore, we decided that the challenge of 'age' is to find roles, training needs of the staff, cross functional roles, reverse mentoring etc. An HR transformation must work on all of these aspects.

Digital Disruptions and Innovations

It was already 7 PM, but no one seemed tired. How to bring digital innovations brought comments only on incremental functional improvements and speed of processing. No one talked of using AI for managing postings or using analytics for skill mapping and job-family inventory. There was no comment on robotic process automation for processing self-appraisals. Nor there was any discussion on employee lifecycle management using past data. HRMS was considered a function that involved only salary payment, leave management and keeping database of employees. A new-age bank requires digital platforms, digital innovations and a fintech mindset of constant experimentation with ideas. Innovation required acceptance of failures, which is nearly absent in PSB ethos. So, we decided that in-house expertise and knowledge may not be enough. This specific area needed professional consultant support.

Skill and Fit

I remembered my morning discussion. Many of our senior-level talks lamented this as well. All my CEO friends in the PSBs had this refrain of large number of staff being 'promotable but not post-able'. The genesis of this is not recognizing the length of the process and the search for instant solutions. For example, risk management and IT were recognized as critical and fundamental skills for the running of banks about a decade back. But we, in the PSB banking industry, persisted with producing more and more branch banking and traditional administrative roles. The solution is to lay down a skill gap projection for the next 10 years in different areas and at different levels of seniority. Probably in blocks of three years. Recruitment, training and promotions must align with the future needs of the organization, not the current ones. As we work on putting together a robust process, we must have a limited lateral hiring plan and policy, so that we stay aligned with the market best practices and through the lateral hires, begin a change of our own practices, where necessary.

Collaboration and Friendship

The value of friendship and collaboration is foundational today to organizations, in general, and PSBs, in particular. Raman was not very enthusiastic, given his private sector experience. My own team members were confused.

'What does friendship have to do with HR?' someone asked half-heartedly.

I explained, 'Today, individuals and organizations can hardly complete anything entirely on their own. They have to depend on vendors, service providers or consultants. Inside the organization, most things depend on joint efforts between departments. And collaboration begins with friendship. The challenge is that it is left as an unmeasured and unstructured activity rather than a positive intervention. When a thing is critical, you put resources and tools to take it forward. For example, in appraisals, do we give credits to joint projects? Do we take 360-degree feedback on collaborative quotient of seniors?'

The Millennial Workforce

The youngsters in the group were excited. Many of them advocated faster career track. Seniors were airing the difficulty in understanding what millennials want. I pointed to the HBR study (Figure 19.2). 'Look, this proves that the key is to appreciate mindset gaps which is anchored in the generation gap.'

The common practice is to put millennials into the drill of routine and asking them to climb the ladder of hierarchy. As the study showed, millennials are impatient to contribute, influence and be part of strategic projects,'

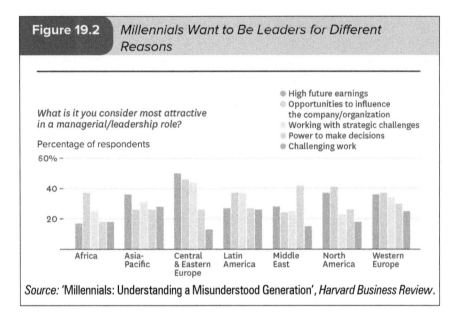

Figure 19.2 *Millennials Want to Be Leaders for Different Reasons*

What is it you consider most attractive in a managerial/leadership role?

- High future earnings
- Opportunities to influence the company/organization
- Working with strategic challenges
- Power to make decisions
- Challenging work

Percentage of respondents

Source: 'Millennials: Understanding a Misunderstood Generation', *Harvard Business Review*.

I added. In PSBs, structures should be changed so that design of projects, drawing and executing them must include millennials based on transparent management of aptitude and abilities.

Challenge of Productivity

Raman began the topic by provocation to the group that PSBs are the worst in per branch, per employee business and profits. Their lack of productivity is the main cause for their stock market performance. As expected, there were roars of protest in the room. 'What about social banking, doing government sponsored projects, being unable to act on non-performers, lack of incentivization for good work in PSBs?'

Raman said, 'But is it not a fact that most PSBs have made very little formal effort to improve and measure productivity?'

I had to agree. We had problems on two fronts. Productivity initiatives including reward and recognition were not just sporadic but were discontinuous. The staff incentive permitted in PSBs as a percentage of operating profits are hardly ever utilized, not even 25 per cent. Budgeting for productivity, which should be potential, and target based for operating units is often arithmetical and does not attract attention from the senior management.

'The problem of productivity is one of governance and modernization, not of lack of intent or energy. Let us design our HR transformation for that,' I concluded.

Social Justice and HR

Traditional PSBs face discords and disruptions because the DNA of HR is moored on male-centric, English-speaking, upper-class sophistication. As the women in the workforce increase rapidly, as the lower strata of society get to be aware of their workplace rights and positive discrimination, the traditional HR machinery fumbles. The transformation required is to make policies transparent and implementing them whole heartedly. Policy-formulation empathy for women with young children, for onboarding, skill development and promotion of the underprivileged is a must. Budgeting for HR for social justice must be specific and action oriented.

Discipline

We deliberately kept it for the last. Discipline, or the lack of it, has always been a major issue. Discipline, in fact, could lead to major operational risks due to loss of customer goodwill, fraud losses and productivity leaks. Should employees not be self-disciplined? Should banks need the discipline of the army? Discipline, as a basic hygiene, is illustrated by George Washington: 'Discipline is the soul of any unit. It makes small numbers formidable; procures success to the weak, and esteem to all.'

Everyone was very enthusiastic at this nuance of discipline being at the core of team building and mentoring. Discipline is, therefore, not about disciplining but building disciplines through organization, collaboration and the spirit of speed and focus on execution. We decided to build a few disciplines and integrate it with HR policies. To begin with, the discipline of giving premium and recognition to the complete transformation of critical projects in or ahead of time. A collaborative project with the CFO was to be started to make the delivery units like IT or recovery notionally responsible for opportunity loss of money due to delays or botched up executions. Also, a process of quantifying and relating frauds to lack of discipline in reporting and due diligence and aligning with budgetary achievements was to be introduced.

Epilogue

The exercise of HR was exhaustive. That day, I returned home well after my favourite BBC serial at 11 PM was over, but I was happy. We had brainstormed in a manner that was productive and inclusive. Of course, my chapter for Anil's upcoming book, now, was a cakewalk.

A Passionate Journey of Continuous Transformation in HR*

Prakash Ranjan

Early Days

Quitting a plum job in the human resources (HR) function at Daewoo Motors in 1996 to join Bank of Baroda (BOB), a large public sector bank, to do primarily a personnel administration job at a lower salary could, in itself, be termed a suicidal career decision. However, when the landscape is big and the determination to paint a story of your own is in mind, risks can be taken. Working through the dilemmas to arrive at this decision was not an easy one. Being the university gold medallist, with the National Junior Fellowship in hand and having commenced the PhD research work, my journey commenced in BOB with the first posting at New Delhi after a short stint of around five months at Daewoo Motors. The initial feeling after joining the bank was that I had committed hara-kiri in my career. The quagmire of dusty files, settling expense claims, sending routine reminders to submit manpower data, and conducting a pleasing discussion with union functionaries had already taken the lustre and zing out of my new career move. Often, when caught on crossroads, human instinct is to rue and go back. However, to continue on the tough road ahead, one needs to muster courage, determination and purpose and that is emotionally choking at times. I never thought of staying for a decade at BOB; however, the opportunity of rotation every three years from regional to zonal and finally to the corporate office in Mumbai gave me a new context to see the same function from a different lens. In the humdrum of personnel administration job, always seeing the hope of being able to think and do something different was the biggest sense of self-confidence that gave me the golden opportunity in my career, when I was asked by the then executive director and later on chairman and managing director (CMD), Anil K. Khandelwal, to come to Mumbai in 2002 and work with him. All this happened in a five-minute interaction,

---

* Views expressed by the author are personal and experiential and nowhere are reflections of any organizational stance or endorsement of the companies he has worked for.

and I never realized what I had done that made him give me this unique opportunity till he revealed to me at a later point that it was the zeal in my eyes to do something different. What started as experimentation prepared the pitch of my career hitherto. The period of professional acquaintance and working together with him between 2002 and 2006 prepared the foundation of my HR leadership. His inspiration and influence on me have been tremendous and it continues to have an effect on me even now; we interact and exchange our views regularly. Had he not provided the opportunity and nurturing, I would have been deprived of valuable experience in my journey.

BOB is a mega organization and the strategic business transformation programme undertaken by Khandelwal was perhaps a unique experimental opportunity that rarely comes in the life of any organization despite continuous changes that otherwise keep occurring. The leadership style created a safety net for many experiments to be undertaken not only in HR function but in other functions too, which went through the crests and troughs before being successful. It was a *perfect* 'start-up' for its time.

It helped potential champions to shine, it challenged the non-believers to believe in mega outcomes, it demolished the roadblocks and barriers for smooth exchange of information, and the biggest outcome was the restoration of self-belief, trust among people and confidence in the future roadmap of the organization, which proved to be one of the best examples of mega transformation.

It was during the experience of an HR transformation that I got an opportunity to work closely for some time with late Udai Pareek and the best learning that I received is how knowledge and humility can co-exist in a person. He was an apt example of brilliance wrapped into simplicity. No wonder he is regarded as the father of organizational development (OD) and human resource development (HRD) in India and is a respectable name at the global level.

One Gets into a Role, but Expanding and Shaping It Is Always Possible

Everyone gets a job description (JD) in a role but rewriting one's own JD could be an exercise in creativity. It's like challenging oneself and seeing above the wall. Career is always a careful exercise of 'meaning-making'. Upon being selected for Junior Research Fellowship, it was very clear in my mind that my research would not be generic, and thus, I selected the topic of strategic HRD, which had virtually no secondary data or research published during the mid-1990s. Inspired by an article about Eicher Motor's transformation, which appeared in the then *the Economic Times Esquire,*

I picked up ITC, Eicher, Voltas and SAIL as my study organizations, as these companies had just started taking some pioneering steps in aligning their HR practices closer to the business.

At BOB, experimentation continued through creative thinking, shaping some conceptual framework, models and adopting unconventional ways to solve problems for which otherwise there was no scope since the organizational culture was more acclimated to acceptance and status quo. When I think in retrospect, I ask this question—how all these could be possible? I think a leader's expectation from my role to break the traditional barrier and come out with different thoughts, in itself, was a great challenge. Khandelwal's vision created the canvas. Given such a nurturing and challenging environment, I was well-prepared with the agility of mind, and my PhD in strategic HRD gave me the perfect frame to think and contribute tangibly in the transformation journey. There was a compelling need to redefine the new context of HRD and the future course of the function graduating from industrial relations to HR. The chairman's initiative of putting a think tank of senior professionals to create new structures and frameworks around people development was a great morale booster for young professionals like me. I was extremely lucky to be placed in the chairman's office. This gave me the rare chance to meet him daily and present my thoughts and ideas to him. To get such an opportunity so early in the career was indeed a huge one. The daily grind of discussing, questioning, reasoning, rejecting an idea, constructing a new idea, praising, criticizing and still hoping to deliver to the big dream was no less than the symbolic 'crucible experience' which Warren Bennis describes as being key to leadership grooming. It made me tough, realistic and confident to manage through the layers of departmental processes and questioning with a strategic thinking mind. Various outcomes that followed out of this process, such as the HR mission statement, HR operating model, KHOJ (Talent Identification and Development Programme), Sampark (employee helpline), Paramarsh (employees counselling services) and happy hours banking, set the pace for further transformation in HR in the bank and added value.

Persistent thinking and experimentation shape attitudes and a strong determination to undertake risks. In all my roles, subsequently, there has always been some work that would fall outside the written scope. It has always been a dilemma whether to undertake those, however, there is a fine difference between what is called mundane and creative thinking. I also feared, at times, that I would be perceived as being extra-jurisdictional. But then how would one acquire a character of 'thinking beyond'' or thinking 'out of the box'? 'Happy hour banking' is a fine example of it. Being in HR, product design was not within the scope of my role, however, thinking about the business imperative when the bank had embarked upon the 24 × 7 physical branch banking under its transformation programme could not be stopped. How to increase the customers' footfall during the lean banking hours was a constant debate in my mind. I still remember how much joy I felt when I saw the comment 'Excellent idea, let's work on it' on the idea file note that I had sent to the CMD. The joy was further multiplied when the product was launched in 2006 by the then finance minister of India. However, this journey was not that smooth. From ideation to conclusion, I had to go through three rounds of rejection by the bank's product operations team.

Later, the institutionalization of the Engineering Knowledge Group at Alstom, in 2012, was another example of a radical idea that came during a free-flowing discussion with the managing director when we were exploring to hire a new engineering head of department. I offered the thought of dismantling the role and going for a collaborative knowledge-driven platform for stream leaders which was needed to be formed for revitalizing the sagging morale of the team. Even though the proposal was opposite to the hiring mandate, I could get through the approval after many persuasive attempts. Its outcome was extremely soothing; one million euro saving to the profit and loss of the business at zero cost in the first year, and the function continued to be managed for many years.

Innovate, Create and Nurture Brands, Live It for Deeper Business Impact

Although every branch of knowledge inspires the other, one that I have drawn most of my inspirations from is sales, branding and marketing. One of the reasons could be that it has always been very close to my heart for the sheer reason that customer–centricity, positioning and service orientation are best taught in this branch of management science. I worked for a large Indian company in sales before I chose to be in HR. Brands bring freshness to the idea, show commitment and create visibility and recall value. Throughout my career, this has been a unique thought process; otherwise, HR could be a stale affair. The strategic linkage of an intervention with the sense of business impact can be very well conceptualized in a brand. During my career of more than two decades, sensing different opportunities and creating brands or banners have been an exciting experience. These have been shaped with a purpose, for creating an emotional connection with the employee audience. One may debate whether to call these as HR brands. Well, if an intervention is powerful, a credible name and packaging go a long way in establishing it. Brands can be wiped out if there is a lack of intent or purpose for which it has been shaped. If a learning intervention such as Learning@70mm was created, the intent behind it was to deliver a real Bollywood-style learning experience under the thought of giving people 'perspective learning'. If Happy Hour Banking could be created, the genuine intention was to create a brand that promises value to customers during lean hours of branch banking. If SpotOn was created for an effective payroll tool, then the on-time service commitment was the real intent. When an HR brand is built, life can be brought into even routine HR operations and emotional communication with employees become possible. The passionate connection of HR delivery needs to be found with the purpose of people.

Culture Is Not Visible but See It beyond the Issue

It is always a struggle to get out of the transactional mode and see the larger picture and grapple with your own dilemmas to decide something for which you may not have many takers. A conviction for a tough decision for a larger cause would always be the challenge for an HR professional, and to acquire this character, there must be a vision of institution building, there must be a passion to shape the culture. Often, buying peace and agreeing on issues brought in by business could be expected behaviour from an HR professional, but how to influence business with smart strategy and an assertive yet supportive consensus-building is what would differentiate grain from the husk. The setting up of the Engineering Knowledge Group is a very apt example where I could muster the courage to assertively put across a radical idea. One should be of strong heart to absorb the criticisms and rejections so that ingenious ideas can be shared.

In a decentralized matrix reporting structure in companies, functional leaders could drive culture very differently and, believe me, sometimes crazily. The job of an HR professional to bring consensus and convergence could be quite a tough agenda. In one such instance, while working at a large multinational corporation, restoring the diluted authority of the CEO amidst functional leaders was a tough call and the path full of thorns. I have been alleged by my critics of aligning with a person or a group and sometimes portrayed as a person trying to bring instability in organizational status quo, but I remained unfettered because there was a cultural change agenda in my mind. In hindsight, it was a much-needed one. An assertive, business-focused and culture-centric demeanour makes a lot of difference. It is often this difference that earns an HR professional a seat on the table in the boardroom.

Create Sponsors, Build Partnerships

The journey of an HR professional with a transformational mindset is arduous, and often, it can be a loner's journey. It can also remain as an under-accomplished one, provided one creates like-minded sponsors and partners. Is it an easy task? Indeed not. There must be a careful selection of right partners who have unbiased interest for the cause, and it needs to be created at different employee levels, including the one within the core HR team. A shared vision created within the internal stakeholders brings genuineness to the planned interventions and creates a sustainable culture to support the change. Even choosing the worst critic as your partner could be helpful, provided that it has been done with great wisdom, strategy and purpose.

One needs a mentor, sponsor and critics. A mentor could become a lifelong teacher whose teachings can help you navigate through the complex business ecosystem. For me, Anil K. Khandelwal had the greatest influence on shaping me to be an HR professional. Thinking big, believing in oneself, managing dichotomies in an organizational system and keeping personal biases and prejudices behind in the larger transformation agenda have been my greatest leadership lessons. He gave me space and time to think and the opportunity to be part of the transformation journey. What I could do at BOB during the HR transformation could only come to pass due to the confidence he showed in me and encouragement he gave me for my work. His inclusive and peer-style discussions were the biggest opportunity for lessons for me. I still recollect his advice to my functional boss, the GM-HR, in 1996, for not allocating me the rudimentary matters was quite a bold advice, and it challenged me to think and contextualize what I was witnessing from the chairman's office. His expectation from me was high and rigorous. I still recall an instance when I could not go to the National Institute of Bank Management (NIBM) library, Pune, for doing my data research when we were writing a keynote article in the *Economic and Political Weekly*. The peaceful counselling which he gave me and his executive secretary, who later became the CMD of another bank, created a tempest inside me, and the next day, I was in the NIBM campus to complete my assignment. I understood the importance of research and passionate diligence in serious work. The two decades of association with him have been not only professional but also emotional. He was my greatest 'sponsor' too.

I realized that sponsors would only be there if one is worthy of sponsorship, and I have been put to various tests and observations. My thoughts, actions, consistency, diligence, passion, commitment, values, learning agility and toughness to withstand pressure were at test continuously in the professional journey before getting the sponsorship.

A good HR professional also needs to be a discernible and credible sponsor of his/her own work; otherwise, you do not always get sponsors for your good work. Without creating an undesirable hype, doing a right positioning of one's own work, communicating the intent, processes, challenges behind doing so and most importantly communicating effectively about the value created must be a self-humbling but self-sponsoring art, and this needs to be carried out with sensible storytelling. The language of communication must be refined over time. This must be only with the intent of honest visibility rather than any gainful strategy behind it. 'Humility is the best test in self-sponsorship.'

Critics also play a great role in helping gain professional maturity. The hammering effect of criticism should create an echo inside your mind because you might be breaking the inertia, making a cultural shift, resetting the agenda or taking up a cause. Self-doubt, facing a dilemma or a sense of slowing down are common symptoms of maturing, however, maturity is in raising the debate within and continue to take the plan forward with a logical conviction. I have experienced all these things while dealing with a few leaders in my experience journey.

To gain active support of business managers or stakeholders for the HR agenda and interventions, the step of making functional leaders as the sponsors has always worked fruitfully. HR functionaries need not and should not do everything by themselves. Collaborative and facilitative partnership ecosystem like business learning partners gave very satisfying results in shaping up on the learning ecosystem.

Authentic Conversations and Process Centricity Bring Credibility

It is a myth that 'what' is more important than 'why' in HR delivery. We are mostly taught the success mantra that only result matters. There is no denying the fact that results do matter, but in human transactions, intent and process are equally important, as they shape the culture on a sustainable basis. Human emotions cannot be handled in a knee jerk, motivation cannot be addressed with any quick extrinsic solution and relationships cannot be managed without having an authentic dialogue for a trusted relationship.

The Thin Book of Trust: An Essential Primer for Building Trust at Work, by Charles Feltman, beautifully describes the framework of building trust at the workplace through these four key attributes—sincerity, reliability, competence and care. I completely agree with these elements. Not succumbing to any pressure or getting carried away under any emotional influence always comes as a mental challenge and creates inherent stress while dealing with any strategic or even an operational issue of significance.

Once, a global head of sourcing function wanted me to complete an exit action of a few senior managers in two days. I thought it over and it was very clear that human emotions cannot be wrecked overnight. Without any hesitation, I replied that it could only be completed within 45–60 days as I would require a proper business case and notice time would have to be factored in. The advocacy here was not only for the people but also for the right business culture. Pulls and pressures from different stakeholders do come, but conviction must be one's own and needs to be calibrated with fine balancing act among priorities, people, values and culture. One needs to be a strategic negotiator and an empathetic listener.

Once, in a winding up of a business unit, I had to do a tough negotiation with the management team to persuade them for approving the formula suggested by me for severance of contractual staff which was more reasonable than the statutory one for the sheer reason that the long service provided by them deserved a fair and compassionate consideration similar to permanent employees because they too had rendered valuable service for the growth of business. The satisfaction at the end of the day is holistic and complete. Institutions are not built in a day, but a dent to a strong foundation can be made in one stroke.

Passionate Learning and Creative Solutioning Helps in Meaning-making

We all know well enough that learning must be a continuous action plan for any professional. As an HR professional, the delivery of learning agenda also needs to be a passionate effort with insight and wisdom. I believe that the 'content' of learning should be set from a 'context' in mind for tomorrow's business agenda and needs to a very selective effort in 'meaning-making'.

While working on the leadership programme, MEP-TIKSHNA, a mammoth leadership education and transformation agenda for over 200 senior executives of BOB who were trained by the IIM Ahmedabad and the Management Development Institute, Gurgaon, one of the first thoughts in my mind was about what should go in for the programme and how that should go in the content so that the outcome fits into the context of the transformation agenda. Understanding the CMD's expectation and his vision for future leaders of the bank was clear guidance into the design context and that gave all of us the context to co-create this programme. Learning has been a process of engagement rather than only delivery, and it has never completely delegated its delivery, rather it has been passionately involved in the process so that I can see its navigation on the meaningful course to achieve the business purpose. It is a creative work of art. The design of the programme 'I am passionate to act (IMPACT)', at another multinational corporation, came out of a very startling observation of blank walls in the office evoking dry emotions amongst employees when all the posters were being taken out as a preparatory action and were to be replaced in a month's time with new ones after the mergers and acquisitions. Within two hours and after deliberations with my team members, we came with a plan—'My Wall, My Expressions'—and utilized those blank walls to capture thoughts and expectations of employees from the new state of things after mergers and acquisitions, which finally culminated into the programme that focused on open dialogue sessions with the help of an expert facilitator. Its objective was to address the apprehensions of the acquisition process and create a positive mindset for change. Similarly, 'Learning @ 70 mm' initiative is simply an intervention of video-based short learning sessions, however, the creative positioning and tying it up with the theme of a Bollywood experience is the ingenuity and adds value to the initiative. The audience's experience of collecting a ticket from the box office, getting seated in a numbered seat in a theatre and enjoying the learning session live, like a movie experience, is the value addition. Some can question the style, but should the fun of learning be forgotten? Peter Block has rightly described 'the pleasure of learning and joy of teaching' in his book *Flawless Consulting: A Guide to Getting Your Expertise Used*.

Even at personal level, continuous zest for knowing something new and investing time to gain a fundamental base of knowledge has always been the drive and my organization development (OD) certification with NTL is one such immersive experience. Learning and continuous reflection need to be a habit.

Building Team Is Like a Pottery Work

Like a deft potter, a manager needs to prepare his/her team for continuous and appropriate nurturing and transformation. The running of the potter's wheel is the fine balance of challenging, caring, letting them go through the conflicts and yet backing them up solidly in a crisis. The time spent on personal coaching never goes to waste. The mind shift from routine operations to end-to-end thinking does not come easy, and this must be coached through demonstrative practices on a regular basis. Passionate delivery and earning credibility are difficult tasks, and team members can only learn these if there are continuous and ethical expectations from them. Most of the time, whenever I had choices and opportunities to induct a new member in my team, my focus has always been on choosing someone authentic, who brings passion and creativity, rather than someone who just has a certificate for results. Proven result is one indicator, however, what is equally important is the potential that the person holds, what challenges and risks the person has taken. Seldom has this assessment gone wrong, because in most instances, the unleashing of hidden potential has been an interesting and a trust-building exercise. More time needs to be spent on doing and learning together rather than reviewing tasks and goals. I can only say that team building is like a portfolio investment strategy wherein each stock must be carefully selected based on its potential to shine in the medium in the long term rather than for quick returns. 'Secure base leadership' that George Kohlrieser, Susan Goldsworthy and Duncan Coombe describe in their book *Care to Dare: Unleashing Astonishing Potential through Secure Base Leadership* is an apt example of a true leader and how the leader manages his/her team.

Endnote

There are many insights and stories as I reflect upon my journey. I am sure I will have many more in my path forward. However, what I have attempted here is a common theme that has been running across throughout my professional career, and I am sure these will continue to help me connect dots in future. The career of an HR professional has been like a healer, a warrior or a competitive player playing the finals of any game who rejoices when he triumphs but also has an unbearable agony when the results are not favourable; the player vows to rise again with a better game. It is a relay race, but at the same time, it is like a sprint too, however, one should also know how to steeplechase.

It has been a fulfilling experience for me, and what excites me every day is a childlike zeal and the dream of an engineer who keeps going back to his drawing board until the design is perfected.

Once, Mother Teresa was asked to speak in a conference of HR professionals and she just asked two things: Do you know your people? Do you love your people? In my thinking, these two statements summarize everything about what an HR professional should be and what they should be doing. Everything else that comes in between could be debated as either strategy or operations.

An HR professional's role is of high magnitude and is a highly credible role. The onus of keeping its value and dignity intact is not an easy task. It's always a personal struggle to keep it on the mainstream of value addition. What I have experienced is that a professional must develop a great personal insight and that comes by developing a sense of what is called in OD parlance, 'use of self' or using oneself as an agent of change, change within and changing the system. It guides and provides great insights into 'ways of being' and 'ways of doing'. Ways of being describe the presence, self-image, openness, trust and belief in others, whereas ways of doing is the credible delivery, cultivating a relationship, enquiring, listening, giving feedback, nurturing etc.

For an HR professional, humility must be character; passion, the voice; and sensitivity, the action. There is a very apt but anonymous saying, 'If my mind can conceive it and my heart can believe it, then only I can achieve it.'

References

Block, P. (1981). *Flawless consulting: A guide to getting your expertise used* (3rd edn). Wiley.

Feltman, C. (2006). *The thin book of trust: An essential primer for building trust at work.* Thin Book Publishing.

Jones, B. B., & Brazzel, M. (2006). *The NTL handbook of organization development and change: Principles, practices, and perspectives.* Wiley.

Khandelwal, A. K. (2011). *Dare to lead: The transformation of Bank of Baroda.* SAGE Publications.

Kohlrieser, G., Goldsworthy, S., & Coombe, D. (2012). *Care to dare: Unleashing astonishing potential through secure base leadership.* John Wiley & Sons.

Rainey, M. A., & Jones B. B. (2019). *Gestalt practice: Living and working in the pursuit of wHolism.* Libri Publishing.

Ranjan, P. (2004). Learning to change, changing to lead: A journey to leadership excellence. In U. Jain, U. Pareek & M. Shukla (Eds), *Developing leadership for the global era.* Macmillan Publishers.

Schein, E. H., & Schein, P. (2016). *Organizational culture and leadership.* Wiley.

Wellness and Yoga

Investment for the Bankers

Ashish Pandey

Introduction

In India, the banks have been going through enormous changes in the last two decades. Increasing competitive pressure with opening up of the market, emerging new technology, changing organizational structure and processes, new types of jobs and dynamic job demands are causing major changes in the working conditions and daily lives of banking executives and managers. Many studies confirm that stress-related problems have increased in the banking sector (Giorgi et al., 2017). Stress-related issues lead to problems such as anxiety and depression and job burnout (Li et al., 2015). I have worked as an advisor and facilitator with a large private retail bank for its management and leadership development programmes for more than five years. Based on my experience, I can infer that many people succumb to the performance pressure and exhibit the behaviours of abusive supervision, suboptimal customer service, mis-selling of financial products and even unethical business practices. In view of the peculiar work requirements and challenges, the competencies such as communication skills, interpersonal skills, emotional intelligence, ethical clarity, ability to work under pressure, resilience, ability to keep developing new skills, negotiation skills, mentoring and coaching and working with a sense of social responsibility have become critical competencies required among banking employees and managers.

The post-COVID-19 scenario for banks and bankers is going to be even more challenging. Banks have to recover revenue, rebuild operations, deal with further changes in organization design and accelerate the adoption of digital solutions (Sneader & Sternfels, 2020). In India, the government's focus is more on supporting the micro and small enterprises post COVID-19 (Economic Times, 2020). In this way, banks in India now need to strengthen their engagement with the community and the sense of purpose to fulfil a social mission that supports households and small businesses with access to credit.

Consequently, bank employees and managers will have to expand their skill set and the nature of existing roles that will become a part of the 'next normal'. They will need to retrain on the skills necessary for the new roles in response to the post–COVID-19 shifts in the business environment and organization strategy. The report by Banerjee et al. (2020) of McKinsey predicts the formation of and more autonomy to the small cross-functional teams with reinforced accountability and with a mandate for high-quality interaction with regulators, other institutions and key customers. Since a major portion of banking jobs will most likely be delivered by employees 'from home', the banks may also reemphasize the role of community and family as a pillar of culture. The above-mentioned competencies are going to be even more crucial in the post–COVID-19 scenario.

Given that competencies pertain to physical, mental, emotional and spiritual realms of human beings that are required in general and post COVID-19, it is critical to identify an intervention to build and restore these competencies. Additionally, the questions as to what extent will the intervention have a sustainable effect on building these competencies are important in this regard. We draw from the Eastern spiritual tradition of yoga to answer the above questions.

Yoga is a philosophical and technical system which was developed in ancient India. It aims at integrating the physical, mental, emotional and spiritual practices for the realization of moral life, personal well-being, mental peace and spiritual fulfilment. This chapter aims to elaborate on the relevance and potential impact of yoga-based practices (YBPs) among bank executives and managers.

This chapter is divided into four sections. The second section, after the introduction, presents a primer on yoga. The third section has four subsections, which briefly discuss the research findings on the impact of YBPs on physiological, emotional, mental and spiritual health. The fourth section connects the findings of the positive effects of YBPs with the challenges faced by employees of the banking sector in India and a few practical suggestions about how to integrate YBPs in the day-to-day functioning of the banks.

Yoga: A Primer

Yoga is a mind–body practice. Its goals are to cultivate balance, calm, harmony and awareness. In the classic yoga tradition, the objective of yoga is transcending the ego-personality (Feuerstein, 2011, pp. 1). Yoga includes paths oriented to service, devotion, intellectual discernment and meditation, each offering the practices to mitigate suffering and produce spiritual fulfilment and advancement (Feuerstein, 2011). In this chapter though, we focus on *ashtanga* yoga, for this is the most well-known and practised form of yoga in present times. *Ashtanga* yoga, the eight-limbed yoga (*asht* meaning 'eight' in Sanskrit), was systematized by Sage Patanjali during the 2nd century CE (Feuerstein, 2011, pp. 5). The multi-component process of *ashtanga* yoga aims at training the mind to be effortlessly quiet, focused and self-aware. The goals of *ashtanga* yoga overlap with some goals of other meditative traditions such as Buddhism (Feuerstein, 2011), from which the modern concept of mindfulness has sprung (Kabat-Zinn, 1994; Bodhi, 2011).

The eight different groups of practices include moral observances (*yama*—ethics when interacting with others), self-discipline (*niyama*—ethics geared toward the self), physical postures and exercises (*asanas*), breath regulation (*pranayama*), sensory withdrawal (*pratyahara*—minimizing sensory input), concentration (*dharana*—effortful and focused attention), meditation (*dhyana*—effortless and unbroken flow of attention) and self-transcendence and ecstasy (*samadhi*; Stone, 2009). The diversity of limbs allows practitioners to begin yoga by working with practices that are most appealing and accessible. Most students often start with physical postures (*asanas*) and breathing exercises (*pranayama*). According to a study commissioned by the US Department of Health and Human Services, yoga is one of the top 10 complementary approaches to health in the USA, along with usage of natural products, deep breathing, chiropractic etc. (Clarke, 2018).

Impact of YBPs

Although the philosophy of yoga recognizes that physical, *pranic*, emotional, cognitive and spiritual aspects constantly affect each other and make an integrated whole of the human self, I am separately presenting the impact of yoga on different aspects of the human self for the need of simplicity and easier comprehension.

Impact of YBPs on Physical Health

Working for long hours, sitting and working in the wrong posture, inadequate sleep and irregular and unhealthy food intake result in diminishing people's energy levels, their ability to manage their emotions and their ability to focus attention and perform cognitive tasks. This may also result in long-term health ailments. YBPs can be a useful intervention to regain physical energy.

YBPs help in synchronizing the daily routine with the natural body cycle, which gets disturbed due to the stress caused by job demands. For example,

YBPs can be performed in the morning or evening hours with an empty stomach. That means YBPs help in bringing self-discipline in eating, waking up, sleeping and managing working hours. Intermittent breaks during work are essential for renewal and result in higher and more sustainable performance. However, most of the executives and managers either do not take a break or rely on eating or drinking unhealthily during the breaks. YBPs can make people aware of the importance of taking intermittent breaks and inculcating a few healthy habits, such as stretching, light yogic postures called Up yoga and light *pranayama*, for enhancing energy.

YBPs enhance the awareness about the stress experienced in different parts of the body due to incorrect postures of sitting and standing. Some of the yogic postures help in controlling and reversing the negative impacts of working for long hours in the wrong posture. For example, Bālāsana helps in relaxing the shoulder and neck area, Trikonasana stretches and strengthens the spine, inner thigh, abdominal and side muscles and Markatasana helps in keeping the lumber area and backbone healthy (Stiles, 2000; Coulter, 2004).

Another significant impact of YBPs is enhancing the quality of sleep. There are statistically robust studies showing that sleep deprivation affects cognitive functioning and emotional resilience (Karatsoreos & McEwen, 2011), which negatively impacts decision-making capabilities (Killgore et al., 2006). YBPs enhance sleep quality by regulating several hormonal parameters of the hypothalamus–pituitary–adrenal axis and reducing blood cortisol levels (Vera et al., 2009).

Impact of YBPs on Emotional Health

Competitive pressure, changing organizational structure and job demands combined with fast-changing technology are causing stress and negative emotions among managers and executives. Naturally, they frequently resort to the fight-or-flight mode during the job. Moreover, workplace incivility, workplace loneliness and workplace fear are also the causes of suffering at the workplace, and banks and financial institutions are no exception. Schwartz and McCarthy (2007) pointed out that people become irritable and impatient, anxious and insecure. Such states of mind drain people's energy and cause friction in their relationships. These disturbances can also result in weakening of the organization as affected employees will give reduced output. In addition, affected employees may resort to deviant behaviour to retaliate against perceived organizational injustice. By its very design, yoga interventions are not only relaxing and energizing, however, they are also reflexive and self-examining in nature. Hence, YBPs are the ideal healing intervention. In a PhD level work in our school, we examined the potential of YBPs as a healing intervention in a privately held commercial port on the Eastern coast of India. We found it effective not only as the healing process after major industrial unrest but also as a supportive intervention for organizational transformation.

Yoga practices (by Iyenger) are found to be effective in enhancing positive affect while reducing negative affect in daily smokers, women with menopausal symptoms and school children respectively (Elibero et al., 2011; Elavsky & McAuley, 2007; Halliwell et al., 2018). In our research programme on the impact of YBPs on positive psychological outcomes, we have consistently found the impact of YBPs on two core aspects of our day-to-day experience: subjective vitality and self-transcendence.

I will explain the nature and impact of self-transcendence in the next sub-section. Here, I will briefly explain the nature and impact of subjective vitality. Subjective vitality is a self-reported feeling of aliveness and the energy available to the self and is reflected in the experience of a sense of and activated positive affect. Subjective vitality is positively toned and represents energy that one can harness for purposive actions unlike other forms of activation such as anger, anxiety or arousal (Ryan & Frederick, 1997). The notion of subjective vitality can be compared with the yogic concept of *prana*. Subjective vitality is the source of many positive emotions such as vigour and enthusiasm (de Zavala, Lantos, & Bowden, 2017) and is robustly associated with both behavioural and objective health outcomes. It has been linked to specific configurations of brain activation and positive response mechanisms (Barrett, Della-Maggiore, Chouinard & Paus, 2004; Rozanski, Blumenthal, Davidson, Saab, & Kubzansky, 2005). Greater subjective vitality also accompanies the experience of autonomy and integration (Deci & Ryan, 2000).

Impact of YBPs on Mental Health

Due to the combined effects of new technology, globalization and regulatory environment, a new management model has emerged in the banking sector wherein a large proportion of employees have become bank sellers rather than banking professionals in the traditional sense. They have to work with clients to meet the bank's targets in areas spanning credit (loans) to a wide range of debit requirements such as insurance, mutual funds, life insurance and so forth. The volume of work has effectively increased due to the considerable reduction in job positions (Silva & Navarro, 2012). This situation is going to continue or will, even more, intensify post COVID-19. Most studies showed that mental health problems have increased in the banking sector and that they were stress-related (Giorgi et al., 2017). Generally, mental health issues start with anxiety and depression, resulting in maladaptive behaviours such as a tendency to multitask and end up in job burnout. Cognitive anxiety also relates to psychological complaints, which in turn lead to health complaints. Extant literature suggests that YBPs can improve mental health symptoms such as depression, anxiety, stress, post-traumatic stress disorder and others (Balasubramaniam et al., 2012).

I would like to furnish examples from the findings of my research team about the impact of YBPs on mental health. The first example is the impact of YBPs on the tendency of multitasking. Multitasking is one of the common responses to stress at the workplace. Existing research suggests that multitasking does not improve productivity in the long term, rather it reduces the accuracy of performance even in the short term among the software and medical professions (Adler & Benbunan-Fich, 2012; Singh Kc, 2014). In our field study, we found that multitasking causes faster dissipation of energy and reduces engagement in the medium and long term. Our findings suggest that mindfulness arising out of YBPs help in retaining attention to one task or a lesser number of tasks at any moment. This prevents the dissipation of energy and increases emotional and mental engagement in the medium term (Kudesia & Pandey, 2017).

We have also found that YBPs enhance self-transcendence, interoceptive awareness and self-regulation. Self-transcendence refers to the awareness of being an inherent part of nature and the universe at large, or the experience of cosmic unity (Johnstone et al., 2016). Interoceptive awareness refers to bodily awareness or the conception of one's body with respect to space. Self-regulation concerning executive functioning involves the development of agentic control on attention, inhibitory control and working memory (McClelland et al., 2010). It is a higher-order concept than self-control that results in enhanced flexibility for adaptation (Kopp, 1982; McClelland et al., 2018). Cognitive-affective processing or simply speaking our response to the different stimulus is affected by interoceptive awareness in such a way that meditation practitioners are better equipped to detach the (negative) emotional reactions from their behaviour (Dunn et al., 2010; Kirk et al., 2011). The findings of my research team show that YBPs enhance both self-regulation and self-transcendence of the participants. YBPs augment self-transcendence that result in flourishing positive emotions, engagement, relationships, meaning in life and accomplishments by enhancing mindfulness metacognition. Self-regulation resulting from YBPs enhances learning at work and a sense of vitality (Dagar et al., 2018).

Impact of YBPs on Spiritual Health

Spirituality is the sacred aspect of the human self and is a form of human potential (Gupta, 1996). If we reflect on our most cherished experiences at work, we find two distinct things about them: first, feeling effective, effortlessly absorbed, inspired and fulfilled, and second, work and activities are consistent with what we value most and what gives us a sense of meaning and purpose. Finding meaning and purpose at work, recognizing and nurturing one's inner life, sense of community, interconnectedness and experience of transcendence or self-transcendence are reflections of spirituality at the workplace (Pandey, 2017). On the one hand, business organizations are sites of production and delivery of material and services, however, on the other hand, they are also sites of living, where individual meaning and purpose are created, shaped and shared among the organizational members (Pandey et al., 2009). Management, spirituality and religion (MSR) is an interdisciplinary and multidisciplinary domain catering to psychology, education, ethics and so forth (Dean & Fornaciari, 2007) and it aims to study the relevance and impact of spirituality in management, organizations and society.

If work really matters to the executives and managers, they typically feel more positive energy, focus better and demonstrate greater perseverance. Regrettably, the high demands and fast pace of corporate life don't leave much time to pay attention to these issues, and many people don't even recognize meaning and purpose as potential sources of energy. Moreover, Cohn et al. (2014) report that when the professional identity of the bank employees is rendered salient, a significant proportion of them become dishonest. Thus, their results suggest that the prevailing business culture in the banking industry weakens and undermines the honesty norm, implying that measures to re-establish an honest culture are critical.

The evidence shows that spiritual practices such as YBPs weaken ego-centric bias, expand consciousness and make one more open to the rich and vivid experience of reality beyond one's narrow and conditioned patterns (Brown et al., 2007; Pavlovich & Corner, 2014). One of our studies demonstrates that mindfulness arising from YBPs helps in developing the level of moral reasoning by increasing compassion and decreasing ego-centric bias in a few weeks of practice. Moral reasoning is the precursor of ethical behaviour.

The self-transcendence aspect of YBPs can enhance the spiritual health of executives and managers of the banks. A vast body of research demonstrates the impact of transcendental meditation on the spiritual and emotional well-being at the workplace (Tischler et al., 2002; Alexander et al., 1993).

Self-transcendence at the workplace is identified as a developmental 'engine' that fuels the search for connectedness with the larger social and natural environment (Pandey & Gupta, 2008), a purpose beyond self-interest (Pawar, 2009), and a sense of meaning by offering service to others (Neal & Vallejo, 2008).

A Framework for Implementation of YBPs in Banks

Millions of people are benefitted by following the YBPs in their personal life. Many simple and effective YBPs can be followed even in the workplace. For integrating YBPs in banking organizations, efforts are required at all three—individual, branch and organization—levels. Moreover, this change requires investment—an investment of time and effort.

Although ultimately, individual executives and managers have to take responsibility for their well-being and make way to include YBPs in their schedule, the organization and branches can play a vital role in integrating yoga in the organization. Some of the ways to promote YBPs at the organizational level comprise celebrating World Yoga Day, supporting employees in the form of paid leave to attend yoga retreats for a few days in a year, organizing online courses on yoga and giving some form of non-financial recognition for completing the courses. There are examples of organizations where meetings start with meditation for a few minutes. Rituals like these can be developed in the banks with inspiration and support from the top-level management.

The dropout rate of people doing yoga practices is very high. People learn and start practising by attending a course and may continue for a few days, however, after it is over, they go back to their normal routine and stop practising. Branch-level intervention becomes very important in this regard. The branch is the immediate social network for most of the bank employees. Most studies agree that social support and YBPs complement each other. Branches can set a routine for the employees, for example, doing YBPs together for 30–40 minutes at least 1–3 days in a week. A shorter protocol of YBPs can be developed to be followed in the branches, where even the customers can be invited for these sessions. My research team has developed a protocol of 25 minutes, which can be practised in the classroom and office setting. Our findings suggest that participants should be introduced to a comprehensive protocol in the beginning and should be encouraged to follow that at their places, while a short protocol should be carried out in the office or classroom. Our findings also indicate that positive psychological outcomes such as psychological capital and thriving significantly go up even by practising YBPs in the classroom for two days in a week and encouraging the participants to practise the long protocol at home.

My doctoral research at Management Development Institute, Gurgaon, was about the impact of branch climate on customers' experience (Pandey, Gupta, & Arora, 2009). That research clearly demonstrates that in the same region of the same bank, the branches can have a different climate. The branch climate is affected by branch-level leadership and created by the nature of interaction among the employees of the branch. In a bank, even if the core product or offering, core technology and service space may be the same, the branch climate may differ across the branches, which can potentially affect the customers' experience. These findings suggest that branches can establish the ritual of following YBPs and be open to people sharing their experience of the job and the impact of YBPs.

Organizational support, leadership and the branch climate are certainly important to instil YBPs in banks, but ultimately following YBPs is an individual choice. Individuals turn towards yoga primarily for two reasons: curiosity and for dealing with a crisis. They do not follow YBPs for two reasons: lack of time and the lack of belief. Hence, the key to start following YBPs in daily life is to try a little bit when one is not facing a health or emotional crisis and pay attention to and reflect on the experience and acknowledge the positive feedback loop. Acknowledgment of the energizing and positive experience helps in developing the habit of following YBPs. There are many organizations that have decades of experience and hundreds and thousands of affiliated teachers. Individuals need to listen to yoga masters, their philosophy and approach towards yoga before taking their tutelage. The Ministry of AYUSH, Government of India, has prepared a common yoga protocol in consultation with the renowned yoga gurus. It is easy and clear to follow, scientifically designed and tested and freely available in the form of booklet and demonstration video over the Internet. Figure 21.1 summarizes the requisites and the impact of YBPs on different organizational levels of a bank.

The benefits of yoga are beyond doubt, however, the number of regular practitioners of yoga is much lesser than the number of people aware of its benefits. YBPs can be integrated into banking organizations and financial institutions only when the time spent on these is perceived as an investment and not as a cost. There is enough research evidence to suggest that time investment in yoga pays back not only in the long term but also in the short term, and sometimes, immediately. The advice of Caroline Webb (2016) is very practical and valuable in this regard that a shift in the mindset is

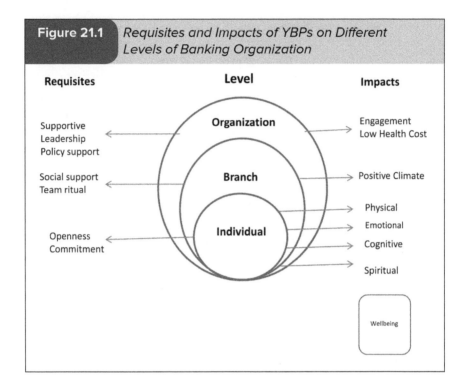

Figure 21.1 *Requisites and Impacts of YBPs on Different Levels of Banking Organization*

required to see and recognize that the practice of yoga and mindfulness is not downtime, it is simply investing in your ability to have more uptime to make a positive difference in the way executives and managers are living their lives and also in the way that their teams around them are living their lives.

References

Adler, R. F., & Benbunan-Fich, R. (2012). Juggling on a high wire: Multitasking effects on performance. *International Journal of Human–Computer Studies, 70*(2), 156–168.

Alexander, C. N., Swanson, G. C., Rainforth, M. V., Carlisle, T. W., Todd, C. C., & Oates Jr, R. M. (1993). Effects of the transcendental meditation program on stress reduction, health, and employee development: A prospective study in two occupational settings. *Anxiety, Stress and Coping, 6*(3), 245–262.

Balasubramaniam, M., Telles, S., & Doraiswamy, P. M. (2013). Yoga on our minds: A systematic review of yoga for neuropsychiatric disorders. *Frontiers in Psychiatry, 3*, 117.

Banerjee, I., Jacobson, R., Krivkovich, A., Libotte, G., & Rambachan, I. (2020). Shaping and safeguarding the banking workforce after COVID-19. McKinsey Insight. https://www.mckinsey.com/industries/financial-services/our-insights/shaping-and-safeguarding-the-banking-workforce-after-covid-19

Barrett, J., Della-Maggiore, V., Chouinard, P. et al. (2004). Mechanisms of action underlying the effect of repetitive transcranial magnetic stimulation on mood: Behavioral and brain imaging studies. *Neuropsychopharmacol, 29*, 1172–1189.

Bodhi, B. (2011). What does mindfulness really mean? A canonical perspective. *Contemporary Buddhism, 12*(1), 19–39.

Brown, K., Ryan, R., & Creswell, J. D. (2007). Mindfulness: Theoretical foundations and evidence for its salutary effects. *Psychological Inquiry, 18*, 211–237.

Clarke, T. C., Barnes, P. M., Black, L. I., Stussman, B. J., & Nahin, R. L. (2018). *Use of yoga, meditation, and chiropractors among US adults aged 18 and over.* US Department of Health and Human Services, Centers for Disease Control and Prevention, National Center for Health Statistics.

Cohn, A., Fehr, E., & Maréchal, M. A. (2014). Business culture and dishonesty in the banking industry. *Nature, 516*(7529), 86–89.

Coulter, D. (2004). *Anatomy of hatha yoga: A manual for students, teachers, and practitioners.* Motilal Banarsidass.

Dagar, C., Pandey, A., Navare, A. V., & Pandey, N. (2018, July). How yoga based practices result in human flourishing? In *Academy of management proceedings* (Vol. 2018, No. 1, p. 16300). Academy of Management.

Dean, K. L., & Fornaciari, C. J. (2007). Empirical research in management, spirituality & religion during its founding years. *Journal of Management, Spirituality & Religion, 4*(1), 3–34.

Deci, E. L., & Ryan, R. M. (2000). The 'what' and 'why' of goal pursuits: Human needs and the self-determination of behavior. *Psychological Inquiry, 11*, 227–268.

de Zavala, A. G., Lantos, D., & Bowden, D. (2017). Yoga poses increase subjective energy and state self-esteem in comparison to 'power poses'. *Frontiers in Psychology, 8*, 752.

Dunn, B. D., Galton, H. C., Morgan, R., Evans, D., Oliver, C., Meyer, M., Cusack, R., Lawrence, A. D., & Dalgleish, T. (2010). Listening to your heart: How interoception shapes emotion experience and intuitive decision making. *Psychological Science, 21*(12), 1835–1844.

Economic Times. (2020). *Micro enterprises best placed to help economy come out of COVID-19 crisis.* https://economictimes.indiatimes.com/small-biz/sme-sector/micro-enterprises-best-placed-to-help-economy-come-out-of-covid-19-crisis-report/articleshow/75599693.cms?from=mdr

Elavsky, S., & McAuley, E. (2007). Physical activity and mental health outcomes during menopause: A randomized controlled trial. *Annals of Behavioral Medicine, 33*(2), 132–142.

Elibero, A., Van Rensburg, K. J., & Drobes, D. J. (2011). Acute effects of aerobic exercise and hatha yoga on craving to smoke. *Nicotine and Tobacco Research, 13*(11), 1140–1148.

Feuerstein, G. (2011). *The encyclopedia of yoga and tantra.* Shambhala.

Giorgi, G., Arcangeli, G., Perminiene, M., Lorini, C., Ariza-Montes, A., Fiz-Perez, J., Fabio, A. D., & Mucci, N. (2017). Work-related stress in the banking sector: A review of incidence, correlated factors, and major consequences. *Frontiers in Psychology, 8*, 2166.

Gupta, R. K. (1996). Is there a place for the sacred in organizations and their development. *Journal of Human Values, 2*(2), 149–158.

Halliwella, E., Jarmana, H., Tylkab, T. L., & Slatera, A. (2018). Evaluating the impact of a brief yoga intervention on preadolescents' body image and mood. *Body Image, 27*, 196–201.

Johnstone, B., Cohen, D., Konopacki, K., & Ghan, C. (2016). Selflessness as a foundation of spiritual transcendence: Perspectives from the neurosciences and religious studies. *The International Journal for the Psychology of Religion, 26*(4), 287–303.

Kabat-Zinn, J. (1994). *Wherever you go, there you are: Mindfulness meditation in everyday life.* Little, Brown Book Group.

Karatsoreos, I. N., & McEwen, B. S. (2011). Psychobiological allostasis: Resistance, resilience and vulnerability. *Trends in Cognitive Sciences, 15*(12), 576–584.

Killgore, W. D., Balkin, T. J., & Wesensten, N. J. (2006). Impaired decision making following 49 h of sleep deprivation. *Journal of Sleep Research, 15*(1), 7–13.

Kirk, U., Downar, J., & Montague, P. R. (2011). Interoception drives increased rational decision-making in meditators playing the ultimatum game. *Frontiers in Neuroscience, 5*, 49.

Kopp, C. B. (1982). Antecedents of self-regulation: A developmental perspective. *Developmental Psychology, 18*(2), 199–214.

Kudesia, R. S., & Pandey, A. (2017). Is attention scarce or sufficient? A field experiment of mindfulness training in task environments. In *Academy of management proceedings* (Vol. 2017, No. 1, p. 13411). Academy of Management.

Li, X., Kan, D., Liu, L., Shi, M., Wang, Y., Yang, X., Wang, J., & Wu, H. (2015). The mediating role of psychological capital on the association between occupational stress and job burnout among bank employees in China. *International Journal of Environmental Research and Public Health, 12*(3), 2984–3001.

McClelland, M. M., Geldhof, G. J., Morrison, F. J., et al. (2018). Self-regulation. In *Handbook of Life Course Health Development,* 1st edn. Springer International Publishing.

Morrison, F. J., Ponitz, C. C., & McClelland, M. M. (2010). 'Self-regulation and academic achievement in the transition to school'. In S. D. Calkins & M. A. Bell (Eds.), *Human brain development. Child development at the intersection of emotion and cognition* (pp. 203–224). American Psychological Association.

Neal, J., & Vallejo, M. C. (2008). Family firms as incubators for spirituality in the workplace: Factors that nurture spiritual businesses. *Journal of Management, Spirituality and Religion, 5*(2), 115–159.

Pandey A. (2017). Workplace spirituality: Themes, impact and research directions. *South Asian Journal of Human Resources Management, 4*(2), 212–217.

Pandey, A., & Gupta, R. K. (2008). Spirituality in management: A review of contemporary and traditional thoughts and agenda for research. *Global Business Review, 9*(1), 65–83.

Pandey, A., Gupta, R. K., & Arora, A. P. (2009). Spiritual climate of business organizations and its impact on customers' experience. *Journal of Business Ethics, 88*, 313–332.

Pavlovich, K., & Corner, P. D. (2014). Conscious enterprise emergence: Shared value creation through expanded conscious awareness. *Journal of Business Ethics, 121*(3), 341–351.

Pawar, B. S. (2009). Workplace spirituality facilitation: A comprehensive model. *Journal of Business Ethics, 90*, 375.

Rozanski, A., Blumenthal, J. A., Davidson, K. W., Saab, P. G., & Kubzansky, L. (2005). The epidemiology, pathophysiology, and management of psychosocial risk factors in cardiac practice: The emerging field of behavioral cardiology. *Journal of the American College of Cardiology, 45*(5), 637–651.

Ryan, R. M., & Frederick, C. (1997). On energy, personality, and health: Subjective vitality as a dynamic reflection of well-being. *Personality, 65*(3), 529–565.

Schwartz, T., & McCarthy, C. (2007). Manage your energy, not your time. *Harvard Business Review, 85*(10), 63.

Silva, J. L., & Navarro, V. L. (2012). Work organization and the health of bank employees. *Revista Latino-Americana de Enfermagem, 20*(2), 226–234.

Singh Kc, D. (2014). Does multitasking improve performance? Evidence from the emergency department. *Manufacturing & Service Operations Management, 16*(2), 168–183.

Sneader, K., & Sternfels, B. (2020). *From surviving to thriving: Reimagining the post-COVID-19 return.* McKinsey and Company.

Stiles, M. (2000). *Structural yoga therapy: Adapting to the individual.* Weiser Books.

Stone, M. (2009). *Yoga for a world out of balance: Teachings on ethics and social action.* Shambhala.

Tischler, L., Biberman, J., & McKeage, R. (2002). Linking emotional intelligence, spirituality and workplace performance. *Journal of Managerial Psychology, 17*(3).

Vera, F. M., Manzaneque, J. M., Maldonado, E. F., Carranque, G. A., Rodriguez, F. M., Blanca, M. J., & Morell, M. (2009). Subjective sleep quality and hormonal modulation in long-term yoga practitioners. *Biological Psychology, 81*(3), 164–168.

Webb, C. (2016). *How to have a good day: Harness the power of behavioral science to transform your working life.* Currency.

PART 2

Case Studies

- State Bank of India
- Bank of Baroda
- ICICI Bank
- Union Bank of India

HR as Strategic Business Partner in SBI Transformation

Alok Kumar Choudhary and M. Jayashree Reddy

Background

With a legacy of over 214 years, State Bank of India (SBI) is the oldest commercial bank in the Indian subcontinent. It is an Indian multinational, public sector banking and financial services conglomerate headquartered in Mumbai. SBI is also the largest commercial bank in India in terms of assets, deposits, branches, customers and employees. The aggregate business size (advances and deposits) of SBI as on 31st March 2020 was more than ₹56.6 trillion (approximately $756 billion). As on 31st March 2020, the bank operated through its correspondent network in more than 56 countries, employed nearly 250,000 employees and served a total customer base of more than 448.9 million.

Scale, Range and Complexity of Businesses

SBI offers a wide spectrum of products and services to different segments of customers. The full range of SBI operations is shown in Annexure C1.1. Its main businesses are described in brief below.

'The retail and digital banking group' is the largest business vertical of SBI and constitutes 94.31 per cent of total domestic deposits and 58.14 per cent of total domestic advances (as of 31st March 2020). Within the retail portfolio, SBI is the leader in the home loan market with a share of 30.62 per cent. It has a 32.93 per cent share in the auto loan segment. The bank takes pride in being the largest education loan provider in India with a market share of approximately 34.72 per cent. The retail and digital banking group comprises eight strategic business units.

'The wholesale banking business' focuses on servicing corporate clients through customized financial solutions such as working capital finance, export finance, trade transactions and foreign currency loans. The Corporate Accounts Group is dedicated vertical handling the 'large credit portfolio' of the bank. Corporate Accounts Group has been a partner in the industrial growth of the country, especially in the creation and development of critical infrastructures such as roads and highways, ports, power, telecom and petrochemicals.

'Small and medium-sized enterprises (SMEs) financing' has over one million customers across the country. SBI is a pioneer in this segment. By providing capital to these enterprises, SBI enables businesses to grow in new markets, especially the currently unexplored/underexplored Tier 3 and Tier 4 regions. The bank's SME portfolio accounts for 12.96 per cent of the bank's total advances. Leveraging state-of-the-art technology and branch network, SBI has emerged as a major player in supply chain finance.

'SBI's treasury operation' is the largest among all banks in the country. It is carried out through the Global Markets Unit to manage liquidity in compliance with regulatory requirements, mitigate various risks such as market risk, liquidity and operational risk. The investment book under Global Markets Unit records at ₹10580 billion as on 31st March 2020.

SBI: The Economic, Social and Public Policy Context

SBI has also traditionally been the banker of choice to the government and continues to be the accredited banker to the major central government ministries and departments. It has a market share of more than 80 per cent in government commission. Being a leading public sector bank, SBI plays a key role in implementing the economic and socially beneficial priorities of the Indian government.

Few such initiatives are outlined further.

SBI played (and continues to play) a key role in building momentum for transforming India through 'digitalization of the economy'. The bank expanded its digital footprint across the length and breadth of the country. As on 31st March 2020, 59 per cent transactions are carried out through digital channels. The digital platform 'YONO', the flagship customer-facing digital bank of SBI, caters to various banking, financial services, lifestyle requirements and delivers world-class customer experience.

The bank is at the forefront in the adoption of e-Solutions of both central and state governments in the Indian financial ecosystem. SBI is an active stakeholder in the government's initiatives, namely government e-Marketplace and continuously engaged with technology solutions such as e-Tendering, e-BG and e-Trade.

'Rural banking' is a critical component of the Indian economy as nearly 68 per cent of the Indian population still lives in rural areas. SBI's contribution has been, and continues to be, key for rural India's development. New products for dairy, fisheries, poultry, sheep rearing, goat rearing, piggery, beekeeping, sericulture and mushroom cultivation have been introduced, and the bank has implemented the retail asset credit centres for centralized sanction of loan proposals in rural and semi-urban branches. The bank has launched 'YONO Krishi' mobile app for sanctioning of agri gold loans, and the digitalization of agri products will help the bank to expand its customer base in rural areas.

As a part of a mission to provide the entire gamut of financial services across India, the SBI Group, through its various subsidiaries, provides a whole range of financial services, including life insurance, merchant banking, trustee business, mutual funds, credit card, factoring, security trading, pension fund management, custodial services, general insurance (non-life insurance) and primary dealership in the money market. The SBI Group structure is shown in Annexure C1.2.

SBI has the highest market share in self-help group loans among all the banks. This includes more than 5 million women community members.

SBI believes in 'sustainable banking'. SBI understands the importance of integrating environmental, social and governance screening and evaluation parameters into its credit/lending decision-making process. SBI has integrated its digital strategy with its overall sustainability strategy.

Human Resources (HR) in SBI

In view of its scale, complexity and diversity, SBI relies on its employees to fulfil its mission and enable operations to run smoothly. These employees are supported by a strong HR function, culture and processes. SBI has consistently promoted a performance-driven culture based on ethically and financially sound business practices. The bank has also been awarded the Business World Award for 'Excellence in Learning and Development'.

HR Structure

The key aspects of HR structure are briefly described below. The full HR structure in SBI is shown in Annexure C1.3.

The HR at SBI is a functional unit supporting other strategic business units with the vision to help them in achieving their strategic objectives. The head of the HR function is the deputy managing director (DMD) HR and chief development officer (CDO) operating from the corporate office at Mumbai.

All new HR initiatives and policies are presented to the Central Human Resource Committee comprising two managing directors, DMDs and chief general manager (CGM) HR. This body scrutinizes the applicability of the policies at SBI and then decides or recommends to the executive committee of the central board/central board of directors of the bank.

All HR activities from hire to retire and beyond are governed by the HR handbook, standardization of all key policies that impact the organization. In addition, there are policies for specific HR areas such as promotion policy, whistle-blower policy, transfer and placement policy, succession policy and vacation policy.

SBI's HR function, in total, has 2,413 officers across the country that add value to the business. The total strength of employees is shown in Annexure C1.4.

Strategic and Transformational HR Initiatives

Banking is a complex, fast-changing and critical industry. It depends on trust from the people, its depositors, government and various other stakeholders to perform the role in an ethical, proactive and engaging manner. Public sector banking in India is additionally complex because of its social priorities, complex governance and large scale.

The employees at SBI are at the heart of SBI's performance in navigating this complexity and doing the right thing. These challenges and complexity are reflected in the various strategic initiatives that the HR function undertakes on a periodic basis to ensure that it is able to hire the best talent, training and engage them well and create the right culture.

HR function at SBI has in the past reinvented itself through HR transformation. It also played a key role in implementing strategic business (such as mergers and digitalization) and HR initiatives (such as fostering employee appreciation, performance management and changing culture). This case discusses six such strategic HR initiative and interventions. Specifically, this case shines a light on the strategic HR role at the SBI in the form of and through the following initiatives.

- HR transformation to revamp and rationalize various HR sub-functions
- HR transformation initiatives covering employee engagement, grievance redressal and recognition
- Transformation of training in SBI

- Corporate communication and mindset transformation: 'Nayi Disha'
- HR role in the merger of five associate banks and Bhartiya Mahila Gramin Bank (BMBL)
- HR role in the digital transformation at SBI

HR Transformation: Project 'Saksham'

SBI undertook HR transformation in 2014–2015 through 'Project Saksham'. The main idea was to transform established transactional activities to improve, accelerate and optimize HR processes to build positive employee experience. This section discusses the transformation in key HR areas.

Manpower Planning

SBI has a talent pool of nearly 250,000 across India and abroad. Since manpower planning is directly linked to business planning and strategy and is also the start point for HR lifecycle, this was identified as an important area for HR transformation.

A new approach to manpower planning was required to address the complexity and business diversity that came up with SBI growth. This exercise was also needed to review and validate assumptions on the adequate staff/manpower levels and address the conflict between qualitative and quantitative approaches. The new approach involved developing a manpower model, which can determine the baseline staffing activity for any branch. Additionally, the new model also aimed to facilitate the distribution of manpower in a uniform manner, allocation of new hires to branches in an equitable way and assess the need for transfers.

This was a comprehensive exercise that involved a wide range of inputs, including 82 work drivers covering various operations. The exercise also used various other productivity drivers at the branch level to ascertain manpower requirements. This model allowed uniformity in staff assessment in a circle and ensured that no branch is understaffed due to extraneous considerations such as geography and location.

Recruitment

Recruitment is the process of attracting good candidates for manning the vacancies in the organization. SBI realized around 2014 that despite having the highest salary structure up to the level of assistant general manager (AGM) in the banking industry, positioning of opportunities in SBI was not getting a vantage point in the recruitment market. To overcome this challenge, SBI set to itself the goal to attract and recruit the best talent in the market by capturing the mindspace of the talent pool available in India.

SBI redesigned its career portal, rebranded it (grow everyday) and also launched a marketing campaign at select 150 top colleges using various channels such as brochures, social media marketing (e.g., career page in LinkedIn and Facebook) and sending 0.8 million (0.008 billion) direct emails to potential candidates.

The impact of this part of the transformational process has been well recognized. In 2016, SBI received 12,000 applications for the recruitment of probationary officers (POs) from the identified institutions, besides millions of applications from the wider market. Anecdotal evidence from interview boards and State Bank Learning Centre also indicated improvement in the quality of recruits.

Career Progression

SBI employs a large number of officers and staff to manage its diverse and complex businesses. The bank, therefore, needs both specialized and generalized skills. While specialization promotes functional knowledge, generalization have a better appreciation of the overall functioning of the bank, which is essential for promotion to top management positions. The legacy system of posting of officers did not encourage specialization and promoted generalization.

The HR function decided to 'upgrade' the career planning system to address the needs of SBI as well as the career progression that employees wanted. To achieve this, it introduced a system of job families. It designed and implemented seven job families (namely credit and risk; sales, marketing and operations; HR; information technology [IT]; analytics; finance and accounts and treasury and forex). These job families enabled the identification of role that required deep functional expertise, training and exposure over a long duration.

All eligible employees (i.e., their roles) were assigned a job family. This encouraged their development as employee became aware of the progression requirements like certifications needed. Job families also gave officers a clear sight into their future career paths and postings.

Performance Assessment

Performance appraisal is one of the key HR processes that provides information and insights on how individual employees have performed as well as the overall performance trends. It is also one of the principal means to align business objectives of the bank with the employee objectives. With this in mind, SBI looked at transforming performance assessment programme and make it strategic in nature.

Previously, the performance assessment at SBI was about traits, suitability and business goals achievement with selectively more emphasis on attributes. However, it was found that the performance assessment process must give more say to operational excellence and output coupled with strategic orientation; hence, the transformation process started with few following ambitious aims:

- Increase business orientation through business-linked key result areas (KRAs) for officers and clerical staff
- Fairness and consistency in the appraisal, through standardization of KRAs across officers and clerical staff in the same role
- Accurately measure performance based on objective criteria and create differential amongst employees based on that
- Increase objectivity in key HR decisions (e.g., promotions, postings and recognition) through objective evaluation of metrics

The new initiative which renamed the performance management system as career development system (CDS) was implemented from FY 2015–2016 for associates up to CGMs. The changes covered the design as well as the process of the assessment system and include the following:

1. Increase in the number of budgetary and measurable roles.
2. Employees posted in business units at local head office and corporate centre were given budgetary/measurable goals to improve collaboration between the operating units and the administrative offices.
3. Employees given grades (AAA, AA, A, B and C) instead of marks (on 100).
4. Evaluation of performance driven by objective metrics for budgetary and measurable roles, with IT systems used to calculate the score.
5. CDS grades were calibrated, that is, a quintile curve used for the distribution of grades within a group of employees.
6. The score given by the reporting authority was subject to review (by the reviewing authority) while the KRAs score calculated by the system was not subject to review.
7. All employees were divided into groups (cohorts), and the grade was based on the relative performance within the cohort. Cohorts were based on the common role, scale and geography, etc.
8. Besides promotions, CDS grades were also used for considering extension in service for officers.

The new CDS system was a transformational step forward from the then existing performance assessment system. Its impact can be highlighted in terms of the following contributions:

1. CDS has promoted the culture of business orientation amongst the staff.
2. Collaboration between the staff for improving the overall performance of the branch has improved because a percentage of KRAs covered unit-level (branch) performance.
3. Collaboration between business units (at administrative offices) and the operating units has improved, given that business units have budgetary KRAs.
4. CDS has made performance evaluation more transparent. Since the scores (in respect of budgetary and measurable roles) are calculated by the system, the scores are shown to the staff at monthly intervals, so that corrective steps, if required, can be taken by them.

Career Movements

Career postings are important for the employees for both career development and personal reasons. The legacy system of career movements/postings for employees was manual and decentralized (Scale VI and above officers are posted by corporate centre; Scale V, IV and III officials are posted by the local head offices, and Scales I and II are posted by regional business offices). It has other challenges as well. It led to inefficiencies, involved large number of HR officials (around 400) and the manual system made it difficult to implement the job family concept.

SBI developed and implemented a system-based IT platform called Prosper to automate the postings for officers up to Scale V. Prosper addressed the challenges that the legacy career posting system had and added further value to it by including the following design features:

1. Comprehensive employee profile in one place
2. Easy and online availability of data of manpower requirement of branches
3. Data of officers due for transfer (based on the transfer policies of the bank)
4. Employees due for retirement
5. Job family to which employee belongs
6. Job rotation/transfer history of each employee

Based on the above data, Prosper identifies and makes recommendations for transfers. The process requires approval by the appropriate authority as in the past. This platform is being used by circles for the posting of officers. However, a latitude has been provided to controlling authorities for making deviations in a few cases after documenting the overriding reasons.

Prosper has made the process efficient and also reduced the number of transfers as well as number of HR officials involves in the postings.

Succession Planning

SBI upgraded its succession planning as part of the HR transformation process. The main objective of the new process was to ensure that there are no gaps in filling up the critical positions of top management.

The process design classified all top management positions as critical. This was followed by a scientific approach that used job families, data on a various amount of time spent in feeder roles for each critical position and analysis of various leaders in the pipeline to draw the succession plans. The board approved the succession plans for the roles of CGMs and DMDs.

HR Transformation: Employee Engagement, Grievance Redressal and Recognition

Given its large-scale, complexity and continuous growth, it was felt necessary that not only there are good people in various roles but also they are fully engaged and recognized. Additionally, in the event of any grievances, employees should have the opportunity to get them redressed in a timely and fair manner. With this big picture in mind, SBI undertook three major initiatives, namely 'Abhivyakti' (employee engagement survey), Sanjeevani (employee grievance redressal) and SBI Gems (employee recognition platform). These three are detailed below.

'Abhivyakti': Employee Engagement Survey

The bank launched an employee engagement survey 'Abhivyakti', which is among the largest such surveys held in a big bank. The objective of 'Abhivyakti' was to identify the factors that actually drive employees to perform their best and also the ones that limit their performance. The survey drew the participation of nearly 95 per cent of the employees covered. The surveyed employees were asked far-reaching questions regarding the most important workplace values, job satisfaction, culture, etc.

The survey results provided comprehensive information regarding opinions of SBI employees on performance, culture, relationships, processes and policies and also on how they go about doing their work. The results showed that 63 per cent of SBIs employees are engaged in contributing to its growth and finding satisfaction in their work.

Most respondents favoured the following statements that highlight SBI as a brand of choice:

- Pride of working in SBI is very high.
- Good and approachable management and employee–manager relationships
- Good infrastructure and welfare facilities
- High employee motivation and satisfaction and various drives conducted
- Freedom to learn and innovate
- Women safety

The participants were also asked to agree or disagree with statements to find out the satisfaction levels with their jobs. Some of the concerns that surfaced from the survey were as follows:

- Low work–life balance leading to job stress
- Promotion and transfer policies
- Regular feedback from managers

The survey report and its findings were analysed by the bank under various parameters using appropriate contexts. The feedback received from the survey was utilized in redesigning the established policies and implement key changes to increase the efficiency, output, involvement, dedication and productivity of the employees.

Engagement scorecards were prepared for the various employee groups. The bank also prepared action plan for the various areas of concern that involves, among other things, implementation of 'work–life balance initiatives', improvements in policies on promotion and transfer and implemented mid-year and full-year check-in feedback process.

Sanjeevani: Employee Grievance Redressal

To build an engaged workforce, SBI also looked at the process for addressing employee grievances in a timely and efficient manner. Before the launch of 'Sanjeevani', there was a very basic and limited system to formally keep track of grievances and their closure. This made it difficult to find out how well employees' concerns and grievances and redressals system is working.

SBI's HR helpline—Sanjeevani—was an online grievance redressal portal available to employees to express their grievances. It replaced the online grievance redressal portal available to employees to express their grievances previously. 'Sanjeevani' can be reached by every employee and pensioners through voice (dedicated landline), SMS and mail. The time for redressal of grievances on HR matters was T + 2 days. All grievances were allotted a ticket number and acknowledged through the mail. The grievances lodged in 'Sanjeevani' were handled effectively and promptly to ward off any dissatisfaction among the employees on HR matters.

Encouraged by the success of Sanjeevani, Sanjeevani–II was launched in July 2019 to handle grievances received directly at HR departments by post, email and by other means.

Additionally, the bank engaged the services of trained counsellors at Sanjeevani. The employees are encouraged to contact the counsellors to share their issues and concerns for getting help in easing stress, coping with work and societal pressures and enable them to perceive the issue in a better way.

Sanjeevani also proactively makes suo-motu calls to the staff posted at difficult centre branches, enquiring about any HR-related issues faced by them. The staff posted in more than 950 branches across Pan India were contacted at the time of case writing.

The impact of Sanjeevani can be summarized as follows:

- Since its inception, Sanjeevani has handled more than 30,000 staff grievances/queries.
- Around 1,400 staff pensioners have utilized the Sanjeevani services since July 2018.
- More than 99 per cent of all the queries/grievances have been responded/resolved at the time of case writing.

Employee Recognition Platform: SBI Gems

Employee recognition is a key component of employee motivation and the psychological contract between SBI and its employees. Previously, there was no formal mechanism available to a senior executive to provide positive feedback to an employee who are not their direct reports. There was also no 'organizational memory' of the appreciation letters sent occasionally.

The purpose of the 'SBI Gems' platform was to enable on the spot recognition and building an 'organizational memory' for them. Senior employees are allowed to award a fixed number of gems a year (e.g., a currency of 10–15 gems was made available to a DGM). An awarder cannot award more than one gem to an employee in a year.

The employee recognition platform led to positive reinforcement through recognition and also reinforced positive behaviour in employees.

Transformation of Training in SBI

The concept of training in SBI is nearly a century old (circa 1922, courtesy Sir Dinshaw Edulji Wacha). SBI established a very elaborate training network comprising 51 learning centres christened as 'State Bank Institutes of Learning and Development (SBILDs)' at the regional level and six top-notch 'apex training institutes (ATIs)' were developed over the years to cater to the competence building of its nearly 250,000 employees. The evolution of training infrastructure is shown in Table C1.1.

The training institutes of the bank have a combined classroom capacity of 4,200 participants per day. In addition, they are International Organization for Standardization certified and equipped with state-of-art facilities that include Wi-Fi campuses, single/twin sharing hostel rooms at par with industry standards, conference halls/computer labs with MS utilities, library facilities that include digital contents and repository of books/magazines/periodicals on a variety of subjects/topics in English, Hindi and local language. The faculty at ATIs and SBILDs comprises experienced bankers with a passion and flair for teaching with requisite domain expertise. The faculty members are inducted through an intensive in-house selection process.

The training philosophy of SBI is stated as follows:

> Training in the State Bank is a proactive, planned and continuous
> process as an integral part of organizational development. It seeks
> to impart knowledge, improve skills and reorient attitudes for
> individual growth and organizational effectiveness.

Table C1.1	*Evolution of Training in SBI*

- **1922:** First training for probationary assistants of Imperial Bank
- **1961:** First residential training college— State Bank Staff College, Hyderabad
- **1961–2020:** Around 6 other ATIs and 51 regional learning centres (SBILDs) across states
- Our ATIs:
  - o State Bank Institute of Consumer Banking (SBICB), Hyderabad (1961)
  - o State Bank Institute of Rural Business (SBIRB), Hyderabad (1981)
  - o State Bank Institute of Credit and Risk Management (SBICRM), Gurugram (1982)
  - o State Bank Institute of Information Technology (SBIIT), Hyderabad (1987)
  - o State Bank Institute of Human Resource Development, Indore (2011)
  - o State Bank Institute of Leadership (SBIL), Kolkata (2017)

Table C1.2	Four-pillar Approach to Revamped Training Structure	
Pillar 1	**Resource Optimization**	
	1.	Domain-specific ATIs
	2.	Transfer control of regional SBILDs centrally to STU
	3.	Selection of right faculty
Pillar 2	**Capacity Building**	
	1.	Revision of training programs for recruits
	2.	Leverage digital modes of learning
	3.	Create role relevant certifications
	4.	Training to senior executives
	5.	Leadership development
Pillar 3	**Marketing of Training**	
	1.	External collaborations
	2.	Paid programmes for external organizations
Pillar 4	**Research**	
	1.	Conduct empirical research

Creation of Strategic Training Unit (STU) and Four-pillar Approach

Strategic training unit (STU) of the bank was created in 2011 to bring the entire training system under a unified training command headed by a CGM (STU structure as mentioned in Annexure C1.5). In 2018, it revamped the training architecture with the following objectives:

- To make employees future ready
- To enhance knowledge, skills and right attitude
- To make them effective at their respective roles
- To align training with corporate priorities
- To establish a culture of self-learning
- To introduce global best practices in the learning

The training model adopted by STU can be pictorially represented as in Annexure C1.6. At the heart of the revamped training structure was a four-pillar approach, which is shown in Table CA.2.

Over the last two years spanning 2018–2019 and 2019–2020, several initiatives were conceptualized and implemented based on the above four-pillar approach. These four pillars are described below.

1. Pillar 1: Resource Optimization

ATIs were repositioned as caches of high-quality speciality training in the areas of credit, international banking, risk, retail banking, marketing, rural banking, IT, leadership and HR. They also served as umbrella institutes for the regional SBILDs.

For direction-setting and internalizing best practices in the learning and development eco-space, each ATI is mentored by hand-picked advisory council members comprising top management and eminent academicians/experts from various sectors. An apex advisory council at the corporate level has been established to set the direction for the training and align training goals with corporate priorities/concerns and emerging trends/changes in the banking industry. The six ATIs and their areas of specialization are shown in Table C1.3.

Under the four-pillar approach, ATIs were entrusted with various roles, which are discussed below.

Design of training programmes: The ATIs were entrusted with the design of training programmes based on the need identified by business units. Under this remit, the training content and role manuals prepared at ATI formed the basis of training programmes conducted pan India. The ATIs also drive the e-learning initiatives of the bank and make available e-repository of knowledge 24 × 7 to over 0.24 million (240,000) employees of the bank

Table C1.3	ATIs and Areas of Specialization
S. No.	**Apex Training Institute (ATI)**	**Area of Specialization**
1.	SBIL, Kolkata	Leadership, management & banking research
2.	SBICB, Hyderabad	Consumer markets/marketing & retail banking
3.	SBICRM, Gurgaon	Risk, forex, credit & compliance
4.	SBIRB, Hyderabad	Rural banking & financial inclusion
5.	SBIIT, Hyderabad	IT innovation & technology products
6.	State Bank Institute Human Resource Development, Indore	Onboarding, orientation and induction programmes for POs/trainee officers (TOs), employees recruited laterally and contractual employees

worldwide. Approximately, 1,000 hours of e-learning content was developed by these ATIs. The ATIs also developed a repository of over 1,329 case studies based on real-life banking cases, which formed an important pedagogy tool for imparting training to its employees.

Training of participants: The ATIs conduct around 1,500 classroom training programmes and train around 30,000 participants annually. The participants to ATIs training programmes are mostly officials from senior management grade and above. The ATIs also train and mentor the faculty members of the 51 SBILDs enabling them to provide training at the regional level to employees up to middle management grade. In view of mobility and social distancing issues due to COVID-19 pandemic, training at ATIs and SBILDs has seamlessly transitioned to a virtual 'webinar' mode in lieu of classroom training. In Q1 of FY 2020–2021, more than 3,400 webinar-based programmes were used to train 91,000+ employees.

Training for banking, financial services and insurance (BFSI) sector: The ATIs design and conduct customized training programmes for BFSI sector and their clientele spanning several sectors and organizations including various government agencies, domestic and international banks and corporates.

Collaboration with academia and industry: The ATIs collaborate with reputed institutes and organizations on various projects and programmes. The ATIs provide a platform for interchange of ideas through hosting of workshops and conclaves on themes of importance to the industry.

Think tank: The ATIs are the think tanks for SBI. There is a research wing at each ATI, which carries out studies of operational significance on product and processes of strategic importance. They also provide policy support for various government initiatives through their domain-specific analysis. For example, SBIRB provided key inputs in government originated 'Pradhan Mantri Fasal Bima Yojana'.

Role of SBILDs: Under SBI's operational map, the entire country is divided into 17 'circles'. The 51 regional SBILDs function under the administrative control of STU. While the ATIs conduct training for officials in senior management grade and above, SBILDs in each circle is predominantly engaged in imparting training to employees up to middle management grade.

2. Pillar 2: Capacity Building

The capacity building covers a range of training initiatives as well as interventions such as training of recruits, designing training programmes for various purposes, creation of knowledge repository, developing digital training approach and building leadership. These aspects are covered in brief below.

Holistic grooming and onboarding of recruits: Every year around 3,000 POs and TOs (junior-most level officer) embark on two-year on-job training during the probation period before being confirmed as permanent officers in the bank. The training curricula enables skilling of POs and training officers in all areas of banking through multi-level two-year continuous assessment process under the monitoring of branch managers and STU at the corporate centre. The training curriculum for junior associates (frontline clerical staff) was designed with an emphasis on enriching the digital knowledge and soft skills of clerical staff recruited as junior associates. Every year around 7,000 junior associates are also trained in-house.

- **Capacity building for the employees:** There are three main kinds of training programmes that are designed and delivered, which are as follows:

    (i) **Mandatory training:** It includes in-house role relevant certifications, RBI mandated programmes as well as other external courses, including e-lessons created in-house and external massive open online courses. As a part of the annual appraisal criteria, all employees from clerical staff to the senior executive level must complete their prescribed mandatory learnings within the stipulated time frame. All role relevant certifications are completely digitalized and available online for anywhere learning ease.

    (ii) **Specialized programmes:** These comprise institutional training designed in co-ordination with business units or requisitioned by controllers to supplement the domain learning for officials working in niche areas, including training for DAPs (visually impaired/ hearing impaired/D&E recruits) and Visiting Faculty Scheme, where faculty from SBILDs visit branches and participate in regional performance review meetings to address knowledge pain points gaps of staff members.

    (iii) **Electives for pull factor programmes:** These include skill-building or learning reinforcement tools, which are self- assigned. These also comprise select webinars on trending topics, power talks by eminent experts, etc.

- **STU's unique capacity building (training) initiatives:** A unique initiative of STU was the creation of 'role relevant certification programmes'. Under this initiative, 59 critical roles have been identified, which required precise skills to enable holistic customer service, build a digital mindset and reduce operational and other risks. For each such role, mandatory in-house grade-level certifications were designed with an aim to equip/upskill the employees performing distinct roles across all levels with exception of a few roles, which are covered through RBI mandated and other external certifications. The introduction of role-based certification has resulted in:

o   Acquisition of at least one role-based certification by the entire workforce
o   Alignment of the learning strategies with business objectives of the bank
o   Creation of a learning culture across the organization
o   Effective execution of work by upskilled employees enhancing productivity

As the leading bank in India, SBI also pioneered the implementation of 'youth apprenticeship training' in SBI to lend a thrust to the Government of India's Skill India Mission. The objective was to help in the creation of a pool of skilled workforce and enhance the employability of youth seeking jobs in the banking sector.

Knowledge repository for continuous learning: SBI created various knowledge and training resources to facilitate training and self-development. These included various role manuals, case studies, booklets, knowledge documents and in-house publications. These include role manuals, case studies (more than 1,329 were prepared), booklets (713 booklets available to help frontline operators), knowledge documents and question bank (over 24,000 help documents created) and in-house publications (such as Gurukul by SBICRM and e-Buzz by SBICB).

Digital learning tools: SBI training strategy leverages the potential of digital technology to offer training programmes to its large number of employees in varied places, diverse businesses and at different levels. It continuously invests and builds a portfolio of various training programmes and choices to meet the various needs of the business and employees. These include e-lessons (754 e-lessons m 477 e-capsules and 725+ mobile nuggets), askSBI (and online search engine and platform for real-time query resolu-tion), Play2Learn (a quizzing app with 21,250+ questions), MyQuest today (a daily quiz platform) and case-study discussion board (a virtual platform to promote peer group learning).

Building leadership: Leadership training is an integral part of the capacity-building programme. All newly promoted DGMs and GMs are provided business and strategic leadership training. Bank officers are routinely trained in different leadership skills at different stages of their career paths.

In addition, a basket of about 125 edX certification is also made available in addition to other internal and external certifications.

The leadership interventions are broader than just routine training. SBI makes use of cross-functional readiness through online assessment centre and practice coaches. It also builds and delivers a high-end training for potential leaders in the chosen areas of expertise and sends executive to external, including international, training programmes.

3. **Pillar 3: Marketing of Training**

The training approach at SBI emphasizes the need to interact with external organizations for cross-pollination of ideas and two-way exchange of policy and practices. To this end, it also organizes events, such as Conclaves of Chief Financial Officers of premier BFSI organizations and National Conference on inclusive growth.

SBI has opened up its training system to train bankers and financial sector professionals from the industry. Owing to a gradual shift to a virtual platform, the spare capacity and infrastructure is being used for revenue generation by offering BFSI sector-specific customized paid programmes. Conducting paid programmes for external organizations also provide an opportunity for elevating the professionalism of SBI's own in-house faculty and builds a pool of highly skilled trainers. The bank has also licensed the use of its learning management system and e-content to select external organizations and partnered with BFSIs in sharing customized e-lessons developed internally for revenue generation.

4. **Pillar 4: Research and Development**

SBI believes that research and development help in making training programmes relevant, useful and cutting edge. It is for this reason, SBI specifically takes initiatives to encourage and build on its research activities. SBI uses post-doctoral fellows as well as summer interns to provide specialist and/or project-based assistance. It also created research wings at all ATIs to address business-related concerns. Rigorous selection criteria were introduced to ensure selection of bankers having in-depth knowledge in operation as research officers. In order to create an environment for conducting research studies in a focused and meaningful manner, business units (BUs) identifies the area/subject of the study and nominate project owner from the department. The project owner periodically monitors the progress and direction of the study and also vets the final report together with recommendations before putting it up to the BU head. A mechanism for review of these studies by the user department was introduced.

Corporate Communication and Mindset Transformation: 'Nayi Disha'

SBI has always been thought of as the nation's bank, one which is pre-eminent. However, in the recent past, new players entered in nearly every segment in the BFSI sector. This meant that unless SBI changes its mindset, it may find its pre-eminent position threatened. The vast changes in Indian financial space along with changes in the global landscape also necessitated that employee's mindset are aligned with the changing times in the banking industry.

A need was felt to supplement the conventional learning and development approach by other transformational initiatives to bring about an organization-wide mindset change. With an aim to achieve this objective, SBI took off on a multi-phased transformational journey named as 'Nayi Disha' (new direction).

Nayi Disha was conceived with an intent to share key macro concerns of the bank with its huge workforce. Through this intervention, the bank encouraged its employees to shed fixed mindset and consider adopting alternative modes of thinking to meet organizational goals.

Design and Process

The programme was conceptualized by STU of the bank after an exhaustive onsite diagnostic study conducted across bank branches and CPCs located in the diverse geographical regions. In addition to one-to-one interactions with the staff members at these units, random mystery audits were conducted by the external vendor wherein the customers and staff touchpoints were observed with a view to identify the areas requiring improvement. Besides the above onsite diagnostic study, the extensive offsite study was conducted by devising a detailed questionnaire, which was published on intranet seeking feedback from the entire workforce of the bank.

Nayi Disha was designed as comprising two discrete phases, namely Phase I and Phase II. The programme covered 2.5 lakh (a quarter of a million) employees.

Phase I of the intervention was an employee-centric and self-reflective programme inspiring employee to align with values of the bank. Phase I comprised two distinct versions: Version I (all employees up to SMGS-V) and Version II (executive leadership team/DGM and above).

Phase II of the intervention was a customer-centric and toolkit-driven programme enabling the translation of the organizational vision and values into action. It was mainly centred around building customer relations, selling solutions, service with compliance and growing bank's service reputation.

Programme Content and Delivery

The programme content and collaterals were made available from one centralized location to ensure utilization of a uniform format and consistency in the delivery of the program. To ensure that language barriers did not impact the programme delivery, vetted version of the translated programmes were made available across all regions. The translated programme collaterals, handouts and videos with regional superscripts were utilized for an inclusive and self-explanatory delivery.

The facilitator pool was drawn out of the serving as well as retired officials of the bank after a preliminary shortlisting of the interested officials. Over 500 facilitators found suitable post-evaluation were certified and designated fit for delivery of a specific version of the program.

Programme Sustenance Bytes

Sustenance of a transformation initiative is essential to deeply embed the learnings in the minds of employees. The reinforcement of learning was made through communication to circles, provision of micro–booklet/card containing entire programme content and fortnightly reinforcement mailers focused on learnings of Nayi Disha.

Implementation

'Phase I' of the programme was delivered onsite at the branch locale wherein all the members of a unit attended six hours workshop together. 'Phase II' of the programme was delivered at offsite locations where the employees were gathered from different units to create a collaborative learning environment.

Impact

The outcomes of Nayi Disha programme involved inculcation of pride among employees for being a part of SBI (a Fortune 500 company), encouraging employees to see their roles in the context of the big picture. Similarly, Nayi Disha Phase II enabled employees to identify the key 'Nayi Disha' behaviours, practice the skills required for great customer service and help employees to understand that great customer service is umbilical to the growth of SBI's reputation.

Role of HR in Merger at SBI: Birth of a Global Giant

In May 2016, the consolidation of subsidiary banks under SBI was accorded in-principle approval of the chairman, SBI. The project was code-named 'Project Numero Uno'. This merger involved five associate banks, namely State Bank of Travancore, State Bank of Mysore, State Bank of Bikaner and Jaipur, State Bank of Patiala and State Bank of Hyderabad. In addition, the merger also included BMBL.

This merger posed a significant number of challenges such as rationalization of administrative offices/branches, huge stressed assets, difficult organizational issues and HR concerns.

Merger: The HR Framework

At the time of the merger, a major challenge for SBI was to manage the heterogeneous workforce in associate banks and address issues such as employee engagement, morale and career progression. The merger made many employees concerned and anxious about the change and what it could mean for them. SBI decided to address this challenge on a pro-active basis through well-designed HR interventions.

Two main aspects of the mergers involved manpower optimization and employee development and engagement. Initiatives taken to address these two main areas of HR are discussed below.

1. **Manpower optimization:** Integration of treasury operations, risk management departments, key administrative functions and other centralized cells led to excess staff, which needed to be redeployed to meet the efficiency norms of the merged entity. Redeployment of staff involves large-scale transfers to harmonize operations and optimize efficiency. To address such changes in a humane, fair and transparent manner, the following HR interventions were used.

   a. **Creation of 'Employee Gratification Gateway' portal:** Majority of the employees of associate banks (ABs) expressed anxiety regarding relocation after the merger. Based on such feedback, SBI launched a portal called 'Employee Gratification Gateway' for collecting preferences of employees. It was designed to capture the inter-circle transfer preferences online from employees and officers of Associate Banks to assess the total numbers of requests for relocation.

   This online portal was made available to all employees of ABs from 30 September 2016 to 10 October 2016, during which time the bank received an overwhelming response, and a total of 14,909 requests were registered online. Preliminary scrutiny revealed that out of the total requests received, 6,011 requests were for intra-circle transfers. This exercise helped in building transparency and alleviating employees' anxiety towards their relocation.

b. **Voluntary retirement scheme (VRS):** Based on discussions with top management of the ABs and also the employees' representatives, a need was felt to initiate measures aimed at increasing productivity and also to offer an opportunity to senior employees of ABs who genuinely wanted to take an exit option on account of uncertainties related to possible relocation and change of job profile, post-merger.

This led to the design of VRS, which was approved by the respective boards of ABs and board of SBI in December 2016 in anticipation of excess employees that would result from the rationalization of branches/processing centres/administrative offices, after the merger. VRS was made available to all permanent award staff and officers of the Bank, who had put in 20 years of service or had completed 55 years of age as on 28 February 2017. The bank paid an ex-gratia amount of ₹473.4 crore to the 3,569 eligible employees under VRS.

2. **Employee development and engagement:** The HR approach to the merger stressed the need for engaging employees and focus on their development at the same time when the 'hard' aspects (such as VRS and relocation) were also being implemented. The HR team considered it a priority that the employees should feel positive about the changes brought about by the merger. This involved initiation of general engagement programme as well as re-energizing the training systems.

Sangam Initiative for Employees of ABs Post-merger

The bank launched the 'Sangam' initiative for e-ABs employees to create a conducive environment and a growth-oriented culture. A dedicated 'Sangam' team was set up in the bank to handhold the e-AB employees. The team shared information on the bank's people policy, work culture, operating style and opportunities in the future.

A booklet was circulated by the HR Department, Corporate Centre, Mumbai, to share information on the organization structure, employee benefits, SBI officers service rules, award staff service conditions, disciplinary proceedings, promotion policy, group mediclaim policies for SBI retirees, HR initiatives, etc.

Training Requirements

In view of the acquisition of ABs, STU was assigned the task to sensitize the employees of ABs/BMBL with SBI methods and impart preliminary awareness of SBI products and processes.

STU addressed these issues by designing suitable programmes to train erstwhile associate bank employees in the following areas:

- Orientation programme for senior management of ABs
- One-week CBS training for all front-line employees
- Role-based programmes for officials of agriculture and SME branches
- Training to familiarize with the usage of loan sanction portals

SBI Digital Transformation

SBI is the largest bank in India with over 448+ million customers, 22,000+ branches, 58,000+ ATMs and over 670,000 point-of-sale machines. The bank accounts for nearly 30 per cent market share in debit card spend. SBI has 73.5 million internet banking and 16.8 million mobile banking customers as on 31 March 2020.

The bank realized early on that despite being in such a good position, there is a need to make a big bet on digital mainly because of the following three factors:

- A growing realization that increasingly customer interface is shifting from traditional product silos·(e.g., insurance, utilities, retail, banking, etc.) towards ecosystems. Digitalization provided SBI with an opportunity to integrate across these different ecosystems and find newer and better ways to serve customers.
- Despite a strong legacy, there was a need to reach out to youth/new-age customers, who preferred more new-age propositions.
- Finally, SBI saw huge potential to transform their core business itself and digital gave them the power to re-think of models they had not considered before.

Initiative

Given this context and a strong belief in digital, SBI launched an effort by the name YONO which stands for 'you only need one' and invested significantly in it. YONO was launched with 4 key aspirations in mind:

o Deliver world-class customer experience through distinctive, omnichannel and seamless customer journeys

o   Achieve disproportionate growth digitally by increasing share of wallet
    and acquiring scale
o   Move to a dramatically different S curve on carrier-to-interference (C/I)
    ratio targeting productivity gains of 20 per cent through digital end to
    end redesign of processes
o   Orchestrate the digital ecosystem by partnering with players and our
    joint ventures (JVs) in it to serve core customer needs.

YONO enabled customers to open an account digitally and do banking
transactions on a mobile app or website; get advice on and purchase a host
of non-banking financial services products such as mutual funds and insurance; withdraw cash/shop at more than 0.297 million customer touch points
across the country without any physical debit/ATM cards, and get the widest
variety and lowest prices beyond banking products, across 80+ merchant
partners across 21 categories on the platform.

Preparing Talent for the Digital Future

Across the banking sector, one of the big challenges that most organizations face is access to superior talent with required digital capabilities. This,
however, did not deter leading technology firms and digital incumbents to
grow continuously and access digital talent as they grow. This led SBI
to ask itself: What is it that the digital disruptors do differently? Whom do
they hire and how do they adapt?

   SBI realized that to attract and retain digital talent, it needed to address
issues such as:

*   What is the 'value at stake'?
*   What types of digital talent does SBI need?
*   What does SBI have to offer to attract them?

Observations and Core Beliefs on Digital Talent

SBI defined digital talent as the human capital needed to accelerate and
deliver on an organization's digital aspirations. To fulfil its digital ambitions,
SBI made digital talent a core component to the success of SBI. SBI started
to define these areas as core enablers for success to build major digital transformation platforms. Through its own research, SBI found that the most
sought-after digital talent typically refers to areas such as:

*   Software development, consisting software developers, product owners,
    UX/UI designers, etc.

- Analytics, consisting data analysts, data scientists, etc.
- Digital marketing consisting of digital marketing channel specialists and content marketing specialists/copywriters
- Strategic roles like digital leadership (e.g., chief digital officer)

Ways to Make Them Work

In order to make it work, SBI looked at imbibing digital talent through the implementation of multiple initiatives, such as:

- **Launch of an innovation department:** The purpose of this department was to be continuously in touch with the FinTech and leading innovators in the industry.
- **Digital lab setup:** The digital lab function role was to act as an enabler to digitization.
- **Digital readiness assessment:** This was an important HR area as it covered skills inventory and taxonomy and locational assessment for digital readiness.
- **Digital talent strategy:** This involved design and delivery of digital talent sourcing strategy and build-up of scouting capabilities. This initiative also involved the design of effective performance management.

Challenges

Digital recruiting is challenging and requires opening up a broad set of new recruiting channels proactively to gain access to excellent digital talent. For example, while setting up the project for YONO, SBI went through multiple experimentation and options to on-board some of the best brains in the industry.

SBI experimented with the recruitment process to access new digital capabilities in a faster and more candidate-friendly manner. This led to onboarding of approximately 150 lateral hires for roles such as product owners, marketing executives, full-stack developers and data analysts. It also experimented with using digital platforms to explore specific talent pools from the industry.

Impact

Since its launch, YONO generated significant value for the bank in terms of business growth, new customer onboarding and customer engagement.

- YONO has achieved ~46+ million downloads and ~21+ million registrations by the end of March 2020. Over 6.0 million user's login daily to meet their banking needs.

- SBI saw significant momentum on new customer onboarding with ~21,000 digital accounts opened per day which was over 65 per cent of all eligible accounts being opened by the bank with 30–40 per cent higher balances than regular accounts
- YONO turned out to be the fastest-growing and a major channel for personal loans. It disbursed ₹138 billion worth of pre-approved personal loans, with over ~0.73 million disbursements through a completely paperless and 4-click process.

Concluding Note

SBI is the largest bank in India, and one of the largest in the world. The role of HR at this scale of size and complexity is crucial to the success of the bank. Additionally, in the last decade, SBI has gone through various strategic and business changes. These include mergers with associate banks and digitalization process within the tight time constraints. HR played an important role by addressing the behavioural aspects of these strategic challenges through the design of appropriate processes and processes to facilitate the achievement of business goals. The case study showcases these approaches, processes and challenges.

HR at SBI also looked at its own functioning in a strategic manner and transformed its processes in areas, such as manpower planning, recruitment processes, performance appraisal, career and succession planning. These change processes required a keen appreciation of not only the scale and complexity of the bank but also how the business is operating and its effect on the engagement and mind-sets of the employees. SBI undertook large-scale interventions through its 'Nayi Disha' programme as well as climate survey to ensure that the growth, scale and changes in SBI do not impact the employees and the business.

As the future of banking unfolds, possibly in uncertain and unexpected ways after COVID-19, there will be additional challenges for HR to address and support the businesses. The role of HR and its contributions to SBI is, therefore, ongoing on nature.

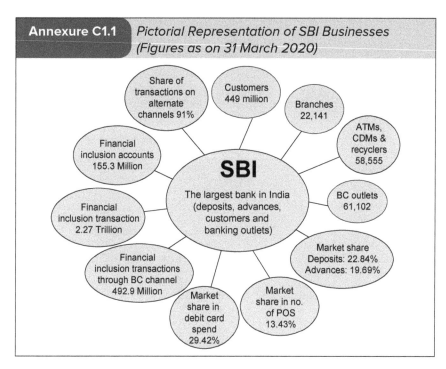

Annexure C1.1 — Pictorial Representation of SBI Businesses (Figures as on 31 March 2020)

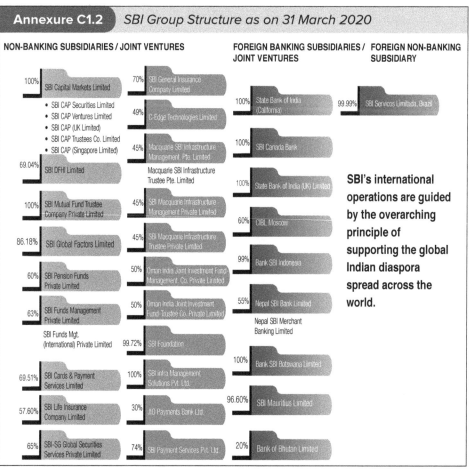

Annexure C1.2 — SBI Group Structure as on 31 March 2020

NON-BANKING SUBSIDIARIES / JOINT VENTURES

- 100% SBI Capital Markets Limited
  - SBI CAP Securities Limited
  - SBI CAP Ventures Limited
  - SBI CAP (UK Limited)
  - SBI CAP Trustees Co. Limited
  - SBI CAP (Singapore Limited)
- 69.04% SBI DFHI Limited
- 100% SBI Mutual Fund Trustee Company Private Limited
- 86.18% SBI Global Factors Limited
- 60% SBI Pension Funds Private Limited
- 63% SBI Funds Management Private Limited
  - SBI Funds Mgt. (International) Private Limited
- 69.51% SBI Cards & Payment Services Limited
- 57.60% SBI Life Insurance Company Limited
- 65% SBI-SG Global Securities Services Private Limited

- 70% SBI General Insurance Company Limited
- 49% C-Edge Technologies Limited
- 45% Macquarie SBI Infrastructure Management. Pte. Limited
  - Macquarie SBI Infrastructure Trustee Pte. Limited
- 45% SBI Macquarie Infrastructure Management Private Limited
- 45% SBI Macquarie Infrastructure Trustee Private Limited
- 50% Oman India Joint Investment Fund Management. Co. Private Limited
- 50% Oman India Joint Investment Fund-Trustee Co. Private Limited
- 99.72% SBI Foundation
- 100% SBI Infra Management Solutions Pvt. Ltd.
- 30% JIO Payments Bank Ltd.
- 74% SBI Payment Services Pvt. Ltd.

FOREIGN BANKING SUBSIDIARIES / JOINT VENTURES

- 100% State Bank of India (California)
- 100% SBI Canada Bank
- 100% State Bank of India (UK) Limited
- 60% CIBL, Moscow
- 99% Bank SBI Indonesia
- 55% Nepal SBI Bank Limited
  - Nepal SBI Merchant Banking Limited
- 100% Bank SBI Botswana Limited
- 96.60% SBI Mauritius Limited
- 20% Bank of Bhutan Limited

FOREIGN NON-BANKING SUBSIDIARY

- 99.99% SBI Servicos Limitada, Brazil

SBI's international operations are guided by the overarching principle of supporting the global Indian diaspora spread across the world.

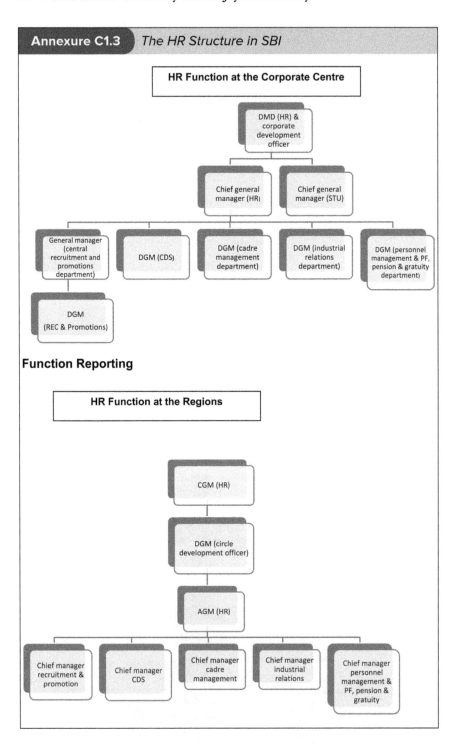

Annexure C1.3 *The HR Structure in SBI*

HR Function at the Corporate Centre

DMD (HR) & corporate development officer

Chief general manager (HR)

Chief general manager (STU)

General manager (central recruitment and promotions department)

DGM (CDS)

DGM (cadre management department)

DGM (industrial relations department)

DGM (personnel management & PF, pension & gratuity department)

DGM (REC & Promotions)

Function Reporting

HR Function at the Regions

CGM (HR)

DGM (circle development officer)

AGM (HR)

Chief manager recruitment & promotion

Chief manager CDS

Chief manager cadre management

Chief manager industrial relations

Chief manager personnel management & PF, pension & gratuity

Annexure C1.4	SBI Manpower Strength as on 31 March 2020		
Staff Category	Male	Female	Total Count
Officers	85,973	23,010	108,983
Clerical	61,668	35,671	97,339
Subordinates	35,523	3,679	39,202
Contractual	841	162	1,003
Medical	58	42	100

Annexure C1.5 *Strategic Training Unit: Structure*

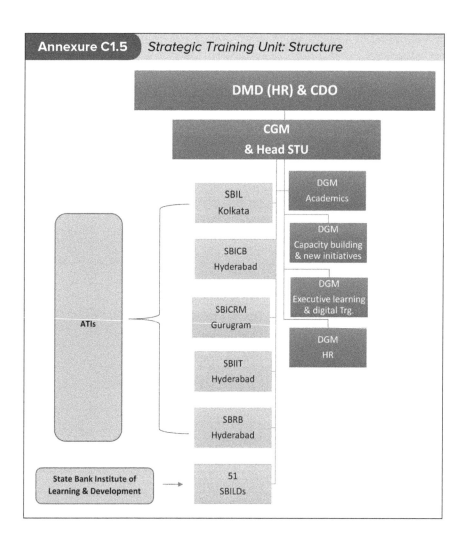

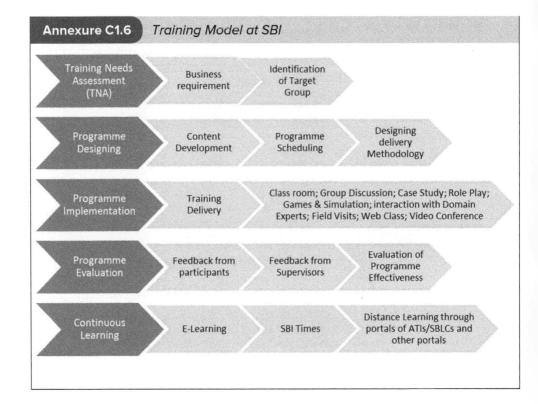

Annexure C1.6 *Training Model at SBI*

List of Abbreviations

Abbreviations	
MD	Managing Director
TEGSS II /DMD	Deputy Managing Director
TEGSS I/ CGM	Chief General Manager
TEGS VII/GM	General Manager
TEGS VI/DGM	Deputy General Manager
SMGS V/AGM	Assistant General Manager
SMGS IV/CM	Chief Manager
MMGS III	Manager
MMGS II	Deputy Manager
JMGS I	Assistant Manager
Associate/junior associate	Clerical Staff
TO	Trainee Officer- promoted from clerical to officer grade

PO	Probationary Officer- directly recruited to officer grade. On confirmation, they become Scale 1/ JMGS I officers
AB	Associate Bank
BMBL	Bharatiya Mahila Bank Limited
STU	Strategic Training Unit
HR	Human Resources
SME	Small & Medium Enterprises
KRA	Key Responsibility Areas
LHO	Local head office
AO/module	Administrative office
RBO	Regional business office

2

Sustainable People Processes and Leadership Development in Bank of Baroda

Joydeep Dutta Roy

Bank of Baroda (BOB) is an Indian state-owned international banking and financial services company, headquartered in Vadodara in Gujarat, India, having its corporate office in Mumbai. It is among the top three banks in India in terms of business size. The bank was founded by the illustrious and visionary Maharaja of Baroda, Sir Sayajirao Gaekwad III on the 20 July 1908. The bank, along with 13 other major commercial banks of India, was nationalized on 19 July 1969 by the Government of India and has been designated as a profit-making public sector undertaking. Professor Dwijendra Tripathy in the history book of the bank *Dynamics of Ascent* mentions that it has been a long and eventful journey of the bank for more than a century across 21 countries. Starting in 1908 from a small building in Baroda to its new hi-rise and hi-tech Baroda Corporate Centre in Mumbai, the bank stands as a saga of vision, enterprise, financial prudence and corporate governance. Seeped in the progressive ideals of its founder, Sir Sayajirao Gaekwad III, the bank also imbibed a progressive and forward-looking outlook.

When the government decided on consolidation in the Indian banking industry in 2018–2019 in order to create bigger banks of global size which could not just handle bigger banking business but also manage risks better due to improved controls, risk practices and governance mechanisms, BOB was an obvious first choice for the first-ever three-way amalgamation of erstwhile Vijaya Bank and erstwhile Dena Bank with it. This amalgamation has made BOB an even bigger entity and the second largest public sector bank (PSB) after State Bank of India. Post amalgamation, BOB has an even larger geographical reach with ~9,500+ branches, ~13,500+ ATMs, ~85,000 employees, nearly 130 million customers and a business size of ~₹15,000 billion.

This new BOB has now become a truly pan-India financial services conglomerate dominating key economic clusters of Gujarat (22% market share), Maharashtra, Karnataka, Rajasthan and Uttar Pradesh (~10% market share in each of these key states). It is now in a position where it can leverage cutting-edge technology and operating platforms, serving customers in India and globally with its international presence, and now the vision is to create an institution of global scale and size, building upon the strength of the three institutions further, and facilitate deeper outreach to be able to compete with the best banks globally.

As the bank evolved from being a small provincial bank into one of the largest banks of the country today, it also simultaneously developed a culture of innovation, customer centricity and being people friendly. The culture and the growth of the bank complemented each other to further evolve. The bank's diversification into different geographies and even into overseas locations helped it develop not only a cosmopolitan outlook but also helped the people within the organization to appreciate diversity and different cultures which in turn helped develop the bank's customer orientation.

The progressive outlook and innovation culture in the bank and among the bank's leaders helped develop very progressive HR practices. As one of the earliest banks in the country to recognize and evolve a professional cadre of specialist HR people (then known as personnel officers), the bank's special focus on its HR function began way back in the late 1950s when the bank recruited a labour welfare officer L. B. Bhide to look after employees- and trade unions-related matters. Bhide carved out a professional approach in dealing with and replace by the word these matters.

The progressive management led by N. M. Choksi, CEO, deputed Bhide to London School of Economics for a one-year full-time programme on labour welfare. This was a rare and pioneering step during those days to recognize the importance of personnel function, even though the bank was small. Bhide set up a professional personnel department and recruited some qualified personnel specialists. This is how the legacy to recognize personnel function as a professionalized and specialized function began, a legacy that has continued till date. Over the years, BOB has reaped the benefits of this approach. Some of the HR professionals have become industry icons. With this sustained recruitment of HR specialists over the years, the bank now boasts of almost 400 odd HR specialists at different levels who handle the HR matters of its 85,000 strong employee base resulting in an HR to employee ratio of around 1:200. Although this ratio is not among the best as per best practices standards, BOB is still better in this respect than most other PSBs. Such a high number of HR specialists is not there in any other Indian bank to the best of my knowledge. These specialist HR officers man the HR departments at regional level, zonal level, HR back offices and at corporate office.

It's a gradual ascend and career path for the HR folks as they move through administrative HR functions at the junior level to handling and implementing strategic and developmental HR initiatives getting launched regularly by the corporate HR team and, with the exposure at the ground level, then graduate to more senior and strategic roles. The bank has been able to implement multiple and best-in-class HR initiatives over time (some of which are covered in this case study) largely because the bank had a professional breed of HR specialists who understood the HR nuances of the initiatives and did not allow them to be frittered away. The conceptualization as well as the implementation both required specialist skills and BOB had built a cadre of HR officers capable of doing both.

However, given this brief history of the bank and the bank's HR personnel, let me now talk about some of the pioneering work done by BOB in the area of HR. I would like to start from the time BOB really broke out from the league of PSBs in India in the area of HR and darted off with a newfound mission of sorts to professionalize its HR function. This was around 2005–2008 when Anil K. Khandelwal, an HR stalwart himself, came to head the bank as its chairman and managing director (CMD). Khandelwal, in his book *Dare to Lead,* has beautifully captured the transformation of BOB during this period. He rightfully brought out the aspects of building human capital and building of people processes as the real engine of growth for the bank. By the time he left the bank on the 31 March 2008, he had left not just a transformed bank but also left an indelible mark on various aspects of how the bank would function in the years ahead. This account takes that story ahead and looks at how the HR function, which at the time of Khandelwal became a pivotal point in the whole transformation story of the bank, evolved itself in the decade thereafter and made itself more relevant not only to the changing times but also for the organization as it underwent multiple changes in its top leadership.

The Khandelwal Legacy

Khandelwal is a man who dreamt big and who dared to convert those dreams into reality. No wonder that the Personnel Department at BOB got its nomenclature change under him as the Human Resources Department. He was instrumental in converting what was once largely an administrative function into a more development-oriented function. While he streamlined the industrial relations (IR) and personnel administration functions, he also laid the foundation for the development side of HR in BOB.

Khandelwal started this HR transformation exercise in BOB in his earlier tenure as executive director of the bank during the period 2002–2003 when he had undertaken a major initiative to restructure the IR scenario in the bank from a crisis and ad hoc mode to a more structured pattern, clearly defining the role of trade unions and improving management control over employee matters, empowering operating managers. A major diagnostic exercise of HR through the HR audit concept, which was introduced for the first time in the industry, revealed the inconsistencies in policy implementation and thereby enabled streamlining of various HR processes. This course correction in the IR scenario in the bank and also in the HR admin processes actually enabled a full focus on development aspects in his later tenure in the bank as the CMD.

Khandelwal envisioned the revamp of the training system to meet the new competency requirements, introduced a scientific process of talent management through an organization-wide talent search exercise called 'Khoj', developed leaders for the future through a very futuristic leadership development programme called 'Leadership Enhancement and Appreciation Programme (LEAP)', organized succession planning for key positions, redesigned the performance appraisal system, put in focused programmes for developing a pipeline of young managers, started what can be called the first steps for an organization-wide employee engagement programme through the 'Baroda Manthan' or Employee Conclave concept, a first of its kind, employee assistance programme called 'Sampark' and years ahead of its time psychological counselling programme for employees called 'Paramarsh'. He put in place a comprehensive HR policy document which for the first time documented what the HR Vision was and what policy and direction HR was going to take in the coming years. This enabled a clear roadmap for HR for the first time in the bank and probably for the first time in the industry as well. He set up a board-level committee on HR as a pro-active measure to bring the focus on HR from the very top and engaged as the bank's HR and organizational development (OD) advisor, Professor Udai Pareek, a giant in the area of HR to help the Bank professionalize its HR function. An HR specialist was brought into the CMD secretariat itself so that certain innovations in HR could be piloted directly from his office. Initiatives such as the Khoj, Sampark, Paramarsh and project LEAP programmes were run right from his office only so that the vision and execution remained undiluted. This was also the time when the HR structure was properly laid out with different HR divisions such as human resource accounting (HRA) and human resource development (HRD) carved out clearly and different specialists heading different subsystems. The belief was the principle that structure follows strategy.

All of these initiatives apart from bringing HR from the periphery to the centre of things and making it a part of the board governance process through the creation of the steering committee of the board on HR are what defined the HR transformation in BOB during his time. Those were heady times for HR in the bank when so many things happened, all in the space of just around three years. This phase also strongly demonstrated the strong connection between HR and business outcomes. During a short period of three years, the business of the bank was doubled, and many qualitative initiatives were implemented such as technology, rebranding and overseas expansion. The credibility of the HR function was firmly established.

As I start writing this account almost a decade later, I am tempted to pose the following questions:

- Post Khandelwal, did all of it last and were all of those HR initiatives sustained over time?
- What impact did some of those initiatives have on the HR personnel and the HR fraternity in the bank?
- Could those HR initiatives, later on, be used as stepping stones to do further work in the area of HR in the bank for employee and company benefit?
- Was there any impact on the culture and organizational climate in the post-Khandelwal years?

As I ponder over these questions and reflect back on the journey of the last few years from 2008 onwards to 2020 now, the HR journey in BOB indeed looks fascinating and worth recounting. I am sure this will have insights and research material for academics and also for HR professionals who can pick up a few of the things attempted in BOB to base newer ways of rethinking the HR function.

Let me start by acknowledging that the HR initiatives taken during Khandelwal's time were really far reaching and left a lasting impact on the way HR in BOB functioned in the years ahead. For one, it left the bank with the whole notion of how important this function was and how it could no longer be relegated to being on the sidelines. Giving this function its due importance under the 'sun' was very important as without that, the tendency of leadership, coming in from a business role, is largely to give prominence to business functions, sidestepping HR, hardly realizing that HR and people are the ones that can build or break businesses. BOB was lucky in that respect in getting successive CMDs who recognized and gave this function its due importance and place in management, thereby allowing the function to steadily keep enlarging its mandate to take on a key and a central role.

Role of the Board-level Committee on HR

The steering committee of the board on HR, started by Khandelwal, became a key body pushing for HR reforms in the bank over time and thereby brought board-level involvement and the entire HR reform agenda to be driven from the very top. What once started as a once-in-a-quarter meeting during the Khandelwal's regime gradually became a monthly meeting and sometimes was held even twice a month. This punishing periodicity almost forced the HR team to be on its toes always and be at the forefront of the reform agenda as they knew that the board was following up on the same. This forum thereby became a key driver for the BOB HR function to continuously evolve and redraw the boundary lines for the HR function. Gradually, from being an HR advisory body, this forum actually became a very active sub-committee of the board, which tracked and reviewed the efficacy of various HR initiatives, helped formulate new ones and also gave new ideas to HR.

This board committee always had people of eminence from among the directors, people who had an academic lineage or came from an eminent B-school who could discuss contemporary ideas with the latest case studies, etc. During his time, Khandelwal brought in advisors from the industry who could help bring an outside perspective and also the latest trends in HR to the bank. Here, people of eminence were brought into the committee, people of the likes of late Professor Udai Pareek, the father of psychometrics and organization behaviour in the country; Professor T. V. Rao, widely regarded as the doyen of the modern HRD movement of the country; Professor Pradip Khandwala, former director, Indian Institute of Management Ahmedabad (IIMA); Professor B. L. Maheshwari, Director Centre for Organizational Development, Hyderabad; Arvind Agarwal, head HR from RPG enterprises, etc. With such luminaries in the HR committee, no doubt, the bank's HR reforms and HR activities stood out in the industry. Although there was a brief period when this HR committee of the board was inactive for around two years in between, it was again revived and the practice of bringing in outside experts to the committee to bring in the best practices from outside continued. The bank brought in heads of HR from other industries like the head of HR from Infosys or the head of HR from one of the leading search firms of the country or people of eminence like former non-executive chairman Ravi Venkatesan or the current non-executive chairman Hasmukh Adhia into the committee, all of whom not only brought outside perspective but also had the ability to view everything from an altogether different lens and contributed significantly in guiding the new HR vision. This helped us shape some of the industry's first and far-reaching HR initiatives in the bank.

The board committee very closely reviewed and tracked some of the leading development interventions initiated by us like the leadership development programme, the employee engagement programme and the total overhaul of the performance management system in the bank. We shall talk about these initiatives in the paragraphs below. This close tracking and review at the board level helped us to continuously refine and hone these programmes to a new level of quality, not seen in the public sector space. Therefore, one big success factor in the gradual professionalizing of the HR function in BOB has been this board-level HR committee. Top-level involvement in the development of the HR function cannot just be undermined, and the BOB experience just proves that.

HR Transformation through Human Touch

The bank embarked on a massive HR transformation programme called 'Project Sparsh' in the year 2011 under which various HR initiatives were launched. This project was based on the premise that one-off HR initiatives could not really break the jinx, and there was actually a requirement of looking at a wholesale transformation of the HR function in various dimensions in order to really reap the right benefits. The common realization was that HR and was crucial for success in business, and the objective was to achieve business excellence through HR transformation. The human touch enveloping the bank's logo gave rise to the Sparsh logo, and this actually heralded a new chapter in the HR journey of the bank.

The bank's annual report of 2012–2013 stated,

> This journey of HR Transformation was started in August'2011 and over the last one year, various landmark HR initiatives have been launched in the Bank which are futuristic and designed to make Bank of Baroda one of the best places to work for its employees, create cutting edge HR policies and processes through which we can be a role model for all other Banks and in the process, leverage the full potential of the Bank's human capital to substantially improve employee productivity.

The following initiatives formed part of the Sparsh programme (Figure C2.1):

1. Onboarding of directly recruited officers and clerks
2. A revamped HR structure
3. Talent management programme
4. Tool to optimize postings
5. Large-scale product training campaign—Ascend
6. Rewards and incentives
7. Online performance management systems
8. Manpower planning
9. Recruitment strategy
10. Employee engagement
11. Career path
12. Launch of e-learning capability and processes in the bank
13. Strengthening the mentoring process in the bank
14. HR automation

This was in continuation of the seats of HR transformation laid during 2005–2008 and many elements of HR were taken up and implemented across the bank. This programme brought many of the industry's best practices into the bank and made BOB's HR processes in many areas match up to what

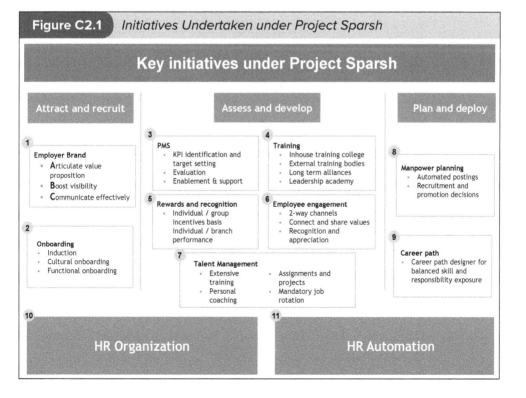

Figure C2.1 *Initiatives Undertaken under Project Sparsh*

Key initiatives under Project Sparsh

Attract and recruit

1 **Employer Brand**
- **A**rticulate value proposition
- **B**oost visibility
- **C**ommunicate effectively

2 **Onboarding**
- Induction
- Cultural onboarding
- Functional onboarding

Assess and develop

3 **PMS**
- KPI identification and target setting
- Evaluation
- Enablement & support

4 **Training**
- Inhouse training college
- External training bodies
- Long term alliances
- Leadership academy

5 **Rewards and recognition**
- Individual / group incentives basis individual / branch performance

6 **Employee engagement**
- 2-way channels
- Connect and share values
- Recognition and appreciation

7 **Talent Management**
- Extensive training
- Personal coaching
- Assignments and projects
- Mandatory job rotation

Plan and deploy

8 **Manpower planning**
- Automated postings
- Recruitment and promotion decisions

9 **Career path**
- Career path designer for balanced skill and responsibility exposure

10 **HR Organization**

11 **HR Automation**

the best-in-class organizations were doing. While we shall cover the talent management piece in more detail, a brief on the other initiatives undertaken during the almost two and half years of this project is given below.

1. **Onboarding of new hires:** This was also a period when the bank was undertaking huge recruitments to match up with the huge retirements and exodus from the bank, a legacy of the post-nationalization era. Almost 4,000–6,000 new people were entering the bank as officers and clerks every year. They required a systematic onboarding to make sure that the recruitment efforts were not wasted. Therefore, a structured programme was put in place to ensure both functional and cultural onboarding, provided new hires in both officers and clerical cadre a pleasant joining experience and also to make them work-ready quickly. This was enabled by technology-enabled tracking of their exposures and training to ensure that everyone's experience was uniform and met the desired objectives.

2. **Strategic workforce planning:** A scientific model of manpower planning was developed for assessing manpower requirements based on activity and transaction levels of various units linked to time and motion studies and using them for making manpower projections and forecasting with built-in linkages to recruitment, promotions, transfers and deployment in the bank.

3. **Performance management:** Strengthening the processes of the performance management system (PMS) and developing various IT tools to make the processes and the system more robust, objective and quicker. Also, PMS was made online to bring in more process discipline. This was probably just the beginning of the reforms in the area of PMS, where the bank broke new milestones with its Baroda GEMS initiative some years down the line.

4. **Training and development (Baroda Academy):** The entire training and development efforts of the bank were then brought under one focused vertical of 'Baroda Academy' (Figure C2.2). All training and developmental initiatives/activities being carried out in the bank, covering both internal training and external training and also covering tie-ups with external training institutes for carrying out dedicated training programmes for targeted groups of people from the bank were now brought under this focused vertical of Baroda Academy. The objective behind this initiative was to enhance (a) the learning experience and development opportunities for employees, (b) help in better grooming and development of people in the bank, (c) create a learning organization and (d) significantly improve organization performance.

Figure C2.2 *Baroda Academy Logo*

The bank always had a very strong training wing—one of the first PSBs to develop its own training infrastructure and undertake various training interventions. Hence, this further revamps into the Baroda Academy branding, which was meant to consolidate all training activities under a single umbrella and set the stage for learning and development (L&D) becoming a separate independent vertical in the bank, led by a chief learning officer. The further sub initiatives that were taken under the broad Baroda Academy initiative were as follows.

a. Publication of a comprehensive annual training calendar
b. Introduction of self-nominations by employees as an additional channel of training nominations
c. Introduction of the system of training credits
d. Introduction of tests at the end of every training programme
e. Creation of a pool of expert practitioners as associate faculty
f. Enhancement of course content through in-house case studies
g. Training policy and training manuals put in place
h. Launch of large-scale product training campaign called 'Ascend' covering all officers and front-line staff of the bank
i. E-learning design and structure created which envisaged implementation of a complete learning management solution, development and hosting of various e-learning content, enabling access through structured interventions and devices, driving adoption and enrolment through building awareness, communication, linking mandatory completion to other HR activities, monitoring and tracking

5. **Rewards and incentives:** Developing a sound and comprehensive policy for rewarding the best performers by formulating a comprehensive incentive policy for the bank covering all staff and using various IT tools to track performance against targets seamlessly across all levels.

6. **Career path and postings:** A career path policy was developed for ensuring various exposures for different types of officers at different stages

| Figure C2.3 | *Employee Value Proposition (FIRST)* |

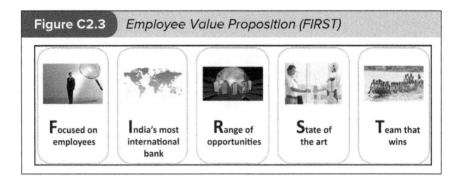

| **F**ocused on employees | **I**ndia's most international bank | **R**ange of opportunities | **S**tate of the art | **T**eam that wins |

of their career to meet with their grooming and development requirements and ensuring right skills at different stages of their career.

7. **A new recruitment strategy:** Strategies were developed for employer branding, and an employer value proposition was created. A focused career portal was created to communicate the bank's value proposition to prospective new hires. A new resourcing channel, namely the 'Baroda Manipal School of Banking' was developed to meet with the recruitment objectives. The bank also articulated, for the first time in its history, a clearly defined employer value proposition with the acronym 'FIRST' (Figure C2.3). This value proposition with each letter signifying a specific reason to prospective applicants as to why BOB should be the preferred choice for them by projecting the different facets of working at BOB. These strategies provided a huge impetus to the 'employer branding' of the bank and gave a significant push in these years of high recruitment by attracting quality talent.

8. **Employee engagement:** Various initiatives were formulated to keep employees motivated and engaged. Engagement of employees was targeted at engagement with the job, engagement with colleagues and engagement with the organization through different initiatives such as improving employee–HR connection, faster and effective grievance redressal mechanisms, focused employee communication and building loyalty and building pride and commitment through a defined set of reward and recognition measures.

9. **Revamp of the HR structure:** A revised HR structure was put in place through clearly defined front-office HR, back-office HR and a mid-office HR (centre of excellence) concepts to bring in desired focus and effectiveness in the delivery of various HR programmes. Centralizing various routine HR issues at the HR back office was taken up to free HR time for development and engagement activities. The HR back

office was christened as the Human Rights and Consumer Protection Cell (HRCPC) where all the employee claims processing including travel bills, medical bills, benefit payments, staff loans processing, etc., for all employees and branches/offices across the country got centralized. This immediately had a great impact of not just reducing turnaround time through an assembly line working process and checking revenue leakages by ensuring uniform implementation of rules and guidelines, but the biggest benefit of it was the freeing up of HR time for more developmental activities. As the drain of these activities on precious HR time got reduced, HR was immediately able to focus on many developmental initiatives that the bank was simultaneously unleashing. This enabled better execution and implementation of the new-age HR reforms and contributed to the overall HR transformation in the bank.

10. **Postings optimization tool:** It is one of the key HR activities revolved around the right placements of manpower. To help in this process and help the bank to place the right people at the right place and thereby improve the productivity level of employees, a postings tool was implemented which was a technology solution to facilitate and arrive at better postings decisions. This tool gave recommendations for ideal postings taking into account various reasons for transfers and matching candidates to available positions. The tool also provided different management information system (MIS) and functionalities at each step for informed decision-making.

11. **HR automation:** Large-scale HR automation was initiated in this programme through a variety of IT tools to enable reaching out to a large, geographically dispersed workforce and ensure the desired effectiveness and impact. These included creations of the following IT tools:

- IT tool for manpower planning
- Onboarding tracking tool to centrally monitor rotations and training of new recruits
- Talent management system to support the logistics of the system and output capture for creating an organization memory
- Strengthen online learning management system: Introduction of annual training calendar, a system for self-nominations and training credits
- Online PMS tool
- IT tool for business planning and incentives
- Postings tool for optimizing various constraints and arriving at best-fit recommendations for placement

The Good People, Bad People Syndrome

The often-quoted Pareto's law about 80 per cent of the work being done by 20 per cent people and the remaining 80 per cent being the free riders rang true for a bank like BOB too. Most organizations struggle to find that 20 per cent and somewhere this 20 per cent gets lost in the crowd, leading to a gradual fading out of the talent and wasted opportunities. We are still not there as an organization which knows all its 'good people'; in other words, the bank's true talent. But BOB was one of the first banks in the public sector space to start some serious work on the talent management front.

Khandelwal inspired and initiated with an ambitious nation-wide talent search programme in the bank called 'Khoj' in the year 2005. That was the first time when people in the bank were tested on psychometrics, and a combination of skill, aptitude and personality assessment tests were used to shortlist talent in various categories. The Khoj programme identified 'talent' in different areas, and this helped in their beneficial placements and utilization. However, this was just a start, and there was lot more to be done in the area of managing that talent and linkage to other sub-systems such as training and development, rewards and succession planning. But a start had been made and the seeds got sown for a more robust talent management programme in the bank to emerge and get implemented in later years. There were some HR functionaries in the bank like me who received a hands-on experience with this whole new concept of talent management in the Khoj exercise, and this helped spark off later initiatives.

Structured Talent Management Initiative Implemented in the Bank under Project Sparsh

To identify and develop top talent and also undertake succession planning in a structured way, 'talent committees' were formed at various levels for identifying top talent, and for the first time, there were focused committees discussing only 'talent' and nothing else. This talent management programme consisted of the following (see Figures C2.4 and C2.5):

1. **Talent pool identification:** Through a systematic and structured process of talent committees, the bank was able to clearly identify around 15–20 per cent people in specific scales of officers, namely Scales III, IV, V and VI (senior managers, chief managers, assistant general managers [AGMs] and deputy general managers [DGMs]) as the future leaders.

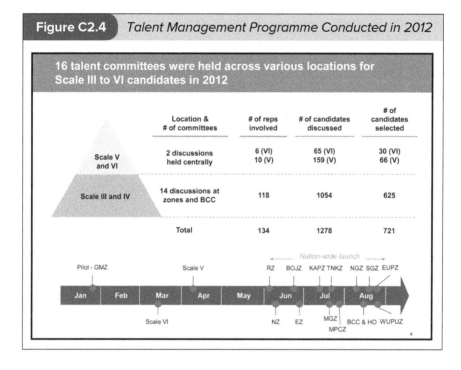

Figure C2.4 Talent Management Programme Conducted in 2012

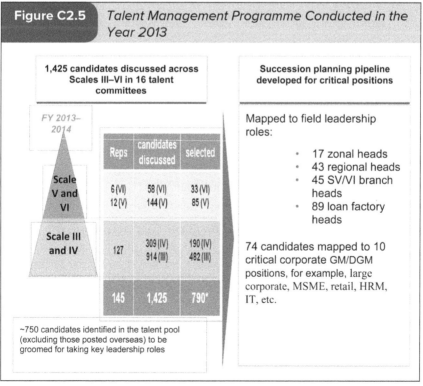

Figure C2.5 Talent Management Programme Conducted in the Year 2013

The mechanics of the process was fine-tuned through IT enablement and run across the bank.

2. **Talent development:** This includes the following:

- Differentiated development agenda for grooming candidates: job rotations, mentoring, training, etc.
- The output feeds into various HR systems such as promotions, selection exercises and postings.
- Leadership conclaves and leadership training for the top talent.

3. **Succession planning:** This includes the following:

- Identification of candidates with the potential to succeed in critical positions in higher scales

   - Identification of candidates in AGM and DGM level with the potential to succeed in critical positions in DGM and general manager (GM) level respectively
   - Identification of candidates in chief manager level with the potential to succeed as regional managers/deputy regional managers

- Postings and grooming path tailored to succession needs
- Multiple new candidates identified for critical positions.
- Bank-level focus on areas having succession gap

At each level, the top talent was now getting discussed, their future postings, exposures required, training required were being discussed and getting recorded, paving the way for the bank to also do a very structured succession planning exercise. This exercise changed the perception of operational functionaries towards HR and brought renewed focus into talent management in the bank in a very structured and strong manner. 'This initiative radically changed how "talent" and HR was being handled and brought the spotlight on people. In a way, this programme took off from where the earlier Khoj programme had left and taken it to another level.'

Getting First-day, First-hour Productive Resources

Given the pressure on recruitments, the bank was at that time hiring large numbers almost to the extent of 4,000–6,000 people annually. The bank had implemented a very exhaustive onboarding programme for all the new hires which ensured not only a uniform joining experience but also enabled them to undergo defined training and exposures in different areas of banking as per set schedule which was tracked meticulously and at scale through the help of technology. However, this still meant that the bank could get the services of the new hires as fully productive resources of the bank only much later, after completion of their detailed onboarding programme in the bank, almost six months to one year later. Given the large retirements, the bank had this huge necessity of making the resources fully productive much faster.

To tackle this problem, the bank then put in place an innovative 'Train-Hire-Deploy' model, which was but an inverted model of the usual 'Hire-Train-Deploy' model. Under this model, the bank selected candidates with requisite norms and put them through a focused one-year postgraduation diploma programme (in banking and finance) first before hiring them in the bank. The entire one-year course was tailored to meet with the bank's specific requirements with the overall objective of making the students 'first-day first-hour productive'. This was done through the 'Baroda Manipal School of Banking' (BMSB) set up by the bank in association with the Manipal Global Education Services group, a first such initiative by any PSB.

Later on, realizing the advantages of this model, many other PSBs set up similar banking finishing schools replicating almost all the processes put in by our bank in BMSB. But the rigour and intensity of our programme remained unmatched as the bank put a lot of focused effort in not only the training and course curriculum at the school but also in the co-curricular activities, building a Baroda culture in the campus even before the formal entry of the candidates into the bank and investing heavily into the personality development, grooming and communication skills of the candidates. The candidates were trained on the bank's core banking system in the campus itself so that when they were formally inducted into the bank, they could get down to work as a full-fledged resource right from day one.

The course was designed in a way that every three months, a fresh batch of students was inducted into the course who graduated after undergoing the focused one year programme, and thereby, it ensured that every three months, the bank was also receiving a batch of fully trained officers who were ready to contribute and face customers from the day one. This greatly helped the bank to meet not only the requirement of officers numerically but also the quality aspects. In the approximately six years of its existence, the school had given almost 6,000 fully trained officers to the bank.

Bringing in the Science of HR

For long, HR had been run as an administrative function and people believed that anyone with common sense, a set of right values, ability to put the right people in the right jobs and with a good sense of organization and administration could run HR. This often resulted in HR being run by Generalists who administered the function with the eyes of a banker and whose main interest was to ensure that the systems were kept up and running. Often the head of HR was a generalist banker who, with the exception of a few, was more concerned about business being run without disruptions and manpower being available at all times. This approach somewhat curtailed the professionalization movement and did not allow the function to focus on skills, talent and efficiencies. However, what helped BOB was the breed of specialists in the bank who slowly but surely played a part in gradually bringing in the science of HR in the bank. This was where other PSBs faced a disadvantage and it helped BOB take the lead in professionalizing HR.

Defining a Leadership Competency Framework

Apart from bringing in the modern concepts of psychometrics for assessment for various selections/recruitment exercises, BOB also became one of the first PSBs to adopt full-fledged assessment/development centres for various selection/promotion/development exercises that it was undertaking. To aid in these exercises, the bank put in place a detailed 'leadership competency framework', again a first in the PSB space. This was a total in-house development by the bank's HR team in a very scientific manner, where even big organizations use the services of consultants to help them draw up such frameworks. This framework culled out six leadership competencies which were agreed to be critical for the bank's managers and leadership at various levels. Each of the competencies had behavioural descriptors with five levels of proficiency or competency standards built in to be used at different levels of leadership. The linking of the competency framework to various interventions in the bank like the leadership programme, individual development plan for executives, succession planning and even for selection/promotion assessments made the HR practices more focused and reliable.

Launch of Bank's Core Values

At some point in time, as the HR team started working on the cultural aspects in the bank, it was felt necessary to bring out the bank's core values; values which form the cornerstone of its existence and success. Articulating the values clearly known to all employees would not only help strengthen the culture but also help the organization reap the benefits of common practice and have a commonality of approaches towards achieving the bank's goals.

This finalization of core values was also done after an organization-wide study, finalizing descriptors and also stating the conforming behaviours and non-conforming behaviours for each core value. Once finalized, the same was then socialized across the organization and through various interventions, employees were sensitized on the behaviours. This is a continuous process and regularly used even now in multiple interventions for achieving cultural assimilation amongst employees.

Introduction of the Annual Employee Engagement Survey, 'Voice of Barodians'

So long, HR was always operating in the dark with its own notions of what was right or wrong. This sometimes brought about a power overhang in HR people, an attribute often criticized by line people. On many occasions, HR went with its own gut feeling or instinctive call on people which could go either way. A key criticism of HR was that it often used its power for the wrong reasons. Therefore, having in place robust feedback mechanisms which not only brought out the ground-level feelings but also analysed the efficacy of various HR interventions was definitely something that was long overdue.

This gave rise to the annual 'Voice of Barodians' (VOB) survey, which was launched to gauge employee satisfaction and engagement on various parameters. The first such survey was conducted in the year 2017, and it showed around 55 per cent employee engagement scores. Based on the results of the survey, various interventions were carried out, and in the second year in 2018, the survey showed a substantial improvement to around 63 per cent. The survey enabled having a hard look at existing HR interventions based on the feedback from employees and take corrective steps.

A Composite-branded Employee Engagement Programme: 'Baroda Anubhuti'

Certain employee engagement initiatives were undertaken as a part of the Sparsh project in the year 2012, but over time, they gradually lost focus. One of the important feedbacks from the VOB survey of 2017 was the inefficacy and inadequacy of the employee engagement programmes in the bank leading to low-engagement scores. This enabled a hard look at the existing initiatives and helped refine the whole concept of employee engagement in the bank.

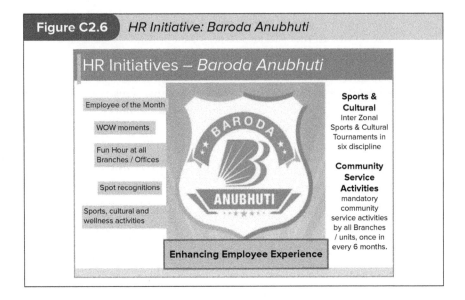

Figure C2.6 | *HR Initiative: Baroda Anubhuti*

The bank brought out a composite and branded employee engagement programme named 'Baroda Anubhuti', covering a wide range of initiatives under it (Figure C2.6).

- The employee of the month
- Celebrating 'wow' moments
- Celebrating 'zero hour/fun hour' at branches/offices
- Mandatory community activity by all branches/offices
- Restarting of sports activities in the bank and also the introduction of inter-regional and inter-zonal tournaments in various sports disciplines
- Starting the concept of an annual sports day for the bank on the second Saturday of November of every year (day of sports and fun and fairs with families)

The Baroda Anubhuti programme helped improve engagement levels substantially as reflected from the improvement in the engagement scores in the VOB survey done in the succeeding year. Certain activities such as the community service activities mandated to be done twice every year by the entire branch team helped greatly in making teamwork stronger in the bank, better bonding among employees, bringing in a service orientation and a healthy feeling of care for the society in employees.

Baroda GEMS

One of the biggest forward movements made by BOB HR has been the introduction of the scientific and system-based performance management system, Baroda GEMS. GEMS, being an acronym standing for growth and empowerment management system, stands out uniquely, not only in the PSB space but also among private peers and has been widely acclaimed not just by the government but also by the regulator and many others as a very forward-looking and progressive system.

Developing Leaders for the Future

One of the most progressive works done by the HR team of BOB was to institutionalize the system and process of leadership development in the bank. Leadership development as a concept and as a good practice may be often spoken about in management circles, but there are only a handful of institutions in India that can really boast of a really robust leadership practice which is carried out on a continuous basis in the organization. And in the banking sphere, there may actually be none, with the exception of one organization, BOB. The leadership development that I am talking about is not a programme that is delivered in a classroom or a simple week-long programme, etc. BOB understood many years ago that leadership development is not a simple skill-building programme, it is about building character, personality and certain innate characteristics which sometimes takes years to hone and polish. This is about a long-term investment in an individual to slowly but surely inch their progress up the leadership development charts.

Project LEAP

Leadership development is also another reason why I would like to bring back Khandelwal's legacy and the vision that he had. It was his futuristic vision that way back in 2007 when banks had not even ventured properly into the soft skills training area, the bank started its first-ever expansive and customized to BOB leadership development programme called project LEAP. LEAP, short for 'leadership enhancement and appreciation programme' brought to the bank, its first ever taste of a leadership development programme. To enable this first of its kind project to be handled professionally, the bank had engaged one of the leading HR consultants of that time, M/s Grow Talent for this assignment. Khandelwal was so passionate about this programme and the change it could bring in that even with his responsibilities as the CMD, he personally took out time and spent long hours discussing the nitty-gritty of this project to help the consultants understand the thinking, the concept, the strategy, the leadership gaps and the execution of this programme in BOB. The methodology brought out was 10 per cent learning in classroom mode, 20 per cent through coaching and

70 per cent through live projects and action learning. It was a model that bore the stamp of time. As the years went by and we learnt with many other experiences of conducting leadership development programmes, we kept refining the model and progressively kept improving upon it with each programme.

The LEAP programme was a watershed programme not only for BOB but also I would dare say that it gave a model to the industry as well. At that time, there were hardly any instances of such long drawn leadership development programmes. Around 300 executives of the bank got selected for this programme right from chief manager grade to DGM grade, and a multi-stage process was put together where the participants underwent two modules of classroom training of around 10 days each at an interval of around 5–6 months. The intervening period was spent on action learning projects. Coaching was held on the competency gaps of participants which were revealed from psychometrics and 360-degree feedback by expert facilitators. This was an altogether new experience for participants, and none of them had ever experienced such a program ever before. The feedback was revealing, and most of them said that it helped them realize their leadership capabilities to which they had not paid any attention at all in their lives and career. For the first time, the bank's chosen executives underwent leadership training which gave them new insights on managing people and managing their leadership challenges.

What many thought was a one-off programme by the bank, Project LEAP, however, became a trailblazer of sorts for igniting the leadership development process in BOB. The flame had been lit, and the spark became an integral part of the HR DNA of the bank.

Project UDAAN

The bank ventured into another focused leadership development programme, named as Project UDAAN, first conducted in the year 2010 and the second time in the year 2012, in partnership with M/s Mckinsey. This comprehensive leadership development programme with the tagline 'flight to the top' was conducted through a field and forum approach and was structured around three modules of leadership, namely 'leading self', 'leading others' and 'leading business'. Each of the three modules was addressed through a combination of off-site forum events, coaching clinics and on-site field and project activities that were designed to enable focused development of leadership capabilities.

Project UDAAN received excellent feedback, and we could observe the unlocking of mindsets in many participants through a tracking of their post-programme behaviour and business performance. It helped the bank in meeting with the objective of creating leaders for the future.

The first edition of Project UDAAN covered almost 1,500 people, 300 AGMs/DGMs and around 1,200 branch heads of all urban/metro branches of the bank. The second edition of Project UDAAN covered around 960 participants across seven zones of the bank during the year FY 2012 and an additional 760 more participants in another five batches in FY 2013. Such a massive and comprehensive leadership development effort is unparalleled in the industry and was definitely a first of its kind for an Indian state-owned bank.

The WELEAD Programme

After each successive Leadership program conducted in BOB, there was a lull of around three–four years after which another programme was unleashed. It was almost like the participants of one programme carried on the torch of leadership in the bank for around three–four years before a new batch of incoming candidates from the junior scales got elevated who required to be also taken through a rigorous course of leadership to make them fit for the senior levels. Hence Project LEAP in 2007–2008 was followed by Project UDAAN in 2012–2013. By 2017–2018, new people had come up and there required another edition of the leadership programme in a new avatar to build a further pipeline of leaders for the future.

The bank was fortunate to have at that time P. S. Jayakumar, as its MD and CEO and Ravi Venkatesan as the non-executive chairman. Both Jayakumar and Ravi Venkatesan came in from the private sector, a first such move by the government with the idea of pushing technology further to bring BOB at par with its private counterparts. Both of them were clearly men of ideas and their vision enabled the bank to kickstart many initiatives in a very short time which may have taken years to create in the normal course. Jayakumar was also someone who really believed in HR as a key change maker for the bank and that led to a plethora of HR initiatives getting unleashed during his tenure. Many of the initiatives that I have described above under the heading of 'bringing in the science of HR' were accomplished during his time and under his stewardship. But the biggest of them all was the initiation of the WeLead programme in 2017 (see Figure C2.7). Venkatesan, at the helm at the board and in the board's HR committee, ensured that HR initiatives always remained the first priority in the overall scheme of the bank's transformation. When we were actually toying with the design of the Welead programme, it was Venkatesan who spent multiple

Figure C2.7 *WeLead Logo*

days with us exclusively to help us firm up our design, continuously giving inputs to hone it further. All of this involvement from the leaders helped us create the program that was finally implemented and became an industry standard of sorts.

WeLead came to be developed as a comprehensive and distinctive leadership development program with the objective of building leaders for the future. It envisaged comprehensive grooming of specially identified high potential talent of the bank who are most likely to don leadership positions in the bank in the future. In that sense, this became a very important program for the bank, which had significant implications for the bank for the future. It also laid the groundwork for a resurgent BOB which was going through an all-round transformation under the then MD and CEO, Jayakumar to take its rightful position as the premier bank of the country.

The tagline was chosen as the 3 Is: Ignite, Innovate and Inspire. Leadership in BOB was thought of as something that 'ignites' passion, 'innovates' continuously by being a progressive organization and 'inspiring' people into action and results. This tagline resonated well with the participants and made this programme a very aspirational one. People tried hard to get onto the programme, and it became almost a symbol of being chosen into an elite club.

The primary objectives of this programme were (Figure C2.8):

- Using internal leadership to make a difference to the bank's transformation efforts
- Creating a bank for the future
- Building on the individual's capabilities as a leader
- Focussing on the collective teamwork for success in the workplace
- Defining success from a six-pronged angle of bringing in change, personal leadership and ownership, execution excellence, leading change, skills of the future and accelerated business results

Figure C2.8 *Objectives of WeLead Programme*

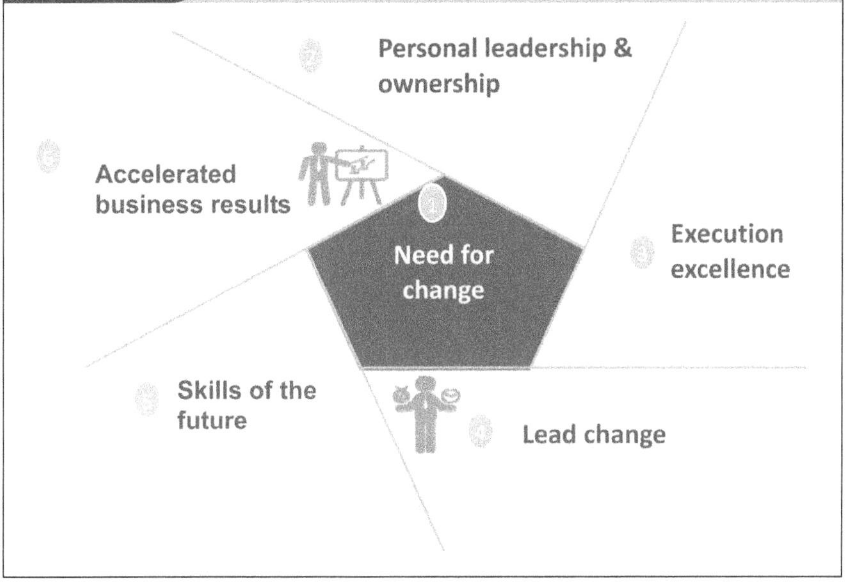

Personal leadership & ownership

Accelerated business results

Need for change

Execution excellence

Skills of the future

Lead change

Recognizing the differences in the leadership requirements at different levels of officers, this programme was conceptualized for developing leadership at four different levels. The four levels of leadership targeted under the broad ambit of the Welead programme are shown in Figure C2.9.

A typical 'WeLead' programme journey looked somewhat as shown in Figure C2.10.

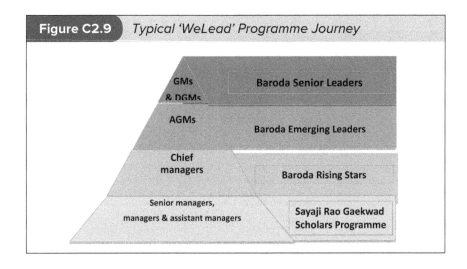

Figure C2.9 *Typical 'WeLead' Programme Journey*

GMs & DGMs — Baroda Senior Leaders

AGMs — Baroda Emerging Leaders

Chief managers — Baroda Rising Stars

Senior managers, managers & assistant managers — Sayaji Rao Gaekwad Scholars Programme

Figure C2.10   Typical Journey Overview

Typical Journey Overview

| Month 1 | Month 2 | Month 3 | Month 4 | Month 5 | Month 6 | Month 7 | Month 8 | Month 9 |

Self Excellence: Learning Workshop

People Excellence: Learning Outbound

Business Excellence: Strategy & Change With INSEAD

Wellness Session (Month 2)

Wellness Session (Month 5)

Program Kickoff

Baselining assessments
• 360 Degree Survey
• Hogan Personality Inventory
• Wellness Survey

Team Learning Project (TLP) Launch

IDP Finalization

1st Coaching Connect: In Person

2nd Coaching Connect: Virtual

3rd Coaching Connect: Virtual

4th Coaching Connect: Virtual

ELP Leaders As Mentors: 1 mentoring session every month with each mentee

TLP Connect 1

TLP Mid-Project Review

TLP Connect 2

TLP Final Presentation

1st Webinar

2nd Webinar

3rd Webinar

4th Webinar

5th Webinar

External Speaker/Study visits

External Speaker/Study visits

External Speaker/Study visits

Learning Challenge: One Challenge Every Month for BELP Leaders

Aon Lead App: Live during the 9 months of the learning journey

After 12 months, 360 Degree Re-assessment

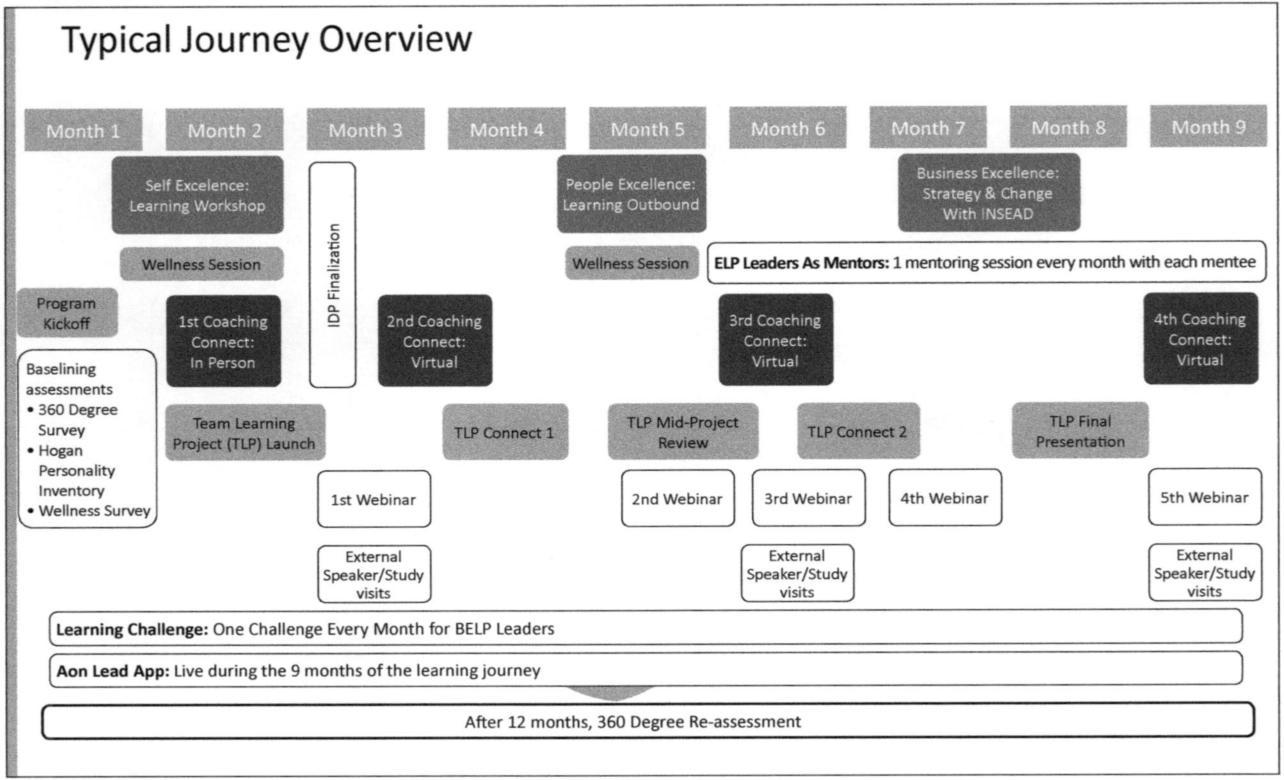

There were two other aspects that made the WeLead programme as very distinctive, which are as follows:

- Tracking progress of the individual development of participants
- Overall participant engagement throughout the programme

By the time, the bank embarked on the WeLead programme, we had realized through our past experiences that tracking of progress and keeping participant engagement throughout in such a long-term developmental intervention was very important. Participant engagement was done through a variety of ways: generating competition amongst participants and publishing of leader boards, declaring of learning champions, stars, etc., digital nudges, fortnightly or monthly learning challenges, ready reckoners, monthly programme newsletters and pushing a variety of content through the learning app. There were flip sessions kept for revision of concepts done earlier, and this helped hardwire some of the key concepts. These initiatives on participant engagement not only kept the participants engaged through the entire journey but also enabled them to pick up the threads quickly even if they fell behind at any point in time.

Tracking of participant progress was done through multiple data points such as supervisor feedback, coaches' inputs, performance in various learning challenges, progress in projects, involvement and participation in various interventions and all these got mapped and tracked. These were all fed in a tracking tool and statistically analysed with pre-programme scores to track progress on various dimensions. This led us to continuously refine strategies and program interventions and even enabled classifying participants into different buckets of progress leading to differentiated treatment and actions for different groups. As we tracked participants at periodical intervals, they were segmented into different segments with each segment getting a different treatment on the basis of bank's requirements as well as the individual's requirements:

Prioritize: Provide special attention and support
Invest: Provide with additional support
Maintain: Continue level of support
Needs more development: Review level and nature of support

These interventions made the WeLead programme a continuously moving programme and not a static one and enabled substantial forward movement in participants. At the end of the programme, that is, after a year or so of the participants having undergone this intensive development journey, there was another 360-degree assessment which was compared with their pre-programme assessment and showed the actual progress made by the participants in various dimensions. The results were indeed encouraging and even though, we cannot expect a huge shift of almost 80–100 per cent in behaviours in a leadership programme anywhere in the world, we saw an average of almost 50–60 per cent in all participants taken together with those in the star category showing progress of nearly 80 per cent and above. Almost 40 per cent of the total participants, that is, around 1,100 persons who underwent the programme got categorized into the 'star' (prioritize) or 'invest' category, in other words, the leaders of the bank for the future.

This vindicates our belief in the leadership development effort and sets the stage for more innovations in the leadership development space in future. We have now started yet another edition of the WeLead programme in 2019–2020, which is currently underway for an even larger number of participants. This edition brings in high potential people from erstwhile Dena and Vijaya Banks also, banks which were recently merged with BOB, to enable them also to come up to speed in the area of leadership development and scale up the leadership index ladder.

Covering such a large number of people under such a comprehensive and long-term development intervention is unprecedented not just in the banking space but also beyond. In just around three years, the bank would have made 7,600 chosen high potential people undergo a very comprehensive and long-term leadership development programme. No other bank, whether public or private or for that matter, any other organization in India can match this effort of BOB in the area of leadership development. It is, therefore, a landmark exercise that BOB has made its raison d'être of its HRD movement. This entire leadership development effort carried out by BOB proves that professionalization of any activity/function does happen if the effort is sustained. Sustenance of the initiatives over the long term is what brings in long-term results.

By this time, the industry was also realizing the importance of a comprehensive leadership development effort and talks were going on at the government level and other forums to develop leaders in the banking industry as well and therefore kickstart a leadership programme for the banking industry. The Banks Board Bureau (BBB) was mandated by the government to design a leadership development programme, which could serve the banking industry as a whole. However, while the BBB was still doing its surveys to arrive at the right design and approach for the leadership programme for the industry, BOB, by virtue of its past experience in this area, had already taken a head start by initiating its own version of a Leadership Development program, 'WeLead'. The BBB team, which incidentally also had Khandelwal as one of its distinguished members, had come to BOB as part of its design interactions and we were delighted to present them our thinking, processes adopted and the implementation of our Leadership Development program. It was a proud moment for us to present the updated version of the program to a person who had initiated it all. The BBB team, including Khandelwal, were very happy with the way BOB had shaped its leadership development interventions and took a lot of notes and inputs from us.

Lessons Learnt

Over this journey of professionalizing the HR function in BOB, there were a few aspects which stand out as the real pillars on which this magnificent edifice of HR in BOB was created.

- Continuity and development of HRD initiatives are somewhat connected to the continuity of CEOs with at least three+ years of tenure.
- Supportive board and CEO who believe in the relevance and importance of HRD initiatives.
- Continuity of professionally qualified and trained chief human resources officers or heads of HR.
- Continuous recruitment of a cadre of professionally qualified and trained HR specialists, recruited in successive batches to enable not only succession line in HR but also taking forward the mantle in times of transition of top management changes.
- Need for imparting professional training to the HR cadre on a continuous basis to enable them to keep abreast of the latest trends and modern practices of HR.
- Giving operational exposure to senior HR professionals for all-round exposure and thereby creating CEOs out of them like in the case of Khandelwal, who at the helm, could further herald the HRD movement in the bank.

BOB has been somewhat lucky in that respect in having got all the above pillars in place. The professionalizing of the HR function enabled not only multiple business benefits but also numerous awards and recognitions, some of which are given below.

- Golden Peacock Award for Training, 2014, instituted by Institute of Directors, New Delhi
- BML Munjal Award for best HR practices in 2015
- National Prize for (first) for innovative training practices

- Best Innovative Training Practices by ISTD in 2015–2016
- Brandon Hall Group (USA) HCM Excellence Award for Best Advance in Mobile Learning Technology 2019 for Baroda Gurukul Mobile Application
- World HRD Congress National Awards 2019 for best use of technology for Baroda Radio
- World HRD Congress National Awards 2019 for innovation in training for the programme 'Life Begins at Sixty'
- The L&D Innovation and Tech Summit and Awards 2020 for best use of online Learning—'Baroda Radio'
- The L&D Innovation and Tech Summit and Awards 2020 for Best Learning Platform Implementation of the Year—'Baroda Gurukul'
- Global Training and Development Leadership Award 2020 by World HRD Congress
- Golden Peacock National Training Award 2020

BOB has also been recognized in 2019 for the third consecutive year as one of the top 50 companies in India under the 'People Capability Index' or the PCI Index, which is an index based on the perception of internal and external stakeholders on the people practices of a company. The PCI index is carried out through a detailed assessment, done by a leading HR assessments firm, M/s Zombay in association with the British Standards Institute.

These recognitions are pointers to the substantive progress made by BOB in professionalizing its HR function and making it 'state-of-the-art'. As we speak, there are a host of other initiatives underway which will propel the next wave of HR reforms in the bank with the aim of creating the future-ready workforce and processes in BOB. The journey of HR professionalization thus continues...................

The Human Resources Story of ICICI Bank

T. K. Srirang and Soumendra N. Mattagajasingh

History and Evolution of ICICI and Its DNA

History and Evolution

ICICI was born to serve the nation and serve the society. Its birth and evolution are closely entwined with that of India in the post-Independence era. After 1947, India embarked on a mission to lay the foundation of a strong and stable economy, powered by robust industrial growth. India needed to develop industries and large-scale infrastructure projects. To support this dream, on 5 January 1955, the Industrial Credit and Investment Corporation of India Limited (ICICI Limited) was born. At a time when economic development was administered by the government, our founding fathers asked how we could become a partner in nation building. With this purpose in mind, they envisioned a new model to create the first private sector development finance institution (DFI) and thus began the creation of ICICI's unique and defining DNA.

1955–2001

ICICI was formed as an innovative experiment—a DFI in the private sector, in a newly independent nation. Over the next few decades, a number of visionary leaders shaped the organization into a premier provider of finance to Indian industry, actively participating in the creation of industrial capacities and providing resources to support India's entrepreneurs.

During its initial years, ICICI participated in the rapid industrialization of the country with a focus on basic and heavy industries. ICICI was among the world's first development banks in the private sector. It quickly emerged as an important source of foreign currency loans in the country and facilitated the import of industrial machinery and technology. ICICI partnered over 400 companies during the first decade.

By the mid-1960s, having set the course for industrial development, the country then focused on other sectors as well. This resulted in the green revolution for food sufficiency, rise in exports to earn foreign exchange, development of industries in the backward areas to broad-based growth, and encouragement to small enterprises. Responding to the emerging needs, ICICI started export finance, concessional funding in industrially backward areas and loans for small enterprises. In the period from 1965 to 1974, over 1,000 enterprises and 2,000 projects were assisted by ICICI.

ICICI grew steadily and set up its first two regional offices in Madras and Calcutta, as they were then called. With broad-based economic growth underway, India continued to consolidate and enhance self-sufficiencies to counter intermittent obstacles such as the oil shock of the 1970s. ICICI was closely involved in building institutions and also in developing the financial markets in India. ICICI was instrumental in setting up a number of financial institutions for the country, including the country's first specialized housing finance company, a credit rating agency, stock exchange and state-level institutions, and has also been closely involved in policymaking over the years. ICICI's role in building institutions continues even today.

In 1988, ICICI set up one of the first venture capital providers of India—ICICI Venture. In the early 1990s, it also set up ICICI Securities and Finance Limited (a joint venture between ICICI and JPMorgan Chase & Company) and ICICI Asset Management Company.

ICICI retained the values on which it was formed—a passion for nation building, deep-rooted belief in meritocracy, care for employees and a commitment to innovation. ICICI prepared itself to partner a resurgent India. It foresaw the changes in the existing economic order and prepared itself for the new economy. It invested in the raw talent of youth who learnt with humility, worked with passion and innovated with boldness.

In the 1990s, the Indian economy was going through a makeover like never before. Economic liberalization was taking root. World-class technology was becoming available. ICICI's vision changed from a dream for India to a dream for every Indian. The process of diversification in the 1980s was the initiation of ICICI's move towards universal banking. This gathered momentum in the 1990s with the setting up of ICICI Bank in 1994, and ICICI's entry into insurance (both life and non-life) a few years later.

ICICI received a banking license from RBI in May 1994. In the late 1990s, ICICI signed an MOU with Prudential Corporation PLC, United Kingdom, to set up a life insurance company. In 1999, ICICI Bank became the second Indian company (the first being ICICI) and the first bank from non-Japan Asia to be listed on the New York Stock Exchange (NYSE) and raise capital through American depository receipts (ADRs). ICICI Lombard General Insurance Company was set up in 2001 as a joint venture with Fairfax Financial Holdings.

In October 2001, the boards of directors of ICICI Limited and ICICI Bank approved the merger of ICICI and two of its wholly owned retail finance subsidiaries—ICICI Personal Financial Services Limited and ICICI Capital Services Limited—with ICICI Bank. These four institutions merged in April 2002.

2002 and beyond

The merger created an organization that combined the complementary strengths and capabilities of the different entities. This enabled seamless delivery of the complete range of banking solutions to corporate and retail clients. It integrated the retail asset and liability businesses to leverage the combined product suite and distribution network. With a strong heritage and the confidence of a formidable cultural core, ICICI Bank ushered in a host of convenient services for the Indian consumers. Aspirations such as a home, a car, a credit card and a host of other desires became a reality for the average Indian. ICICI Bank further enabled the Indian entrepreneur to compete globally. ICICI's core cultural values morphed from serving Indian industries to serving every Indian in fulfilling their dreams.

Over the next few years, ICICI rapidly grew its retail banking franchise and made retail credit available to a large customer base, thus giving an impetus to economic growth by supporting long- and medium-term asset creation by Indian consumers. The vision that led the bank to foray into retail was twofold. The primary belief was that the Indian diaspora needed retail services for economic growth and prosperity. Second, the large scale use of technology was the key to success in this business. The bank introduced the Indian consumers to an array of products and services which, until then, were not available to them. From ATMs to internet banking to phone banking, ICICI Bank was instrumental in changing the way Indians banked.

With the same spirit of serving India and Indians, ICICI Bank expanded its footprints into rural markets at one end and international geographies at the other. The country had a large unbanked rural population. With a focus on comprehensively covering the rural areas, the bank rolled out what was then called the 'no white spaces' strategy. ICICI Bank's international foray followed the Indian diaspora and gradually expanded to several countries across the world.

With the evolution of technology and deep penetration of mobile telephony, ICICI Bank launched a unique mobile banking app in early 2009.

This app is today popularly known as iMobile, the first mobile banking app in the country. It may be noted that iMobile was launched before the launch of the android operating system.

As we stand today in 2020 and reflect back on our journey over the last 20 years, ICICI Bank has built capabilities that can serve the customer anytime or any place and has learned to build scale at speed. Team ICICI has been ICICI's biggest strength. In the last two decades, ICICI Bank's employee strength has multiplied a hundredfold from about 1,000 to about 100,000. In the next few pages, we attempt to highlight a few aspects of this hundredfold journey. Towards the end, we will also speak about some key aspects of our current work in preparing the organization for the future.

Guiding Principles of Human Resources (HR) Function

ICICI Bank's HR strategy has been guided by the overall philosophy of the bank and is characterized by certain guiding principles and core beliefs.

- **One bank, one team:** A common notion and term called 'HR-business partnership' has long defined the HR framework in many organizations. The word 'partnership' in itself indicates two separate entities. In ICICI Bank, that term loses its meaning as everyone has one defined goal of doing business and serving the customer. At ICICI, the HR function is the responsibility of all business heads and managers and not limited to the HR department. Similarly, HR is responsible for understanding customers, knowing banking and doing sales calls so as to ensure that HR philosophies and practices are oriented to deliver value to our customers. The entire bank, thus, collectively works as one team towards the defined goal of doing business and serving the customer.
- **First principles and indigenous solutions:** In ICICI Bank, there is a firm conviction that no problem is insurmountable. One has to remain humble, keep learning and work towards developing a solution from scratch if none exists in the first place. The bank thrives on professional excellence, innovative thinking and big impact agendas. 'Challenging status quo' is encouraged and valued in order to continuously improve systems and processes and take them to the next level. All challenges are approached from first principles. The basic idea is that if we have not found a solution to a problem, we have not tried enough in a creative way.
- **Humility and service orientation**: ICICI has been one of the most successful DFIs that has continuously evolved and morphed itself to

serve the emerging needs of its customers and the country. Humility, sensitivity and service orientation are threshold behaviours expected from all employees at ICICI. The HR function serves the institution and its employees. Reaching out to employees and proactively serving the needs of various businesses is essential to this service delivery.

The Starting Point: ICICI Bank's Organizational DNA

In ICICI Bank, all functions work towards one common objective of delivering value to its stakeholders. In fact, we believe this alignment is as important as the strategy itself. The core purpose of the HR function is to enable people and to facilitate the cultural alignment process to achieve this shared goal. ICICI has always been known as a company with a distinct culture and a belief that that culture guides the thoughts and actions of all employees. Hence the core cultural ethos of the Bank is the starting point and guiding principle for all HR policies. At ICICI Bank, this ethos is commonly known as the DNA of ICICI Bank.

Simply put, DNA anchors are the expectations of employees. They guide our thought and action. It is interesting to note that they are both co-created and experienced by employees. Hence, aligning all people-related policies and practices to these behaviours and expectations is very crucial.

Our HR practices work towards bringing these tenets of our culture to life. While recruiting, we look for people who will inherently align with our cultural ethos. Our learning and development interventions are geared towards building skills and perspectives to help employees demonstrate these behaviours. The employees' relations practice acts as propagator and custodian of this ethos. Our compensation design and the performance management architecture reflect these ideologies and align the organization towards the common objective.

ICICI is a progressive and dynamic organization which has evolved with the changing needs and demands of society. Recalibrating our cultural ethos and redefining our DNA with the growth of the organization remains at the heart of this evolution (Figure C3.1).

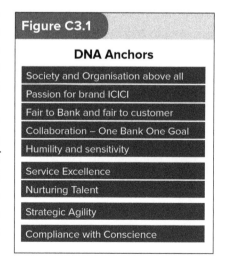

Figure C3.1

DNA Anchors

Society and Organisation above all

Passion for brand ICICI

Fair to Bank and fair to customer

Collaboration – One Bank One Goal

Humility and sensitivity

Service Excellence

Nurturing Talent

Strategic Agility

Compliance with Conscience

HR in ICICI Bank: A Glimpse into Few Practices

The HR function at ICICI Bank plays a pivotal role in its business delivery and growth by embedding the cultural anchors in all people processes, acquiring the right talent and grooming leaders for tomorrow. Our people practices have evolved over the years to cater to the rapidly changing business environment. Aligning organization structure to bring about synergies, leveraging technology to re-imagine processes and building capabilities are at the centre of the bank's people strategy. The bank ensures that every employee upholds the ethos of the bank to serve as 'one team' with humility, sensitivity and responsibility.

The HR team comprises around 200 professionals based across the country. The team is organized in an agile matrix structure to support the business functions and also create deep expertise through centres of excellence.

True to the bank's DNA, the HR function has always focused on identifying the next big opportunity, innovating new practices and leveraging technology to enable solutions in order to drive scale with speed and execution. In the following pages, we will focus on some of our practices in the areas of talent acquisition, learning and development, industry–academia partnerships and the work of cultural integration during mergers and amalgamations.

Talent Acquisition

Our talent acquisition and development are closely intertwined with the core ethos of the organization nurtured over the last six decades. Two key events define this. In the year 1955, when ICICI was set up, development finance was new to India. The country did not have skills which could further the organization's objectives. The nation needed capital sponsorship of enterprise and entrepreneurs. How would ICICI engage with these conditions? The skill was nurtured, developed and ICICI slowly emerged as a model DFI. It was a journey of learning, forging partnerships, experimenting and developing expertise. Numerous examples elucidate this belief, some of them being ICICI's entry into lease finance, venture funding, capital market, insurance and asset management. The second defining event unfolded when the parent institution set up a commercial bank and the subsequent reverse merger of the parent institution with the newly set-up bank. The expertise needed to run a commercial bank was different from that of a DFI. Commercial bankers were required, and initially, ICICI hired some of the finest leaders from the public sector banks. However, the growth aspiration of the bank, especially after the reverse merger, required us to hire a large number of employees with skill sets that were very different from those available within ICICI, as well as in the established banking industry dominated by public sector banks.

The banking model envisioned by ICICI was very different from that of the existing commercial banks. While in the prevailing model customers walked into bank branches for various services, ICICI envisioned a model where bankers were required to proactively reach out to customers and offer banking services. They were expected to engage with the clients, uncover latent needs and offer banking solutions. This was unheard of at the time. Given this new model of banking, the supply pool of bankers was limited. This was an adaptive challenge which required a reorientation of beliefs and values.

The bank responded to this challenge in the typical ICICI way by working from first principles to find a solution. The core belief of the institution around 'talent and human capability' remained unchanged, but the solution was innovative. ICICI believes in unbounded human potential and capability. It has always relied on building and nurturing talent to support its growth aspirations rather than buying ready talent.

ICICI broke the tradition and started hiring some of the best talents from outside the banking industry. This was in keeping with its new banking model that required bankers to go to the customers rather than customers reaching out to banks. ICICI Bank started hiring raw talent from across industries—fast-moving consumer goods, auto, pharma, manufacturing, consumer durables and many others. This infusion of industry-agnostic raw talent was of course backed by a robust capability development strategy.

ICICI's approach to the selection of talent was also different from standard industry norms that relied on typical competitive examination style tests. The selection was based on alignment to ICICI DNA—our cultural anchors (commonly known as competencies). This cultural anchors' driven framework created a common view, and all selections were made based on an ICICI 'fit', and then, placement was across various domains/functions. In fact, the belief of the bank was that if the competencies were present in the applicant, then they can be groomed for any job with the right training, managerial support and guidance. Hence, in the true spirit of synergy and collaboration, it is quite a common practice that an individual was selected for a branch manager role by the product head of an assets team. That did not mean that the bank did not recruit those with specialized knowledge. Such profiles were the most preferred subject to their meeting the competency requirements. The entire process was built around positive selection rather than rejecting applicants on account of lack of domain knowledge or prior experience. This philosophy can be distilled into two phrases—'hire for cultural fit and train for technical skills', and 'select for 'fit' as opposed to 'rank and reject'.

The principles of hiring remained the same even while recruiting students from campus. The selection was degree agnostic—that is to say that ICICI, once again, broke away from the convention of hiring from finance/accounting background, instead foraying into engineering, humanities, arts, science, economics and management backgrounds for fresh minds.

Over the last two decades, the resource strength of the bank has grown a hundredfold, from about 1,000 to an organization of 100,000 employees spread across its numerous branches and offices. In the last 15 years, many market dynamics have changed. Today, the private sector banks employ over 400,000 employees, a significant shift to what it was in the mid-2000s. There is market depth in banking skills though at a premium. Employees have a choice amongst banks as well as competing industries such as e-commerce, start-ups and retail amongst others.

ICICI Bank's talent acquisition practice is developed against this backdrop. The core pillars of the model are as follows:

- **Recruitment ecosystem for job applicant:** ICICI Bank is a preferred organization to work for. It is the favoured career choice for job applicants across varied education and experience backgrounds, segments and geographies. In this aspect, it is crucial that the bank is available to the aspirants through their lifecycle and journey. ICICI was an early adopter of technology and digital solutions in this practice. www.icicicareers. com[1] was created for candidates as early as 2001. Applications moved digitally, through defined journeys. The core belief of the institution was ease and transparency for job applicants. It brought scale and predictability to our process.

- **Operationalizing the selection philosophy:** ICICI Bank as a brand has always attracted a large pool of applicants. How would the selection process identify the right applicant? How will we ensure a high degree of reliability and validity in the process? In a large distributed system, how will this get implemented? A superficial construct of the job would set up markers such as skills needed to perform the job. Of course, the selection process would positively consider skills where available. But the methodology put primary emphasis on identifying the key traits and competencies needed to work at ICICI Bank. The approach included personality profiling using psychometric tools such as the occupational

[1] https://www.icicicareers.com/website/

personality questionnaire, in-house developed tool called the personality profiler followed by a behavioural event interview.

- **Applicant experience:** ICICI Bank has always believed in creating a brand presence and high-quality service experience for its prospective employees. Take the example of the campus segment. ICICI Bank runs a programme called 'Beat the Curve', which offers a unique platform for campus students to showcase their thinking and ideation to create new business lines. At the same time, it creates a brand presence for ICICI Bank amongst the campus applicants. It gives ICICI Bank an opportunity to convey key institutional values to the applicants and attract like-minded students. ICICI Bank has always believed in providing a superior customer experience. Same is true of recruitment and selection. We have always focused on creating a system which is available 24x7, a system which provides information symmetry and helps applicants make the right decision. Currently, the full recruitment journey is available on a new-age bot, a unique offering based on natural language processing (NLP) with which applicants can engage to clarify their queries. It is available on four platforms: WhatsApp, Google Assistant, Amazon Alexa and web/mobile browser.
- Backward integration of talent supply through 'industry–academia partnerships'. This is addressed in detail in a separate section.
- **Use of new-age data science and technology tools:** It is to create scientific rigour, scale and applicant experience: co-creating cutting-edge products through partnerships with technology start-ups and design thinking. Machine learning algorithms like neural networks are used to score resumes and recommend applicants who are more suitable for a role. Semantic testing platform (STEP), an in-house cognitive testing platform, is configured to administer adaptive testing with advanced features such as image recognition, text analytics, language check, emotion and tone analytics and security check systems. It uses a combination of in-house artificial intelligence (AI) and machine learning (ML) algorithms as well as solutions offered by IBM Watson, Readable, AYLIEN Text Analysis, Microsoft Video Indexer and Amazon Rekognition and Comprehend among others.
- A state-of-the-art platform—iStudio—enables virtual interviews and limits the challenges of distance and time.

Today, ICICI has built the capability to hire tens of thousands of people in a matter of months if needed. The talent acquisition strategy of ICICI Bank, which saw the bank grow multi-fold in a matter of years was part of an integrated strategy of people capability. A robust learning and development platform was equally critical.

Learning and Development

Investing in the learning and growth of its employees has been one of the defining features of ICICI's DNA. The company has always believed in giving jobs ahead of time, trusting human potential and providing employees with all the necessary learning support. From equipping individuals with functional knowledge and skills to grooming employees to take on larger roles and mentoring leaders for tomorrow, ICICI Bank has always prioritized the learning and growth of its people. 'Trust human capability to deliver extraordinary results' has been the credo. The cultural emphasis on learning and development is underscored by the fact that at ICICI Bank, training is rigorous work. If one is nominated for a programme, one is expected to attend it without fail, barring any serious emergency.

The exponential growth of ICICI Bank and the talent strategy supporting this growth require the in-house capability to train employees in a fast-paced manner. The idea was to make employees productive from first-day first-hour.

In 2002, the original parent company ICICI Ltd, along with ICICI PFS and ICICI Capital Services merged with ICICI Bank. This was a landmark event not only for the ICICI Group but also for the entire corporate world. Overnight, thousands of employees from three different organizations were to be trained in banking regulations and operations. Any instructor-led training programme would have taken months if not years. The innovation and technology gene of ICICI took over and ICICI Bank launched a comprehensive e-learning platform called the 'The Learning Matrix'. The name was inspired by the Hollywood movie 'Matrix' since the vision was to conquer the constraints of time and space. Dedicated time for learning, separate from the performance was to come to an end. People would learn at their workplace in their own time. ICICI Bank visualized its own learning management system and developed it with a local partner. Programmes were designed internally by pooling in subject–matter experts and instructional designers from the HR team.

While well-designed programmes were made available over The Learning Matrix, adoption of this initiative by employees was a more complex adaptive challenge. It required a change in the behaviour of employees who have been trained since childhood to learn in a classroom setting. Various measures, from reward and recognition to mandating completion with certification in a time-bound manner, were used. Throughout this process, the standards were kept high. For example, for an employee to pass the certification test at the end of a module, a minimum of 80 per cent score was required. Today, The Learning Matrix offers a repository of more than 300 modules providing well over 800 hours of content with new courses being created continuously.

The channel strategy for learning and development was two pronged. Functional knowledge was provided through the e-learning platform while behavioural programme and skill building happened through classroom programmes. Various developmental programmes were launched to cater to the emerging needs of personal effectiveness, managerial effectiveness, team effectiveness and other similar areas. The programmes were internally designed keeping in mind the cultural values of ICICI bank and specific business nuances. Soon, ICICI Bank started experimenting with blended programmes where the programme had both in classroom as well as e-learning sections. The first such programme was launched in 2004 with 'selling skill for bankers' and a complementary technology-based simulator for honing skills over e-learning.

Gradually, the bank started experimenting with new technologies for capability building in the areas of gaming and simulation.

ICICI Bank launched its 'gaming- and simulation-based learning tools' to accelerate the development of superior customer service skills amongst its retail branch banking workforce. The gaming modules were designed by replicating a specific transaction into an interactive storyboard—featuring an engaging user-interface and providing a non-threatening environment to practice skills with immediate performance feedback. For example, in a game called 'Cash Detectives', learners could practise the detection of fake currency from a given set of currency notes by evaluating the features of the currency note. Similarly, another game 'Cheque Mate' challenged the learner to tag a series of correct and incorrect cheques with respect to an identified discrepancy in a limited time.

While gaming offered game play-based skill building, simulators were developed for training branch service staff on various complex banking transactions by replicating the real-life branch environment. In this branch banking simulation, a learner could handle hundreds of scenarios/transactions by applying their product/process knowledge and customer service skills. The simulation focused on providing a real-time yet risk-free environment, where the employee enjoyed complete freedom to experiment, make mistakes and absorb new knowledge.

With advancements in technology, voice-based 'mobile learning' was made available to employees. This added another layer of convenience by making learning truly self-paced and taking away the limitations of time and space completely. In line with the technological innovations, ICICI Bank also introduced a 'virtual classroom' platform in 2006–2007.

While these interventions provided threshold level functional knowledge and skill, there emerged a need to create academies that would provide expertise in a specific domain. This led to the formation of the internal functional training academies that focused on the next level of practical and technical skills. These institutions are unique in the sense that they are designed and delivered using internal subject–matter experts and in–house trainers. ICICI Bank has a pool of more than 1,000 certified trainers drawn from various business teams. They are the best performers in those teams and have a passion for training. This practice also helps the bank in building a learning culture in the company, since business leaders at all levels are also trainers in the classroom.

Various 'functional academies' were created to cater to the needs of employees in various roles and business groups (Figure C3.2).

ICICI Bank also conducts a massive annual banking knowledge test. This proctored test ensures that the employees are fit to service the customers with adequate knowledge of products, processes and regulation. It also serves as a barometer for how well the functional inputs have been imbibed in the various business teams/staff members.

The exponential growth in business and the consequent rapid growth in employee strength saw the emergence of another challenge. The bank identified young managers and gave them the responsibility of managing large businesses and teams. The bank internally referred to this practice as 'the young leading the young'. The challenge was to build perspective and wisdom that comes over years of experience. How do you expedite the maturation process? How do you create a development process which would have normally come through a lifetime of experience?

Figure C3.2 *Indicative List of Flagship Academies and Programmes*

The bank then designed its flagship 'Leadership Mentoring Programme', an in-house programme conducted by practising leaders for budding leaders. It uses peer mentoring methodology and action–consequence model to provide perspective on 'adaptive' leadership challenges through discussions, case studies, structured experiences and case-in-point methodology. The programme is intense and brings out the risks and challenges of exercising leadership and provides perspective and ideas to deal with them.

Employees are also exposed to thought leaders and practitioners who have weathered many adaptive challenges in their own work/profession. Leadership engagement sessions are conducted with thought leaders from various domains and some of the most outstanding leadership experts from across the world such as Ronald Heifetz, Peter Senge, Ram Charan, Wayne Brockbank, Phil Rosenzweig, Mike Useem, Professor Jeffrey Pfeiffer, Roger Martin, Mark Inglis, Captain Jim Lovell, K. Balachandar, Martina Navratilova, Sir Clive Lloyd, late C. K. Prahlad, Vishwanathan Anand, Rahul Dravid and Dan Ariely.

ICICI: The leadership Factory

ICICI has often been referred to as the 'leadership factory'. It has not only produced thousands of leaders for itself but has also produced numerous chief executive officer (CEOs) and chief experience officer (CXO) for the entire banking, financial services and insurance industry.

ICICI has long been known for its deep leadership bench and its ability to spot and groom leaders. Over the years, ICICI Group has filled its Board level positions and CEOs from within the group. In the last two decades, more than 20 CEOs and many Board level leaders for its various companies and subsidiaries have emerged from its ranks. This philosophy of grooming leaders from within its fold has not only helped ICICI to remain true to its core purpose but has also helped to strengthen its cultural alignment as the organization evolved. These leaders have lived and breathed the bank's cultural values. In the face of change, they know what to conserve and what to disrupt, what to retain and what to let go of. As ICICI progressed, they have shaped and upheld ICICIs cultural ethos and philosophy.

At the heart of ICICI Bank's leadership development philosophy is a belief that 'good leaders produce more leaders'. Developing and grooming leaders for the future is a leadership responsibility. This approach goes beyond structured leadership potential identification and development programs. Nurturing leaders is cultural to ICICI. It is part of its DNA. ICICI Bank takes a risk on people and supports them with an enabling work environment. It gives people large jobs ahead of time that stretch their capability beyond their own aspiration. In the process, individuals discover themselves and their potential. In order to build perspective and expose employees to complex leadership challenges, ICICI Bank gives its young employees access to board meetings and board-related projects. They are also exposed to investor meetings to get a direct perspective from the investors. Meetings and reviews by managers are seen as an opportunity for leadership development. The top management also spends considerable time in nurturing young minds. The supportive work culture provides the necessary freedom and autonomy to experiment. All this converges to create industry leaders of the future. The tag 'leadership factory' given to it by the media quite aptly summarizes this culture and legacy of ICICI.

Leadership development programmes as well as other learning interventions are run at the iconic ICICI Learning Centre at Khandala near Mumbai. To the employees of the bank, this centre is what NDA is to its cadets. It is where several ideas are brought to life, where innovations are unleashed and strategies are formulated, and where individuals continue to be groomed to emerge as leaders, not just for the Bank but for the industry.

Industry Academia: A New Dimension to Talent Acquisition

In the early 2000s, as the financial sector in India was expanding in leaps and bounds, a common topic of discussion among business and HR leaders across industry was 'war for talent', 'dearth of skilled manpower' and related subjects.

With the bank's aspiration for exponential growth, it was vital for the HR function to find an answer to this acute shortage of skilled manpower. In 2005, as the leadership team of HR department met at Kolad, in coastal Maharashtra, for their annual strategy meeting, this was on top of everyone's mind. They realized that the problem had to be looked at with a radically different lens. India, with a population of over 1 billion, had the largest pool of people under the age of 30. It was producing the highest number of graduates in the world. Hence, to even suggest that there was a shortage of manpower seemed absurd. But the fact remained that this was exactly what the sector was experiencing. True to its ethos, ICICI Bank approached the problem from first principles and with a strong determination to challenge the status quo.

What emerged from this deep introspection was a realization that everyone in the industry was defining 'talent' in a very narrow way. The team found two fallacies in the existing definition: (a) an extreme bias for fluency in English and urban etiquette and (b) using functional knowledge as a key indicator for selection. The first was a prejudice that needed to be overcome, and the second was a completely trainable attribute. These fallacies were severely reducing the total pool of manpower available to organizations to draw from. ICICI chose to fundamentally challenge both these biases that were prevalent at the time.

By expanding the definition, ICICI suddenly found an abundance of talent that it could draw from. The focus shifted from 'finding the talent' to 'honing the talent to meet our needs'. Two strengths came in handy during this time: (a) The well-oiled and battle-tested recruitment machinery that had been built in the previous years and (b) the world-class learning and development capability of ICICI. The bank created a unique programme where it went to the hinterlands of India, to the Tier III cities and rural areas and found candidates who were just waiting for someone to give them a chance so that they could prove themselves. These were youngsters who were passionate, achievement-oriented and eager to learn. All they needed was someone to believe in them and their capabilities.

ICICI set up the initial two institutions with two like-minded and progressive partners. ICICI Manipal Academy (IMA) was set up in partnership with Manipal Academy for Higher Education and Institute of Finance, Banking and Insurance (IFBI) in partnership with NIIT. Substantial effort went in to designing the entire supply chain, right from reaching out to potential candidates across every nook and corner of the country to selection effectiveness to training at these academies and then onboarding them to the bank. Considerable investments were also made in setting up the training infrastructure and designing path-breaking programmes. These programmes have an extreme bias for vocational pedagogy instead of taking the cognitive approach prevalent in educational institutions. The thrust of the programme is to orient students to the culture of ICICI Bank and to impart functional knowledge in banking and related subjects. Participants were put through rigorous training with an emphasis on application of knowledge and overall development of personality. The tutoring at the academy was supplemented with practical training in various branches of the bank through structured internship modules. A simulated bank branch was set up on campus to provide an experience of real-life banking operations with access to the core banking software used by the bank.

Two primary factors led to the growth of these partnerships. First, the relevance of the content in grooming talent with industry-specific skills. Second, the acculturation of the participants, not just to the corporate and professional way of work, but to the context and culture of ICICI Bank. This helped bring about 'first-day first-hour' productivity from graduates passing

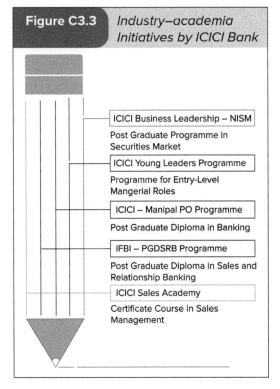

Figure C3.3 *Industry–academia Initiatives by ICICI Bank*

ICICI Business Leadership – NISM
Post Graduate Programme in Securities Market

ICICI Young Leaders Programme
Programme for Entry-Level Mangerial Roles

ICICI – Manipal PO Programme
Post Graduate Diploma in Banking

IFBI – PGDSRB Programme
Post Graduate Diploma in Sales and Relationship Banking

ICICI Sales Academy
Certificate Course in Sales Management

out from these training academies. Names such as IFBI, ICICI PO programme or IMA have become common terms among young graduates across the country (Figure C3.3).

Industry–academia Partnership: The Impact

What started out in 2005 as an attempt to challenge the status quo and relook at the supply side problem from first principles, went on to become a major recruitment channel for ICICI Bank over the next 15 years. In due course, the bank expanded its partnership with few more premier and progressive institutions such as Narsee Monjee Institute of Management Studies (NMIMS), National Institute of Securities Markets (NISM), Institute of Technology & Management (ITM) and TVS Academy. The industry–academia initiative by ICICI Bank fundamentally altered the recruitment landscape for the banking industry. In the years to come, several banks would set up similar supply-side interventions—a testament to the strength of this model and also of ICICI's ability to reshape an ecosystem. But perhaps, more importantly, what this initiative achieved was to provide an avenue to students from small towns and rural areas to join the mainstream financial sector. It offered opportunities to youngsters across the sociological and geographical spectrum of the nation. Through this, ICICI, in its own small way, continued to partner the nation in its growth.

Mergers: A Cultural Confluence

The growth and evolution of ICICI Bank have been organic as well through multiple mergers and amalgamations. Mergers are commercial decisions.

However, the success of mergers is highly dependent on the integration of people and their willingness to embrace a new culture. The adaptive challenge of this assimilation makes mergers sensitive and vulnerable. In many ways, 'how' we deal with this challenge, decides the success or failure of mergers. In 2002, ICICI Ltd, ICICI PFS and ICICI Capital Services had merged with ICICI Bank, and the workforce was effectively retrained and integrated. In the case of amalgamations with other banks, the primary task was that of cultural integration. In the decade 2000–2010, ICICI Bank had three mergers—Bank of Madura (2001), Sangli Bank (2007) and Bank of Rajasthan (2010).

All three banks had a very rich tradition and culture. The employees of these institutions not only carried expert knowledge in banking, outstanding customer connect and pride in their culture, but they also had strong unions and associations. Further, most of the HR policies of the three banks were decided through negotiations and settlements between the union and the management. ICICI Bank is a professional organization. It works as one team. The concept of dual interest groups, that is, management and employees, doesn't exist. ICICI Bank believes in taking care of its personnel in a proactive and transparent manner. It encourages direct and open communication. It has always believed in discussing matters directly and only between the parties involved. Employees of the bank trust the institution and have faith in its leadership to act in everybody's best interest.

The primary task at the heart of this adaptive challenge was to build this direct trust between employees and the institution. Employees joining from the merging entities should trust the new institution and have faith that their issues and concerns will be dealt with in a fair manner.

Building this trust is easier said than done. When a merger is announced, people worry about various issues, and this leads to anxiety. The loss of identity and association with a brand cultivated over the years is indeed painful. Along with it also comes the fear of the unknown and uncertainty in the environment.

ICICI Bank team recognized and acknowledged this anxiety. The starting point was to understand where people are and to take note of their unspoken fears. Communicating and listening to the prospective employees joining ICICI Bank from the merged entities was critical in this trust-building process. In each of these mergers, almost immediately after the announcement of intent to merge, ICICI Bank reached out to the employees of the merging entity through various means. Emails, magazines, video addresses and extensive open house meetings were conducted. The idea was to start a dialogue with the incoming team members as well as highlight the culture and ethos of the organization. It was also necessary to listen to their thoughts and concerns and clarify their doubts. To many employees, these open forums were the start of a direct channel with the organization. Presence of and access to senior managers of the bank at these meetings was vital in creating a supportive holding environment.

For the employees of the merging entities, these communication forums were the first taste of the culture of ICICI Bank. The bank was aware of the importance of these meetings in setting the tone and tenor of this emerging relationship. Meticulous planning was carried out in deciding the content, language, tone and people who were best suited to conduct these meetings.

The essence of ICICI Bank's culture was the respect and dignity of every employee in all circumstances. Caring and standing by them at their time of need—professionally as well as personally. And fairness in all its dealings with the workforce. This philosophy was reiterated in all the communication meetings. Doubts around the policies of the bank were clarified. Assurances of skill development to cope with the technological environment of ICICI Bank were also provided. Simultaneously, expectations of the bank from its employees were also reinforced during these discussions. ICICI Bank expects all its personnel to be committed and passionately work towards achieving the goals of the organization. It expects its employees to value the brand and deliver high performance. At ICICI Bank, care and meritocracy go hand in hand. This mutual responsibility was made clear repeatedly to all employees of the merging entities.

ICICI Bank has always acted in a very fair manner towards its workforce. Hence, it didn't need to do anything special for the employees of the merging entities. It knew, once the incoming team members start experiencing the culture of ICICI Bank, they will understand the genuine care it has for them. However, some vested interests could have derailed this process. Whenever such situation arose, ICICI Bank dealt with it in a very firm manner. All through the merger process, we always believed in discussing matters directly only between the parties involved.

Communicating with employees of the merging/merged entities was not good enough. Once the merger is approved by the RBI, a large number of employees start working with each other on a daily basis. It was essential that the frontline managers and employees of ICICI Bank welcomed their new colleagues with respect and warmth. Communication meetings and sensitization sessions were held with the managers of ICICI Bank.

Once the employees of the merged entities started experiencing the culture of ICICI Bank, it gradually became clear to them that ICICI Bank truly meant what we had asserted before the actual date of the merger. After the merger, we did not have employees of two different organizations anymore. Very specific training programs were launched to bring the incoming staff up to speed with the business context as well as the systems and processes of ICICI Bank.

In each of these mergers, after the initial discomfort, employees of these entities did realize that ICICI Bank is indeed a fair organization. The most significant and symbolic gesture came from the union of Sangli Bank Ltd when they invited the HR leaders to its general body meeting. These meetings are typically forums for members of the union to discuss and draw out their charter of demands to be placed in front of the management. However, in this case, the office bearers of the union invited the senior leaders of the Bank to directly engage with the employees. The act was not only unprecedented but also symbolic of the cultural transformation that had taken place.

This trust in the relationship only grew over time. Employees were directly dealing with the institution, like everybody else. Their own managers and local HR managers championed the cause of the employees and brought them to the attention of policymakers. Gradually, the need for unions was not felt. In due course, all these associations approached the registrar of trade unions and dissolved the bodies.

Many of the office bearers of the erstwhile unions express their deep sense of satisfaction and gratitude.

Dharmendra Rao, President of the erstwhile All India Bank of Rajasthan Employees Federation says that the 'merger of eBoR and ICICI, is heralded as the best merger ever in the history of Banking. ICICI Bank is truly a Bank that cares for its employees. All the promises that the Bank made before the merger, were not only kept but much more was made available to us. Above all, what stands out is the respect and dignity with which every employee is treated.'

Subash Pareek, joint secretary of the former All India Bank of Rajasthan Employees Federation echoes the same sentiments. He says 'the respect and love that ICICI gave to all the employees is truly praiseworthy. Regardless of their origin, everybody is respected. At ICICI, whatever is fair comes without asking. This is a truly professional organization. One cannot imagine the professionalism, respect and care of ICICI Bank unless you experience it.'

M. S. Sopal, general secretary of the erstwhile Sangli Bank Employees Union concurs. He says 'ICICI Bank reached out to different employees and solved their problems. Be it payment of full pension, which was pending for long, to a fair review of the transfers and disciplinary processes which were initiated under the last management, from promoting clerks to officers or standing by employees during times of emergency, ICICI Bank is always proactive in reaching out to its employees and very fair in dealing with issues. Above all, ICICI Bank treats all employees with great respect and dignity. All employees of Sangli Bank are fortunate that we merged with ICICI Bank.'

Slowly, but steadily, the employees coming into ICICI bank started recognizing that at ICICI Bank everybody is an employee, and everybody has the opportunity to exercise leadership. Today, the employees of the merged entities are proud ICICIans and flag bearers of brand ICICI.

Crafting Today to Create the Future

Since its inception, one of the defining strengths of ICICI Bank has been its ability to shape the future. In today's rapidly changing environment, this inherent ability of the bank is one of its biggest strength. By using the most advanced technologies and digital capabilities available anywhere in the world, the bank continues to reimagine new solutions for customer convenience and superior service. The HR function is constantly engaged in facilitating the required culture and in building the skills and capabilities not only for today but also for the future. The objective is also to provide best-in-class service to employees so that they further create excellence in service for the customers.

The unrelenting obsession with technology is another DNA attribute of ICICI, which one will find in full bloom within the HR function. The skills required in the future will be heavily inclined towards technology, data sciences, design thinking and use of AI and ML, to significantly improve customer experience. ICICI Bank is heavily invested in building these capabilities and is also providing top of the range service to its employees using new-age communication platforms, predictive data science, AI algorithms and chatbots.

A mobile application 'Universe on the Move', popularly known as UoTM, brings all HR services under a single integrated platform. Employees can access all the HR services like marking attendance through GPS-based attendance system, accessing salary slip, applying for leave, learning the newest video modules, responding to snap surveys, other policy information and service request through the UoTM. This unified mobile application also serves as the umbrella app for all other employee service-related apps. UoTM is also powered by a new age chatbot, called Zeno that responds to employee queries and also helps in resolving their doubts about products and processes.

Integrating and aligning an organization of around 0.1 million employees requires robust communication systems and practices. ICICI Bank's in-house communication platform called 'iStudio' serves as a virtual town hall that can connect the entire organization in a two-way video engagement process. From virtual branch visits to open house discussion forums to learning engagements with thought leaders across the world, ICICI Bank has been able to connect and communicate with speed and scale using this platform. It has further integrated this communication platform with chatbot and cloud telephony facilities to enhance the experience of employees.

Even prospective employees of ICICI Bank experience its culture and technological prowess from the time they apply to ICICI Bank. The recruitment journey of ICICI Bank is available on a new-age bot, a unique offering based on NLP wherein applicants can clarify any queries they may have. Candidates can engage with the bank anytime and from anywhere, be it telephone, WhatsApp, Google Assistant, Amazon Alexa, web and mobile browser, in a seamless manner. ICICI Bank's recruitment machinery is powered by the use of new-age data science and technology tools to ensure scientific rigour, scale and smooth applicant experience. It has co-created cutting-edge products through partnerships with technology start-ups and through design thinking. ML algorithms like neural networks are used to score resumes and suggest the applicants who are most suited for a specific role. We have already mentioned about adaptive testing through STEP, and the work we are doing using new-age technologies such as image recognition, text analytics, emotion and tone analytics, remote security check systems and a combination of AI and ML algorithms. This is an ongoing body of work and our attempt is to remain at the forefront of innovation so that we provide an outstanding experience to our prospective employees and build effective and efficient selection tools for the organization.

Investing in employees to prepare them for the future and building leadership capabilities has been a hallmark of ICICI's DNA. The bank is working tirelessly to usher in a new era of digital banking with speed and swiftness to augment personal convenience as well as business delivery of customers. In this journey, the HR function is investing in the capability building of employees and its leadership team. New-age skills in the domain of data sciences, design thinking and behavioural economics are the principal areas of focus. Deep expertise in the fields of artificial intelligence, machine learning, virtual connectivity and media integration, voice and video analytics, design thinking and behavioural economics is being pursued to create new customer solutions for tomorrow. All employees are being trained in data science, data analytics and the usage of new-age technologies as they are no longer the purview of a few or an island of excellence. Technology, data and design are now part of the ICICI fabric, and employees are encouraged to conduct micro experiments using these tools. International experts and academicians from around the world are spending time with employees across the bank to inculcate this thinking and aptitude within the organization.

New-age technology solutions are being leveraged across every function of ICICI Bank to bring convenience to customers. Similarly, the internal operating system and organizational software is being carefully rewired. Creating the right culture and an enabling work environment has always been the top agenda for the bank.

In the last couple of years, ICICI Bank has been carefully reshaping its culture. A radical transformation is underway with an eye on the future and a deep desire to serve the society. The aim is to bring a high degree of 'speed of delivery', design innovative solutions and services and create the ability to bring the entire bank to the doorstep (or rather in the palm) of the customer, thereby developing a culture where the entire organization comes together to serve one client, every employee attending to the 360 degree needs of that client. They are expected to take the full bank to them rather than being caught in the narrow definition of any role. The rallying call is 'one bank, one goal'. This is no longer wishful thinking or sloganeering. Decisive actions are being taken to foster this philosophy. For example, the top 400 executives of the organization (leadership group) carry one single goal unlike the usual practice of each department having separate departmental goals.

Innovative solutions require less hierarchy and greater structural agility for it to fructify. The organization is moving away from the traditional, hard-coded, lines and boxes structures to agile networks where cross-functional teams work together to solve customer pain points. Many symbols of the hierarchy have been decimated. The identity of the top 400 executives is no more based on their grade (general manager, senior general manager, etc.) but by their roles and responsibilities. Authority manuals, policies, systems and work practices have been reworked to operationalize this cultural intervention. Not just that, symbols such as large cabins on separate floors and exclusive lunchrooms for a select set of senior managers, which indicated hierarchy, have given way to a more open culture. A work environment where both vertical hierarchy and horizontal hierarchy cease to exist—creating an open, empowered and customer-focused organization. No individual, team, group or department has primacy or can claim supremacy. It is a culture that encourages actions which are fair to the Bank and fair to the customer.

The front line is being empowered, within the guard rails of compliance, to facilitate faster decision–making and customer response. Requisite capabilities are being created in line with these expectations. The typical business targets have given way to total opportunity focus. All these changes are ushering in an environment that is less hierarchical, synergistic and agile.

ICICI Bank is not only busy infusing technical skills among its employees but is also working on developing and honing leadership capabilities. At the heart of this agenda is the necessity to equip senior managers with the ability to deal with the leadership dilemmas and 'adaptive challenges' coming their way. Dealing with adaptive challenges that confront deeply held values and beliefs requires the capacity to reflect and the courage to intervene, despite personal risk. ICICI Bank is building this capability in multiple ways from intense structured classroom programmes, peer-mentoring workshops, cross-functional on the job assignments to exposing employees to thought leaders from across the spectrum from professors at Harvard, MIT and Wharton to astronauts and army generals. Many employees from the leadership group are invited to attend board meetings and investor meetings to build perspectives. Further, all training programs within ICICI focus on the cultural ethos of the organization. Similarly, orientation to the cultural ethos of the organization is a primary focus of all industry–academia courses. These tenets also get reiterated through thousands of communication meetings, branch visits and other similar modes of employee engagement.

Building leadership capacity to future proof the organization and to continuously reimagine the organization is an enduring task. At ICICI Bank, we are deeply aware of the value of our history and heritage and the value of openness to embrace the new. Conservation and exploration go hand in hand. What remains unchanged is our unwavering focus on serving society and serving every customer. The ongoing narrative of the HR function in ICICI continues to be the story of passion for service, humility to unlearn and learn, challenging the status quo to keep reinventing and above all a commitment to the duty of serving the organization, the brand and the society.

Digital Transformation of HR at Union Bank of India

Brajeshwar Sharma

With its hundred-year legacy, pan-India presence and being the fifth-largest bank in the country, Union Bank of India is uniquely positioned to leapfrog growth in the coming years. While the bank has already initiated some pioneering changes across functions, the next five years promise to be transformative in its journey. With a clear vision to become one of the 'top places to work in India', human resources (HR) is going to play a key role in ensuring an engaged, skilled and agile workforce in the future that will help shape the bank's growth and digital agendas. With this goal in mind, a range of initiatives has been undertaken to provide the best employment experience to its employees.

Legacy in Brief

Union Bank of India was established on 11 November 1919 with its head-quarters in the city of Bombay.

The roots of Union Bank of India lie to the credit of one of the great visionaries, Seth Seetharamji Kisondayal Podar, who was able to bring together people of the business community so as to join hands to set up a bank in Bombay after the end of the First World War (1914–1918). He had carefully handpicked prominent business personalities of the time to become the bank's founder directors.

The registered office of the bank was located at Fort, Bombay, where the business operations of the bank commenced, following a grand ceremony on 3 March 1920.

The head office building of the bank was inaugurated by Mahatma Gandhi, the father of the nation, in the year 1921, and he had said on the occasion that,

> We should have the ability to carry on a big bank, to manage efficiently crores of rupees in the course of our national activities. Though we have not many banks

amongst us, it does not follow that we are not capable of efficiently managing crores and tens of crores of rupees.

His prescient words anticipated the growth of the bank that has taken place in the decades that followed. The bank's core values of prudent management without ignoring opportunities are reflected in its 100-year journey.

Union Bank of India has been playing a very proactive role in the economic growth of India as it extends credit for the requirements of different sectors of the economy. Manufacturing, exports, trading, agriculture, infrastructure and the individual segments are sectors in which the bank has deployed credit to spur economic growth and to earn from a well-diversified portfolio of assets.

On the technology front, Union Bank of India was among the first to computerize all its branches. It has been a pioneer to introduce 100 per cent core banking solution with connectivity between all its branches making it a leader among its peers in infusion of technology. Innovations like the debit/credit card limit setting are forever being added to its offering, extending choices to customers, adding speed and convenience to transactions.

The amalgamation of Union Bank of India with Corporation Bank and Andhra Bank has made Union Bank of India the fifth-largest public sector bank of the country by making it stronger and sustainable with the business of ₹14,000 billion and 75,000+ employees, more than twice its earlier size. Further, it has strengthened the bank's presence in southern India with a substantial market share in this region, making it India's fourth-largest banking network.

HR Management at the Bank

The HR function is one of the most crucial functions of the bank. Over the years of its existence, HR has played a key role in shaping the cultural fabric of the organization. Like all other critical functions, the HR portfolio lies with one of the bank's executive directors, with the HR department being headed by a chief general manager, who is assisted by two general managers, one each for admin and operations and learning and development (L&D).

At the board level, there exists an HR sub-committee of the board, which deliberates and decides on all matters of HR policy. This committee is constituted by experts in the field of HR management and government nominated director among others. The subject–matter experts in this committee bring to the table a wide range of their practical industry and academic experience.

HR teams at various controlling offices comprise a good mix of HR specialists who have been hired specifically for HR and team members who aren't specialists. The bank has taken to inducting bright and enthusiastic employees who show potential as good HR managers into the HR job family for the past two years. Many of them hold qualifications in people management or have proven their aptitude through their work. Fresh specialists are also hired from time to time to make sure the bank's HR philosophy stays relevant to the changing times.

In the recent decade or so, the HR department has had a major facelift. It no longer is constrained and defined by the administration of people processes; rather, it has evolved into a key facilitator and partner of business strategy. Today, who should be doing what, where and how are all questions that are answered by the bank's HR strategy. Innovations in digitizing HR processes have reduced not just the time taken to deliver on services but also the grievances related to many an administrative function.

In the post-amalgamation scenario, with the significant increase in the size of its human resource base and geographical playing field, the bank shall witness significant changes in people management strategies, enhanced use of technology as well as expansion in the span of control.

Transformation across Six Key Levers of HR

The HR team is focused on the objective of complete digitalization of processes to make them more people friendly, transparent, simpler and quicker.

Digitization of all employee interface processes and the use of technology in critical functions such as disciplinary matters are all a result of design thinking keeping in mind the end use and needs of the end users.

In addition to centrally designed systems, suggestions and ideas are welcomed from across the field and incorporated towards this end. Accordingly, six key levers of HR have been identified across the bank, and transformation initiatives have been planned across them (Figure C4.1).

1. **Way of working:** One of the primary objectives has been to create efficiency and agility in the HR 'way of working'. Some of the key initiatives undertaken for the same are as follows:

   a. **Digitization of key applications and processes:** Union Bank of India has increasingly digitized more and more processes through its human resource management system (HRMS) portal. All employee-related activities are carried out and processed online. This includes disbursing salaries and allowances, making leave applications, annual

Figure C4.1 *Transformation across Six Key Levers of HR*

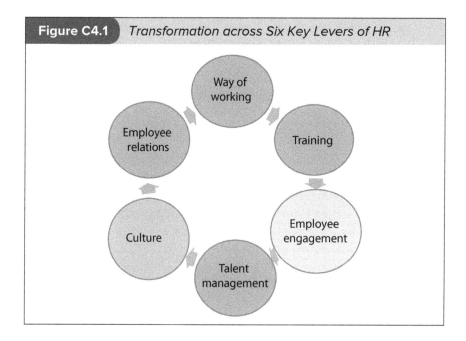

appraisals and promotions processes. Even transfer request applications are received and processed online as against the erstwhile physical form submission to eliminate all loss in transit as well as lower the lead time in communication to all relevant parties.

b. **HR Suvidha—centralized processing hub:** Concerted effort has been made to centralize grant of increments and fitment, as well as all reimbursements such as travel allowance, leave fare concession (LFC) and monthly bills such as conveyance, cleaning, entertainment and liveries to name a few.

HR Suvidha not only simplified the process for sanctioning claims but also led to 91 per cent reduction in turnaround time (TAT) to the delight of employees and HR managers alike. Uniformity in the interpretation of guidelines and procedure further reduced grievances related to claim processing as well as brought substantial savings to the bank.

The commencement of HR Suvidha is a shining example of the use of technology to achieve efficiency and customer delight. This was achieved through:

- Three-tier sanctioning procedure for travelling expenses/travelling advance bills (recommender, approver, sanctioner) being reduced to two stages of sanctioning, that is, approver and sanctioner.

- Two-tier sanctioning procedure (approver and sanctioner) is reduced to one stage of sanctioning of bills other than travelling expenses/travelling advance on a reimbursement basis.
- Enabling verified scanned copies of supporting documents to be uploaded with the claims.

c. **Technology for communication and collaboration:** An extensive network of video conferencing infrastructure has been created to be able to reach out to a larger number of HR managers for simultaneous communication of any changes, updates, chain messages, etc.

d. **HR analytics:** The bank is using spreadsheets and statistical software suite as part of HR analytics in order to take more informed decisions and not rely on the traditionally uneven method of 'intuitions'. The bank has undertaken meaningful studies on performance management, stagnation analysis, absenteeism, women in the bank and attrition analytics—to name a few which have brought valuable insights to light.

2. **Training:** Union Bank of India is committed to increasing the knowledge and skill base of employees and has made long strides toward this endeavour. During FY 2018–2019, the bank has conducted over 814 in-house training sessions, 197 vocational programmes and 68 workshops covering approximately 29,000 employees and sent another 548 employees for external training covering different programmes to gain industry-wide exposure. Twenty-six new programmes focusing on credit, forex, rural and agri-business, credit monitoring and restructuring/credit recovery, information technology, etc., have also been added in 2019.

Techniques such as gamification and interactive e-learning modules are used for training purposes.

By making the learning resources easily available to employees at all times, there has been an increased interest in acquiring new skills and keeping up to date with policy changes/industry trends/ etc.

This commitment to L&D has been well recognized by the industry in the form of awards and accolades received from prestigious quarters such as the Golden Peacock Awards, World HRD Congress, Indian Society for Training and Development, Times Ascent and ET Now among others.

Some key L&D initiatives undertaken by the bank are:

a. **Prajna—the e-learning portal:** The bank has a dedicated e-learning portal with ~28,000 registered users and over 10,000 monthly active users for modules covering a wide array of training content across functional areas as well as soft skills. With the e-learning modules made available for employees 'on the go' through the Union Prajna mobile application, ease of usage as well as accessibility to the training content has been enhanced for anytime-anywhere learning.

Union Bank of India's policy to include a stipulated number of mandated e-learning hours per employee as a part of the promotion and appraisal key performance indicators for each job role for continuous knowledge enrichment has made e-learning a crucial part of the career progression framework.

b. **Induction and onboarding:** Onboarding today has been made very interesting for a new recruit and easy to manage for the bank with the use of technology. Not only recruits are able to learn through the e-learning resources available to them, but they are also able to get updates and feedback on their progress through the induction portal specifically designed for this purpose.

During the 52-week induction and onboarding programmes, the new recruits are rotated in 12 different specialized branches for 'on-the-job training'. Their movements are tracked through an application made for the purpose.

c. **Imparting online training at the training centres:** Digitization of the overall learning experience has also been a focus area for the bank and building the right infrastructure to impart knowledge has been given utmost importance.

Union Bank of India has built a capacity of ~590 personal computers in over 20 classrooms to impart hands-on learning through animation, interactive modules, gamification, etc.

Dedicated L&D website U-learn and a learning radio broadcasting podcasts/episodes on recent changes in standard operating procedures and revised banking guidelines.

3. **Employee engagement:** Studies have shown that employees who have invested in their roles are more productive than those who haven't. Union Bank of India has recognized this well and come up with multiple means to boost employee engagement as well as productivity. The core of the engagement programme aims to improve involvement and ownership, hygiene factors, strengthen team bonds and increase group cohesion.

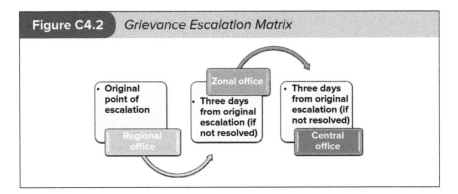

Figure C4.2 *Grievance Escalation Matrix*

Digitization has been at the heart of most employee engagement initiatives, including the following:

a. **HR Aapke Dwar—solutions at your doorstep:** This online portal helps employees raise any concerns that they might have during their day-to-day jobs. The unique and automatic escalation matrix makes the portal highly efficient as it ensures employee queries are resolved within a pre-set TAT. In addition, the portal is well monitored to be able to effectively capture employee pulse on recurring concerns (Figure C4.2).

b. **Query corner—how may I assist you:** The live website to answer any queries helps in timely resolution of questions raised by employees. The process has been streamlined such that an employee receives a response to any query on the website within 48 hours. All queries raised are captured on the website anonymously along with responses for other employees to view in case they have similar queries. With this initiative, Union Bank of India has created a safe, transparent space for employees to engage in community discussions. Additionally, all queries raised are stored as a repository of frequently asked questions for future reference (Figure C4.3).

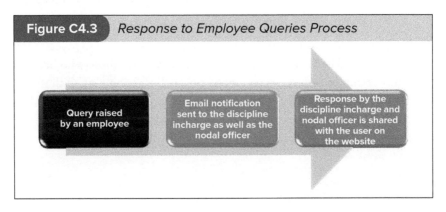

Figure C4.3 *Response to Employee Queries Process*

In case frequent queries are raised on similar topics, staff college collaborates with the respective business vertical to create a case study on the subject, which is then leveraged during classroom training sessions.

c. **Innovation portal—ideation invited:** The Innovation portal invites suggestions from employees on how to improve day-to-day working using novel or technology-based solutions. These suggestions are processed through a feasibility study as well as a cost–benefit analysis and are taken up very seriously for implementation. 'Innovation' has led to numerous process improvements for the benefit of customers and employees alike as well as helped the bank easily comply with certain statutory guidelines with the development of special reports or flagging mechanisms. Consistent efforts have been made to improve upon hygiene factors and increase motivators at the workplace. Employee satisfaction surveys have been conducted to gain insights into the motivations of employees in the bank, and as per their findings, HR decisions are taken to further improve the employment experience. For example, policy change as a direct result of employee feedback led to an improvement of 15.5 per cent in the number of stagnating employees in the bank.

4. **Talent management:** Union Bank of India is committed to engage, develop and retain its most talented employees, and this strategy is reflected in the initiatives that have been taken in this sphere. Managing talent is an art that needs constant re-inventing at each stage of the employee lifecycle. The bank has developed the following initiatives for the same:

a. **Sparks:** The Spark programme is an initiative to target high potential individuals early on so as to fully hone their talent. The programme is initiated at the training level, assessing the employees during their probationary period to identify 'Sparks' or 'high performers'. A list of 'Spark' employees is shared with the central office and aids in the process of designating roles and responsibilities thereby matching the right job for the right person.

b. **Bhavishya programme:** Bhavishya is a comprehensive year-long, leadership development and capacity-building programme aimed at shaping future leaders of the bank. Union Bhavishya groomed over 1,000 employees in FY 2017–2018, and covered another 294 in FY 2018–2019, including a special batch for women employees with an emphasis on providing a fillip to women leadership at the top. During the course of this programme, applications have been developed for tracking the progress of participants online.

c. **Performance management and succession planning:** Digitalization of the performance management package has brought greater credibility to the annual appraisal activity as for the first time in 2010–2011, employees were able to see the remarks against their performance by their supervisors as well as the scores they received. Over the last decade, innumerable changes have been made to the performance management system (PMS) with bringing in management by objectives, the in-built scope of setting individual development plans (IDPs) by the employee as well as capturing employee aspirations and potential. Objectivity has been enhanced with auto-population of targets for budgetary roles.

The bank is already in process to further strengthen PMS to make it completely digital with auto generation of scores, cohort comparisons and real-time performance feedback.

The performance management process has been key to succession planning. With objectivity and automation being brought in by the PMS, it becomes easier to rate performance and assess potential of candidates. The bank is on the verge of creating an inventory of competencies which shall aid in further refining the succession planning process.

d. **Leadership development strategy:** The bank has been consciously focused on creating a strong line of future leaders. Towards this end, the performance management and training systems have been leveraged to identify consistently high performing individuals with the potential to lead. These individuals have been specifically selected for leadership development programmes and exposed to the best-in-industry L&D interventions, including but not limited to human process labs, assessment centres, psychometrics, etc. During the course of this one-year programme, the participants also undertake their personal and professional growth journey by setting up and creating their own IDPs. Participants of this programme have shown evident improvement in soft skills and have been chosen for higher assignments.

This model by the bank has received widespread recognition and accolades from the industry, that have brought with them numerous leadership development awards.

In the post-amalgamated scenario, the bank has plans to extend this model specifically to develop successors for identified key positions, through IDPs focused on preparing the candidate for those positions.

5. **Culture:** Organizational culture is a critical element of ensuring an innovative, agile working environment. The culture at Union Bank of India is a manifestation of the core values and the overall vision of being 'good people to bank with'.

The use of technology in the day-to-day work has led to more emphasis on customer-service, innovative thinking and problem-solving attitude. These have had a positive impact on the work ethos of the bank as a whole while giving employees the platform to voice their ideas as they are encouraged by implementation of those ideas.

a. **HR day and HR week:** HR day and HR week offer employees a plethora of systematically planned activities and initiatives ranging from grievance redressal, open doors with leadership, compliance awareness, contests, etc.

   These activities play the dual role of employee engagement as well as sourcing of new ideas from employees to effecting positive changes and improvements.

b. **Union Parivar:** Union Parivar is a fully digitized HR portal and HRMS for employees to access, with individual employee profiles including details such as personal information, family and dependent details, education and career progression information and work history. It forms the cornerstone of the employment experience for the whole 'family' as it is through this alone that all processes are routed, and all records are kept. This portal has recently been given the shape of a mobile app to enable the fastest delivery on employee-initiated activities.

6. **Employee relations (ER)/disciplinary action:** ER has made formidable strides in the direction of becoming a fully digitized ecosystem while complying with the requirements of maintaining timely records across the bank.

a. **Central portal for maintaining all ER records:** Since April 2012, the department has moved to a completely digital platform to maintain all information on disciplinary actions being taken at the bank. It has been ensured that records are completely comprehensive so that while seeking any clearances, filing applications or searching digital records, all information has been made available using the central portal. All details are made available to the concerned authorities at regional/zonal level, through individual user IDs created for the purpose.

   Since the portal is updated on a real-time basis to reflect the latest update on each action initiated, employees are able to seek clearance in as low as 48 hours from the time of a request. Additionally, during the promotion season, using the bulk clearance functionality, teams are able to provide clearances at a much quicker TAT as compared to the hitherto manual system.

    b. **Online Disciplinary Action at Local level (DALL):** DALL portal facilitates monthly updation by the department to maintain a progress report on the disciplinary actions initiated.

    c. **Inquiring authority/inquiry officer (IA/IO) log:** This initiative of 100 per cent digitization of the inquiry function has significantly streamlined the overall process and saves considerable manual effort. The IA is able to track and provide real-time updates on all activities such as pre-hearing meetings, schedule of the hearing, any potential delays, sharing of the case brief with the IO, etc. The time saved has helped the bank reach an all-time low number of cases pending for more than six months.

Looking Ahead

These technological innovations have all made the organization more agile and processes more fluid. For example, there are thousands of e-learning modules available anywhere anytime which can be used to gain knowledge of processes/functions that an employee may need in order to deliver in a stop-gap role; similarly, policies and circulars on specific standard operating procedures are now available on the go.

The only challenge in bringing in new technology is the initial resistance to change, which is temporary. Once the teething troubles are over, there is quick and easy acceptance. This is only obvious since the majority of the workforce, just like the majority of the population of the country, is between the 25 and 35 age bracket. Therefore, the adoption of technology is not a problem.

The positive impact of digitalization can be gauged through the reduction in grievances on account of bills processing or other admin functions, the incredible improvements in TAT of some of the key functions, uniform interpretation of policies and procedures and the increased ability to track progress.

Communication technologies have also made it easier to gather feedback and keep a tab on the pulse of the organization.

In the wake of the recent amalgamation, with the expansion of its human capital base and geographical reach, the HR journey ahead shall have to include cultural integration and process synergies.

The process of rationalization of benefits and procedures has already been accomplished. Technological integration is underway, and the future shall see continued improvements in the same.

Defining the culture of the new entity is a work in progress, which has assumed a place as one of the top priorities.

The bank now stands at the cusp of a major transformation. As it embraces a more digital- and analytics-driven approach, it stands ready for the change that will allow it to win in this redefined playfield. Union Bank of India has set a clear vision for 'being a trendsetter in ensuring an excellent employee experience while becoming the bank of choice for customers'.

The near future shall witness HR transformation in the form of an unbiased, digitally-backed PMS to enable suitable recognition and reward of top performers as an effective tool for retention. Coupled with a mindful succession strategy which draws an inference from both the quantitative and qualitative data points, it is intended that the art of deployment that is placing the right person at the right job could be mastered.

In addition to this, the bank is working towards an overall revamp of recruitment and career planning processes to make these activities completely digital.

Looking further ahead, the bank would start building its own unique position in the digital ecosystem leveraging partnerships with key fintech players, redesigning customer and employee journeys as well as creating analytics-driven intelligence across the current value chain. While a lot of ground has been covered for automation and digitization, leveraging available artificial intelligence technology and social media platforms furthermore is on the cards for improving engagement and creating an overall more agile and empowered workforce.

The progress made by Union Bank of India has been truly commendable and is reflected clearly across both improved processes and employee satisfaction. With its current momentum and in the context of the newly amalgamated entity, there is scope to move only upwards and onwards from here on. Union Bank of India is ready to embrace change and undertake a revolutionary journey towards realizing its mighty aspirations.

PART 3

Perspectives from Experts

'An area of grave concern is the fear psychosis in the executives.'

Kewal Handa*

AK: You came from a multinational background; how was your experience in a public sector bank (PSB)? Was it a culture shock?

KH: I had some experience of working in a joint public sector and also in a promoter-driven company prior to my innings in a multinational. I was also on the board of ING Vyasa before its merger with Kotak Bank. What was, however, a shock, in some sense, was the prevailing culture of a high degree of hierarchy over administration, a culture where one felt the luxury of people as perquisites—a lot of people looking after the convenience of operating management and the board, the ritual of being seen off and being received by a number of people. I found this very embarrassing and quite unnecessary.

AK: Did you have any brief from the government about your role as the non-executive chairman in Union bank of India?

KH: The government had high expectation from us and expected us to improve governance by bringing professionalism and giving strategic direction. I received a notification about my appointment and a note on dos and don'ts for the role. However, I did not feel constrained deploying myself completely in understanding the bank, its business, its customer franchise, strategies and its people.

AK: How did you do it? Did you do it before joining or during the process of your work as the non-executive chairman (NEC)?

KH: For the first few months, I organized—almost on alternate days—presentations from different functions to understand the bank and its business, what they do and how they do it. I wanted to familiarize myself with the banking operations, how risk is being managed, internal controls, appraisal and monitoring, retail and treasury business and the reason for the high-level

*Kewal Handa, Former Non-executive Chairman, Union Bank of India.

non-performing asset (NPAs). This was very useful in building a relationship with the department and exposing them to the outside competitive world.

AK: So how was your experience in the board? How did you feel about the issues and challenges?

KH: I was quite daunted by the sheer number of persons in the board room. I was told that apart from board members all general managers also attend board meetings. I was not comfortable for the simple reason that there was no privacy of discussions amongst the board members, and there was always a possibility of a discussion leaking out in the bank even before minutes were ready. I also observed that most of the time of the board was spent on routine and statutory agenda items.

Additionally, I observed a strong pecking order of hierarchy. Even the members would not talk until there was a signal from the managing director.

However, now I am very happy to say that the board is very agile, competitive, professional and business oriented.

Recommendations from the department on many occasions have been sent back, as they lacked depth in data analysis and fresh thinking. The board actively participates in the discussion on all issues, strengthening areas such as audits, risk, monitoring, retail business, and in evolving new systems and procedures.

AK: How did you go about changing the board culture?

KH: I did not want to sound like a restless and an overwise soul, and therefore, I followed a self-inflicted protocol for myself to openly raise issues including whether we needed every general manager (GM) in every board meeting, and invited suggestions of other board members and built a consensus that board meetings will be attended by board members; whenever any particular items came up for discussion, the concerned GM was invited.

We also ensured that there was wider participation by the full-time directors as well as the other board members in various discussions. As a matter of routine, we ensured that before the actual taking up of agenda items, business presentations were made, followed by functional department presentations. All the important aspects of the information item were covered in the presentation. Benchmarking has now been not only with peer PSBs, but also with private sector banks. I ensured that I reviewed the board agenda before it was released and the board minutes captured the essence of the discussions.

Besides my role in the board, I also attended many town hall meetings, sometimes with the chief executive officer (CEO) and sometimes singly, which gave me a good idea about the issues at the operating level. I may have attended more than 30 meetings in my three years' tenure. It was amazing to get ideas from below and observe their motivation.

AK: Normally, it is the role of NEC to be visible at the field level. How did it work? Did it not create any problem?

KH: It was done in the interest of creating a new future for the bank and to bring insights from the field to develop new strategies and bring a change in culture. I was open and transparent and ready to meet and take comments or questions; this helped bring about an inclusive culture. In no way did this create any role erosion of the CEO, and in fact, board and CEOs were seen pursuing a common agenda. I would like to compliment CEO Rajkiran for working to bring about change in the bank culture and opening up to new ideas, taking the chairman and the board not as competitors or hindrance but as partners to build a great bank.

I never got involved in operational issues, however, I had built a lot of trust and respect amongst the board members and bank colleagues. In partnership with the CEO, we initiated a strategic exercise involving more than 70 senior managers who worked along with their team members to define the strategy for the bank. This process took six months and we were able to build a robust strategy and at the same time change the culture of the bank as the team started taking responsibility and there was a sense of pride associated with the future of the bank. This open transparent culture and owning responsibility by involving people to take their decision brought the best amongst the employees.

AK: As you know that the banking industry is facing difficulty on various parameters and is seen to get stuck in one problem or the other whether NPA or capital or leadership, what do you think are the major challenges before PSBs?

KH: In spite of the fact that the staff of PSBs and especially senior executives work diligently and with passion, the banks do not seem to come out of problems. They seem to be in some kind of *chakravyuh* (labyrinth). There are areas that require critical attention by the government to face the competition and transform banks as full-range technology-smart entities.

AK: Could you please elaborate?

KH: The most critical issue is the type of talent gaps at every level. Banks are not allowed campus recruitment at entry level because of some Supreme Court judgement delivered a couple of years ago. We expect the government to help the banking industry on this. If at the entry level you are able to get some good talent, you can groom them and pull them through the pipeline of leadership faster. Recruitment at the lateral level has not worked well for various reasons. First, you don't get the candidates willing to work in the public sector and then there are problems of compensation. Even though we are allowed to pay differential compensation, it disturbs the existing system and retention is a big issue. At the clerical level, the system of the interview has been discontinued by the government. If any organization with market orientation recruits in a routine manner, there are serious problems of maintaining a level of talent required for a digital environment. You cannot manage a commercial business in an administrative manner.

The other issue is that of autonomy. Practically, all decisions in human resources (HR) are standardized through government notifications like recruitment and promotions (especially at GM/chief general manager [CGM] levels). The system of any reward at any level is practically non-operational because the criteria set by the government hardly make any personnel in senior management eligible in the present circumstances. Frankly, it is the job of the board to decide the criteria for rewards. The board has no role to play in the selection of senior executives and the pro-motions of senior executives are undertaken as per the criteria laid down by the government. Thus, practically, banks have very little say in devising their own HR policies in consonance with their unique problems, capacity to pay and other criteria.

An area of grave concern is the fear psychosis in the executives, including senior management, on account of the criminal investigation of commercial decisions. Some recent incidents of bank executives and even directors being questioned, and in some cases arrested, have had a negative impact on the morale of decision-makers. The problem is serious enough to deserve some solution that can heighten the morale and confidence of the banking community. The low credit growth, which is often com-mented upon in spite of soft interest rates, in my opinion, is an outcome of decision paralyses resulting in files being pushed upwards.

AK: While I understand your viewpoint on some of the above issues, I think that many of the human resource issues can possibly be improved at the bank-level. What do you think?

KH: You have a point. *HR today needs a highly professionalized approach and competent professionals who understand the core purpose of human factor and its possibilities and potential. Such qualified professionals can align HR to business strategies, manage talent, innovate in the behavioural side and design modern sys-tems. This is what is done by leading successful corporations both in private and multinational corporations.* HR in my opinion is a strategic function. In banks, I observe this function is largely administrative and busy with recruitment, training, placement and promotions, union-management relations, etc. This function, with minor changes here and there and mostly handcuffed by government guidelines, often performs its tasks in a routine manner.

There are hardly any HR professionals at the senior level. The HR cadre is not developed. There is also no continuity in the HR function.

There are occasional flirtations within the training system to offer courses in managerial skills or leadership, but largely, they do not make much impact.

AK: What inhibits a bank from hiring professionals or the HR committee of the board from taking a long-term view and laying a plan for HR transformation?

KH: Some banks have experimented with hiring professionals from outside to head the departments, particularly in areas of digital and retail. However, I'm afraid they were culturally misfit in the hierarchal set-up and as they were not supported by the mid-level talent they faced the execution challenges. The solution is to have business units who are made accountable and also given the responsibility to develop talent. We, at the Union Bank of India, now, are experimenting with a different structure making the CGM responsible for the business unit having its own vertical business teams. Today, the banking business has moved out of the branches and some of the private sector banks are doing almost 60–70 per cent of the business outside the branch. We need to build strong professionals in HR, digital and retail, and additionally, have strong mid-level professionals.

AK: How do you see the process of reforms—Indradhanush, Gyan Sangam, splitting the CMD position as part-time chairman and managing director (MD) and CEO, BBB, Ease 1,2,3, and the amalgamation of some smaller banks into large banks? How does it add up to reforms? Is there something more that the government needs to do to make PSBs vibrant and strong?

KH: Within the existing structure, these reforms are making a marginal impact. However, if we want to compete with the private sector banks and make public sector banks global, then we need to make changes in the existing structure. *The Nayak committee had proposed a holding company concept whereby the government shares would be vested in the holding company having its own independent board. Given the size of the amalgamated banks, it's time to have this model in place, whereby it will have its own free and independent board, top management being accountable to the board, market-driven salaries and compensation, and hiring the professionals from outside.* The holding company can oversee and guide the bank but not interfere in the operations; these public sector banks can still continue to play an important role in government schemes.

AK: Overall, what has been your learning in this role? What are your views about the future of PSBs?

KH: The future of PSBs depends on how independent and flexible they are in terms of hiring and compensating people and creating the performance culture. Leadership can do only so much within the existing structure, but freeing the bank will make them a global player and contribute immensely to the government. I see that PSBs are not just followers of digital, but are also taking a quantum leap in technology and breaking the bureaucratic shackles, becoming the master of their destiny.

2

'You need best-in-class leaders to shift the titanic.'

Ajay Nanavati*

AK: Ajay, the Government of India appointed you as a non-executive chairman of Syndicate Bank for a three-year term, which ended recently. You came from 3M, a leading multinational corporation of the world and it must have been quite an experience. How was it different?

AN: Since my background was with a global industrial multinational corporation, I had no prior experience with the public sector, and more so, a financial services company. My focus, therefore, was both to learn and share some best practices from the private sector, especially with regard to building customer franchises in a competitive environment, and on developing leadership and executing strategy.

The one thing that positively surprised me was the commitment of the people in the public sector banks (PSBs). Most of the people I met have spent 30+ years with the bank and have a strong desire to succeed.

On the other hand, what concerned me was a lack of outcome-based thinking. The focus is on activities rather than results. For example, numerous new products were launched regularly with much fanfare, but there was little emphasis on measuring the outcomes in terms of impact and profitability.

Similarly, although extensive data is available, the ability to glean the data for insights is limited. Also, the emphasis on routine compliance at various level leaves very little time for innovations. As a result, a culture of experimentation, which is a key prerequisite for innovation, is lacking. The entire ecosystem is of cautious decision-making and compliance. The spirit of risk taking and aggressive marketing is missing.

AK: What challenges are PSBs facing currently and what kind of culture, do you think, can be conducive to transform the banks?

AN: In my opinion, the primary challenges PSBs face are (a) building a customer orientation, (b) creating a meritocratic environment, (c) introducing

* Ajay Nanavati, Former Non-executive Chairman, Syndicate Bank.

appropriate rewards and recognition systems, (d) inculcating good govern-ance practices, (e) using analytics more effectively as a marketing tool, (f) inculcating a culture of accountability, and (g) a strategic orientation (versus a short-term tactical approach).

For example, at one of my first board meetings, I asked the group of general managers how many of them had called upon a customer in the last six months, and to my utter surprise, not one hand went up. Subsequently, I learnt that there was a fear that if they were seen soliciting clients and if the account goes sour or becomes a non-performing asset, they would be potentially accused of being in collusion with the client.

Another example that surprised me was that there was no attention given to the competitive landscape. The idea of market share was an alien concept. Most of the financial reporting revolved around measuring performance versus our own past performance rather than industry performance or plan targets. This was probably a conscious decision to avoid being held accountable.

AK: To operate in a digital environment, what kind of leadership mindset needs to exist in the banks?

AN: *In an increasingly competitive world, adopting a strong data-driven decision-making process is essential. This includes using analytics more effectively as a customer acquisition and retention tool as well as a risk assessment tool. In an era when power-ful tools like artificial intelligence can be utilized to assess risk (and adopt risk-based pricing), they are, unfortunately, inadequately leveraged.*

Similarly, using data to segment the market to identify areas of focus and building unique strengths as a competitive advantage is not used.

For example, the ability to look at trends (as compared to a snapshot at a point in time), understand the implications and take appropriate actions was not in the DNA.

AK: What were your key challenges in the board and how you mobilized the board for a transformation programme? Can you list some key challenges? What challenges existed for implementation?

AN: Although we had a very competent board with great experience/expertise, historically, boards of PSB's had largely played a compliance role.

My job, as the chairman, was to encourage them to get more deeply engaged in the business aspects (without, of course, stepping on management toes).

Some of the steps we took were to create empowered committees to drill down into granular aspects, so that the board discussions were more focused on critical issues rather than mundane matters. As a result, what used to be a two-hour rubber stamp meeting transformed into one and half-day session with deep deliberations.

Many of the board members either came from government or academia (and largely with finance backgrounds) with very few having real-life industry experience. Over time, the board started getting more engaged in asking difficult questions and keeping management on their toes.

AK: What new skills and leadership competencies are required in banks to face challenges of future banking? What should be a prioritized agenda for change?

AN: *The most urgent need is to build a customer-centric mindset with an intense focus on acquiring customers, growing the relationship with and retaining customers. To do this, the entire ecosystem needs to be aligned with a culture of customer service. It also means prudent risk-taking, which, after all, is at the very heart of a bank's operations.*

What I observed was that PSBs, in general, prefer to maintain the status quo rather than rock the boat, and our bank was no exception. This seems to have percolated across the organization and inhibited the willingness to try new things. The fear psychosis is palpable in the system.

The second problem in PSBs is the lack of specialized professionals with deep domain expertise in areas such as digital, risk management, marketing, analytics and technology. We pioneered, on an experimental basis, in inducting some senior professionals in digital and risk management areas, but inevitably, there was significant push back for a variety of reasons.

The third problem in PSBs is a lack of deep leadership bench strength with appropriate cross-functional experience to produce well-rounded general managers.

Last, the appraisal processes are suboptimal, and an absence of a rewards and recognition system does not drive the right behaviour.

AK: Can you elaborate on some of the issues that were mentioned, especially in the area of talent management and leadership?

AN: PSBs require flexibility in recruiting the best-in-class talent. The rigidities of the system are a major stumbling block for banks to be able to respond to volatility, uncertainty, complexity and ambiguity world, which is disrupting the traditional banking and the level of services expecting expected from a bank.

Many of the traditional functions in the banks, such as credit, treasury, customer service and compliance, are now getting highly specialized, and banks require good talent in these areas. Digital disruption is also necessitating a new kind of leadership that is agile and bold.

The recruitment methodology, performance management systems and reward mechanisms need to be urgently addressed to ensure that they contribute to motivation and engagement of people.

The compensation mechanism, which currently has a vanilla flavour (standardized across all PSBs), need to be reviewed to link compensation to performance and energize high performers.

The biggest issue, however, is the continuity of leadership at the top level. I was quite surprised to note that our bank had 16 CEOs (chief executive officers) in 24 years! Even in my short tenure of a little less than three years, I would have worked with three CEOs. If there is no continuity of CEOs, how does one undertake long-term measures of transforming their organizations? How does one create a leadership pipeline? How does one create a culture for innovations and experimentation? How does one take bold initiatives?

AK: What is the role of the board of directors in architecting it transformational agenda and implementing the same?

AN: Boards need to get more involved in evaluating strategy (not developing), become empowered in succession and leadership planning and more actively engage with the senior executives within the ranks. Boards should also include industry sectoral domain experts beyond just chartered accountants. This lack of outside-in perspective is a handicap. For example, one of the most critical committees—the Remuneration and Compensation Committee—doesn't even exist.

Beyond being custodians of compliance to fulfil fiduciary responsibilities, boards need to hold management accountable. In PSUs (public sector undertakings), there is a tendency to ignore minority shareholder rights as management perceives the entity is an arm of the government even though in reality it is a publicly listed company.

AK: What do you think are the major challenges for the HR function in the banks?

AN: I do believe that HR has to prepare for the new environment and needs of modern digital banking. It needs transformation.

The biggest challenge I see is the need for HR leaders to themselves be deep domain experts with professional backgrounds in HR. The new millennial generation has very different wants/needs than historical hires. Unfortunately, they have very little leeway in where they can source hires. There is an urgent need to dramatically transform with a far greater focus on talent acquisition, talent development and succession planning, that is, building a deep pool.

The other major handicap HR faces is the flexibility they enjoy to set up appropriate reward systems relevant to their context. The current one-size-fits-all approach is no longer meaningful.

Finally, the appraisal systems being used are obsolete and do not drive appropriate behaviour.

AK: Can you elaborate on this?

AN: Even now, the HR function is mostly saddled with mostly routine administrative functions such as promotions, transfers, placement, industrial relations and training. Certainly, they are responding to changes but in a marginal manner. The HR transformation will require the professionalization of HR function in terms of professional competencies and the manning of HR by professionally qualified persons as well as talented operational executives in order to bring a flavour of understanding the context of business. This will help continuity in HR apart from domain knowledge of various HR functions. *HR needs rebirth in terms of its orientation and shifting its focus from maintenance to development as well as deep work to seek employee learning and engagement. It also needs to be decentralised and each operating manager has to accept responsibility for people processes.*

The board committee on HR has to function to set the vision for effective engagement of human capital, digitalisation and its effective use for various HR sub-systems. It needs to look at leadership gaps, succession on critical functions etc., and oversee effective implementation of various HR policies.

AK: What future do you see for PSBs?

AN: Despite the challenges I have outlined above, I am quite optimistic. Today, although PSBs are not in the best of the health, they have a huge reach, extensive infrastructure and brand equity developed over decades. Additionally, ever since nationalization, they have played a significant role in contributing to national development.

So what needs to change? They need (a) empowered, independent boards, (b) CEOs with a minimum tenure of 4–5 years, (c) a board which decides differentiated policies for compensation, rewards and recognition, and (d) autonomy for lateral recruitments at senior levels.

An organization is only as good as its leaders, managers and employees. Banking is in a perpetual state of transformation, and it has a strategic role in national development. Therefore, you need the best-in-class captains (leaders) to shift the titanic. This, to me, remains a major challenge. Everything begins with the quality of leadership, and I must say with some concerns that this is still not understood in the manner it should be.

'Unless management has sufficient autonomy in HR and governance structure, PSBs will move from one problem to another.'

Ravi Venkatesan and Biju Varkkey*

AK: Ravi, you came from a multinational (Microsoft) and private sector (Tata Cummins) background to Bank of Baroda (BOB), a public sector bank (PSB), as a non-executive chairman in 2015. This is something rare. How did it happen?

Ravi: Well, sometime in February 2015, I got a call from the then Reserve Bank of India (RBI) Governor, Raghuram Rajan, advising that they are trying to fix the public sector banking system and persuading some talent from the private sector to create a model of success for transformation. He requested me to accept the position of a part-time non-executive chairman in one of the large banks.

Around that time, the Finance Minister, late Arun Jaitley, had announced the scheme of banking reforms titled 'Indradhanush', which articulated several reform measures including bringing chief executive officers (CEOs) to some large PSBs from outside the banking system, splitting the position of chairman and managing director (CMD) into non-executive chairman and managing director (MD) and CEO, creation of Bank Board Bureau for appointing full-time board members. The vibes for reform measures were positive.

Although I did not have either any background as a banker or experience in the public sector, I accepted the offer purely as a call of duty. I believe that when you get a chance, it is your opportunity to deploy yourself to straighten the system. In August 2015, I was informed by then secretary DFS, Adhia, about my nomination as the non-executive chairman of Bank of Baroda. I received an appointment letter which mentioned more about what I could

*Ravi Venkatesan, Former Non-executive Chairman, and Biju Varkkey, Member of the Board, Bank of Baroda.

not do. On a lighter note, I wondered how is it that the oral briefing is to reform the system and the appointment letter speaks the opposite!!

AK: How did you prepare for the role?

Ravi: Remember when I met you over dinner and read your book *Dare to Lead*—a story of the transformation of BOB? (Laughs)

I decided to just listen to and understand the bank's top executives in the first few meetings. When I attended my first board meeting, for several months, there was no CEO, and the affairs of the bank were run by an interim CEO, an existing executive director, who was to retire in next few months. My first board meeting (which I attended as an observer) was a rather disappointing one. It was horrifying to see 50 executives (all general managers [GMs] and even some deputy general managers [DGMs]) around the table. It was a sheer waste of their time. They were required only during the time of discussions of their agenda item. The board papers were carried in thick files. Mostly routine items occupied a major time of the board, and discussions were often dysfunctional.

Next time, after a few weeks, when I chaired the board meeting, I made sure that only the members of the board were present, and concerned GMs were called only when the item sponsored by was taken up for discussion. Each board member who already had a tablet was requested to use the same during meetings, and the system of physical board papers was dispensed with. We also changed the organization of board papers into three categories, namely strategic issues, approvals and items for noting. This helped us spending about 50 per cent of the time on strategic issues. We also activated and reorganized various committees of the board such as human resources (HR) committee, risk committee and technology committee, and inducted outside experts and advisors to these committees. Elaborate discussions took place in these committees and decisions were made. This helped the board focus on its transformational agenda. All these changes happened over two or three months.

AK: How did you conceptualize your vision for the bank? Where did the issue of HR and technology fit in?

Ravi: About three months after my takeover, Jayakumar (Ex-Citi Bank) joined in as CEO and MD. We both came from a private and multinational background and decided to put our collective intellectual muscle to prepare the bank as a robust financial entity using state of the art technology and building leadership bench strength.

I was very clear that I would stay for only three years, and I was positively impatient to achieve the four goals by the end of my tenure in 2018. These were:

1. To establish the brand reputation as a modern and tech savvy PSB
2. To clean up the balance sheet and reduce the non-performing asset (NPA) levels

3. To get back to an industry leadership role by improving profit and achieve a 15 per cent return on equity (ROE) by 2018
4. To be seen as a leader in technology especially in Fintech within the PSB space

To achieve all this, we had to relentlessly focus on the people side and building leadership across the organization. Talent and leadership were high on my priority as a lever of change and transformation. We spent a good deal of time in the HR committee to discuss these issues.

AK: Did the public sector culture overwhelm you in any way? What elements of culture were positive and negative?

Ravi: While there are many good aspects of the BOB culture (warm, relative openness to outsiders/new ideas, better than average customer focus and best effort), there are many aspects of a public sector undertaking (PSU) bank culture that, I think, are hugely problematic when it comes to their ability to compete.

1. It's a low trust system. The government doesn't trust bankers and has designed rules based on low trust.
2. Risk results in an unwillingness to take the necessary risk with good judgment.
3. Not many are willing to take ownership, let alone initiative; there are few consequences good or bad, resulting in a culture of low accountability.
4. Hierarchical—kiss up and kick down.
5. Application of mind.
6. Learning/continuous improvement.

AK: Ravi, how did you leverage the diversity in the background, experience, bandwidths and preferences of the board members? How did you achieve the buy-in for the above vision?

Ravi: I strongly believe in building relationships with strategic individuals. I developed a personal one-to-one relationship with all the directors, and more particularly, with directors representing the government and the regulator (RBI). On all important matters, I took them into confidence, explained the logic of our proposals and understood the other point of views. I also met DFS secretary and RBI governor/deputy governor quarterly and briefed them about the progress of the bank and took their feedback. I enjoyed the access and the trust of the government and the RBI, and this was very important for my role effectiveness.

AK: Biju, how has your experience been in the BOB board?

Biju: I joined the board after about nine months of Ravi's takeover. I must say that he was a hard taskmaster and was in full control. Ravi focused a lot on aspects of board effectiveness. He would take pre-meeting consultations on important issues to ensure that discussions during the board were focused on strategic issues, and that decisions were taken. He also introduced good procedures by bringing in a qualified company secretary on the board who could take care of all regulatory issues. Besides this, Ravi had to manage executive leadership issues and he would organize team dinners, he even engaged a coach for the top executive team. He also engaged an international consulting firm to undertake a board evaluation exercise and improve the effectiveness of the board. Many of these initiatives were foreign to the public sector, and this is where we developed a good alignment for hassle-free decision-making in the board on crucial issues.

AK: In undertaking any major transformation like digitalization or entering new lines of business, specialized talent is required. How did you go about?

Ravi: In BOB, the management hired some specialized talent laterally in senior positions on market-related compensation. It is never easy to integrate them culturally, and sometimes, it creates an emotional issue for the insiders impacting their motivation and morale. We too had our problems on this count. The board engaged itself with this issue. The induction of highly specialized individuals in technology and for promoting new business lines on contractual appointments with high compensation was endorsed by the board in principle. In the HR committee, we engaged with this issue, and I must say that Professor Biju helped in putting together procedure and policy, terms and conditions, including compensation structure in case of lateral hires. The process was made transparent and the issue was contained.

Biju: *Frankly, in these times of change and transformation, new talent at different levels are required for agile and technology-driven transformation to exploit new business opportunities. There are areas such as digital, analytics, risk management, HR, economic research, where you need high-quality professionals both at senior and middle levels.* With restrictions on campus recruitment of talent, PSBs are in a great disadvantageous position compared to private sector banks. Compensation is another handicap in hiring professional talent. Today, scarcity of strategic talent is a key constraint in undertaking any major transformation, and the banks have to hire consultants in many areas at a very high cost. If you do not have in-house trained talent, even the consultant's contribution is marginal, and after their departure, the implementation process suffers.

The BOB board supported the policy of lateral hires at senior levels, but we also worked out a policy framework to avoid any ad hoc-ism.

AK: What would be the future industry-level big picture for HR look like? What should the regulators, government, future CEOs and researchers start thinking about and working on it right now?

Ravi: Today, human capital issues are very central to the growth aspirations of any company. In fact, this is the most critical and strategic issue to ensure whether you have critical talent both, in technical and leadership and in combination. *An unpalatable truth is that while PSBs have a lot of good, bright and hardworking people, the lack of investment in developing talent for a really long period and constraints on changing HR rules in fundamental ways have created an acute shortage of specialists with expertise in areas such as technology, risk management, fraud control or internal audit, and faces an even bigger scarcity of leaders who are able to drive performance and change.* Lateral hiring is not a solution for even select lateral hiring faces major resistance and challenge of integration.

Weak leadership and culture make it a monumental challenge to create a meritocracy or hold people accountable for performance and compliance. This is despite tons of policies and rules and the fear of Central Vigilance Commission/Central Bureau of Investigation, punishing the perpetrators is hard. Fixing this requires a very fundamental overhaul of the HR system.

AK: Biju, do you agree with Ravi?

Biju: Ravi is right. I too believe that unless management has substantial autonomy in the HR and governance structure, PSBs will move from one problem to another. Management autonomy is needed in areas such as in deciding compensation in its executive cadre (Scale IV and above), incentivization, recruitment, management structure at the top, selection of board members, CEO and compensation for board members and CEO. These are fundamental issues. The Khandelwal Committee appointed by the government had also mentioned many of these issues to strengthen the HR systems.

PSBs also require professionally qualified and trained HR cadre to build a partnership between HR and business and initiate meritocratic systems of assessment, placement and career development. HR in large systems, like PSBs, also extensively need to use data analytics and other tools to develop the credibility of HR decisions. All this requires a complete overhaul of the HR function and the attention of the board to human capital–building issues.

In BOB, we have experienced professionalization of the HR function with a good amount of talent and continuous hiring of HR laterally at middle and senior level. This has helped the bank to consistently innovate, and I can say with some confidence that BOB is a leader in HR in the industry.

It has also provided a CEO from the HR stream, and it has an excellent system to rotate their mid- and senior-level HR functionaries in business roles.

The board committee on HR has been very active, which I understand was created pro-actively in 2002. Right from the beginning, the HR committee had some great academics and professionals, who contributed significantly to developing a policy framework for HR work. Its meetings have been regular and engaging. I was happy to chair this committee and am happy that the committee laid a policy framework for developing leadership across the cadre.

You would thus note that emphasis on human capital issues has to be substantial and knitted through the policy framework and appropriate strategies.

AK: Ravi, would you like to comment?

Ravi: I could not agree more. I am very proud to say that the steps initiated for leadership development will bear fruits in times to come. The HR committee of the board has spent an extraordinary amount of time in taking major strategic initiatives in the matters of policies with regard to lateral induction, leadership development, performance management system, promotions and succession planning. I can confidently say that in the next few years, it will create leaders for other banks as it has done in the past. The bank will be known as a leadership 'factory for bankers'.

Having said that, I must add that the journey ahead for digitalization will require new competencies at various levels and total culture change. Banking skills will become subordinate to digital implications of business and potential of digital play to innovate new products and new lines of businesses and create a new culture of risk taking and speed up decision-making. You will need a board, which is digitally well informed to perform its function of oversight and guidance in a digital environment. You will have to select CEOs and other full-time directors who can lead in a digital environment and are supposedly trained to do this. HR, technology and leadership issues will require most strategic attention.

AK: Why do analysts and the market not give the deserved valuation in spite of many reform measures?

Ravi and Biju: Analysts often take short-term focus because the reforms are cosmetic rather than addressing the core issues of governance and HR policies that do not allow accountability and meritocracy. The measures so far are akin to 'rearranging deck chairs on the Titanic'. Right in the thick of transformation, two PSBs were amalgamated into BOB. Will it create

synergy for the integrated entity? What has been the HR and cultural implications of amalgamation? Unlikely, as someone remarked, it is difficult to
call the merger of two or three unreformed banks as reform.

**AK: Is the present system in PSBs geared for this transition? Are
we ready for the desired direction?**

Ravi: To be honest, my answer is negative. *It is your serendipitous luck to get a
good CEO and inspired board members with whom you can undertake the journey of
transformation. PSBs in the current form are fragile. Any weakness at any level, any
dysfunctional individual can cause the transformation stonewalled, or transformational
efforts can face premature death.* The system does not ensure you to have a top
team relevant in your context, competent to take the bait, motivated to
deploy emotionally in the transformation journey. Full-time directors look
at their assignment as a bird of passage until they reach their aspired goal
to be a CEO and move to another bank. Such short tenures of CEOs and
full-time directors is a serious issue.

Biju: I, too, feel that the present system is not facilitative of institutionalization of initiatives taken during a particular tenure of the board.

**AK: As you are aware that the government has taken many initia-
tives in the direction of reforms such as splitting the chair between
the part-time chairman and CEO, creation of Banks Board Bureau
and recent autonomy measures such as the board to evaluate the
performance of full-time directors and lateral appointment of risk
chief on market compensation, do you think these measures are
adequate?**

Ravi: The answer is not incremental reforms as they do not produce desired
outcomes. When the situation is difficult, you require fundamental reforms.
The state of PSBs is critical. The measures taken from time to time are barely
adequate. The PSBs are in the ICU. Look at the various parameters such
as ROE, price to book and market capitalization. They are way behind the
private banks. The market capitalization of one of the large private banks'
set-up only 26 years ago is twice the market capitalization of combined PSBs.

Time and again, the government has recapitalized the banks, however,
the situation has hardly improved. Besides, *there is no animal spirit in PSB
bankers to lend as the system is gripped with fear. Commercial decisions cannot be
scrutinized through the prism of criminality. Every credit and investment decision on
some criteria can be considered a breach of rules. All this calls for some fundamental
shift in the way we run PSBs. The best way is to either privatize some large banks or*

implement the Nayak Committee's recommendations, which has provided a creative mechanism to run PSBs with the required autonomy. India's PSBs are accident-prone by design, and therefore, the government should not wait—like in the case of Air India—and should take a prompt and bold decision before it is too late. The banking system is too critical to ignore.

Biju: I largely agree. There are no short cuts to reforms. The government should consider bold measures like the one suggested by the Nayak Committee. I am of the view that by retaining its social concerns, some major restructuring of the banking system can be undertaken.

INTERVIEW

4

'Bank directors require training in specific areas of technology.'

H. Krishnamurthy*

AK: Over the past three decades, we have seen many changes in a society driven by the adoption of technology. What do you see as the main technology trends now and in the near future for the banking sector and its customers?

HK: Yes, we have seen many changes in the past four decades. Let me briefly list out the technology interventions in the banking sector chronologically.

The 1980s belonged to the period of banks implementing the advanced ledger posting machines in the branches based on the directive from the regulator, Reserve Bank of India (RBI). In order to process inter-branch reconciliation requirements and a few other applications required at the administrative level, some of the public sector banks (PSBs) had invested in the mainframe computing environment.

It is to be noted that the personal computing platforms were available during the mid-1980s, and the banks started implementing the total branch automation.

The 1990s was a period which saw major initiatives in computerization of banks to address both customer service and internal housekeeping require-ments. Deployment of ATMs and networked applications and services using the very-small-aperture terminal (VSAT) technology was the beginning of the focus towards customer service. Multi-branch banking services were made available to customers. ATM connectivity was using VSATs and ter-restrial lines with low bandwidth. From a network traffic point of view, ATM traffic is categorized as short and busy traffic, and therefore, VSAT technology was able to meet this requirement.

At the turn of the century when the Y2K problem was being tackled, banks still had the branch-based computerization framework. Some of the banks implemented cash management services, which turned out to be a very viable business option. This decade also saw the implementation of the

*H. Krishnamurthy, Chief Research Scientist (Retired), Indian Institute of Science, Bengaluru.

core banking platform by many of the banks and the delivery of networked applications and services.

Bank of Baroda, under the leadership of Anil K. Khandelwal, implemented a major information technology (IT) initiative called Project Shikhar, which is appropriately termed as the technology-enabled business transformation. I was a part of this journey as an IT advisor to the bank for about five–six years. The key takeaway from this solution design was to come out with the integration and interface layer across multiple applications which enabled the bank to comprehensively look at the transaction audit of all the applications. It has to be noted that not having a comprehensive audit of all transaction-oriented application leads to situations that could further lead to frauds not drawing the attention of the system.

It is important to note the role played by RBI in coming out with strategies and directions from time to time. Some of the key initiatives are:

- The Rangarajan Committee report in the early 1980s was the first step towards computerization of banks with a major focus on branch computerization.
- The Vasudevan Committee report in the 1990s was focused on technology upgradation in the banking sector, and the major emphasis was to look at networked applications and services with appropriate levels of security.
- The *Gopalakrishnan Committee Report* in the next decade was a fairly comprehensive exercise, which covered information security, electronic banking, technology risk management and cyber frauds.

I was privileged to be a member of the Vasudevan Committee and the Gopalakrishnan Committee, and these initiatives gave me an insight into how the core networking and security technologies (which was my focus area) need to be understood and addressed in the context of designing, implementing and delivering highly mission-critical customer-oriented services in the banking sector.

To answer your question, *I am of the view that major focus in the banking sector will be to understand the new technology offering by the industry in the areas of artificial intelligence (AI) and machine learning (ML), robotic process automation, big data and decision science high-performance computing with both central processing units (CPUs) and graphics processing units (GPUs) and many other evolving technologies.*

These technologies need to be examined very carefully with reference to the capability, limitation and more importantly applicability in the context of delivering applications and services in the banking sector.

Just to touch upon one example, AI and ML technologies will play a clear role in the next-generation security operation centres not only to generate alerts and alarms in the event of a security breach but, more importantly, to forecast and predict the possibility of impending attacks if left unattended. The data collected as the logs for analysis increases in size and complexity, and therefore, we need to arrive at solutions which can process huge data which is both structured and unstructured within a reasonable period of time.

I have dwelt upon this technology as an answer to another question later.

AK: Banks, at least the bigger ones, have now begun their digital initiatives.

- Could you please advise as to how this is different than technology track (introduction of core banking)?
- What are the differences that you see in the objectives, agenda and implementation process between the past (core banking) and future?
- How do you assess the progress so far, particularly in PSBs? What should the existing banks be doing further in this regard also?

HK: Good question. First, you need to understand the objective behind setting up the core banking platform. In my view, core banking is popular terminology. From a technical standpoint, core banking is the centralized database and application architecture. All the applications and services will be driven from the data centre, and the service delivery architecture is the key to ensuring round the clock uninterrupted services to all the stakeholders. The metrics of relevance to deliver state of the art services are:

- Performance and scalability
- Availability and fault tolerance
- Robustness and maturity
- Security and access control
- Conformance to standards and interoperability

The above metrics have to be kept in mind while designing the core banking platform as more and more innovative customer-oriented services need to be introduced from time to time.

Therefore, a centralized service delivery architecture design and implementation required a centralized database and application framework, which is commonly known as the core banking.

New digital initiatives starting from the internet and mobile banking are deployed on the same base architecture, and going forward, we will see many more applications rolled out based on business requirements on the underlying core banking platform.

The implementation philosophy and the process continue to be the same approach, but requirements in terms of performance and security are redefined. For example, you will understand that the turnaround time of a transaction is completely different across delivery channels, and customers are looking for almost instantaneous response, especially while using mobile banking platform for either funds' transfer or utility payments. One of the areas which has really come of age is the delivery of payment services for utility payments, and several players from the private sector and start-up have made significant progress over the last couple of decades.

I used to work with PSBs for almost 20 years as an advisor and found that they are moving in the right direction and do have a road map with reference to implementing technology solutions from time to time. You may be aware of the EASE reforms. It is a responsive and responsible PSBs banking reforms' roadmap, and the Department of Financial Services of the Ministry of Finance has come out with this excellent initiative and the bank boards are responsible for driving this initiative to ensure 'clean' and 'smart' banking.

In short, designing and implementing the core banking technology platform, and more importantly, conforming to standards and the best global practices is an investment for the future and several new initiatives have been built on this platform to deliver the services.

AK: The public sector banking in India is also entrusted with advancing the societal/social agenda, which private banks are not obliged, at least in the same way and to the same level.

- **How do you think digitalization would help in this dual challenge of profitability and meeting social objectives/banking?**
- **How can digital be used to make banking services available at a lower cost to the poor and farmers? What should be the banks' strategy?**

HK: I agree that the PSBs do have social and societal obligations as they are government-owned banks and are supported by the government whenever there is a requirement. If we look at the EASE reforms, which are aimed at ensuring that the internet banking and mobile banking channels are very effectively utilized by the customers, the cost per transaction will come down once a large number of customers start using these delivery channels. It is also to be noted that at the beginning of this decade, RBI, Unique Identification Authority of India, National Payments Corporation of India and Indian Banks' Association came out with an excellent idea of designing and implementing the micro ATM-based services through the business correspondent model to ensure that direct benefit transfer programmes are effectively implemented to ensure that the funds reach the intended beneficiary. Implementation of the financial inclusion schemes across the country undoubtedly needs a digital backbone to deliver services to the beneficiaries, and to that extent, the technology investments are playing a meaningful and purposeful role. I would urge the readers of this interview to look at the progress and road map of this excellent initiative.

I understand that after a period of three years wherein the banking system has gone through a lot of stress, we find that performance of a large number of PSBs in the last fiscal is a turnaround scenario, and therefore, we can safely assume that the PSBs' downward trend is behind them, and they will see positive growth in future.

If we look at the initiatives of the Government of India in the agricultural sector and specifically to the farming community, it is heartening to note that several steps in the right direction are taken. I understand that digital technology, with support from remote sensing and geographic information system, is playing a key role in this space. The announcement by the government with reference to the agricultural infrastructure fund to the tune of ₹1,000 billion will help the agriculturists and the farming community to take advantage of the platform, once created, to arrive at meaningful and productive investments from time to time.

AK: We hear a lot about new terms such as AI, ML, cloud computing, big data and decision science as the emerging technologies which will play a dominant role to come out with innovative technology solutions in the future.

- **How do banks, particularly PSBs, keep at the top of it, and decide what to use?**
- **How all this can be integrated and used for operational excellence, cost reduction and business growth?**
- **Are there differences between the approaches used by private and public sector banks in how they see and use technology?**

HK: I would like to make a few observations regarding the above technologies before answering your questions.

AI and ML, along with deep learning (DL), are the hot topics of discussion in the industry today, specifically with reference to applicability or otherwise in the banking, financial services and insurance (BFSI) sector. Please note that DL is a subset of ML, which is a subset of AI.

AI as a field existed for quite long, and we did not find much use several years back as the technology was not in a position to address large complex problems in the real-life scenario. Developments in big data, cloud computing and high-performance computing with specific reference to GPUs has enabled researchers to look at real-life problems which are complex and arrive at meaningful and acceptable solutions.

Technology forecasting is exciting if one is passionate about learning about technologies of the future and the possibility of solving the unsolved real-world problems. Gartner is a well-reputed international organization which specializes in this aspect and comes out with a critical analysis of some of the areas of interest in the BFSI sector. The report from Gartner last year gave a glimpse of the new technologies and their availability through algorithms and software to address complex problems.

For example, the Gartner Hype Cycle for AI, 2019, clearly comes out with technology forecasting to address the building blocks in the broad area of AI.

It can be seen from the data given below that the following three areas that are reasonably well understood today and developed to deliver value to practical problems.

- Robotic process automation
- Speech recognition
- GPU accelerators

It can also be seen that the technology forecasting with reference to the following areas is in the band of 5–10 years and beyond.

- Artificial general intelligence
- Quantum computing
- Autonomous vehicles

Therefore, it needs to be looked at as the field of AI is still evolving and will take a considerable amount of time before one can look at aspects such as common sense, reasoning and other areas where humans are good at to be modelled.

When we teach neural networks to students, I mean the artificial neural networks, we always say that our modelling of the human brain is limited today by our understanding of the same.

In short, AI, ML and DL are able to solve a few real-world problems and applications and services in the BFSI sector. Moving forward, we will see a few deployments.

To answer your questions, banks are currently looking at the possibility of using AI algorithms for problem-solving in these domains. One application that we are currently looking at is in the area of designing and building the next-generation cybersecurity operation centre. Based on the guidelines and framework with reference to cybersecurity from the RBI, the PSBs have already implemented the Cyber-Security Operation Centre (C-SOC). The current implementation is to collect the logs and analyse them to arrive at any security breach that has taken place in the environment. Therefore, based on the data collected, the observations will be made, and it does not help in forecasting. AI and ML algorithms are currently implemented in the next generation C-SOCs, and they are in a position to look at possible attacks in the near future if appropriate preventive steps are not taken immediately. This is just one example.

Well, this is a difficult question to answer at this stage. It is well known and understood that technology investments would continue to happen in the banking sector, and they are required to survive in the competitive scenario. I have not come across any clearly defined mathematical model which can be applied effectively to prove that the technology investments indeed were the only reason for operational excellence, cost reduction and business growth. As I always state, appropriate and cost-effective technologies, clearly defined processes which are implementable and enforceable, along with competent and capable manpower to administer and manage the resources, is the ecosystem for success.

One of the major concerns that I see is the outsourcing of highly mission-critical services by the banking system as they do not have the technical expertise, and more importantly, are not in a position to hire and retain the resources. It is to be noted that the responsibility, accountability and ownership rest with the bank, and in the event of a major disruption in service delivery, they are answerable to all stakeholders. Therefore, apart from just looking at investment in technology, it is also important to look at appropriate resources and train them adequately to handle this portfolio.

One of the justifications that we come across is the reduction in the manpower requirements to address banking services if appropriate and cost-effective technology is deployed. If the productivity per employee of the bank is on the increase year after year, definitely the contribution from technology investments has played a role towards the same.

I do not think there are differences in the technology deployed between the PSBs on one side and the private and new generation banks on the other. Probably the new generation banks, for example, take the decision to absorb technology quicker than the PSBs, but that gap is also narrowing.

It is to be noted that the technology investments need to be also looked at from the opportunity-lost-cost, in the event a decision is taken not to deploy appropriate technology at the right time.

From the manpower angle, I think, a requirement of specialized manpower in niche areas of technology will be required to ensure that appropriate selection of technology and that effective management is carried out within the organization.

AK:

- **What is the role of the board and CEO in the digital transformation process?**
- **What are your observations on how banks have adapted their leadership attributes over the past decade, and how these need to change in the years ahead for the digital age?**
- **What kind of leadership and skills are required by the board, CEO and other members of top management?**

HK: The digital transformation process is said to be complete in all respects if and only if all the processes that are required to be implemented in the overall ecosystem of the bank are fully digitized. I do not think that this has happened. We are on the right track and maybe, sooner rather than later, some of the banks will definitely fall under this category. If we can look at this as a first step, there is absolutely no need for the customer to visit any of the branches or the controlling offices for any requirement. It is another question whether it is a prudent idea to implement branchless banking. I do not think so.

One of the advantages that the PSBs even today enjoy even today is the excellent customer service through human touch and interaction. Maybe this will have to continue. But the next generation of customers may not require this as a differentiator as most of the younger generation do not visit the branches. Therefore, technology and digitalization to address a maximum number of customers with innovative applications and services with a critical mass of branches to address specific segments and undoubtedly the home banking services for the senior citizens who bank with the PSBs are the future directions.

Coming to the board and the constitution of the board, it is definitely important to bring specialists at the board level. For example, banks today are having technology specialists and human resources specialists as members of the board who can bring in tremendous value addition for strategic decision-making.

There is an absolute need to look at focused short training programmes for the bank directors in specific areas of technology. One example that I can bring out is the certification course by the RBI through the Institute for Development and Research in Banking Technology for the board directors and senior management in the area of cybersecurity. Some of us who are members of the Standing Committee on Cybersecurity of RBI participate in this programme as faculty along with senior professionals of RBI. This is just one example. I would like to state that, especially in the last few years, steps have been taken to induct specialists from academic institutions and industries in the board, and this has enhanced the quality of the discussions and, more importantly, the decision-making.

Being a technology professional for the last three–four decades and having had the opportunity to work closely with many of PSBs and the RBI, I would like to submit that it has been a great learning experience to look at the application of technologies in my area of expertise to solve problems in the technology landscape.

I am of the view that many of the steps taken by the MOF, RBI and the Government of India, from time to time, have enabled the banking ecosystem, especially the PSBs to deliver services to the customers almost on par with that of the private banks. It is not out of place to mention here that the customer profiles of the PSBs are different than that of others. This trend is changing, and with the younger generation of the customers and bank employees being more techno savvy across the industry, the service delivery paradigm will also have to change.

'HR function requires huge transformation in terms of its structure, processes and competencies.'

T. V. Rao*

AK: Late Professor Udai Pareek and you have been pioneers of the human resource development (HRD) movement in this country since the mid-1970s. Your pioneering work at Larsen & Toubro (L&T) and subsequent books have given impetus to setting up of HRD function in several companies. How do you reflect on the growth and changes in HR in the Indian industry over the last 40 years?

TVR: The journey over the last several decades had been the journey of both high points and low points. It started in 1974–1975 when L&T took the first step towards implementing an integrated human resources (HR) system that was designed based on inputs from L&T's managers themselves. When we recommended the system, L&T board accepted it in entirety and immediately appointed a task force to implement the same. None of us had any idea about the time it is going to take to implement the full HRD system, which included performance appraisal, feedback and counselling, potential appraisal, training, career planning and organization development. Later on, functionalities related to worker affairs and personnel administration were also included.

It took more than three years to stabilize the performance appraisal system along with its linkages. The high point was developing over a hundred L&T managers in skills, such as performance analysis, feedback and counselling. L&T University started then and offered many train-the-trainer programmes. The low point was the difficulty in ensuring that every supervisor and manager understood the system and implemented it in its true spirit. The change required a change in mindset because appraisal, performance and rewards are a complex process and could be a political one also.

* T. V. Rao, Former Professor, IIM Ahmedabad.

Around that time, Professor Udai Pareek, Indian Institute of Management Ahmedabad, was invited by R. K. Talwar (then chairman, State Bank of India [SBI]) who wanted to implement a similar HRD system in SBI. The SBI also took some quick steps like creating a new HRD department and position of chief general manager (HRD). SBI also started a new performance appraisal system, which it first tried in the Ahmedabad circle with tremendous success. Associate banks also created a dedicated HRD department, and many of them took initiatives, such as organizational climate surveys, organizational development (OD) and culture building.

In the early stages of HRD movement, we worked hard to impress on people to separately structure HRD and give it a mandate of competence-building (those days it was called 'attribute analysis'), commitment-building and culture-building, using a performance appraisal system, potential appraisal, feedback and counselling, training, career planning as well as development and OD. Many companies started implementing the same. The low point, however, was several of them have established HRD departments, but recruited HRD managers without really understanding the principles and philosophy behind HRD. In many organizations, the title changed from the personnel department to HR department in effect, replacing development with the department. Such experiences resulted in my starting a centre for HRD Xavier School of Management Jamshedpur, the National HRD Network and the Academy of HRD with which you have been associated.

An important high point today is wide recognition, in India as well as abroad, that there can be no business without good HR. Those who understood this as chief executive officers (CEOs) or chief human resources officers (CHROs) have made a difference and built their organizations. You are one of them. The low point is that still many look at HRD as a department and not a philosophy or a system with principles and a way of life.

AK: What are your reflections in terms of boards' and CEOs' perception of HR over the last couple of decades? Did you see it change from decade to decade or industry to industry?

TVR: In 1991, post-liberalization and later with technological changes and the internet becoming the common, organizations, especially technology and also a few manufacturing and service firms, prioritized attention to talent acquisition and development, leadership and succession issues. Some management institutions have now started an MBA in HR, apart from Tata Institute of Social Sciences (TISS) and XLRI, which always supplied the qualified HR to companies.

Traditionally, multinational corporations (such as Hindustan Unilever Limited) and leading Indian businesses (such as TATA, Birla, TVS Group

Sundram Fasteners, Murugappa Group and Mahindra groups) have positioned their HR functions quite strategically with top-class HR professionals driving the function. Their growth and diversification are supported by very smart HR policies using modern management tools in selection, promotion and leadership development. Many senior executives of these organizations have also been deputed to long-duration leadership programmes at Harvard, Stanford and similar institutions. With the exception of a few private and public sector banks (PSBs), other firms in the banking, financial services and insurance sector continued with the traditional ways of managing HR with some tinkering.

In conclusion, the CEOs of progressive companies recognized the need and the importance of development-focused HR and implemented the right kind of HRD. To many other CEOs, however, HRD means the HR department and a support function. 'That it is a leadership function which is recognized by very few even today.'

AK: PSBs have witnessed significant changes in post-liberalization and technology and competition from private banks. How do you describe the emergence and development of the HR function in PSBs?

TVR: The record of PSBs in remodelling HR functions is not very encouraging. Except for some prime banks such as SBI and Bank of Baroda, one does not come across an inspiring story or innovations in HR functions. HRD in banks has also suffered ups and downs with the change of CEOs. For example, SBI took some major initiatives way back in the 1970s, including setting up of the HRD function. In fact, SBI's associate banks created a position of manager HRD for the first time in the banking industry and initiated some innovations in HR functions. SBI also undertook OD work in the early 1980s, followed by some innovations in their promotion system by using assessment centres. Way back in 1978, Bank of Baroda set up an exclusive HRD function under a professional which mainly focused on bringing a new performance appraisal system and some other initiatives.

Post liberalization, the attention of the banking industry shifted to reorganization and rationalization of structures and systems, and in that context, people-related issues did not remain in focus, except for building capacity through training systems. Throughout the decade of 1980s and 1990s, PSBs have been overwhelmed by their IR functions and did not pay as much attention to the HRD function as was perhaps required. There was also functionally a lack of integration between IR and HRD. Overall, the HR journey in banking has been choppy.

AK: Obviously, the role of HR in strategy formulation and implementation remains a less chartered and less attempted area.

What are your perspectives on this process? What can boards, CEOs and HR can do to facilitate this process?

TVR: Banks, being essentially commercial organizations, are number-driven. Traditionally, the orientation has, in most cases, remained short term. With the growth of banking and banks over a period of time, this orientation, unfortunately, has not undergone much change. Added to this is the problem of short tenures of PSBs' CEOs, who are always overwhelmed with myriads problems of commercial banking, and in the process, the people process initiatives have been quite marginal. The HR function has remained merely administrative in terms of recruitments, promotions, placements, performance appraisal etc.

If you could recollect when you chaired the Khandelwal Committee, of which I was a member, we elaborately dealt with this issue and suggested a number of measures, including putting in place a boards committee on HR, an exclusive position of executive director of HR, development of a five-year plan for HR, the professionalization of the HR function through recruitment of HR specialists and many other measures. Although the Government of India accepted many recommendations, the initiatives at the bank-level have not been inspiring. Having said this, I should add that some banks in the public sector such as SBI and Bank of Baroda have taken a good number of initiatives in building a leadership pipeline, rehashing HR function and introducing many innovations encouraging staff. The board's and CEO's involvement is very vital in building the HR function. Barring some exceptional CEOs, who are HR-driven have demonstrated their commitment to navigating people processes for transformation, the track record of HR in banking has been anything but inspiring. This is a worrying situation because banks are driven by people.

My own impression is that senior and top bankers are not trained during their career in this vital function, and they are recognized only on the basis of their number-crunching capabilities. *Great organizations are not built on this strength of commercial orientation alone but on their propensity to strengthen the human potential and taking steps to develop future leaders.*

I feel quite concerned that this aspect is missing in the banking industry. Neither the government nor the boards of the banks are able to pursue this. I wonder how the government as well as banks have not been able to take advantage of the Khandelwal Committee recommendations, which are so relevant even after 10 years.

My own experience as a member of the Board of the Advisory Committee of a large bank is not very much different. I am convinced that the CEO is the driving force for building the talent and leadership pipeline and can build the future of the bank. This is a task which cannot and should not be delegated. I am also convinced that we need professionally qualified and trained HR professionals both at the middle and senior level to build continuity. This is what industrial houses of repute have done, and HR professionals have contributed a great deal in these organizations to facilitate their growth through expansion and diversification. We need, in the banking institution, bankers such as Talwars, Vaghuls and Khandelwals.

AK: In a highly competitive and digital world, how should the HR function be organized in banks in terms of structure, processes and HR functionaries?

TVR: Given the size of some of our big banks having a large staff (ranging from 1 lakh to 2.5 lakhs), the HR function requires a huge transformation in terms of its structure, processes and competencies. Currently, the functionaries deployed to manage HR function are far more limited in number as well as in their orientation and training. To enable HR to make any significant contribution in mobilizing the potential of employees, develop capabilities and build a leadership pipeline, the function would require clear segregation into its administrative dimension and developmental dimension. While each bank, depending on its size and the context, may require a different structure, broadly, the function may be divided into HR operations (wages, service conditions, terminal benefits, pension, etc.), industrial relations and industrial law and HRD, including learning and development, performance management, HR research, leadership development, HR innovations, employee wellness and culture building.

In addition to this, the HR function should be set up and headed by a professionally qualified specialist, who can provide continuity, research support and use of the latest methodology to strengthen the core of the HR work. The CHRO and every HR person should be professional and work with a missionary spirit because HR is a function that requires passion and humanistic thinking.

In addition, I believe that one of the key roles of HR should be to uplift the spirit of employees and shape a positive attitude. This can be done by building a cadre of counsellors, coaches and mentors to help people take charge of their self-development and growth. In short, we require (distinct somehow) who are, in a way, intellectual capital builder. This is not esoteric but a necessity when human problems post-pandemic is on the rise, and we need to build confidence around.

AK: What should be the best way to build leadership bench-strength in banks? What is your concept of a future banking leader in the top who can steer the process of transformation?

TVR: I think we expressed a clear strategy in the *Khandelwal Committee Report*. Building leadership is quite a serious business. It, however, needs a commitment to have intrinsic faith in the people and take right steps such as giving individuals opportunities at the right time in handling variety of jobs, supporting them at critical times, broadening their vision and perspectives by giving them special projects and helping them through mentors. The process of leadership development is largely accomplished on the job, and of course, supplemented through a variety of training exposures. Even at the cost of repetition, I mention that the engaged attention to leadership development is a missing link. In the public sector, there are added problems. *We look upon the government to take initiatives while I believe it is decidedly the job of the board and the CEO to lead the leadership development process. Leaders with vision in spite of their short tenures are able to do it, but leaders who lack vision often fail to accomplish this even with long tenures. As I mentioned earlier some leaders both in industry and banking have demonstrated this, but such a tribe is in short supply. To address this, we need to set our priorities right.*

AK: Increasingly, the economy and the society are subject to unexpected risks such as global financial crises 2008, COVID-19, and in the future, hopefully, no other big risks such as global climate could surface. What can HR do to prepare organizations to deal with such eventualities and what kind of leadership is needed? What kind of employee engagement strategies will work?

TVR: I think in the years to come, HR will be on the front-lines of any banking or organizational response to any crises. Each crisis brings with it new and unknown challenges for which no rules or processes exist. Therefore, in any crises, employees need to come up with a solution and to implement them. If boards and CEOs realize this, it will be an important first step towards preparing banks to deal with eventualities. I think developing employee-centric culture is one of the best ways to enable employee engagement for this and any other purpose. What would such a culture look like? This culture should be based on empowerment, trust, risk and taking initiative, collaboration, experimentation and learning.

Unfortunately, these are also the features, which are in short supply in banks, particularly PSBs. Excessive and complex regulation and bureaucracy have led to a culture, which is based on rules, control and compliance. Crises means something unforeseen and unexpected; rules and control processes are for expected situations, and therefore a culture based on rules and control is itself a risk in changing times. We have to bear in mind that culture change needs leadership. So to build culture, banks need leaders, and for that, banks need a leadership pipeline, career planning, succession planning, mentoring, and in fact, the whole of HR. We do not know what the next crises will be, but we know that building an employee-centric culture will be part of the solution in every case.

AK: What are your perspectives on digitization, HR and banking?

TVR: Digitalization presents a unique opportunity to banks and HR in banks to leapfrog many constraints for the development of employees, culture, leadership and customer service. The value of digitalization has become self-evident during the current COVID-19 crises. I am encouraged by the way a few banks have embraced technology in the last couple of years to offer choices and services to customers. Much more needs to be done at these banks and other banks that are behind. And the same digital spirit needs to be adopted for using it in HR. Digitalization provides cost- and time-effective ways to offer training, opens up access to a multitude of internal mentors and coaches, builds collaboration and problem-solving and commitment to the purpose. It could help in employee engagement, deep HR analytics and research and getting good performance data. Digital technology also needs to be used in new ways to world-class HR strategy and governance.

Unfortunately, digitization is used for target setting, monitoring and accountability fixing. This, in my view, is a short-sighted approach and not enough. We have hardly scratched the surface in this rare—possibly once in a lifetime—resource. Digitalization also has other implications for HR. Digital skills and training will emerge a key success area for banks, more so because technology keeps changing fast. Cyber and privacy risks are big threats, and HR needs plans to address them proactively and strategically. *Many of our HR processes are still old-fashioned, analogue or paper drive. We can accelerate efficiency in HR areas by making HR processes digital in nature. Digitalization is changing the way leaders need to engage, influence and empower employees. Banking is a fast-changing industry and increasingly led by technology. Its leaders need to be trained in digital leadership.*

To me, digitization is a powerful tool to be used to remain in touch with the changing world of practice and problems and to solve them. Digitalization is the best tool for development.

6

'Boards must objectively hold mirror to themselves, reflect on their own capabilities and contributions.'

Arun M. Kumar*

AK: You have seen, up-close, all major disruptive changes. What do you see as some of the crucial challenges for the boards and chief executive officer (CEOs) currently? Are some of these challenges going to change, get more accentuated or side-lined in the post-COVID-19 context?

AMK: In the context of the COVID-19 crisis, CEOs and boards must prioritize how they weather the storm and what they need to do to have their firms emerge stronger as we emerge from the current situation.

The crisis has made us re-think ways of working and accelerated the momentum of trends that were latent prior to the pandemic. For instance, digitization and remote working had been gaining attention over the last two years. COVID-19 crisis hastened change in these areas.

Board agendas, the world over, will also need to address environmental and social issues, corporate culture and diversity. There is an increasing focus on the multiple stakeholders of a corporation and an acceptance that a board must not focus solely on shareholders. Issues of climate change and the common good are seen as a high priority, especially by the younger generation of employees and shareholders. Cultures that are inclusive and fair are valued more than ever.

Combined with concerns about the economy—mounting trade tensions, resurging debt and a looming market correction—and political gridlock in USA, the UK and elsewhere, the year ahead will require a careful balance of near-term focus, agility and long-term thinking.

Boards will have to spend more time on strategy, risk and global disruption—especially now in light of the crisis. An element of strategy will be overseeing the impact

*Arun M. Kumar, Chairman, KPMG, India.

of digitization; boards will need to oversee their impact and ensure that firms take advantage of the opportunities and do not get left behind, and also keep an eye on increased risk in cybersecurity that comes with an expanded digital footprint. New demands of the market and new ways of working impact the workforce. Boards must look to ensure that firms focus plans that include developing new skills and capabilities for strategic execution.

And in times of disruptive change, CEOs and boards must promote the purpose and the values of the firm to strengthen its culture, competitiveness and resilience.

AK: In general, how do you see the priorities of boards and CEOs changing in response to the economic slowdown, COVID-19 virus and so on? Do you see them making fundamental shifts in terms of strategy, business models, digitalization and so on?

AMK: *Never before have CEOs and their teams been more in need of the foresight and seasoned judgment that a well-functioning board of directors can provide. Likewise, never before have boards needed more carefully to balance providing support to management teams operating in highly stressful conditions with challenging them to ensure that they make the best decisions throughout a crisis for which no playbook exists.*

Just as every organization faces different challenges during this crisis—some are reaching new levels of growth, while others are struggling to survive—there is no one-size-fits-all answer for what a board should do.

The word 'crisis' has two meanings, one being 'danger' and the other being 'chance.' Boards must consider both.

Many organizations will have to rethink their product–market focus, customer engagement or pace of technological innovation. During this period, a board should encourage management to undertake a broad strategic revaluation that could entail embracing bold moves.

AK: To deal with current and emerging challenges, what should the transformation agenda now be like?

AMK: Digital is everything. For instance, in the case of banks, where the physical mode of banking has been challenged more than ever, in addition to new platforms for customer engagement and lending, important considerations would include data governance and cybersecurity.

This is a good time to refocus on core competencies and build on strengths. Areas that are not core to the strategy of a firm may be considered for disinvestment or refocus.

Boards must also objectively hold a mirror to themselves, reflect on their own capabilities and contributions. There are gaps which need to be filled with regard to composition, capabilities, perspectives and diversity.

AK: Can you share your perspective on how the current uncertainty, challenges and new transformation agenda will change the type of leadership and talent that boards and CEOs will need going forward? In your opinion, will the current context change the way HR is perceived by the boards and CEOs?

AMK: One of the learnings from the current crisis is that as human beings, we are all in this together. This was a health crisis, first and foremost. It was a pandemic that hit the powerful and the powerless all at the same time. We, all of humanity, all members of an enterprise, are in this together.

That sense of being in this together meant that we reemphasize that our first priority is the health and well-being of our people. If they are healthy and feel supported, they will do their best for our clients. That approach has worked. We have done our best to keep our people safe. They have done their best to work insane hours from home to meet the needs of our clients and their jobs.

The empathy induced by the pandemic, thus, fostered a sense of unity. I hope this feeling of being together and looking out for each other stays with us.

HR has a big role to play to foster and advance the agenda of keeping people at the centre of a firm's considerations. And likewise, HR must ensure, working with other functions and business lines, that employees imbibe the purpose, culture and values of the organization.

CEOs must be supported by HR in shaping and executing the firm's strategic agenda.

Ways of working will change as more employees can work from home or remotely. HR will have to be at the forefront of making this a productive transformation.

AK: What could boards and CEOs do to ensure that the firm has a talent advantage, particularly when there is going to be a premium on it?

AMK: *The pandemic is a dress rehearsal for a more turbulent world ahead. To meet the challenges of an uncertain landscape, leading CEOs will perforce retool their firms.*

To begin with, they must re-define mission-critical roles. And revisit the delivery agenda, what is needed to fulfil existing customer and stakeholder commitments. A 'development agenda' must be pursued to discover and define future business needs. Employees must be encouraged and empowered to experiment, learn, adapt and innovate for success. The best learnings of the lockdown—the ability to team, communicate and motivate remotely and to stay focused on objectives in an uncertain environment—must be preserved.

AK: Banking influences the functioning of all sectors of the economy in various ways. What are your perspectives on the changes, trends and challenges before the banking sector—globally and nationally? Are they very different from what other sectors/industries are experiencing?

AMK: Three implications seem to emerge for the future of banking.

First, banks will operate in a financial system that is awash with liquidity and with low-interest rates but added risk aversion.

Second, the government will be a key player in the financial sector, both as a borrower to fund its deficits and as a 'risk absorber' providing guarantees, back-stops and more direct fiscal support for borrowers whose businesses and cash flows bear the brunt of the virus.

Third, with reduced customer spending, retail bankers could end up with a bounty of deposits but with limited demand for loans.

Major economic upheavals invariably lead to an escalation in risk perception and a flight to quality. This means that banks will prefer to give loans to borrowers whose cash flows are visible and strong. Clearly, sectors such as pharmaceuticals and health care, which are likely to see an increase in business volumes in the battle against the pandemic, will be on the list of preferred borrowers.

Banks will have to find ways of gauging risk better and dive deep into the risk profiles of borrowers, both retail and corporate, to enhance lending. This calls for a major upgrade in analytical tools and data that build more complete risk profiles of borrowers. Fintech, whether in-house or outsourced, is likely to grow in the post-COVID world.

We should expect that a market for financial products that help hedge against future crises will develop.

The appetite for complex instruments, particularly for corporate entities, will abate. Simple and transparent structures will command a premium. This demand for simplicity will result in reducing the margins for banks.

The coronavirus quite literally makes money 'dirty', in that banknotes and coins become potential fomites that can carry the virus. Thus, the fear of infection will drive the next wave of digitalization and a flight from cash. This will buttress the rapid digitalization that India has seen over the last few years.

AK: In your public- and industry-level roles, you have seen the relationships between government and industry up close. Are there any relationship models, case studies, recommendations and

examples, which you want to share to provide insights on how the relationship between the government and private sector (e.g., public sector banking) can become even more productive? What should that partnership look and work like?

AMK: In my view, there should be an exchange of personnel between the public and private sector. The USA does this successfully as each president brings in a number of senior-level leaders into the administration; many of these are drawn from the private sector. In France, there is a tendency for senior government officials to move to the private sector for senior roles. These kinds of personnel movements catalyse creativity and fresh thinking in both the public and private sectors.

AK: In India, public sector banks (PSBs) cover 70 per cent of the banking. PSBs operate under governmental context and controls. This includes CEO appointments, controls, governance, culture, recruitment and compensation. KPMG's CEO survey emphasizes the importance of agility. Could agility be a factor that will help bridge the gap between public and private sector banks? What can the boards and CEOs in public sector banking do to embrace agility and what could be the role of HR in it?

AMK: India's growth ambitions and imperatives demand a larger number of banks that belong in the top 100 globally.

Agility is more in demand than ever in the context of the uncharted waters we are operating in today. Public and private sector entities need to extend to embrace agility and resilience.

Banks should consider applying the tenets of design thinking. Leading practitioners in 'experience design' are applying product design rigour to the new discipline of customer journey architecture. Long-established 'product push' processes in banks can be replaced with engaging and targeted customer-centric processes.

A new approach to IT engineering is being adopted by leading banks that recognize that their legacy mainframe IT systems are hard to change, expensive to run and ultimately slow down innovation. Cloud adoption has enabled leading banks to add agility, where it once wasn't possible. This technology can significantly improve and simplify back-end operations in banks.

Mergers, acquisitions and divestments provide pathways to enhancing competitiveness. In particular, banks are learning that they can become leaner, less complex enterprises by selling non-core assets or businesses.

Privatizing PSBs is no panacea. Many intricate sector-specific reforms must also be carried through to get useful results. For instance, the governance and management of PSBs need to improve. The way to do this was outlined by the Nayak Committee, which recommended distancing between the government and top public sector appointments (everything the Banks Board Bureau was supposed to do but could not).

It would be worth considering the privatization of a couple of mid-sized banks to take government ownership to below 50 per cent. This will result in three types of ownership: wholly government-owned, majority government-owned and large minority stakes held by the government. Attempts at better governance across these can yield valuable lessons on what works and what does not.

There is a need to de-risk banks which handle too many risks, by letting them handle what they can and transferring the rest to non-banks and the market.

AK: Talent and culture are frequently cited in various surveys and research studies as the secret sauce behind the success of a firm. In Indian PSBs, there is large untapped human potential. In your view, what could be some of the blind-spots, priorities, information gaps etc., that could be preventing boards and CEOs from transforming HR and tap the full potential of employees?

AMK: Treating HR as an administrator, acting principally as an agent implementing processes on behalf of the top management or a moderator responsive to the needs of all stakeholders is not adequate. For HR to make a true contribution, it needs to be an agile business partner.

Talent initiatives that generate real-business value must be created. Many business leaders today do not look to HR teams as drivers of value; they continue to see them as administrative personnel managers. This must change.

Talent and culture are frequently cited in various surveys and research studies as the secret sauce behind the success of a firm. In Indian PSBs, there is large untapped human potential.

AK: From the perspective of CEO and HR leaders, what should a business case include to transform HR function in order to convince boards of PSBs that despite regulation, governance and short-term earning pressures, HR is an area of strategic advantage for the bank?

AMK: *HR is a serious functional area of expertise. It is important that the function is staffed by experts. They should also be provided intensive exposure to and develop a keen understanding of the banking business.*

The entry of new players into the banking sector armed with innovative products has created a demand for new skill sets that an agile HR function must facilitate in terms of recruitment and training.

AK: Where and how should boards and CEOs start if they want to unleash the HR potential within their banks?

AMK: HR needs to be the CEO's and the board's priority. The HR team may need to be supplemented with contemporary skills, sometimes by hiring from the outside.

The performance management system and links to promotions and compensation should be reviewed. Training would need to be given a high priority. The recruitment policy of the banks should be oriented towards having a right-sized and right-skilled workforce in tune with their medium to long term business plans.

In a service-oriented industry like banking, the quality of human resources has to be the central consideration; recruitment, training, promotion and compensation practices must all be aligned with the bank's strategies and values.

AK: From your perspective, are there any specific areas that you see firms struggling with the most? Are there areas of HR where you think the 'knowing–doing' gap exists the most, and what, in your opinion, needs to be done about it?

AMK: There appear to be more gaps than ever these days, and for HR professionals, one that is particularly haunting is the distinction first made by Jeffrey Pfeffer and then Robert Sutton, who asked, 'Why do we know so much, yet can't turn this knowledge into better practices?'

Their book emphasizes the importance of execution. Similarly, Ram Charan and Larry Bossidy are strong advocates for the discipline of getting things done; Stephen Covey echoes this perspective by saying that we don't need organizations with more intelligent quotient (IQ), but rather, greater execution quotient (XQ).

Knowing–doing gaps that we see include the inertia of translating ideas into action. We over-intellectualize change, focusing on the technical aspects, forgetting that change is about people. And our message is often incomplete and ineffectual, missing the why behind the what.

It is important, therefore, to always keep purpose at the core, ensure that all parts of an organization, including HR, are aligned and accountable for strategy execution.

AK: The world is experiencing perhaps the biggest economic crises in our living memory, and we do not know what and how it will change the business and economies. What would be your advice to HR leaders and professionals on navigating the change, when what will change itself is not known? What kinds of perspectives,

mindsets, approaches and any other resources could they lean on to help CEOs and banks?

AMK: Almost every HR policy and practice has been affected by this crisis. There are no easy answers or precedents in this pandemic, yet CEOs and C-suite leaders are looking to CHROs to solve problems such as keeping people safe and pivoting an entire workforce to be able to work productively from home when feasible.

HR leaders must stay not only visible and positive, but also authentic and sincere, as many colleagues are looking to them for cues during this uncertain time. HR leaders equip other leaders to cope and ensure that they have what they need to support their teams, especially those working remotely for the first time.

Along with other leaders, they must reinforce the company's mission and a higher calling. People at organizations with a clear purpose make better decisions and are more engaged in their work.

Communications, frequent, transparent and realistic but not alarmist, are of critical importance. This can be achieved through frequent community calls or virtual town halls.

This is a time of stress for many. It is important to acknowledge this and empathize with employees and find ways to reframe thinking and replenish energy.

During this time, organizations are moving from the traditional design for efficiency to design for resilience. Roles and structures will need to be redesigned around outcomes to increase agility and flexibility. While undertaking such redesign, consideration should be to provide employees with varied, adaptive and flexible roles, so they acquire cross-functional knowledge and training.

Companies are mapping the competencies of their employees and exploring the possibility of transferring or re-skilling where there is a shift in demand due to the economic impact of COVID-19.

About the Editor and Contributors

Editor

Anil K. Khandelwal, PhD, is a thought leader, author, international speaker on leadership and governance. An acclaimed authority on HR and leadership in the banking sector, he is a rare transformation leader who moved from HR specialization to the chief executive officer (CEO) position in two large public sector banks (PSBs). He was featured amongst the 100 most powerful CEOs in India by the *Economic Times* for three consecutive years between 2005 and 2008. Transforming Bank of Baroda (BOB) (2005–2008), in particular, from a staid PSB to one of India's most valuable international banks won him many awards, including the Asian Banker Singapore's Lifetime Achievement Award. His brand of human resources (HR) leadership and its application in business turnaround also won him the Lifetime Achievement Award from the National HRD Network. He chaired the government-appointed committee on HR in PSBs and was a member of the first Banks Board Bureau appointed by the government for banking reforms and selection of whole-time directors. He has been a UNDP consultant to banking reform commission in Tanzania and also a short-term visiting professor, at Asian Institute of Management, Manila. He has been an advisor and board member to several corporates. He is an internationally recognized keynote speaker and has trained over 5,000 leaders in India and abroad.

Peter Cappelli (Wharton) calls him an HR Hero, Dave Ulrich (Michigan) describes him as an exceptional CEO and Tom Peters (author of *In Search of Excellence*) rates him as a 'very wise leader'.

He has authored/co-authored/edited seven books, including the bestselling *Dare to Lead* (SAGE, 2011) and *CEO, Chess Master or Gardener* (2018). He has been advisor to international consulting firms such as Accenture, Booz and Company, Hewitt and KPMG.

He has travelled to 80 countries and lives in Mumbai. He can be reached at akk1948@gmail.com

Twitter handle: @anugyaan

Website: www.anilkhandelwal.in

Contributors

Late N. Balasubramanian, having had more than half a century of work experience behind him, had a unique blend of exposure to the industry and academia that is not easily found. 'Bala' had three and a half decades of experience in senior- and board-level responsibilities in companies such as ICI, Britannia and Wipro, complemented with teaching and research activities at Indian Institute of Management (IIM) Ahmedabad and IIM Bangalore over the last two decades.

A non-practising-chartered accountant with a PhD in business finance, his interests spanned corporate governance, business ethics and board-level counselling. He had been on the statutory and advisory boards of the listed companies and had served as a member of various government-sponsored bodies and also on the advisory committee of National Stock Exchange's centre for excellence in corporate governance. He had served on the editorial and advisory committees of some Indian and international scholarly journals and authored many books on corporate governance and business ethics.

Asha Bhandarker is currently a distinguished professor of organizational behaviour at IMI, New Delhi. Prior to this, she worked for many years with Management Development Institute (MDI), Gurgaon. She has been a Senior Fulbright Fellow and is currently the director of PNB Board and director of the Institute of Management Technology, Ghaziabad. Bhandarker has worked closely with the corporate sector for the last 38 years and has contributed significantly to bring corporate transformation and develop better quality leaders in many companies and banks in India. She is well known for her contributions to research and teaching in the field of leadership, competency assessment and potential identification. She has published eight books with reputed publishers along with Late Dr Pritam Singh. She has also published 40 research papers, articles and cases in peer-reviewed journals both nationally and internationally. She is a psychologist by training and a coach, and counsellor by temperament who is passionate about academic excellence and scholarship.

Prasenjit Bhattacharya is a man with a mission to help enterprises in India create high trust cultures that deliver sustained business results. He is the chief executive officer (CEO) of Great Place to Work® Institute in India, whose vision is to 'make India a great place to work'. Prasenjit is the co-founder and director at Great Manager Institute whose mission is to enable individuals to be great people managers who deliver sustained results by building trusting relationships.

He has close to three decades of experience in Indian and multinational corporations such as HSBC, Eicher Consultancy Services (ECS Ltd), Siemens and Crompton Greaves. In his previous stint in consulting, he has worked widely in various areas in HR and service quality and total quality management in industries ranging from telecom, cement, heavy engineering, automotive components, dairy products, software and hotels.

He has done his MA in personnel management and industrial relations from Tata Institute of Social Sciences (TISS).

Raj Bowen is a seasoned business leader with around 36 years of experience across consumer products, durable goods, education, learning and leadership consulting. He has launched and led the rapid growth of start-ups in corporate learning and leadership consulting sectors. His deep study of the domain and his expertise in learning and development provide him with impeccable coaching credentials. He is a senior executive coach and leadership development facilitator. His clients are business leaders seeking personal and professional excellence.

Raj's last full-time assignment was as the managing partner, EMA Partners (a global executive search firm), leading the talent advisory practice, through a joint venture with Decision Dynamics AB, Sweden.

Raj has been the managing director of PDI Ninth House (a Korn Ferry company), and earlier, he was the CEO of Dale Carnegie Training, India. His other career stints have been at Blow Plast Ltd, NIIT/NIS Sparta and Geep Industries.

Alok Kumar Choudhary is currently deputy managing director (HR) and chief development officer in State Bank of India (SBI). He has over 33 years of distinguished experience in a variety of roles in diverse locations ranging from branch banking to retail to commercial banking. He has also headed some of the largest branches of SBI and has headed regions and zones of strategic importance. He has been recognized for his people management skills early on in all his assignments. In his present policymaking role, he steers the most critical function of HR for developing and engaging a workforce of about 250,000 as well as building capabilities for the new generation banking in SBI. He is passionately engaged in redefining the boundaries of HR through the reengineering of processes and envisioning the new normal in a digital environment.

Akhil Handa is the head of Fintech, Partnerships, Mobile Banking and Digital Lending Department at BOB. He is driving the digitization of the bank with a view to transform the bank into a leading digital bank of the country.

He has set up fintech, partnerships and mobile banking at the corporate office of the bank which is leading the charge to partner and co-create with fintech across India and is considered an early mover in fintech in India. This was the first fintech vertical among all PSBs in India. His role has expanded to re-imagine digital lending journeys to create a digital lending ecosystem that enhances the customer experience through customized digital products. His areas of expertise include digital banking, payment solutions, contactless cards, algorithmic underwriting, advanced analytics, application programming interface banking, etc.

Handa has spent over a decade with varied emerging digital technologies. He started a fintech and a mediatech company, donned the analyst hat at JP Morgan and led some of PM Modi's digital initiatives. By training, he has a BTech in chemical engineering from the Indian Institute of Technology (IIT) Delhi.

Kewal Handa is a former non-executive chairman of the Union Bank of India. He has also been the managing director of Pfizer Limited, India, from 2005 to 2012. He is a qualified management accountant and company secretary and has a master's degree in commerce. He has completed the Pfizer Leadership Development Programme from Harvard University and the Senior Management Development Programme from IIM Ahmedabad. He has also completed a certificate course on marketing strategy from Columbia Business School, New York. In addition to having a diverse experience in finance, commercial, strategy, business development, merger and acquisition, banking, corporate affairs, he has experience in sectors such as engineering, consumer and project finance. He is a former president of All India Management Associations and a board member of IIM Ahmedabad and IIM Raipur. He has also been the member of the board for many leading companies such as Alfa Laval Ltd, ING Vyasa Bank and has been the executive director at Parke Davis and managing director of Wyeth Ltd.

Rajiv Jayaraman has, over the last few years, built a high-octane global team at KNOLSKAPE that helps organizations accelerate employee development using an integrated learning and assessment platform. Under his leadership, KNOLSKAPE has delivered durable business outcomes for 300+ leading organizations across 25 countries and has won numerous industry awards.

Rajiv, a TEDx speaker, has a keen interest in the psychology of learning, design and technology. He is the author of the book *Clearing the Digital Blur* (2019). He has deep expertise in digital transformation and its impact on capability development across industries. He has been widely quoted and featured in the *Economic Times, Mint, Business Standard*, CNBC Young Turks, ET Now, *digitalLEARNING, Entrepreneur* and Yourstory.in. Prior to KNOLSKAPE, he worked at Oracle, USA, in the server technologies division, where he led numerous product development efforts from the ground-up.

Anujayesh Krishna is currently a board advisor with Institute for Advanced Studies in Complex Choices, Hyderabad. Prior to that, Krishna has worked in different industries, such as consumer products, industrial engineering, information technology (IT), pharmaceutical and financial services in the UK and India. In the recent past, he has worked in the financial services sector in the UK with leading banks.

Krishna has also been a visiting faculty at IIM Udaipur, and he writes regularly on organizational topics. Prior to joining the industry, Anujayesh completed his Fellow Programme in management (equivalent to a doctorate in management) from IIM Ahmedabad.

Krishna's current areas of interest cover the effects of digitalization on organizational leadership, culture, change and strategic human resources (HR).

H. Krishnamurthy has more than 40 years of experience (1975–2017) in teaching, research and consulting. He has been associated with the Indian Institute of Science (IISc), Bengaluru, since 1983 as a scientist and retired as a chief research scientist in 2017. He had a brief stint in Defence Research and Development Organisation before joining National Institute of Technology, Warangal, as a lecturer in electronics and communication engineering (1977–1983). Krishnamurthy's main focus areas of interest are design and implementation of IT solution architecture in the BFSI sector, data and information security. He has been on the boards of Canara Bank, Indian Institute of Banking and Finance, and Institute for Development and Research in Banking Technology. He currently serves on various boards including National Institute of Securities Markets of Securities and Exchange Board of India. He has been a pioneering consultant on behalf of IISc in helping many banks to plan and implement technology solutions.

Arun M. Kumar, chairman and CEO of KPMG, India, is an accomplished global executive with experience spanning multiple sectors from high technology to the government and many geographies from Silicon Valley to India. He serves on the global board of KPMG.

Previously, Kumar served in the Obama Administration as the Assistant Secretary of Commerce for Global Markets and Director General of the USA and Foreign Commercial Service. He oversaw teams located in 78 countries and across the USA, and engaged in commercial diplomacy and advocacy worldwide—for exports and FDI—on behalf of the US government and industry.

Before his tenure in public service, Kumar was a partner and member of the board of directors at KPMG, LLP; he led the firm's West Coast Management Consulting practice.

Kumar has authored a book of poetry, *Plain Truths* (2010), and has co-edited a book, *Kerala's Economy: Crouching Tiger, Sacred Cows* (2007). Arun received an MBA from the MIT Sloan School of Management.

Atul Kumar, Chief Ethics Officer and Chief General Manager in SBI, has nearly 33 years of distinguished banking experience by means of holding strategically significant positions. A certified banking compliance professional, associate of Chartered Institute for Securities and Investment, London, and a certified associate of Indian Institute of Banking and Finance (IIBF), he is known in banking for his experience in managing conduct failings, ethics risks and behaviour modifications around nudge principles. Having handled more than 9,000 ethical violations and conduct-related matters including investigations, he has been in several policymaking committees of Central Vigilance Commission, Working Groups of Indian Banks' Association and chaired a Committee on Ethical Banking in PSBs formed by the government of India (GOI). Honoured with 'Vigilance Excellence Award—Individual' by Institute of Public Enterprise, Hyderabad, he is a member of Confederation of Indian Industry's (CII) National Task Force on Integrity and Transparency. Kumar frequently takes ethics sessions at Centre for Advanced Financial Research and Learning, Reserve Bank of India, NPA, Hyderabad, Indian School of Business (ISB), Hyderabad, IIBF, banks and insurance companies. Also, he was invited by IIM Bangalore and IIM Ahmedabad for sessions on ethics for MBA students.

M. Mahapatra joined SBI in 1982 as a probationary officer. He had several assignments in India, UK and USA. He set up new businesses such as leasing, private equity and insurance for SBI. He was a deputy managing director in SBI leading global strategy, marketing, new businesses, digital, analytics and IT initiatives. As a chief information officer, he established the innovation, data analytics, enterprise architecture verticals which were instrumental in creating many path-breaking products such as You Only Need One (YONO), loan life management system and SBI Chatbot.

Later, he became the CEO of Syndicate Bank, leading the transformation and repositioning of one of India's oldest and largest banks.

As a writer in leading newspapers and a known public speaker, he is regarded as a thought leader in the Indian banking, financial services and insurance sector. He has won several awards and accolades and has served in various Reserve Bank of India (RBI) and government committees besides being a member of corporate boards.

Kuriakose Mamkoottam obtained post graduate and doctoral degrees in sociology from the Delhi School of Economics, University of Delhi. He taught post graduate students of management (MBA) at the Faculty of Management Studies (FMS), University of Delhi, from where he retired as Head and Dean in 2011. Dr Mamkoottam has carried out extensive research, corporate training and consultancy work in the area of human resources and industrial relations. His publications include *Labour and Change* (SAGE, 2004), *Trade Unionism: Myth and Reality* (1982) and many articles in international and domestic journals.

He was the founding Dean, School of Business, Public Policy and Social Entrepreneurship; Dean, Student Services, Ambedkar University Delhi (AUD) during 2011–2016, and also the Executive Chairperson, AUD Centre for Incubation, Innovation and Entrepreneurship which he helped to set up at AUD. He is Professor Emeritus, Business, Public Policy and Social Entrepreneurship, AUD.

Soumendra N. Mattagajasingh is an HR professional with more than 23 years of experience. He is currently responsible for the HR function of the retail banking group of ICICI Bank. He is also responsible for employee relations practices. He joined ICICI Bank in 2002 and has worked in various areas of HR, including learning and development, leadership development, recruitment, employee relations and performance management. Soumendra holds a master's degree in industrial relations and personnel management and worked at Hindustan Petroleum Corporations Ltd before joining ICICI Bank.

Ajay Nanavati is a seasoned global executive with over 35 years of multi-country, multi-business and cross-functional experience. He joined 3M in India in 1988 as its first employee and was responsible for forming the joint venture. In the subsequent 28 years with 3M, he held positions of increasing responsibility in Singapore, APAC; Austin, Texas; St. Paul, Minnesota and Israel. He returned to India in 2008 as the first Indian managing director of 3M's only public company outside the USA. He retired as chairman of Syndicate Bank and is on the board of Alicon Castalloy Ltd, Livinguard AG (Zug) and Quantum Advisory Services Ltd (a Fairfax company). He is an active innovation evangelist and mentors start-ups as an angel investor. Co-chair of CII Directors Guild on Corporate Governance, a member of the CII Start-up Council and on Advisory Board of Israel Centre, IIM Bangalore, Ajay holds a degree in chemical engineering from Virginia Technology, USA.

Rajeshwari Narendran, an alumnus of IIM Ahmedabad and Harvard Business School, is currently the Head of Department of Business Administration and Director, Master of Human Resource Management (MHRM) in Mohanlal Sukhadia University, Udaipur. She is also a visiting faculty member at IIM Ahmedabad, IIM Udaipur and many universities across the globe. She was the youngest and first woman president of Indian Society for Training and Development (ISTD) and has been a board member to International Federation of Training and Development Organizations. Additionally, she had represented in UNO for the emancipation of women as initiator of 'make a difference'. Rajeshwari has been a popular counsellor, motivational speaker and trainer of international repute and has trained around 65,000 aspirants. Her psychodynamic assessment and deep research has made her help many public sector undertakings, corporates and micro, small and medium enterprises to hire the right leaders and move in transformational HR/OD.

She is also the chief editor of the *International Journal of Technology Diffusion* and a member of the editorial team of the *International Journal of HRD Practice, Policy and Research*, UK, ECNR, Canada. She is a recipient of Women Super Achiever Award by World HRDC, Exceptional Leader Award by World Women Economic Forum, Fellow ISTD, NEBAA UK International Best Paper Award, to quote few.

Abinash Panda is an associate professor in organizational behaviour at MDI, Gurgaon. Prior to this academic assignment, he has worked with IIM Kashipur and Xavier School of Management, Jamshedpur, as a faculty member. His corporate stint includes assignments such as Associate Vice President, Learning and Development with Adani Group; General Manager, Leadership Development and Talent Management with Suzlon Energy; and Senior Consultant with Tata Management Training Centre, the learning hub of Tata Group. He has published more than 50 academic research papers in peer-reviewed journals of international and national repute. He was the principal co-investigator of Lessons of Experience, India study, jointly conducted by Tata Group and the Centre for Creative Leadership, USA.

Ashish Pandey is an associate professor and teaches organizational behaviour, organization development and human resource management related subjects at IIT Bombay. His research is in areas of positive psychological outcomes of yoga and mindfulness, the interface of business and society, and spirituality at the workplace. Recognition to his research comes from the awards conferred to his work in the forums such as Academy of Management, Indian Academy of Management, IISc (Bengaluru), Infosys Leadership Institute and Case Western Reserve University (Cleveland). His research papers, inventory and approach notes have appeared in several leading international journals and periodicals. Along with research and development, Ashish has been regularly involved in training and consulting work in the areas of leadership, organization development and institution building across industries and institutions.

Prakash Ranjan is a senior HR professional with around 23 years of experience. He has worked in companies such as Daewoo Motors, BOB, ITC Infotech and multinational corporations such as Areva, Alstom, General Electric and SUEZ. He currently heads the HR function for South Asia at SUEZ Water Technologies and Solutions and is based out of Bengaluru. He has done his MA in personnel management and industrial relations and is a gold medalist, a PhD in strategic HRD and an NTL certified organization development practitioner.

T. V. Rao is currently the chairman of T. V. Rao Learning Systems Pvt. Ltd, Ahmedabad. He was a professor at IIM Ahmedabad between 1973 and 1994, and subsequently, adjunct/visiting professor until 2014. He is the founder president of the National HRD Network and the first honorary director of the Academy of HRD, India. He was also the president of the Indian Society for Applied Behavioral Science (ISABS). Rao has worked as an HRD advisor to the RBI, assisted the administrative reforms commission in reviewing the personnel management practices for civil services and also served as a member of the HRM Review Committee of Nationalized Banks set up by the Ministry of Finance. He has worked as a short-term consultant to the United Nations Educational, Scientific and Cultural Organization; the Ministry of Health, Indonesia; National Entrepreneurial Development Association, Malaysia, and the Commonwealth Secretariat, London. Rao has over 50 books to his credit, out of which 15 are authored jointly with Professor Udai Pareek.

Jayashree Reddy has been with SBI since 1987, shouldering diverse roles of business planning, personal banking operations, administration and HR development. In her banking career spanning over 33 years, she has handled several challenging assignments at branches, zonal offices, apex training institutes and corporate centres.

In her current role as head of strategic training unit, the training vertical of SBI, she is responsible for crafting training strategies, overseeing designs and administration of training programmes to equip over quarter million employees with requisite skill and knowledge to create future ready workforce for the bank.

Ms Reddy holds a master's in agriculture economics and is a certified associate of the Indian Institute of Bankers. She has conducted several research studies in the field of retail and investment credit in agriculture during her stint as a faculty member at the State Bank Institute of Rural Banking.

Joydeep Dutta Roy, a career banker for around 25 years, is currently the chief general manager in charge of strategic HR, subsidiaries and joint ventures at BOB, one of India's premier PSBs. Having joined BOB as an HR specialist, he has handled a variety of HR functions in the bank, across levels, and has been instrumental in spearheading many marquee HR projects and initiatives for the bank. Joydeep has also successfully handled various banking assignments, such as being the regional head of the bank at Dehradun and Bareilly Regions, implementing various business projects.

He loves to read, take tranquil walks in the midst of nature and enjoys good company. He is passionate about people and mentions people development as one of his fortes. Joydeep holds an honours degree in economics from the University of Delhi, besides having a law degree and an MBA in HR from the Narsee Monjee Institute of Management Studies (NMIMS) in Mumbai. He is also a certified assessor for CII's annual HR Excellence Awards.

Anil Sachdev is the founder and CEO of Grow Talent Company Limited and the School of Inspired Leadership (SOIL).

In October 2008, Anil and the other co-founders of Grow Talent entered the field of education by creating SOIL. This innovative school has been co-created by a consortium of 32 leading firms. In 2019, SOIL launched its second campus in Manesar—the SOIL School of Business Design.

Anil's experience in India and across the world covers areas such as talent management, strategic change and organizational transformation.

Anil is a member of the academic committee and a faculty member of the European Centre for Executive Development, the leading leadership institute of Europe, located in the INSEAD campus, Fontainebleau. He is a member of the World Compassion Council, Seattle, a trustee of the Chinmaya Mission and serves on the Global Board of Shizenkan University in Tokyo.

Gordhan K. Saini is an associate professor at the School of Management and Labour Studies at TISS, Mumbai. Prior to joining TISS in 2010, he completed his postdoctoral fellowship from the Indira Gandhi Institute of Development Research, Mumbai. His areas of interest in research include employer branding, social marketing and consumer behaviour. He has published more than 25 research papers in national and international journals. He has co-authored chapters in two edited volumes, including *India Development Report 2011* and has one book to his credit. He has taught at premier management institutions such as IIM Indore, IIM Kolkata, IIM Kozhikode, IIM Rohtak and NMIMS, Mumbai, and has also taught in various executive training programmes/workshops. He has consulting experience of research projects for corporates and research projects of government and non-government organizations.

Sushil Saluja is a senior international business leader and a government advisor based in London, with over 30 years' experience at Accenture in Europe, Asia and the USA. His career has focused on international business, technology-led transformation and education.

Within Accenture, Sushil ran the Financial Services EMEA business unit based in London and prior to that, Asia Pacific from Hong Kong. Before that, he led the financial services to the UK/Ireland business unit and personally led several major industry transformations in the UK.

Half of his time has been spent working directly with clients to advise and execute their digital-led transformations, including clients in Asia, Europe, the Middle East and the UK. He has launched fintech accelerators in Hong Kong and Dubai as well as overseen the same in London.

Sushil is currently a corporate advisor in the private equity/investment industry as well as a non-executive director on a lot of charity and non-commercial boards. He is an alumnus of Cambridge University, UK.

Brajeshwar Sharma started his career as a banker in 1986 and over his tenure of 34 years, he has played his part in all the major turning points in banking history, be it liberalization, computerization or spearheading globalization as the managing director and CEO of the bank's London subsidiary.

His role as the head of the HR vertical has been no less exciting. He has brought cultural transformation, changing perspectives and giving direction during the seamless integration of three big PSBs—Union Bank of India, Andhra Bank and Corporation Bank—as also an effective crisis manager during the present international pandemic.

Identified by McKinsey as one of the future leaders of the bank, his quest for knowledge and perfection define him. Under his leadership, Union Bank of India continues to garner awards and accolades at national and international forums.

Late Pritam Singh was a distinguished scholar, thinker, academic leader and role model. He had been a director with the Midas Touch, and transformed IIM Lucknow, MDI, Gurgaon and IMI, New Delhi. He is well known as an inspiring and wise Guru to chairmen and managing directors of companies, top directors of organizations and academic leaders heading the prestigious IIMs. He had served on more than 20 boards of leading Indian companies. He had authored 10 academically reputed books (three of which are award winning) and published 60 research papers. He had served on many important government committees. He was the chairman of the Defence Acquisition and Procurement Committee (2016) and Member of the prestigious Prime Minister's Committee on Institutions of Excellence (2017–2020).

He was the recipient of more than a dozen prestigious national and international awards. He was the first Padmashri awardee in management education for his work in transforming management institutions.

M. S. Sriram is currently a faculty member and chairperson at the Centre for Public Policy, IIM Bangalore. He is also a distinguished fellow at the Institute for Development of Research in Banking Technology, Hyderabad.

Prior to this, he was an ICICI Bank Lalita D. Gupte chair professor of microfinance at IIM Ahmedabad. He has worked as vice president (finance) at BASIX and was a faculty member at the Institute of Rural Management Anand. In addition to the academic work, he has been active in the policy space, chairing the Expert Committee on Kerala Co-operative Bank, being a member on the Financial Inclusion Advisory Committee of the RBI and the External Advisory Committee of RBI to licence small finance banks and on the Vaidyanathan Committee on co-operative reforms. He graduated from the Institute of Rural Management Anand and is a fellow from IIM Bangalore.

T. K. Srirang, group chief HR officer, heads HR function and infrastructure management services group for ICICI Bank. He also oversees the HR function for ICICI group companies. He is a member of the research advisory council of IIT Bombay, Monash Research Academy; member of the society of IIM Ahmedabad; member of the governing body of the International Institute of Information Technology Bangalore, and former board member of the National HRD Network.

Srirang holds an MBA degree in personnel management and industrial relations and a bachelor's degree in industrial engineering. He has been with the bank since 2001.

In his 25 years of work experience at organizations such as Coca-Cola India Limited, Ford India Limited, ICI India limited and ICICI Bank, Srirang has handled industrial relations, mergers, capability building, leadership development, performance management, talent acquisition and employee engagement processes.

Nishchae Suri is the president, Asia Pacific, the Middle East and Africa at EdCast Inc. Prior to EdCast, Nishchae was a senior partner with KPMG in India. With over two decades of experience in consulting and academia, he has worked with a wide array of clients in 25 countries across Asia and the Middle East. Prior to joining KPMG, Nishchae was managing director and CEO at Mercer India and held several leadership positions with Hewitt Associates (Aon) where he also achieved the feat of becoming the youngest ever global partner.

Nishchae has led some of the largest organization transformation engagements working with public sector enterprises, Indian and foreign multinationals and family-led businesses. In 2005, CNBC recognized him by conferring on him with the title 'Young Turk', an award for young achievers who were helping shape and transform businesses.

A teacher at heart, Nishchae is often invited as a speaker to several national and international conferences. He is also the founding president of SOIL. Nishchae holds an MBA in finance from the Symbiosis Institute of Business Management, where he was awarded a gold medal and several scholarships for academic excellence.

Biju Varkkey is currently a faculty member at IIM Ahmedabad. He is a fellow from National Institute of Bank Management, Pune. Earlier, he has taught at IIM Lucknow and MDI, Gurgaon. He has been on the board of many companies and a consultant to several organizations. He has contributed several research papers both in Indian and international academic journals.

Ravi Venkatesan has done BTech from IIT Bombay, MS from Purdue University and MBA from Harvard Business School, where he was a Baker scholar. He has spent three decades leading organizations in the private, public and social sectors across three continents and multiple industries. He is a former non-executive chairman of BOB, co-chairman of Infosys Ltd, chairman of Cummins India Ltd and chairman and CEO of Microsoft India. He is currently UNICEF's special representative for young people and innovation as well as the founder of the Global Alliance for Mass Entrepreneurship (GAME), a multi-stakeholder coalition which aims to create 10 million entrepreneurs in India by 2030. He is the director of Hitachi Ltd, a trustee of Rockefeller Foundation and a partner at impact investor Unitus Ventures. He is the author of the acclaimed book, *Conquering the Chaos: Win in India, Win Everywhere* (2013).

Shyam Viswanathan is an electrical engineer and an MBA from Faculty of Management Studies, University of Delhi. He has four decades of experience in configuring and delivering solutions to large corporations in India, West Europe, Asia Pacific as well as in the USA, in areas as diverse as process design, knowledge management and technology-based training.

He has been a consultant and faculty in personal effectiveness, leadership of teams, leadership of change, new initiatives and innovation, and design thinking. He has also been a subject-matter expert with the Society for Human Resource Management and an empanelled faculty with Harvard Business School Publishing.

Shyam works with the leadership teams of business organizations and educational institutions to help them articulate, deploy and leverage their vision, strategic roadmap and cultural DNA.

He was the first associate dean of executive education at ISB. He has led the design and delivery of leadership development initiatives for 120 different organizations worldwide.

Index

The solutions Acharya offers are many, and policy-makers would do well to have a closer look at the fairly long list provided in the various chapters of the book... a must for students of finance and banking, academics, market participants, policy-makers and the informed citizen.

Dr Usha Thorat
Former Deputy Governor, Reserve Bank of India
The Hindu Business Line, 3 August 2020

Pursuit for financial stability in India

For special offers on this and other books from SAGE, write to marketing@sagepub.in

Explore our range at
www.sagepub.in

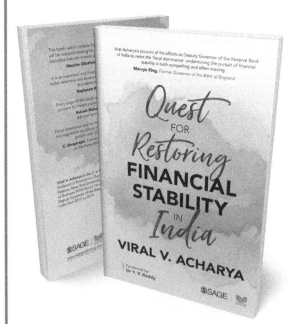

PAPERBACK
9789353884895

Lightning Source UK Ltd.
Milton Keynes UK
UKHW012213110521
383564UK00002B/114